# William Beveridge

William Beveridge in 1942

# WILLIAM BEVERIDGE

## A Biography

JOSÉ HARRIS

CLARENDON PRESS · OXFORD
1977

*Oxford University Press, Walton Street, Oxford* OX2 6DP

OXFORD LONDON GLASGOW NEW YORK
TORONTO MELBOURNE WELLINGTON CAPE TOWN
IBADAN NAIROBI DAR ES SALAAM LUSAKA ADDIS ABABA
KUALA LUMPUR SINGAPORE JAKARTA HONG KONG TOKYO
DELHI BOMBAY CALCUTTA MADRAS KARACHI

**British Library Cataloguing in Publication Data**
Harris, José
  William Beveridge
  1. Beveridge, William Henry, *Baron*
  *Beveridge*   2. Economists, British – Biography
  330'.092'4    HC252.5.B45 *H 37*

ISBN 0–19–822459–1

921
B57/A

*Printed in Great Britain
by Cox & Wyman Ltd
London, Fakenham and Reading*

# Acknowledgements

MANY people have helped me in the preparation of this book, by sharing their recollections of Lord Beveridge, by the loan of private correspondence and by commenting on the various stages of my manuscript. I am particularly grateful to the members of Lord Beveridge's family, Mr. and Mrs. Philip Mair and Professor Lucy Mair, for letting me loose on their family archives and for many helpful criticisms and suggestions. I also received valuable assistance from Miss Enid Chambers, Sir Norman Chester, Lord Chorley, Mr. Martin Collier, Dame Marjorie Cox, Mr. and Mrs. John Dodd, Miss Eve Evans, Professor Arthur Goodhart, Sir Edward Hale, Professor Lancelot Hogben, Professor R. Klibansky, Lord Longford, Miss Muriel Ritson, Professor Philip Sargent Florence, Lady Stocks, Messrs. Frank Thorold, Professor Richard Titmuss, Mrs. Kay Titmuss and Mrs. Lucia Turin.

I am grateful also to the following for permission to refer to unpublished copyright material deposited in libraries: Mr. Derek Clarke of the British Library of Political Science; the Controller of HMSO; the Cabinet Office; the English Speaking Union; Mr. S. H. G. Barnett; Lady Henderson; Mrs. Margaret Lloyd; the Hon. Godfrey Samuel; Mr. A. J. P. Taylor; Mr. Michael Vyvyan; the Royal Economic Society; the Principal and Fellows of Newnham College, Cambridge; the Provost and Fellows of Corpus Christi College, Oxford; and Mrs. Diana Wills.

The book was started while I was a research fellow at Nuffield College, Oxford, and completed with the help of a research fellowship from the Centre for Studies in Social Policy. I am indebted to both those institutions for encouragement and support. In addition the Nuffield Foundation kindly gave me a grant from their 'small grants' scheme to assist with the costs of research. I should like also to thank colleagues at the London School of Economics and elsewhere for their helpful comments on earlier drafts, particularly Professor Brian Abel-Smith, Professor Garth Plowman, Dr. Pat Thane and Dr. J. W. Harris. I am very grateful to Mrs. Rose Parton and Miss Jean Seddon for their inexhaustible patience in typing a much-revised manuscript, and to Mrs. Freda Chambers for help with indexing and correction of proofs.

One fact that rapidly emerged from my research was that no two people held the same opinion of Beveridge. I doubt whether any of those named above will entirely concur in my interpretation—the responsibility for which is of course mine alone.

# A Note on Sources

THE most important source for this book is the collection of nearly five hundred boxes of personal papers amassed by Lord Beveridge and deposited in the British Library of Political Science. A collection of such size presented major problems of selection; and many topics covered at length in the primary sources are dealt with only superficially, or not at all, in the pages that follow. In so far as I pursued a guiding principle in selecting material, it was that Beveridge's chief interest for both the historian and general reader lay in his many and varied contributions to modern social policy. However, history has a habit of up-staging this kind of assumption; and I shall be the first to admit that an entirely different book might have been written by someone who sifted the sources in a different way.

In spite of the wealth of material available, the Beveridge collection proved to be incomplete. Beveridge's own rudimentary card-index to his papers referred to extensive correspondence with the other members of the Committee on Social Insurance and Allied Services, who helped to produce the famous Beveridge Report of 1942. On 9 April 1953 Beveridge wrote a long note to Lady Beveridge, advising her on manuscript sources for her book *Beveridge and his Plan*. In this note he referred to two boxes which contained his correspondence with the Social Insurance Committee, together with other correspondence relating to the Beveridge Report. These letters were not, however, used by Lady Beveridge in writing her book, nor were they found among the Beveridge papers when these were placed in the British Library of Political Science in the 1960s. The correspondence undoubtedly existed, because Beveridge himself listed the individual letters and made extracts from them (see his 'Working Notes and Materials' in BP, IXa 37). A few of the missing letters were also referred to in his Autobiography, *Power and Influence* (pp. 305–8), although it was clearly his intention that the detailed account of the Beveridge Report should be included in his wife's book rather than his own. In spite of extensive inquiries I have been unable to discover what happened to these letters. The loss was not irreparable, as it was possible to make use of Beveridge's manuscript copies and to supplement them with a great deal of further material on the Social Insurance Committee available both among Beveridge's own papers and in the Public Record Office. However, it should be noted that the source material was defective in this important respect.

# Contents

# Abbreviations

| | |
|---|---|
| ASB | Annette Susannah Beveridge. |
| HB | Henry Beveridge. |
| WHB | William Henry Beveridge. |
| AHBP | Annette and Henry Beveridge Papers. |
| BP | William Beveridge Papers. |
| Bev. Coll. B | Beveridge Collection on Unemployment. |
| Bev. Coll. Misc. 9 | Beveridge Collection on Family Allowances. |
| Bev. Coll. Misc. f. 11 | Beveridge Collection on Tariffs. |
| Bev. Coll. Misc. 144 | Beveridge Collection on Munitions. |
| *BFC* | W. H. Beveridge, *British Food Control*. |
| *ICT* | W. H. Beveridge, *India Called Them*. |
| *MP* | *Morning Post* |
| *PI* | W. H. Beveridge, *Power and Influence*. |
| RC | Royal Commission. |

William Beveridge at the Board of Trade

# Introduction

IN August 1938, Sir William Beveridge spent a week-end in Hampshire at Passfield Corner, the home of his old friends, Sidney and Beatrice Webb. The famous partners were now both in their eighties, and Sidney was too tired to talk. With the indefatigable Beatrice, however, Beveridge went for two long walks and talks upon the downs. Their conversation ranged over a number of topics that they had been arguing about for the previous thirty years—the ideal organization of society, methods of economic and social research, questions of social welfare and the problem of the unemployed. 'His conclusion is that the major if not the only remedy for unemployment is lower wages,' recorded Mrs. Webb;

. . . if this does not happen the capitalist will take his money and his brains to other countries where labour is cheap. . . . He admitted almost defiantly that he was not personally concerned with the condition of the common people. . . . He declared that he had no *living philosophy*—he was a thoroughgoing materialist agnostic about man's relation to the universe; and he had no particular credo or ideal as to man's relation to man.[1]

Four years later Beveridge became the author of the most popular blueprint for social reform ever produced in Britain, the *Report on Social Insurance and Allied Services* of 1942. Published shortly after the battle of Alamein this report was seen by many people as the light at the end of the tunnel of war, and as a promise of 'social justice' for the post-war world. Beveridge himself was widely acclaimed as the prophet of peaceful social revolution, as the champion of new forms of collective altruism and as the characteristic philosopher of the British 'welfare state'. These two pictures of Beveridge—both of them exaggerated but both basically authentic—give some idea of the complexities that lay beneath the ideas and character of this rather baffling man. These complexities are reflected in the recollections of people who knew Beveridge and their assessments of his work. To some he seemed wise and lovable, to others overbearing and vain. To some he was a man of dazzling intellect, to others a tedious bore. To some he was endlessly generous and sympathetic, to others harsh and self-centred to the point of complete insensitivity. By some he has been seen as a humane, radical and visionary reformer, by some as a dangerous bureaucrat, by some as a sentimental idealist with his 'head in the clouds and his feet in the pond'.[2]

[1] Passfield Papers, Beatrice Webb's diary, 10 Aug. 1938.
[2] Dalton Papers, Hugh Dalton's diary, 24 Apr. 1942.

He has been described to me personally as 'a man who wouldn't give a penny to a blind beggar' and as 'one of the kindest men who ever walked the earth'.

This book is the first full-length study of Beveridge that has appeared since his death in 1963. I have tried to make it both more and less than an orthodox historical biography. It is less than a full biography because although it covers the whole span of Beveridge's personal and intellectual life, it concentrates particularly on certain aspects of his public career—on his ideas about social welfare, his work as a social and educational administrator, and his wider influence on the making of social policy. At the same time it goes beyond conventional biographical questions and embraces certain wider issues in social and administrative history. These wider issues are of four main kinds. Firstly, an attempt is made to analyse the underlying assumptions of Beveridge's social philosophy, and to dispel the familiar image of Beveridge as a straightforward collectivist liberal whose famous Report sprang fully-armed out of his experiences forty years before as sub-warden of Toynbee Hall.[3] That there *was* an intellectual connection between the social planner of the 1940s and the young social worker of the 1900s is undeniable but the progression from the one to the other was much more devious and erratic than is usually supposed. Nor can Beveridge's contribution to welfare be ascribed, as it has sometimes been, to the 'politics of conscience' tradition that derived from the teachings of T. H. Green.[4] That Beveridge whilst at Oxford was influenced by the Idealist school is again undeniable; but there were other and more important components in his social philosophy—most notably the scientific empiricism of T. H. Huxley, the positivist tradition of the liberal utilitarians, and the Spencerian conception of social evolution. As a social and political theorist Beveridge was in fact highly eclectic and frequently self-contradictory. Between 1900 and 1942 there was scarcely a point upon the compass of liberal philosophy through which he did not travel, and at times he went far beyond the bounds of what is conventionally thought of as 'liberalism'. Far from being a consistent 'welfare-collectivist', he veered between an almost total commitment to the free market and an equally strong commitment to an authoritarian administrative state. At times he favoured generous social welfare and radical redistribution of resources; but at other times he favoured 'the whip of starvation' as a necessary precondition of economic advance.

Secondly, these underlying assumptions of Beveridge's philosophy will be considered, not in isolation, but within a context of continuous social

    [3] Janet Beveridge, *Beveridge and his Plan* (1954), pp. 53–7; Maurice Bruce, *The Coming of the Welfare State* (1961), p. 165.
    [4] Melvin Richter, *The Politics of Conscience, T. H. Green and his Age* (1964), p. 294.

and structural change. Beveridge was born in India in 1879, the son of a high-ranking official in the Anglo-Indian hierarchy, into a household staffed by twenty-six servants. As a young man he lived through what he himself described as 'the ball before Waterloo'—a time for the upper and middle classes of 'unexampled spending and luxury'.[5] He survived until 1963, the lonely, servant-less and slightly bewildered spectator of a pattern of social change that he himself had helped to create. His life spanned the 'discovery of poverty' in the 1880s and 1890s, the rise of a politically significant labour movement, the inter-war depression and revival, and the post-war era of full employment, mass consumption and planned obsolescence. He himself was profoundly conscious of living in an 'age of revolutions'—of revolutions in methods of production, techniques of government, political loyalties and spiritual aspirations, which he ascribed partly to the inevitability of 'progress' but much more fundamentally to the cataclysmic impact of two world wars. This sense of instability filled him sometimes with optimism and sometimes with despair, but in either case it was of great importance in shaping his perspectives on society and his ideas on social reform.

The third focal point of this study will be Beveridge's role in the process of governmental growth and administrative rationalization. A great deal of historical literature over the past twenty years has been devoted to the role of the professional bureaucrat as the protagonist of governmental change—as the mediator of political ideas and scientific expertise, as the guardian of class and professional interests, and as the conscious or unconscious instrument of functional responses to social change. Much of this literature has been concerned with the mid-nineteenth century 'revolution in government'; and in spite of a number of more modern studies we still know far more about the bureaucratic revolutionaries of the 1840s, 50s and 60s than about their more anonymous and less flamboyant heirs and successors. Yet, as Beveridge's own career shows, the ideas and perspectives of a dynamic civil servant could still be of crucial importance in shaping policy and administration, even within the context of the much more formal structure of government that evolved in Whitehall after 1870. Moreover, Beveridge's administrative philosophy was in itself highly revealing of some of the competing principles that were locked in the struggle for government growth. Viewed objectively, Beveridge may perhaps be seen as a typical example of the classic Weberian bureaucrat.[6] He was convinced of the need for an 'appointed' bureaucratic élite to balance the corruptions of popular democracy. He was personally responsible for greatly extending the

---

[5] *Unemployment: a Problem of Industry* (1930 edn.), p. 387.
[6] *From Max Weber: Essays in Sociology*, ed. H. H. Gerth and C. Wright Mills (1948). pp. 200–1, 228–9.

scope of officialdom, and for shifting the balance of social arrangements away from the small, intimate 'community' and towards the large anonymous 'society'. He was unusual amongst administrators of the pre-1914 generation in favouring centralization as a matter of political principle and not merely as a matter of reluctant pragmatic necessity. Above all, he was an exponent of administrative rationalization—of policies which substituted routine and uniformity for the waste and inefficiency of archaic tradition and unplanned organic growth. Para-doxically, however, Beveridge's subjective preferences and personal beliefs by no means consistently conformed to those of the archetypal rational bureaucrat. He himself positively disliked working in a formal administrative context. He conducted business in a highly personal and autocratic fashion, and throughout his career he frequently kicked against the pricks of bureaucratic machinery that he himself had created—a fact which may account for Harold Wilson's comment that Beveridge was 'probably the greatest administrative genius of this century', but 'almost certainly the worst administrator'.[7] Tempera-mentally he belonged with the 'zealots' and 'stormy reformers' of the high Victorian period rather than with the 'mandarin stereotype' of the modern civil servant.[8] This ambivalence was reflected, moreover, in Beveridge's views of social organization, and throughout his life his conception of welfare was torn between two mutually antagonistic administrative models. On the one hand he was strongly attracted by a pluralistic model of welfare—organized by numerous small societies, which would be subsidized by government but allow a great deal of scope for autonomy, group solidarity and individual choice. And, on the other hand, he was equally attracted by a monolithic model, in which the inefficiency and injustices of pluralism—its duplication of functions, its failure to cope with deprived minorities, its sheltering of vested interests—were cancelled out or superseded by an impersonal, 'im-partial' administrative state. Beveridge himself aspired to achieve a compromise between these two models; and it was largely due to forces outside his control that in the history of British social administration the former model has been eclipsed or has survived only in a residual form.

The fourth and most important theme of this study will be Beveridge's influence on the history of social policy. As with the wider issue of government growth, the development of social policy has been the subject in recent years of widely varying historical interpretations. Innovations in social welfare have been seen by different writers as the

[7] Harold Wilson, *Beveridge Memorial Lecture* (1966), p. 7.

[8] Henry Parris, *Constitutional Bureaucracy: The Development of British Central Administration since the Eighteenth Century* (1969), ch. 5.

product of reforming ideologies, as the result of conflict between competing interest groups, and as part of a process of spontaneous adjustment to the pressures of industrialization. Many attempts have been made to uncover the ways in which social policy is formed, and to weigh the comparative influence of politicians, administrators, specialists, social theorists and private commercial or charitable organizations. Some general hypotheses have been put forward, though none that seems to dispense with the need for further analysis and research. In such a far-reaching area of discussion the biography of a single social reformer is clearly of limited relevance, and it would be absurdly pretentious in a work of this kind to attempt to resolve such basic questions of historical causation. Nevertheless, the life of Beveridge closely relates to such questions at a number of crucial points. Beveridge himself was at various times a social worker, a journalist, a permanent civil servant, an academic theorist and a professional politician. In each of these roles he put forward a wide range of ideas about social welfare and tried to influence the ways in which social policy was made. In the following chapters Beveridge's ideas and practical influence will be analysed in considerable detail and an attempt will be made to assess his work within the wider context of general policy-formation. No general explanation will be offered for how social policies have historically come about, but it is hoped that Beveridge's ideas and work will help to illuminate this wider context and provide relevant material for continuing historical debate.

# I

# A Late Victorian Childhood

## I

THE upper grades of the Indian Civil Service during the late nineteenth century embodied, perhaps more clearly than any domestic institution, the characteristic Victorian ideals of morality, government and social organization. The Benthamite principles of utility, efficiency, impartiality and open competition were incorporated into the Indian Civil Service much earlier and more systematically than in the home departments; and the service attracted into its ranks men who formed a new model army for the Victorian administrative state.[1] Drawn mainly from the ancient universities, many of these officials were administrators and lawyers of remarkable calibre who, within the rather narrow bounds of the British vision of India, devoted themselves to public service of a high order. Inspired in many cases by the twin ethics of utilitarianism and evangelical Christianity, they were deeply committed to bringing justice, rationality and true religion into a dark continent where injustice, unreason and impiety had previously prevailed. This sense of mission was reinforced by extreme geographical and social isolation. In the cities I.C.S. officials mixed to a certain extent with army officers, merchants and educated Indians; but outside Madras and Calcutta the average Anglo-Indian civil servant and his family enjoyed the lonely eminence of a feudal lord.

It was into this hybrid layer of Anglo-Indian society—highly traditional in its functions but reformist and bureaucratic in attitudes and ideals—that William Beveridge was born at Rangpur on 5 March 1879. He was the first son and second child of Henry Beveridge, a district sessions judge in the Bengal section of the Indian Civil Service, and of Henry's second wife Annette. His forbears on either side were modestly middle-class and had been so for four generations—masons, master-printers and publishers on his father's side, farmers and clothiers on his mother's.[2] The Beveridge parents shared many of the social assumptions of their class and generation, but they were in certain respects critical of and out of sympathy with the Anglo-Indian establishment of the day. The history of their marriage has been chronicled in *India Called Them*;

[1] Eric Stokes, *The English Utilitarians in India* (1959), esp. parts III and IV.
[2] *ICT*, pp. 377–8.

but it is worth inquiring in some detail into their ideas and antecedents, since many of their views—and some of the contradictions between their views—were subsequently reflected in the character and philosophy of their son.

Henry Beveridge—shy, gentle, introspective and self-deprecating— was by temperament a scholar and antiquarian rather than a lawyer or public functionary. His judicial pronouncements were studded with references to classical mythology, and he seems to have been less at home in a court-room than in translating Persian and Hindi texts. Beneath a bashful and rather austere manner he concealed a nature that was passionate and idealistic in both private life and public affairs. He had inherited strong anti-imperialistic views from his father, a Scots presby- terian bookseller and publisher who had written a history of India that was highly critical of the British regime.[3] The chronic bankruptcy of his father's business had forced Henry Beveridge to enter the employment of the East India Company when he graduated from Belfast University in 1857; but service with the company, and subsequently with the Indian Civil Service, did nothing to diminish the radicalism of his views. He was strongly opposed to the crude 'Europeanization' of the Macaulay school of Anglo-Indian administrators; and throughout his time in India he took an active interest in preserving and reviving Indian customs, languages and institutions. Shortly after his arrival in Bengal he shed the beliefs of his Presbyterian upbringing and, unlike many of his I.C.S. contemporaries, did not regard evangelical Christianity as a necessary instrument of British rule. He greatly admired the writings of Auguste Comte, although his sceptical mind baulked at the religion of humanity —indeed, he seems to have had an almost physical distaste for all organ- ized religion, whether Christian, positivist, Muslim or Hindu.[4] Through- out his career, he strove to make contact with 'native gentlemen' and to promote multi-racial cultural institutions such as the Asiatic Society of Bengal.[5] He was highly critical of the system of recruitment to the I.C.S. whereby, even under open competition, the service was effectively closed to all but the wealthiest Indians; and he looked forward eagerly to the supersession of British by native administrators and to Indian Home Rule. These views almost certainly damaged his professional career and were eventually responsible for blocking his promotion to the Indian High Court. By comparison his views on English politics were much more conventional, for he was an orthodox Gladstonian Liberal, passion- ately committed to civil freedom but strongly opposed to paternalistic

---

[3] Henry Beveridge, *A Comprehensive History of India* (3 vols., 1858–62).

[4] AHBP, Mss. Eur. C. 176/16, HB to Dr. Congreve, 4 June 1884.

[5] H. Beveridge, *Presidential Address to the Asiatic Society of Bengal* (Baptist Mission Press, Calcutta 1891).

control by the state. Throughout his life he was a cautious and some-what pessimistic utopian idealist. 'That there will some day be a new religion, a new heaven and a new earth, so to speak, is what I hope and expect,' he wrote. 'But I doubt its arrival in this generation. Perhaps my children will see the dawn.'[6]

Annette Beveridge, *née* Ackroyd, whom Henry married in 1875, was a less attractive but at the same time more subtle and complex figure than her earnest, well-meaning, free-thinking husband. Her domestic back-ground was more secure, her expectations more ambitious, her tempera-ment altogether more imperious than those of Henry Beveridge. Bernard Shaw once described her as 'the cleverest woman of my acquaintance and the wickedest in her opinions';[7] and, if certain conjunctions of circumstance had been different—or if Annette's talents and strength of character had been matched by a more realistic sense of judgement—she might well have figured in Victorian history as another Miss Hill or Miss Nightingale, instead of as the wife of a minor Anglo-Indian judge. The daughter of a self-made Worcestershire businessman, Annette had been reared in an atmosphere of Cobdenite politics, Unitarian theology and the 'high-toned teaching' of Harriet Martineau.[8] In the early 1860s she studied with distinction at Bedford College, London, and soon dis-covered within herself an unusual capacity for leadership and organiza-tion. It proved difficult to find a professional opening for her talents, however, and for several years after leaving college she confined herself to voluntary social work—the conventional outlet for over-educated, under-occupied, middle-class women of her generation. She cherished a rather vague ambition to 'be a manufacturer or to marry one who would let me help on the social and all sides of his factory'.[9] Not until after her father's death in 1868 did she think seriously of a full-time career, becoming a lecturer at a London working women's college in 1871.

At this stage Annette's views were every bit as progressive as those of her future husband; and they also took a more proselytizing turn. Miss Ackroyd in her late twenties desired, not merely to 'think rightly', but to be a positive 'influence for good'. She found in teaching grammar to schoolgirls that 'each driest rule became to me instinct with life, because by the true and clear teaching of it I hoped to work a moral good'; and like George Eliot's Dorothea Casaubon she 'longed to widen the skirts of light'.[10] It was this yearning for practical reform that brought her into contact with a group of educated Indians who visited England in the early 1870s under the leadership of the Hindu reformer, Keshub

[6] AHBP, Mss. Eur. C. 176/16, HB to Dr. Congreve, 4 June 1884.
[7] *PI*, p. 110.
[8] *ICT*, pp. 66–9; AHBP, Mss. Eur. C. 176/14, ASB to HB, 12 Sept. 1882.
[9] BP, IIa, ASB to WHB, 1 Jan. 1903.
[10] AHBP, Mss. Eur. C. 176/14, ASB to HB, 12 Sept. 1882.

Chunder Sen. Sen, who preached the abolition of the caste system, the emancipation of Hindu women and the fundamental unity of all religions, appealed for English governesses to go to India to spread liberal education among Indian women, without propagating the doctrines of any particular sect. Annette Ackroyd, looking for a vocation, responded eagerly to this call.[11] She set herself to learn Bengali, and sailed for Calcutta in 1873 convinced, as Henry Beveridge was, of the basic equality of all races, the inherent dignity of many Indian institutions, and the damage done by imperialism to both the subduer and the subdued.

As we have seen, life in India merely tended to confirm Henry in his radical prejudices. But for Annette the next decade was a period of disillusionment with India and its people—a disillusionment brought about at least in part by the almost insuperable nature of the task she had set herself in attempting single-handed to bring education to the women of Bengal. A 'little soft white-skinned wee woman', she rapidly succumbed to the Calcutta climate, and was stricken with a recurrent fever that left her increasingly and incurably deaf. Unsupported by any English institution, she was forced to start by finding premises and raising funds for her venture, and she soon found 'her mission to Indian women becoming a drab affair of spoons and forks and filters, and drunken landlords and absconding servants . . .' More dispiriting than any mere physical difficulty, however, she found the constant quarrels between her Indian patrons, the contempt for the position of women displayed even by educated Indians, and the unresponsiveness of the Indian women whom she was trying to teach. Most shocking of all was her discovery that Keshub Chunder Sen himself kept his womenfolk in subjection and had given his daughter in child marriage. Annette persevered with the founding of her school, which opened with a dozen pupils in November 1873, and she continued to despise the arrogance and ignorance of the Anglo-Indian ascendancy. But in her private spectrum of opinions, distaste for the racial tyranny of the British began to pale beside the sexual tyranny of Indian men.[12] In a reaction that was more emotional than intellectual she came over the next few years to regard Hinduism as 'repulsive, childish and degraded', to denounce male Indians as 'savages' and 'murderers of women and children' and to conclude that 'breed is breed in men and horses . . . The real fact is—the substance of England in India—that race for race superiority is on our side.'[13]

It was with something of a sense of relief that Annette encountered

    [11] *ICT*, pp. 82–9.          [12] *ICT*, pp. 89–92.
    [13] ASBP, Mss. Eur. C. 176/59, ASB's diary, 30 Jan. 1883; C. 176/17, ASB to HB, 22 Sept. 1884.

Henry Beveridge, a member of her school management committee, whom she married in a Calcutta registry office in March 1875. For both of them it was in the first instance a marriage of convenience rather than of passion. It rescued Henry, still mourning the death of a much-loved first wife, from a lonely widowerhood and it rescued Annette from what was proving to be an impossible vocation.[14] Both of them subsequently admitted that it was only after marriage that they came to love each other; and both of them were inclined for many years afterwards to kick against the pricks of their new situation. They were in many ways an ill-matched pair. Annette—gregarious, practical, extravagant, and domineering—was nearly always convinced that she was right; Henry—solitary, frugal and diffident, with an 'immense capacity for self-worry' —was more often than not afraid that he was wrong.[15] Moreover, their views on Indian society tended to diverge rather than converge as the years went by—Henry remaining obstinately loyal to the Bengalis, Annette becoming more and more convinced of the inherent superiority of her own race and class.[16] These differences of opinion in the Beveridge parents were never entirely resolved; and it is clear from their surviving correspondence that their fifty-three year union was often lacking in harmony and sometimes actively unhappy. Nevertheless, in the early years of their marriage, these latent conflicts were submerged by other more immediate interests in their everyday lives. Annette renounced entirely her inclination for good works, and immersed herself in her husband's passion for oriental scholarship, eventually becoming herself an authority in this field. Henry retained what seemed to his wife an unrealistic sense of mission to India; but as their family expanded and as Henry's prospects of promotion faded, the emotional pull of India and the Indians began also to fade. In the mid-1880s it was Henry rather than Annette who first began to think wistfully of retirement to a life of scholarship in Europe;[17] and, at the same time, he became increasingly caught up in her maternal preoccupation with houses, governesses, illnesses and schools.

## II

The young Beveridges, of whom there were four by 1885, were therefore brought up in an intellectual and political atmosphere that was rather unusual for children of the Raj. In spite of this, however, the life of the Beveridges at Rangpur, and at the other stations to which Henry was

[14] *ICT*, ch. 7.
[15] BP, IIa, ASB to WHB, Feb. 1907; HB to WHB, 20 July 1916.
[16] AHBP, Mss. Eur. C. 176/16, HB to ASB, 23 Aug. and 13 Sept. 1884; C. 176/17, ASB to HB, 22 Sept. 1884.
[17] AHBP, Mss. Eur. C. 176/16, HB to ASB, 23 Aug. 1884.

subsequently appointed, was in many ways typical of the experience of the Anglo-Indian establishment of the day. They enjoyed social pre-eminence and an artificially high standard of living, the price for which was the constant threat of discomfort, squalor, disease and death. Rangpur was 'a far off, malarious, lonely station' with a 'very limited society',[18] but even so the territory in which Henry Beveridge dispensed imperial justice covered several thousand square miles. As a relatively minor member of the Indian judiciary his salary was more than twice as high as that of a senior official in the Home Civil Service; and his wife managed their mansion-bungalow with a staff of no less than twenty-six Indian servants, together with a succession of European nannies.[19] As with other British households in India, however, the pattern of their family life was dominated by annual irruptions of heat and monsoon. Rangpur was surrounded by flood-plains and snake-infested swamps, and each summer Annette Beveridge was driven to take refuge with her children in the holiday resorts of the Himalayas or Assam. This annual migration of mother, children and servants—together with cows to ensure a fresh milk supply—involved journeys of almost unimaginable difficulty. In 1879 the railway was just penetrating the plains of Bengal, but the normal methods of transport were still bullock-carts, package steamers and mule-drawn 'palkis'. Consequently, the journeys to and from the mountains might take weeks or even months to plan and exe-cute. The family life of the Beveridges in India was therefore a continual round of preparation and migration, separation and reunion.[20] Out of these recurrent separations came a correspondence between Annette and Henry which formed a day-to-day commentary on the upbringing of the Beveridge children and the development and interplay of their parents' ideas.

The first long separation occurred in 1879, when Annette, still convalescent from childbirth, retreated to Shillong in the hills of Assam with her two-year-old daughter Laetitia and her son William, aged three months. Shortly after her arrival Annette wrote a severely critical account of hill-station society, commenting adversely on the malicious gossip, the squabbles between civil and military and the 'depth of imperialism and caste feeling' which she heard expressed.[21] But she was soon caught up in that 'strong light-brigade of sportive matrons of all ages' enshrined by Kipling in *Plain Tales from the Hills*.[22] She took part in balls, dinner parties, skating and badminton; and two months later she was clearly rather reluctant to leave Shillong for the 'solitude à deux'

[18] BP, IIa, ASB to WHB, 5 Mar. 1912; *ICT*, p. 209.
[19] *ICT*, p. 195.        [20] *ICT*, ch. 9.
[21] AHBP, Mss. Eur. C. 176/11, ASB to HB, 18 and 28 Sept. 1879.
[22] Charles Carrington, *Rudyard Kipling, His Life and Work* (Pelican edn., 1972), p. 100.

of Rangpur. Of her children she reported that Laetitia—Letty—was 'sensitive, loving and humorous', already developing a 'moral sense' but inclined to be jealous of her brother. William had nearly perished through an overdose of brandy and laudanum, administered by a zealous nurse; but at six months old was 'red as a rose' and with an 'ineffable look of being the world's pivot'. He was clearly 'to be the wicked one of the family—he is so strong and full of life'.[23]

In 1880 Henry was transferred to Bankipur in the Patna district of Bengal, where the climate was sufficiently temperate to live all the year round. Here a second daughter, Jeannette or 'Tutu', was born in September 1880. Bankipur was a large station with a cosmopolitan society and, in spite of her growing antipathy towards the Bengalis, Annette here did her best to promote the multi-racial social intercourse cherished by her husband. She took her Hindi-speaking children to Indian open-air theatres, and organized 'international parties' at which special arrangements were made to conform to the customs of Christians, Muslims and Hindus. 'I even feel these people may like one when I see their smiles at my bairns,' she recorded, '. . . I wish they knew how friendly one feels to them and how one joins in their pleasures.'[24]

The next family separation occurred in 1882, when the illness of her younger daughter forced Annette to take refuge in the hill station of Mussourie, leaving Letty and William in their father's care. Henry wrote critically of William that he was 'jolly but somewhat stolid . . . [he] will not be the comet of the season but he will be a pleasant thought and perhaps a shelter in a weary land . . . he will float downstream and perhaps go over the cataracts unless some kind fairy pluck him aside'.[25] Annette replied defensively: 'You do not do my boy justice. He makes no noise but he has no lack of strength of mind.'[26] From this time may be dated William's own first fragile awareness of the outside world of India. In later years he had a vivid though almost certainly imaginary recollection of 'being carried in my bearer's arms to see a tiger looking in through a window in the outer wall of the house'.[27]

In 1883 the whole family sailed to Europe on Henry's first home leave since 1876. They rented a house near Dunfermline, and paid visits to their numerous Beveridge relations and to Annette's elder sister Fanny, who was married to an aspiring Liberal politician, James Mowatt. William at this stage was an earnest and bookish child, at once both chivalrous and pedantic towards his sisters. 'He is slim, compact and

[23] AHBP, Mss. Eur. C. 176/11, ASB to HB, 16 and 18 Sept., 5, 8, 23 and 28 Oct. 1879.
[24] *ICT*, pp. 210–12; AHBP, Mss. Eur. C. 176/12, ASB to HB, 3 Oct. 1881.
[25] *ICT*, p. 219.
[26] AHBP, Mss. Eur. C. 176/14, ASB to HB, 12 Sept. 1882.
[27] BP, IXa 35, 'Anglo-Indian Childhood', typescript by WHB, n.d.

tall—has very fair hair and large loving blue eyes,' wrote his mother, shortly after her son's fifth birthday. '. . . He spends much play-time in writing series of arithmetical and multiplication statements very neatly. . . . One of the distinct traits of Willie's character, is his accuracy of statement. He speaks deliberately and requires it in others. One critical ear is always open for Tutu's correction. He allows no lapses into mistake. . . .'[28]

At the end of the year in Dunfermline Henry returned to Calcutta, while Annette remained behind to settle her children in a school. The establishment chosen was a small Unitarian boarding-school in Southport, owned by a family connection of the Ackroyds, Mrs. Fanny Lewin. The children were to be chaperoned by a German governess, Fraulein Emma Vögel, who taught them to speak fluent German and whom William remembered in later years with great admiration and love. Annette felt herself 'reft in all directions' at leaving her children, and took them first on an educational tour of the museums and galleries of London.[29] They arrived in Southport at the end of September 1884, and Annette recorded hopefully that Letty, William and Tutu rapidly adjusted to the unfamiliar experience of playing with other children. William 'got knocked down but screwed up his face and didn't cry—like the well-plucked boy he is in spite of his sparrow-like appearance'.[30] The ages of the three children when their mother left them were seven, five and four.

A month later Annette sailed to join her husband in his new appointment at Faridpur, where their fourth child, Hermann, was born in October 1885; and there is little record of the experiences of the three elder children for the next two years. When Annette returned to England in 1886, however, she was forced to admit that the boarding-school experiment had not been a success. Mrs. Lewin's school had sadly deteriorated during her absence, and she found three thin, subdued and undernourished children with dangerous coughs. Fraulein Vögel flatly refused to return to Southport, Letty 'cried and seemed to have been rather unhappy', and William 'complained about food' and told his mother 'a story of how he had been so frightened that he had once told a lie'.[31] 'I remember most poignantly of all,' he wrote later of this period, 'my bitter grief when another little boy had a birthday to celebrate on the same day as I had, and I was made, in my mother's absence in India, to go to the other boy's party instead of having one of my own.'[32]

[28] *ICT*, p. 238.
[29] AHBP, Mss. Eur. C. 176/60, ASB's diary, 31 May–5 Aug. 1884.
[30] AHBP, Mss. Eur. C. 176/17, ASB to HB, 28 Sept. 1884.
[31] AHBP, Mss. Eur. C. 176/19, ASB to HB, 5 July 1886; C. 176/62, ASB's diary, 21 April 1886.
[32] BP, IXa 35, 'Anglo-Indian Childhood', typescript by WHB, n.d.

Annette therefore severed her connection with Mrs. Lewin, engaged a private tutor and sent the children to fashionable German gymnasium classes to improve their strength. She recorded with pride that they were academically advanced, particularly William who was already doing mathematics in his head. Annette herself undertook their literary education, introducing them to Lamb, Wordsworth and Cervantes; and the three children 'cried' and 'trembled' together over the sad and improving tale of Lucy Gray.[33]

In the summer they rented a house in Epping Forest, where the two elder children were deeply shocked by their first close contact with the English working class. Letty wept at the sight of the poor, Annette recorded, and William ran about the forest trying unsuccessfully to give help to starving children who wandered there 'bonnetless, shoeless and in a most abject state'. Annette did not encourage these stirrings of social conscience in her offspring. 'Sometimes,' she wrote, 'I feel as though, if I had no other mission, it might not be an unworthy one to potter about in this forest and do trifling acts of kindness to the poor;' but after taking her children on a workman's train she recorded that they had encountered many people 'whose clothes were certainly objectionable . . . it was really not nice . . . I shall not risk it again'.[34] It may seem strange that during an upbringing in Bengal the young Beveridges had never before encountered the existence of poverty; and it is significant that their parents at any rate thought that poverty in England at this time was much worse than in India. 'Poverty in Calcutta bears a much less dread aspect than it does in London or Edinburgh,' recorded Henry. 'There are no gin palaces (their places being apparently supplied by sweet-meat shops) and not so much terrible squalor.'[35]

After some hesitation Annette decided to take her family back to India, and she looked around for a governess who would give 'good elementary education' and 'keep up English ways' but without imparting 'missionary tendencies'.[36] The question of the children's religious education was a further source of contention at this time between Henry and Annette—a difference of opinion which again was never entirely resolved. Beveridge in later life described himself as a person of 'wholly non-religious upbringing' but family records show that this was incorrect.[37] At the time of their marriage, Annette, like Henry, had declared that she professed no religion; but this declaration was not strictly true since, although she shared her husband's dislike of the evangelical character of many Western churches in India, Annette never

---

[33] AHBP, Mss. Eur. C. 176/19, ASB to HB, 28 May 1886.
[34] AHBP, Mss. Eur. C. 176/19, ASB to HB, 11, 18 and 28 July 1886.
[35] *ICT*, p. 114.
[36] AHBP, Mss. Eur. C. 176/19, ASB to HB, 13 June and 18 July 1886.
[37] BP, IIb, WHB to Sir Robert Greig, 2 May 1923.

entirely abandoned some kind of religious faith. 'I do believe in a great unknown which through us makes for righteousness,' she confessed to her husband in 1882. 'I do not care what it is called. I can call it God and I could, if you would let me, teach our children to pray—to lay open their hearts—for moral strength to such a God.'[38] Henry's response to this suggestion was presumably unfavourable, because religious instruction seems to have played little part in their upbringing until they were left at Mrs. Lewin's in 1884. There they were sent to church and taught to pray, and Annette in 1886 was surprised and gratified to discover the extent of their interest in the existence of God. Daily prayers thereafter became a regular part of the Beveridge children's routine; and when they returned to Calcutta Annette sent them to Sunday school and to the Anglican cathedral.[39] Henry protested and suggested that Annette read *Robert Elsmere* as an antidote to religiosity, but Annette as usual had her way, claiming that Letty, William and Tutu loved listening to sermons and reading 'Sunday books'.[40] Thereafter the religious education of the young Beveridges became outwardly indistinguishable from that of many conventionally religious late-Victorian households, although Annette never forgot what she regarded as her duty to teach them about non-Christian and secular points of view. On general moral education her views were a curious mixture of liberality and puritanism. 'We will not let them read evil books or associate with doubtful children,' she insisted; but she thought that 'boys should be told as a matter of fact of their physical appetites so as to divest them of the charm of mystery—certainly they should be told to look forward to happy and early marriage'.[41]

Annette and her three eldest children departed for India—without having found a suitable governess—in the autumn of 1886. They travelled by way of Germany and stayed for a time in Holstein with the widow of a German count who had shared Annette's interest in oriental translation. During their absence Henry had at last despaired of advancement to the High Court, when a much less experienced man was promoted over his head. He had been transferred, however, to an appointment in Calcutta; and on Annette's arrival the whole family settled in a house on the outskirts of the city. This reunion, intended to be permanent, was in fact short-lived, for within a few weeks the youngest child Hermann contracted a paralytic fever that caused severe damage to his brain. Three months later Annette carried off her children

[38] AHBP, Mss. Eur. C. 176/14, ASB to HB, 24 Sept. 1882.

[39] AHBP, Mss. Eur. C. 176/14, ASB to HB, 28 May 1886; C. 176/62, ASB's diary, 26 Nov. 1887.

[40] AHBP, Mss. Eur. C. 176/24, HB to ASB, 24 Aug. 1889; C. 176/23, ASB to HB, 8 May and 1 July 1888.

[41] AHBP, Mss. Eur. C. 176/14, ASB to HB, Sept. 1882.

to Darjeeling in the foothills of the Himalayas, where—except for short visits to their father in the cool season—they lived for the next three years.

In Darjeeling Annette determined that the children should continue to be reared as far as possible in European style. She rented a large house with an 'English garden'; and, after a series of unsatisfactory governesses, the care of the children was resumed by Fraulein Vögel, who sailed to India in the summer of 1888. For Letty, William and Tutu specialist tutors were engaged in mathematics, Latin, music and drawing; and they learned to dance, to ride ponies and to play tennis, badminton and cricket. Darjeeling was a sociable resort, and Annette's diary registered a constant round of balls and receptions for herself, and sports, theatricals and fancy dress parties for the children. She wrote proudly of their scholastic progress, remarking that they excelled more in 'freedom of expression' than in the formalities of spelling and grammar. Of William she recorded that he was very persevering, that he strove again natural timidity and that he flung himself eagerly into all boyish pursuits. At the same time he was 'very tender hearted and of tender conscience'; and he had begged to be punished when discovered doing wrong.[42] His favourite game was editing a toy news-sheet, which displayed a rather macabre preoccupation with illness and death. 'Miss Ruth Christmas living at Fairyland has whooping cough but will probably survive,' he recorded, 'Katy Beauty Christmas is half mad of sorrow for the death of her child. Clarence Beauty Christmas born the 21st of August, very deformed and ill and probably will not live long.'[43]

In spite of the separation from her husband and the backwardness of her youngest child, the three years in Darjeeling were probably Annette's happiest period in India; but, even so, her mind was constantly turning to the time when the whole family could leave India for good. When Henry in 1884 had first proposed an early retirement, Annette had discouraged him, arguing that they had not yet saved enough money to buy a 'gay and pretty home' in England and to pay for the children's education.[44] Four years later, however, it was Annette who was urging retirement, whilst Henry was having second thoughts. '. . . I feel as if it would be ungrateful to leave India as long as she will have me,' he wrote in May 1888. 'When my hour of service is up, I can feel that I go away with a good conscience.'[45] They disagreed also about where they should live on retirement. Henry favoured Edinburgh, close

---

[42] AHBP, Mss. Eur. C. 176/25, ASB to Maggie Beveridge, Oct. 1889.
[43] BP, Ib 1, 'News', n.d. (*c.* 1888–9).
[44] AHBP, Mss. Eur. C. 176/17, ASB to HB, 23 June 1884.
[45] AHBP, Mss. Eur. C. 176/22, HB to ASB, 6 May 1888.

to his friends and relations, or else a continental town like Geneva, within easy reach of many European libraries and centres of learning. But Annette objected that she always felt a stranger in Scotland, and that 'I should not like to go to Geneva as I do not wish to cultivate Bohemianism in the children'.[46] She favoured instead an English provincial town with good schools for both sexes, such as Oxford, Clifton or Bath.

This controversy came to a head in 1889, when William fell ill with a fever that was variously diagnosed as malaria, typhoid and dysentery. Tended by his mother, two physicians and a nursing-sister, the child hovered for fourteen days on the brink of death. A local priest offered baptism—an offer which Annette refused, although she later recorded that her child's ultimate recovery had confirmed 'in a very real sense' the gradual revival of her 'early faith in God'.[47] William lay in bed for over two months, and during that time Annette resolved that never again should a child of hers set foot in the plains of Bengal. She wrote to Henry announcing that she had reached the end of her tether in India and that she was determined to take the children home and to settle permanently in England. Henry in reply was rather reproachful, pointing out that he himself could not leave India for several years and painting a gloomy picture of life in an English provincial town. But Annette was adamant. 'I quite agree with you about my not living in a street,' she replied, 'I have never thought of such a thing, but I must settle near a town which gives all educational advantages. . . . I feel I must live in a beautiful place. An ugly town suburb would be a perpetual sore after this beautiful home.'[48]

Having failed to persuade Henry to accompany her, Annette sailed for England with her children and landed at Plymouth in April 1890. During the next few weeks she made a rapid tour of towns in southern England and eventually settled on Eastbourne—hoping that the bracing climate would be good for her children's health. While the family was moving to Eastbourne, however, a great blow fell. The four-year-old Hermann was stricken with influenza and died after an illness of twenty-four hours. The shock of his death seems to have healed the slight estrangement that had arisen between Annette and Henry, and finally severed Henry's sense of overriding commitment to India. He applied for special leave to join his family and decided that he would definitely retire in 1891 or 1892. Thus ended what Annette once sadly described as 'all these vagrant years'.[49]

[46] AHBP, Mss. Eur. C. 176/17, ASB to HB, 23 June 1884.
[47] AHBP, Mss. Eur. C. 176/25, ASB to HB, 23 Nov. 1889.
[48] AHBP, Mss. Eur. C. 176/25, ASB to HB, 24 Nov. and 9 Dec. 1889; C. 176/24, HB to ASB, 12 and 22 Nov. 1889.
[49] AHBP, Mss. Eur. C. 176/23, ASB to HB, (? 8 July) 1888.

## III

In Eastbourne the Beveridges acquired a lease on a house named Woodholme Croft, and the three surviving children settled down to regular education. On reflection Annette decided that William was not yet ready for the pressures of public school. 'I feel a great desire to give him a leisurely and scholar's education,' she wrote to Henry in defence of this decision. '[I am] most averse from haste and from great competition.' William was therefore sent to a small private school catering for only ten boys; and when this turned out to be an unimaginative cramming establishment, he was transferred as a weekly boarder to Kent House, a preparatory school on Beachy Head. The teaching at Kent House was much more in accord with Annette's ideas of a liberal education, but she continued to be troubled about her son's health, particularly when well-meaning friends 'made insinuations about "overstrain" and hinted that he was less well cared for than his sisters'. 'Will is a little skeleton . . . looking about seventy,' she recorded; and on medical advice she decided to send him to school only in the mornings and to engage a private tutor for evening lessons at home.[50]

William's adjustment to school life seems to have been initially rather painful. Early in 1891 Annette recorded that he was over-burdened with homework and that she had been forced to intervene to protect him from bullies.[51] Two months later, however, he was top of his class and had gathered a circle of Kent House friends—among them Morgan Forster, the future novelist, who at twelve years old was known as 'Saint Forster' for his 'astonishing wickedness' and terrifying practical jokes.[52] At the end of the year William won prizes for 'remarkable progress', and was so attached to school life that he could scarcely wait for the holidays to end. In regular letters to his father he wrote enthusiastically of the new-found pleasures of science and Greek, the joys of playing 'spoof-golf' and 'cock-alorum', and the *uninterpretable, intolerable, inexplicable bore* of learning to dance quadrilles.[53]

In the summer of 1892 he won a scholarship to Charterhouse, where he was to be a pupil for the next five years. In view of Annette's educational ideas, this was in many ways a curious choice, for Charterhouse in the 1890s was almost entirely devoted to worship of athletics. Moreover, in so far as scholarship was encouraged, it was scholarship of the cramming, place-hunting, examination-passing kind of which Annette

[50] AHBP, Mss. Eur. C. 176/27, ASB to HB, 30 June, early Oct., and 10 Dec. 1890.
[51] AHBP, Mss. Eur. C. 176/67, ASB's diary, 29 and 31 Jan. 1891.
[52] BP, IIa, WHB to Laetitia Beveridge, 10 July 1892.
[53] BP, IIa, WHB to HB, 30 Nov. 1890 and 11 Jan. 1891.

so much disapproved. Whereas Annette herself and Fraulein Vögel had encouraged original composition, play-acting, natural history and wide reading in several languages, the education at Charterhouse was primarily designed to produce what William himself described as a 'Latin-verse-grinding-machine'.[54] The curriculum centred almost exclusively on classics and mathematics, to the neglect of 'modern studies' such as history and natural science; and looking back on his public school career in after years, William was highly critical of its intellectual sterility and the lack of encouragement given to creative thought. 'I can't trace anything which I particularly value in myself of mental or moral development to Charterhouse,' he confessed to Annette in 1907. '. . . With the exception of the remote voice of the headmaster, all the voices—masters and all—were rather in a conspiracy to make one think meanly of oneself if one wasn't good at games.'[55] Although his own athletic prowess was mediocre, William himself became partially caught up in the mania for sport, and letters to his family were full of detailed descriptions of games of football, hockey, cricket, tennis and squash. He was desolate when for several terms he was forbidden to play games after straining his heart in a running race; and overjoyed when temporarily promoted to a 'house eleven'.[56] On at least one occasion his lack of sporting ability caused him acute distress and embarrassment. This was in 1895 when his housemaster, Mr. Girdlestone, offered to make him a house monitor, but hinted that he should stand aside in favour of one of the 'muscular babies who are the idols of the great body of Charterhouse'. William took the hint and declined the honour. Several terms later he became captain of his house and head of the school. But the slight secretly rankled within him, and fifty years later his chief recollection of Charterhouse was of having felt inferior and unfit to take responsibility because he was not good at games.[57] This 'sense of inferiority' was reinforced by a certain sense of isolation from other boys. As at other schools, it was the custom for boys to go around in pairs, and 'to walk alone was the mark of the outcaste'. For several terms William found himself without a bosom friend, and he would hide from other boys and creep into chapel late, in order to 'escape the public shame of walking openly alone'. 'One extremely strong boy made my life unpleasant for me by physical bullying and jeering,' he recorded. 'He nicknamed me "May Yohe" after an American beauty of that day, and cheered me on by that name when I was playing football. Years later I met him in London and he asked me to his house to meet his wife. I went prepared to feel very sorry

[54] BP, IIa, WHB to HB, 29 Nov. 1896.
[55] BP, IIa, WHB to ASB, 23 Feb. 1907.
[56] BP, IIa, WHB to ASB, 28 June 1896.
[57] BP, IIa, WHB to ASB, 10 May 1895 and 9 Nov. 1896; Ia 36, WHB's 'Notes on School', n.d.; 'From my Family Album', interview with WHB, *John Bull*, 18 Oct. 1952, p. 26.

for the wife. I found that my bully friend trembled at her nod. I felt
assuaged for my boyish sufferings.'[58]

Nevertheless, it would be wrong to imply that he was uniformly
unhappy at Charterhouse—at least in so far as can be judged from the
letters which he sent to his parents and his sister Jeannette. He eventually made two close friends—Hugh Bell, who was studying to become a
regular army officer, and C. F. Ryder, another 'old boy' from Kent
House. Mr. Girdlestone's house was renowned for its liberal food supplies, its 'Saturday night entertainments', its frequent 'outings' and—
by the standards of the rest of Charterhouse—its relative freedom from
'police supervision'.[59] In spite of the narrow curriculum William enjoyed
his studies and it was at Charterhouse that he first acquired the habits
of hard work, early rising and meticulous accuracy that became almost a
fetish with him in later life. In the fifth form he discovered a passion for
astronomy, and began to study 'higher dynamics' with the aim of
becoming a professional astronomer. With this end in view he spent
much of his spare time reading books on astronomy and recording the
incidence of meteorites and eclipses of the sun and moon. At night he
would lie in bed, awake whilst other boys slept, observing through a
telescope the movement of the stars.[60] In 1896 he was urged by his
masters to sit for Oxford scholarships in both classics and mathematics,
and it was almost certainly his interest in astronomy which made him
decide to aim for the latter. He was awarded a mathematics exhibition
at Balliol in the November of that year; and in the spring of 1897 he also
obtained a 'Founder's Kin Scholarship' from an Ackroyd family trust
established in the eighteenth century by one of the forbears of Annette.[61]

## IV

William left Charterhouse in the summer of 1897, with his character
and interests still largely unformed. Outwardly he was a model schoolboy—cheerful, polite, unquestioningly conforming, and anxious to avoid
giving offence. He was inclined to be censorious and priggish, and yet at
the same time was disarmingly aware of these faults in himself. His upbringing had been in many respects unusually sheltered, even by the
standards of the day, and he appears to have been alarmed and

[58] BP, IXa 37, typescript on 'Charterhouse', by WHB, n.d.
[59] BP, IIa, WHB to ASB, 2 Oct. 1892, 9 Nov. 1896 and 28 June 1897.
[60] BP, IIa, WHB to Jeannette Beveridge, 21 May 1895.
[61] His acquisition of the Ackroyd Scholarship caused a permanent breach between Annette
Beveridge and her sister Fanny Mowatt. It was Fanny who had discovered the existence of the
scholarship and had proved her own descent from the seventeenth-century founder, hoping
thereby to benefit her own children. The scholarship was in fact awarded first to William and
subsequently to the sons of Annette's younger sister, Kate Norton. Fanny never spoke to
either of her sisters again.

disturbed by his occasional encounters with the 'common people'.[62] While
he was in his first year at Charterhouse his elder sister Letty died from
influenza at the age of fifteen; and her death seems to have driven the
depleted Beveridge family even more closely together. William's own
feelings at the time were not recorded but the death of a sister following
so closely on the death of a brother perhaps helps to explain the unusually close relationship which thereafter developed between William
and his younger sister Jeannette. Temperamentally they had little in
common, for Jeannette was as vague and insouciant as William was
practical and precise. But nevertheless from the age of thirteen onwards
he was Jeannette's protector and confidant, and showed an almost
paternal concern for her welfare which lasted for the next sixty years.
Letty's death also helps to account for the increasing possessiveness and
protectiveness of Annette, whose hopes and ambitions now centred
around her two surviving children, and in particular upon her only son.
Both in private and public she proclaimed him the apple of her eye, and
caused him acute embarrassment by 'trumpeting the paragon' to total
strangers.[63]

Early in 1894 the Beveridge parents purchased Pitfold, a modern
country house near Haslemere and within easy reach of Charterhouse
so that William could come home for week-ends. Pitfold was often
referred to by the Beveridges as a 'little' house, but in fact it had seventeen rooms, servants' quarters, stabling for three horses and twelve acres
of land.[64] To run it Mrs. Beveridge employed four living-in servants—a
parlourmaid, housemaid, kitchen maid and cook—together with a
variety of handymen, grooms and gardeners. It was a substantial property, even by the spacious standards of the 1890s, and was a reflection
of the comfortable standard of living to which the Beveridges had
become accustomed during their years abroad. It was an extravagance
which Henry's retirement income could ill afford, and they were to find
some difficulty in meeting the expenses of such an establishment. But
Annette insisted that she must have a house to which her children could
return frequently and invite their friends.[65] Her wish was to be fulfilled,
for it was to be the scene of many social events and week-end houseparties, and her son was to see it as his home for the next twenty years.

[62] BP, IIa, WHB to ASB, 3 Feb. and 29 Aug. 1895.
[63] BP, IIa, WHB to Jeannette Beveridge, 8 Sept. 1897.
[64] Lady Beveridge, *Beveridge and His Plan*, p. 39; *ICT*, p. 350; BP, IIa, Giddy & Giddy's
advertisement for the letting of Pitfold, 1903.
[65] BP, IIa, ASB to WHB, 2 Oct. 1905.

# 2

# Beveridge at Oxford

## I

AFTER the narrow athleticism of Charterhouse and the protective atmosphere of Pitfold, Oxford in the late 1890s appeared to the young William Beveridge like the threshold of a new and rather shocking world. It was in many ways a reversal of all that he had previously known and believed. The average undergraduate seemed irreverent where Beveridge was earnest, idle where he was industrious, endlessly sociable where he was shy and withdrawn. Amongst intellectuals the tone was set by young sophisticates like Raymond Asquith—son of the future Prime Minister—to whom provincialism was the only crime and originality the only god.[1] In Balliol, that celebrated forcing-ground for the nation's future leaders, the Master Edward Caird preached the philosophy of 'practical idealism' to those who cared to hear. But the Idealist school had passed its zenith by the time Beveridge went up to Oxford. The prevailing attitude was one of extreme philosophic dilettantism, peculiarly distasteful to Beveridge's practical and rather literal mind; and he was disturbed by the fact that religion, ethics and philosophy were seen, not as guides to moral action, but as subjects for endless metaphysical debate. 'The whole place abounds with cliques, scandal, envy,' he recorded, 'pervaded by a refining atmosphere of atheism, cynicism, militant agnosticism and affected indifference to all things in heaven and earth.'[2]

Beveridge entered Balliol as a mathematics exhibitioner in the autumn of 1897. His first year at Oxford, he later recalled, was 'the most miserable that I remember'.[3] He was a shy, self-conscious and sensitive youth, young for his age in knowledge of the world and almost morbidly anxious to avoid giving offence. He had still not finished growing and photographs of him with his Balliol counterparts show a slight, gangling figure with a solemn, rather foxy face—a lone schoolboy in a group of young men. His letters to his family at this time were, as always, conscientiously cheerful, but they nevertheless suggest that he was going

[1] Ensor Papers, Raymond Asquith to R. C. K. Ensor, 10 June 1904; BP, IIa, WHB to ASB, 30 May 1898.
[2] BP, IIa, WHB to ASB, 30 May 1898.
[3] BP, IIb, WHB to A. C. Carré, 20 Feb. 1902.

through a period of prolonged nervous agitation, teetering between over-excitement, disillusionment and acute depression. 'I don't think you know me at my worst,' he wrote to his sister in a moment of despair. 'I can be far more despondent than Father without any of his sweetness; and the unfortunate part of it is I see through my own folly the whole time, which only makes me think worse of myself and the whole human race.' And to his father he confessed that he had been 'looking at everything through a pair of spectacles of the most violent blue'.[4]

These feelings of despondency stemmed from a variety of sources. They arose partly from a loss of confidence in his mathematical ability, partly from a recurrence of the strained heart which had troubled him at Charterhouse, and partly from a secret fear that he would never be popular with his Oxford contemporaries. He was slow to make friends, and his social contacts during his first term at university were largely confined to other old Carthusians, lonely foreigners and friends of his parents living in Oxford—though he was understandably horrified when Annette thought of moving the family home to Oxford to promote his social life.[5] Nevertheless, the chief cause of his misery was not so much lack of friends as the tortuous nature of his relationship with the friend whom he preferred above all others, namely Arthur Collings Carré, a Balliol classicist and the 'strangest and rarest creature' in Beveridge's 'new world'.[6]

Beveridge met Carré late in 1897 and fell instantly and painfully under his spell. They had many intellectual interests in common, partnered each other in the Balliol tennis team, spent several vacations together and shared lodgings during their final year as undergraduates in 1900–1. From the start, however, it was a rather stormy relationship, for Carré was Beveridge's opposite in almost every possible way. In taste and temperament Carré was an aesthete and dilettante, with a penchant for Roman Catholicism and a rather sentimental hankering for the 'contemplative life'.[7] Gifted with great personal charm and poetic talent, he was looked upon as something of a 'prophet' by his Balliol circle, and as a connoisseur of manners and literary style. He was at the same time 'flighty', unreliable and totally lacking in sense of purpose or ambition.[8] Chronically depressive, he was by the age of twenty heavily addicted to opium. Blithely iconoclastic, he constantly mocked Beveridge's nebulous and half-formed beliefs in the existence of 'conscience' and 'practical morality', and he was coldly disparaging of those who believed in

[4] BP, IIa, WHB to Jeannette Beveridge, 8 June 1898; WHB to HB, 7 June 1898.
[5] BP, IIa, WHB to ASB, 27 Feb. 1898.
[6] BP, IIb, WHB to A. C. Carré, 21 Feb. 1902.
[7] BP, IIb, A. C. Carré to A. W. Pickard-Cambridge, n.d. (Dec. 1901).
[8] BP, IIa, WHB to ASB, 12 June 1899 and 13 Nov. 1900; WHB to Jeannette Beveridge, 9 Sept. 1901.

'assisting the poor [and] becoming a great light among the unenlight-ened'.[9] At the same time he opened up for Beveridge 'new comprehen-sion and fresh modes of thought', by giving him for perhaps the first time in his life a direct insight into the world of creative imagination.[10] He was casual where Beveridge was formal, averse to concepts whereas Beveridge was always conceptualizing, vague and intuitive where Beveridge was logical and precise.

Beveridge's affection for Carré was undoubtedly the most profound emotional experience of his youth. It was a 'state between love and despairing hate', in which he longed to perform some sacrifice for Carré and was insanely jealous of Carré's other friends. He was thrown into despair by the suspicion that he was not first but a 'poor third' in Carré's regard, and he was tortured by 'the accursed shyness on my part . . . which lay like a mist between us, lifting only at rare and glorious inter-vals'.[11] On several occasions he was reduced to secret tears by some casual sign of affection on the part of his friend. He consciously modelled himself on Carré's tastes, reading books which he thought Carré would have read and aspiring to write poetry because Carré wrote poetry. His poems turned out to be 'rambling' and 'languorous . . . very uncharacter-istic and much more like Carré than me'.[12] 'I think that I had for you,' wrote Beveridge early in 1902, 'what six months ago I would have scouted as impossible in any man—a love that regarded neither what you did nor what you were but simply yourself, and yet was not mere feeling.'[13] Towards the end of their relationship, Beveridge's devotion was increasingly tinged with frustration and despair as he watched help-lessly while his friend slowly poisoned himself with opium; but the strength of his attachment and its rather obsessive character may be measured by the fact that he continued to address long and passionate letters to Carré after the latter's premature death.[14] In after years Beveridge could scarcely bear to speak of Carré and referred to him simply as 'my closest friend of those days'.[15] It is difficult for the bio-grapher to assess the full impact of this relationship upon his sub-sequent development; but Beveridge himself was in no doubt about its influence. To Carré he ascribed the emergence of that part of his character ruled by emotion rather than intellect, by feelings rather than 'formulae'; without having known Carré he believed that he would

[9] BP, IIa, WHB to Jeannette Beveridge, 1 June 1898; IIb, A. C. Carré to W. A. Pickard-Cambridge, Dec. 1901.
[10] BP, IIb, WHB to A. C. Carré, 20 Apr. 1902.
[11] BP, IIa, WHB to Jeannette Beveridge, 16 July and 4 Nov. 1898; IIb, WHB to A. C. Carré, 20 Feb. 1902.
[12] BP, IIa, WHB to ASB, 18 May 1901.
[13] BP, IIb, WHB to A. C. Carré, 21 Feb. 1902.
[14] BP, IIb, WHB to A. C. Carré, 20, 21 and 22 Feb., 9 Mar. and 20 Apr. 1902.
[15] *PI*, pp. 9–10.

almost certainly have been happier, but 'poorer in soul to the end of my time'.[16]

Beveridge was made periodically miserable by Carré throughout his time at Oxford, but the general sense of isolation which he had felt during his first terms at Balliol was partially dispelled during his second year. He became friends with H. W. Garrod, the future poet and classical scholar; with Richard Denman, a young historian with ambitions to enter Liberal politics; and with the violently disputatious B. P. Moore, who loved an intellectual argument as much as Beveridge himself. Through the generous and sociable Denman he was admitted to a wide circle of like-minded acquaintances, among them Jimmy Palmer, the Balliol chaplain, and Augustus Andrewes Uthwatt, the future judge. And in November 1899 he met for the first time and made friends with a Balliol history scholar, R. H. Tawney—a friendship apparently founded on a common devotion to George Eliot and cemented by the discovery that they shared a growing interest in social reform.[17] It was Tawney who invented the nickname 'Drink'—an appellation that stuck to Beveridge for the rest of his time in Oxford.

It was amid this circle of friends that the main developments in Beveridge's character and attitudes at Oxford took place. Under their influence he began to shed at least temporarily some of the puritanical habits acquired at Charterhouse. He abandoned cold baths, philosophized or played billiards far into the night and rose at ten instead of six in the morning. He overspent his comfortable income of £290 a year, and stocked his wardrobe with extravagant neck-ties and dandified clothing. He developed a passion for 'gadgets' of the kind increasingly popular in Edwardian England—self-developing cameras, collapsible umbrellas, automatic coffee-machines and other 'ingenious domestic devices' that were 'an amusement and a terror to his university friends'.[18] With Carré he went to concerts and theatres, heard Paderewski play at Oxford Town Hall, and explored Hardy's Wessex on a bicycle. With Carré and Denman he passed the summer of 1899 on a fishing and reading holiday in Norway, where they attempted to penetrate the 'real truth' of classical civilization. With Denman he visited 'low jingoist music-halls', and with Tawney and Denman he spent July 1901 canoeing dangerously up the Wye valley.[19] Communication with females he found difficult, and dances and other 'social occasions' even more so. 'Harry knew everyone, danced all night, boasted about all his flirtations and girls he rejected but never thought of introducing me to anyone,' he

[16] BP, IIb, WHB to A. C. Carré, 20 Feb. 1902.

[17] BP, IIa, WHB to HB, 3 Jan. 1903.

[18] *Bristol Times*, 4 May 1921 (press-cutting in BP, XII, 5).

[19] BP, IIa, WHB to ASB, 5 Sept. 1901 and 1–3 July 1902; IIb, A. C. Carré to WHB, n.d. (1899); R. Denman to W. A. Pickard-Cambridge, 24 Apr. 1900.

recorded sadly, during a visit to some sociable Edinburgh cousins. 'Harry expressing condescending surprise that I danced five times with the poker-like Mary, who seems when dancing to possess such a super-fluity of knees, or the elderly Miss Mott who was always having to sit down, is not a subject that I can at present contemplate with philosophic equanimity.'[20] In 1899, however, when Jeannette Beveridge went up to Somerville, his social life markedly improved and he found himself increasingly in demand as a spare escort and doubles partner. In June 1899 he even took his sister to a Balliol commemoration ball—carefully and rather incongruously chaperoned by an ever-protective Annette.

It was during this period that Beveridge first became aware of the unimaginative narrowness of his public school education, and of how little he had read by comparison with most of his friends.[21] He began to study non-classical literature, and devoured the works of nineteenth-century English poets and novelists, and of continental authors like Goethe, Schiller, Zola, Ibsen and Maeterlinck. His literary judgements were often highly revealing. He liked works which were either socially informative or morally uplifting, and had little sympathy with the con-temporary vogue of 'art for art's sake'. Hence he dismissed Byron and Hardy as 'disgustingly coarse', but solemnly approved of Tennyson's *Princess*.[22] Above all he admired George Eliot, in whose novels he per-ceived certain philosophic principles which he sought to make his own; namely, an understanding of and commitment to science, an intellectual desire for progress tempered by an emotional feeling for history, and a belief in the 'absolutely serious and relentlessly moral' nature of every-day life.[23]

## II

Apart from the development of personal friendships, Beveridge took little part in the non-academic side of Oxford life. He never spoke at the Union—preferring the informality of small college-based societies like the Arnold and the Fodringaye, which met in Balliol to discuss political and literary topics. Even more he preferred the intimacy of a small group of friends; and it was in this context, rather than in the wider context of Oxford, that he began to formulate opinions on religion and morality, politics and society and on his own future career.

The attitude to religion which Beveridge adopted in early manhood

[20] BP, IIa, WHB to Jeannette Beveridge, 15 Jan. 1899.

[21] BP, IXa 35, 'Autobiography', pp. 1–3. This unpublished work was written by WHB in 1912. References cited are to the typescript copy.

[22] BP, IIa, WHB to ASB, 15 May 1898; WHB to HB, 7 Nov. 1898.

[23] BP, IXb 1, 'The George Eliot Aspect of the Absolute', paper by WHB to the Fodringaye Society, 1900–1.

seems to have remained more or less unaltered for the rest of his life.
'Though Christian dogma has never meant much to me,' he recalled
fifty years later, 'the personality and spirit of Christ have meant much.'[24]
As we have seen his early religious upbringing had been a curious mixture of agnosticism and orthodoxy—a compromise between the rather
confused religious convictions of Henry and Annette. For most of his
time at Charterhouse he had thought little about religion, except that
he had conceived a mild distaste for the lengthier parts of the Anglican
liturgy and a violent dislike of the Salvation Army and other extreme
evangelical sects.[25] In his last year at school, however, he had come
across Arthur Winnington-Ingram's *Work in Great Cities: Six Lectures on
Pastoral Theology*—a book which was to have notable repercussions on
his subsequent outlook on the world. Written by a parish priest in the
East End of London, *Work in Great Cities* was significant not only as
Beveridge's introduction to modern theology but as his introduction to a
work of social science. Winnington-Ingram described, not merely the
spiritual desolation of the East End, but its 'vast population', its poverty,
its 'sickness and great distress' and 'the tremendous pressure under
which many of the people work, in order to keep their heads above
water'. He emphasized the need for clergymen and for Christians
generally to involve themselves in social reform, to understand without
condemning the traditions of working-class life, and to learn 'the necessity of governing by influence, not authority'.[26] Beveridge was deeply
impressed, not so much by Ingram's theological arguments as by his
analysis of social problems and by his description of the 'practical and
social duties' of a clergyman. 'I liked it very much,' he wrote to his
mother, '. . . it seemed to be a thoroughly earnest book.'[27] The emphasis
on 'influence' rather than 'authority' ground itself very deeply into his
consciousness; and it is significant that when writing his memoirs fifty
years later Beveridge saw this emphasis as the unifying theme of his own
career.[28]

The transition from conventionally Anglican Charterhouse to the
theological hothouse of Oxford forced Beveridge to examine more
seriously the claims of religion. In Oxford, remarked his friend Tawney,
'beneath the sun of philosophy the wax of settled conviction flows hither
and thither'.[29] Beveridge was deeply shocked by the 'atheism and pro-
fanity' of many Oxford undergraduates; and he was conscience-stricken
during his first term at Balliol by a sermon given by Canon Gore,

[24] BP, IXb 63, 'This I Believe', transcript of a B.B.C. broadcast by WHB, 2 Oct. 1953.
[25] BP, IIa, WHB to Jeannette Beveridge, 12 Mar. 1895 and 1 July 1897.
[26] Arthur Winnington-Ingram, *Work in Great Cities, Six Lectures on Pastoral Theology* (1895),
pp. 49–50.
[27] BP, IIa, WHB to ASB, 13 June 1897.          [28] *PI*, p. 3.
[29] BP, IIb, R. H. Tawney to A. W. Pickard-Cambridge, 30 July 1906.

denouncing the 'hypocrisy with which people made themselves appear less serious about religion' than they actually were. 'My inherited fondness for the weaker side often almost makes me wish I was a Christian, for one could certainly have work here to do in plenty,' he wrote to his father.[30] At the same time, however, he was increasingly sceptical of theological inquiry, impatient with the failure of modern churchmen to distinguish clearly between history and mythology, and repelled by the claim of orthodox Christianity to be the sole repository of religious truth. He was horrified by reading a best-selling evangelical work, *Master Christian*—'an astounding mire of howling dullness'—whose popularity made him fear that the 'under-educated middle classes of England' wanted a religious revival of the most fanatical kind.[31] Equally he was unimpressed by Oxford Christians, whose 'ways are mostly the ways of tract-giving, of bible-reading and of adorning their walls with texts'.[32] His own inclination was for a religion that would combine scientific credibility with a philosophy of good works; and in pursuit of such a creed he attended meetings of the 'philosophically religious' Martineau Club, and studied the works of the German radical theologian Harnack, of Christian Socialists like Gore and Scott Holland, and of scientific theorists like Darwin, Huxley and Alfred Russel Wallace. At the suggestion of Edward Caird he began work on an 'independent study of Christianity', and in March 1902 he recorded that he was 'studying the New Testament with great perseverance and an entirely open door'.[33]

The conclusions that Beveridge drew from these inquiries were outlined in a series of letters to his family between 1898 and 1903. In thought and feeling his position was very close to the 'positive agnosticism' of Thomas Huxley—the modern thinker whom he was coming to admire above all others.[34] He accepted in entirety the Darwinian analysis of evolution, with the sole reservation that he preferred Russel Wallace's doctrine of a separate evolution for the 'higher parts of the mind'. The God of the Old Testament he dismissed as tribal and barbaric, no more worthy of worship than the gods of the Norse sagas. The doctrines of the trinity and eucharist he believed were arbitrary, allegorical and totally irrelevant to 'practical religion'.[35] He was infuriated by the tendency of broad churchmen like his friend William Temple to assume that 'every good man is necessarily and unconsciously a Christian'; and he accepted Harnack's attack on formal church organization

[30] BP, IIa, WHB to ASB, 15 Nov. 1897; WHB to HB, 7 June 1898.
[31] BP, IIb, WHB to W. A. Pickard-Cambridge, 11 Apr. 1901.
[32] BP, IIa, WHB to ASB, 30 May 1898.
[33] BP, IIa, WHB to ASB, 29 Nov. 1898 and 9 Sept. 1901; IXb 63, 'This I Believe', by WHB, 2 Oct. 1953; IIb, WHB to W. A. Pickard-Cambridge, 9 Mar. 1902.
[34] BP, IIa, WHB to ASB, 19 Jan. 1902.
[35] BP, IIa, WHB to Jeannette Beveridge, 14 Mar. 1898.

as 'most interesting and reasonable'.[36] He thought that 'most of our thought and activities are beyond the range of Christianity', and that 'the other-worldliness and simplicity of Christianity make it a standing paradox as the religion of the bustling west'.[37] At the same time, however, he 'came to feel' that Jesus Christ 'was one of the greatest personalities in human history—with a greatness the more impressive because it had to be seen through the eyes of very ordinary men'; and he rejected the certainties of dogmatic atheism as 'untenable' and 'absurd'.[38] He was greatly influenced by the writings of Samuel Butler, and in the fly-leaf of his copy of *The Way of all Flesh* he inscribed Butler's prayer to 'cleanse him not from secret sin but from faults which others could see and criticise'. He was strongly attracted by Butler's notion of 'vicarious immortality'—of immortality not through personal survival but 'as the prophetic consciousness in supreme moments of one's continuing activity through one's surviving works'.[39] 'In conclusion I will just give the main heads of my beliefs,' he wrote to his sister at the end of a long letter on metaphysical questions in 1898.

(1) I believe in a God; but I do not believe he troubles himself in the least as to the action of nature's laws, etc., merely confining himself to supporting and influencing the minds of men. (2) I believe that the mind of man has a separate creation. (3) I do not believe in the God of any particular religion for my God is just and fair. As a consequence I do not say that any particular belief is worse than mine; I merely say it cannot be the whole truth in that it tries to cut out the rest of the world. (4) I believe in the immortality of some part of us but I believe neither in Heaven which would be insipid nor in Hell which would be ridiculous. . . . Personally I see no more reason for troubling about the beginning of the world than I do about the end; I look back to eternity in the past as I look forward to eternity in the future. I believe that there is something, a spirit of some sort, which has existed always and will exist always and that is practically all one can say.[40]

Beveridge's political views when he entered Balliol were even more indefinite than his views on religion. As we have seen, the Beveridge parents had disagreed strongly about Indian politics and society; and the antinomy between their attitudes—between humanitarian and authoritarian liberalism—was to be clearly reflected in their son's subsequent career. Both Henry and Annette Beveridge, however, were much less involved in English politics than they had been in the politics of India. Annette, like many members of the English upper classes,

[36] BP, IIa, WHB to Jeannette Beveridge, 15 June 1903; WHB to ASB, 9 Sept. 1901.
[37] BP, IIa, WHB to HB, 19 Nov. 1904.
[38] BP, IXb 63, 'This I Believe', by WHB, 2 Oct. 1953; IIa, WHB to Jeannette Beveridge, 6 July 1898.
[39] BP, IIa, WHB to HB, 19 Nov. 1904; E. M. Forster to WHB, 13 Mar. 1908.
[40] BP, IIa, WHB to Jeannette Beveridge, 16 Mar. 1898.

ceased to regard herself as a Liberal soon after Gladstone's first Home Rule bill, whereas Henry continued to give at least token support to the Liberals until 1924. But discussion of party politics, and of English politics generally, had little place in the Beveridge home; and when Beveridge went up to Oxford in 1897 he was almost entirely ignorant and uncommitted on every major political question of the day.

Beveridge's understanding of party politics, as I shall show in later chapters, was never very acute, and his awakening to political consciousness was slow. His first expressions of political opinion were the conventional responses of an upper-middle-class child of his time. He defended the British annexation of Egypt, supported a 'forward policy' in India and 'believed that the state of human nature as exhibited in the British workman' was an 'insurmountable obstacle' to the extension of democracy, 'at least at the present time'.[41] During the South African war he was strongly opposed to the Liberal pro-Boers, of whom there was a large contingent in Balliol headed by Edward Caird. He followed with a certain amount of hero-worship the military exploits of his fellow Old Carthusian, Lord Baden-Powell; and in common with many of his contemporaries, he 'mafficked' through the streets of Oxford after the relief of Ladysmith and Mafeking in the spring of 1900.[42]

Nevertheless, Beveridge was not really interested in 'high politics'; and about political leaders and their machinations he wrote that 'I care little and know less'.[43] Nor was he interested in 'party politics', regarding the two main parties in English political life with equal disfavour. 'Perhaps by the time it matters to you and me there will be a more respectable party to belong to,' he wrote to Jeannette.[44] His chief political interest, from the time when he first went up to Oxford, lay not in foreign and imperial affairs, but in the study of the 'big modern social questions of the day' and in the field of social policy.[45] He was increasingly critical of the traditional curriculum of Oxford education, and greatly impressed by a lecture given by Bernard Shaw advocating technological universities open to all classes in the community.[46] He strongly supported the campaign of Liberal radicals for the taxation of urban site values, and was very critical of the Liberal ex-Premier, Lord Rosebery, for rejecting such a policy as impractical. 'He may be right,' wrote Beveridge to Annette, 'but the one justification for a statesman is that he should be able to deal with practical difficulties.'[47] In January 1901 he was contemptuous of Rosebery's famous Chesterfield speech, regarding

[41] BP, IIa, WHB to ASB, 2 Nov. 1897, 4 Mar. and 21 Nov. 1898.
[42] BP, IIa, WHB to ASB, 22 Feb., 24 Mar. and 20 May 1900.
[43] BP, IIa, WHB to ASB, 29 Jan. 1901.
[44] BP, IIa, WHB to Jeannette Beveridge, 3 Mar. 1902.
[45] BP, IIa, WHB to ASB, 19 Jan. 1902.  [46] BP, IIa, WHB to ASB, 8 Feb. 1900.
[47] BP, IIa, WHB to ASB, 14 Mar. 1902.

its call for 'national efficiency', as 'utterly vague and indefinite'.[48] On
the other hand he warmly approved a speech at the Oxford Union by
the Reverend G. S. Horton, arguing that social reform was an urgent
'imperial necessity'.[49] This was a central theme of much political debate
in the post-Boer War period, but it seemed to Beveridge that a major
stumbling block to such reform was lack of precise sociological information. After attending a debate on social reform and democracy he came
away 'clamouring for statistics'; and early in 1902 he and Tawney
resolved to remedy this lack of information by founding a society.

Its object is to be the writing of papers on social questions from a matter of
fact and as far as possible practical point of view [recorded Beveridge].
Theories are to be eschewed as far as possible while facts (in theory at least)
are to abound in the society. It has only two members at present but hopes to
expand; the only way to learn about things is to write about them.[50]

This society does not seem to have been very active—in fact its only
recorded meeting was to hear Tawney read a paper on the 'Taxation of
Site Values' in June 1902.[51] But it was indicative of Beveridge's growing
interest in the interrelation between social research and social reform.
This interest was closely bound up with a general re-orientation of his
intellectual interests and with the gradual evolution of his choice of a
future career.

### III

Beveridge's first academic leanings had been not to mathematics but to
natural science—expecially to physiology in which he had been passionately interested since the age of thirteen. This interest was intensified by
his growing admiration for the philosophy of Thomas Huxley; and in
particular he was impressed by Huxley's contention that the inductive
method peculiar to biological sciences could ultimately be applied to all
areas of human knowledge. 'I think Huxley is the modern whom I am
most inclined to make my hero,' he wrote in 1902.[52] At one time he
considered studying medicine, in the hope of becoming 'a great surgeon';
and much of his spare time at school and university was taken up in
reading popular scientific works.[53] He was, however, turned away from
the study of physiology by a peculiarity of his own temperament: he
found that, although he was passionately curious about biological

---

[48] BP, IIa, WHB to ASB, 29 Jan. 1902.        [49] BP, IIa, WHB to ASB, 24 Feb. 1902.
[50] BP, IIa, WHB to ASB, 24 Feb. 1902; AHBP, Mss. Eur. 176/193, R. H. Tawney to R.
Denman, n.d.
[51] BP, IIa, WHB to ASB, 8 June 1902.
[52] BP, IIa, WHB to ASB, 19 Jan. 1902; WHB to HB, 2 Feb. 1902.
[53] BP, IIa, WHB to ASB, 27 Jan. 1899; WHB to Jeannette Beveridge, 3 Dec. 1896.

theories, he was constitutionally incapable of stomaching certain kinds of biological fact. On at least three occasions in his youth he actually fainted when confronted with some distasteful physiological detail— once when visiting a sick friend in Germany, once when told that his pet dog must be destroyed, and once when he heard that his mother was losing the sight of an eye.[54] And, although for many years he continued to hanker after the possibility of biological research, he gradually became reconciled to the fact that he was himself 'physically incapable' of pursuing such research in any practical way.[55]

Beveridge's next scientific enthusiasm was for astronomy, and it was partly with the hope of becoming an astronomer that he went up to Oxford to study mathematics. He was soon conscious, however, of a growing dissatisfaction with the study of mathematics—a dissatisfaction which appears to have stemmed from a number of causes. The mathematical teaching in Balliol at the time was singularly uninspired— consisting largely of copying out the tutor's lecture notes—and Beveridge soon felt that mathematicians were very much cut off from the mainstream of Oxford's intellectual life.[56] Secondly, he suffered from a certain 'loss of nerve' after failure to convert his exhibition to a scholarship in a Balliol mathematics examination in November 1897; and he gradually came to the conclusion that he would never make a first-rate speculative mathematician.[57] Thirdly, he began to read Homer and Virgil for pleasure with Carré and, fired by Carré's infectious imagination, he discovered for the first time a 'real delight' in the study of the classics.[58] And, finally, he decided that mathematics was irrelevant to the study of real life. In spite of getting a 'first' in mathematical moderations he therefore transferred to the Oxford classics school in 1898, where he studied under A. L. Smith, A. W. Pickard-Cambridge and Edward Caird. The 'Greats' course, which included logic and modern philosophy as well as classical studies, he found much less difficult than mathematics and 'quite as interesting as reading novels and trash and much more improving'.[59] It also left him time to pursue his old interests in biology and astronomy and his new interests in modern literature and works on social reform.

Nevertheless, the study of classics at Oxford, although the gateway to many different kinds of occupation, was not in itself a choice of profession; and for the next four years Beveridge was rather self-consciously searching for a vocation. Edward Caird advised him to concentrate on

[54] BP, IIa, WHB to ASB, 14 Oct. 1901 and 11 Jan. 1909.
[55] BP, IIa, WHB to Jeannette Tawney, 16 Aug. 1912.
[56] BP, IIa, WHB to Jeannette Beveridge, 31 Oct. 1897; WHB to ASB, 30 May 1898.
[57] BP, IIa, WHB to ASB, 24 Apr. 1898.
[58] BP, IIa, WHB to Jeannette Beveridge, 22 Feb. and 8 June 1898.
[59] BP, IIa, WHB to Jeannette Beveridge, Feb. 1898.

acquiring a general philosophical education, without concerning himself too much about his future career;[60] but although Beveridge followed
the first half of this advice he was unable to accept the second. He was
suspicious of minds which were 'too broad and philosophic . . . to do
anything effectual'; and although he enjoyed philosophy he was irritated, as with mathematics, by its divorce from 'practical life'.[61] He
remarked of himself that, 'I should be much happier if I knew that
what I was doing would be directly useful.'[62] This search for a practical
vocation gradually brought to light certain hitherto unsuspected facets
of his character—a consciousness of power in himself to do something
important, a stubborn preference for his own judgement over that of
other people, and a growing conviction that obsessive single-mindedness
was an essential prerequisite of constructive social reform. 'Putting
aside the word fanatic, as liable to misinterpretation,' he wrote to his
sister in July 1898.

'I really do think that no man can do really progressive work who has not one
idea carried to excess. It must be rather excessive to counter-balance the
conservative forces of society which tend to retard the carrying out of the idea.
The man must have one great ideal to aim at, to a certain extent excluding all
else, and his convictions must be very strong.'[63]

As Beveridge himself recognized, however, he was 'slow of invention
and in getting convictions',[64] and for some time he was clearly torn
between several competing interests and ambitions. 'I don't know
whether to try to learn astronomy or get some understanding of social
questions, or merely to go in for "general culture",' he confessed to
Annette towards the end of his second year in Oxford, just after he had
been awarded a first in classical moderations.[65] The attractions of astronomy faded as he became increasingly dubious of its status as a science;
but it is clear that he was still considering the possibility of a scientific
career for some time after he had given up the formal study of mathematics.[66] An obvious alternative to science for someone of Beveridge's
educational background was the Civil Service; and his tutor, A. W.
Russell, told him that his methodical habits and well-ordered mind were
ideally suited to a career in public administration.[67] But Beveridge himself was doubtful, fearing that life as a career civil servant would be
neither interesting nor remunerative nor intellectually challenging. In
this he was supported by his mother, who drew a dismal picture of 'the

[60] BP, IIa, ASB to HB, 19 May 1899.
[61] BP, IIa, WHB to ASB, 20 June 1898; WHB to Jeannette Beveridge, 7 Feb. 1899.
[62] BP, IIa, WHB to ASB, 13 Feb. 1898.
[63] BP, IIa, WHB to Jeannette Beveridge, 6 July 1898.
[64] BP, IIa, WHB to ASB, 25 Jan. 1903.         [65] BP, IIa, WHB to ASB, 7 Mar. 1899.
[66] BP, IIa, WHB to ASB, 28 Apr. 1899.
[67] BP, IIa, WHB to ASB, 26 Jan. 1898.

long hours of desk-work—with so little holiday—and a prospect of being
a poor man for life'. She suggested instead that he might go into business,
with the long-term aim of a public career modelled on that of Joseph
Chamberlain.[68] Beveridge in reply was unenthusiastic. He was convinced that an Oxford education was a singularly bad preparation for a
business career and 'highly deleterious of business capacity . . . which
last I am sure I never possessed or possess!'[69]

The alternative to science which Beveridge found increasingly attractive was not business or public administration but involvement in social
reform. While still at school his attention had been drawn to the social
problems of great cities; and in his second term at Balliol he spoke of his
desire to do some 'practical social work'—a desire reinforced by his
interest in the study of social questions and his friendship with Tawney.[70]
In October 1899 he went to a recruitment meeting conducted by representatives of Toynbee Hall, the university settlement in Whitechapel;
and he was impressed by what he heard of the non-sectarian character
of the settlement and its efforts to bring 'education and civilisation' to
East London. He recorded rather diffidently that 'I should like to do
something for them but I seem incapable of teaching anything that is
wanted except perhaps swimming'. In the following winter he paid a
vacation visit to Toynbee Hall—a visit which seems to have met with
some opposition from Annette, perhaps with an anxious premonition of
the way in which her son's career was tending. At Toynbee Beveridge
spent two days being whisked around 'like an American tourist doing
Whitechapel', accompanying a caseworker on family calls, and visiting
a boys' club, a school board, and the local Charity Organisation Society.
In June 1900 he helped to entertain a party of working-men on a visit
from Toynbee, taking them on a tour of the Oxford colleges, punting
on the Cherwell and ending with 'a solid meat tea in my rooms'.[71]

Nevertheless professional openings in social work were at the time
few and far between, and although Beveridge was fascinated by social
problems he was for a long time by no means clear how, if at all, he
could devote himself to their solution. He obtained a first in Greats in
the summer of 1901—his third first in four years—and in the autumn
he returned to Oxford to study law, still undecided whether to enter the
Civil Service, to try for a 'prize fellowship' or to read for the bar. With a
view to becoming a barrister he set about mastering the art of public
speaking, by reading papers to the Arnold Society and taking part in
college debates. He found the law much less 'crabby and cranky' than

[68] BP, IIa, WHB to ASB, 26 Jan. 1898; ASB to WHB, 20 Oct. 1900.
[69] BP, IIa, WHB to ASB, 23 Oct. 1900.
[70] BP, IIa, WHB to ASB, 13 Feb. 1898 and 24 Feb. 1902.
[71] BP, IIa, WHB to ASB, 29 Oct. 1899, 10 and 16 Jan. and 5 June 1900.

he had expected, and he won the favourable notice of Alfred Dicey, the Vinerian professor of law.[72] Nevertheless, he soon began to find the law just as unsatisfying as he had found philosophy and mathematics, and in particular he was troubled by the vast chasm between theoretical jurisprudence and the practical working of the law.[73] He found, moreover, that the university itself was no longer the exciting place that it had once been. Of his close friends only Tawney remained at Balliol, and the centre of his social life had shifted to London, where Denman and Carré had set up home in the Temple—Carré to write poetry, Denman to work as an insurance broker at Lloyds.

Beveridge's doubts about his future were revealed in a letter to his mother in January 1902, in which he tried to explain why he could not devote himself to the life of scholarship which seemed the ultimate satisfaction to Henry and herself. 'I have always seen two possible ways before me,' he wrote, 'one that of scholarship with the certainty of making some progress . . . the other the chance of doing something immediately for this age.'[74] In February he received two severe emotional blows. His friend Carré was 'led into disaster by reading and following De Quincey', and Richard Denman, returning one evening to their flat in the Temple, found him unconscious from an overdose of laudanum. He died soon afterwards. Carré had been for some time 'in a great state of mental distress' and at the inquest a verdict was returned of suicide during temporary insanity. Beveridge was distraught with grief—a grief made worse by the rather heartless censure passed on Carré by Annette.[75] The second shock came three days after Carré's death, when the Balliol law tutor, Edward Jenks, indicated that he did not consider Beveridge suitable for life as a practising barrister—owing to a 'certain excitability which seems to have lurked in me unawares for many years'.[76] Coming at such a moment, Jenks's warning had the effect of increasing rather than allaying this element of excitability, and for several months afterwards Beveridge was simultaneously haunted by doubts about his future and by disturbing memories of his dead friend. He took refuge in hard work and in mournful lyric poetry. 'I feel rather insane and I don't mind who knows it,' he wrote to Jeannette in March 1902.[77]

From this time onwards Beveridge seems to have lost any personal desire for a career at the bar; but he was dutifully aware that Henry

[72] BP, IIa, WHB to ASB, 30 Aug. and 22 Oct. 1901.
[73] BP, IIa, WHB to HB, 30 Aug. 1901 and 25 Jan. 1902.
[74] BP, IIa, WHB to ASB, 19 Jan. 1902.
[75] Turin Papers, WHB to Lucia Turin, 14 Mar. 1943; BP, IIa, WHB to ASB, early Mar. 1902.
[76] BP, IIa, WHB to ASB, 24 Feb. 1902.
[77] BP, IIa, WHB to Jeannette Beveridge, 3 Mar. 1902.

Beveridge had set his heart on seeing his son become a judge or jurist, and he therefore resolved at least to be called to the bar and to obtain his degree in law. In May 1902 he rejected Jenks's suggestion that he should become a legal antiquarian; and in July he turned down the offer of a position at Toynbee Hall—although the fact that he did not tell his parents of this proposal suggests that he found it attractive.[78] Instead he arranged to study in the chambers of H. W. Loehnis, a leading London barrister and expert on marine insurance. At the same time he gave up living in Oxford, and moved to London to take Carré's place in Denman's flat in the Temple. In the autumn of 1902 he sat for several prize fellowship examinations and was awarded the Stowell Civil Law Fellowship at University College—a non-resident seven-year fellowship which would enable him to live and work in London while drawing a stipend of £200 a year.

London opened up to Beveridge new opportunities for finding out about social questions. His friend Tawney, who graduated in the summer of 1902, became a caseworker with the Children's Country Holiday Fund, and Beveridge accompanied him on some of his visits to parents whose children were being sent to the country. With Denman and other Balliol contemporaries he helped to run a boys' club in the Elephant and Castle. He was invited to give classes at a working-men's college; and he became a founder-shareholder in the Garden City Company, set up to implement the social philosophy of Ebenezer Howard.[79] At the same time three months in chambers confirmed his distaste for legal practice, and in January 1903 he informed his parents that he had definitely decided not to practise at the bar. His reasons for this were emphatic. He perceived the work of a barrister as 'solitary', 'self-centred' and intellectually trivial: 'It has nothing to do with any real problems and difficulties and does not go about slaying any dragons.' It offered a prospect of twenty years of overwork and penury, with the ultimate possibility of becoming a politician or a judge. For neither of these prizes did Beveridge think the effort worthwhile. 'The successful barrister who goes into politics,' he wrote, 'must really be a tool in the hands of others; he cannot of his own knowledge form his own opinions because he has never had time to acquire that knowledge.' And the work of a judge he dismissed as a glorified game of chess.

In view of these objections, Beveridge argued that it would 'be the wildest conceivable paradox for me to become a barrister'. About alternatives to the law he was not yet certain. He still intended to be called to the bar, in order to comply with the conditions of his fellowship; but after that he was hoping to find work in central or local government,

[78] BP, IIa, WHB to ASB, 21 May 1902; IIb, W. H. Forbes to WHB, 23 July 1902.
[79] BP, IIa, WHB to ASB, 10 July 1902; WHB to HB, 9 Sept. and 16 Oct. 1902, 3 Jan. 1903

possibly as a local organizer for the Board of Education. About one thing, however, he was now quite clear:

I think I may take it that the one thing in which I am interested wholly and completely is the getting to know something about human society and working at some part of its machinery. (I avoid 'social problems' because it always suggests 'slumming' and drink and I mean something wider—simply the question of under what conditions it is possible and worthwhile for men as a whole to live) . . .[80]

At the time when this letter was written the Beveridge parents were in Florence, where Jeannette was recovering from a major operation. Their reactions were in many ways characteristic. Annette was initially sympathetic. She agreed that her son had in no way committed himself to a life-long career at the bar; and, with typical lack of insight, she urged him to make a commercial fortune in South Africa instead.[81] Henry, bitterly disappointed, wrote to Beveridge accusing him of 'hereditary instability of purpose' and suggesting that he was quite unsuited to the strain and financial insecurity of 'organization, municipal socialism . . . politics or a heated civic life'. He sympathized with his dislike of legal practice, but urged him instead to become an academic lawyer: 'Stick to the shady bypaths of the Law, there are such bypaths as well as the dusty highroad, and you will do well.'[82]

Beveridge in reply was reasonable but resolute. He admitted that he was unsuitable for professional politics; but 'neither an education inspector nor a county council organizer nor a municipal official nor a paid official at an East End settlement (which I mention merely as instances) are "politicians", just as they all get more pay than the student of law'.

Furthermore, he firmly rejected the idea of a career in academic law.

My interest in law is neither historic nor scientific—I care for it first and foremost as an instrument of practical justice and to know it in that light far more knowledge of what is outside law books is wanted than what is in them. . . . I have the conviction that in times such as these it is necessary for every man who possibly can to be out in the storm to some extent. The times seem stagnant; people seem to sit waiting to see in what direction things will move and therefore now above all there seems need of an effort to make them move in a direction dictated by reason rather than by the line of least resistance. The last is the inevitable tendency under the guidance of the rich who pursue politics but have been too busy becoming rich to have political ideas. My one

[80] BP, IIa, WHB to ASB, 25 Jan. 1903.
[81] BP, IIa, ASB to WHB, 28 Jan. and 2 Feb. 1903.
[82] BP, IIa, HB to WHB, 29 Jan. 1903.

desire is to experience the actual working of the πόλις in the hope of finding such an idea.[83]

For a time the family argument simmered. Beveridge was working hard for the Vinerian law scholarship and had little time to write to his parents about his plans. Annette wrote to reproach him for neglecting them, and in particular with being callous about his sister's illness—a letter which so distressed him that it effectively sabotaged his work for the Vinerian exam.[84] Henry wrote offering to pay for lessons in elocution —an offer which Beveridge rejected as a sign that his father had not really accepted his decision to abandon the bar.[85] Early in April he reported that he had discussed the possibility of employment with the Board of Education and with the head of a suburban teachers' training college—in both cases with negative results.[86] Then on 18 April he disclosed that he had had an interview with Canon Barnett, the warden of the Toynbee Hall settlement, who was looking for a sub-warden and had invited him to apply for the post. In describing the attractions of this position Beveridge was at pains to play down its 'social work' elements; he would have little to do with the trivial routine of running clubs and classes, the results of which he thought were not worth the labour involved. Instead he hoped to acquire 'immediately practical experience in management, organisation, talking to and talking over people and the chance of really learning what I want to know about— the state of other kinds of people from my own kind'.

In addition he pointed out that he would receive a salary of £200 a year—considerably more than the average newcomer to the bar—and come into contact with many influential people and opinions.[87] Nevertheless, his parents were resolutely unimpressed and resorted to extreme emotional blackmail to persuade him to change his mind—hinting strongly that Annette's health and Jeannette's convalescence were being undermined by his obstinacy and lack of filial feeling.[88] Annette, completely reversing her previous position, declared that having accepted financial support from Balliol, the Ackroyd trustees, the Stowell fellowship and herself, he was morally bound to continue with the bar.[89] Henry wrote scathingly of 'horny-handed mechanics', 'soup-kitchens for the proletariat' and 'trying to be genial to people with whom you have little in common'. He maintained that 'any plan is a good one as long

[83] BP, IIa, WHB to HB, 3 Feb. 1903.
[84] BP, IIa, ASB to WHB, 27 Feb. and 6 Mar. 1903.
[85] BP, IIa, HB to WHB, 21 Feb. 1903.
[86] BP, IIa, WHB to Jeannette Beveridge, 8 Apr. 1903.
[87] BP, IIa, WHB to ASB, 18 Apr. 1903.
[88] BP, IIa, ASB to WHB, 16 Feb. 1903; HB to WHB, 21 Apr. 1903.
[89] BP, IIa, ASB to WHB, 21 Apr. 1903.

as you stick to it', and urged his son to follow in the footsteps of Jeremy Bentham by devoting himself to reform of the law.[90]

Beveridge needed all his not inconsiderable reserves of willpower to resist this onslaught from those on whose judgement he had always previously relied. After 'three days of much mental perturbation', and long discussion with Denman, Tawney, Palmer and a new friend Robert Ensor, he resolved to 'present Florence with an accomplished fact'.[91] At a further interview with Barnett on 27 April he agreed to accept the subwardenship if it were offered him—an offer subject to confirmation by the Council of Toynbee Hall. Justifying this decision to his parents, Beveridge adopted three lines of self-defence. Firstly, he denied that he was either financially or morally committed to the law. If he had unwittingly taken money under false pretences then he would certainly refund it; but he hoped that he would 'never grow old enough to consider "any plan will do if you stick to it" as anything but pernicious doctrine when applied to plans of life'. Secondly, he rejected the model of Bentham, arguing that the work of the exclusively legal innovator was now almost complete and that the modern need was for social rather than legal reform.

It is the adaptation of law to a new order of society and is a matter neither for Jeremy Bentham nor the Law Lords—but for a combination of political philosopher, economist and (moderately learned) lawyer. . . . I shall be in a better position to have an opinion on this form of legal question by living the practical rather than the legal life.

Thirdly, he argued that his parents had utterly misinterpreted the functions of a sub-warden of Toynbee Hall. These functions were not to waste his energies on magic-lantern lectures and social evenings, but to organize adult education, to supervise the work of other residents, to involve himself in local government and generally to influence public opinion and to formulate policies on social affairs. 'I have a vision,' he wrote to his father, 'of Toynbee speaking one day with a voice of thunder and I have a vision of myself (if I prove capable of it) among others directing that voice's utterance.'[92]

Beveridge's appointment to Toynbee was confirmed in May 1903. In June he took his B.C.L. examination and was placed in the second class. In going to Toynbee he was particularly anxious to avoid 'all appearance of "self-sacrifice" and "renunciation" and other such gear'; and he successfully persuaded University College that he should keep his Stowell fellowship for the full period of seven years.[93] His parents

[90] BP, IIa, HB to WHB, 21 and 24 Apr. 1903.
[91] BP, IIa, WHB to ASB, 28 Apr. 1903; Ic 1, WHB's diary, 25 Apr. 1903.
[92] BP, IIa, WHB to ASB, 24 Apr. 1903; WHB to HB, 28 Apr. 1903.
[93] BP, IIa, WHB to ASB, 15 May 1903; WHB to Jeannette Beveridge, 15 June 1903.

were still opposed to his decision, but they were partially reconciled by the intervention of Sir William Markby, an old family friend and fellow of All Souls, who was Treasurer of Toynbee Hall's Oxford committee. Markby assured Annette that Beveridge would be working on 'the best philanthropic work which has ever been done in London' and that it was 'most important that these posts should be filled by the best men'. Moreover, her son was 'not an ordinary man, either in ability or character. Besides his university distinction he has won the friendship of some of the very best men of his time. . . .'[94]

## IV

Beveridge's decision to go into social work was not unique, but it was sufficiently unusual in the context of its time to require some further consideration. In his autobiography Beveridge ascribed his interest in social reform to the influence of Edward Caird and to Caird's injunction to the young men of Balliol 'to go and discover why, with so much wealth in Britain, there continues to be so much poverty and how poverty can be cured'.[95] This is an attractive and simple explanation but it contains at least an element of pious exaggeration. It was not Caird but E. J. Palmer, the Balliol chaplain, who recommended Beveridge to Samuel Barnett.[96] Beveridge's interest in social questions antedated his connection with Caird, and his relationship with the Master though cordial was never very intimate. In his last year of classics he was tutored by Caird in Greek philosophy, but Caird was a notoriously uncommunicative tutor; he merely 'smiled all the time', remarked Beveridge, 'till I really thought he would petrify into a smile for the rest of his life'.[97] Moreover, Beveridge was in many ways out of sympathy with some of Caird's most basic ideas. As we have seen, he disagreed with Caird politically and was critical of his ideal of a general, philosophical, non-vocational education. Although he greatly admired Caird's essays and addresses—regarding the latter as one of the great events of life in Balliol—their tortuous Hegelianism was fundamentally alien to his own rather literal mind. He regarded Caird's quest for moral absolutes, and his pre-occupation with paradoxes like 'unconscious consciousness', as unnecessary and mildly absurd. 'The fact is that one can in various ways swallow one's difficulties and get on without any Philosophy in the Master's sense,' he observed to Annette; and certainly it could never be said of Beveridge that 'his intellect worked like a

[94] BP, IIb, Sir William Markby to ASB, 12 May 1903; ASB to WHB, 13 May 1903.
[95] *PI*, p. 9.
[96] BP, IIb, Sir William Markby to ASB, 12 May 1903.
[97] BP, IIa, WHB to ASB, 23 Oct. 1900.

conscience', as was said of Caird.[98] All this is not to deny that Caird exercised an important formative influence on Beveridge's life. His example undoubtedly reinforced Beveridge's youthful belief in 'earnestness' and 'social morality' against the Oxford fashion of the day. Almost certainly it was from Caird, and from the philosophical tradition of which Caird was an exponent, that Beveridge derived his conception of society as an 'organism', which was to be an important feature of his ideas on social reform.[99] And Caird's concern for poverty and connections with the settlement movement helped to give a practical focus to Beveridge's awakening interest in problems of social structure. But Caird's influence does not account for the peculiarly inductive approach which Beveridge sought to bring to bear on social questions. Nor does it explain why at the age of twenty-three he experienced a passionate desire to devote his whole life to the understanding of social questions and the promotion of social reform.

For a fuller explanation we must therefore look elsewhere—to Beveridge's own personality and to other intellectual influences. Firstly, for all his rational and rather matter-of-fact exterior, Beveridge was throughout his life a profoundly emotional man, who was happiest when devoting himself to a person or a cause. Early in his undergraduate career he had spoken of his need to attach himself to some overriding ideal, but for most of his time at Oxford his deepest and most idealistic feelings had been engaged by his friendship for Carré. The death of Carré in February 1902 left an emotional vacuum in his life which at the time no other human being was able to fill; and into this vacuum flowed his new-found commitment to social investigation and social reform.

Secondly, it must be remembered that from a very early age he had been a natural scientist *manqué*. The lack of science teaching at Charterhouse and his own squeamish nature had shifted him away from science to mathematics and classics; but he still felt himself to be a scientist, and certainly he had many of the qualities which are necessary if not sufficient for scientific research—methodical habits, patience with repetitive detail, meticulous accuracy and ability to handle quantitive data. As we have seen, he greatly admired the work of Thomas Huxley, and it was the writings of Huxley that first introduced him to the idea of a 'science of Society or Sociology' and suggested to him how his education in the humanities might be turned to scientific account.[100] On more

---

[98] BP, IIa, WHB to ASB, 27 Jan. and 3 Feb. 1901; H. Jones & J. H. Muirhead, *The Life and Philosophy of Edward Caird* (Glasgow 1921), p. 143.

[99] Edward Caird, 'The Problem of Philosophy at the Present Time', *Essays in Literature & Philosophy*, vol. I (1881), p. 204. For Beveridge's comments on this essay, see BP, IIa, WHB to ASB, 27 Jan. 1901.

[100] T. H. Huxley, 'On the Educational Value of the Natural History Sciences', *Lay Sermons,*

than one occasion Beveridge specifically contrasted the minute empirical inquiries conducted by Huxley with the vast metaphysical speculations of Caird—very much to the latter's disadvantage. He greatly admired Huxley's capacity to mediate scientific ideas to a popular audience and to 'express the new discoveries in a clear and forcible manner'.[101] And certainly it was the spirit of Huxley rather than Caird which rang through his impassioned defence of his decision to study social problems and to go to Toynbee Hall:

I wish to go there because I view these problems in a scientific way—as hindrances to the future prosperity of the state. I utterly distrust the saving power of culture and missions and isolated good feelings as a surgeon distrusts 'Christian Science'. If I had been brought up in science you could not call me a sentimentalist for devoting myself to the investigation of a destructive disease, or unambitious because I thought I should rather pursue that investigation in all the time at my disposal instead of in half-hours spared from doctoring. Will you not believe that the parallel holds? My motive is that which I have stated to you—to study certain branches of the state as a scientist studies his subject matter . . . please do try to think of me in the light of that parallel to the scientist. It is absolutely true.[102]

[101] BP, IIa, WHB to ASB, 27 Jan. 1901; WHB to HB, 2 Feb. 1902.
[102] BP, IIa, WHB to ASB, 11 May 1903.

---

*Addresses and Reviews* (4th edn., 1872), p. 88. On the subsequent influence of this essay on Beveridge's ideas, see below, Ch. 12.

# 3

## Toynbee Hall

### I

THE Universities' Settlement in East London had been founded at Toynbee Hall by a group of dons and clergymen in 1884. Located at 28 Commercial Street, Whitechapel, Toynbee Hall in the 1880s was centrally poised between two worlds. The immediate neighbourhood of Whitechapel was a wilderness of crowded tenements, common lodging-houses, crumbling warehouses and workshops for sweated labour. Its crime rate and infant mortality rate were the highest in London. A third of its labour force was casually employed, and over 40 per cent of its population lived below Charles Booth's definition of subsistence level. Yet a mile to the north of Whitechapel lay the prosperous new suburbs of Hackney and Islington; fifteen minutes' walk to the west brought one to the greatest financial centre in the world; and along its southern boundaries flowed the commercial history of the nineteenth century.[1]

It was to bridge the gulf between these two worlds that the founders of Toynbee Hall first thought of establishing a settlement, as a place where professional men could live among the poor—not as missionaries but as neighbours and friends. The underlying philosophy of the settlement was derived from various sources—from Octavia Hill's desire to 'elevate' the lives of the poor, from Matthew Arnold's belief in the civilizing power of 'culture', from T. H. Green's doctrine of 'personal service' and from the Christian socialist emphasis on 'social reconciliation'. Its practical objectives were originally threefold; to spread education and culture, to discover facts about social problems, and to enable middle-class people to establish personal relationships with members of the working class.[2]

In pursuit of these aims, young men from many different professions—civil servants, lawyers, doctors, and clergymen—were attracted to Toynbee Hall; and in the 1890s many other settlements were founded on the Toynbee model in London, the provinces and the United States. There was no formal requirement that Toynbee residents should engage in

---

[1] *Toynbee Hall, Twenty-First Annual Report* (1904–5), pp. 11–18. The best account of the early history of Toynbee is E. K. Abel, 'Canon Barnett and the First Thirty Years of Toynbee Hall' (unpublished London Ph.D. thesis 1969).

[2] Abel, op. cit., pp. 95–105.

social work, but new recruits tended to be selected with reference to their enthusiasm for social service. As a result Toynbee Hall in the 1890s became a centre for experiments in education, philanthropy and social investigation. Toynbee residents organized local clubs and societies, conferences on social problems, University Extension lectures and many other forms of recreation and education. They served on local school boards, vestries and boards of guardians, and helped to promote local trade union organization. They gave free legal advice, pressed for the improvement of local amenities, and conducted pioneering surveys of homelessness and unemployment. In spite of all these activities, however, Toynbee in the 1880s and 1890s was in many ways a conservative, even reactionary institution, implicitly committed to the superiority of upper-class values, and at the same time looking back wistfully to the social harmony of a pre-industrial age. The very buildings of Toynbee were an architectural embodiment of this outlook, for the settlement was designed as a 'manorial residence' in a 'nineteenth-century Elizabethan' style more commonly found in North Oxford than East London.[3] With its gatehouse and courtyard and mullioned windows, its great common-room stuccoed with the armorial bearings of its academic patrons, Toynbee Hall was a direct reflection of the paternalistic vision of its founders; and the warden's lodgings and residents' quarters—each with his own private bathroom—were deliberately designed to simulate the conditions of Oxford college life.

Toynbee Hall was therefore a rather unlikely centre for radical reform. But by the early 1900s its character and philosophy had been subtly modified by changes in the outlook of its warden and chief founder, Canon Samuel Barnett. Canon Barnett was a devout, self-effacing, deceptively mild-mannered little man, who believed that social progress must be founded in a 'sense of sin'.[4] He was married to Henrietta Barnett, a strong-willed, practical, rather overbearing woman, who had been one of Octavia Hill's lady visitors and who subsequently founded Hampstead Garden Suburb. According to Beatrice Webb, Barnett was intellectually undistinguished, a poor preacher, weak in his grasp of theoretical principles and often hopelessly confused in practical affairs.[5] Throughout his life he clung to the belief that 'character' was the clue to social distress and the key to social reform.[6] Yet, as contemporaries noted with some perplexity, he inspired a whole generation of reformers who rejected personal explanations of social problems; and he seemed to be at the centre of every movement for

[3] J. A. R. Pimlott, *Toynbee Hall: Fifty Years of Social Progress, 1884–1934* (1935), p. 37.
[4] B. Webb, *My Apprenticeship* (1946 edn.), p. 155.
[5] Ibid., pp. 180–1.
[6] *Toynbee Hall, Nineteenth Annual Report* (1902–3), p. 14.

institutional reform. The secret of Barnett's influence is difficult to recapture, but it seems to have rested on three main grounds. Firstly, he had a quality of personal saintliness which impressed itself profoundly on people of widely differing views. Secondly, he combined deep convictions with an unusual facility for changing his mind; indeed, in his inconsistency lay much of his strength for, caught in the cross-current of competing social policies, he found no difficulty in holding and acting upon mutually incompatible points of view. And, thirdly, he had a talent for capturing the confidence of great men. Many of his Toynbee protégés—such as Alfred Milner, Robert Morant, Arthur Salter and Beveridge himself—subsequently advanced to very influential positions; and throughout his time at Toynbee Barnett was regularly consulted by Conservative and Liberal leaders about conditions in East London and social questions of the day.

Barnett had originally gone to Whitechapel as vicar of St. Jude's in 1869. He was first drawn to social work by the influence of Octavia Hill; and his thinking always bore the stamp of her highly personal approach to social problems. As a local guardian he had been instrumental in getting rid of outdoor pauperism in Whitechapel, and in imposing upon applicants for poor relief the strict character investigation advocated by the Charity Organisation Society. The settlement at Toynbee Hall was very much Barnett's own individual creation, and its paternalistic philosophy and emphasis on personal relationships were a clear reflection of his own early views on reform. By 1900, however, Barnett's views on social questions had perceptibly evolved. Twenty years of residence in Whitechapel had convinced him of the economic as well as personal causes of social distress—a conviction reinforced by Charles Booth's revelation that the chief cause of poverty in London was low or irregular wages.[7] By the turn of the century Barnett had dramatically broken with the Charity Organisation Society over its obsession with inquiry into 'character' and its indifference to economic facts. While retaining a fairly orthodox attitude to the Poor Law, he had come to the conclusion that there should be other forms of state provision for the destitute, such as pensions for the elderly and training schemes for the unemployed.[8]

Barnett was, moreover, increasingly dissatisfied with the role of Toynbee Hall. By 1900 the first flush of enthusiasm for 'slumming' had subsided, and it was becoming difficult to attract suitable settlers to the East End. Those who came tended to be more sceptical and scientific than their predecessors, and to look with suspicion on anything savouring of sentimentalism and self-sacrifice.[9] Whitechapel too was changing.

---

[7] Charles Booth, *Life and Labour of the People in London*, vol. I (1902–3), pp. 146–9.
[8] B. Webb, pp. 178–80.
[9] *Toynbee Hall, Nineteenth Annual Report* (1902–3), p. 8.

The extension of the underground railway to Stepney had helped at least superficially to reduce the physical segregation of East and West. 'Rookeries' were giving way to model dwellings and the casual labourer was under increasing pressure, on the one hand from a higher grade of workmen and on the other from Russian and Polish immigrants who looked for assistance to the Jewish Board of Guardians rather than to Toynbee Hall. In Toynbee itself there were signs that the clubs and classes were becoming 'cliquish', that they were failing to attract new members, and that their educational function had declined.[10] This loss of a sense of purpose was reinforced by the knowledge that other and more important social movements were abroad. A Labour Representation Committee, to promote the election of independent working-class M.P.s, had been founded by the labour movement in 1900. During the Boer War a group of progressive Liberals—many of them closely connected with settlement work—had published a bitter indictment of *laissez-faire* capitalism, and called for a new approach to social reform that would recognize the fundamental interdependence of the problems of unemployment, bad housing, squalid cities, deserted villages and enormous inequalities of income and wealth. Official inquiries into 'physical deterioration' after the Boer War convinced reformers of all parties of the causal link between poverty and malnutrition, and at the same time the Conservative demand for a tax on imported food forced the 'condition of the people' question once again to the forefront of public affairs.[11] Faced with movements such as these, an institution such as Toynbee, with its emphasis on personal rather than collective action, began to look suspiciously irrelevant. Barnett from about 1900 onwards seems to have been aware of this danger, and he became increasingly interested in political aspects of social reform and in 'putting forward the rights of labour as against those of property'.[12] At the same time, however, he was convinced that a new role could be found for Toynbee which would be of some significance in a rapidly changing world. 'The war has encouraged a spirit of impatience and of masterfulness in all classes of society,' he wrote in 1903;

. . . a critical spirit has put to the test many theories and institutions and found them wanting. There is much zeal but no sense of direction; the world does not know where it is going. The moment seems one of crisis. Old things are passing away; there is a sound in the air as if a better time was coming, but as yet its character is hidden . . .[13]

[10] Abel, op. cit., pp. 120–2.

[11] C. F. G. Masterman *et al.*, *The Heart of the Empire* (1901); Bentley B. Gilbert, 'Health and Politics: the British Physical Deterioration Report of 1904', *Bulletin of the History of Medicine* (1965), pp. 143–53; Barnett Papers, F/BAR/302, S. Barnett to F. Barnett, 12 June 1903.

[12] Barnett Papers, F/BAR/286, S. Barnett to F. Barnett, 28 Feb. 1903.

[13] *Toynbee Hall, Nineteenth Annual Report* (1902–3), p. 8.

It was the duty of Toynbee, Barnett believed, to capture and interpret this new spirit and to give a lead in the direction of social reform.

## II

It was in order to discover and implement this new role for Toynbee that Barnett invited Beveridge to become sub-warden in the spring of 1903. Now aged twenty-four, Beveridge was in many ways a very different person from the shy and self-effacing youth who had gone to Balliol five years before. Inwardly he was still troubled—as he was to be periodically throughout his life—by feelings of self-doubt; but outwardly he was confident, even conceited, about his own abilities, convinced that he was on the track of a new approach to social problems and increasingly impatient of those who stood in his way. Barnett, in looking for an assistant to take some of the burdens of Toynbee off his shoulders, had been hoping for a man 'who thinks with his heart';[14] and for some time he was uneasy about whether Beveridge was really the right man for the job: 'We have been weighing a man as sub-warden,' he recorded.

He is very able—a whale for work—with definite views of filling up his life in social service, but not very patient with his tools, not a lover of the man in the fool—I hardly know what to say—he might draw together a more intellectual set, but what about dear boys such as Douglas . . .[15]

The 'dear boys', as Barnett called them, were those residents engaged in the traditional functions of Toynbee such as the running of classes and clubs. There is, however, little evidence to suggest that they resented Beveridge's presence at the settlement; and, although there was much disagreement about tactics, there seems to have been little resistance at Toynbee to the development of a more impersonal approach to social reform.[16] Beveridge went into residence in September 1903. He was allocated a room on the ground floor so as to be 'in the middle of things',[17] and he was soon directing the educational activities of Toynbee, presiding at conferences, addressing recruitment meetings in Oxford and Cambridge and taking a large share in the settlement's administration. He took over the editorship of the *Toynbee Record*; and with Barnett's approval he resolved to purge the journal of its 'parish magazine' approach and to develop it into a forum for discussion of social reform.[18] In the winter of 1903–4 the Barnetts spent four months

[14] *Toynbee Record*, May 1902, p. 107.
[15] Barnett Papers, F/BAR/298, S. Barnett to F. Barnett, 9 May 1903.
[16] Though conflict was to occur on this issue at Toynbee in later years: Abel, op. cit., pp. 196–9.
[17] BP, IIb, S. Barnett to WHB, 29 Aug. 1903.
[18] BP, IIa, WHB to ASB, 22 Sept. 1903.

in Italy, leaving Beveridge at Toynbee in charge. Between Barnett and Beveridge a close sympathy developed—a sympathy quickened by each one's awareness that the other's qualities were very different from his own. The Canon came to care very deeply for Beveridge, 'expecting of him great things'. Beveridge in turn much admired Barnett's 'everlasting youthfulness and infinite sanity', his talent for political manipulation and his openness to new ideas.[19]

Nevertheless, although there was much sympathy between them, it was soon clear that they had very different views of Beveridge's role at Toynbee Hall. Barnett was anxious for Beveridge to 'develop a policy' and for Toynbee to acquire a character that was 'scientific' as well as humane. But he believed that this could best be done by attracting dedicated men to Toynbee, by 'uniting people in one another's service' and by promoting the interests of 'the House'. 'It is the instrument—the House itself—rather than the things it has done for us, for which I care,' he wrote to Beveridge in March 1904. 'Are you men at the centre conscious of a policy? Do you see more clearly what there is to be done? . . . If Toynbee is known to be strenuous it will surely lead . . .'[20]

Beveridge on the other hand felt unable to gather round himself the group of dedicated reformers envisaged by Barnett. As he recorded many years later:

> I have never found it easy to ask anyone—man or woman—to do things, even things that they desired to do. I was not, I think, a sufficiently good mixer of others to do for the House what the Canon desired.[21]

He found it difficult, moreover, to share Barnett's vision of Toynbee as not merely a means to an end but an end in itself. As we have seen he was sceptical of the immediate value of many Toynbee activities, and this attitude was strengthened rather than otherwise by his experience in the East End. His family, although acquiescing in his new appointment, continued to be highly critical of settlement ideals. Jeannette found Toynbee 'rather appalling', and Annette after a visit to Whitechapel cryptically remarked that 'people gathered together to do good are not clothed'.[22] Beveridge as a consequence was rather exaggeratedly anxious to dissociate himself from the 'social work' aspects of Toynbee life. 'I don't think social work activities worth much study in themselves,' he commented, 'but useful first and foremost as themselves means of knowledge.' After a lecture on 'social service' he recorded contemptuously

[19] Henrietta Barnett, *Canon Barnett, His Life Work and Friends*, vol. II (1918), p. 245; BP, IIa, WHB to ASB, 20 Apr. 1904.
[20] BP, IIa, WHB to HB, 28 Apr. 1903; IIb, S. Barnett to WHB, 28 Apr., 13 and 26 May 1903, 30 Jan. and 19 Mar. 1904.
[21] *PI*, p. 37.
[22] BP, IIa, Jeanette Beveridge to ASB, 23 Jan. (?1904); ASB to WHB, 18 Dec. 1903.

that 'it seemed to typify all that is worst in philanthropic social
reformers. It was all about doing things for other people and other
people's children.'[23] With Harry Tawney he joined a local working-
men's club, but he formed no close relationship with any local working-
man. On one occasion he recorded a long and interesting conversation
with an old sailor, but he was shocked and acutely embarrassed when
the sailor asked him for a threepenny loan.[24] He never became an official
of any of the numerous Toynbee-based clubs and societies, and regarded
their existence as a source of weakness rather than of strength—as things
which stamped Toynbee with the hallmark of charity rather than of
social change. To his friend Ensor he confided that Toynbee Hall
'simply isn't an address that one can give to one's fellowmen—it stigma-
tises one definitely as a gentleman come to do good, and the fact that
one does good only to oneself doesn't remove the stigma . . .'[25]

Beveridge's own view of Toynbee was in many ways an extension of
Caird's view of Balliol; it was a place of education which existed primarily for the benefit of the inmates—a place which shattered their
preconceptions of society and produced 'a sort of general culture in
political and social views'.[26] In a recruiting address to the Cambridge
Nonconformist Union he described Toynbee as 'an extraordinarily
interesting place with plenty of chances for the purely selfish (as I fear I
told them all reasonable men must be)'.[27] His own position at Toynbee
he interpreted in three ways. Firstly, as an opportunity for scientific
analysis of social problems and for treating them as 'business problems
concerning the welfare of the state'. Secondly, as a position from which
to 'develop authoritative opinion on problems of city life'. And, thirdly,
as a means of advancing his own self-education and of extending his
knowledge of men and public affairs.[28] In pursuit of these aims Beveridge held himself aloof from much of the daily round at Toynbee.
Occasionally he took part in a debate, or worked the magic lantern for
someone else's lecture; but his main interests lay in work which brought
him into contact with local politics and administration and with the
wider social questions of the day. In particular, he became actively
involved in four main aspects of local affairs—in juvenile and adult
education, in canvassing for local elections, in the Stepney Council of
Public Welfare, and in provision of relief for the East End unemployed.
The last of these—his involvement in the Mansion House Relief Scheme
of 1903 and the London Unemployed Fund of 1904–5—will be discussed in a later chapter, since they carried Beveridge far beyond settle-

[23] BP, IIa, WHB to ASB, 10 July 1904 and 1 Oct. 1905.
[24] BP, IIa, WHB to HB, 10 Feb. 1905.
[25] Ensor Papers, WHB to R. C. K. Ensor, 14 July 1904.
[26] BP, IIa, WHB to ASB, 28 Nov. 1904.            [27] BP, IIa, WHB to ASB, 28 Feb. 1904.
[28] BP, IIa, WHB to HB, 28 Apr. 1903; WHB to ASB, 11 May 1903.

ment work in East London; but the other three will be considered in some detail, since they demonstrate very clearly Beveridge's own conception of the nature and purpose of his work at Toynbee Hall.

## III

Barnett was urging Beveridge to involve himself in local educational plans even before he went into residence—hoping that out of such activities would come the 'nucleus of a body of men who will build up your work in East London'.[29] As we have seen, one of the main original purposes of Toynbee Hall had been to promote adult education; and public lectures and University Extension classes had been given at Toynbee since 1885. In the early days they had attracted star speakers like Leslie Stephen and Frederick Harrison but by the early 1900s both the quality and popularity of these lectures were in decline.[30] The Canon was anxious to revive the lectures and had a vision of establishing a working-class 'College of Humanities' in the East End. Beveridge was at first enthusiastic. He allowed himself to be co-opted on to the Toynbee Hall Education Committee, and became Censor of Studies at Balliol House—one of two halls of residence for part-time students attached to Toynbee Hall. He volunteered to give a course of lectures on Wordsworth and to tutor students in advanced Greek. But he soon became rather sceptical of Barnett's educational dreams. He found that no money was available for an education programme of any kind; and he was 'flabbergasted' by the ambitious and unrealistic plans being considered by the Education Committee—plans which were 'appallingly learned and literary' and 'about two and a half miles above the head of any possible audience'. He discovered also that, although Balliol House had originally been founded for working-class students, 'the artisan is conspicuous by his absence and the men are most superior and educated people—second-class Home Civilians, electrical engineers, elementary or secondary schoolmasters, etc.—all of whom one addresses as Esq!'[31]

It was soon obvious to Beveridge, and to other young residents like Tawney and H. R. Maynard, that Toynbee Hall was utterly failing to make any significant educational impact on the Whitechapel working class. It was easier, however, to diagnose this fault than to prescribe a remedy, and in the summer of 1904 Beveridge tried to sound out the views of London trade unionists and local working-men. On 14 July he recorded that he had been discussing working-class education with Isaac Mitchell and other labour members of the L.C.C.:

---

[29] BP, IIb, S. Barnett to WHB, 29 Aug. 1903.     [30] Abel, op. cit., pp. 204–14.
[31] BP, IIa, WHB to Jeannette Beveridge, 8 Sept. 1903; Ensor Papers, WHB to R. C. K. Ensor, 14 July 1904.

Mitchell made the following practical suggestion: many of the trade union branches devote a part of their regular meetings to having an informal lecture plus discussion of half or three quarters of an hour; they cannot always get lecturers—they do not want academic people and they are sick of socialists who in reply to any practical question 'always fly to the referendum'. Accordingly if we can suggest to him any people who can be trusted to be neither professional nor frothy, Isaac Mitchell offers to introduce them to these branch meetings to lecture and discuss. The subjects should naturally be something modern—social, industrial, historical . . .

As a result of this discussion a new type of lecture course was introduced into Toynbee in the autumn of 1904. Beveridge, Maynard and Tawney gave a series of lectures on modern industrial and social history, deliberately designed to attract the politically conscious but not very literate working-man. In the following year Beveridge lectured on 'Labour and the Law' and Tawney on 'Social Aspects of Industry', and they both contributed to courses on 'The Governors of England' and 'Crime and Punishment'. Moreover, in October 1904 a Toynbee Hall Enquirers' Club was founded, for reading and discussion about social problems and visits to agencies of social reform. It was hoped that the Club 'may go beyond mere self-education, may develop practically or may conduct original research'; and by the end of 1905 the Club under Beveridge's guidance had carried out pioneering surveys on 'Children in Industry' and 'The Homeless Man'.[32]

Beveridge's involvement in local juvenile education was less ambitious. He became a manager of two elementary schools, and was soon involved in a protest of local school managers against the implementation of one of the provisions of the London Education Act of 1903. This Act transferred responsibility for education in the metropolis to the London County Council, but control over appointment of school managers was given to borough councils. The Stepney borough council decided to confine school management to its own elected members instead of, as under the previous system, drawing upon the services of local persons experienced in education. This decision was strongly condemned by a conference of Stepney school managers in April 1904, on the ground that it would make school management a shuttlecock of local party politics; and after intervention by the Board of Education it was for a time postponed.[33] Beveridge was an extremely conscientious manager, and took parties of Whitechapel children to the Tower of London and the Zoo. Through Harry Tawney, who was now secretary of the Children's Country Holiday Fund, he arranged for many of them

[32] *Toynbee Record*, Nov. 1904, p. 23; Jan. 1905, pp. 59–66; June 1905, pp. 151–61.
[33] *Toynbee Record*, May 1904, pp. 110–11; BP, IIb, William Bousfield to WHB, 28 Mar. 1904; C. A. Elliott to WHB, 21 Apr. 1904.

to pay visits to the country—some being sent to Haslemere to neighbours of Henry and Annette. Beveridge was surprised to find that, for all their poverty, the children of the East End seemed 'dreadfully intelligent and full of knowledge'; and their generosity gave him some inkling of that 'charitable force—the gifts of the poor to those poorer—which is seldom sufficiently recognised'.[34] He discovered also that he had a talent for getting on well with children. On one occasion his mother found him 'seated on the lawn with a tiny girl's arms clasped from behind round his neck and a closely ranged circle chatting round him'. And the pupils at his schools often waylaid him in the Whitechapel streets and 'babbled to him of their dinner hour affairs'.[35]

One of the most significant areas of educational reform in which Toynbee Hall was involved at this time was the debate on free school meals for children suffering from malnutrition. Charitable societies for the provision of free school meals in poor areas had existed in London since the 1860s; and since 1889 an attempt had been made to co-ordinate their activities under the London School Dinners Association, founded by the Fabian Graham Wallas. Their impact on the physical condition of London schoolchildren appears, however, to have been slight; and in the early 1900s many East End children were still unable to derive any benefit from their education because of sheer physical weakness and lack of food.[36]

The spearhead of the attack on this situation came initially from theoretical socialists and from organized labour. Since 1883 the programme of the Social Democratic Federation had called for free school meals financed out of local rates, and this demand was taken up by the T.U.C. and the Labour Representation Committee during the depression of 1903. The need for such a service was strongly endorsed by medical evidence to the Interdepartmental Committee on Physical Deterioration early in 1904.[37] Nothing, however, could more directly have challenged the fundamental principles of Victorian social policy than the demand for public provision of free school meals. To bodies like the Charity Organisation Society it was an inviolable axiom that— whatever the state might do to improve the environment or to lay down conditions for industrial safety—the basic unit of social security for the individual should always be the family, and the head of a household should always be exclusively responsible for maintenance of his children. To provide rate-aided school meals, it was argued, would undermine

[34] BP, IIa, WHB to ASB, 13 Dec. 1903; *Toynbee Record*, Feb. 1905, pp. 81–4.
[35] 'Lessons from Holiday Children to a Country-Woman', *Toynbee Record*, Nov. 1905, p. 24.
[36] Bentley B. Gilbert, *The Evolution of National Insurance in Great Britain, The Origins of the Welfare State* (1966), pp. 104–6.
[37] Ibid., pp. 88–9, 108; J. D. Hirst, 'The Campaign for the Provision of Free School Meals'. I am grateful to Mr. Hirst for allowing me to consult his unpublished paper.

family independence and individual responsibility and lead to a dangerous increase in the power of the state.[38] Against this view it was claimed
by socialists—and increasingly by non-socialist reformers influenced by
the revelations of Booth and Rowntree—that there were many families
who, even in times of full employment, were simply too poor to fulfil
the Charity Organisation ideal. Hence, the superficially straightforward
demand for the feeding of starving children was fraught with ideological
controversy about the causes and effects of poverty and the nature of the
relationship between the individual and the state.

The demand for free school meals was taken up by Sir John Gorst,
the 'Tory Democrat' and M.P. for Cambridge in 1903. Gorst was a close
friend of the Barnetts, and in May 1904 the Canon asked Beveridge to
arrange a conference of working-class organizations to discuss Gorst's
proposals.[39] The conference, consisting of 'trade union secretaries, co-
operators, friendly society men, labour borough councillors etc.', met
at Toynbee on 9 June 1904. The first speaker was Gorst himself who
outlined a scheme whereby local authorities would provide dinners for
all children at elementary schools and then recover the cost from parents
who were able to pay. Gorst was followed by Dr. Lister, one of the
medical inspectors of the Local Government Board, who urged that
schoolfeeding should be followed up by a system of compulsory medical
inspection in all state schools.[40] These speeches evoked a torrent of
further proposals, most of them far more ambitious than the scheme
envisaged by Gorst. The conference, Beveridge reported to his mother,
was

predominantly socialistic and of course socialists are the people who tell you
whatever you do that you are only touching the fringe of the problem. Most
of the speakers by way of practical suggestions for the feeding of underfed
schoolchildren, demanded housing reform or the repudiation of the national
debt or the resuscitation of the schoolboard or indiscriminate outdoor relief of
paupers!!!

He himself spoke in favour of a plan devised by Barnett and E. J. Urwick
for

providing a free breakfast of porridge and milk and treacle to every child at 8
in the morning and severely punishing the parents of all children who should
neither avail themselves of this nor feed the children properly themselves.

Privately, Beveridge agreed with neither Gorst's nor Barnett's proposals. His own view was in fact much closer to the socialist panaceas
of which he had written with such scorn, for he was coming round to the

---

[38] *Charity Organisation Review*, n.s., vol. XX (July–Dec. 1906), pp. 121–4.
[39] BP, IIb, S. Barnett to WHB, 28 May 1904.
[40] R. H. Tawney, 'Report of a Conference on Underfed Schoolchildren', *Toynbee Record*,
July–Sept. 1904, pp. 141–4.

view that the best solution was neither free school dinners nor charitable breakfasts but a redistribution of national income to make such measures unnecessary. 'Really I don't want anything done at all by the State,' he recorded after the conference.

Many children of course are quite unable to profit by their education because physically unfit by underfeeding, but I would rather let charity come in as a present palliative and re-organise society if necessary as a complete remedy. Granted that many parents have now the responsibility of feeding their children without the power of doing so (through low wages) the remedy is not to remove the responsibility but to give the power.[41]

This view was subsequently to become a corner-stone of Beveridge's social philosophy. It was the first clear expression of his deeply-held conviction that adequate income maintenance for all rather than selective welfare services for the very poor should be the basis of social policy in a rationally organized society.

## IV

One of Beveridge's main tasks in Whitechapel was to organize local election campaigns for candidates sponsored by Toynbee Hall. The settlement was in the parliamentary constituency of Whitechapel, but for local government purposes it came under the Stepney Borough Council. Because of the area's large alien population, the local electorate was very small and local politics tended to divide on ethnic or religious rather than class or party lines.[42] When Beveridge went to Whitechapel in 1903 the borough council was dominated by a majority of Moderates consisting mainly of brewers, licensed victuallers and other local tradesmen. Council meetings were held in the daytime, which virtually precluded attendance by working-men. The council conspicuously failed to use its powers under the Housing Acts, or to enforce its own bye-laws about paving, street lighting and sanitation. In spite of a general improvement in living standards in the area over the previous twenty years, some parts of the borough were still notoriously neglected. Limehouse in particular had an infant mortality rate of 210 per thousand and fewer sanitary inspectors than any other area in the country.[43] Canon Barnett was anxious for Toynbee Hall to take a lead in remedying this situation, and to put forward candidates for the council who were not necessarily members of any one political party, but who were prepared to commit themselves to measures of local reform.

Borough elections were scheduled for November 1903, and one of

[41] BP, IIa, WHB to ASB, 12 June, 1904.
[42] Henry Pelling, *Social Geography of British Elections 1885–1910* (1967), p. 42.
[43] *Toynbee Record*, Oct. 1903, p. 10.

Beveridge's first tasks on going to Toynbee was to familiarize himself with the law on local elections and the powers of local councils.[44] The settlement decided to put up four candidates, all Progressives, and to support a number of others, Progressive, Labour and Independent. In October 1903 the residents of Toynbee drew up a 'Programme for the Borough Council Election', which closely followed the Progressive programme for London as a whole. It called for improved public health regulation; more slum clearance and rehousing; better street paving, cleaning and lighting; direct employment of labour by the borough council at trade union wages; and the levying of higher rates on local commercial property. The council was urged to hold its meetings in the evening, and to promote legislation for the amendment of the Housing Acts, the improvement of public transport, and the pooling of the rate-yield between rich and poor local authorities.[45] Beveridge himself was put in charge of canvassing and spent the last week of October either deploying other canvassers or canvassing himself. He drew up a series of 'notes for canvassers', which gave advice on methods of canvassing and summarized the views of candidates on such issues as temperance, vaccination and alien immigration. On the day of the election he acted as counting agent for Mile End Central Ward. All four Toynbee candidates were returned, and the Moderate stranglehold on the Stepney council was replaced by a coalition of Progressives and Independents.[46]

In Whitechapel, the central theme of the election—and the issue with which Beveridge had been most personally concerned—was the question of alien immigration. One of Toynbee's protégés, T. E. Williams—a ship's chandler and the only Labour member of the outgoing council—had recently given evidence to the Royal Commission on Alien Immigration, opposing the exclusion of aliens except in the case of criminals or persons suffering from infectious disease. As a consequence he had become a target for attack from Major Evans Gordon, Whitechapel's notoriously anti-semitic Unionist M.P.; and this attack was echoed by some of the Moderate candidates in the Stepney local elections.[47] Beveridge's own views on immigration exactly coincided with those of Williams, and he spent the day before the election trekking the streets of Whitechapel on the latter's behalf.[48] Williams was defeated, but he was successful a fortnight later at a council by-election in the Shadwell ward. On this second occasion Beveridge composed his election address,

[44] BP, IIa, WHB to Jeannette Beveridge, 8 Sept. 1903.
[45] *Toynbee Record*, Oct. 1903, pp. 8–11.
[46] BP, IIa, papers relating to borough council election, 2 Nov. 1903; WHB to ASB, 3 Nov. 1903.
[47] BP, IIa, WHB to ASB, 1 Nov. 1903.
[48] W. H. Beveridge, 'The Aliens Bill', *Toynbee Record*, May 1904, pp. 116–20; BP, IIa, WHB to ASB, 3 Nov. 1903.

which admitted that Williams was opposed to exclusion of aliens, but emphasized also his hostility to sweating, overcrowding, the keeping of 'disorderly houses' and other social evils for which immigration had often been popularly blamed.[49]

A more serious test of Beveridge's electioneering capacities came with the County Council elections in 1904. Barnett wrote to him in January, asking him to organize support for four Progressive ex-residents of Toynbee—G. L. Bruce in Whitechapel, Henry Ward in Hoxton, Arthur Leon in Limehouse and Harold Spender in Stepney.[50] Beveridge spent much of February canvassing for all four candidates, pressing his own friends into service as canvassers, and acting as election agent for Arthur Leon. On the day of the election he was put in charge of the Progressive Committee Rooms in Whitechapel, and spent the day restraining the enthusiasm of drunken Progressive supporters and arranging for systematic last-minute canvassing of local workshops and model dwellings. In London as a whole the central issue in the election was the Education Act of the previous year, but in Whitechapel it was again the question of alien immigration. On this occasion the chief threat to the Progressives came not from anti-semitic Moderates but from Independent contestants for the Jewish vote—in particular from H. H. Gordon, a Jewish Independent member of Stepney borough council. Because of the immigration question the Progressives, who won a major victory elsewhere in London, were relatively much less successful in the East End. Of the Toynbee candidates only Arthur Leon was elected—almost certainly not because of Beveridge's efforts but because there were fewer Jews in Limehouse than elsewhere in East London. G. L. Bruce was heavily defeated by Gordon and Harold Spender in Stepney came bottom of the poll. Beveridge welcomed the overall Progressive victory with some misgivings. He rejoiced at what seemed to be a sign of popular support for non-sectarian education, but he was rather disillusioned with the caprice and vulgarity of democratic politics. He was mistrustful of many of the successful Progressives, seeing them as sentimental radicals of 'a rather foolish and philanthropic type'. In particular he was saddened by the defeat of G. L. Bruce, a man of 'lifelong experience and complete devotion to national education'; and he was disgusted by the success of H. H. Gordon, whose 'ambitions [had] outrun and guided the development of his principles' and who had consorted with Moderates, brewers and publicans to smash the Progressive vote.[51]

[49] BP, IIa, T. E. Williams' address to the electors of Shadwell, enclosed with WHB to ASB, 15 Nov. 1903.
[50] BP, IIb, S. Barnett to WHB, 30 Jan. 1904.
[51] BP, IIa, WHB to ASB, 2 and 6 Mar. 1904.

V

The Stepney Council of Public Welfare had been founded early in 1903 under the chairmanship of Canon Barnett. It was mainly composed of local clergymen, and its aims were to promote co-operation between voluntary social work agencies, to encourage 'temperance, public health and public morality' and to 'watch all matters of civil interest in Stepney and to take action where need be'.[52] In theory it was designed as a counterweight to the excessive influence in the East End of the Charity Organisation Society.[53] In practice—and particularly in its emphasis on the moral aspect of social problems—the council shared many of the characteristic attitudes of 'organized charity'; but it went much further than the C.O.S. in its involvement in local politics and its support for statutory reforms.

Beveridge first came into contact with the council in September 1903, when he attended one of its meetings to discuss the sponsoring of candidates in the forthcoming borough elections. He was amused and rather irritated to discover that, although anxious to influence local politics, the members of the Council were almost uniformly ignorant of local political structure and electoral affairs.[54] However, early in 1904 he was co-opted on to the Council as 'municipal secretary'; and he determined to 'educate' the other members, to 'broaden their interests beyond [their] present ones of temperance and morality' and 'to produce informed public opinion on local government'.[55] The issue with which he was particularly concerned on the Council was restriction of Sunday trading in the East End. Opening on Sundays had become increasingly common among traders in Stepney—ostensibly in response to the competition of Jewish shopkeepers who opened on Sunday having closed for the Jewish sabbath. It was a trend of which Beveridge strongly disapproved—not on sabbatarian grounds but because of the loss of the weekly holiday to shop employees. In March 1904 he compiled a report for the council on existing 'Lord's Day' legislation, showing that most of it dated from the seventeenth century, and bore little relation to modern commercial conditions.[56] On the rare occasions when tradesmen were prosecuted under these Acts, the fines imposed were 'ridiculously low', usually amounting to less than twenty shillings. In April 1904 a bill was introduced into Parliament by Lord Avebury restricting Sunday trading to vendors of perishable goods; but the bill was strongly criticized on the ground that there was no support for such legislation among the trades-

---

[52] *Toynbee Hall, Twentieth Annual Report* (1903–4), p. 12.
[53] Abel, op. cit., p. 293.    [54] BP, IIa, WHB to ASB, 24 Sept. 1903.
[55] BP, IIa, WHB to ASB, 20 Apr. 1904.    [56] BP, IIa, WHB to HB, 10 Mar. 1904.

men concerned. The Stepney Council of Public Welfare therefore
decided to sound out opinion among local shopkeepers; and a survey
was carried out under Beveridge's supervision in three parishes of Limehouse during May and June 1904. He discovered that, out of 313
tradesmen canvassed, two-thirds remained open on Sundays, but of
these three-quarters would have preferred to close. Even among Jewish
tradesmen two-thirds favoured Sunday closing; and the survey revealed
an overall preference for Sunday closing by a majority of four to one.
The main reason given for Sunday opening was fear of competition,
and a majority of those canvassed would have been prepared to close on
Sunday if their neighbours had been compelled to do the same.[57] As a
result of this survey the Council of Public Welfare decided to press
Stepney borough council for new trading bye-laws, and Beveridge was
chosen as spokesman of a deputation that waited upon the council on
6 July. Here he pressed for a strict limitation of Sunday opening, with
exemption only for shopkeepers who closed on the Jewish sabbath. 'We
were very well received,' he recorded, '. . . the Jews are the main difficulty, but ought not to prevent something from being done to give one
day in seven (whether the same day or not) to all people. . . .'[58] This
deputation had no immediate impact on borough council policy,
because the problem had become too complex to be dealt with purely
by local bye-laws. It was, however, part of a much wider movement for
the reform of Sunday trading laws, which led to the setting up of a
parliamentary inquiry in 1906. This inquiry recommended stiffer penalties for breach of the law, but much greater flexibility in allowing shops
in poor areas to open for limited hours on Sundays for the sale of newspapers, medicines and perishable goods.[59]

## VI

Beveridge's initial scepticism of the settlement ideal as cherished by
Samuel Barnett was on the whole confirmed and reinforced by his
experiences in the East End—a reaction which was based partly on a
rational assessment of the limitations of Toynbee, partly on a growing
personal distaste for the settlement way of life. During his three and a
half years at Toynbee he was conspicuously successful in convincing
other residents of the need for a broader conception of social work, and
in promoting discussion of several major issues—such as poverty, malnutrition and unemployment—that were to be taken up by the Liberal
government after 1906.[60] But Beveridge himself was increasingly con-

[57] BP, III 2, 'Report of Canvass as to Sunday Trading', by WHB, 3 July 1904.
[58] *Toynbee Record*, July-Sept. 1904, p. 138; BP, IIa, WHB to ASB, 10 July 1904.
[59] *MP*, 6 Aug. 1906.      [60] Abel, op. cit., p. 181.

vinced that settlements were only important, not as institutions in their own right, but as the lodging-place of individuals who incidentally happened to be active in public affairs. Even those aspects of settlement life which he had originally seen as most important—namely social inquiry and the moulding of public opinion—he began to think might just as well, if not so conveniently, be carried on elsewhere. He discovered among local residents in Whitechapel a feeling that settlements devoted to social research were just as implicitly patronizing as settlements devoted to missions and moral improvement.[61] And by 1907 he had come to the conclusion that the concentration in settlements of groups of 'experts in social problems' was in danger of merely perpetuating that unnatural differentiation of function and status in society which the early settlement movement had been specifically designed to avoid. 'There is immense and growing value in the settlement idea pure and simple,' he wrote in the *Oxford and Cambridge Review*. But the settlements of the future he thought should consist not of institutions but of individuals, prepared to live in an 'ordinary street' and to take their place as 'ordinary citizens' in the community at large.[62]

Beveridge's criticisms of the orthodox settlement movement were backed up by a growing consciousness of his own temperamental unfitness for life in an institution which, for all its aspirations to the contrary, was inextricably associated with 'devotion to good works'. He admired but could not share the vocation of those who saw social reform primarily in terms of service to individuals; and he felt little sense of personal identification with the victims of social distress. 'I don't believe that to the generality of people the consumptive appeals more than the healthy man who is temporarily unwell,' he wrote to Annette; 'while for myself I must admit that neither appeals so much as the man who is well physically and morally, but from whom I may hope to learn something or to whom I may hope to teach something.'[63] Moreover, practical experience of social reform movements tended to harden rather than soften that inability to suffer fools gladly, which Barnett had anxiously detected in Beveridge early in 1903. 'You snub people whose interests are not your own,' he was warned by Cosmo Gordon Lang, the Bishop of Stepney; '. . . you are narrow in your view of the life which is not purely intellectual.'[64] Beveridge was conscious of this fault in himself, but was increasingly unable to conceal his impatience with people who thought or acted slowly. This was a characteristic that was to bedevil his public and professional relationships throughout his life, but

[61] BP, IIb, M. Catmur to WHB, 11 Dec. 1904.

[62] W. H. Beveridge, 'Settlements and Social Reform', *Oxford and Cambridge Review*, Michaelmas 1907, pp. 108–17.

[63] BP, IIa, WHB to ASB, 5 May 1904.

[64] Quoted in BP, IIa, ASB to WHB, n.d. (*c.* Aug. 1907).

it was especially inappropriate in an institution such as Toynbee Hall. He lost pupils from his classes who objected to being 'targets for his sarcasm',[65] and he offended local residents by his contempt for in-efficiency and apparent assumption of intellectual superiority. 'You must watch and pray,' admonished a local Toynbee supporter, com-menting on a report in which Beveridge had written scathingly of conventional good works and religious enthusiasm; '. . . there is danger that cold logic is terribly misleading you.'[66]

From a personal point of view Beveridge had always seen Toynbee mainly as a stepping-stone to more influential positions, and from mid-1904 onwards he began to project his ideas and activities on to a wider stage. His articles in the *Toynbee Record* were well-received in the national press, and the publisher Julian Dent urged him to expand them into a book for circulation among social workers and prospective Liberal poli-ticians.[67] At the same time the economic historian W. T. Ashley sug-gested that he should write a theoretical analysis of the problem of the unemployed.[68] Encouraged by this reception he began to write for a wider audience, producing articles on unemployment for the *West-minster Review* and on trade union law for the *Economic Review*. Early in 1905 he gave two courses of extension lectures on labour law and prob-lems of unemployment; and in June he gave a widely acclaimed public lecture at Oxford, in which he deplored the eclipse of political philo-sophy by classical economics.[69]

It is clear that from about the middle of 1904 onwards Beveridge was anxious to leave Toynbee for some other more intellectually challenging sphere. Barnett quickly recognized that this was so, and appointed Edmund Harvey as deputy warden, leaving Beveridge more time for lecturing and public affairs. For some time Beveridge seems to have been torn between posts in public administration and a return to aca-demic life. In the winter of 1904–5 he was offered the job of secretary to the London Unemployed Fund, but eventually rejected it as the post was not permanent. In 1905 he became secretary to a C.O.S. inquiry into problems of unskilled labour, but although he was paid a salary this was in no sense a full-time job. For a time he toyed with the possibility of acting upon his ideal of settlement life by buying a house and setting up home in the East End; and in the summer of 1905 he negotiated for a lease on an eighteenth-century villa in Limehouse, which he planned to share with a local clergyman, the Reverend T. C. Witherby. Profession-ally, however, he was no longer really interested in work in the East End. To his mother he confided that he was tired of lecturing to 'ethical or

[65] BP, Ic, WHB's diary, 19 Feb. 1904.    [66] BP, IIb, M. Catmur to WHB, 15 Jan. 1905.
[67] BP, IIb, Julian Dent to WHB, 6 Oct. 1904.
[68] BP, IIa, WHB to ASB, 10 Dec. 1904.    [69] Below, p. 87.

self-improvement societies', that he was determined 'to be a professor some day', and that his gradually unfolding ambition was to become 'a scientific economist'.[70]

In October 1905, however, another opening presented itself. The influential Conservative daily, the *Morning Post*, inaccurately reported that a registry for unemployed workmen had been opened at Toynbee Hall. The settlement was flooded with applications from men looking for work, and Beveridge therefore wrote to the paper, asking it to publish a correction of the error. In reply he received a telephone call from the editor, Fabian Ware, inviting him to lunch to talk about 'things generally'. It turned out that the new owner of the *Morning Post*, Lord Glenesk, was anxious to develop Conservative opinion on social reform, and that Beveridge had been recommended for this purpose by Edward Caird.[71] Ware himself belonged to the social imperialist wing of the Conservative and Unionist party. He was a disciple of Chamberlain and Milner, a 'reforming Radical forced into the Tory ranks by his vision of imperial greatness', who believed that 'imperial reconstruction depends on social reconstruction at home and the creation of a true imperial race'. On 25 October Ware tentatively invited Beveridge to join the staff of the *Morning Post*, and to take over responsibility for all articles on questions of social policy. 'I should have nothing to do with politics,' reported Beveridge to Annette:

I should not have to write to order about extraneous subjects—but simply to stick to social questions, formulate a policy, [and] bring a scientific understanding of these questions home to the ordinary comfortable public. I told him of course that in party politics I was certainly not a Conservative and that in speculative politics I was a bit of a Socialist. He rather liked that than the reverse. He wants to make the 'Morning Post' an independent organ for moving the intellectual part of the wealthy classes. He believes them to be all patriots at heart, willing to do their duty in social matters if only it is brought home to them. . . . Shortly: it's a great opportunity to preach to the comfortable classes doctrine which they wouldn't stand for a moment in the 'Daily News'.[72]

On this occasion there was no family opposition to Beveridge's change of career, and his parents tactfully admitted that the £500 a year he would earn on the *Morning Post* was considerably more than the income of a junior barrister. Annette in particular was overjoyed that her son would have a chance to 'exercise his statesman's mind' and to come into

---

[70] BP, IIa, WHB to ASB, 4 Mar., 25 Oct., and 27 Oct. 1905.
[71] BP, XII 2, ms. note by WHB, attached to 'Contributions to Morning Post', vol. I, f. 8; *PI*, p. 34.
[72] BP, IIa, WHB to ASB, 25 Oct. 1905.

contact with a 'really good and nice class of people'—though she warned him that 'you may have to speak in a language somewhat conventional —that is the oil on the wheel'.[73] Barnett was strongly in favour of the project, seeing it as an opportunity for radicalizing middle-class public opinion.[74] Beveridge himself was more cautious, foreseeing problems in adjusting to the paper's Tory philosophy; but his doubts were soon outweighed by the obvious advantages of a post which would give him, not only a voice in public affairs, but leisure for private research. 'Just think,' he wrote to his mother, 'of all the people I should see, and the wisdom I, and the Canon through me, should pump into the comfortable public about Poor Law, Trade Union Law, Unemployed, Garden Cities, Locomotion and Decentralisation—everything in fact that wasn't for the moment a *burning* party question.'[75] His appointment was confirmed early in November, and he became the first and most important of a group of young writers whom Fabian Ware gathered round himself, in a more or less deliberate attempt to rival the influence of C. P. Scott's *Manchester Guardian*. A few days later Beveridge resigned his position as sub-warden. Although he remained in residence for over a year afterwards, this was the end of his career in Whitechapel and of his formal relationship with Toynbee Hall.

[73] BP, IIa, ASB to WHB, 26, 27 and 28 Oct. 1905.
[74] BP, IIa, WHB to ASB, 27 Oct. 1905.
[75] BP, IIa, WHB to ASB, 25 and 27 Oct. 1905.

# 4

## Beveridge and his Circle

### I

WHEN Beveridge resigned from Toynbee Hall he was still only twenty-six years old, but he was already recognized as a leading figure in London social administration—as was shown when the newly-established Central (Unemployed) Body elected him at the head of its poll for co-opted members in December 1905. Physically he was still very youthful in appearance, about five feet ten inches tall, with a 'boyish face, clear complexioned and fair, a pair of steady grey eyes, and the quiet clear-accented speech of the Balliol graduate'.[1] Contemporaries noted that he had a powerful social conscience and 'high ideals';[2] but they noted also that there was something 'un-English' about him, something rather Germanic in his passion for precision and contempt for inefficiency. 'Mr. Beveridge, as Englishmen go, is very free from either sentimentality or partisanship,' commented Robert Ensor; 'he clings almost ruthlessly to facts and logic.'[3] 'He is very systematic,' wrote another observer; 'he can seldom be caught out on a point of logic . . . but he underestimates the human factor.'[4] When Beatrice Webb first met Beveridge she commented rather caustically on his 'ugly manners', by which she almost certainly meant, not that he was discourteous, but that he was dogmatically convinced that he was right.[5] To his intimate circle of friends he was boyish and exuberant, but to outsiders he was rather reserved and gave the impression of being cold and overbearing. In private life he was affectionate and tender-hearted, the 'slave and jester of small children', with a fondness for dogs, old ladies and romantic novels;[6] but he was very severe on any signs of 'sentimentality' in public affairs. A few years earlier he had criticized himself for an excessive 'desire to please',[7] but this characteristic was evident only to his closest friends. In public life he showed little talent or inclination for ingratiating himself with persons in power, and he was 'shockingly bad at

[1] *Daily Mail*, 13 Oct. 1909.
[2] BP, IIb, Henry Goudy to WHB, 22 Apr. 1906.
[3] *Manchester Guardian*, 9 Feb. 1909, review by R. C. K. Ensor of WHB's *Unemployment: a Problem of Industry*.
[4] *Economist*, 27 Feb. 1909.     [5] B. Webb, *Our Partnership* (1948), p. 309.
[6] BP, IIa, WHB to ASB.
[7] BP, IIa, WHB to Jeannette Beveridge, 6 Mar. 1898.

recognising great men'.[8] He found it difficult to hide his impatience with people who thwarted or opposed him, and was constantly 'wondering why sensible people can be so stupid on committees at all times'.[9] As he admitted to his mother, there was some justification for 'all the unkind remarks that people are beginning to make at me about being egotistic and monomaniac'.[10] He was also obsessively single-minded. As he recalled twenty years later he spent the years before 1914 'wholly almost to the exclusion of other interests and with a full share of priggishness', devoted to the task of converting other people to his idea about social reform.[11]

As in his Oxford days he was a voracious reader of literary, scientific and political works; but—except in his studies of unemployment—there was rarely an obvious connection between his reading and the development of his attitudes and ideas. 'I do not remember ever reading anything specially for the purpose of my writing, except out of books of reference at the office,' he recalled of his days at the *Morning Post*.[12] He was becoming convinced that economic problems could best be studied by observation of facts, and he was increasingly irritated by the predominantly deductive approach in traditional methods of analysing society. Political science, economics, law—even biology—were all, he believed, corrupted by the 'taint' of metaphysics; and the aim of 'sociology' should be, not to provide an alternative set of theories, but to correct all these abstractions by empirical studies.[13] In matters of taste he was attracted by 'artistically unusual people'; but he saw himself as a 'broad-minded Philistine'—a judgement that is largely confirmed by many of his comments on books, people and ideas.[14] The letters that he wrote whilst on holiday in Germany, Switzerland, Ireland and Italy were full of rather monotonous descriptions of mountains and scenery; they rarely referred to people and never to a work of art. He liked stories and plays that were cheerful and instructive and had happy endings, and he found a biography of Napoleon 'much more interesting' than *War and Peace*.[15] After seeing a production of Hedda Gabler he 'very nearly made a vow never to go near anything so ugly again'.[16] He found the writings of Thomas Hardy 'enormously long and hard to get through', and after struggling with a work by Henry James he wrote despairingly, 'I can't make head or tail of it. Life is too short.'[17] His

---

[8] BP, IIa, WHB to ASB, 28 Nov. 1904.     [9] BP, IIa, WHB to ASB, 12 Dec. 1906.

[10] BP, IIa, WHB to ASB, 13 Feb. 1908.

[11] BP, Ic 50, notes for WHB's diary, 29–30 Dec. 1934.

[12] BP, XII 2, ms. note by WHB, n.d., attached to vol. I of 'Contributions to Morning Post', f. 8.

[13] *MP*, 5 July 1906.

[14] BP, IIa, WHB to ASB, 6 Dec. 1909; WHB to R. Denman, 20 June 1903.

[15] BP, IIa, ms. conversations with ASB, n.d. (*c.* 1913).

[16] BP, IIa, WHB to ASB, 13 Mar. 1907.

[17] BP, IIa, WHB to ASB, 16 June 1907 and 30 Sept. 1909.

favourite poet was Wordsworth—a taste that seems to have derived from his fondness for climbing mountains; and his favourite novelists, apart from George Eliot, were George Meredith and the Irish female Macgonigle, Amanda McKittrick Ros.

Another of Beveridge's most striking characteristics was his passion for hard work—a passion that he retained throughout his life. He would arrive at the *Morning Post*'s office in the Strand at nine in the evening and work on leaders and feature articles until one or two o'clock. He then walked home through the deserted streets and went to bed at dawn. He spent about five hours every day on work for the Central (Unemployed) Body, the Stepney local distress committee and the Charity Organisation Society's inquiry into problems of unskilled labour. He never lost an opportunity of propagating his ideas on social questions, and between 1905 and 1908 gave an average of three public speeches and lectures a week. At the same time he was collecting statistics of the trade-cycle, writing numerous free-lance articles, organizing classes for the Workers' Education Association, and preparing a full-length academic study on the problem of the unemployed. This energetic routine was punctuated by equally vigorous leisure activities—by tennis-parties, mountain-climbing, motoring, ski-ing, and long-distance walking holidays with his sister and friends. 'He eats and drinks and sleeps like a savage and appears bubbling over with energy,' recorded Jeannette when they were on holiday together on Lake Como in 1906.[18] And he himself recorded that the 'prevalent note' of this period of his life was a note of feverish activity—'activity in play as intense as activity in work'. 'I'm amazed retrospectively,' he wrote in 1912, 'at the strenuous life I appear to have lived in 1905, 1906, 1907, and the flood of talk, talk, talk, write, write, write, that I poured out into every unwilling ear and suitable or unsuitable chance' on social reform and the organization of labour.[19]

## II

For a time Beveridge planned to stay on at Toynbee Hall, but he found himself increasingly cramped for time and space in the bustling atmosphere of a university settlement. He considered the possibility of moving back to Paper Buildings, but decided that 'I can't cut myself off from reality by living in the Temple just yet'.[20] He was in any case still strongly attracted by the prospect of living as an ordinary citizen in a

[18] BP, IIa, Jeannette Beveridge to HB, 4 Oct. 1906.
[19] *PI*, p. 94; BP, IIa, WHB to Jeannette Tawney, 16 Aug. 1912.
[20] BP, IIa, WHB to ASB, 18 Mar. 1906.

working-class street. His plans to share a villa in Limehouse had fallen through, but early in 1907 he took a lease on a four-roomed flat in Park Mansions, a group of rather notorious bachelor dwellings over-looking Vauxhall Park. Here he lived alone for the next four years, looked after by a daily 'treasure', carefully selected for him by the local C.O.S.

Throughout this period, however, Beveridge saw Pitfold rather than Lambeth as his main home, and his family continued to play an important part in his personal and social life. Henry Beveridge was now over seventy years old, a benign and rather eccentric old man almost totally immersed in oriental scholarship. His political interests were now confined to symbolic actions—such as burning Shaw's *Candida* in the garden at Pitfold, as a protest against the heroine's 'unwomanly disposition'.[21] He showed little interest in the details of his son's work, but in 1904 he again offered to pay for elocution lessons—an offer which this time Beveridge gladly accepted, as a sign of Henry's acquiescence in his Toynbee career.[22] Annette Beveridge like her husband had acquired a reputation as an oriental scholar—in particular for her translation of *Tales for the Hearts of the Beginners*, a series of Turkish stories for children. Unlike Henry, however, she was greatly interested in current events and took a lively and sometimes active interest in her son's affairs. Beveridge wrote to her regularly about his ideas on politics, his articles for the *Morning Post* and his work on unemployment; and Annette in return favoured him with her own forthright and often provocative opinions on politics and social reform. She had soon been reconciled to his work at Toynbee, and in general strongly approved of her son's commitment to reform, urging him to follow his ideals and to have 'personal detachment and faith in the victorious power of the clearly seen principle'.[23] On specific issues, however, she was often aggressively anti-reformist, denouncing free public education, subsidized school meals, old-age pensions and anything which involved 'interference with individuals—for no man is worth anything who does not stand on his own feet un-propped'.[24] She was particularly critical of the contemporary movement for women's enfranchisement, and was a leading member of the Shotter-mill branch of the Anti-Suffrage League. 'I am becoming entirely averse from "women of causes" as companions,' she recorded. 'There is much to say in favour of social and non-political women as home companions and refreshment for weary workers. . . . Now so many women have taken to play the political game, they are very dull.'[25]

[21] *PI*, p. 110.     [22] *PI*, p. 36.
[23] BP, IIa, ASB to WHB, 24 Nov. 1906.
[24] BP, IIa, ASB to WHB, 2 May 1904, 18 Mar. 1906 and 4 Mar. 1914.
[25] Lady Beveridge Papers, ASB to J. Mair, 23 Dec. 1911.

Beveridge had great respect for his mother's opinions, and his ideas on many aspects of policy were to a certain extent coloured by her views. Nevertheless, by this stage in his career Annette's influence was domestic rather than intellectual. She gradually ceased to be his main confidante on political questions, but throughout the 1900s she continued to make Pitfold the centre of his social life. By 1908 she was almost totally deaf and was troubled by blindness in one eye; but she was as vigorous and sociable as ever, and Pitfold was the scene of many houseparties, dances, musical evenings, long week-ends and sporting events. Beveridge recalled this period in later years as 'an episode of unexampled spending and luxury; as the time when we saw our roads beset by motors, our countryside by golfers . . . our dancing-rooms and dining-rooms by every form of extravagance';[26] and although the Beveridges were not a wealthy family they enjoyed a comfortable position in this panoply of affluence. Annette kept virtually open house for her children's friends, and frequent guests at Pitfold included Denman, Tawney, E. M. Forster, A. W. Pickard-Cambridge, Andrewes Uthwatt, Arthur Leon and many of Beveridge's colleagues from the Central (Unemployed) Body and from Toynbee Hall. With several of these visitors Annette herself kept up a regular correspondence—discussing Christian Science and Buddhism with E. M. Forster, democratic politics with Denman, and Platonism and the Poor Law with Tawney.[27] In the mid-1900s she was particularly pre-occupied with Christian Science, seeing it partly as a potential cure for her deafness and partly as an expression of that 'practical mysticism' which she had been seeking for the past thirty years. She became a regular attendant at Christian Science meetings, and unsuccessfully urged her children to follow her example in pursuing 'the religion of the healthy mind'.[28]

As in earlier years one of Beveridge's closest friends and confidants was his sister Jeannette, and they frequently took their holidays together —in Wales in 1905 and Italy in 1906. Jeannette Beveridge was a plump, fair, striking girl with an insatiable 'appetite for seeing new things'[29]—a good-natured scatterbrain with none of her brother's intensity or desire to change society. After reading French at Somerville she had studied music for a while in Italy, but her studies were interrupted by a severe illness early in 1903. When she returned to England she made no secret of the fact that her main ambition was to have a gay social life. 'Don't be hard on me for frivolity . . . it's going to be such fun,' she wrote dis-

---

[26] *Unemployment: a Problem of Industry* (1930 edn.), p. 387.

[27] AHBP, Mss. Eur. C. 176/197, R. H. Tawney to ASB, 19 Feb. 1906; E. M. Forster to ASB, 3 Oct. 1906 and 23 Nov. 1906; Mss. Eur. C. 176/183, R. H. Tawney to ASB, 26 Dec. 1906 and 20 Jan. 1907; Mss. Eur. C. 176/184, G. A. S. Northcote to ASB, 18 Aug. 1909.

[28] BP, IIa, ASB to WHB, 30 July and 5 Sept. 1906.

[29] BP, IIa, ASB to WHB, 18 June 1907.

armingly to her serious-minded brother.[30] In 1904, however, Beveridge persuaded her to take part in running a club for female factory hands, and in 1905 she was taken on by Harry Tawney as a part-time organizer for the Children's Country Holiday Fund. 'I have had such a frantic time with those C.C.H.F. children,' she confided to a friend, 'and unfortunately I can't put the blame of it on Harry because he never asked me to do it; it was Will and Will argues!'[31]

Jeannett's involvement in social work was in fact almost certainly due, not to the persuasions of her brother but to her affection for Harry Tawney, whom she had secretly preferred to all other men since she first met him in Paper Buildings in 1901.[32] From family correspondence it seems clear that Beveridge knew nothing of his sister's partiality for Tawney for several years. Tawney himself affected to be a misogynist, claiming that 'women are all fools, that all women over thirty are damned fools and that anyhow injustice is the best policy'.[33] Jeannette herself said nothing, being 'too uncertain of Harry's feelings' to reveal her own;[34] but in 1906 and 1907 she refused two offers of marriage, one from a wealthy businessman and another from a regular army officer. Annette on both occasions was greatly upset, and tried to persuade her daughter that she 'did not know her own mind'; but Jeannette insisted that she 'cared for someone else'.[35] Tawney eventually proposed in June 1908, and Jeannette was so delighted that she 'lost her head' and announced their engagement before she had told her parents—a rather shocking misdemeanour by the standards of the day.[36] Henry and Annette reacted strongly not merely against Jeannette's misconduct, but against the prospect of Tawney as a son-in-law. When Tawney visited Pitfold Annette took to her bed and refused to see him, objecting partly to the precariousness of his prospects (Tawney was at this time a junior lecturer at Glasgow University) and partly to the fact that there was a history of insanity in the Tawney family. Beveridge himself intervened at this stage, in one of the sharpest letters he ever wrote to Annette. He insisted that there was no medical objection to the marriage, and that Tawney was a man of 'unimpeachable character' and 'great abilities', whose education and social position were just as good as his own.

You have not had a pair of children to deal with but a pair of absolutely determined grown people. The parents cannot surely under such circumstances refuse assent because of their own personal likes or dislikes or on any

[30] BP, IIa, Jeannette Beveridge to WHB, n.d.
[31] BP, IIb, Jeannette Beveridge to W. A. Pickard-Cambridge, 17 July 1905.
[32] BP, IIa, Jeannette Beveridge to ASB, n.d. (*c.* July 1908).
[33] AHBP, Mss. Eur. C. 176/193, R. H. Tawney to R. Denman, 27 Dec. 1902.
[34] BP, IIa, Jeannette Beveridge to ASB, 24 June 1908.
[35] BP, IIa, ASB to WHB, 23 Apr. 1906; Jeannette Beveridge to ASB, 24 June 1908.
[36] BP, IIa, Jeannette Beveridge to ASB, 24 June and 7 July 1908.

ground except absolutely definite ones of health or character. . . . I do entreat you to consider for a moment how you would regard any lady of your acquaintance who treated my proposal for her daughter's hand as you have been treating Harry's. . . . I quite realise that announcements of this sort appear at first rather as shocks. I was much surprised myself when the possibility of feeling between Harry and Tutu was first suggested to me some time ago. But such doubts as I have had on the matter have been entirely the opposite of you i.e. whether she was the person to make *him* happy—In view of his long determination—and really in view of hers—there is no room left for doubting by third parties.[37]

The Beveridge parents were eventually reconciled to the engagement, and Jeannette and Harry Tawney were married at Haslemere by Canon Barnett in the summer of 1909. To the possibility that her son might also marry, Annette's attitude was even more ambivalent—she often advised him to choose a wife, yet became distraught and hysterical whenever it seemed possible that her advice might be taken. During week-ends at Pitfold she introduced him to 'more than one girl who seemed . . . to have promise of what I wish for you'—to such an extent that Beveridge angrily accused her of 'matchmaking'. Annette strongly denied that this was so, but she protested that he was 'looking in woman for what can only be found in God'. She urged him to be less severe in his intellectual judgements of women, and to choose a 'calm and tranquil' wife with strong religious convictions, who would complement his own rather assertive and tempestuous personality.[38] Several months later, however, when she heard a rumour that her son was about to marry, she wrote very disparagingly of the lady in question, insisting that his future wife must have 'savoir faire and the habit and ease of good society. You will by and by belong to the *best* society—the real best—and must not be hampered by an unfitting wife—who could not join in the best and would inevitably feel this and be sad and perhaps angry.'[39]

The identity of the unfortunate woman who attracted such disparagement is not known, since Annette tantalizingly referred to her only as Miss ——. Nor is it clear whether on this occasion Beveridge himself really had any intention of proposing marriage. Certainly his transition to the *Morning Post* had made it financially possible for him to do so, since he was soon earning about £600 a year. He undoubtedly pondered a great deal upon marriage. He thought that 'it would be nice to see girls quietly' without fuss and social formality; and he dreamed of meeting a George Meredith heroine, with whom he was sure he would 'certainly fall into immediate and irreparable love'.[40]

[37] BP, IIa, WHB to ASB, 23 June 1908.
[38] BP, IIa, ASB to WHB, n.d. (*c.* Aug. 1907), 10 June 1909, 4 Mar. 1915.
[39] BP, IIa, ASB to WHB, 21 Oct. 1907.
[40] BP, IIa, ASB to WHB, n.d. (*c.* Aug. 1907); WHB to Jeannette Beveridge, 16 Apr. 1903.

He had several female friends, whose letters suggest that they were eager to further his acquaintance; and on several occasions between 1906 and 1911 his father and close friends hinted at the possibility of an engagement.[41] What does seem clear, however, is that on none of these occasions were his affections deeply involved; none of the young ladies of his acquaintance came up to the standards of Meredith, none were so clever as Diana of the Crossways, none of them sparkled like Clara Middleton, none sat in a tree like Carinthia Jane. Moreover, in spite of his defence of Jeannette's engagement, Beveridge believed that marriage should have parental blessing and that 'relations count for much in choosing a partner'.[42] Such a blessing was unlikely to be given when even the rumour of a future daughter-in-law threw Annette into a fever and caused her to have 'visions of mistaken marriages' and 'sleepless nights'.[43]

Beveridge's lack of resentment at Annette's interference was perhaps surprising, in view of his often peremptory dismissal of opposition in public life. But apart from his decision to work at Toynbee and his defence of Tawney, he was almost invariably an exceptionally dutiful son. He wrote to his mother nearly every day, consulted her on most important decisions, and filled voluminous notebooks with written conversations in an attempt to keep her in touch with the outside world. Far from resenting her possessiveness he seemed to view it as a normal and valuable aspect of family life, and only on very rare occasions did he complain against her intrusion into his private thoughts and feelings. Throughout his twenties and thirties he continued to idealize his mother in much the same way as he had done as a small boy.

You are as much my mother and my ideal mother to me at 33, as at 32, 31 . . . and all the way back to my first remembrance [he wrote to her in 1912].
. . . In growing up as everyone must into my own way of life, I've never grown out of the feeling (and never shall, I hope, grow out of the feeling) that if in any way I can be like my Father and Mother as regards all the most important points of character and attitude to life, I'll do all that can be required of human nature. And, of course, I'd like you to be an ideal grandmother too, but these things are not in one's own hands . . .[44]

### III

Nevertheless, Annette was no longer the sole or even the main confidante in Beveridge's life. During his period at Toynbee and on the *Morning Post* he made many new acquaintances—some of them prominent

[41] BP, IIa, ASB to WHB, 18 Mar. 1906; IIb, Helen Sutherland to WHB, 1 Apr. and 1 Aug. 1911.
[42] BP, IIb, Mary Gardner to WHB, 2 and 14 Jan. 1913.
[43] BP, IIa, ASB to WHB, 21 Oct. 1907.
[44] BP, IIa, WHB to ASB, 10 Mar. 1912.

in public life, like Sydney Buxton, Nathaniel Cohen and Sidney and Beatrice Webb. He conceived a great admiration for the Webbs, and was for several years a frequent guest at their notoriously spartan dinner parties at 41 Grosvenor Road. He strongly approved of their earnestness, their contempt for 'sentimentality', and their belief in the possibility of purposive social change. At the Webbs' house he took part in discussions on unemployment, on techniques of social investigation, and on the latest iniquities of H. G. Wells. On one such occasion he caught a unique glimpse of the Webb partnership in action.

I made some remark about unemployment which Beatrice tore to pieces, with an eloquent expression of her own views. At the end of her harangue, I heard Sidney pipe up from the other end of the table: 'You are absolutely right my dear, and I agree with every word that you have said. But—there is just this in what Mr. Beveridge has said!' There followed an exposition of my own views in Sidney's language, and a complete acceptance of them by Beatrice. She had a mind so full of its own ideas that often she could take in other people's ideas only after predigestion by Sidney.[45]

From Sidney Webb himself Beveridge received tactful advice about the selection of projects for social research. Webb cautioned him not to be over-ambitious and to select problems that were 'manageable'. 'I always cite Darwin's Monograph on the Barnacle which long preceded the Origin of Species,' he wrote warningly on one occasion, when Beveridge had suggested a 'stupendous' study of cyclical depressions of trade.[46]

Beveridge's relationship with the Webbs, however, was primarily cerebral; and the most intimate of his new friends were his colleague on the Central (Unemployed) Body, Mrs. Rose Dunn Gardner, and his cousin and cousin-in-law, David and Jessy Mair. David Mair, whom Beveridge met for the first time at the Mairs' home in Banstead in 1904, was the son of a first cousin of Henry Beveridge. He was a distinguished mathematician and former Cambridge don, who had given up his fellowship and entered the Civil Service in order to support a family of young children. He was now a senior official in the Civil Service Commission, but he appeared to move more easily in the world of science and mathematics than in the world of public administration. Much of his spare time was spent in writing books on new methods of teaching mathematics; and he had a rather reserved and hermit-like personality with 'an infinite capacity for silence'.[47] He was closely acquainted with the biologists, Karl Pearson and Francis Galton, and with the sociologists, Victor Branford and Martin White. In 1905 he had been with them

---

[45] *PI*, p. 62.    [46] BP, IIb, S. Webb to WHB, 21 Feb. 1909.
[47] Lady Beveridge Papers, draft fragments of autobiography; J. Mair to WHB, 10 Dec. 1907.

one of the Founder members of the Sociological Society, where he tried to interest his colleagues in linking up sociological theory with empirical social science.[48] In 1907 he and Beveridge spent a holiday together climbing in Wales—during the course of which their contrasting personalities were graphically demonstrated, when Beveridge was mistaken by a party of businessmen for 'an irresponsible undergraduate', whilst David Mair was mistaken for a minister of the Scottish Kirk. 'It's quite a fairly accurate picture of you both,' commented Jessy Mair to Beveridge; 'you know you're nothing like grown up, and David is the most dogmatically constructed human being I've ever known.'[49]

Jessy Mair, *née* Philip, had married David Mair in 1897, and when Beveridge first met her in 1904 she was a forceful young woman of twenty-eight years old. She was the daughter of a Scots businessman and philanthropist, and throughout her life she gave the impression of being 'very much a Scot in manner and speech, and in her ambitions and domineering temperament'.[50] Her photographs suggest that she had been rather a plain young girl, but by her late twenties she was developing into a strikingly handsome, statuesque figure of a woman. Her father had been 'a passionate Gladstonian Liberal and a passionate teetotaller . . . a creature of almost fanatical religious and political opinions, absorbed in reforming everything and everybody, and altogether unaware of the individuals as humanity in general he sought to improve'. As a schoolgirl she had experienced a curious mixture of parental encouragement and neglect; she had been taught to believe that she should always 'come first in everything', and yet at the same time she was painfully conscious of being her parents' least favourite child.[51] Possibly for these reasons she had as a grown woman a compulsive desire for flattery and attention, combined with a dread of criticism and rejection. Her letters and diaries convey the impression of a highly contradictory personality—a continual mixture of generosity and rancour, shrewdness and silliness, extravagant idealism and nagging fear of material insecurity. At the same time she had a quick intelligence, a strongly practical turn of mind, a discerning judgement of other people, and a keen interest in public affairs. Before her marriage she had studied mathematics at St. Andrew's University, and as the mother of several young children she was 'oppressed by the fear that my mind will cease to be able to tackle any intellectual pursuit because I am almost entirely unable to keep it in practice'.[52] She fretted against life in suburban

[48] Lady Beveridge Papers, note by J. Mair, 30 May 1939; D. Mair to WHB, 23 Oct. 1907.
[49] BP, IIa, WHB to ASB, 20 and 21 May 1907; Lady Beveridge Papers, J. Mair to WHB, 21 May 1907.
[50] Passfield Papers, B. Webb's diary, 14 May 1922.
[51] Lady Beveridge Papers, draft fragments of autobiography, n.d.
[52] AHBP, Mss. Eur. C. 176/197, J. Mair to ASB, 11 Dec. 1906.

Banstead, where she had a depressing picture of herself as 'a professional Hausfrau', surrounded by 'children rampant'.[53] Beveridge found in Jessy Mair a sympathetic confidante for his dreams and ambitions; and she in return found Beveridge himself in many ways a more stimulating companion than her rather aloof and abstract-minded husband. 'It was . . . congenial to me,' she later recalled, 'to form an audience on labour exchanges and the decasualisation of dock and other labourers.'[54] Through Beveridge she began to live vicariously in the world of administrative and social reform, and became herself increasingly ambitious to take part in public affairs. To Beveridge she gave a domestic milieu that he would otherwise have lacked. She furnished his rooms for him and chose his servants, while he in turn arranged holidays, cricket matches and pantomimes for her children. She and Beveridge read poetry together, and went to concerts, public lectures and matinées; and this period saw the beginning of a partnership that was eventually to lead to their marriage nearly forty years later.

Mrs. Rose Dunn Gardner was a member of the Chelsea Board of Guardians, and of the Chelsea and Lambeth branches of the London C.O.S. Beveridge met her through the Central (Unemployed) Body at the end of 1905, and he was soon a frequent visitor at her house in Bruton Street and often accompanied her to theatres and social gatherings. A wealthy and fashionable widow in her early forties, Mrs. Dunn Gardner seems to have exercised a good deal of intellectual influence over Beveridge at this stage in his career. She deliberately set out to counteract what she saw as the dangerously 'socialistic' influence of the Barnetts, George Lansbury and Sidney and Beatrice Webb, and she strongly discouraged his penchant for universal panaceas. '*Don't* want to live in an age when things have been settled,' she begged him, shortly after they had first met. 'It is far better to have a chance of making a difference to the solutions of problems.'[55] Decisive, autocratic and doctrinaire, she had certain characteristics in common with Annette Beveridge, and it may have been this similarity that prompted Beveridge to call her his 'London mother' and to treat her with an intimacy which he had previously reserved for Annette.[56] There the resemblance ended, however, for Mrs. Dunn Gardner was fashionable and urbane, with a fondness for theatres, witty conversation, intimate dinner parties and 'high class bridge'. She suffered from a weak heart and spent part of every year on a ritual visit to one of the European spas, interspersed with trips to Paris for the purchase of clothes and hats. Intellectually she was

[53] Lady Beveridge Papers, J. Mair to Florence Philip, n.d., and J. Mair to WHB, 8 Aug. 1912; BP, IIb, Phyllis Gardner to WHB, n.d. (1912).

[54] Janet Beveridge, *Beveridge and his Plan*, p. 59.

[55] BP, IIb, R. Dunn Gardner to WHB, 21 Apr. 1906; 1 Apr. and 30 May 1907.

[56] *PI*, p. 47; BP, IIb, R. Dunn Gardner to WHB, 14 Sept. 1906.

shrewd but narrow, with an ironical contempt for pomposity, vulgarity and all kinds of social Utopianism. She sat on numerous charitable committees, but with no conviction that they did any positive good—seeing them merely as protective barriers against more dangerous social alternatives. On these committees she had brought to a fine art the power of getting her own way. 'First teach a thing to a person—who will entirely . . . oppose it,' she advised Beveridge; 'then wait *quite* a short time and *he* will discover the thing and bring it up as his new idea and expound it to you. It is the right way to accomplish much.'[57] She was highly critical of contemporary proposals for integrating and rationalizing the different branches of social welfare, believing that this would abolish competition and 'where there is no competition I don't think things ever get so well done'.[58] Her husband, Arthur Dunn Gardner, had belonged to the most conservative wing of the Charity Organisation Society; and in the mid-1900s she was the friend and confidante of J. S. Davy, the chief inspector of the Local Government Board and a leading opponent of relaxation of the Poor Law. In politics she was an extreme theoretical individualist, believing that institutions could be changed only 'by carefully and thoroughly dealing with the individuals who compose them' and that individuals could be changed only by learning 'true principles' of self-help.[59]

Mrs. Dunn Gardner was almost certainly a major influence in holding Beveridge back from a commitment to Fabian Socialism, to which he was strongly attracted during the mid-1900s.[60] She worked with him closely in local administration, discussed in detail many of his ideas on unemployment, counselled him against loveless marriage, and soothed and cajoled him in moments of depression.[61] They were on close terms until the middle of the First World War—after which their friendship became more intermittent and, as will be seen in later chapters, Beveridge's social life was increasingly taken over by Jessy Mair. It was probably no coincidence that as the influence of Mrs. Mair waxed that of Mrs. Dunn Gardner waned. Nor is it surprising that Beveridge seems never to have introduced them to each other, since it is difficult to imagine that these two strong-willed ladies could ever have hit it off together—the one so sceptical of all forms of social action, the other so ambitious to make her mark in public life.

[57] BP, IIb, R. Dunn Gardner to WHB, 9 July 1912.
[58] BP, IIb, R. Dunn Gardner to WHB, n.d. (*c.* June 1910).
[59] Rose Dunn Gardner, 'The Training of Volunteers', *Charities Review* (New York, Feb. 1895), pp. 191–7.
[60] See below, ch. 5.
[61] BP, IIb, R. Dunn Gardner to WHB, 30 June 1910, 21 June 1912, 26 May 1913.

## IV

Throughout the 1900s Beveridge continued to see a good deal of Denman and Tawney, and with them was involved in various projects for reform. Tawney was living at Toynbee during much of Beveridge's period as sub-warden, and together they toured the churches, chapels and wayside pulpits of East London 'in search of a new religion'.[62] Beveridge recoiled in disgust at the prevalence of 'brass bands', 'universal handshaking' and 'nursery theology', while Tawney sadly recorded the almost total failure of the London churches to make any spiritual impact on the lives of the working class.[63] East End evangelicalism inspired them both with exaggerated irreverence and anticlericalism, although Beveridge subsequently subsided into tolerant indifference towards organized religion, while Tawney became a lifelong member of the Anglican Church. Richard Denman, now a stockbroker, had married in 1904 and his new home in Swan Walk, Chelsea, became the scene of many discussions on the future of social reform. His wife, Helen Sutherland, was the daughter of a prominent shipowner; and through this contact Beveridge learned much about experiments in decasualization and methods of employment in the London Docks.[64] At the end of 1905 Denman became personal secretary to the new Postmaster-General, Sydney Buxton, and he was henceforth able to keep Beveridge informed about trends of opinion in the new Liberal government. Beveridge rejoiced at his friend's appointment, seeing it—like his own work on the *Morning Post*—as a chance for influencing the Liberals in the direction of reform. 'The post office is the one socialist experiment,' he wrote to Denman. 'Sydney Buxton's main interest is social reform and you'll get lots of that to do . . . I am glad to think that both Balliol and T. H. will do a very fair share towards running this blessed government, while I pat it on the back and insidiously undermine the foundations of Toryism.'[65]

Early in 1906 Beveridge became closely involved with Tawney and Denman in what they called 'the Great Conspiracy'—a movement for the reform of Oxford University inspired by Samuel Barnett.[66] During the nineteenth century Oxford had twice been investigated by a Royal Commission which had on each occasion swept away many abuses and led to important innovations in University administration. Religious tests had been abandoned, some of the most notorious sinecures had

---

[62] BP, IIa, WHB to ASB, 6 Mar. 1904.

[63] BP, Ic 2, WHB's diary, 7 Feb. and 6 Mar. 1904; R. H. Tawney, 'The Daily News Religious Census of London', *Toynbee Record*, Mar. 1904, pp. 87–91.

[64] BP, IIb, R. Denman to WHB, 30 Apr. 1905; WHB to R. Denman, 8 May 1905.

[65] BP, IIb, WHB to R. Denman, 18 Dec. 1905.          [66] BP, IIa, WHB to ASB, 26 Mar. 1906.

been abolished, new faculties had been established and competitive examinations had replaced the sale of degrees. By the 1900s, however, there were many critics who argued that the reforms of the mid-nineteenth century had singularly failed to bring Oxford into contact with modern life. Endowments were still used to maintain luxurious living-standards, rather than for the promotion of education and research; most of the subjects taught were strictly non-vocational and, unlike the new provincial universities, Oxford made no attempt to meet the needs of modern industry and commerce. Most serious of all, in the eyes of many reformers, the innovations of the mid-nineteenth century had made the colleges more rather than less exclusive in terms of social class. Competitive entrance examinations, reinforced by the traditional emphasis on Latin and Greek, meant that scholarships were nearly always awarded to candidates from public schools, rather than to the persons of low income for whom the colleges had originally been endowed. The needs of the latter were met only by Ruskin Hall, founded by the trade union movement in 1899, and by local branches of the Workers' Education Association, founded in 1903. This situation was increasingly criticized as not merely socially inequitable but politically dangerous—particularly after the emergence of a significant parliamentary labour movement in the general election of 1906. 'The working people have now become the governing class of the nation,' argued Samuel Barnett; and, as such, he claimed that they needed an education appropriate to the powers and duties of a governing class.[67]

Beveridge himself had been highly critical of the rather lackadaisical character of college administration ever since he took up his fellowship at University College in 1903.[68] Whilst at Toynbee Hall he seems to have become increasingly conscience-stricken about his tenure of a fellowship whose only duty was the collection of a stipend of £200 a year; and in 1904 he was involved in an unsuccessful movement to limit the award of prize fellowships to scholars engaged in full-time research.[69] The wider movement for University reform did not get off the ground, however, until Samuel Barnett published an article on 'Labour and Culture' in the radical journal *Tribune* early in 1906. Barnett had been striving for many years to bring the universities to the working class; his aim now was to bring the working-class to the universities. He called for a 'new alliance' between working men and the ancient seats of learning —the aims of which would be to save both parties to the alliance from a merely 'materialist' view of social progress. He urged the Oxford colleges to finance seminars in working-class areas, to provide scholarships for

[67] Tawney Papers, 21/1, item 1, typescript article by S. Barnett on 'Oxford University and the Working People', Feb. 1909; *Canon Barnett, His Life, Work and Friends*, II, pp. 105–14.
[68] BP, IIa, WHB to ASB, 1 Nov. 1903.    [69] BP, IIa, WHB to ASB, 28 Nov. 1904.

elementary schoolteachers and to set up hostels in Oxford where working men could live cheaply and study, not the traditional academic subjects, but 'their own interests from a university point of view'.[70] Barnett's
arguments were amplified a month later by Tawney in a series of articles
in the *Westminster Gazette*. Commenting on these articles to Annette
Beveridge, Tawney claimed that his underlying purpose was to defend
rather than attack the University, and that the demand for reform was a
constructive alternative to the views of those who thought Oxford 'too
far gone' to be worth saving. 'They do not always realize,' he remarked,
'what a revolution in English thought and manners the abdication of
Oxford and Cambridge will mean. . . .'[71]

Beveridge meanwhile began to collaborate with Tawney, and with a
New College classics don, Alfred Zimmern, 'in an assault on our University'.[72] At the end of March 1906, he, Tawney and Zimmern—
together with E. J. Palmer, W. A. Pickard-Cambridge, William Temple
and R. W. Livingstone—spent a week-end in Oxford discussing a programme of University reform. They decided to divide the subject into
specialist topics, and to spend the next six months gathering ideas and
information.

I have to tackle finance and the relation of Oxford education to the Professions [recorded Beveridge]. Others have Oxford and secondary schools,
The Teachers, The Teaching, The Taught, Government, Research, etc. Our
general line is tremendously revolutionary conservative, i.e. we want to con-
serve the humane education of Oxford against the . . . mainly technical education represented by Birmingham, etc., and to do this we have to turn the
Government and the Finance of present day Oxford upside down . . .[73]

Throughout the summer and autumn of 1906 the 'conspirators' were
in constant correspondence with each other about University reform.
Their aims were not in each case precisely identical. Tawney was perhaps most concerned with working-class higher education for its own
sake, whilst Zimmern laid more emphasis on making Oxford relevant to
modern life and Beveridge on the need to educate the new holders of
political power. In September Zimmern published an article in the
*Independent Review*, condemning the 'idleness and excessive expense' of
Oxford life, the 'deadness of classical teaching', the 'lack of touch with
professions' and the premium placed by the Oxford examination system
on qualities of 'journalism' rather than 'research'.[74] On 15 September

[70] *Tribune*, 18 Jan. 1906.
[71] R. H. Tawney, 'The University and the Nation', *Westminster Gazette*, 15–17 Feb. 1906;
AHBP, Mss. Eur. C. 176/197, R. H. Tawney to ASB, 19 Feb. 1906.
[72] BP, IIa, WHB to ASB, 31 Jan. 1906.
[73] BP, IIa, WHB to ASB, 18 and 26 Mar. 1906.
[74] BP, IIb, A. Zimmern to WHB, 4 July 1906.

Beveridge in the *Morning Post* called for the representation of 'outside opinion and unacademic ideas' in University government, and on 26 October Tawney in the same paper denounced the compulsory entrance requirement of Latin and Greek—both for its effect in excluding working-class students, and for its cramping influence on the curricula of the public schools. Behind the scenes Barnett urged his young disciplies that 'Oxford has to be reformed by the public for the public'; and he advised them to draw up schemes for 'subsidising lectures in industrial centres' and opening up Oxford to working men.[75]

The full programme for the new movement was not published until early 1907, when a series of articles by 'some Oxford tutors' appeared in *The Times* under the title 'Oxford and the Nation'. Since the articles were published jointly and anonymously it is impossible to ascribe to Beveridge any particular part of them—but there was an unmistakable ring of Beveridge's prose style in the introductory essay, which proclaimed that the authors were 'neither so young as to think that they have found a final solution nor so old as to believe the problems insoluble'. The articles defined two closely interrelated goals for reform— the promotion of 'educational efficiency', and the realization of Mark Pattison's ideal that the university should become 'co-extensive with the nation'. For the achievement of these goals they recommended the following programme. Firstly, the abolition of pass degrees and the exclusion of the 'ignorant idler who has won for Oxford such a disastrous reputation in the eyes of practical men'. Secondly, the preservation of 'liberal' and 'cultural' undergraduate courses, combined with a much more 'vocational' component in higher degrees. Thirdly, the limitation of prize fellowships to two-year periods, and the creation of studentships for postgraduate research. Fourthly, the conversion of 'scholarships' into merely honorific titles, and the use of scholarship funds for bursaries awarded solely on the basis of financial need. Fifthly, a reform of the teaching system, with less emphasis on college-based tutorials and more emphasis on university-based lectures and seminars. Sixthly, a reconstruction of university government, limiting Congregation to University teachers and abolishing the power of non-resident M.A.s. Finally, the articles called for the setting up of a Royal Commission to inquire into problems of university administration, to abolish the 'suicidal competition' which had grown up between colleges, and to 'emancipate our University from the domination of the public schools and of the unemployable rich'.[76]

These articles created a considerable stir in Oxford, and to a lesser

[75] BP, IIb, S. Barnett to WHB, 31 Oct. and 14 Nov. 1906.
[76] *The Times*, 3 Apr.–11 May 1907, reprinted as *Oxford and the Nation*, by some Oxford Tutors (1907).

extent in the national press. Their theme was taken up by Bishop Gore in the House of Lords, and in June the articles were re-published as a book. In July 1907 several of the reformers met together at Barnett's house in Little Cloisters, Westminster, to draw up a private member's bill appointing a Royal Commission on University reform.[77] In Oxford itself, however, there was little enthusiasm for the idea of a Royal Commission, even among those who favoured reform; and in the summer of 1907 a movement for 'reform from within'—inspired by Gore and initiated by the Chancellor of the University, Lord Curzon—began to ward off the demand for more drastic structural change. Barnett and his followers were doubtful whether internal reform could ever be successful, but Curzon's initiative robbed them of much of their academic support. From this time onwards the main focus of Barnett's movement was diverted from the reformation of Oxford to the promotion of nationwide adult education classes, under the auspices of the University Extension Delegacy and of the W.E.A.[78]

Beveridge himself was unable to attend the meeting of the conspirators at Little Cloisters, but early in 1907 he offered to give up his prize fellowship for the endowment of working-class higher education—an offer which was refused by University College. Beveridge was very 'down in the dumps' at this refusal, and in June 1907 he recorded that he was 'rather disgusted' with Oxford life.[79] Thereafter he took a less active part in organizing the reform movement, though he continued to write articles on modernizing the Oxford curriculum, on the need for subsidizing poor students, and on the dangers of an uneducated governing class.[80] He gave several courses of unpaid lectures to students for the economics diploma at Ruskin, acted as treasurer for the South London branch of the W.E.A., and eventually in 1909 persuaded the fellows of University College to support local tutorials for working-class students.[81] For the rest of his life Beveridge gave generous financial support to the workers' education movement; and many of the views which he first acquired in the Oxford reform movement during the 1900s were to re-emerge in his policies as a leading educational administrator two decades later. He consistently opposed narrowly 'vocational' training, believing that this was inconsistent with the fast-changing character of modern society. But he was sceptical of the value of purely 'cultural' disciplines; he believed that technical subjects required academic analysis; and, rightly or wrongly, he was convinced that 'modern sub-

[77] Tawney Papers, 21/1, item 19, A. Zimmern to S. Barnett, 17 July 1907; 'Suggested Petition to the Hebdomadal Council', by A. Zimmern, 26 Sept. 1907.

[78] *Canon Barnett, his Life, Work and Friends*, II pp. 112–13; Bev. Coll. B, 'Oxford and Working-Class Education', vol. III, item 2, May 1908.

[79] BP, IIb, A. Farquharson to WHB, 21 Mar. 1907; IIa, WHB to ASB, 23 June 1907.

[80] *MP*, 15 July 1907.  [81] BP, IIa, WHB, to ASB, 25 Mar. 1909.

jects'—such as government, economics, statistics and sociology—could provide an education that was much more directly useful and just as broad and rigorous as the classics themselves.[82]

## V

The portrait of Beveridge that emerges from this period is of an intensely active, gregarious, yet basically rather lonely youth. He was filled with half-formed visions of the future of society, yet he seems rarely to have shared these visions even with his closest friends. Although outwardly of a cheerful and rather extrovert disposition, he suffered secretly from lack of self-confidence and from occasional moods of black depression.[83] He was troubled also by 'nerves', which he consciously tried to overcome by pursuing many interests and leading a healthy life.[84] In 1910 and again in 1912 he had a recurrence of the strained heart that had afflicted him at Charterhouse, and for several years he was in the hands of heart specialists who subjected him to a series of cures at fashionable spas. It is perhaps fanciful to suggest that his heart trouble had a nervous basis, but he himself noticed that it occurred mainly when he was feeling bored or underoccupied and that it miraculously disappeared during the pressures of the First World War.[85]

Beveridge's loneliness seems to have increased as one by one his friends married. From the extent to which he thought and wrote about marriage it is clear that he hoped to follow them; but he was restrained from doing so, partly by his mother's possessiveness and partly by his own quest for a feminine ideal. During the summer of 1910 he appears to have been contemplating matrimony, so as to have his 'off times made pleasant' and as an antidote to boredom; but he was strongly counselled against such a move by Mrs. Dunn Gardner.

It is folly [she wrote] to waste the one chance you have of making life real happiness by using it up just to escape boredom. You are a good respectable boy and will stick to the wife you marry and make the best of her and never 'let on' even to yourself that things might have been so far different. But you will miss the best in life I think if you marry on these lines.[86]

Whether this was good advice to give to the young Beveridge is open to question. As will be seen in later chapters he himself bitterly regretted that he had not married;[87] and it seems probable that a man of

[82] See below, ch. X.

[83] BP, IIb, R. Dunn Gardner to WHB, 30 June 1910; Lady Beveridge Papers, WHB to J. Mair, 9 June 1907, 19 Aug. 1914.

[84] BP, IIa, WHB to ASB, 11 Jan. 1909; Ic 50, notes for WHB's diary, 29–30 Dec. 1934.

[85] *PI*, p. 101.

[86] BP, IIb, R. Dunn Gardner to WHB, 30 June 1910.

[87] Below, p. 277.

Beveridge's temperament, with his rather rigid sense of propriety, his fondness for children and his deep attachment to family life, might well have been happier married to a less-than-perfect partner than not married at all.

Beveridge's conception of the ideal woman, and his views on women in general, were spelt out most clearly in his one published excursion into the writing of fiction—*John and Irene: an Anthology of Thoughts on Woman*, compiled while convalescing from his strained heart in 1912. As a work of literature *John and Irene* belongs to the sentimental scrap-book genre; it was admired for its ingenuity, but was virtually unreadable and largely unread. Nevertheless, the book was highly revealing of Beveridge's own attitudes towards the female sex. It consisted of a brief fictional preface, followed by several hundred quotations from a wide variety of literary sources, illustrating the virtues, vices and aspirations of women, and their relationships with men. The preface told the story of a young man called John, who was *en route* from University to Settlement and was 'more or less consciously seeking for a cause'. After exhausting various causes, he fixed upon the feminist question and thereafter devoted himself to studying and denouncing the subjection of women to men. In this choice of a cause there was more than a hint of irony, since John was firmly under the thumb of mother, sisters and assorted landladies, and invariably 'did at once what any woman, old or young, good-looking or bad-looking, told him to do'. Indeed, Beveridge suggested, the attraction of the subject may well have lain 'in the contrast afforded between his personal experiences and his theories, between his own observations and the facts that he learned from books. . . . He probably rather liked to look upon himself as Grand Hereditary Oppressor.' Some two years after John's conversion, he fell in love with Irene Middleton, a sprightly young woman with a strong, vigorous but uneducated mind—the kind of mind, Beveridge implied, most ripe for the reception of all forms of prejudice. Irene had never heard of the feminist cause, but John proceeded to educate her on the subjection of women. Irene proved an apt and eager pupil. She supported female suffrage, studied feminist literature and frequented the drawing-rooms of a 'Mrs. Oscar Delaney, that talented lady who, by precept and example, has done so much to establish among us a new conception of marriage'. As a result Irene had the temerity to disagree with John, who was greatly distressed and was found in a garden under a copper-beech tree burning the works of Mr. Bernard Shaw. The precise cause of their quarrel was not revealed, but almost certainly it stemmed from that 'new conception of marriage' that Irene had learned from her feminist friends. 'Irene may have proposed a terminable arrangement,' Beveridge concluded, 'or entirely separate establishments; or she may simply have asked him for a salary as wife and mother larger than he was able to afford.'[88]

Not surprisingly, many of Beveridge's friends were curious to know who had been the prototypes for John and Irene. It was hinted that John was Harry Tawney;[89] but it seems more probable that—in character if not in emotional experience—John was more closely based on Beveridge himself. Like Beveridge, John lived in a settlement before eventually entering the Home Civil Service; like Beveridge, he allowed himself to be domineered by strong-minded females; and like Beveridge he thought that 'a life not devoted to a purpose was no life at all'.[90] The character of Irene was not drawn from life, but was a blend of two high-spirited fictional heroines—Meredith's Clara Middleton and the Irene Iddesleigh of Amanda McKittrick Ros. Irene was undoubtedly Beveridge's favourite name: it seems to have conjured up for him the quintessence of mysterious femininity—a conception that was possibly inspired by the famous heroine of John Galsworthy, although Beveridge left no record of having read *The Forsyte Saga*.[91] Irene's story, and Beveridge's reflections upon it, may have been suggested by the fate of Richard and Helen Denman—who parted in 1909, apparently for no more concrete reason than that Helen could no longer bear the spiritual suffocation of marriage.[92] The book-burning incident was based on Henry Beveridge's burning of *Candida*, and the copper-beech tree beneath which it took place grew upon the Pitfold lawn.[93]

The moral that Beveridge drew from his story was that

woman's real problem, on which she has yet to settle her account with man and with society, lies not in any question of Education or Work or Wages but in the conditions of the marriage relation and all that springs from it; and that, until these last points are settled, women's and men's aspirations for true companionship will, as in the case of John and Irene themselves, be again and again defeated.[94]

The radical tone of this conclusion was to a certain extent belied, however, by the quotations that Beveridge chose to accompany his story. In selecting these quotations he reflected some of the dominant themes in the Edwardian feminist movement—the demand for women's education, for political equality, for improved working conditions and for financial and social support for mothers as the biological 'guardians of

[88] *John and Irene: an Anthology of Thoughts on Women* (1912), pp. vii–xix.
[89] BP, IIb, F. Darlow to WHB, 27 Nov. 1912.
[90] BP, IIa, WHB to ASB, 29 July 1912.
[91] His and Lady Beveridge's papers for this period contain numerous ms. fragments of short stories, all with a beautiful heroine called Irene. It was also the name of a sailing-boat that he shared with Richard Denman.
[92] BP, IIb, Helen Sutherland to WHB, 1 Sept. 1912.
[93] *PI*, pp. 110–11.
[94] *John and Irene*, p. 18.

the race'. Yet the dominant flavour of his quotations was not radical but highly traditional; and for every literary extract portraying women as 'equal partners' he chose ten portraying them as household goddesses, as amiable scatterbrains, or as beautiful, scheming, treacherous and unattainable coquettes.

# 5

## Labour Imperialist
## and Revolutionary Conservative

I

BEVERIDGE's three years as a leader-writer on the *Morning Post* coincided with many important developments in British politics and social policy. These years—late 1905 to mid 1908—saw the emergence of a significant parliamentary labour movement, the redefinition of pauperism and poverty by the Royal Commission on the Poor Laws, the spread of new concepts of fiscal redistribution, and the beginnings of non-stigmatic state welfare policies in the form of old-age pensions and subsidized school meals. Throughout the period there was an upsurge of interest in social policy questions—an interest that to a certain extent transcended the conventional boundaries of party, ideology and social class. It was within this context that Beveridge began to formulate his mature political beliefs—some of which were later modified, whilst others were to underpin his social philosophy for the rest of his career. It was during this period that he came close to embracing, and then eventually rejected certain principles of theoretical socialism. It was during this period that he first acquired a commitment to reform not merely as an end in itself but as an instrument of social and political integration. It was during this period that he first acquired his lifelong mistrust of all forms of direct democracy, and his preference for a centralized, enlightened and supposedly impartial administrative state. It was during this period that he first acquired his characteristic dislike of means tests, selective welfare, and discretionary official inquiry into private lives; and, finally, it was during this period that he first developed a deep suspicion of theory and an abiding preference for what he described as 'opportunist common sense'. To illustrate and illuminate these attitudes this chapter will look closely at three main aspects of Beveridge's ideas during his *Morning Post* period. Firstly, at the growth of his political convictions; secondly, at his responses to some current social and political issues; and thirdly at the development of his views on questions of social reform.

## II

As was shown in an earlier chapter Beveridge was slow to acquire political consciousness and he was suspicious and critical of conventional party politics. He has sometimes been referred to by historians as an archetypal representative of the 'new' or 'advanced' liberalism of the Edwardian era; but this view exaggerates both the degree and the certainty of his convictions at this time. He belonged to no Liberal Party organizations and on only one occasion in his correspondence of the pre-1914 period did he describe himself as a Liberal—and then it was in qualified and rather deprecatory terms.[1] He knew several members of the Rainbow Circle, the intellectual nucleus of 'new Liberalism', but he was never himself a member of this clique.[2] Nor can he be identified with the Liberal wing of the Edwardian 'progressive movement', since his attitudes both to war and to state power seem clearly to mark him off from this radical group.[3] When he joined the *Morning Post* in 1905 he described himself as 'a bit of a Socialist in speculative politics' and his practical views as 'strongly radical or socialist', but he was persuaded by his mother that there was nothing in his principles that need honestly prevent him from writing for a Tory paper.[4] Over the next few years he described himself at various times as a 'Labour imperialist', a 'Tory democrat' and as a 'tremendously revolutionary Conservative'; and he constantly disparaged the Liberals for what he perceived as their obsession with individualism and outworn constitutional freedoms. 'The Liberal Party . . . is sick to death,' he wrote in August 1906, '. . . it desires nothing . . . it is a party of negations.'[5]

These references all suggest a basic lack of commitment on party-political questions, and it is necessary to look beyond the confines of 'new liberalism' to understand fully the development of Beveridge's political beliefs at this time. He admired certain features of each political tradition—the collectivist liberalism of the *Daily News* radicals, the social imperialism of Chamberlain and Milner, and the non-revolutionary state socialism of Sidney and Beatrice Webb. But with none of these groups could he identify himself completely, and between 1904 and 1908 he was struggling to work out in his own terms a set of ideas about democracy, 'progress', the individual and the state. The changing

[1] BP, IIa, WHB to ASB, 24 Jan. 1910.      [2] BP, IIa, WHB to ASB, 23 June 1914.

[3] On Edwardian progressivism, see P. F. Clarke, 'The Progressive Movement in England', *Transactions of the Royal Historical Society*, 5, vol. xxiv (1974), pp. 159–81.

[4] BP, IIa, WHB to ASB, 25 Oct. 1905; ASB to WHB, 27 Oct. 1905; IXa, 35, ms. autobiography (1912), p. 12.

[5] BP, IIa, WHB to ASB, 26 Mar. 1906; IIb, R. Denman to WHB, 26 Nov. 1905, WHB to R. Denman, 18 Dec. 1905; E. M. Forster to WHB, 17 Mar. 1907; *MP*, 27 Aug. 1906.

contours of these ideas can be seen very clearly in his flirtation with theoretical socialism—a flirtation which in 1906–7 brought him, in his own words, 'very nearly' into the 'socialist fold'. His interest in socialism seems to have begun in 1904, shortly after he had first met the Webbs. He later recorded that

as any intelligent person of my age and interests must have been, I was deeply impressed by the Fabian movement. Sidney Webb and his associates gave one the sense that by taking sufficient thought one could remedy all the evils in the world, by reasoned progress.[6]

He began to attend Fabian meetings and made a detailed study of the Webbs' works on trade unionism—where for the first time in his life he encountered the socialist critique of capitalism and the free market.[7] In December 1904 he gave a lecture at Toynbee on 'Socialism in Books and in Facts', during the course of which he defined socialism as 'the right of society to override all private individual interests' and the 'power of society as an organism to make itself fit to survive'.[8] In June 1905 he denounced economic individualism before an audience at All Souls, and argued that collectivism was both ethically and functionally desirable in complex industrial societies.[9] Early in the following year he gave a paper on the 'Economics of Socialism' to the Oxford University Social Sciences Club; and this paper was highly significant, both for its favourable account of certain types of socialist theory and as an expression of Beveridge's own beliefs at the time. The view of socialism that he outlined was gradualist, bureaucratic and philosophically utilitarian. He carefully distinguished 'socialism' from 'communist, Anarchist, equalist utopias . . . [socialism] does not postulate altruism . . . it is not based on any fundamentally new or absurd view of human nature'. Nor did socialism necessarily entail equality or democracy or abolition of private property; instead it would simply subordinate the interests of individuals to those of the nation at large. This, he argued, was likely to be done only by 'a strong government, a remorselessly unsentimental government' and it would involve 'the extension of deliberate social action— in a word, organization—over fields hitherto left to the blind play of conflicting interests. It replaces the rule of natural law by the rule of the expert'. In practical terms, socialism would consist, not of 'social welfare' but of public control over production—not through nationalization, but through factory acts, organization of the labour market and other measures to compel economic efficiency. A 'socialist' social policy would

---

[6] BP, IXa 38 (1), WHB's notes on 'Relation to Webbs & Socialism', n.d.
[7] BP, III 1, ms. notes and statistics by WHB, c. 1904.
[8] BP, IXb 2, ms. Lectures and Addresses, 1904–10.
[9] BP, IXb 1, untitled ms. lecture on Plato and Aristotle.

mean, not transfer of responsibilities from the individual to the state but draconian measures against social failures and misfits—against 'the loafer, the criminal, the vicious and the unemployable', to stop them being a 'prey' upon the rest of society.[10] 'I preached a brand of socialism which I think some would-be critics found disappointingly like individualism,' Beveridge recorded afterwards. 'In my eyes socialism is not "doing things for people" or the assertion of the interests of the poor and the weak; it is an association of the interests of the state, viz. those interests of the citizens collectively which individually they are apt to forget, e.g. the individual sacrifices the future of the race to his present needs; the state by forbidding overwork, unemployment, etc. would be defending the future of the race.'[11]

The general tone of this paper, and Beveridge's subsequent comments upon it, suggest that it was in many respects not just an academic exercise but a statement of belief. The paper suggests also that at this stage in his career there was little to choose between Beveridge's political philosophy and that of the Fabian variant of socialism represented by the Webbs. From this time onwards, however, Beveridge's writings suggest a gradual retreat from socialist doctrines—a retreat expressed by his growing impatience with the ideas and policies of some leading left-wing groups. He had joined the Fabian Society as an associate member in 1904 and lectured for several years to Fabian summer schools. On one occasion in Cambridge he 'stormily' defended the Fabians against criticism from Alfred Marshall, who had accused them of 'jeering at orthodox economics' and 'posing' as friends of the working class.[12] Nevertheless, Beveridge never became a full member of the Fabian Society, and eventually resigned his associate membership in 1907. His attitude to the Labour Party was even more ambivalent. In January 1906 he welcomed the success of labour in the parliamentary election; but he was highly critical of the newly-formed Labour Party, partly because of its strong working-class bias and partly because of its commitment to restoring the privileged status of trade unions—a policy which Beveridge himself regarded as a 'profoundly anti-Socialist' measure.[13] In 1906 and 1907 he wrote several articles on the Marxist-inclined Social Democratic Federation; but although he approved the Federation's demand for more state welfare, he dismissed the rest of its programme as sectarian, utopian and basically irrelevant to the English political scene.[14] In August 1907 he reported a meeting of the International Socialist Congress and denounced its obsession with 'relics of

[10] BP, IXb 4, ms. lecture on 'Economics of Socialism', 1 Feb. 1906.
[11] BP, IIa, WHB to ASB, dated 31 Jan., but from the context clearly 1 or 2 Feb. 1906.
[12] BP, IIb, Alfred Marshall to WHB, 1 Mar. 1908; IIa, WHB to ASB, 4 Mar. 1908.
[13] *MP*, 1 Feb. and 9 Apr. 1906.          [14] *MP*, 15 Apr. 1906, 1 Apr. 1907.

Marxist dogmas' and the doctrine of class war. 'It is obvious,' he wrote, 'that this theory of the "class war" . . . is in the nature of a pious dogma. It has no importance for any practical question. Its consideration may be safely postponed for some two thousand years to come.'[15]

As Beveridge's enthusiasm for socialism waned, so did his never very powerful belief in the virtues of popular democracy; and, in particular, he was disturbed by what he believed was the growing trend for politicians to act, not as individual representatives, nor even as members of a party, but as the docile instruments of a particular faction or class.[16] This suspicion of popular politics was reinforced by his personal experience of working with distress committees in East London—by the 'costly red tape . . . lucrative contracts to local tenderers and soft jobs to local workmen', and by the ignorance and ineptitude which he perceived in the vast majority of local councillors and guardians.[17] It was strengthened also by reading works on American politics, in particular the studies of Ostrogorski and Graham Wallas, which he described as presenting 'truly a vivid picture of corruption and perversion of democratic institutions'.[18] This mistrust of direct democracy was implicitly or explicitly apparent in many of Beveridge's writings of the time—in his dislike of civil disobedience and popular demonstrations, his opposition to referenda, and his resistance to enfranchisement of paupers and other recipients of public relief.[19] He repeatedly advocated greater central control of local authorities, more power for non-elected 'experts' and more effective sanctions to enforce the law.[20] And in a long article in August 1907 he defended the need for paternalistic legislation, denounced 'extreme democracies' both ancient and modern, and concluded that 'one of the lessons that democracies learn unwillingly, but have to learn at last, is that in the last resort they must trust somebody or other with great and continued power if government is to be carried on at all'.[21]

Another important feature of Beveridge's ideas at this time was his growing belief in the value of policies designed to promote social cohesion and ward off political conflict—a belief that was almost certainly influenced by his study of the social institutions of Imperial Germany. It was most apparent in his passionate advocacy of contributory social insurance, which will be considered in more detail below. But it can be seen also in his dislike of 'class politics', his criticism of attempts to divide Liberals from Labour and his fear that Labour would become

[15] *MP*, Aug. 1907.          [16] BP, IIa, WHB to ASB, 22 Jan. 1910.
[17] *MP*, 13 Mar. 1906; BP, IIa, WHB to ASB, 18 Mar. 1906.
[18] BP, IIa, WHB to AJB, 11 June 1907 and 25 Feb. 1909.
[19] *MP*, 25 Aug. 1906. W. H. Beveridge, 'The Question of Disfranchisement', *Toynbee Record*, Mar. 1905, pp. 100–2; BP, IIa, WHB to ASB, 31 July 1911.
[20] *MP*, 9 May and 19 June 1906.          [21] *MP*, 13 Aug. 1907.

exclusively a party of the working class.[22] Instead he argued that the working class should be deliberately integrated into the existing socio-economic system; and with this end in view he supported state assistance of friendly societies, the growth of profit-sharing schemes, and the promotion of public companies. Such policies, he argued, would muffle the cleavage between capital and labour, divert capital into the hands of the working classes and 'give a large and growing proportion of the people an interest in at least the fundamentals of the existing order'. They would also help to obviate 'the absence of contact—the separation of classes', which he believed was 'the greatest source of weakness in the modern state'.[23]

## III

As the employee of a Conservative paper there were clearly constraints on what Beveridge could say about current politics, at least when writing in the *Morning Post*. Nevertheless, he certainly did not feel himself to be a retained party hack and he claimed that he 'never wrote anything that I did not at the time of writing sincerely believe'. His brief from his Editor was merely to write on social problems; and when he wrote on wider issues it was because he deliberately chose to do so. There is therefore little reason to suppose that Beveridge's frequent *Morning Post* articles on current political topics did not represent his own views at the time. He himself recorded that 'the only way in which the political complexion of the *Morning Post* consciously affected my writing, was that while I might be as rude as I liked to the Liberal leaders I had (except in regard to Mr. Balfour) to be polite and reasonable in admonishing or arguing with the Unionist leaders. In fact there were of course many points on which I (and the Liberals) cordially disagreed.'[24]

Beveridge's views on specific political issues were in many respects as revealing as his more general political beliefs; and the characteristic ambivalance of his views can be seen in his commentary on many current issues—such as imperialism, femininism, temperance, local government reform, the status of trade unions and the rise of labour. In foreign affairs he was at this time undoubtedly an imperialist. He believed that as a matter of historical necessity 'progressive nations' would increasingly dominate undeveloped nations; and on this ground he supported the world-wide export of British institutions, condemned

---

[22] See below, p. 94.

[23] BP, IIa, WHB to ASB, 16 May 1906; *MP*, 13 Mar. 1907, 16 Apr. 1908.

[24] BP, IXa 35, 'Autobiography', pp. 13 and 15; XII2, ms. note attached to vol. III of 'Contributions to Morning Post', p. 106.

the Liberal 'little-Englanders' and defended the American annexation of Cuba in 1906.[25] On the feminist question his publicly-expressed opinions may well have been inhibited by the views of his mother, who was a militant Anti-Suffragette. Early in 1906 Beveridge defended the principle of women's suffrage in the *Morning Post* but he implied that there were major practical objections to giving women the vote—in particular, that extension of the existing 'head-of-household' suffrage would merely enfranchise a few middle-class, property-owning females, while the introduction of 'universal' suffrage would enfranchise many vicious and socially-undesirable property-less males. He suggested that, in any case, the vote was much less important than involvement of women in public life, and that neither was so important as the need to buttress the family and to encourage wifehood and motherhood with financial support from the state.[26] Throughout 1907 he condemned suffragette violence, but he was equally appalled by the hysterical behaviour of a vocal backbench minority who repeatedly 'talked out' a woman's suffrage bill in the House of Commons.[27] He was finally converted to votes for women by a massive peaceful suffrage demonstration in June 1908—after which he rather grudgingly conceded that female suffrage might be a useful 'educational measure' and that the rearing of children was not 'necessarily done best . . . by people taught to regard themselves and agreeing to regard themselves as fitly ranked with aliens, criminals, lunatics and paupers'.[28]

It was on the issue of temperance and licensing reform that Beveridge's views most strongly differed from *Morning Post* editorial policy, and on this question he rather daringly trailed radical notions under the very noses of his Conservative employers. 'I only hope Drink, i.e. Licensing Reform, won't be my ruin,' he recorded; 'I don't like brewers a bit and shall have to tread warily.'[29] His position was perhaps partially secured by the fact that the *Morning Post*'s proprietor, Lord Glenesk, belonged to the Chamberlainite wing of the Unionist Party, which had sponsored a limited measure of licensing reform in 1904. Beveridge was, however, highly critical of the 1904 Licensing Act, arguing that, by merely limiting the number of liquor licences, it had increased the monopoly value of those that remained. On the other hand, he was equally opposed to the total abstinence school still prominent within the Liberal Party—not on grounds of principle, but because he thought that very severe temperance legislation would be impossible to enforce. Instead he advocated what he claimed was a policy of compromise,

---

[25] *MP*, 21 June, 27 Sept. 1906.
[26] *MP*, 21 May, 18 June, 19 Sept. and 19 Nov. 1906.
[27] *MP*, 8, 9, and 21 Mar. 1907.          [28] *MP*, 15 June, 1908.
[29] BP, IIa, WHB to ASB, 20 Feb. 1907.

though to some at least of his readers it must have seemed very extreme—namely, municipal ownership of public houses, transfer to the state of the monopoly value of all licences, severe limitation of opening hours and abolition of profit from all retail sales of drink.[30]

If 'drink' divided Beveridge from his Tory readers, his views on local government divided him even more sharply from the radical wing of the Liberals. Since the 1890s many advanced Liberals had been pressing for drastic reforms in the financing of local government—for redistribution of income between rich and poor localities and for much larger subsidies to local authorities from the State. Beveridge agreed with the radicals that there was a real problem, and that in poor areas something should be done to relieve local rates. But he claimed in rather Gladstonian terms that it would be fatal to local efficiency and integrity to divorce local management of services from local obligation to pay. His own preference, which reflected his more fundamental distrust of the pressures of local democracy, was for fewer, larger, local authorities and for the creation of large-scale regional authorities to supply specialist services, such as transport, water, electricity and gas. Such authorities, he argued, could make intelligent use of expert advisers, they could be free from the constraints of local democracy, and they could with their own resources equalize the burden of the local rates.[31]

Beveridge's interest in industrial relations dated back to his period as a law student in 1902. He had studied trade union law, and this was the one specialist area of law that continued to interest him after he had abandoned the bar. His interest was aroused by the major political controversy that surrounded the unions in the early 1900s, after a series of judicial decisions had overturned or reinterpreted existing trade union Law. Between 1899 and 1901, a court of appeal decision in the case of *Lyon* v. *Wilkins* had challenged the legality of peaceful picketing, the House of Lords in the Taff Vale judgement had revived trade union liability to damages arising from actions of union members; and a further appeal decision in the case of *Quinn* v. *Leatham* had called in question the right to strike. These decisions had caused a furore throughout the industrial world, and between 1902 and 1905 a series of private members' bills was introduced into Parliament, which tried unsuccessfully to restore the earlier law.[32] Beveridge whilst at Toynbee gave a series of lectures on trade unionism, in which he criticized the 'individualist' bias of the judicial bench;[33] and in 1904 he wrote a long article setting out his own views on reform of trade union law. In this article

---

[30] *MP*, 16, 17, 19 Apr. and 26 May 1906.

[31] *MP*, 9 May, 2 and 9 July 1906; 18 Jan., 13 Feb. 15 and 22 Apr. 1907; 3 Apr. 1908.

[32] Henry Pelling, *Popular Politics and Society in Late-Victorian Britain* (1968), pp. 74, 76–8.

[33] BP, IXb 2, ms. Lectures and Addresses, 1904–10.

he argued that *Quinn* v. *Leatham* should be instantly reversed by statute; but on the other two cases his proposals were much more cautious. The right of peaceful picketing he thought should be restored, but only for trade unionists 'acting in parties of not more than two together'. The Taff Vale judgement he thought should be retained; but he proposed that registered unions should be specifically excluded from liability for damages in respect of non-criminal actions 'in direct furtherance of a trade dispute'. Except in this respect, trade unions should be bound by law like other corporations and should operate within a framework of legal rules. These reforms, he argued, were all that was necessary to restore to the unions 'that powerful but entirely peaceable force of con-certed action which is part of the accepted order of our great industries'. Anything less would rob the unions of their recognized *raison d'être* but anything more would 'open the door to persecution and organized violence', and place trade unions outside the law.[34]

Beveridge's views fell far short of the most advanced labour and radical thinking on this issue, as he found when he tried to get his article published in various progressive magazines. He submitted it to Edward Jenks, his old Balliol law tutor, who was also editor of the *Independent Review*. Jenks showed it to several leading trades unionists, who advised unanimously against publication, on the ground that Beveridge's pro-posals constituted an irreducible minimum of labour demands, which should only be put forward when all else had failed.[35] His transition to the *Morning Post* however, gave him a ready-made platform on indus-trial questions, and in a long series of articles over the next two years he proceeded to elaborate his ideas on trade union law. He pressed for much wider recognition of trade unions, for development of female unionism, and for state assistance to the unions' welfare functions; and by early 1906 he had come round to the view that both *Quinn* v. *Leatham* and *Lyon* v. *Wilkins* should be totally repealed.[36] He continued, however, to uphold Taff Vale, and was highly critical of Labour and radical-Liberal M.P.s who were pressing for legislation to revive trade union immunity from damages for tort. He approved the recommendation of the Royal Commission on Trades Unions that, although strikes should be legal, contracts entered into by the unions should be enforceable and binding; and in March 1906 he welcomed the Liberal Trades Disputes Bill which proposed to legislate on these lines.[37] In the following month, however, the government accepted a Labour amendment which virtu-ally repealed Taff Vale—a concession which Beveridge interpreted as

[34] W. H. Beveridge, 'The Reform of Trade Union Law', *Economic Review*, Apr. 1905, pp. 129–49.

[35] BP, IIb, Edward Jenks to WHB, 5 Mar. 1904.

[36] *MP*, 22 Mar., 17 Aug. 1906; 13 May 1907.

[37] *MP*, 21, 29 and 30 Mar. 1906.

the collapse of an 'invertebrate majority' before the onslaught of a ruthless militant sectarian group. Throughout the passage of the amended bill he continued to denounce it for encouraging 'coercive action on the borderline of intimidation' and for placing the unions above the law. In particular he condemned the unions for what he perceived as their indifference to political principle and to any interests except their own. 'They are certainly devoid of any political theory,' he wrote: 'the anarchical proposals of the Trade Disputes Bill are in direct opposition to the only political theory—Socialism—of which they are suspected.'[38]

Beveridge's suspicion of the unions largely accounts for his highly ambivalent attitude towards the Labour Representation Committee, reconstituted as the Labour Party in 1906. He greeted the new party in heavily qualified terms, welcoming its commitment to social reform, but strongly deprecating what he believed to be the sentimental fallacy that a man who had suffered bad social conditions had some kind of special insight into how they should be cured. He believed that poverty, far from broadening a man's political sympathies, tended to make him 'materialist . . . narrow-minded, self-interested, incapable of high political ideals'; and he would clearly have preferred to see Labour, not as an independent party, but as a useful ginger-group, inspired and directed by the radical middle class.[39] For this reason he was highly critical both of Labour leaders for asserting their political autonomy and of right-wing Liberals who tried to dissociate themselves from the independent Labour group. Such a policy, he prophesied, would ultimately lead to an intensification of class conflict and to the eclipse of the Liberals as an active political force.[40] In June 1908 he deplored the transfer of the miners' M.P.s from Liberal to Labour benches, anticipating that this would destroy the two-party system and make it difficult for the Liberals ever again to obtain an absolute parliamentary majority.[41] He deplored also what he regarded as the confirmation of his 'worst fears', when Labour not only secured the repeal of Taff Vale, but began to press for municipal trading and guaranteed public employment—policies which he denounced as fatal to economic efficiency and social evolution. 'The dangerous aspect of English socialism,' he wrote, was not 'revolution or free love', but 'sentiment' and 'overconfidence' in trying to abolish competition and prop up 'the unfit', without making any alternative provision for promoting human progress. 'A state,' he concluded, 'cannot refuse to let the less industrious, the less competent, the less inventive suffer the disadvantages of their inferiority without itself becoming inferior.' The solution, he thought, lay not in political

[38] *MP*, 26 Apr., 27 and 28 July, 2 and 10 Nov. 1906.
[39] *MP*, 1 Feb., 27 and 31 Aug. 1906.     [40] *MP*, 27 Aug. 1906.
[41] *MP*, 6 June 1908.

'sentimentality', nor in a return to free competition, but in 'systematic collective action to protect or limit or adjust the activities of individuals' and in 'measures of social reform so devised as to preserve the essential conditions of progress while mitigating or limiting the painful effects'.[42]

## IV

Whilst at Toynbee Hall Beveridge had come to the conclusion that involvement in social policy was by its nature a highly political activity, and he was very critical of people who tried to divorce social welfare from a much broader context of political action and political debate.[43] Throughout the Edwardian period his ideas on social policy closely mirrored his more general political convictions, such as his belief in the role of the expert, in 'social organization' and in the assertion of national interests over those of the individual, class or group. In particular, he increasingly viewed social policy as a means of promoting social cohesion and of harmonizing the warring forces unleashed by the free market. As with the wider aspects of politics, his views on social policy did not fit neatly into any pre-ordained party categories; they were highly eclectic and idiosyncratic, borrowing from and influenced by many different strands of liberal, conservative and socialist thought. Beveridge's approach to social problems can perhaps most characteristically be seen in his studies of unemployment, his analysis of poverty, his advocacy of social insurance, and his contribution to the prevailing debate on heredity and environment. His views on unemployment will be discussed extensively in a later chapter, since this was the area in which he made his greatest impact on early twentieth-century social policy. However, it is worth looking also in some detail at his ideas on poverty and social insurance and at his views of both the 'eugenic' and 'environmental' schools of Edwardian social reform.

Beveridge first directly encountered the problem of poverty whilst he was employed at Toynbee Hall—as a practical problem through working on local relief committees and as a conceptual problem through reading reports of the Charity Organisation Society and the works of such writers as Charles Booth, Alfred Marshall, and Sidney and Beatrice Webb. In his early days at Toynbee he was strongly influenced by the C.O.S. point of view that poverty was primarily a problem of personal character and lax social administration, and this view was only gradually displaced by a more impersonal conception of poverty as an economic phenomenon largely outside the individual's control. In 1904 he first came across the Webbs' idea of a statutory 'national minimum',

---

[42] *MP*, 18 Apr. 1908.
[43] *Toynbee Record*, July–Sept. 1904, p. 139.

designed to give everyone a basic minimum income calculated in accordance with subsistence needs. This concept has often been seen as of crucial importance in Beveridge's own contribution to theories of welfare;[44] and it is interesting to note that his first reaction to the idea of a national minimum was markedly unenthusiastic. 'The authors disregard here a fundamental difficulty,' he complained.

> Is the minimum to be that which will keep a single person or which will keep a whole family? If it is to be the former the minimum will hardly produce much effect (10s. to 12s. perhaps) and would still allow of sweating where the worker was in fact responsible for a family. Il it is to be the latter . . . it will *enormously* increase the class of 'unemployables'—by all persons who can earn say 20s. but not 25s. a week. It would probably effectually prevent all 'supplementary' wage-earning.[45]

Nevertheless, Beveridge's views on the treatment of poverty developed rapidly over the next two years; and in his lecture at All Souls in 1905 he declared that 'destruction of the monster poverty' had become the first priority of a civilized society, without which all other 'social ideals' were bereft of meaning and value. In the same lecture Beveridge vividly contrasted the view of poverty held by the classical economists with the view that had emerged among economic writers during the previous twenty years. To the orthodox classical economist poverty was not a social problem but an economic fact. It was the inevitable condition of the bulk of the working class, and all attempts at redistribution were both morally wrong and practically self-defeating—wrong because they infringed the rights of property, self-defeating because they depleted the funds available for investment and thus destroyed the sources of wealth. Now, however, Beveridge claimed that 'Economic Science no longer gives sanction to the view that poverty is incurable'. The 'extraordinary fatalism' of the orthodox view of poverty had been exposed as a 'moral error' and the sanctity of property had been exposed as an 'intellectual error'; both were merely 'plastic conventions, which the community makes for its own purposes and may remould at its will'.[46]

From early 1905 onwards Beveridge was convinced, like many other radical thinkers of the Edwardian era, that industrial societies could produce the wealth necessary to abolish poverty, and that the crucial problem remaining for economists was how to devise an effective method of redistribution of resources. In the *Morning Post* he strongly denounced the traditional view that welfare benefits such as pensions or free school

---

[44] e.g. by Beveridge himself in *The London School of Economics and its Problems 1919–1937* (1960), p. 98.

[45] BP, III 1, ms. notes and statistics by WHB, *c.* 1904.

[46] BP, IXb 1, untitled ms. lecture on Plato and Aristotle, 1905.

meals would depress the level of wages; instead he argued that they would boost consumer demand, increase employment and ultimately help to *raise* levels of industrial remuneration.[47] He became increasingly critical of the Charity Organisation view tnat generous welfare payments positively encouraged poverty and social dependence—pointing out that if people could be corrupted by bad social administration then they could surely be corrupted by a harsh industrial environment in a very similar way.[48] At the same time he was increasingly influenced by the marginalist arguments of writers like Hobson and Urwick; and he justified progressive taxation to his *Morning Post* readers on the ground that the 'last pound' of a rich man's income brought him much less happiness than the 'last pound' of the income of the poor.[49]

Nevertheless, although Beveridge was convinced of the need for redistribution he was highly sceptical of many contemporary proposals for bringing this about. In a review of Chiozza Money's *Riches and Poverty* he criticized Money's proposal for an overall equalization of incomes, arguing that some measure of inequality was necessary for economic efficiency.[50] Except in the case of sweated industries he was opposed to a statutory minimum wage, on the ground that this would drive many marginal workers out of the labour force; and he was equally opposed to a guaranteed right to work, on the ground that this would encourage inefficiency and uneconomic production.[51] At the same time he was increasingly critical of relief schemes based on means tests—on the grounds that they were unfair to those just above the poverty-line and likely to destroy incentives among the working class.[52] Most strongly of all he condemned proposals from the C.O.S. for converting the Poor Law into a gigantic system of casework, in which relief would be given only when accompanied by 'advice, encouragement or moral exhortation' from trained almoners and charitable volunteers. Such a system, Beveridge conceded, might achieve the objective of promoting contact between different social classes; but it totally ignored the economic causes of poverty and 'simply stereotype[d] an unhealthy relationship of patron and dependant' between rich and poor.[53]

Beveridge's caution about panaceas for poverty persisted throughout his life, and was central to much of his thinking on social reform. His doubts and hesitations on this subject may be very simply explained in the following way. He believed that capitalist production had resulted in a highly inequitable distribution of resources, but at the same time

---

[47] *MP*, 11 Apr. 1906.
[48] *MP*, 31 Jan. 1907, WHB's review of *The Manufacture of Paupers*, ed. J. St. Loe Strachey.
[49] *MP*, 15 May 1908.          [50] *MP*, 7 Dec. 1905.
[51] *MP*, 14 July and 21 Nov. 1906, 10 Dec. 1907.
[52] *MP*, 11 Apr. and 8 Dec. 1906, 3 Jan. and 11 Oct. 1907.
[53] *MP*, 14 May 1906.

that it was the *only* system capable of producing the wealth that was a prerequisite if poverty was to be abolished. The problem as Beveridge saw it therefore was how to modify the capitalist system of distribution without in any way hampering the process of production. Such a method he believed must continue to reward efficiency, it must continue to encourage personal saving and it must not undermine incentives to work.

These concerns lay at the heart of Beveridge's approach to poverty, and they help to explain his sponsorship of social insurance as the chief if not the only method of relieving financial need. In June 1905 he wrote that 'the danger of weakening the incentive to work, supplied by the institution of property, forms the greatest difficulty in the way of all projects of industrial reform'; and he was highly critical of attempts to 'humanise public relief without first humanising industrial conditions'— on the ground that this would make relief 'unduly attractive to the lowest class'.[54] Redistribution of resources was pointless, if workers were thereby induced to withdraw their services from the labour market; and on this point Beveridge was in complete agreement with the Poor Law Amendment Act of 1834. On the other hand it would be wrong to see Beveridge as subscribing to a mid-nineteenth-century ideal of the so called 'work ethic'. In his lecture at All Souls in 1905 he roundly denounced the 'absurd apotheosis of useful toil', and of 'labour for its own sake', which he believed was dominant in all industrial societies. This doctrine was 'a conscious device of the upper classes for stimulating industry in the lower classes' and was 'both base and false'. On the contrary Beveridge argued, the 'object of life' was 'not labour but leisure'. 'People sometimes talk,' he remarked on one occasion, 'as if all that a man wanted was regular work. It was nothing of the sort. What they really wanted was a regular income. Regular work was of no great value to anyone except as a kind of discipline for the young.'[55] Work for all but the fortunate few who actually enjoyed it was, he argued, a necessary evil; and one of the major objectives of social policy should be to ensure that everyone shared both an adequate amount of leisure and a necessary minimum of work.

As a basis for social policy Beveridge's formula was clearly open to a number of objections—particularly that he nowhere discussed just how much work was 'necessary' nor who was to determine the optimum balance between leisure and work. Nevertheless his views on work have been considered in some detail because they were fundamental to his views on social insurance and on the economic relationship between the

---

[54] BP, IXb 1, ms. lecture on Plato and Aristotle, 1905; Webb Local Government Collection, Coll. V. part II, vol. 297, item B66, WHB to B. Webb, 11 Dec. 1908.

[55] *Daily Chronicle*, 10 Aug. 1910, press cutting in XII4, p. 32.

individual and the state. Underlying all his ideas on welfare was the belief that in the last resort men would not work unless they were compelled to do so—either by economic necessity or by cultural pressures or by the force of law. This was not because they were immoral but because, except in the case of a few exceptional persons, it was 'part of human nature to prefer leisure to work'. Work was a social not a spiritual obligation, and a corollary of this obligation was that people who worked should be adequately paid. A man had no moral duty to work if he could get more from public welfare; and Beveridge specifically stated that it was better for a family to be on poor relief than to live on a sweated wage.[56]

Beveridge's interest in social insurance as a means of meeting financial need was first aroused by the movement for statutory old-age pensions. Since the 1880s there had been a great deal of discussion in England about poverty in old age, and many different proposals had been put forward for some kind of old-age pension. The most important of these were Joseph Chamberlain's plan for contributory old-age pensions insurance, Charles Booth's plan for universal tax-financed pensions, and a scheme recommended by a Select Committee of the House of Commons for paying pensions based on a means test to the 'aged deserving poor'.[57] Beveridge became involved in the old-age pensions movement in 1905; and early in 1906 he outlined four different possible methods of providing state relief for poverty in old age. Firstly, the state could subsidize voluntary superannuation insurance, managed by friendly societies, trade unions and other private institutions. Secondly, the state could compel its citizens to provide against old age by contributions deducted from wages. Thirdly, the state could pay a non-contributory, means-tested pension to those in financial need. And, finally, the state could simply give an old-age pension as a 'free gift to everybody above a certain age who likes to claim it'. To each of these models, Beveridge argued, it was possible to advance certain major objections. Subsidies to voluntary saving would not meet the problem of those who could not or would not save. Compulsory insurance, of the kind introduced into Germany in the 1880s, entailed 'an amount of regulation and identification of individuals entirely foreign to British habits'. Means-tested non-contributory pensions, of the kind already paid in New Zealand and Australia, constituted a disincentive to saving and encouragement to fraud. Free universal pensions of the kind proposed by Booth would be administratively simple and would not penalize thrift; but they would

[56] *MP*, 4 July 1907. He expressed similar views at the time of the Beveridge Report forty-five years later (see below, p. 414).

[57] P. M. Williams, *The Development of Old Age Pensions Policy in Great Britain 1878–1925* (London Ph.D. 1970), chs. 3 and 4.

be exorbitantly expensive and would be paid to many people who were not at all in need.[58]

Early in 1906 Beveridge seems to have been most in favour of a free universal pension of the type sponsored by Booth; but over the next year he gradually shifted his ground, partly in response to the financial realities of the situation and partly because he began to fear that even a *universal* non-contributory pension might discourage voluntary thrift.[59] In April 1907 when the Chancellor of the Exchequer, Mr. Asquith, promised to set aside £2¼ million for an as yet unformulated pension scheme Beveridge in a leading article pressed for adoption of the contributory German system rather than the means-tested New Zealand model.[60] Then in September 1907 he paid a visit to Germany to inspect the social security arrangements set up by Bismarck over twenty years before; and there in the Mecca of national efficiency he found what appeared to be overwhelming practical confirmation of his own ideas. He discovered a network of contributory social insurance agencies, which covered 12 million workers against sickness, disablement and old age. The system was financed by tripartite contributions from workers, employers and the state; and workers were entitled to a wide range of social welfare benefits, which included earnings-related maintenance payments, medical and hospital treatment, and permanent invalidity pensions payable from the date at which each worker individually became medically incapable of work. The economic and political implications of this system were summed up by Beveridge in a series of articles later in 1907. He estimated that social insurance cost German industry £33 million a year—a tax which by British standards was absolutely prohibitive; and yet, he argued, the German economy was apparently flourishing as never before. Administratively the system was a unique combination of pluralism and centralization, since benefits were managed by numerous small, self-governing societies and yet overall principles and financial arrangements were carefully prescribed by the state. The system depended on universal registration of all employed citizens; and it forced the government to become intimately acquainted with a whole range of socio-economic questions—with sickness and mortality tables, prediction of trade depressions and promotion of personal and public health. Moreover, in a strictly political sense, social insurance was of growing importance in the life of the German nation. One of Bismarck's original objectives, Beveridge recalled, had been to use social security to win the support of the masses away from revolutionary socialism; and in this the insurance system had partially succeeded and partially failed. The Social Democratic Party had continued to expand over the previous twenty years and was now the largest single

[58] *MP*, 16 Feb. 1906.          [59] *MP*, 21 Nov. 1906.          [60] *MP*, 20 Apr. 1907.

party in the Reichstag; but at the same time it had become increasingly moderate and revisionist in its aims. An important element in this transformation, Beveridge concluded, had been the institution of social insurance, which helped to promote inter-class collaboration and through its self-governing machinery brought 'men of all sorts into co-operation with one another, in insurance associations, arbitration tribunals, management of sick funds and countless other ways'.[61]

Beveridge from this time onwards became a powerful advocate of compulsory insurance; and he was highly critical of the Liberal government when in 1908 it opted for a selective scheme of non-contributory pensions, confined to deserving citizens of limited means over seventy years of age.[62] The Old Age Pensions Act, he argued, was typical of the government's piecemeal and unscientific approach to questions of social reform; it was both mean and sentimental, it was based on inadequate sociological knowledge and it took no account of undesirable secondary consequences, such as the penalization of thrift.[63] Beveridge himself was convinced that the Act would prove a disincentive to saving, and he cited the case of the Leicestershire miners, who were abandoning their voluntary superannuation scheme because it would disqualify them from the statutory old-age pension.[64] He strongly attacked Lloyd George's argument that a contributory system could only pay benefits after twenty years—pointing out that in Germany pensions had been paid within a year of the first contributions.[65] He was convinced also that the qualifying age for the government pension was much too high—arguing from the evidence of trade union records that the average age of working-class retirement was sixty-three and a half.[66] In general he condemned the scheme for projecting the image of 'the State as Lady Bountiful' and for degrading its citizens by forcing people to 'declare themselves as poor'.[67] Above all he was scornful of Asquith for putting forward what he described as 'the orthodox Whig excuse' that no machinery was available for contributory insurance. 'The want of administrative machinery,' Beveridge argued, 'far from being an objection—is in reality the main reason in favour of the contributory scheme. Half the virtue of such a scheme lies in the machinery which it compels the state to establish, and which when established serves many purposes besides its immediate one. It affords the basis of knowledge and organization, which is essential if social reform is to be something other than chaotic philanthropy.'[68]

[61] 'Social Reform: How Germany deals with it', series of articles in *MP*, Sept. 1907.
[62] P. M. Williams, op. cit., pp. 218–19; Bentley B. Gilbert, *The Evolution of National Insurance in Great Britain, The Origins of the Welfare State*, pp. 215–26.
[63] *MP*, 28 May 1908.   [64] *MP*, 14 Dec. 1907.   [65] *MP*, 21 May 1908.
[66] *MP*, 4 June 1908.   [67] *MP*, 14 Dec. 1907.   [68] *MP*, 8 and 29 May 1908.

Beveridge's espousal of contributory insurance has been seen as 'entirely pragmatic'; and on one level this is correct.[69] Certainly he had come to see insurance as the most effective method of relieving poverty, and the one least likely to have harmful long-term repercussions in the form of personal stigmatization or discouragement to thrift. On another level, however, his choice was not pragmatic; it coincided with some of his most deeply-held assumptions about the ideal relationship between the individual and the state. As we have seen, he was anxious that social policy should palliate conflict between the classes; and he believed that the complex nature of advanced industrial societies required a much higher degree of 'social organization' than had been seen as desirable in the age of *laissez-faire*. By 'social organization' Beveridge meant, literally, the promotion and enhancement of the 'organic' nature of society; and he suggested that this could be brought about in three practical ways. Firstly, the state itself should take a much more positive role in regulating the lives of its citizens—in eliminating inefficiency, laying down minimum standards and identifying needs. Secondly, citizens themselves should play an active part in day-to-day management of social welfare services—not through political parties or through local government but through voluntary bodies like friendly societies, trade unions and organizations of consumers. And thirdly, the vast network of voluntary self-help organizations should themselves no longer be seen as alternatives to state action but should be brought into co-operation with the machinery of the state. Such policies Beveridge believed, were consistent with the mutual interdependence of men in complex modern societies and with the need for social and political integration. Only by intervention in individual lives could the state acquire the necessary knowledge for scientific social reform. Only by integration in the state could potentially selfish pressure groups be tamed and harnessed to public ends. Only by taking part in provision of public services could individuals be forced 'to know more of the state, and to know it not as an abstraction, but as an organisation of which they form a part and to which they owe duties'.[70] Beveridge's commitment to social insurance was therefore more than merely pragmatic; it stemmed from a much wider conception of the nature of society, as an increasingly complex organism in which it was desirable to foster social solidarity and feelings of identification with a benevolent state. This vision of society was in many ways strikingly similar to that of the contemporary French sociologist, Emile Durkheim, although there is no evidence to suggest that Beveridge read any work of Durkheim either at this or any later stage of his career. It was similar also to the organic Liberalism preached by L. T. Hobhouse, although again there is nothing to suggest that Bever-

[69] P. M. Williams, op. cit., p. 203.          [70] *MP*, 8 Feb., 8 May and 8 July 1908.

idge was consciously influenced by Hobhouse's ideas. The belief in 'social organisation', not merely as an instrument of welfare but as centrally important to the cohesion of modern societies, provides a vital clue to the whole of Beveridge's thinking and was to be the chief corner-stone of his approach to social policy from his time at Toynbee until his authorship forty years later of the Beveridge Report.

## V

Beveridge's interest in poverty also brought him into contact with the contemporary debate on heredity and environment and their relevance to issues of social reform. This controversy had been brought to the fore-front of political discussion by the famous interdepartmental inquiry into 'physical deterioration' at the end of the Boer war.[71] A majority of witnesses before the inquiry ascribed physical deterioration to the environmental effect of life in great cities—to overcrowding, deficiencies in diet, and unhealthy conditions of work. A minority of witnesses claimed, however, that physical deterioration should be ascribed to eugenic factors—that social and medical progress had upset the process of natural selection and were producing a race of the mentally and physically unfit. Reviewing the committee's report in the *Toynbee Record* Beveridge remarked that the relative influence of environment and 'congenital weakness' was not yet clear; and he suggested that, to test the validity of both positions, detailed research should be carried out on representative working-class families and 'their development, history, decline and fall'.[72] A year later, however, in a series of articles on infant mortality, he came down firmly for an environmentalist approach to reform. Infant mortality, he argued, varied throughout Britain between town and countryside, between different social classes and between rich and poor areas, in a way that was manifestly related to external physical conditions. 'Infant mortality is neither a symptom nor a result of racial degeneration,' Beveridge concluded, '. . . the vast bulk of all children are born physically sound—the national stock is *not* tainted, it is the environment before and after birth that counts.' More-over, he challenged the view that infant mortality was a form of healthy natural selection—claiming instead that the very same conditions that killed off some children also injured those who were left. 'The same environment—bad food, bad air, bad clothing—that kills the unfit must inevitably cripple and stunt the more fit, and can be shown to do so in many cases by positive observation.'[73]

Nevertheless, Beveridge's views on heredity were no less complex and

[71] Bentley B. Gilbert op. cit. pp. 88–95.     [72] *Toynbee Record*, May 1905, p. 126.
[73] *MP*, 15 June 1906.

ambivalent than on other social questions; and although he continued to deny its significance in relation to infant mortality it is clear that he did not exclude it from other comparable issues. On one occasion he shocked R. H. Tawney by expressing the view that the upper classes 'represent on the whole a higher level of character and ability than the working classes because in the course of time better stocks have tended to come to the top'.[74] In 1907 he ridiculed the views of a certain Doctor Reich that alcoholism was an ineradicable genetic condition, that temperance merely transmitted the disease to future generations, and that alcoholics should therefore be positively encouraged to drink themselves into extinction. But at the same time Beveridge was clearly concerned that alcoholism *might* be hereditary; and he concluded that 'the moral of the theory is not to let the inebriate drink himself to death but to shut him up where he can leave no posterity'.[75] He expressed similar views about criminals, vagrants, and the unemployable, arguing that the habitual criminal and vagrant were 'diseased with a disease which may be transmissable at birth'.[76] He was alarmed also at the dysgenic effects of sweated industries and one of his chief reasons for supporting the campaign against sweating was that long hours, low wages and bad conditions would combine to produce a 'degenerate posterity'.[77] The area in which he was most strongly influenced by eugenic arguments, however, was in his attitude to treatment of mental subnormality. Commenting on the opening of a school in Whitechapel for mentally handicapped children he remarked that many handicapped people could acquire 'special skills'—that much so-called handicap was merely 'late development'. Nevertheless he questioned whether there might not be a residue of incurably 'feeble-minded persons' for whom remedial treatment in childhood 'would ultimately bring more harm than good'.[78] He was similarly disturbed by a report from the medical officer of the Metropolitan Asylums Board, describing the case of a boy of weak intellect, who had one insane parent, one paralytic parent, three insane grandparents, and nine brothers and sisters, all but one of whom were 'paralysed, psthisical, epileptic or dull'. The medical officer lamented the fact that the parents had removed the boy from an M.A.B. home, and concluded that the case suggested that the Board should have powers of compulsory detention in such cases for a 'fairly long period'. 'It certainly does suggest that,' Beveridge caustically remarked. 'Does it really suggest nothing more? Is the whole conclusion of this family history nothing more than the suggestion that the victims of it should be

[74] R. H. Tawney's *Commonplace Book*, ed. J. M. Winter and D. M. Joslin, Economic History Review Supplement 5, 1972, p. 26.
[75] *MP*, 18 Feb. 1907.
[76] *MP*, 23 May 1906; *Unemployment: a Problem of Industry* (1910 edn.), p. 134.
[77] *MP*, 4 May 1906.          [78] *MP*, 14 Apr. 1908.

kept under treatment for a few years rather than a few months? . . . The suggestion to which such a history leads is *not* that its victims might be set right by staying "for a fairly long period" under special treatment in a home. The suggestion is rather the opposite one that they cannot be set right at all.' The arguments that Beveridge used to justify such a conclusion were derived without dilution from the eugenics school: 'If the science of heredity has any lesson for practical statesmen,' he claimed,

it is that abnormalities so marked can never be trained out of the individual. They can only be eliminated from society by eliminating the tainted stock. It is morally certain that if the boy who is the hero of this history survives to marriageable age his descendants will be as uniformly deficient and unsatisfactory as his ancestors and brethren. . . . That is the trouble of it all. . . . There is much talk of increase of lunacy. Much that is said is no doubt mere exaggeration. But granted that there is a real increase . . . could anything else be expected? It is so much more possible now . . . for people of weak mind to be partially cured by careful treatment and sent out again—free to marry— than in former less skilful days.[79]

On remedies for such a situation Beveridge was considerably less dogmatic. He thought that probably the 'best thing for society as a whole' would be simply to withhold treatment from severely subnormal cases in the hope that 'diseased stocks' would eventually die out. But he recognized that 'whether right or not' this doctrine was probably 'too brutal for modern times'. A second alternative was 'permanent detention for the irredeemably abnormal . . . except for its permanence made as happy and humane as possible'. Clearly Beveridge himself had no personal objections to such a policy; but he recognized that again it would meet with much public hostility and that, in any case, it could only be applied to the tiny minority of patients for whom there was 'irrefutable evidence of incurability'. He concluded therefore that the only viable policy would be to promote more research into eugenics and more publicity about 'bad family histories', in the hope that this would eventually lead to 'the formation and strengthening of individual opinion against the continuance of diseased stocks'. For those who *were* curable Beveridge himself was strongly opposed to institutional treatment—arguing in surprisingly modern terms that institutions were in themselves frequently the cause of mental illness and often reinforced the pathological conditions they set out to cure. Instead he advocated 'guided treatment in their own homes or in special foster homes'; and he claimed that 'for disease and abnormality in general—whether it be moral, mental or physical—there is one remedial agent distinguished from all others by its strength and simplicity. This is the equal companionship of normal

[79] *MP*, 14 June 1907.

people; the being treated so far as possible as a healthy and respectable person . . . the unconscious tonic of a normal environment.'[80]

## VI

Beveridge's underlying views on politics and society during the Edwardian period have been considered in some detail, because an analysis of his social philosophy is essential if we are to fully comprehend his contribution to specific areas of policy. It is important also if we are to move beyond a merely sentimental or cliché-ridden interpretation of the origins and principles of the welfare state. Moreover, although he subsequently changed his mind more than once on many major issues, Beveridge seems during this period to have acquired certain fundamental attitudes and intellectual predilections that were to underpin his more practical activities for the rest of his life. These fundamental attitudes may be summarized as follows. Firstly, it is clear that in spite of his frequent emphasis on pragmatism and empiricism, Beveridge was not exclusively either a pragmatist or an empiricist; his views and reactions on a wide range of issues were held together by a prior theoretical commitment to social evolution—by a belief that societies evolved towards higher and more complex types and that social institutions should be re-arranged accordingly. This view can most clearly be seen in his dislike of policies that might impede social progress, his espousal of a programme of 'social organisation' and his anxiety about people who were evolutionary failures. A second characteristic was his highly optimistic view of the nature of the state and of its identification with the interests of the whole of society—a view which may perhaps be ascribed to the influence of Caird and which seems to have been typical of a whole generation of Balliol-educated bureaucrats with an interest in social reform. A third fundamental belief was his conviction that in the economic sphere the average human being was indeed primarily an 'economic man', who responded rationally to rewards and incentives, and that no system of social welfare could afford to disregard this fundamental fact. A fourth characteristic of Beveridge's ideas was his belief in the almost unlimited possibility of 'social engineering' or rational social planning. 'It is highly refreshing,' wrote his closest friend, Richard Denman, 'to read about a state in which particular social results are achieved by the deliberate and wilful contrivance of the citizens;'[81] and this was a view that Beveridge himself wholeheartedly endorsed. A fifth characteristic was his belief in the need for 'social solidarity' as a prerequisite of national progress and ultimately of national survival—a view which he perceived as being typically em-

---

[80] MP, 1 Jan. 1907.    [81] AHBP, Mss. Eur. C. 176/194, R. Denman to ASB, 29 Aug. 1905.

bodied in the social institutions of Imperial Germany, and to which similar contemporary parallels may be found in the corporate state movement in North America and in 'l'école de l'intervention et de la solidarité' in early twentieth-century France.[82] A final and more practical attribute was his irritation with piecemeal reforms, his concern about the unintended consequences of ill-thought-out legislation and his preference for a 'grand design of welfare' on the Imperial German model.[83] As will be seen in subsequent chapters, these attitudes were to be of crucial importance in determining his approach to social insurance, his analysis of the labour market and his proposals for dealing with the unemployed.

[82] James Weinstein, *The Corporate Ideal in the Liberal State: 1900–1918* (Boston 1968); Charles Brouilhet, *Le Conflit des Doctrines dans l'Economie Politique Contemporaire* (Paris, 1910).

[83] P. M. Williams, op. cit., p. 219.

# 6

## The Problem of Unemployment

### I

BY far the most important of Beveridge's activities in the 1900s, in terms of both personal development and influence on policy, was his involvement in schemes for relief of the unemployed. It was in the promotion of policies for unemployment that he saw most clearly the possibility of making Toynbee Hall a force in national politics. After he left Toynbee it was in the discussion of unemployment that he tried most systematically to educate public opinion through the medium of the *Morning Post*. And it was in the empirical and theoretical study of unemployment that he hoped to establish a reputation as a professional economist. This chapter will consider three different aspects of Beveridge's involvement in unemployment questions. Firstly, his role in the planning of charitable relief schemes; secondly his share in the campaign to promote state intervention; and, thirdly, the development of his ideas about the organization of the labour market and provision of relief for the unemployed.

### II

The unemployment problem in East London centred chiefly upon the phenomenon of casual labour—of men hired by the day or by the hour, who were the first to be dismissed when trade was slack and who even in prosperous times could never be sure of a continuous week's work.[1] Since the 1880s there had been numerous schemes for assisting the unemployed—labour colonies, emergency funds, local authority public works—but these had scarcely scratched the surface of the problem of casual labour. Samuel Barnett had been searching for many years for new ways of relieving casual unemployment; and nothing more clearly demonstrated the mixture of radical and conservative in Barnett's philosophy than the development of his attitudes towards the unemployed. He was equally opposed both to the extravagant relief funds of 'sentimental philanthropy' and to the mainly negative view of unemployment adopted by the C.O.S. Trade was slack in the Port of London at the end of the Boer War, and early in 1903 there had been

[1] Gareth Stedman Jones, *Outcast London, A Study in the Relationship between Classes in Victorian Society* (1971), esp. ch. 5.

serious unemployed riots in the East End—evoking the customary response of ill-planned relief schemes and panic-stricken charity.[2] When Beveridge arrived in Whitechapel several months later, Barnett was already determined that Toynbee Hall should take the lead in devising some more rational and systematic method of relieving the unemployed, and in solving the problem of casual unemployment.

Barnett's first action was to convene a conference of social workers and settlement residents to plan 'a really sensible and non-philanthropic way of dealing with the problem and abolishing street processions' and 'to find relief work for the unemployed outside London'. At this conference he outlined a programme for relieving distress in the forthcoming winter, which he hoped would avoid the waste, chaos and demoralization of earlier charitable schemes. Local committees were to be set up throughout London to co-ordinate policies and receive applications for relief. Applications would be considered only from unemployed workmen settled in London—thus excluding vagrants and people who might migrate to the metropolis specifically to get relief. The men chosen for assistance would be set to work in agricultural labour colonies, and their wives and children would receive a maintenance allowance in London. The men would be free from the 'degrading' and 'harassing' restrictions imposed by the Poor Law, and would be allowed to leave the colonies to visit their families or to apply for jobs. It was hoped that the offer of continuous work would successfully deter 'the workshy', and that some at least of the men relieved would proceed to permanent settlement on the land. The whole scheme was to be financed in the traditional manner—by charitable funds raised through a Mansion House committee under the patronage of the Lord Mayor of London.[3]

A Mansion House committee on the unemployed had been in existence, though dormant, since the early 1890s; and it was now revived under the chairmanship of Cosmo Lang, the progressive Bishop of Stepney. After some debate it was decided to adopt Barnett's scheme, though confining it initially to the East End boroughs. About £4,000 was raised by public subscription, and arrangements were made to send unemployed workmen to the Salvation Army's labour colony at Hadleigh, and to an estate on Osea Island in the Thames estuary, owned by Frederick Charrington, the Mile End brewer, temperance reformer, evangelist and Conservative M.P.[4] A Toynbee resident, H. R. Maynard, was appointed secretary, and Beveridge himself became a member of the committee in December 1903. Beveridge at this stage knew virtually

[2] José Harris, *Unemployment and Politics, A Study in English Social Policy 1886–1914* (1972), pp. 111–14, 136–7, 152–3.
[3] *The Times*, 25 Nov. 1903.
[4] *Mansion House Committee on the Unemployed, Report of the Executive Committee*, 1903–4.

nothing about the unemployment problem, but during Barnett's absence in Italy he was forced to take over a large share of responsibility for promoting the Canon's scheme. As he recalled in his autobiography, he was 'set to learn about the main economic problem of those days, not from books, but by interviewing unemployed applicants for relief, taking up references from former employers, selecting men to be helped and organising the relief work'.[5] With a local Stepney priest, Father Higley, he drew up a report on the Salvation Army colony at Hadleigh; and with H. R. Maynard he inspected the colony on Osea Island—recording with approval that it was 'a sufficiently depressing place not to make the life of the unemployed too attractive'. On 10 December he addressed a meeting on the colony scheme at the Browning Hall settlement; and he was disturbed to discover that the atmosphere at Browning Hall was 'dreadfully soft-hearted' and ridden with the kind of 'purely philanthropic sentiment . . . which loves to give doles no matter how injurious'.[6]

Beveridge was aware that Barnett was anxious for the scheme to be not merely an end in itself but a model for future policy. He was soon convinced, however, that the attitudes of many of the Mansion House organizers were not in accord with Barnett's original plan. Early in December 1903 he observed that the committee was 'drawing back into the old grooves of hopeless and injurious philanthropy',[7] and he soon found himself in conflict with several of its leading members. These conflicts arose mainly over the question of determining which of the unemployed should be eligible for relief. Barnett had originally envisaged that the scheme should be confined to men normally in regular work: it was soon flooded out, however, by chronically irregular workmen, who saw it as merely another source of temporary casual employment. Beveridge's view and that of other Toynbee residents was that local committees should refuse all applications from purely casual labourers, in order to concentrate on those with a chance of regaining regular work. But in this they were strongly opposed by the Reverend Peter Thompson, minister of the Stepney Wesleyan Temple, who persisted in sending to the colonies men with no experience of regular employment who were totally unsuited for work on the land. 'They are in clover at Hadleigh,' commented Maynard to Beveridge, 'and their search for work in the intervals is a farce'.[8] Thompson, however, was a man of considerable power in the East End—a power exercised through hell-fire sermons against High Churchmen and Roman Catholics—and he had a large following on the Mansion House committee. Beveridge and Maynard worked hard to detach this following from him; and although the committee refused to exclude casual labourers they eventu-

[5] *PI*, p. 23.     [6] BP, IIa, WHB to ASB, 13 Dec. 1903.     [7] Ibid.
[8] BP, IIb, H. R. Maynard to WHB, 3 Jan. 1904.

ally agreed to 'give a preference to men with good employers' references, who were likely to regain regular work if tided over the bad season'.[9] For Beveridge, Peter Thompson and his followers came to represent all that he most disliked in traditional social work—sectarian zeal, the use of charity to maintain a network of paternalistic relationships, and a style of argument both in committee and in the pulpit that Beveridge likened to a 'performing God'.[10]

Beveridge's conflicts with other participants in the Mansion House committee also had semi-religious overtones. In his report on Hadleigh he had advised the committee to make no objection to the Salvation Army's requirement that colonists should attend compulsory 'religious entertainments'.[11] But further contact with the authorities at Hadleigh seems to have revived his earlier prejudice against the Salvation Army. He became convinced that the Army's officers were abusing their position of influence over the unemployed; and on reading General Booth's plans for expanding the colony system he remarked cynically—and quite unjustifiably—that the Army extended forgiveness to economically-productive workmen but not to those too weak for useful work.[12] Nevertheless, the controversy about religious influences came to a head, not with the Salvation Army, but with Frederick Charrington. Charrington, the founder of the Tower Hamlets Mission, was suspected of using for evangelistic purposes money paid to him by the Mansion House committee for giving work to the unemployed. Charrington himself, however, was a munificent contributor to charitable schemes, and the other members of the Mansion House committee appear to have been reluctant to offend him. Beveridge in opposing Charrington found himself in a minority of one, and was forced to resign from the committee in February 1904.[13] Thereafter he concentrated on working for the local Stepney committee of the Mansion House scheme—a committee organized by Tawney and dominated by representatives of Toynbee Hall. Here strict administrative principles were enforced, an attempt was made to exclude chronically irregular workmen and there was 'a continuous check on fraud and waste'.[14] Even so, the results were depressing. A 'follow-up' of cases relieved in Stepney was carried out by Beveridge and Maynard in the summer of 1904. They found that of men who had worked satisfactorily in the labour colonies only a third

[9] *Mansion House Committee on the Unemployed, Abstract of the Report of the Executive Committee,* 1903–4.

[10] BP, Ic 2, WHB's diary, 6 Mar. 1904.

[11] BP, III 3, Rev. Father Higley's and Mr. W. H. Beveridge's Report on the Industrial and Land colony Hadleigh, n.d.

[12] Bev. Coll. B, vol. III, item 38, annotations by WHB on General Booth's *The Vagrant and the Unemployable* (1904).

[13] BP, Ic 2, WHB's diary, 27 Jan. and 3 Feb. 1904; IIb, S. Barnett to WHB, 13 Feb. 1904.

[14] BP, IIa, WHB to ASB, 2 Mar. 1904.

regained regular work; another third remained unemployed throughout the summer, while the rest had obtained only occasional casual jobs.[15]

By this time Beveridge had captured some of Barnett's enthusiasm for
solving the apparently intractable problem of how to deal with the
unemployed. In the winter of 1903–4 he had begun to study the causes
of unemployment and convened a small committee of Toynbee residents to consider possible remedies. In June 1904 this committee discussed methods of improving the previous winter's experiment and it
gave its support to a bill recently introduced in Parliament by Sir John
Gorst, providing for detention in labour colonies of 'criminal vagrants'
and 'habitual paupers'.[16] In August 1904 Barnett himself wrote to
Beveridge prophesying a further unemployment crisis in the coming
winter, and urging him to develop a policy based on experience of the
previous winter's scheme.[17] Barnett's own ideas on unemployment were
evolving at this time along characteristically ambiguous lines. He
believed that, contrary to orthodox economic theory, the vast majority
of unemployed workmen were genuinely unable to find work; and yet
he was increasingly convinced that the problem could only be solved by
penal detention of the 'workshy'—so as to make possible more generous
treatment of the 'genuine unemployed'. He was alarmed lest a sense of
panic should produce hasty and unwise legislation; but at the same time
he was increasingly sympathetic to labour militancy, and he hoped that
the unemployed agitation would force the apathetic Balfour government
into measures of radical reform.[18]

Toynbee Hall was not the only organization which was pressing at
this time for government action on behalf of the unemployed. The
T.U.C. and local authorities throughout the country were demanding
an emergency session of Parliament; and it was their pressure rather
than that of Toynbee that forced the Local Government Board to take
action in October 1904.[19] Nevertheless, the new policy announced by the
President of the Board, Walter Long, followed very closely the scheme
originally propounded by Barnett and Beveridge the year before. 'Joint
Committees', representing borough councils, guardians and charities
were to be set up throughout London to receive applications for relief
and to segregate the 'respectable, temporary out of work men' from the
'ordinary pauper'. These committees were to appoint delegates to a

[15] W. H. Beveridge and H. R. Maynard, 'Unemployment in London', *Toynbee Record*, Oct.
1904, p. 13.
[16] BP, III 1, minutes of the 'Committee on the Unemployed', 1903–4; and BP, III 3,
'Report of the Proceedings of a Small Informal Committee', June 1904; IIa, WHB to ASB,
26 June 1904.
[17] BP, IIb, S. Barnett to WHB, 20 Aug. 1904.
[18] BP, IIb, S. Barnett to WHB, 6 Sept. 1904; Barnett Papers, F/BAR/329, S. Barnett to F.
Barnett, 29 Oct., 26 Nov., and 9 Nov. 1904.
[19] Harris, op. cit., p. 152.

central committee which would raise subscriptions for a 'London Unemployed Fund' and devise a 'common policy for London'. Employment in labour colonies and on local authority relief works would be given to unemployed workmen with a record of regular employment; and preference would be given to 'persons who have established homes with wives and families'.[20]

The leadership in devising unemployment policy now passed out of the hands of Toynbee Hall; but nevertheless, the Canon and his subordinates continued to play an important role in pressing for more permanent measures. In December 1904 H. R. Maynard became secretary of the London Unemployed Fund, and Beveridge privately prophesied that the Fund would become the nucleus of a new government department.[21] Beveridge himself took charge of the local Stepney committee, brusquely recording that it had been 'very badly arranged . . . I have had to try to produce some sort of organisation in chaos at a moment's notice'.[22] His main role in the experiment, however, was one of devising and publicizing ideas on policy rather than practical administration. In the winter of 1904 he discussed unemployment with groups of workmen, clergymen and voluntary workers all over the south of England; and in a series of articles in the *Toynbee Record* he urged that support of workmen during periods of depression could no longer be left to 'private organisation or philanthropy' but should be dealt with by government like questions of industrial safety and public health.[23] In February 1905 he and Maynard dined with the Barnetts at their home in Hampstead, and there they planned a draft 'Unemployment Bill, to be suggested first to Mr. Long and then (if he wouldn't take it) to some Liberal M.P.'[24] No record exists of the details of this discussion, but its results were apparent three weeks later, when Barnett and Beveridge addressed a meeting of Liberal M.P.s in one of the committee rooms of the House of Commons. On this occasion Barnett outlined proposals for legislation that went considerably beyond his earlier plans for relieving the unemployed—pressing for local authority labour exchanges, emergency relief works, penal labour colonies for 'vagrants and idlers' and agricultural training colonies for the 'genuine unemployed'. After the meeting Barnett and Beveridge were invited to tea on the House of Commons terrace with John Burns, Herbert Samuel and other progressive Liberals, and Beveridge seized the opportunity of discussing not merely unemployment but a whole range of current socio-political questions from the national efficiency movement to infant mortality and

[20] PRO, HLG 29/85, vol. 77, papers relating to 'The Unemployed—Mr. Long's scheme', Oct. 1904.
[21] BP, IIa, WHB to HB, 10 Feb. 1905.  [22] BP, IIa, WHB to HB, 21 Jan. 1905.
[23] W. H. Beveridge, 'The Preservation of Efficiency', *Toynbee Record*, Dec. 1904, pp. 43–7.
[24] BP, IIa, WHB to HB, 10 Feb. 1905.

physical deterioration.[25] In terms of policy, however, the immediate influence of the meeting seems to have been slight. It served merely to reveal the lamentable ignorance of most parliamentary Liberals on unemployment questions. And as Barnett later remarked to his wife, their audience had been most interested in agricultural labour colonies, which he and Beveridge regarded as the least important and most peripheral aspect of their scheme for the unemployed.[26]

Definite proposals for legislation eventually came, not from the Liberal opposition, but from Walter Long and the Local Government Board. Since the setting up of the London Unemployed Fund, Long had been under continual pressure not merely from Toynbee Hall but from local authorities, trades unions, and Poor Law guardians to convert the machinery of the fund into a permanent, statutory institution. The need for such an institution was underlined by the extreme distress that prevailed in many areas in the winter of 1904–5 and by the accompanying public disorder. The L.G.B. therefore published a bill which proposed to place Long's scheme on a permanent footing, to extend it to all urban areas, to raise charitable funds for provision of relief works, and to finance labour colonies and labour exchanges by a subsidy from the rates. The bill was immediately denounced by Conservative backbenchers as a dangerous concession to the right to work, and the government showed no great enthusiasm for its enactment. It was strongly supported, however, by the Liberal opposition and was eventually passed as the Unemployed Workmen Act for a limited three-year period in August 1905. In London the Act established a two-tier system of administrative machinery for assisting the unemployed. As in previous years applications for relief were to be examined by local committees; but co-ordination of policy and management of relief schemes were to be in the hands of a Central (Unemployed) Body—an *ad hoc* organization representing distress committees, the L.C.C. and the L.G.B., together with several co-opted experts. The Body was set up in October, and Beveridge—supported by both Socialist and C.O.S. representatives—was elected at the head of the poll for co-opted members in November 1905.[27]

### III

By the end of 1905 Beveridge had clearly become recognized as a leading authority on unemployment questions, and his election to the Central (Unemployed) Body gave him a chance of directly influencing future government policy. Nevertheless, his views on unemployment were still

[25] BP, IIa, WHB to ASB, 4 Mar. 1905.
[26] *Canon Barnett, His Life Work and Friends*, II, p. 244.
[27] BP, IIa, WHB to ASB, 20 Nov. 1905.

in a state of flux; and before looking further at his involvement in policy more must be said about the development of his theoretical analysis of unemployment and his proposals for reform.

At the time when Beveridge first became interested in the problem, very little was known about the causes of unemployment, the structure of the labour market and the social and economic characteristics of the unemployed. The mainstream of English economists had dismissed unemployment as a function of inelastic wages; and it was a cardinal principle of the 1834 Poor Law that genuine unemployment amongst able-bodied workmen did not really exist. Throughout the nineteenth century there had been few attempts either to explain or quantify the problem of surplus labour; and such studies as were carried out tended to emphasize the moral delinquency of the unemployed. Since the 1880s, however, several new schools of explanation had begun to emerge. The under-consumptionist school, headed by J. A. Hobson, reinterpreted unemployment as a problem of maldistribution of income and inadequate consumer demand; and socialist writers began to suggest that 'surplus labour' was in some sense an inevitable corollary of capitalist production. At the same time an entirely new approach to the problem was pioneered by Hubert Llewellyn Smith, head of the Labour department of the Board of Trade, who eschewed general theory and began to collect empirical data about unemployment—based chiefly on the records of certain leading trade unions, which organized unemployment insurance and paid benefits to their members whilst 'out of work'.[28]

Beveridge from the start of his interest in unemployment attached himself, not to the tradition of speculative economics, but to the new empirical school. His manuscript notebooks for the Toynbee period suggest that he read few works of economic theory, and the same was true of his time on the *Morning Post*. Instead he concentrated on the study of statistical bluebooks, on analysing case-histories of applicants for relief, and on the works of historical and descriptive writers like Charles Booth, Llewellyn Smith and Sidney and Beatrice Webb.[29] The inquiries of the committee on unemployment which he convened at Toynbee in 1903–4 were firmly focused on practical and quantitative aspects of the problem rather than theoretical analysis, and the lectures which he gave on aspects of the labour market were always squarely based on a preliminary survey of 'the facts'.[30] In March 1904 he recorded

[28] Harris, op. cit., pp. 1–2, 9–33; on the statistical work of the Board of Trade's Labour department, see Roger Davidson, 'Llewellyn Smith, The Labour Department and Government Growth', *Studies in the Growth of Nineteenth Century Government* ed. Gillian Sutherland (1971), pp. 227–62.

[29] BP, III 1, and III 3, ms. notes and statistics by WHB.

[30] e.g. BP, IXb 5, ms. lectures on 'Unemployment in Germany (and Utopia)', Oct.–Dec. 1907.

that he was studying the subject 'theoretically', but it is clear from the context of this remark that he meant he was collecting statistical data rather than studying economic theory. He began to fashion 'glorious curves representing seasonal variations of employment, the effect of frost, statics, etc.'; and it was at this time that he first conceived what was eventually to become a lifelong ambition—namely, the hope of extrapolating the causes of unemployment from a wide range of empirical data, relating to climate, wages, prices, births, deaths, marriages and crime.[31]

Beveridge's views on unemployment were first spelt out in articles for the *Toynbee Record* in 1904. In these he defined the main practical problem of unemployment as the 'maintenance of efficiency' amongst unemployed workmen during trade depressions; and the remedies he proposed added little to those advanced by reformers over the previous twenty years—namely, temporary relief works, backed up by labour colonies, emigration and strict inquiry into personal character.[32] Early in 1905, however, he came across two works which were to have profound repercussions on his views of the unemployed. Firstly, he read the evidence of Charles Booth to the Select Committee on Distress from Want of Employment in 1895.[33] In this evidence Booth had pointed to the existence in the Port of London of a permanent margin of semi-employed labourers—a margin created not by trade fluctuations, but by the fact that there were several thousand small riverside employers, each drawing upon his own separate reserve of casual workmen. If dock labouring were 'decasualised', Booth argued, then two-thirds of London's waterside labourers could be employed on a permanent basis; and the rest would lose all chance of dock employment and would be forced to look for work elsewhere. The second work which influenced Beveridge's thinking was *The Unemployed: A National Question*, by Percy Alden, the warden of the Mansfield House Settlement in Canning Town. Beveridge wrote a rather supercilious review of Alden's book, criticizing its lack of economic perspective;[34] but, nevertheless, Alden suggested a number of methods of dealing with unemployment that Beveridge had not been aware of before. In particular, Alden drew attention to various continental schemes for subsidizing trade union insurance out of public funds; and he described the national network of 'labour exchanges', which had been established in Germany to register and publicize job-vacancies and to bring potential employers into contact with the unemployed.

[31] BP, IIa, WHB to ASB, 2 Mar. 1904 and 23 Feb. 1907; W. H. Beveridge 'The Pulse of the Nation', *Albany Review*, 2 (Nov. 1907), pp. 160–70.
[32] *Toynbee Record*, Dec. 1904, p. 45.
[33] BP, III 1 and III 3, ms. notes and statistics by WHB.
[34] *Toynbee Record*, Feb. 1905, pp. 75–7.

The insights of Booth and Alden made an immediate impact on Beveridge's own ideas. In a series of lectures at Bristol in the spring of 1905 it was clear that his emphasis had shifted from the occasional problem of trade depression to the chronic problem of casual labour.[35] And a few months later his appointment as joint secretary of a C.O.S. Committee on Unskilled Labour gave him a chance to study questions of labour organization in considerable depth. The C.O.S. committee was set up to examine the phenomenon of casual employment and 'the extent to which casual employment habituates men to a casual life'.[36] The inquiry included several representatives of the most conservative wing of the Charity Organisation Society—including C. S. Loch, who acted as joint secretary with Beveridge, and who was convinced that unemployment could only be dealt with by reviving the deterrent Poor Law of 1834. Beveridge was much impressed by Loch, who for many years had been the leading administrator of the London C.O.S.[37] He greatly admired Loch's powerful and dedicated personality and the strict logic of his socio-economic views; and it is possible that, if Loch had been more active on the Unskilled Labour inquiry, Beveridge's own views might have evolved along very different lines. Loch was a sick man, however; he rarely attended committee meetings and left Beveridge to organize the Committee's research. This Beveridge did with characteristic thoroughness, studying the records of the Board of Trade's Labour department, collecting information from census authorities and school attendance officers, and sending out questionnaires to employers of casual labour. In particular he concentrated on the structure of employment among waterside labourers—dockers, lightermen and stevedores—whom Charles Booth had identified as the archetypal 'casual class'. He compiled statistics of fluctuations in dock employment, studied experiments in voluntary 'decasualisation', compared dock organization in London, Bristol, Liverpool and Manchester, and travelled around centres of industry cross-examining witnesses on how to diminish the struggle for employment at the dock gate.[38] Significantly, most of his evidence was gathered from employers, shipowners, and trade union officials rather than from the casually-employed themselves. 'I did not . . . then see the actual taking on of a dock or wharf labourer,' he later recorded, 'and I had not seen this when I wrote my book, which deals at such length with casual employment. I first saw a dock labourer engaged in the summer of 1911.'[39]

[35] BP, IXb 1, ms. lectures on 'The Problem of the Unemployed', Mar. 1905.
[36] *Report of a C.O.S. Special Committee on Unskilled Labour*, 1908.
[37] BP, IIa, WHB to ASB, 4 Mar. 1905.
[38] C.O.S. Papers, Minutes of Committee on Unskilled Labour, 20 Oct. 1905; BP, IIa, WHB to ASB, 23 Sept. and 1 Oct. 1905; IIb, WHB to R. Denman, 8 May 1905.
[39] BP, IXa 35, 'Autobiography', p. 11.

As a result of these inquiries Beveridge concluded that unemployment should be seen no longer as a problem of social distress or personal character but as a problem of industrial organization; and he identified three main types of unemployment that were characteristic of the existing organization of industry. Firstly, redundancy caused by decay of a particular industry or by technical innovation. Secondly, occasional unemployment caused by seasonal or cyclical fluctuations in demand. And, thirdly, the chronic 'underemployment' of the casual labour market, caused by lack of communication between employers and workers, by the deliberate harbouring of a margin of surplus labour, and by the constant downward pressure of competition from workers squeezed out of more regular occupations. These economic and structural factors, Beveridge argued, were far more significant than traditional explanations based on lack of skill, thrift and moral character among the unemployed. He did not deny that as a cross-section of the labour-force the unemployed were probably less efficient than the average worker—indeed, his study of case-histories of applicants for relief strongly reinforced this view. But he cut across the contemporary debate on 'character' and 'environment' by arguing that moral improvement without industrial re-organization would not create a single new job, and that it was adverse industrial conditions that largely determined the character of the unemployed.[40]

Beveridge's research was very closely linked to his quest for a new policy; and he gradually became convinced that 'unemployment'—which he defined as 'the inability of a willing and fit person to find work'—could not be relieved without the prior abolition of 'underemployment'—which he defined as less than adequate employment 'but sufficient to keep the man attached to the firm, trade or district concerned'.[41] He gradually relaxed his earlier insistence on strict character-inquiry—though he continued to advocate investigation of personal case-histories, not as a means of weeding out the 'undeserving', but as a method of obtaining sociological information about the unemployed.[42] Throughout 1905 he was considering various new methods for dealing with the 'unemployed', the 'unemployable', and the 'underemployed'. As we have seen, he had derived the idea of 'decasualisation' from Charles Booth and the idea of German-style labour exchanges from Percy Alden; and he increasingly linked these two ideas together, suggesting that exchanges might be used to organize and regularize the employment of casual labour. He also considered schemes for reform of the Poor Law and for making treatment of able-bodied paupers positive

[40] *MP*, 2 Jan. 1906.
[41] BP, IIIa, ms. notes on Central Unemployed Body, by WHB.
[42] *MP*, 14 Dec. 1905.

and reformatory rather than negative and deterrent. In a lecture to the Bristol Board of Social and Economic Studies he outlined a plan for a tripartite system of labour colonies—protective colonies for the medically unfit, punitive colonies for the work-shy and training colonies for the genuine unemployed. 'In reforming the Poor Law,' he told his audience, 'he did not want to relax it or make it more attractive; but it was easy to make it less degrading without making it more attractive. They needed to change the whole policy of doing as little as possible for these people.'[43]

The policy implications of Beveridge's new analysis were not fully apparent until April 1906, when he gave a paper to a conference of the Sociological Society held at the London School of Economics. In this paper, which had been drafted in consultation with Sidney and Beatrice Webb,[44] Beveridge advanced his threefold interpretation of the unemployment problem and proposed a fourfold solution. Firstly, an 'organised system of labour exchanges' for redeployment of men made redundant by industrial progress. Secondly, the concentration of public expenditure into periods of depression. Thirdly, the provision of state-subsidized out-of-work insurance and temporary relief works for victims of trade fluctuation. And, fourthly, the regularization of employment and expulsion of surplus workmen from casual trades. Of these proposals, Beveridge singled out labour exchanges and decasualization as 'the most important industrial reform already within the range of practical politics'. He hoped that most of the excluded surplus would be helped by labour exchanges to find alternative work; but for those who were not ultimately re-absorbed his plan was stern, simple and inexorable. Those who, because of physical or mental defect were 'unemployable' would become 'the acknowledged dependants of the state, removed from free industry and maintained adequately in public institutions, but with complete and permanent loss of civil rights—including not only the franchise but civil freedom and fatherhood'. To those who 'may be born personally efficient, but in excess of the number for whom the country can provide, a clear choice will be offered; loss of independence by entering a public institution, emigration or immediate starvation. The slow starvation of the casual labourer, like that of the sweated worker, must become impossible'.[45]

Beveridge's paper provoked a heated discussion among delegates to the conference, and he was variously criticized for basing his argument on inadequate statistics, for ignoring 'underconsumption', and for

[43] *Western Daily Press*, 24 Mar. 1905.
[44] Webb Local Govt. Coll. vol. 297, item 14, H. R. Maynard to B. Webb, 8 May 1907.
[45] W. H. Beveridge, 'The Problem of the Unemployed', *Sociological Papers*, vol. III (1906), pp. 328–31.

neglecting policies of 'back to the land'. 'After your paper I do not think you are what I mean by a Socialist,' commented Mrs. Dunn Gardner approvingly. 'You looked horridly young to have to fight against all the lions who roared against you. But you did it beautifully.'[46] Perhaps surprisingly only one member of the conference, Edmund Harvey, strongly dissented from Beveridge's harsh and pessimistic prescription for the long-term unemployed;[47] but nevertheless it is clear that his analysis of the unemployment problem was by no means universally acceptable to the world of Edwardian social reform. What is less clear, however, is how far this paper accurately reflected Beveridge's own convictions at the time and how far it was merely an academic exercise designed to provoke thought and discussion. Certainly Beveridge himself was confident that in a well-organized economy there need be no real shortage of labour demand, and he predicted that, as had happened in the past, industrial development would always keep pace with growth of population. It therefore seems unlikely that he seriously envisaged that his draconian plan for the decasualized residuum would ever have to be practically enforced. On the other hand, even as a purely intellectual exercise, Beveridge's paper provides some interesting pointers to the nature of his socio-economic beliefs at the time. Of these perhaps the most significant was the extent to which, for all his emphasis on empirical inquiry, Beveridge's views on the unemployed were hedged about with certain fundamental presuppositions about the nature of economic activity and the structure of society. These presuppositions were of four main kinds, each of them deeply embedded in the mainstream of late-nineteenth-century social philosophy. The first was the belief that, whatever its apparent deficiencies, the free market was in the last resort sacrosanct and the aim of rational state intervention should be, not to constrain the free market, but to liberate it from obstructions and if possible to render it freer than ever before. Secondly, there was the belief—held not only by Beveridge but by Booth, the Webbs and many Edwardian social theorists—that shackled to the wheels of the free market was a class of 'surplus' or 'unfit' or parasitical persons with primitive social habits and archaic industrial practices, who not only refused to obey the laws of evolution but inhibited the rest of society from obeying them as well. A third belief, though one that was increasingly challenged by the labour movement, was the belief that political emancipation should go hand-in-hand with capacity for independent work, and that the unemployed like the pauper should have no active role in the political nation. And, finally, there was the belief in residual institutions for the misfits of civilization—a belief that had been steadily

---

[46] BP, IIb, R. Dunn Gardner to WHB, 4 Apr. 1906.
[47] *Sociological Papers*, vol. III (1906), pp. 335–6.

growing throughout the nineteenth century, and reached its zenith in the 1900s when proposals were advanced to extend powers of detention, not merely over criminals and lunatics, but over the unemployable and the unemployed.[48]

The development of Beveridge's views on unemployment between 1903 and 1906 was therefore in many respects ambivalent. On the one hand he was intellectually committed to a purely inductive approach to social problems; yet many of his conclusions about unemployment were clearly derived not merely from facts but from contemporary social theory. He believed that many irregular workmen were inferior industrial specimens; and yet at the same time they were victims of blind impersonal forces—of trade fluctuations, technological progress and the chaotic irrationality of the so-called 'market for labour'. He concurred with the view of the C.O.S. that nothing should be done to relax the principle of deterrence, but he strongly dissented from the traditional view that nothing could be done by government either to regulate the labour market or to reduce the number of unemployed. He was increasingly convinced that an administrative prerequisite of both these objectives was the setting-up of an organized network of labour exchanges, both to assist men in finding work and to test the genuineness of the unemployed. It was as champion of labour exchanges that he went on to the Central (Unemployed) Body, and it was in the planning of labour exchanges under the new Unemployed Workmen Act that he hoped to influence future government policy.

## IV

As a remedy for unemployment the Unemployed Workmen Act was very limited in aim and scope. It was designed to co-ordinate the work of borough councils, guardians and charitable organizations; but in terms of policy it went little further than the numerous *ad hoc* relief schemes of previous years.[49] Moreover, the Central (Unemployed) Body, which was set up to administer the Act in London, was in many ways peculiarly ill-fitted to assist the urban unemployed. Apart from a small handful of trade unionists and East End guardians it was a predominantly upper-class body, composed of clergymen, philanthropists and charitable volunteers. The fact that the Body held all its meetings in the daytime effectively precluded the attendance, not merely of working-class representatives, but of most business and professional men. The general orientation of the Body, as Beveridge soon disapprovingly observed, was almost exclusively towards 'charity' and not towards

---

[48] e.g. Cd. 2852/1906, *Report of the Departmental Committee on Vagrancy.*
[49] Harris, op. cit., pp. 165–210.

business or public administration. He himself would greatly have preferred a committee of 'businessmen and workmen, to consider methods of engagement and remuneration with a view to some more stable organisation of industry'.[50]

The first meeting of the C.U.B. was held in November 1905, and Henry Russell Wakefield, the Vicar of St. Mary's, Bryanston Square, was elected chairman. Regular meetings were held once and sometimes twice a week thereafter. Other leading members included Thomas Hancock Nunn, one of the more progressive members of the C.O.S. and founder of the Hampstead Council of Social Service; Nathaniel Cohen, the Jewish philanthropist and pioneer of private labour exchanges; Edmund Harvey, who had recently succeeded Barnett as warden of Toynbee Hall; George Lansbury and Will Crooks of the Poplar guardians; and C. H. Grinling, the socialist editor of the *Woolwich Pioneer*. Seven executive committees were set up to deal with different aspects of unemployment relief, and the Body began to receive applications for assistance in January 1906.

Beveridge was usually occupied at the *Morning Post* from nine in the evening until two in the morning. He was therefore able to devote a good deal of time to the C.U.B. and to combine administering the Unemployed Workmen Act by day with writing about it by night. It was here that he met Mrs. Dunn Gardner, who sat on the Body as representative of the Chelsea guardians. Mrs. Dunn Gardner soon became Beveridge's chief confidante in C.U.B. affairs, and together they discussed all aspects of general policy and the day-to-day problems of the various executive committees. In particular, they became deeply involved in the two committees responsible for employment exchanges and 'working colonies'. It was these two committees which embodied the major differences of reforming opinion in the C.U.B., and which were to have most impact on the direction of future policy.

The chairman of the Working Colonies committee and chief protagonist of labour colonies on the C.U.B. was George Lansbury—a self-educated man of great humanity and integrity, who since the 1890s had been a leading figure in working-class politics in the East End. Lansbury had become convinced that the cause of unemployment was inadequate demand in the 'Home Market' and that the remedy lay in the resettlement of surplus urban workmen on self-sufficient co-operative agricultural estates.[51] Lansbury, in fact, linked together under-consumption theories with the 'back to the land' movement in much the same way that Beveridge had linked labour exchanges with the idea of decasualization. Under Lansbury's influence the Poplar guardians had set up an

---

[50] *MP*, 29 June 1906; *Toynbee Record*, Dec. 1904, p. 46.
[51] BP, IIb, G. Lansbury to WHB, 18 Sept. 1905.

agricultural colony at Laindon in Essex; and in 1905 he had persuaded the London Unemployed Fund to lease an estate at Hollesley Bay, with a view to training unemployed workmen for permanent settlement on the land. 'The two of us, George Lansbury and I, each wanted something different,' Beveridge recalled many years later. 'We were the two wild young men of the C.U.B., he urging back to the land and I urging Labour Exchanges; the minister in charge of us at the time—John Burns of Battersea—thought us both equally foolish. . . .'[52]

Beveridge's own views on agricultural labour colonies when he first went on to the C.U.B. seem to have been distinctly ambivalent. Eighteen months earlier he had written that '"Back to the Land" is . . . an impossibly cry; the London unemployed, as he is, will not go back to the land from which he never came, and if he does go he very soon returns or is returned by the farmer who tries him.'[53] He had supported Barnett in his attempt to sponsor labour colonies among the Liberal opposition; but in December 1905 he wrote in the *Morning Post* that 'in respect of the problem of unemployment . . . neither home colonisation nor emigration can claim to be more than palliatives'.[54] Early in 1906, however, he had apparently come round to the view that colonies could play an important role in catering for workmen made redundant by decasualization. He was warned against Lansbury, and against the Poplar guardian's 'sentimental' principles, by Mrs. Dunn Gardner. But, as he later recalled 'in practice, George Lansbury and I made a deal; he was ready to support my Employment Exchanges, so long as I supported his Farm Colonies for the unemployed, like Hollesley Bay'.[55]

This was an uneasy alliance, tactically of more benefit to Beveridge than to Lansbury. There seems to have been no personal animosity between the two men; but Beveridge was deeply suspicious of 'Poplarism', whilst Lansbury was equally suspicious of the paternalistic influence of Toynbee Hall.[56] Moreover, Beveridge's conception of a labour colony was very different from Lansbury's. The Poplar guardian hoped to create permanent communities which would provide a model for the eventual eclipse of capitalism by co-operative production. Beveridge on the other hand saw colonies as useful but residual institutions for the misfits of the economic system—for those expelled from the labour market by systematic decasualization.

Nevertheless, Beveridge became an active member of the Working Colonies Committee and spent many days in 1906 inspecting colonies

[52] BP, III 34, 'The Birth of Labour Exchanges', by WHB, *c*. Feb. 1960.
[53] *Toynbee Record*, Dec. 1904, p. 43.
[54] *MP*, 21 Dec. 1905.
[55] BP, III 34, 'Employment Exchanges Jubilee. Speech by Lord Beveridge', 1 Feb. 1960.
[56] *MP*, 28 Nov. 1906; George Lansbury, *My Life* (1928), pp. 130–1.

in the London area—although he was highly critical of an administrative system that left the supervision of what were potentially large-scale productive enterprises to amateurs like himself.[57] Often he was accompanied by Mrs. Dunn Gardner who would borrow a motor-car, pack a picnic lunch and characteristically transform their tours of inspection into gay social events. 'Do let us make a scheme and you do me the honour of conducting me to see all the Labour colonies we can find and let's look up some Church Army shows—and generally enjoy ourselves,' she wrote in anticipation of one such occasion.[58] In March 1906 they visited the colony at Hollesley Bay, which had been taken over from the London Unemployed Fund and to which the C.U.B. had sent several hundred of the metropolitan unemployed. Beveridge reported with obvious surprise that 'the superintendent had the highest praise for the aptitude of the Londoners under his charge' and that the combination of abundant food and regular work was having a remarkable effect on the morale and physique of the labourers employed. He was sceptical, however, about whether life at Hollesley Bay—with its large meals, games rooms, and remoteness from normal economic constraints—was in any sense a realistic preparation either for agricultural work in England or for emigration overseas.[59] In May 1906 he reported that 'Hollesley Bay has not yet, after a year's working, placed a single man "back on the land" . . . as a self-supporting agriculturalist'; and he concluded that 'farm colonies are really no solution of the chronic unemployed problem. They can only remove the individual casual labourer from poverty; they do not touch the causes of his poverty or prevent others from succeeding to his place of irregular work.'[60] In an article on possible amendments to the Unemployed Workmen Act he proposed that in future more emphasis should be placed on labour colonies; these were not, however, to be colonies of the kind at Hollesley Bay, but institutions under a reformed Poor Law for 'compulsory detention over long periods of men proved to be unemployable through vice or disease'.[61] Beveridge's doubts about the vision of labour colonies cherished by Lansbury were reinforced by Mrs. Dunn Gardner, who was highly critical of Hollesley Bay for undermining the colonists' habits of independence. 'The men were treated as children rather than as reasonable adults,' she complained; and to Beveridge she wrote that it would be preferable to use the colonies for training boys and youths rather than for adult workers who had become hardened in their social and industrial habits. 'Then those who had the taste for the Country could marry country girls and live in the cottages which someone is to

[57] BP, IIa, WHB to ASB, 18 Mar. 1906.
[58] BP, IIb, R. Dunn Gardner to WHB, 31 Aug. 1906.
[59] *MP*, 3 and 5 Mar. 1906.          [60] *MP*, 31 May 1906.          [61] *MP*, 22 June 1906.

build. Or even Family Colonies would be better than what we are doing now, which is it seems to me quite childish.'[62]

Mrs. Dunn Gardner's criticisms were echoed by other members of the Working Colonies Committee, and the only member who whole-heartedly supported Lansbury was C. H. Grinling, who withdrew from the C.U.B. after his defeat in the borough elections of November 1906. Controversies arose within the committee not only over general princi-ples but over day-to-day management and industrial organization. Lansbury was convinced that colonies should be seen as a social service, run by men whose main function was to build up a community without regard to economic constraints.[63] Beveridge on the other hand was equally convinced that they should be run by men with business exper-ience on primarily commercial lines; while Mrs. Dunn Gardner argued that there should be a clear division of responsibility between the produc-tive side of a colony's work and its social and domestic arrangements.[64] Lansbury as a consequence felt himself increasingly estranged from his colleagues, and admitted to Beveridge early in 1907 that 'the men with real brains on the committee are against me either in principle or in detail and a Chairman can never run a committee properly when such is the case'.[65]

Nevertheless, it was not so much opposition inside the Working Colonies Committee as external factors which ultimately led to the failure of Lansbury's plans. John Burns, the new President of the L.G.B., was sceptical of the value of colonies; but he sanctioned the use of Hollesley Bay for temporary relief employment in the spring of 1906. Lansbury was anxious, however, that Hollesley Bay should also be used for the creation of permanent smallholdings, which would form the nucleus of a co-operative estate. Burns prevaricated for many months over this decision and spent the summer of 1906 inspecting labour colonies in England and abroad. In July 1906 he received a report from his chief inspector, J. S. Davy, on Poor Law administration in Poplar, which roundly condemned both the management of the Poplar labour colony and the extravagant policies of the Poplar guardians with which Lansbury was closely associated. This report seems to have confirmed Burns in his dislike of the colony movement.[66] In October 1906 he refused to allow Hollesley Bay to be used for permanent settlement; and when Parliament voted £200,000 towards the expenses of the

[62] Cd. 5068/1910, *RC on the Poor Laws, Minutes of Evidence*, para. 19; BP, IIb, R. Dunn Gard-ner to WHB, 3 June 1906.

[63] BP, IIb, G. Lansbury to WHB, 11 Jan. 1907.

[64] BP, IIa, WHB to ASB, 18 Mar. 1906; Cd. 5068/1910, *RC on the Poor Laws, Minutes of Evidence*, statement of Mrs. Dunn Gardner, para. 21.

[65] BP, IIb, G. Lansbury to WHB, 1 Feb. 1907.

[66] BP, IIb, postcard from John Burns to WHB, n.d. (1906).

Unemployed Workmen Act, he refused to allow any of this money to be used for consolidating the colony movement on the lines suggested by Lansbury. Lansbury resigned from the Working Colonies Committee in February 1907; and thereafter labour colonies were used by the C.U.B. merely as a form of rural relief-employment, in aim and principle indistinguishable from other methods of temporary relief.[67]

V

Labour exchanges unlike labour colonies had received relatively little attention from English reformers before 1905. Several private labour bureaux had been in spasmodic operation since the 1880s, and since 1902 municipal authorities had been empowered to support labour exchanges out of the rates.[68] At the time of the passing of the Unemployed Workmen Act, however, there was no significant body of support for labour exchanges, and little was known about this method of assisting the unemployed. Beveridge himself was coming to be recognized as an authority on labour exchanges, but he had by no means fully formulated his ideas on their role in a rationalized economic system. In November 1905 he referred to labour exchanges as a central feature of 'the final solution of the unemployed problem'.[69] But at this stage he was mainly interested in using them to promote decasualization, and since the Unemployed Workmen Act was not supposed to refer to casual workmen there was no *prima facie* reason why exchanges set up by the C.U.B. should realize this aim. A year later he still thought that skilled workers could be left to make their own arrangements for finding work and that 'the most important object' of public exchanges was dealing with unskilled and casual labourers.[70] Not until early 1907 did he come to the conclusion that 'the universal application of the principle of the Labour Exchange' was a vital prerequisite, not merely of decasualization, but of the prediction and prevention of trade depressions and the maintenance of labour mobility throughout the economy.[71]

Beveridge's conception of labour exchanges was therefore not clearly defined for well over a year after he went on to the C.U.B. Nevertheless, from the start he began to press the idea of labour exchanges upon his colleagues, and he submitted a plan for a metropolitan system of exchanges in February 1906. He proposed that the system should consist of twenty-five local exchanges, coinciding with areas covered by borough

[67] Harris, op. cit., pp. 107–8.          [68] Ibid., pp. 199–200, 279–81.

[69] *MP*, 6 and 15 Nov. 1905.

[70] Bev. Coll. B, vol. XVI, item 10, memorandum on 'Relation of Employment Exchanges to Trade Unions', by WHB, 17 Dec. 1906.

[71] W. H. Beveridge, 'Labour Exchanges and the Unemployed', *Econ. J.*, XVII, no. 65 (Mar. 1907), p. 76.

councils. Every exchange would have a professional staff to interview applicants for work, to make contact with employers and to register vacant situations. To each exchange would be attached an advisory committee representing employers and workmen; and the system would be co-ordinated by a Central Employment Exchange, supervised by the Employment Exchanges committee of the C.U.B.[72] Among members of the C.U.B. there was some criticism of Beveridge's scheme—in particular from Grinling, who objected that exchanges might be used to recruit blackleg labour unless they were placed under direct democratic control.[73] Nevertheless, Beveridge won the powerful support of Charles Booth and Hancock Nunn, and his plan was approved by the C.U.B. in March 1906.[74] The Employment Exchanges Committee began work under Beveridge's chairmanship a month later. A protégé of Sidney Webb, H. J. Stone, was appointed superintendent of the Central Exchange; and by January 1907 exchanges had been set up in nearly all the London boroughs.[75] Registration was free, and workmen seeking employment were required to register weekly at their local exchange. Special provision was made for women and juveniles, and vocational guidance for school-leavers was made available through exchanges in conjunction with the Education Department of the L.C.C. The staff of the exchanges had access to the records of local distress committees; but at the insistence of Mrs. Dunn Gardner, it was laid down that in other respects employment exchanges and distress committees should be entirely separate, so as to convince employers that exchanges were 'business' and not 'charitable' institutions.[76] Officials were instructed to refer men for situations solely on the grounds of industrial capacity and not of personal need; and the character and skill of applicants were supposed to be carefully vetted so as 'to offer to the employer a better sort of man than he would be able to get in the ordinary way'.[77]

Throughout 1906 Beveridge was publicizing the labour exchange experiment in the *Morning Post*, and he travelled throughout the country expounding the principles of 'labour organisation' to audiences of employers, trade unionists, academics and persons interested in social reform. He did much of the work of the Employment Exchanges Committee single-handed and made himself personally responsible for acquiring premises, appointing staff, promoting good relations with

[72] Bev. Coll. B, Vol. XVI, item 2, draft memorandum on 'Employment Exchanges', by WHB, 14 Feb. 1906.
[73] BP, IIb, C. H. Grinling to WHB, 16 Mar. 1906.
[74] BP, IIa, WHB to ASB, 26 Mar. 1906.
[75] W. H. Beveridge, 'Labour Exchanges and The Unemployed', loc. cit., pp. 66–81.
[76] BP, IIb, R. Dunn Gardner to WHB, 16 Apr. 1906.
[77] Bev. Coll. B, vol. XVI, item 2, draft memorandum on 'Unemployment Exchanges', by WHB, 14 Feb. 1906.

employers and encouraging schemes of decasualization. He persuaded John Burns to summon a conference of employers to discuss casual labour problems; and through his friend, Richard Denman, he persuaded the Post Office to engage its Christmas workers through the labour exchanges of the C.U.B.[78] He lectured local advisory committees on labour exchange principles, urging them that exchanges were 'not machines for pushing incompetent men into a job, but for putting a competent man into touch with the demand for him'.[79] And in private, he later recalled, he 'never stopped talking about labour exchanges' and was 'a terrible bore to my friends'.[80] He was increasingly convinced that he had discovered in labour exchanges the kind of social reform for which he had been searching since first he went to Toynbee—a reform which would improve the lot of individual workmen and at the same time enhance rather than detract from general economic efficiency; a reform, moreover, which was based on scientific inquiry into the structure of the labour market and which would itself make possible further empirical research.

Beveridge like Barnett before him was anxious that his experiment should be seen not merely as an end in itself but as a model for innovations in public policy; and from the spring of 1906 onwards he began to view the C.U.B.'s labour exchanges as the potential core of a future national system. Such a system, he thought, should be controlled by a central government department and should be linked with measures for the provision of public works.[81] For a time he considered the possibility of making the use of exchanges compulsory; but he eventually concluded that, at least in the short term, a system based on persuasion would be more politically acceptable.[82] Within the C.U.B., however, there was little enthusiasm for extension of labour exchanges except within Beveridge's immediate circle; and Lansbury in particular was convinced that exchanges could do nothing to reduce the total number of the unemployed.[83] Moreover, the small trade union contingent on the C.U.B. regarded labour exchanges with extreme suspicion. Many unions already operated an informal job-information service for their members, and they saw the new system as a potentially threatening source of cut-price and black-leg labour. In November 1906 Beveridge recorded that the exchanges were 'in a critical position between being accepted and being violently opposed by the Trade Unions';[84] and in the following

---

[78] BP, IIb, John Burns to WHB, 21 Mar. 1906; WHB to R. Denman, 8 Sept. 1906.
[79] Bev. Coll. B, vol. XVI, item 49.
[80] BP, III 34, Lord Beveridge's address on the 50th anniversary of Employment Exchanges, 1 Feb. 1960.
[81] *MP*, 22 June 1906.                          [82] BP, IIb, J. Carter to WHB, 9 May 1906.
[83] BP, IIb, G. Lansbury to WHB, 1 Feb. 1907.
[84] BP, IIa, WHB to ASB, 23 Nov. 1906.

month he drafted a memorandum which laid down that exchanges should be 'markets for labour in time of peace rather than time of war' and should therefore avoid registration of vacancies caused by strikes and lock-outs. He refused to concede, however, that exchanges should advertise only vacancies which conformed to the standard rate—arguing that it would not be legal for an institution 'established for common purposes' to insist on privileges which were enjoyed by only a minority of the work force.[85] Some months later he had a long meeting with representatives from the T.U.C., but no agreement was reached on this highly controversial issue.[86] The fears of the unions were partially allayed by allowing them to use labour exchange premises and facilities for continuing with their own system of private registration; but the dispute over standard rates was never satisfactorily settled throughout the period in which labour exchanges were managed by the C.U.B.[87]

A few months later Beveridge encountered further opposition to his policies—this time from William Stutchbury, who had succeeded H. R. Maynard as clerk to the C.U.B. in November 1906. The post had first been offered to and refused by Beveridge; and possibly for this reason Stutchbury displayed considerable personal hostility towards Beveridge, by rejecting his candidates for labour exchange appointments, by criticizing him to other members of the C.U.B., and possibly also by fomenting hostility to exchanges among the trade union representatives.[88] Beveridge fumed against Stutchbury in private but took no action to defend himself until May 1907, when he discovered that one of Stutchbury's nominees, H. W. Fordham, was conspiring to replace H. J. Stone as superintendent of the Central Exchange. Fordham was a self-educated man of working-class origin who had been involved in labour exchange administration since 1902, and he was greatly embittered at the takeover of exchanges by men whom he regarded as 'idealists' without practical experience—men whose 'idea of the working-classes was a working man in his Sunday best, not in his actual work and his ordinary everyday conditions'. He was also highly critical of Beveridge's refusal to comply with trade union opinion on the issue of the standard rate.[89] Early in May Beveridge interviewed Fordham, accused him of 'intriguing to supplant his chief' and asked him to resign. Fordham complained to

[85] Bev. Coll. B. vol. XVI, item 10, Memorandum on 'Relation of Employment Exchanges to Trade Unions', by WHB, 17 Dec. 1906.

[86] BP, IIa, WHB to ASB, 23 Feb. 1907.

[87] Harris, *op. cit.*, pp. 203–4.

[88] BP, IIb, R. Dunn Gardner to WHB (? Sept.) 1906, 8 and 13 Jan. 1907; BP, IXa 35, 'Autobiography', p. 25.

[89] Cd. 5066/1910, *RC on the Poor Laws, Minutes of Evidence*, statement of H. W. Fordham, paras. 3 and 9, and QQ.81, 265–6.

Stutchbury, who responded by giving Fordham a post in his own office and commissioning him to write a critical report on all the London exchanges—the results of which Fordham on his own initiative submitted to the President of the L.G.B. Beveridge was incensed at what he regarded as Fordham's gross disloyalty, and summoned a meeting of the Employment Exchanges committee which demanded Fordham's dismissal. Stutchbury in reply circulated a hastily composed paper, purporting to come from the Finance Committee, in which he denounced labour exchanges in general, and accused Beveridge as chairman of the Employment Exchanges committee of having greatly exceeded his financial powers. A special meeting of the C.U.B. was called to thrash the matter out on 7 June. Beveridge was distraught at the personal charges made against him. He spent a sleepless night beforehand and at the meeting made an incoherent speech, in which he defended himself at excessive length but failed to make clear the grounds of his complaint against Stutchbury and Fordham. The feeling of the meeting turned against Beveridge, and Lansbury—who had promised to speak in his favour—withdrew his support. As a result the Employment Exchanges committee was defeated and Fordham retained his post. The Finance Committee proceeded thereafter to exercise rigorous control over labour exchange expenditure, and several hostile motions demanding independent inquiries into the work of the Exchanges were put forward by other committees of the C.U.B.[90]

Beveridge was more shattered by this apparently trivial episode than he cared to admit to any but his closest friends. 'I contemplated suicide all Friday night,' he wrote to Jessy Mair.[91] He blamed himself for 'want of imagination' and for having been more concerned with defending his own integrity than with the cause he was trying to promote.[92] For a few days he contemplated giving up his campaign for labour exchanges and going to America as special correspondent for the *Morning Post*. Just when the fortunes of labour exchanges seemed at a low ebb, however, there were signs of interest in other quarters. Through the influence of Denman he was invited to draft a clause in the government's Port of London Authority Bill, giving the new authority 'power to set up labour exchanges . . . in co-operation if it likes with the C.U.B.'[93] Cyril Jackson, an assistant commissioner to the Royal Commission on the Poor Laws, sought his advice on the use of exchanges in dealing with juvenile employment.[94] Mrs. Dunn Gardner wrote to her friend, J. S. Davy,

[90] BP, IXa 35, 'Autobiography', pp. 20–4; III 5, printed letter from WHB to the Chairman and members of the London C.U.B., 5 June 1907; C.U.B. minutes, vol. II, 7 and 21 June 1907.
[91] Lady Beveridge Papers, WHB to J. Mair, 9 June 1907.
[92] BP, IXa 35, 'Autobiography', pp. 23–4.       [93] BP, IIb, WHB to R. Denman, n.d.
[94] BP, IIa, WHB to ASB, 2 Aug. 1907.

urging him to warn John Burns that Fordham was an unreliable source of information;[95] and as a result of her intervention Beveridge was invited to prepare a memorandum on labour exchanges for the President of the L.G.B. This memorandum was submitted to the President at the end of June 1907. 'Dear Mr. Burns, Here's a case for Labour Exchanges —what's the alternative?' scribbled Beveridge challengingly in a covering note.[96] His memorandum was an implicit condemnation of the amateur and a quasi-charitable system of social administration prevailing under the C.U.B. In it Beveridge argued that labour exchanges should be 'recognised, industrialised, nationalised', and that 'as instruments of industrial organisation they need industrial management'. He suggested three alternative lines of future policy in order of preference. Firstly, the setting-up of a national network of exchanges under direct supervision of the Board of Trade. Secondly, the creation of a special department within the Board of Trade to supervise exchanges set up by local authorities. And, thirdly, 'as second best, except the L.G.B. in place of the Board of Trade. . . . But it has to be remembered that it is the Board of Trade which is in touch with trade unions and employers.'[97] As a result of this memorandum Burns arranged to make an exploratory tour of German exchanges, and Beveridge was interviewed by Davy about the future of the exchanges founded by the C.U.B. Davy was sympathetic but sceptical, and Beveridge left the interview confirmed in his opinion that exchanges more properly belonged to the business and commercial functions of the Board of Trade than to the poor relief and social welfare functions of the L.G.B.[98]

Early in August Beveridge was offered, and refused, a research post in the Board of Trade's Cost of Living Inquiry;[99] but for the time being the Board's officials showed little overt interest in his plans for extending Board of Trade control over labour organization. In the spring of 1907, however, his friendship with the Webbs had brought him into contact with another sphere of influence—the Royal Commission on the Poor Laws, which was beginning to consider the problem of the unemployed. A year earlier Beveridge had been proposed to the Commission as an Assistant Commissioner, but his appointment had been blocked by Lansbury who described him as too 'clever' and 'doctrinaire'.[100] Charles Booth, however, had been greatly impressed by Beveridge's *Morning Post* articles and thought that 'in some form we are sure to look

[95] BP, IIb, R. Dunn Gardner to WHB, 20 May 1907.
[96] B.M., Add. Ms. 46299, p. 313, WHB to John Burns, 11 June 1907.
[97] Bev. Coll. B, vol. XIV, item 20, 'Memorandum as to the Future of Labour Exchanges', by WHB, June 1907.
[98] BP, IIa, WHB to ASB, 3 July 1907.
[99] BP, IIa, WHB to ASB, 2 Aug. 1907.
[100] Webb, Local Govt. Coll. vol. 286, G. Lansbury to B. Webb, 15 Feb. 1906.

to him in later stages of our work'.[101] Beveridge had first expounded to
the Webbs his plan for a national system of labour exchanges in 1906.
They had been intrigued by the idea, but doubted whether it could
succeed without a greater degree of compulsion than Beveridge seemed
to contemplate.[102] Nevertheless, they were searching for policies on
unemployment to lay before the Royal Commission, of which Mrs.
Webb was a forceful and indefatigable member. They were highly
critical of the way in which the Commission's official investigators were
conducting research into labour problems, and in particular they were
afraid that the overwhelming evidence about the futility of relief works
would be used as an excuse for reviving the Poor Law of 1834. They
therefore convened an independent research committee, consisting of
Beveridge, Barnett, Maynard and Ensor, to prepare alternative proposals for dealing with the unemployed.[103] They also introduced Beveridge to Lord George Hamilton, the chairman of the Royal Commission;
and Beveridge spent an evening in Grosvenor Road expounding to this
Whiggish nobleman his ideas on exchanges and decasualization.[104] In
April 1907 Hamilton told Beveridge that he had read the article in the
*Economic Journal* in which Beveridge argued for the 'universal application of the principle of the Labour Exchange'; but Hamilton was convinced that the unions would never co-operate with such a scheme, and
that decasualization would inevitably increase the number of the unemployed.[105] Nevertheless, a few days later Beveridge was invited to
submit evidence to the Royal Commission on 'the question of distress
due to unemployment and the remedies which have been or may be
applied in mitigation of such distress'.[106]

## VI

The Royal Commission on the Poor Laws had been appointed in 1905
in the face of a growing crisis in English social administration—a crisis
brought about partly by the rising cost of poor law services, partly by
growing criticism of the stigmatic way in which the Poor Law was
administered, and partly because traditional Poor Law definitions of
poverty, destitution and 'want of employment' had patently ceased to
fit the economic facts.[107] The Commission covered a wide spectrum of

[101] Ibid., C. Booth to B. Webb, 5 Jan. 1906.
[102] BP, IIa, WHB to ASB, 3 Dec. 1906.
[103] Ensor Papers, B. Webb to R. C. K. Ensor, 4 May 1907; Webb Local Govt. Coll. vol. 297,
item 13, WHB to B. Webb, 7 May 1907.
[104] BP, IIa, WHB to ASB, 12 Dec. 1906.
[105] BP, IIb, Lord George Hamilton to WHB, 21 Apr. 1907.
[106] BI, IIb, R. G. Duff to WHB, 27 May 1907.
[107] Harris, op. cit., pp. 145–50.

opinion on politics, administration and social reform. Apart from Mrs. Webb and Lord Hamilton, the members included Charles Booth, Russell Wakefield, George Lansbury, several leading members of the C.O.S. and the Local Government Board, and the well-known economists, Professor William Smart and Dr. Lancelot Phelps. For the first eighteen months of their inquiry the commissioners had been studying the administration of the Poor Law, and although they were more or less agreed that the traditional structure of the Poor Laws should be abolished they were sharply divided about what should take its place.[108] When the Commission came to the study of unemployment, however, the areas of agreement and disagreement between them were much less clear-cut.[109] Even the Webbs at this stage had few preconceived ideas on unemployment; and, as Beveridge quickly realized, the Commission was ripe for permeation by an expert witness with a plausible plan. '. . . I have been buried deep in the preparation of my Poor Law Commission evidence,' he recorded on 23 June. '. . . I've taken Mrs. Webb's advice to put in everything I know or think and I'm inclined to believe that I've done it rather well.'[110]

The first draft of Beveridge's written evidence was completed early in July. In substance it was an elaboration of all that he had written on unemployment during the previous eighteen months; but the main emphasis of his argument had subtly shifted since his controversial paper to the Sociological Society in 1906. He was no longer so pre-occupied with the treatment of casual labour and the decasualized residuum. Instead he gave as much weight to seasonal and cyclical unemployment and to skilled and regular workmen as to the casual labour market; and he was increasingly impressed with the possibility that labour exchanges might be used for managing a scheme of social insurance on behalf of the unemployed.[111] Much to the disquiet of Mrs. Dunn Gardner his memorandum had been prepared in close collaboration with the Webbs. 'I am very sorry you are going to consult Mrs. Sidney Webb about it,' Mrs. Dunn Gardner had written on 30 May.

In my opinion it will not increase your weight at the Commission to be seen in collusion with her—and also I have no doubt that your evidence and statement will—if you consult with her—not be the same as if you wrote it independently. . . . I have no doubt that a *very* clever and attractive woman who thoroughly understands her subject and thoroughly knows what she is aiming at—and remember you *don't* in detail as she does—will have no difficulty in getting you to unconsciously colour your statement with her views . . . the

[108] S. and B. Webb, *English Poor Law Policy* (1963 edn.), pp. 278–304.
[109] Bryce Papers, Box E. 28, L. Phelps to James Bryce, 29 Mar. 1909.
[110] BP, IIa, WHB to ASB, 23 June 1907.
[111] *MP*, 20 and 23 July 1907.

danger of it lies in the fact that I am sure you will not realise that she has swayed you a bit . . .[112]

Beveridge, however, ignored Mrs. Dunn Gardner's misgivings—confident, perhaps, that the Webbs' power to influence his ideas was no greater than his power to influence theirs. Early in August he visited the Webbs at Bernard Shaw's house in Ayot St. Lawrence and they spent a Sunday morning going through Beveridge's draft statement and rehearsing his oral evidence to the Commission. Beveridge's self-confidence proved to be well-founded, for during this week-end he convinced the Webbs that labour exchanges were both politically practicable and an administrative prerequisite of all other kinds of policy for dealing with the unemployed. The Webbs for their part were full of tactical suggestions about how he should proceed with his labour exchange campaign. They advised him to publish different versions of his proposals, making them acceptable both to Fabian socialists and to the C.O.S.; and they suggested that he should get himself called as one of the first oral witnesses on unemployment, so that all subsequent discussion in the Commission would be dominated by his construction of the problem. Beveridge was greatly impressed by the 'inexhaustible industry and preparedness of the Webbs', and in after years he looked back on this week-end as an object lesson in how to handle a public inquiry. 'They alone of all the Commissioners thought of going through my evidence with me,' he recalled. 'I felt that people who would take so much trouble deserved to succeed.'[113]

The Webbs were most pressing on two specific issues. They urged him, firstly, 'to find evidence of existing effective Labour Exchanges', and secondly, 'to believe in compulsory decasualisation'.[114] Beveridge continued to be doubtful whether public opinion would tolerate compulsion, but he acted swiftly on the Webbs' first suggestion. A few weeks earlier he had received a postcard from Tawney, recording his impressions of the municipal exchange at Strasbourg—then part of the German Empire.[115] Beveridge resolved to follow him and to finance his journey by writing freelance articles for the *Morning Post*. He began to study German sources, and was 'more and more overcome by finding all my own ideas and belief in Labour Exchanges recurring in German blue books . . . if the Germans and I can understand one another at all our unanimity will be quite wonderful'.[116] He left for Berlin at the end of August, armed with introductions from Sidney Webb, Canon Barnett, R. B. Haldane, and C. S. Loch. In the German capital he called on the

[112] BP, IIb, R. Dunn Gardner to WHB, 30 May 1907.
[113] BP, IIa, WHB to ASB, 6 Aug. 1907; *PI*, pp. 62–3.
[114] BP, IXa 35, 'Autobiography', p. 27.
[115] Bev. Coll. B, vol. XVI, item 6, R. H. Tawney to WHB, 9 July 1907.
[116] BP, IIa, WHB to ASB, 22 Aug. 1907.

British Ambassador, who arranged for him to visit the Imperial Insurance Office, the Imperial Statistical Office and the Ministry of the Interior. Everywhere he went he found that 'the name of Sidney Webb is quite a charm',[117] and he spent the next fortnight interviewing trade unionists, leading socialists and government officials. His childhood fluency in German soon revived, and proved of great importance not merely in communicating with German administrators but in enabling him to delve deep into some of the less obvious refinements of German administrative principles. He inspected numerous social institutions, ranging from insurance arbitration courts and workers' hospitals to a 'Charity Organisation Society and a Social Museum'. He examined both public and voluntary exchanges in Berlin, Nuremberg, Cologne, Munich and Frankfurt-on-Main.[118] In Berlin he talked with Dr. Freund, a leading authority on the labour exchange movement, who advised him that 'the most practical measure for promotion of labour exchanges [was] to get the trade union leaders over to Germany to see and talk to German trade unionists and be convinced'.[119]

Beveridge's impressions of German exchanges were subsequently recorded in articles in the *Economic Journal* and the *Morning Post*. He found that there were over four thousand exchanges of various kinds in the German empire, which filled over a million and a quarter vacancies a year. Of these the most important were public labour exchanges organized by the municipality, as in Munich, and voluntary exchanges which received a municipal subsidy, as in Berlin. The exchanges were almost universally accepted by employers and trade unions, and in many cases were managed by joint committees of employers, workers and public officials. During industrial disputes, some exchanges closed down, some carried on business as usual; but the commonest practice was for exchanges to stay open and inform potential applicants which vacancies had been specifically caused by strikes. In the vast majority of cases normal trade union pressure was an entirely adequate safeguard against blackleg labour. In Munich, Beveridge recorded, he 'actually witnessed an unsuccessful attempt by an employer to get two ordinary labourers to fill vacancies created by a dispute. The wages offered were good, and the waiting room full of men, but no-one would put himself forward for the work'. In many cases exchanges were experimenting with the provision of additional specialist services—with supervising apprenticeships, suppressing vagrancy and arranging municipal subsidies to schemes for trade union insurance. These exchanges, Beveridge concluded, were 'still only at the beginning of their development . . . yet

[117] BP, IIa, WHB to ASB, 29 Aug. 1907.
[118] BP, IIa, WHB to ASB, 30 Aug. 3, 4 and 26 Sept. 1907.
[119] BP, IIa, WHB to HB, 12 Sept. 1907.

no-one can doubt that they have come to stay and to grow as the many services they may render come to be more fully recognized. They do not solve the unemployed problem. They simplify it enormously, and are indispensable to a solution.'[120]

Beveridge returned to England in October, and almost immediately was summoned to give evidence to the Poor Law Commission. He submitted two papers—one the general analysis of unemployment that he had prepared with the Webbs, the other a detailed description of German exchanges—and he spent two days expounding his ideas before the commissioners. He maintained that throughout industry and at all levels of skill there was widespread 'overstocking' of the market for labour. This was due, Beveridge argued, not to 'overpopulation', nor to a slowing-down of industrial progress, nor to the personal deficiencies of the unemployed. He agreed with the traditionalists that, as a cross-section of the labour force, the unemployed probably *were* physically and morally inferior; but he claimed that this was the result rather than the cause of irregular employment—the consequence of lack of industrial training, lack of a regular income, and enforced habituation to an irregular pattern of life. The solution, Beveridge argued, lay not in temporary relief nor in uneconomic labour colonies nor in a deterrent Poor Law, but in nation-wide labour exchanges, supervised and encouraged by a small 'propaganda' department of the Board of Trade. Such a system could abolish casual employment, register vacancies, discipline the work-shy, and eliminate the unemployed workman's time-wasting and often futile 'tramp in search of work'. Beveridge admitted that exchanges could not wholly eliminate unemployment caused by trade fluctuations, but he thought that this kind of unemployment could best be dealt with by schemes of contributory insurance. Labour exchanges could perform an essential role in testing the legitimacy of claims to insurance benefit, in subsidizing trade union insurance schemes and in extending the scope of insurance to non-unionized workers. He claimed that insurance was 'one of the great general methods of dealing with this problem', and that the trade union 'out-of-work' donation was 'one of the best instruments' against unemployment 'yet devised'.[121]

Beveridge's evidence both written and oral appears to have made a powerful impact on the Commissioners. Lansbury and Wakefield henceforth withdrew their opposition to labour exchanges in the C.U.B. Dr. Phelps invited him to dine at the Political Economy Club, and assured him that Lord George Hamilton had been very greatly im-

---

[120] W. H. Beveridge, 'Public Labour Exchanges in Germany', *Econ. J.*, XVIII, no. 69 (Mar. 1908), pp. 1–18; *MP*, 5 Oct., 5 and 13 Nov. 1907.

[121] Cd. 5066/1910, *RC on the Poor Laws, Minutes of Evidence*, statements of WHB, and QQ 77, 77,893, 78,014–24.

pressed.[122] Professor Smart told him that all the commissioners agreed with his analysis, and that his evidence was 'by far the best we have had—to say nothing of what I believe is a fact, that your remedy is the one likely to be adopted . . . you are on the top of the flowing tide'. Smart was particularly impressed by the possibilities of state-managed insurance, seeing it as a means whereby redundant workmen might be induced to undergo industrial retraining. He urged Beveridge to press for a new 'civil service department' to deal with labour problems; and a year later both Smart and Phelps wrote many of Beveridge's proposals into the Commission's Majority Report.[123] The Webbs themselves began publicly to press for labour organization, taking over many of Beveridge's ideas and recasting them in a more coercive form. They made compulsory labour exchanges a central feature of the plan for 'organisation of the labour market' outlined in their Minority Report. 'The Beveridge-cum-Webb Complete Plan will I believe get carried out—your part first,' wrote Beatrice Webb to Beveridge early in 1908. 'We will Break Up once and for all that Nasty Old Poor Law.'[124] 'Many thanks for sending me the Utopian plan,' wrote Beveridge to Sidney Webb.

I am very glad to see it and still more glad to think that it will in due course be boomed. I'm much too much in agreement with it to have any criticisms to make . . . I am simply a stage more Utopian than you in that I really hope to divide all provision for the unemployed into 'tiding over' (which will ultimately be done by universal insurance) and training for complete removal to another sphere.[125]

Beveridge's influence on the Royal Commission was not confined to his own personal evidence. In August 1907 he had been asked to prepare several research papers for submission to the Royal Commission on behalf of the Board of Trade. Throughout October and November he was working on these papers, producing one on the history of labour bureaux, one on trade union insurance, and another on foreign experiments in insuring the unemployed. In his paper on trade union insurance he showed that between 1892 and 1907 the hundred leading trade unions in the United Kingdom had paid to their unemployed members an average of £350,000 per annum. More than half this sum had been paid by unions in the building, shipbuilding and engineering industries —sectors where wages were relatively high and the work-force highly organized, but where the impact of trade fluctuations was particularly

[122] BP, IIb, L. Phelps to WHB, 19 Oct. 1907.
[123] BP, IIb, W. Smart to WHB, 23 Aug. 1907; Harris, op. cit., p. 260.
[124] BP, XII 3, f. 56, B. Webb to WHB, n.d.
[125] Webb Local Govt. Coll., vol. 297, item B50, WHB to S. Webb, 16 Feb. (? 1908).

acute.[126] In his survey of foreign schemes, Beveridge looked at voluntary, municipal and state experiments, and classified unemployment insurance into five main types. Firstly, independent trade union insurance, of the kind prevailing in Britain. Secondly, trade union insurance schemes subsidized by public authorities—of which the prototype was a scheme pioneered in the Belgian city of Ghent. Thirdly, municipal subsidies to individual saving, which were available in Ghent, Bologna and La Rochelle. Fourthly, voluntary insurance subsidized by charitable or public subscriptions as in Leipzig and Cologne. And fifthly, compulsory insurance managed by a public authority—of which the sole example was an experiment in the Swiss canton of St. Gall which had gone bankrupt in 1899. Beveridge refrained from saying which of these models he thought the most promising; but he pointed out that none of the variations on the Ghent system had managed to insure unskilled workmen, among whom 'the bulk of distress through unemployment is found'. Moreover, he claimed that the experience of St. Gall could not be regarded as conclusive and that compulsory insurance might well be successful if backed up by a labour exchange to test 'malingering', if contributions were collected from employers rather than workers, and if allowance was made for the varying frequency of unemployment in different trades.[127]

Beveridge submitted these memoranda to the Board of Trade in November 1907. 'Now I have a pleasing sense of being once more ahead of everyone else in regard to the unemployed,' he recorded, 'and have developed any amount of theory as to the possibility and limits of insurance against unemployment.'[128] Throughout the winter of 1907–8 he continued to publicize his unemployment proposals. He gave lectures at the London School of Economics and at the C.O.S. School of Sociology, and he addressed meetings of the Cambridge Fabians, the Association of Labour Exchange superintendents, several working-men's clubs and the Education committee of the L.C.C. In December 1907 he pacified an angry gathering of unemployed workers in Lewisham, who demanded to know why the local exchange had been unable to find them work.[129] And in January 1908 he rehearsed Mrs. Dunn Gardner in her evidence to the Poor Law Commission—evidence which amounted to a damning indictment of relief works and of the inefficient management of the C.U.B.[130]

Nevertheless, it was some time before Beveridge's labours bore practical fruit. He had several interviews with John Burns, but Burns

---

[126] Cd. 5068/1910, *RC on the Poor Laws, Minutes of Evidence*, Appendix XXI (C).
[127] Ibid., Appendix XXI (K).     [128] BP, IIa, WHB to ASB, 20 Nov. 1907.
[129] BP, IIa, WHB to ASB, 11 Dec. 1907.
[130] BP, IIa, WHB to ASB, 19 Jan. 1908; Cd. 5068/1910, *RC on the Poor Laws, Minutes of Evidence*, statement of Mrs. Dunn Gardner, paras. 10–30.

remained 'obdurate' in his dislike of exchanges—seeing them as potentially dangerous machinery for depressing wages and breaking strikes.[131] In February 1908 he had an encouraging talk with Ramsay Macdonald;[132] but the Labour Party was at this time absorbed in promoting its own Unemployed Workmen Bill, which proposed to solve the problem by a municipal guarantee of the 'right to work'. In March 1908, however, the situation rapidly changed. The C.U.B. passed a virtually unanimous resolution pressing for a national system of exchanges organized by central government. Then the Webbs showed their unemployment proposals to Winston Churchill, who wrote a letter to the *Nation* calling for the organization of the labour market and 'the development of certain national industries' as a 'means of counterbalancing the natural fluctuations of world trade'.[133] On 11 March the Webbs invited Beveridge to dine with Churchill, and they spent an evening talking about labour exchanges, decasualization and other means of dealing with the unemployed. 'I have always assumed,' wrote Beveridge in 1912,

that it was that dinner which settled my fate for the next few years. . . . I came away with a feeling that I had made an impression. I had certainly contradicted or criticised Churchill on some point about the Nonconformist ministers as the 'non-commissioned officers of democracy' (the whole conversation was not on unemployment). But beyond this and the impression of Churchill's brilliancy and restlessness I recollect little. . . .[134]

A few weeks later Churchill became President of the Board of Trade; and on 6 April several of his permanent officials gave evidence to the Poor Law Commission in favour of a voluntary system of labour exchanges combined with experimental schemes of compulsory unemployment insurance.[135] Later in the month Churchill himself referred to 'decasualisation' and prevention of unemployment in his by-election addresses at Manchester and Dundee, and the Webbs told him that 'if you are going to deal with unemployment you must have the boy Beveridge'.[136] Beveridge himself was at this time considering an invitation from the Board of Trade to carry out a Cost of Living Inquiry in America, and he had no idea that his cherished schemes were at last receiving serious policital attention. Early in July, however, he was invited to a conference at the Board of Trade, attended by Churchill, Sidney Webb, the Permanent Secretary Sir Hubert Llewellyn Smith,

---

[131] BP, IIa, WHB to ASB, 22 Aug. and 22 Oct. 1907; IIb, Walter Jerred to WHB, 21 Oct. 1907.
[132] BP, IIa, WHB to ASB, 13 Feb. 1908.
[133] BP, IIa, WHB to ASB, 12 Mar. 1908; *Nation*, 7 Mar. 1908.
[134] BP, IXa 35, 'Autobiography', p. 29.
[135] Cd. 5066/1910, *RC on the Poor Laws, Minutes of Evidence*, QQ.98,928–56.
[136] *PI*, p. 68.

and the Comptroller-General of the Commercial, Labour and Statistical department, Arthur Wilson Fox. At this conference Churchill expressed his intention of taking up Labour Exchanges seriously. 'The question turned', Beveridge recalled,

on the prospects of success for voluntary exchanges and I remember Churchill turning to me suddenly and asking me if I could undertake to promise that exchanges on a voluntary basis could succeed—to which I replied that I felt certain that without compulsion exchanges could secure a sufficient volume of general work; whether they could touch the problem of casual employment was another question altogether. Churchill had in mind then the starting of exchanges without a special Act—by a grant from the Exchequer. Webb, though desiring compulsion ultimately, supported a trial on a voluntary basis. Finally Churchill asked me to frame some proposals for the establishment of exchanges. As I was leaving Wilson Fox asked me something about the American project, and Churchill, overhearing, said I must not be allowed to go.[137]

On the following day Beveridge received a telephone call from Wilson Fox, inviting him to become a full-time official of the Board of Trade, for 'work in connection with exchanges' that would be 'both executive and theoretic'. After some negotiation he was offered a salary of £600 a year, and agreed to start as soon as he could leave the *Morning Post*. 'I feel that the change has come just at the right moment,' he wrote joyfully to Annette. '. . . I'm not pensionable at present but I'm quite permanent and in a delightfully new position with any amount of room for expansion.'[138] In retrospect, however, he looked back on this decision in a rather different light. It was, he wrote,

the rashest and most ill-considered act of my life. I became simply a personal clerk on the staff of the comptroller—with no definite position and no claim to do any particular work. I had no guarantee that Labour Exchanges would be established—or had even been accepted by the Cabinet; in the Board of Trade they had no friends except Churchill and Wilson Fox (who died in December). I had no understanding that if they were established I should be put in charge . . . I got no permission then to publish my half-written book. A defeat for Churchill in the Cabinet or a promotion for him to some other office would have left me absolutely stranded . . .[139]

## VII

By mid-1908 Beveridge's analysis of unemployment had developed considerably from the position he had held when he first went on to the C.U.B. in 1905. Firstly, he was increasingly convinced that there were

[137] BP, IXa 35, 'Autobiography', p. 30.
[138] BP, IIa, WHB to ASB, 3 July 1908.
[139] BP, IXa 35, 'Autobiography'. p. 31.

not one but several 'problems of unemployment', some of which could be cured by rational state intervention, whilst others were an inevitable concomitant of modern industrial life.[140] Secondly, he was now much less exclusively concerned with casual labour, and was much more concerned with what he defined as the 'problem of under-employment' throughout the industrial world. He still saw the casual trades, particularly dock labour, as the paradigm example of chronic under-employment; but he believed that the same phenomena could be found to a certain extent throughout modern industry—the phenomena of lack of mobility between different centres of employment, wasteful duplication of the labour force and lack of communication between employers and employed.[141] The cause of this widespread under-employment was to be found in the fact that sophisticated market economies had not developed institutions for the hire of labour comparable with those developed for their other exchange functions, such as the retail sale of goods. 'Everyone has seen in a window at times the notice "Boy wanted",' he wrote. 'No one, it is safe to say has ever seen in a window the notice "Boots wanted". Yet people in fact want to buy boots as much or at least as often as they want to buy the labour of boys. The contrast . . . indicates a deep-reaching difference of economic methods.'[142]

Beveridge rounded off his ideas on unemployment with a series of lectures in Oxford during the Michaelmas term of 1908. With special permission from the Board of Trade these lectures were published as a book, *Unemployment: a Problem of Industry*, early in 1909. The lectures and book largely reiterated Beveridge's articles in learned journals and his evidence to the Poor Law Commission. As in earlier works he identified a range of different causes of unemployment—periodical fluctuations of demand, lack of organization, personal moral inferiority, 'blind-alley' situations, structural decline. The remedies which he proposed were as follows. Firstly, labour exchanges which would eliminate casual employment, promote labour mobility, encourage technical education, divert school-leavers from 'blind-alley' occupations, reserve light employment for elderly and disabled workmen, and weed out the unemployable and the work-shy for 'disciplinary or hospital treatment under the Poor Law'.[143] Secondly, state promotion of unemployment insurance, either directly through exchanges, or indirectly through trade unions—both of which could pay out-of-work benefits and operate a 'test' of willingness to work. Beveridge claimed that the premiums for

[140] 'Unemployment: a Symposium of Platitudes', *Toynbee Record*, Mar. 1908. p. 21.
[141] Webb Local Goct. Coll. vol. 297, item 13, WHB to B. Webb, 7 May 1907.
[142] W. H. Beveridge, *The Organisation of the Labour Market* (pamphlet 1908), p. 1.
[143] *Unemployment: a Problem of Industry* (1909 edn.), pp. 197–216.

such insurance were now within the means of all but a small minority of English workers; and even of these, he argued, 'there are probably few . . . who do not on average spend at least the amount of those premiums on luxuries with which they could well dispense'.[144] Thirdly, he suggested the encouragement of 'short-time agreements' and adjustments in standard wage-rates to meet periods of depression.[145] Fourthly, the regulation of public works programmes so as to concentrate employment into periods when demand was slack.[146] And, finally, reform of the Poor Law and abolition of the prevailing administrative confusion between provision of work and provision of relief. A reformed Poor Law, Beveridge suggested, would perform three main functions for the unemployed. It would provide 'sustenance' for those genuinely looking for work; 'restorative or educational treatment' for those whom hardship had rendered unfit for work; and discipline in penal labour colonies for those who wilfully refused to work and were 'beyond restoration'.[147]

Beveridge's arguments in *Unemployment: a Problem of Industry* were indicative of his wider social beliefs in a number of different ways. His whole programme was rooted in a very ambitious conception of how far social and economic activities were inherently capable of rational administrative control. His defence of labour exchanges reflected his belief in 'social organisation' as not merely useful but functionally necessary to the complex structure of advanced industrial societies; and, similarly, his advocacy of insurance reflected his commitment to policies of 'social integration' discussed in an earlier chapter. In spite of their radical and far-reaching nature, however, none of his proposals was fundamentally inconsistent with mainstream social and economic ideas of the day. R. H. Tawney, reviewing Beveridge's study in the *Morning Post*, observed that it was 'one of those rare books which mark the end of a powerful movement of thought and . . . swing both theory and practice out of well-worn channels into hitherto unexplored fields'.[148] Yet Beveridge's analysis—as he himself subsequently admitted—was firmly based on the traditional economic assumptions that depressions were inevitable and that there could be no such thing as an overall imbalance of labour supply and demand.[149] He explicitly rejected the 'underconsumptionist' argument advanced by radical liberals,[150] and ignored the socialist argument that fluctuations could be abolished by public control of production. Moreover, he saw 'depressions' and 'trade fluctuations' as not merely inevitable but as necessary prerequisites of economic progress—as the means by which sub-standard workmen were expelled

---

[144] Ibid., p. 228.                [145] Ibid., pp. 220–2, 231–2.                [146] Ibid., pp. 230–1.
[147] Ibid., pp. 232–4.             [148] *MP*, 8 Feb. 1909.
[149] *Full Employment in a Free Society, a Report by William H. Beveridge* (1944), pp. 91–2.
[150] *Unemployment: a Problem of Industry*, pp. 59–63.

and obsolete practices abandoned, thus rendering industry more efficient than ever before.[151] Similar 'evolutionary' assumptions can be seen
in Beveridge's whole discussion of casual labour—in his belief that
archaic processes must give way to modern methods, in his fear that
casual employment sheltered 'the unfit', and in his implicit condemnation of the casual labourer's way of life as an economic and cultural
anachronism in the modern world.

*Unemployment* rapidly became the standard work on the subject, and,
unusually for a book of its kind, it ran through three editions in the next
four years. It was widely praised for its lucidity, comprehensiveness and
practical plausibility from all points of the political spectrum, ranging
from the Independent Labour Party to the C.O.S. J. A. Hobson
described Beveridge's proposals as 'humane and reasonable' and C. S.
Loch informed him, 'I am in close agreement with you throughout.'[152]
As an economic work, the book was warmly approved both by free
market liberals like Harold Cox and A. C. Pigou, and by radical collect-
ivists like Leo Chiozza Money and Reginald Bray.[153] Curiously enough,
some of the severest comments on Beveridge's study came from his
personal friends and acquaintances. E. J. Urwick, his predecessor at
Toynbee Hall, wrote rather disparagingly that the work was 'masterly
rather than profound . . . it does not face up to the essential rottenness
of competitive production'.[154] And R. C. K. Ensor in the *Manchester
Guardian* observed that Beveridge was too concerned with logic and not
enough with life. 'Perhaps, indeed, a defect in his mental outfit lies just
there,' wrote Ensor. 'He is too much content to diagnose and prescribe
in a spirit of pure reason; he does not ask himself often enough if the
patients will swallow the remedies; if the physicians can be trusted to
apply them and so on. He reminds one of a geometrician dealing with
straight lines and points and circles, and forgetting that in this actual
world neither straight lines nor points on circles are ever found.'[155]

[151] Ibid., p. 64.
[152] *Nation*, 20 Feb. 1909; BP, XII 3, f. 47, C. S. Loch to WHB, 12 Feb. 1909.
[153] BP, XII, 5, f. 51, T. E. Harvey to WHB, 2 Mar. 1909; *Yorkshire Gazette*, 27 Feb. 1909;
*Daily News*, 11 Feb. 1909.
[154] *St. George*, Apr. 1909.
[155] *Manchester Guardian*, 9 Feb. 1908.

# 7

## Beveridge and the Board of Trade

### I

THE Board of Trade which Beveridge entered in 1908 was one of the most dynamic and expansionist of Whitehall departments. Its traditional role was 'the provision of information and advice to the Government on matters of trade and commerce', but during the previous twenty years its functions had greatly extended into the spheres of social investigation, labour relations and industrial arbitration. Under the presidency of Lloyd George between 1905 and 1908 the Board had introduced a major programme of legislative reforms, dealing with company law, merchant shipping control and nationalization of the Port of London. At the same time the Board took over responsibility for several areas of policy which had previously belonged to other government departments. In 1907 the overseas consular service was transferred from the Foreign Office to the Board of Trade. In 1908 it was the Board of Trade rather than the Local Government Board which began to prepare measures for dealing with unemployment. And in 1909 it was the Board of Trade that introduced 'anti-sweating' legislation—not the Home Office, which was the department of state traditionally concerned with the welfare of employees in factories and workshops.[1]

Historians have put forward a number of explanations to account for this unusual degree of reforming initiative on the part of a government department. Several commentators have ascribed it to the personal initiative of Churchill and Lloyd George—in such marked contrast to the lethargy of the Liberal Home Secretary, Herbert Gladstone, and to the zealous inefficiency of John Burns at the L.G.B.[2] A recent study has suggested that a further crucial factor was the superior quality of the Board of Trade's research and information services, which enabled the Board to expand its administrative functions into areas of policy in which Home Office and L.G.B. statistics were notoriously poor.[3] Beveridge himself ascribed the Board's initiative to the fact that financially it

[1] See J. A. M. Caldwell, 'Social Policy and Public Administration 1909–11', (Nottingham Ph.D thesis 1956), and the same author's 'The Genesis of the Ministry of Labour', *Public Administration*, XXXVII (winter 1959), pp. 367–91.

[2] 'The Genesis of the Ministry of Labour', loc. cit., pp. 376–81.

[3] Roger Davidson, 'Llewellyn Smith, the Labour Department and Government Growth', *Studies in the Growth of Nineteenth Century Government*, ed. Gillian Sutherland, pp. 252–4.

was a 'low status' department, which attracted a series of ephemeral Presidents anxious to move on to more lucrative office. 'This meant,' he recalled, '. . . that the influence of the officials was relatively great, particularly the influence of the Permanent Secretary . . . it was natural that at times we should regard ourselves as the Board, and our Ministers as perhaps pleasant but certainly transient and occasionally embarrassing phantoms.'[4] This tradition of independence was reinforced by the fact that relatively few of the Board's higher officials had entered the Civil Service straight from university through the conventional route of Open Competition. Many of them had prior experience in business, research or trade union organization, and had been specially recruited into the Board as 'experts' on commercial and industrial issues. Throughout the ministry these experts were given a considerable degree of freedom and scope for innovation; and probably for this reason the Board of Trade escaped from much of the 'ossification and the bureaucratic outlook' found in other departments of public affairs.[5]

All these factors help to explain why it was that during the 1900s the Board of Trade became at least for a short time the spearhead of innovation in government social policy—particularly in the introduction of policies for the unemployed. It would be wrong, however, to exaggerate the extent to which this involvement in social policy constituted a fundamental breach with the earlier history of the Board. Many historians have explained the growth of government-inspired social policy in terms of a functional response to increasing industrialization; and it was perhaps inevitable, once belief in unmitigated 'laissez-faire' had faded, that the department most intimately concerned with promoting industrial progress should turn its attention to questions of social and industrial welfare. This growing concern with the 'social' dimension of economic policy had been reflected in the setting up of the Board's Commercial, Labour and Statistical department in 1894. This department had carried out several special investigations into problems of the labour market and policies for relieving unemployment in Britain and abroad; and the head of the department, Wilson Fox, was a firm believer in 'grandmotherly control by the State'.[6] Moreover, there had been continuous if not very powerful pressure for government-sponsored labour exchanges since the 1890s; and this movement had always viewed labour exchanges as an aspect of 'labour information' rather than social welfare, and therefore as a logical extension of the research and

---

[4] *PI*, pp. 72–3.
[5] 'The Genesis of the Ministry of Labour', loc. cit., p. 370.
[6] C. 7182/1893–4, *Board of Trade, Agencies and Methods for Dealing with the Unemployed*; Cd. 2304/1905, *Report ot the Board of Trade on Agencies and Methods for dealing with the Unemployed in Certain Foreign Countries*; Webb Local Govt. Coll., vol. 297, item C 1., Arthur Wilson Fox to S. Webb, 9 Oct. 1907.

statistical services of the Board of Trade. Beveridge himself had been convinced that nation-wide labour exchanges could best be organized by the 'information department of the Board of Trade', ever since he had first considered the problem during his days at Toynbee Hall.[7]

Furthermore, at a purely practical and personal level the staff of the Board of Trade were far better equipped to deal with labour exchanges than the overworked and underpaid officials of the L.G.B. The Permanent Secretary, Sir Hubert Llewellyn Smith, was well known as an expert on unemployment. Wilson Fox had carried out surveys of labour migration for several public inquiries, and Board of Trade investigators compiled regular statistics about unemployment, wages and conditions of labour, which were published monthly in the *Labour Gazette*. Finally, and perhaps most crucially important, the Board of Trade was free from the taint of 'pauperism' and 'charity', which had continually undermined the unemployment policies carried out under the L.G.B. The Board had good relations with both employers and trade unions, and it managed these relations on strictly 'business' lines—its chief aim being simply to promote 'capitalist enterprise' and to secure to industry 'the best possible conditions for industrial progress'.[8] It was mainly for this reason that Beveridge had pressed for a labour exchange system under the Board of Trade rather than the L.G.B.; and the appropriateness of such an arrangement was officially recognized in July 1908, when an interdepartmental conference of senior officials agreed that the 'subject of Labour Exchanges ought to be considered as a question of employment and not of Relief, and consequently should be dealt with by the Board of Trade'.[9]

## II

Beveridge joined the Board of Trade as an unestablished civil servant on the staff of the Comptroller-General of the Commercial, Labour and Statistical Department early in July 1908. His salary of £600 a year was considerably more than that paid to other Board of Trade 'experts' and was a reflection of the Board's anxiety to acquire his services. 'The appointment is a tremendous tribute to Will's peculiar genius,' commented his friend, Andrewes Uthwatt. 'I feel sure that he is the last person to suffer extinction by becoming part of a machine.'[10] Another friend, Helen Denman, confided to Annette Beveridge that she had 'heard this little bit of gossip about Will . . . that when he got his Board

[7] Harris, op. cit., pp. 279–82; *Toynbee Record*, May 1905, p. 126.

[8] 'The Genesis of the Ministry of Labour', loc. cit., pp. 367, 376.

[9] PRO, T. 1/11093/6763/19536, note of an interview with Sir Samuel Provis with regard to status, 29 July 1908.

[10] AHBP, Mss. Eur. C. 176/200, A. A. Uthwatt to ASB, n.d. (1908).

of Trade appointment he went about in the greatest delight because, he said, "now I can write blue-books"!! I think it is very nice and character-istic but I daresay you knew it.'[11] Annette herself was jubilant at her son's success. 'Your news is indeed good and contenting,' she wrote, '. . . various pleasant wishes open out from it—the good society you will enter—the entire withdrawal into the statesman's milieu from what is the party politician's . . . the entry into the continuous government of the nation—the chance of initiating work of which you see the good.'[12] Beveridge himself saw his new position less as an advancement of his personal prospects than as a chance to implement some of the ideas on social policy which he had been evolving since 1904. 'The exact position is that I am not a full public servant,' he recorded:

I am really there . . . to formulate arguments and schemes for national Labour Exchanges with a view to getting them accepted by the Government. If and when that is done there will be a Labour Exchange department and I shall no doubt be there—as a full civil servant, with pension and all the rest of it. If it does not get accepted by the Government (and the Treasury) as soon as we . . . hope, I still go on permanently in the present position and do whatever comes to hand. There is of course any amount to do.[13]

Beveridge's work during his first few weeks at the Board was primarily statistical. Nevertheless, signs of action on labour exchanges came more swiftly than he had originally envisaged. During the summer of 1908 several Liberal ministers publicly committed themselves to new social policies on behalf of the unemployed—probably prompted by rising unemployment and by popular unrest in many industrial centres.[14] Churchill in August warned the Cabinet that 'the amount of unemploy-ment is disquieting for the season of the year' and that 'a period of unusual severity for the working classes has begun.'[15] Towards the end of July Beveridge was summoned several times to the President's office to discuss plans for legislation. He found Churchill 'great fun to work with. He told me then—I think as a reason for getting on quickly with Labour Exchanges—that he had not himself many years to live; he expected to die young like his father Randolph. But this was before he married. Just after, he saw and settled with Clementine and gave up any idea of dying young.'[16] Beveridge also established a good working relationship with the Board's permanent secretary, Sir Hubert Llewellyn

[11] AHBP, Mss. Eur. C. 176/200, Helen Denman to ASB, n.d. (1908).
[12] BP, IIa, ASB to WHB, 4 July 1908.
[13] BP, IIa, WHB to ASB, 4 July 1908.
[14] Harris, op. cit., pp. 273–4.
[15] Board of Trade Reports on Employment and Trade 1905–9, vol. D, W. S. Churchill to the Cabinet, 8 Aug. 1908.
[16] BP, III 34, 'Employment Exchange Jubilee. Speech by Lord Beveridge', 1 Feb. 1960.

Smith, whom he had known since his days at Toynbee Hall. Llewellyn Smith was a brilliant and rather domineering man, with considerable 'inventive genius' in the formulation of policy.[17] He was notoriously impervious to the views of others, and was much more sceptical than Beveridge about the possibility of an organized labour market. Nevertheless, he and Beveridge had much in common and they soon slipped easily into the roles of master and apprentice. Like Beveridge, Llewellyn Smith had graduated from Balliol and Toynbee and had been involved in social investigation in London's East End. Like Beveridge he had been attracted by Fabian Socialism, although by 1908 he was anxious to shed his reputation as an 'ex-Fabian who has become a bureaucrat' and to dissociate himself from the all-pervasive influence of Sidney and Beatrice Webb.[18] Like Beveridge he was strongly committed to empirical methods of social research and to pragmatism in social policy; and he shared Beveridge's rather exaggerated belief in the objective, impartial, administrative state. He was, moreover, a 'master' in the 'technique of legislation'—in preparing detailed memoranda, resisting powerful pressure groups, manipulating difficult ministers and warding off Treasury control. Towards his political superiors he adopted a slightly patronizing air, bordering at times on a suggestion of veiled contempt. 'One of Mr. Churchill's great qualities,' Llewellyn Smith told Beveridge, '[was] that he would listen to reason. He didn't like it at all, but if you persisted it went home in the end.'[19] Beveridge himself regarded Llewellyn Smith as 'one of the ablest and most constructive such officers that can ever have existed. To work under him as I did on Labour Exchanges and Unemployment Insurance was a liberal education.'[20] The two men were soon on friendly terms; Sir Hubert became familiarly known as 'Shubert' to Beveridge's family, and Beveridge was a frequent and popular visitor at the home of the Llewellyn Smiths. As Lord Salter commented many years later, the active support of both Llewellyn Smith and Churchill was to be of crucial importance to Beveridge in implementing the policies for which he had so long pressed. 'It should be noted', wrote Salter,

that in this period he had an unusual combination of advantages to help him; an indisputable pre-eminence in personal knowledge; an appreciative and sympathetic colleague . . . and an imaginative and constructive political chief ready to give him all the support he might need to secure his immunity from any jealous or obstructive critics among those nearest to his work. This was a

[17] W. H. Beveridge, 'Sir Hubert Llewellyn Smith (1864–1945)', *Econ. J.*, LVI, no. 221, Mar. 1946, p. 145.

[18] C. F. Rey, unpublished autobiography, p. 80.

[19] 'Sir Hubert Llewellyn-Smith (1864–1945)', loc. cit., pp. 145–6.

[20] BP, III 34, 'Employment Exchange Jubilee. Speech by Lord Beveridge', 1 Feb. 1960.

happy combination not always available or obtainable, as he was to find later in his career.[21]

As Llewellyn Smith's apprentice, Beveridge composed his first brief for Churchill on 20 July 1908. In this memorandum he reiterated his now familiar argument that there was no general failure of labour demand, but that each trade tended to be overstocked because of inadequate labour information and local hindrances to labour mobility. He proposed that a nation-wide system of labour exchanges should be set up 'for measures of organisation, not of relief', and that central control should be exercised by a 'department of industrial intelligence'. He claimed that exchanges could be used, not merely to promote mobility and to reduce frictional unemployment, but to pursue a wide range of secondary objectives—to manage a system of insurance, to dovetail employment in seasonal occupations, to provide vocational guidance, to encourage technical education, and to re-train workmen who had been made redundant by long-term structural change. At the same time exchanges could detect the work-shy, punish the vagrant, and eliminate the casual labourer 'who remains financially and morally beyond the possibility of thrift and organisation'. The cost of such a system Beveridge calculated at £130,000 a year, and he proposed that a special branch of the Board of Trade should be formed to put it into operation. At a local level control could be exercised either directly, through a national system modelled on the Post Office, or indirectly through local authorities. In principle Beveridge favoured a centrally-controlled, thoroughly nationalized system, as likely to secure greater efficiency and uniformity; but at this stage he recommended a locally-based system, as likely to evoke less suspicion from local workers and employers. 'Local interest may be of great value,' he argued, 'while the danger of local feeling presenting obstacles to the mobility of labour should not prove beyond the powers of control by the grant-in-aid.'[22]

Beveridge's scheme met with some criticism from the Board's permanent officials, but it was nevertheless circulated to several Cabinet Ministers before the end of July.[23] Churchill did not, however, accept all of Beveridge's suggestions. He rejected the idea of a localized system, and opted instead for 'a national scheme directly under the Board'. Almost certainly this decision was motivated by the belief that labour exchanges would soon be followed by a scheme of national insurance, which would necessarily involve a national rather than local system of control. Nevertheless, as Beveridge later recalled, Churchill made the

[21] Lord Salter, 'Lord Beveridge 1879–1963', *Procs. Br. Acad.*, XLIX, 1963, p. 420.
[22] Bev. Coll. B, vol. XIV, item 23, *c.* 20 July 1908.
[23] BP, IIa, WHB to ASB, 21 July 1908; R. Churchill, *Winston S. Churchill*, II, Companion part II (1907–11), pp. 827–31.

decision 'before it was certain that unemployment insurance would become law. . . . It is important . . . to realise how revolutionary a decision this was in expanding the direct functions of Whitehall.'[24]

The decision to proceed with unemployment insurance was taken in the autumn of 1908, and thereafter the two schemes were planned in close conjunction. In October Churchill told the House of Commons that his department was preparing policies to deal with 'the general questions of unemployment, under-employment and casual labour',[25] and in November he dispatched a deputation of trade union officials to inspect the treatment of unemployment in the German empire. The trade unionists, as Beveridge had been advised by Dr. Freund a year before, were greatly reassured by the sight of a successful labour exchange system in action. 'The moral tone of an unemployed workman must be strengthened by regularly visiting such institutes,' they reported in approving tones, 'and his money is not wasted by travelling from place to place and from factory to factory in search of work.'[26]

Meanwhile, Beveridge and Llewellyn Smith began to work out the administrative details of a joint scheme of labour exchanges and unemployment insurance. Consultations were held with the Government Actuary, the Treasury, the trade unions, and with independent experts like Sidney Webb. The main principles of the new scheme were outlined by Churchill in a paper submitted to the Cabinet in December 1908. The chief problem, as Churchill defined it, was to organize simultaneously 'the mobilities and stabilities of labour'—to facilitate the search for work, and at the same time to prevent the economic breakdown of homes and families while this search was in progress. The tone and content of this paper reveal just how strongly at this time Churchill shared Beveridge's vision of the wide-ranging secondary advantages of nation-wide labour organization. 'A system of public labour exchanges,' he argued, 'stands at the gateway to industrial security. It opens the way to all immediate reforms.' Such a system, Churchill claimed, could provide the machinery for unemployment insurance, advise school-leavers on choice of occupation, weed out the inveterate 'loafer', and enable the genuine workman to survey in a single day 'the whole labour market of the United Kingdom'. At the same time it could publish employment statistics, forestall trade depressions and gradually eliminate casual labour. At a more fundamental level it could foster industrial harmony and feelings of political solidarity by forming a

[24] BP, III 34, draft of a speech for the Labour Exchange Jubilee, Feb. 1960.

[25] H.C. Deb., 4 s., vol. 195, col. 492.

[26] Braithwaite Papers, II, b (1) 'Workmen's Insurance Systems in Germany, Report of Deputation'.

'social link' between the potentially warring forces of capital and labour.[27]

The administrative details of the labour exchange scheme were spelt out in a further Cabinet paper, drafted by Beveridge and circulated by Churchill in January 1909. Significantly, the administrative arrangements outlined in this plan were neither purely local nor purely central but regional. It was proposed that the United Kingdom should be divided up on the basis of 'geographical' and 'industrial' characteristics into nine or ten regional divisions, and that the main focus of administration should be in these divisions—subject to overall supervision by the Board of Trade. In the principal town of each division there would be a regional 'clearing-house', controlled by a Divisional Chief who would be responsible for managing local exchanges in that region. Local offices would be graded into first and second class exchanges, according to size of population in the districts which they served; and in remote areas labour exchange facilities would be provided through voluntary agencies or through local post offices, which had 'the advantage of being found everywhere, of being clear of the taints of public relief or politics, and of being places to which everybody goes'. The whole system would be directed by a 'National Clearing House', located in the Board of Trade, which would devise general policy, collect statistical returns from divisional offices, and 'become the centre of general information as to industrial tendencies'. Beveridge envisaged that the 'brains and driving-power ... of the Labour Exchange movement' would be the Divisional Chiefs, who would not only control the regional clearing-houses, but would be in constant touch with labour exchange managers, with the central authority and with each other. They would be recruited from business rather than from social welfare or charitable administration, and would be 'able to hold their own' with both management and trade unions.

At a local level Beveridge envisaged that each first-class exchange would provide separate facilities for skilled and unskilled, female and juvenile applicants, and that accommodation would be spacious enough to allow each registered applicant to call at the exchange every day. Registration would be entirely voluntary and entirely free. Workmen who registered as available for work would be invited but not obliged to give details of previous employment; and applicants would be recommended for situations, not with reference to financial need but solely on grounds of their suitability for the work. Labour exchanges would not lay down conditions about wages, but trade unionists would be allowed

[27] PRO, CAB 37/96/159, 'Unemployment Insurance: Labour Exchanges', by W. S. Churchill, circulated 11 Dec. 1908.

to use the exchanges to advertise their standard rates; and every workman sent to a situation would be informed in advance of the wages
offered, so that the onus of black-legging would fall on the individual
rather than on the exchange. Notice of trade disputes would be publicly
placarded in all exchanges; and at each principle exchange an advisory
committee of employers and workmen would be appointed by the
Board of Trade 'to settle occasional difficulties as to disputes and the
like'. Finally Beveridge recommended that special juvenile employment
committees should be set up, including members of local education
authorities, to advise school-leavers on choice of occupation, to recommend improvements in juvenile employment, and to cultivate 'a public
opinion among employers, parents and children against premature
earning in blind-alley occupations'.[28]

In February 1909 labour exchanges received further support from the
Majority and Minority Reports of the Royal Commission on the Poor
Laws; and on 17 February Churchill's announcement to Parliament
that he intended to introduce a national system of voluntary exchanges
was welcomed by all political parties. 'I see that Austen Chamberlain
blessed Labour Exchanges the other day,' Beveridge recorded, 'and the
Labour Party resolved in their favour at Portsmouth, and the Liberal
Government—so they've hardly an enemy in the world.'[29] He began to
sit in the Officials' gallery at the House of Commons to help Churchill
with answers to hostile parliamentary questions—but found that he had
very little to do.[30] A few months later he composed Churchill's parliamentary brief when the Labour Exchanges bill was introduced into the
House of Commons. In this he claimed that labour exchanges had won
the support of a wide range of political groups—free traders and tariff
reformers, local councils and distress committees, trade unions and
chambers of commerce. He defended the choice of a national system on
the grounds that the market for labour was now nation-wide and that
'local government areas are out of all relation to industrial needs and
structure'. He also put forward a series of hypothetical objections to
labour exchanges and refuted them one by one; labour exchanges would
*not* interfere with employers' freedom of choice, they would *not* depress
wages, they would *not* encourage irresponsible dismissals. They would
*not* undermine trade unionism, but would simply extend to all workers
the kind of information services previously available only to a minority
of highly-skilled men. Above all, Beveridge denied the charge that, by
exposing the true extent of unemployment, labour exchanges would
'give a handle to Socialist agitators to force through the "right to work".'
On the contrary, he argued, they would simply give policy-makers the

[28] PRO, CAB 37/97/17, 'Labour Exchanges', Jan. 1909.
[29] BP, IIa, WHB to ASB, 4 Feb. 1909.          [30] BP, IIa, WHB to ASB, 18 Feb. 1909.

necessary facts on which to act, and would 'so far demonstrate the complexity of the problem as to dispose finally of all rough-and-ready revolutionary solutions'. He recalled that 'at the beginning of the exchange movement in Germany this same objection was raised by the middle class parties—that the exchanges would show an ever-swelling mass of unemployment forcing a revolution. In fact, the exchanges show no such thing, but only a supply and demand not altogether out of relation to one another in amount but differing often in kind.'[31]

The Labour Exchanges bill passed its second reading with scarcely any debate and without a division on 16 June 1909. Its terms were deliberately brief, as Churchill was anxious to leave scope for further amendment once the scheme had come into force. The Bill empowered the Board of Trade simply to establish, take over and maintain exchanges, to collect and publish information about employment, and to frame regulations for labour exchange management—the cost of these services being borne by the national exchequer. Nevertheless, although the bill was an overtly uncontroversial measure it involved delicate negotiations with both sides of industry—particularly with the trade unions who were disturbed by the absence of safeguards against blacklegs and demanded greater union representation on advisory committees. Churchill was anxious to placate the unions, realizing that the business reputation of exchanges would depend on attracting the custom of the higher grades of workmen; and he therefore summoned a series of conferences with the T.U.C. and with representatives of the leading shipbuilding and engineering unions. Beveridge, in preparing the President's brief, advised him that there were three possible ways in which an exchange could deal with vacancies caused by a trade dispute. It could refuse to register them; it could register all vacancies regardless of cause; or it could register strike vacancies, but notify customers of the existence of a dispute, so as to throw the responsibility for strike-breaking 'not on the bureau but on the men'. Beveridge himself recommended this third course, as being the one that had worked most successfully in the German system. Apart from this, Beveridge argued, labour exchange superintendents should be given complete discretion in the selection of men for jobs. Trade unions should be encouraged to use exchange facilities and to deposit their own 'vacant books' at an exchange; but they should not be given special privileges in any other way, and no jobs could be reserved exclusively for union men. Nor could it be guaranteed that working-class representatives on advisory committees would always be trade unionists—although this would almost invariably be the case, since very few non-union workmen were active in public affairs. Beveridge argued, moreover, that such guarantees were strictly unnecessary,

[31] Bev. Coll. B, vol. XIV, item 15, 'Labour Exchanges General Memorandum', Nov. 1909.

since high standards of fairness would be maintained, not by the advisory committees, but by the professional labour exchange staff. 'The permanent salaried public official—with the growth of his business his one principal aim—is the real safeguard for impartial administration. He will know that he simply cannot succeed except by a reputation for strict impartiality.'[32]

These arguments were reiterated by Churchill when, accompanied by Llewellyn Smith and Beveridge, he met a deputation from the T.U.C. on 17 July. Several of the delegates took objection to the fact that the new scheme had been largely drawn up by Beveridge, who two years earlier had been chiefly responsible for the resistance to trade union demands on the Central (Unemployed) Body. 'We asked for certain conditions,' complained W. C. Steadman, a London trades unionist who had taken part in the C.U.B. negotiations. 'Mr. Beveridge . . . absolutely refused to give us those conditions; and if we are going to have our labour bureaux under the Board of Trade run off the same system, then I say the sooner you do away with it the better.'[33] On the following day a deputation from the shipbuilding and engineering unions complained bitterly about the extension to non-union men of privileges which the unions had won by their own efforts; and they denounced the role in labour exchange management of benevolent and supposedly impartial administrators. 'We do not want these benevolent parties at all,' declared J. M. Jack, the Secretary of the Scottish Ironmoulders, '. . . we want men who have come through the rough and tumble of life . . . men who have come through the thick of battle.'[34]

Churchill, however, handled these conferences very skilfully, appearing to compromise with the unions whilst in fact conceding nothing that had not already been accepted in principle by the Cabinet earlier in the year. He told the unions frankly that without their co-operation the labour exchange system would come 'clattering to the ground', and he suggested that exchanges could become focal points for trade union recruitment and the propagation of trade union principles. He convinced the T.U.C. that organized labour would be adequately protected if exchanges gave full publicity to trade disputes and allowed unions to put up notices advertising the standard rate; but, as Beveridge had recommended, he refused to confine workers' membership of advisory committees solely to union men. At the same time he hinted strongly that labour exchanges were merely the first instalment of a much more

[32] PRO, LAB 2/211 LE 499, 'Labour Exchanges. Trade Union deputation', WHB's brief for W. S. Churchill, June 1909.

[33] PRO, LAB 2/211 LE 500, typescript report of first conference with the Parliamentary Committee of the T.U.C., 17 June 1909.

[34] PRO, LAB 2/211 LE 500, typescript report of conference with the Federation of Shipbuilding and Engineering Trade Unions, 18 June 1909.

ambitious programme for dealing with unemployment—a programme which would include not merely insurance, but drastic reform of the Poor Law, expulsion from the labour market of 'the weakling and the feeble and the unstable', and elimination of trade depressions by 'some sort of averaging machinery' to regulate labour demand. The main result of these negotiations was that on 22 June when the Bill came before a standing committee Churchill introduced a new clause, stipulating that no workman who registered at an exchange 'should suffer any disqualification or be otherwise prejudiced' for refusing wages lower than those current in his trade or district or for refusing a vacancy created by a trade dispute.[35] This amendment was accepted by the T.U.C. at a further meeting with Churchill on 8 July, and the President was warmly thanked by the unions for his 'courteous and sympathetic reception' of their complaints.[36] The new clause did not, however, represent any substantive change in labour exchange policy; it merely embodied in the statute a principle which Churchill and his officials had in any case intended to apply by day-to-day administrative regulation ever since the scheme was first planned.

## III

Throughout the summer of 1909 Board of Trade officials were working to bring the new scheme into operation by the beginning of 1910. In August Beveridge paid a further visit to Germany, this time in the company of Llewellyn Smith and Sir George Askwith, the Board of Trade's chief conciliator in industrial disputes. They inspected the details of labour exchange administration in Cologne, Elberfeld, Dusseldorf, Freiburg and Berlin—Beveridge acting as interpreter because neither of his companions was fluent in German.[37] Early in the autumn the final passage of the Labour Exchanges Act and the need to recruit a new body of staff led to some major readjustments in the internal structure of the Board of Trade.[38] Labour exchanges, trade boards, industrial conciliation and the Census of Production were hived off from the Commercial, Labour and Statistical Department and became the responsibility of a new 'Labour Department' headed by George Askwith—not a fortunate choice from Beveridge's point of view, since Askwith was lukewarm about labour exchanges and later became their

[35] PRO, LAB 2/211/LE 733, Report of Standing Committee C, 8 July 1909.
[36] PRO, LAB 2/211/LE 499, William Mosses to W. S. Churchill, 19 June 1909; LE 500, typescript report of second conference with the Parliamentary Committee of the T.U.C., 8 July 1909.
[37] BP, IIa, WHB to ASB, 28 Aug. 1909 and undated letter of same period.
[38] PRO, B.T. 15/57/F6644, Estimates file, a note on the Labour Department, n.d. (1910).

bitter critic.[39] Within the Labour department a new 'Labour Exchanges Branch' was set up at Caxton House, to devise labour exchange policy and to supervise the new regional divisions. Beveridge himself was initially invited to become merely an 'expert advisor' in this new system, without formal executive responsibility; but he protested strongly against such an arrangement, on the grounds that it would lead to a confusion of authority and that 'as an expert cerebrating *in vacuo* I would lack the daily contact with reality to make my ideas practical as well as new'.[40] He was therefore offered the post of administrative head of the new system in September 1909. His appointment was announced in October, and received much publicity and approbation in the press. It was widely regarded as a symbol of the Liberal government's determination to commit itself to a programme of national efficiency; and Beveridge himself was pronounced 'the greatest authority on unemployment of the day'.[41] 'This really seems to be a world on the march,' commented a friend from Toynbee days, 'with everybody provided with a fitting task.'[42] 'You need not be told how glad—how proud and hopeful I am,' wrote Samuel Barnett. 'You have the rare chance of shaping your dreams into facts.'[43]

Beveridge was now a permanent civil servant employed on the same basis as other Board of Trade officials. He was, however, far more suited both by temperament and intellect to general social planning than to routine administration; and this characteristic was perhaps in the minds of his departmental superiors when they also appointed C. F. Rey as 'general manager' of labour exchanges, with particular responsibility for day-to-day affairs. Rey, who had previously been Llewellyn Smith's private secretary, was a bluff, energetic, extrovert character with considerable experience in industrial arbitration. He had little of Beveridge's intellectual power, but he proved to be an extremely forceful departmental negotiator and, like Llewellyn Smith, he was particularly skilful at resisting Treasury control.[44] To work under Rey, three 'upper division clerks' were imported from other Board of Trade departments— Thomas Phillips, Stephen Tallents, and the poet and essayist, Humbert Wolfe. 'Each of these,' Beveridge later recalled, 'in coming to us, gave up his place in the Board of Trade hierarchy, with the prospect of regular promotion there, in order to get an immediate rise of pay and to chance his arm with our venture. They were a strong trio, each with a special gift added to general ability. Tallents was best of the three in

[39] Below, p. 167.                          [40] *PI*, pp. 77–8.
[41] *Daily Chronicle*, 18 Oct. 1909; see also collection of labour exchange press-cuttings in BP, XII 3 and 4.
[42] BP, IIb, H. Lucas to WHB, Oct. 1909.
[43] BP, IIb, S. Barnett to WHB, 19 Oct. 1909.
[44] S. Tallents, *Man and Boy* (1943), pp. 184–5.

judgment, Wolff in speed, Phillips in mastery of detail.'[45] Elsewhere in the Civil Service the new branch was regarded as 'a great gamble . . . a new and wild department . . . a company of pirates'; but as Stephen Tallents later recorded, the young men working in it saw themselves as 'high adventurers giving shape to one of the great social reform measures of that quinquennium'.[46] Outside the central administration Churchill and Beveridge were particularly anxious to recruit men with business experience rather than career civil servants; and for this purpose a special appointments committee was set up, to bypass the normal process of open competition. This unconventional method of recruitment was reflected in the character of the new divisional officers, who included businessmen, trade unionists, a regular soldier, a retired polar explorer, and an American gold speculator who claimed to have 'run a labour exchange in Chicago, with a revolver provided as part of the office equipment in the drawer of his desk.'[47]

Although labour exchanges were now on the statute book, many further negotiations were necessary to translate Beveridge's plan into administrative reality. During the autumn of 1909 the principles of labour exchange management, including the maintenance of neutrality in trade disputes, were laid down in a series of Board of Trade regulations. Arrangements were made to take over control of existing exchanges—including the large bloc of metropolitan exchanges administered by the C.U.B. Special provision was made for dealing with juvenile applicants and for co-operating with local education committees in giving advice to school-leavers.[48] Conferences were held to advertise the new scheme to employers and in particular to make contact with employers of casual labour. New sites were acquired and new buildings erected in areas of casual employment; and elsewhere 'old customs-houses, post-offices, chapels, schoolrooms, business premises, workshops, factories, halls [were] leased for a short term of years, awaiting the construction of model exchanges'.[49] Plans were made at both central and local level to carry out research into the state of the labour market and to compile nation-wide labour exchange statistics, recording the number of situations vacant, applications received, and applicants successfully settled in jobs.

In all these negotiations Beveridge was recognized by other Board of Trade officials as the 'master mind'.[50] Throughout the winter of 1909–10 he was working for twelve hours a day, interviewing and cajoling interested employers, and travelling about the country to explain and

[45] *PI*, p. 78.
[47] *PI*, pp. 76–7.
[49] *Westminster Gazette*, 1 Feb. 1910.
[50] Sir Jameson Adams, 'Reminiscences of a Divisional Controller', *Minlabour*, vol. 14, no. 1, 1960, p. 5.

[46] Tallents, op. cit., p. 180.
[48] Harris, op. cit., pp. 292–5.

propagate labour exchange principles. 'Every few minutes we get telegrams disturbing some cherished and settled plan,' he observed in
January 1910. 'When one is responsible for a big machine which is
beginning to move one can't limit one's hours. It's not a question of
flurrying or pressing unduly. One simply daren't leave the machine any
more than one would a locomotive.'[51] His meticulous thoroughness,
capacity for hard work and intellectual mastery were clearly regarded
by his junior colleagues with a certain amount of awe—although one of
them later recalled that he 'was, strange to say, always easy to do with,
generally very understanding and sometimes quite humorous'.[52] Another
colleague, Stephen Tallents, left a detailed description of Beveridge in
action during this period which is worth quoting at some length—both
for the impression it gives of Beveridge's impact on others and for its
insight into his methods of work:

He still showed traces . . . of the slightly arrogant aloofness of the Balliol man
who had taken successive firsts in Mathematical and Classical Mods. and in
Greats, and had then become a Civil Law Fellow. . . . In those days I found
him occasionally alarming. He would start his major tasks in weekend solitude, generally reclining on the floor with books and papers strewn about
him. On Monday morning he would commit the results partly in manuscript,
partly by dictation, to his meek little stenographer, Batchelor. Having thus
secured a flying start, he would introduce his lieutenants to a voluminous half-
margin draft memorandum. As we floundered through the novel material, he
did not always conceal his impatience. We recognised, however, his leadership in our adventure; and the apprenticeship which I served with him . . .
gave me an exceptional experience of closely knit and accurate work on
material which had largely to be supplied by imagination. He was and is, as
strong and swiftly-flowing a mind as I have ever worked with closely. . . . He
has always had an exceptional capacity for attacking a complex problem of
public administration at speed, and sweeping his way inventively through
daunting perplexities to its solution . . .'[53]

The new exchanges started work in February 1910—their opening
having been postponed for a month so as not to clash with the January
general election. Sixty-one exchanges were opened on the first day and
'great crowds' were reported at Liverpool, Glasgow, Birmingham,
Sheffield and many London exchanges.[54] Beveridge himself spent the
first few months of the experiment travelling around the country, urging
both employers and workers to make use of the new service. During the
spring of 1910 he made speeches on labour exchanges to the London and

---

[51] BP, IIa, WHB to ASB, 24 Jan. 1910.
[52] 'Reminiscences of a Divisional Controller', loc. cit., p. 5.
[53] Tallents, op. cit., pp. 183–4.
[54] *The Times*, 4 Feb. 1910; *Evening News*, 5 Feb. 1910.

Norwich Chambers of Commerce, the Boys' Country Work Society, the South African Colonisation Society, the Army Recruitment Association, and a conference on migrant workers convened by the L.G.B. With a few notable exceptions the exchanges were well received in the press, and several newspapers reported regular 'success-stories' of workers engaged through an exchange—stories which ranged from skilled artisans rescued from the workhouse to a 'two-headed woman' employed in a fair.[55] Among trade unionists, however, reaction to the new system was much less favourable, and union leaders continued to fear that exchanges would encourage strike-breaking and undermine the standard rate. In August Sydney Buxton, who had succeeded Churchill as President of the Board of Trade, interviewed the Parliamentary Committee of the T.U.C. and urged them to rely on the advisory committees to protect trade union interests. Buxton, however, lacked Churchill's skill as a negotiator and the T.U.C. representatives were unimpressed—particularly as the advisory committee had not yet been officially set up, more than six months after the first exchanges had opened.[56] The new system and its authors were strongly attacked by both right and left wing unionists at the T.U.C.'s annual conference in September 1910. 'The Government was either afraid or incapable of putting their own words into execution,' declared Ben Tillett. 'Mr. Beveridge was a very clever University young man, and out of the fulness of his knowledge he was quite prepared to tell them what to do with the economic problem. He was going to abolish casual labour through the Labour Exchange. If ever there was a more cockeyed view of things he did not know of one.' Other speakers claimed that exchanges were depressing wages and exploiting female labour, and the conference passed a resolution condemning the new system by a large majority. This hostility increasingly convinced Board of Trade officials that the better class of workman would not use the exchanges without some form of financial incentive; and it was not until the introduction of insurance benefits three years later that skilled workmen began to use the exchanges in significant numbers and the fears of the unions were to a certain extent assuaged.[57]

## IV

Once the labour exchange system had come into operation Beveridge's attention was increasingly diverted to the planning of unemployment insurance and to schemes of decasualization. 'I've practically no time

[55] BP, XII 4, press-cuttings on labour exchanges and unemployment insurance, 1910–14. The chief press critics of exchanges were the right-wing *John Bull*, the radical *Morning Advertiser*, and later the *Daily Herald*.

[56] *TUC Annual Conference Report*, 1910, report of the Parliamentary Committee.

[57] Ibid., pp. 160–5. See, however, *The Annual Conference Reports* of 1915 and 1916 for evidence of continuing union criticism of labour exchange management.

for Labex proper,' he commented regretfully early in 1911;[58] and the supervision of the labour exchange system was largely delegated to C. F. Rey. Nevertheless, there was one aspect of labour exchange administration in which Beveridge continued to be closely involved— the provision of special facilities for juvenile employees. This area of his interests will be considered in some detail, since it demonstrates very clearly Beveridge's forcefulness and vision as a policy-maker and as an architect of administrative schemes; but at the same time it suggests some of his personal shortcomings in relations with other officials, in coming to terms with determined opposition, and in the handling of day-to-day public affairs.

As was shown above, one of the important secondary functions that Beveridge had envisaged for labour exchanges was the provision of vocational guidance for school-leavers and the diversion of juvenile workers from blind-alley occupations. Churchill, Llewellyn Smith and Askwith were all particularly keen to develop this aspect of labour organization, and the need for such a service was endorsed by the Royal Commission on the Poor Laws in 1909. When Beveridge was drafting the labour exchange regulations he therefore included provision for special 'Juvenile Advisory Committees', composed of 'members possessing experience or knowledge of educational or industrial conditions', who would assist labour exchange managers in vetting suitable vacancies and advising children on choice of employment.[59] The Board of Trade's labour exchanges were not, however, the first administrative agencies to be active in this field. Since the late nineteenth century voluntary Apprenticeship and Skilled Employment Committees had been set up in many areas to promote technical education and to divert school-leavers from dead-end occupations. During the 1900s several local education authorities had begun to provide some form of vocational guidance; and since 1904 the National Union of Women Workers had been urging the Board of Education to set up juvenile employment centres in order 'to humanise the roughest elements in our population'.[60] In 1908 the Education Act (Scotland) had empowered Scottish School Boards to finance a juvenile employment service out of the rates, and this measure had led to renewed pressure on the Board of Education to provide a similar service in England and Wales. The introduction of the Labour Exchanges Bill, and Churchill's declared intention of using the new system for juvenile as well as adult workers, led to a major conflict of principle between the Board of Education and the Board of Trade.

[58] BP, IIa, WHB to ASB, 25 Apr. 1911.
[59] PRO, LAB 2/210 LE 778, Regulations for Labour Exchanges and Draft of special rules made under Regulation 9 with regard to Juvenile Applicants, 1909.
[60] PRO, Ed. 24/246, Maria Ogilvie Gordon to Sir R. Morant, 20 Mar. 1908.

Officials of the Board of Education, headed by the powerful Permanent Secretary, Sir Robert Morant, argued that 'choice of employment' was essentially a part of the educational process and should therefore logically be a function of the department responsible for education. Beveridge and Rey, on the other hand, claimed that existing services provided by local education authorities were hopelessly inadequate, and that juvenile employment services should therefore be concentrated under the Board of Trade—not as a matter of principle but as a matter of efficiency and of sheer practical necessity.

The battle was drawn between the two departments shortly after publication of the Labour Exchanges Bill in March 1909. On 2 March Morant received a protest against the Bill from the chairman of the Education Committee of the National Union of Women Workers, the dynamic and imperious Mrs. Maria Ogilvie Gordon. Mrs. Gordon complained that 'to associate an Employment Bureau for boys and girls under the same management (as Labour Exchanges for adults) would at once brand it as something of a charity, and it would never have the right social standing or become popular among the better working-classes, still less with our great middle-class'.[61] This view was clearly very much at odds with Beveridge's conception of labour exchanges as a strictly 'business' system serving the whole working population. However, Morant urged Mrs. Gordon to seek an interview with Beveridge, to explain the 'educational' point of view;[62] and a meeting was held at the Board of Trade on 31 March. 'Mr. Beveridge was throughout antipathetic', reported Mrs. Gordon,

and had no open mind on the subject of bringing educational benefits to young workers. His mind is entirely 'Board of Trade'. Only *that* Board ought to deal with employers, only *that* Board requires statistics about employment, only *that* Board knows properly about the industrial training of young workers! What little expert knowledge might be required about Continuation Classes and Trade Schools could, in Mr. Beveridge's opinion, very easily be added to the large stock of knowledge already possessed by the Board of Trade . . .'[63]

Nevertheless, as a result of this meeting Mrs. Gordon was invited by the Board of Trade to draft a paper, listing her objections to labour exchanges and suggesting 'some plan of co-ordination' between the exchanges and local education authorities. In reply she argued that labour exchange control of juvenile employment would lead to 'administrative complexity', that a 'spirit of commercialism . . . would be

[61] PRO, Ed. 24/246, Maria Ogilvie Gordon to Sir R. Morant, 2 Mar. 1909.
[62] PRO, Ed. 24/246, Sir R. Morant to Maria Ogilvie Gordon, 5 Mar. 1909.
[63] PRO, Ed. 24/246, Maria Ogilvie Gordon to Walter Runciman, 29 Apr. 1909.

engendered amongst parents and employers', and that 'the Board of Trade was powerless to move a foot towards making a better worker, a better man or a better citizen of the young worker'. Instead she argued that statutory 'information and employment' bureaux should be attached to all local education authorities, to advise on job selection and further education.[64]

Mrs. Gordon's arguments won the support of Walter Runciman, the President of the Board of Education; and Churchill was at this stage very willing to accommodate the education lobby's demands.[65] The Board of Education, however, had no funds available for setting up statutory employment bureaux and no plans for promoting the necessary legislation. The Board of Trade, on the other hand, was pressing on fast with its Labour Exchanges Bill; and a few months later Mrs. Gordon remarked to Sir Robert Morant that 'the wind was now blowing towards the Board of Trade'.[66] The labour exchange regulations, drafted by Beveridge in December 1909, specifically provided for exchanges to assist juveniles with vocational training and to set up Juvenile Advisory committees.[67] This led to renewed protests from Board of Education officials, but still no funds were available for special juvenile employment bureaux; and in April 1910 Morant was forced to issue a circular to local education authorities, advising them to co-operate with the new exchanges set up by the Board of Trade.[68]

Relations between the two departments were, however, far from happy. Beveridge in his travels about the country encountered much hostility from local education officials. He found the Director of Education in Brighton 'very obstinate' and the Director of Education in Liverpool 'very, very, very obstinate' in resisting directives from the Board of Trade.[69] In London the education committee of the L.C.C. was torn into three warring factions—those who wanted a purely charitable system, those who wanted to use the new exchanges, and those who wanted a separate juvenile employment bureau responsible only to the Board of Education.[70] Moreover, it was rumoured in 'educational circles' that labour exchange managers were deliberately sending juveniles to 'blind-alley' situations in order to swell their record of successful placements. 'The Board of Education', recorded Stephen Tallents,

[64] PRO, Ed. 24/246, Maria Ogilvie Gordon to Walter Runciman, 8 May 1909.
[65] PRO, Ed. 24/246, Sir R. Morant to Maria Ogilvie Gordon, 5 Mar. 1909.
[66] PRO, Ed. 24/246, Maria Ogilvie Gordon to Sir R. Morant, n.d. (July 1909).
[67] PRO, LAB 2/210 LE 778, Draft Regulations for Labour Exchanges, 24 Dec. 1909.
[68] PRO, Ed. 24/249, W. Runciman to Sir R. Morant, 3 Mar. 1910, and copy of Circular 743.
[69] BP, IIa, WHB to ASB, 16 May 1910.
[70] PRO, Ed. 24/246, Maria Ogilvie Gordon to Sir R. Morant, 22 Apr. 1908; BP, III 28, Cyril Jackson to Sir H. Llewellyn Smith, 14 June 1910.

. . . resented the whole business as an invasion of their proper field. They attacked us, and Beveridge selected me as his aide-de-camp for the fight. When I came upon the scene I found him locked in a fierce struggle with E. K. Chambers, the well-known Shakespearian scholar, who was determined to secure for local education committees the sole right of advising juveniles and placing them in work. . . . Neither Beveridge nor Chambers was in those days particularly tactful, and there was little pretence to politeness in our discussions. . . .[71]

Matters came to a head between the two departments in July 1910, when the Board of Trade proposed to appoint a nation-wide professional staff to assist the Juvenile Advisory Committees and sought approval from the Treasury for the necessary finance.[72] At this point Morant wrote a long letter of protest to the Treasury, arguing that such work was 'essentially of an educational nature', that many teachers throughout the country were already deeply involved in vocational guidance, and that any additional staff in the field of juvenile employment should be under the control of the Board of Education. He concluded:

The great question at issue is one which the Board feel to be of the first importance in view of its bearing upon the future development of national education, and of the grave administrative dangers which must attend any failure to maintain a clear distinction between the functions of different departments of state.[73]

As a result of this protest the Treasury refused to sanction the Board of Trade's request for additional staff, except in the few areas where Juvenile Advisory Committees had already been set up.[74] At the same time the Board of Education decided to promote its own legislation on the subject; and an Education (Choice of Employment) Bill, empowering local authorities to finance juvenile employment services, was introduced in August 1910. Beveridge was highly sceptical about the new proposals, and continued to argue that 'the risks of feeble methods of registration' outweighed the advantages of a strictly logical arrangement of departmental functions.[75] Between August and November 1910, however, he and Llewellyn Smith attended a series of conferences with Board of Education officials, to work out 'a common policy' between the two departments. At these conferences it was observed that 'the spirit of

[71] S. Tallents, op. cit., pp. 186–7.

[72] PRO, Ed. 24/249, copy of letter from Sir H. Llewellyn Smith to the Secretary of the Treasury, 23 June 1910.

[73] BP, III 28, copy of letter from Sir R. Morant to the Secretary of the Treasury, 18 July 1910.

[74] PRO, Ed. 24/249, copy of letter from Sir George Murray to Sir H. Llewellyn Smith, 29 July 1910.

[75] PRO, Ed. 24/246, Maria Ogilvie Gordon to Sir R. Morant, 13 Dec. 1910.

compromise was shown on both sides, although more markedly by Sir H. Llewellyn Smith himself than by Mr. Beveridge'.[76] As a result of these discussions, it was agreed that primary responsibility for juvenile employment should lie with the Board of Education—except where local authorities chose deliberately not to use their powers under the Choice of Employment Act. In the latter case juvenile employment services would be supplied, as Beveridge had originally intended, by special advisory committees attached to labour exchanges under the Board of Trade. This compromise was embodied in a circular to local authorities and local exchanges, issued jointly by both departments in January 1911.[77]

In principle this decision was a victory for the Board of Education, but in practice it turned out to be an almost complete victory for the Board of Trade. A year later a majority of local education authorities had taken no action under the Choice of Employment Act—thus leaving the way clear for the setting up of juvenile advisory committees attached to local exchanges. Much of the local support for juvenile employment services came not from teachers and education experts but from 'lovely society women' and 'earnest' lady philanthropists, who proved singularly ineffective in making provision for the juvenile unemployed.[78] The administration of the Choice of Employment Act was severely criticized in Parliament; and Morant and Chambers were increasingly embarrassed by the importunity of the 'education' faction and increasingly reluctant to pursue the battle for administrative control.[79] Many large local authorities, including the L.C.C., deliberately opted for a juvenile employment service managed by the Board of Trade—perhaps not surprisingly, in view of the financial advantage which they gained from a scheme financed out of central taxation rather than local rates. Several hundred juvenile advisory committees, attached to local exchanges, had been set up in England and Wales by 1914. In London the juvenile advisory committee, under the chairmanship of Richard Denman, was in close touch with the policy-makers in the Board of Trade; and it pursued an active policy of opening up employment for disabled children, checking medical records with school doctors, promoting technical and further education, and waging continuous war against sweated trades.[80]

[76] PRO, Ed. 24/249, note by E. K. Chambers to the President of the Board of Education, n.d. (Aug. 1910).

[77] PRO, Ed. 24/248, Board of Trade and Board of Education memorandum with regard to Co-operation between Labour Exchanges and L.E.A.s exercising their powers under the Education (Choice of Employment) Act 1910, 3 Jan. 1911.

[78] PRO, Ed. 24/246, Maria Ogilvie Gordon to Sir R. Morant, 24 Nov. 1911.

[79] PRO, Ed. 24/246, E. K. Chambers to Sir R. Morant, 27 Feb. 1911.

[80] G.L.C. Records, EO/WEL/1/6, papers relating to the L.C.C. Education Department's Juvenile Advisory Committee, 1914–18.

Whether these policies were more or less successful than they might have been under the Board of Education is difficult to say. What is chiefly significant about the juvenile employment controversy is the perspective that it gives on social policy-formation during this period, and the picture it reveals of rivalry, conflict and compromise between two departments of state. It is interesting to note that the controversy was never discussed in Cabinet and that even the respective departmental ministers were only very peripherally concerned. The main debate on principles of policy and demarcation of functions was fought out almost exclusively by departmental officials—a fact which demonstrates the remarkably high degree of day-to-day autonomy enjoyed by civil servants in the social policy departments, at least in the period before the First World War. The episode also underlines certain contrasting features in the administrative philosophies of Beveridge and Morant. It is true of course that Morant at this stage was a senior career civil servant, whereas Beveridge had gone into Whitehall merely as a temporary adviser with a specific policy brief. But nevertheless both men have been seen as the greatest administrators of their day, and both were to play an important part in reforming and rationalizing twentieth-century social administration. It is interesting therefore to compare their fundamentally different approaches to a problem of administrative innovation. To Morant the first priority of government was to streamline the administrative machine and to ensure a logical coherence between its functions and its parts. This meant that all educational functions should be concentrated under an education department, all 'labour' functions under a labour department, all health functions under a health department—as in the schemes outlined in the Minority Report on the Poor Laws by Morant's friends and confidants, Sidney and Beatrice Webb.[81] To Beveridge on the other hand, the logic of administrative functionalism made little appeal—at least at this stage of his career. His own approach to the machinery of government was a rather idiosyncratic mixture of principle and pragmatism: in so far as he adhered to any general administrative principle it was to the principle of centralization rather than local autonomy—a preference that was largely derived from his experience of local inefficiency and corruption on the London Unemployed Fund and the C.U.B. Beyond that, however, he saw the main object of government as one of sheer practical expediency; it was simply to 'get things done', as quickly and efficiently as possible, by whatever means and whatever administrative machinery came most readily to hand.

[81] Morant himself subsequently helped to compose what was perhaps the classic statement of this theory of public administration in the *Report on the Machinery of Government*, Cd. 9230/1918.

V

Beveridge in later years looked back on labour exchanges as by far the most important of the social experiments in which he had taken part during the Edwardian period. And in the 1920s and 30s he tended to blame all deficiencies in social and economic policy upon the failure of successive governments to observe the model for labour organization that he had so lucidly and forcibly outlined in 1908. The effectiveness of labour exchanges was undermined, so Beveridge argued, by Treasury parsimony in provision of staff and buildings; by the subordination of 'job-finding' to administration of national insurance; by the weakness of sanctions against the work-shy; and, finally, by the use of exchanges in the 1920s and 30s for the payment of the dole.[82] Even if these dis-advantages had been avoided, however, it is highly unlikely that labour exchanges could ever have evolved into that 'final solution for the problem of the unemployed' that Beveridge had so optimistically pro-claimed in the *Morning Post* between 1905 and 1908.[83] To the historian the labour exchange experiment is chiefly significant, not for its impact on the labour market, but for the light which it throws on certain aspects of Edwardian reforming ideas, and for its role in the genesis of an increasingly centralized and bureaucratized 'administrative state'.

From the start labour exchanges evoked a good deal of criticism and hostility from Beveridge's own contemporaries—including some of those who had been closely involved with him in setting up the new system. 'What do these Exchanges do when a woman enters and states that her occupation is that of wife and mother; that she is out of a job; and that she wants an employer?' scoffed Bernard Shaw in the preface to *Getting Married* published in 1911. The unconventional system of staff appoint-ments was strongly denounced as 'jobbery' and 'patronage' before the Royal Commission on the Civil Service in 1912; and although Beveridge himself defended his recruitment policy before the Commission, he was forced to admit that the new system had been much less successful than he had hoped in attracting men with experience of business and public affairs.[84] Among respectable working-men labour exchanges were for many years looked upon with dislike and suspicion, as the haunt of unemployables and black-leg labour; and within the labour movement there were periodic revivals of the demand for observance of trade union conditions and for greater trade union control.[85] The local advisory committees were not particularly successful in harmonizing the interests

---

[82] BP, IIa, WHB to Jeannette Tawney, 16 Aug. 1912; *Unemployment: a Problem of Industry* (1930 edn.), pp. 303–5; *RC on Unemployment Insurance, Minutes of Evidence*, QQ. 5,853, 5,883–5.
[83] *MP*, 6 and 15 Nov. 1905.
[84] Cd. 6740/1913, *RC on the Civil Service, Minutes of Evidence*, QQ. 16,069–71, 16,078–9.
[85] T.U.C. Annual Conference Report, 1916, pp. 360–4.

of capital and labour, and by 1919 Beveridge himself appears to have come to the conclusion that it would have been better to seek advice from local authorities than from *ad hoc* committees of employers and workpeople.[86] One of Beveridge's fellow officials, C. F. Rey, observed in his memoirs that although the labour exchange principle was 'beautiful in theory', in practice both masters and workmen disliked the depersonalization of traditional placement procedures that registration at a labour exchange inevitably entailed.[87] Such depersonalization was almost certainly preferable to the random and desperate 'tramp in search of work' which Beveridge and other writers, including prominent members of the Labour movement, had so graphically described and denounced; but it was at the same time one more breach in the declining chain of face-to-face relationships between masters and men. Another of Beveridge's colleagues, G. R. Askwith, strongly criticized the labour exchange system in a letter to *The Times* in October 1919. Labour exchanges, he argued, had radically altered relationships between industry and the state, they had undermined feelings of personal responsibility among both employers and trades unionists, and they had been foisted upon an unwilling public ten years earlier by an ambitious and self-seeking President of the Board of Trade. Beveridge angrily retorted on Churchill's behalf that Askwith had put forward none of these criticisms in 1909; but a few months later Askwith returned to the attack by accusing the exchanges of fostering 'ca'canny' and acting as 'props to class war'.[88] Whether or not these criticisms were justified, it was certainly true that during the 1920s many labour exchanges became focal points of alienation and social conflict rather than the organs of rationalization and social solidarity that Beveridge had so optimistically hoped for before the First World War.

[86] BP, IV 27, WHB to Delisle Burns, 26 July 1919.
[87] C. F. Rey, unpublished memoirs, p. 95.
[88] *The Times*, 28 and 30 Oct. 1919; G. R. Askwith, *Industrial Problems and Disputes* (1920), p. 278.

# 8

## Social Insurance and the Organization of Labour

### I

THE Board of Trade's labour exchange scheme had been planned from the start in close conjunction with a scheme for contributory unemployment insurance. As we have seen, Beveridge himself had been a strong advocate of contributory insurance for a wide range of social contingencies since early 1907; and in his evidence to the Poor Law Commission he had outlined five different models of unemployment insurance, ranging from purely voluntary trade union insurance to compulsory universal insurance managed by the state. Moreover, Beveridge was not alone in his enthusiasm for social insurance. Several other witnesses to the Royal Commission had also advocated one or other of the five models. The Commission's Minority Report had recommended state 'subventions' to trade union insurance, and the Majority Report had proposed further consideration of compulsory insurance organized by the state.[1] The Liberal M.P. Percy Alden, had written in favour of the Ghent system as early as 1904, and laudatory reports on German social insurance were published by David Schloss and W. H. Dawson, both of whom were on the research staff of the Board of Trade.[2] Beveridge's advocacy of insurance was therefore by no means unique. His views were remarkable mainly because he had written about them for a popular audience, and because he had seen social insurance not merely as an end in itself but as an instrument in a much wider programme of 'social organisation'.

It is not entirely clear how the decision to introduce national insurance into Britain was taken, since Lloyd George and Churchill each subsequently claimed the credit for himself.[3] Lloyd George as Chancellor of the Exchequer had spoken disparagingly of social insurance during the debates on old age pensions.[4] But in August 1908 he had paid a visit to Germany and returned to England enthused with the possibilities of

---

[1] José Harris, *Unemployment and Politics*, pp. 301–2.

[2] Percy Alden, *The Unemployed, A National Question*; W. H. Dawson, *Bismarck and State Socialism* (1896); Schloss was the author of *Agencies and Methods for dealing with the Unemployed in Certain Foreign Countries*, Cd. 2304/1905.

[3] Harris, op. cit., p. 276.

[4] *MP*, 21 May 1908.

contributory social insurance against sickness, unemployment and death. It was Churchill, however, who first pressed the idea of social insurance on his Cabinet colleagues and persuaded them that he had discovered a 'scientific' solution for the problem of the unemployed.[5] In the autumn of 1908 it was agreed that responsibility for the new measure should be shared between the two reforming ministers; Churchill at the Board of Trade was to prepare legislation on unemployment insurance, while Lloyd George at the Treasury would produce a complementary scheme for sickness and invalidity. In practical terms, however, the two schemes presented very different problems, because of the markedly different character of the private interests already in the field. The only bodies that had previously organized unemployment insurance were skilled trade unions covering only a small fraction of the labour force. In health insurance and life assurance, however, there was a wide range of private institutions—friendly societies, collecting societies and industrial assurance companies—commanding vast capital resources and holding policies on twelve million people. In providing insurance against unemployment, therefore, the problems were primarily technical—the absence of statistical data, the danger of spurious or voluntary unemployment, and the difficulty of predicting the extent of future risk. In the planning of health insurance the main problem was far more overtly political—it was how to placate the powerful voluntary and commercial institutions which already afforded insurance to the working class.

## II

Llewellyn Smith and Beveridge began to prepare details of an unemployment insurance scheme in October 1908. Churchill in later years ascribed the planning of labour exchanges to Beveridge and insurance to Llewellyn Smith, but Beveridge himself claimed that this was a 'mistake' and that in both cases 'neither the schemes nor the minds' could be separated from each other.[6] Beveridge's recollection was substantially correct, since many of his papers at the time dealt simultaneously with both issues. Nevertheless, there was a perceptible difference of emphasis in the approach of the two men—Beveridge seeing labour exchanges as the more important measure, whereas Llewellyn Smith gave priority to social insurance.[7] Moreover, Beveridge was undoubtedly the main architect and apologist of labour exchanges, whereas in the planning of insurance his main role was to criticize and elaborate proposals initially put forward by the Permanent Secretary.

Llewellyn Smith produced his first draft scheme for unemployment

[5] Asquith Papers, vol. 11, f. 252, W. S. Churchill to H. H. Asquith, 29 Dec. 1908.
[6] *PI*, p. 82.
[7] C. F. Rey, unpublished autobiography, p. 87.

insurance in October 1908.[8] No copy of this original draft appears to have survived, but its proposals were summarized in a Cabinet paper prepared for Churchill on 30 November.[9] One of the main principles at issue was which of the various models of unemployment insurance the state should adopt. The Ghent system of state subventions to trade union insurance had the obvious attraction of simplicity, and would clearly have been popular with organized labour. But, as Beveridge had argued before the Poor Law Commission, such a system offered nothing to unskilled non-union workmen, among whom the economic impact of unemployment was probably most severe. Moreover, the Board of Trade was anxious to levy contributions from employers, and it was feared that employers would oppose a system which was confined to organized labour.[10] The scheme which Llewellyn Smith proposed therefore combined elements both of the Ghent system and of direct state insurance, though with a much stronger emphasis on the latter than the former. Compulsory insurance would be provided for all workmen in certain trades which were particularly susceptible to cyclical depression— namely building, engineering and works of construction. Outside these 'insured trades' encouragement to voluntary trade union insurance would be encouraged by subsidies from the state. To administer the insurance funds a Central Insurance Office would be established within the Board of Trade. In the compulsory scheme, weekly contributions would be levied at the rate of 2d. from workmen, 1d. from employers and 1d. from the national exchequer. Benefits would be payable after one week of unemployment and would be graduated downwards from 7s. 6d. to 5s. a week for a maximum of fifteen weeks in any one year. In the event of a deficit the Insurance Office could apply for a Treasury loan, which would be repaid by lowering benefits and raising contributions. Benefits would be paid through a labour exchange, which would ascertain that a man was genuinely unemployed and test his willingness to accept employment. To each exchange would be attached an 'advisory trade committee' composed of representative employers and workmen, which would hear appeals from workmen to whom benefit had been refused.

Llewellyn Smith's proposals were submitted to the Cabinet together with Beveridge's plan for labour exchanges in December 1908; and Churchill in explaining the schemes to his colleagues claimed that they were logically and practically interdependent. Insurance, he envisaged,

[8] Ibid., p. 87. This draft was preserved among Sir Charles Rey's papers and destroyed during the Second World War.

[9] PRO, CAB 37/96/159, 'Unemployment Insurance: Labour Exchanges', 30 Nov. 1908, circulated 11 Dec. 1908.

[10] PRO, CAB 37/99/69, 'Memorandum on a Scheme for Unemployment Insurance', by H. Llewellyn Smith, Apr. 1909.

would support workmen suffering from that legitimate residue of un-employment which would still remain after the labour market had been properly organized. It would harness the 'just and humane' instincts of the majority of employers, and would force employers and workers to collaborate in achieving their common goals. The scheme had been designed, Churchill claimed, to encourage private interests already providing insurance and to promote rather than to replace voluntary thrift. Benefits would be kept low so as to 'imply a sensible and even severe difference between being in work or out of work'. Exchanges and insurance were complementary to each other, since an exchange could test the authenticity of unemployment, whilst insurance payments would provide an incentive to register at an exchange. It was hoped, moreover, that the desire to minimize contributions would encourage many secondary objectives—such as short-time agreements, industrial re-training schemes and concentration of business contracts into periods of slack demand.[11]

Churchill accompanied his memorandum by a draft bill, which pro-posed to introduce exchanges and insurance as a single unified scheme. Later in December, however, he agreed with Lloyd George to postpone the introduction of unemployment insurance until the Treasury had produced its scheme for sickness and disablement.[12] In the meantime Llewellyn Smith's proposals were undergoing modification within the Board of Trade; and Beveridge himself was increasingly involved in working out the administrative details of the scheme, in consulting interested parties and in translating Llewellyn Smith's blueprint into legislation. His reaction to the overall structure of the scheme was highly favourable, but he was critical of some of its detailed provisions. In a paper on 28 October he suggested that in times of high unemployment any deficit should be made up not by lowering benefits but by raising the employers' contribution—in the hope that this would encourage employers to co-operate in measures for keeping unemployment low. He thought also that the proposed rate of benefit was unnecessarily mean, in view of the fact that labour exchanges would keep a constant check on fraud and malingering. At the same time, however, he sug-gested that more stringent methods should be devised to guard against spurious claims and to detect collusion between workers and employers. In particular, he was anxious about the attitude of trade unionists, fearing that they might be less scrupulous about resisting false claims under a state system than when their own funds were at stake. Finally, he was critical of the plan to set up a single unemployment fund, and proposed instead that there should be separate occupational funds, to

[11] PRO, CAB 37/96/159, 'Unemployment Insurance: Labour Exchanges', 30 Nov. 1908.
[12] Asquith Papers, vol. 11, ff. 239–44, W. S. Churchill to H. H. Asquith, 26 Dec. 1908.

harness the sectional self-interest of each insured industry. Both employers and workers, he argued, would be much more willing to support measures of unemployment-prevention if they were thereby sparing their own pockets rather than the funds of a common industrial pool.[13]

None of Beveridge's suggestions was at this stage accepted by Llewellyn Smith. A few weeks later, however, Llewellyn Smith himself devised a list of fifty-two hypothetical objections to his own proposals—including criticisms that had been put forward from many different points of the political spectrum outside the Board of Trade. He attacked the tripartite system of contribution, the flat rate of benefit, and the failure to discriminate between high and low-paid workmen. He suggested that insurance would positively increase unemployment, by encouraging malingering and by relieving employers of moral responsibility for retaining workmen during a recession; and he claimed that state insurance would compete with private saving, reduce the attractions of trade unionism, and was 'fundamentally opposed to English ideas'. He attacked the whole idea of a 'national' system, claiming that it would prop up inefficient industries and incompetent workmen; and he argued that the risk of unemployment should be borne by the individual or by private industry and not by the state.

In reply to these objections Beveridge prepared a thorough-going defence of compulsory contributory flat-rate national insurance. This defence was of considerable significance not merely as a justification of Llewellyn Smith's proposals but as a statement of some of the basic principles that were to dominate Beveridge's own approach to social insurance questions for the next forty years. He justified the levy upon employers, on the grounds that they would benefit from the growth of organization and discipline among their workers and from the prevention of physical deterioration among the unemployed. He justified the state subsidy on the ground that the unemployed were supported by the community in any case, and that a subsidy to insurance would merely be a substitute for less systematic forms of public and charitable relief. He defended the flat-rate principle on the grounds that benefits based on need would involve an undesirable inquisition into a claimant's private affairs, and that benefits related to income were unnecessary, because higher-paid workers could supplement state benefits with savings and private insurance. A compulsory scheme was essential because trade union insurance seemed to have reached the limit of its potential for expansion, and because voluntary schemes attracted only the worst risks. Beveridge denied that insurance would positively increase unemployment, since all parties would have a direct financial

[13] BP, III 37, 'Unemployed Insurance, Notes on Memorandum from Sir H. Llewellyn Smith', by WHB, 28 Oct. 1908.

interest in minimizing claims upon the fund; nor would it displace trade union insurance, because state benefits would merely provide a threshold for additional voluntary thrift. He denied also that insurance would be strictly unnecessary within a framework of scientific 'prevention', of the kind advocated by Sidney and Beatrice Webb. He agreed with the Webbs that there was a need for supplementary schemes of discipline and re-training. But there were also 'men who are not in need of cure or change of any sort', whose main problem was the purely financial one of 'averaging wages over good times and bad'; and to assist men of this sort insurance was cheaper and more efficient than artificial employment, and less demoralizing and 'more honourable' than poor relief. Finally, he strongly defended the proposal that unemployment insurance should be organized on a national basis rather than left to the individual of to private industry. There was, he claimed, a fundamental identity of interest between all different types and grades of workman, and unemployment in one sector had indirect repercussions throughout the whole economy.

The regular workman must admit a certain solidarity . . . with the irregular workman, since without the latter the industry by which the former lives could not be carried on. . . . Different trades are to a very considerable extent dependent upon one another. Each finds its own market in men of other trades. Labour in every trade is depressed by unemployed men from other trades seeking work on desperation terms.[14]

Llewellyn Smith's proposals backed by Beveridge's theoretical arguments were submitted to a variety of critics during the winter of 1908–9. Wilson Fox suggested that there should be an impartial 'umpire' to act as a final court of appeal when right to benefit was in dispute; and Percy Ashley, the Secretary of the Board of Trade's Commercial Intelligence Advisory Committee, thought that the contribution of employers should be raised so as to increase their financial incentive to reduce unemployment.[15] Both these proposals were incorporated into the draft scheme in April 1909. Outside the Board the scheme evoked some of the classic arguments against contributory insurance. The Treasury objected that the levy on employers would raise prices, depress wages and lower demand, thus intensifying 'the very evil it is intended to mitigate'.[16] Mrs. Dunn Gardner objected that guaranteed unemployment benefit would inevitably reduce mobility of labour by removing the harsh necessity of searching for work; and Sidney Webb predicted that, without a framework of 'prevention', the scheme would be flooded with bad

[14] BP, III 37, 'Unemployed Insurance, Objections and Answers', n.d.
[15] BP, III 37, 'Unemployment Insurance: Criticisms', pp. 4–6, 17–20.
[16] Ibid., pp. 1–3.

risks, malingerers and the seasonally unemployed.[17] Sir Benjamin
Browne, the shipbuilder and philanthropist, advanced the case for a
'residual' view of welfare—arguing that insurance was unnecessary for
the skilled worker and that state assistance should be concentrated on
the very poor.[18] Among trade unionists opinion varied widely, some
favouring a purely private system, others a scheme financed exclusively
by the state.[19] One of the most powerful critics of the new scheme was
H. T. Holloway, the President of the Institute of Builders, who represented one of the largest employers' groups in the insured trades. Holloway objected strongly to the employers' contribution as a potentially
disastrous 'tax on industry', but at the same time he thought that the
projected rate of benefit was much too low. He proposed instead that
larger benefits should be paid for shorter periods, and that benefits
should be graduated according to earnings—giving highly-skilled workmen as much as 12s. a week. He urged that benefit should automatically
be withheld from workmen who left their jobs voluntarily or were discharged for misconduct, and he strongly condemned the proposal to
allow trade unions to administer benefits financed by the state. He
thought that 'employers would object to this very much as tending to
strengthen the trade unions', and he feared that money previously spent
by unions on their own 'out-of-work donation' would now be diverted
to support of strikes.[20]

Beveridge composed a detailed reply on Holloway's criticisms, which
further expanded his own views on the role of contributory insurance.
He agreed that both employers' and workers' contributions constituted
a 'tax on industry'; but he argued that this was 'perfectly reasonable',
since each industry ought to take some share of responsibility for its own
unemployed, and since in any case the tax could eventually be passed on
to the consumer. He claimed, moreover, that employers would greatly
profit from the scheme 'because men will be better secured against
destitution and consequent deterioration while unemployed' and
'because unwillingness to forfeit benefits for which they have contributed will improve the discipline of the men and discourage laziness,
bad time-keeping and voluntary discharges'. He strongly opposed
graduation of benefits, arguing that 'the line to take is that the insurance
scheme makes merely a minimum or basis of provision . . . on that basis

[17] BP, IIb, R. Dunn Gardner to WHB, 26 May 1909; BP, III 37, 'Unemployment Insurance: Criticisms', pp. 8–12.
[18] Ibid., Sir Benjamin Browne to Sir H. Llewellyn Smith, 22 Feb. 1909.
[19] Ibid., pp. 12–14, 23–6, 'Unemployment Insurance: Criticisms', by G. N. Barnes, n.d.;
'Criticisms of Workmen's Insurance by Members of the E.C. of the Shipbuilding and Engineering Trades Federation', by D. C. Cummings, 29 May 1909.
[20] BP, III 37, 'Notes of an Interview with Mr. Holloway', and 'Notes on Mr. Holloway's
Criticisms', by WHB, 25 Mar. 1909.

each individual may add according to his means and his personal standard of life'. He agreed with Holloway that no benefit should be paid to those who voluntarily discharged themselves, since this was customary in most benefit-paying unions; but he had apparently changed his mind about the inadequacy of the proposed benefits, arguing that 'until the check upon malingering afforded by a Labour Exchange is perfected the rate of benefit must be kept down'. On the participation of trade unions he wrote that it was not 'politically possible to ignore the trade union funds as Mr. Holloway suggests, nor if this were possible would it prevent the insurance scheme from relieving trade unions at the expense of employers and the state'. He agreed, however, that 'the union system of benefits is a factor to be reckoned with and accepted, rather than one to be welcomed', and that nothing should be done 'to encourage the growth of the system within the insurance scheme or to make that appear as the main object of our scheme'.[21] These adverse comments on trade union insurance seem curiously inconsistent with his claim in the same memorandum that state benefits were merely to provide a foundation for private thrift; and they were indicative of the mixed feelings with which Beveridge viewed not merely the trade unions but voluntary organizations in general—as embodiments on the one hand of personal initiative and freedom and on the other hand of selfish sectional interests threatening and competing with the community at large.

A revised version of Llewellyn Smith's scheme, together with a draft bill for unemployment insurance, was submitted to the Cabinet in April 1909. It was estimated that the compulsory scheme would cover 2¼ million persons, and the cost to the state was calculated at £1,000,000 annually for the first five years. These estimates were based on the expectation that unemployment would fluctuate between 4 per cent and 16 per cent—a prediction which allowed a wide margin for error, since unemployment among trade unionists in the insured trades during the previous decade had been only 5.6 per cent. The draft bill outlined the powers of the Insurance Office, the procedure for payment of benefit and collection of contributions, and the proposed arrangements with trade unions. It defined also the duties of the advisory trade committees, which were to hear appeals against refusal of benefit and to advise the Insurance Office on measures to reduce insurance claims, such as the 'systematic adoption of short-time'. The committees were also to promote industrial harmony and to 'facilitate common action' between employers and employed.[22]

[21] BP, III 37, 'Notes on Mr. Holloway's Criticisms', by WHB, 25 Mar. 1909.
[22] PRO, CAB 37/99/69, 'Memorandum on a Scheme for Unemployment Insurance', by H. Llewellyn Smith, Apr. 1909.

The draft bill and revised memorandum were discussed by the Cabinet at the end of April, and a Cabinet committee was set up to consider the question of insurance against unemployment. This committee was greatly concerned at the prospect of 'malingering and other forms of imposition'[23] with the result that Beveridge spent the next few months closing loopholes and inventing safeguards against bogus claimants, extravagant trades unionists, the unemployable and the wilfully unemployed. He proposed that no benefit should be payable to workers whose unemployment was caused by trade disputes, 'incompetence', 'drunkenness and dishonesty' or 'voluntary discharge'—though they might re-apply for benefit if they had not found work after six weeks. This provision was trenchantly criticized by Churchill, who thought that moral criteria should play no part in contributory insurance; but Beveridge compiled a dossier of trade union rules, showing that the vast majority paid no benefit to workmen discharged for misconduct or who voluntarily abandoned a job which conformed to the standard rate. He also devised further measures to exclude from benefit the habitually unemployed. He proposed that no man should be entitled to benefit until he had worked in an insured trade for a minimum of six months, and that workmen who made few claims upon the fund should be rewarded with a rebate when they reached retirement. At the suggestion of Sidney Webb he abandoned the clause enabling a workman to draw fifteen benefits in any one year and substituted instead the 'one in five rule,' whereby a man's entitlement would be limited to one benefit for every five contributions. Such a rule, Beveridge hoped, would exclude the chronically irregular workman who would otherwise always apply for his statutory fifteen weeks of benefit every year. He also tightened up the financial arrangements with trade unions—laying down that state subsidies to union benefits should always be retrospective, so as to deter union officials from being extravagant with public funds. Finally, he carefully defined the conditions under which a workman drawing benefit could refuse an offer of work. All competent workmen, he suggested, should be entitled to refuse work at wages below those prevailing in their district; sub-standard workmen could refuse work at wages inferior to those paid in their previous position; and trade unionists who managed their own funds within the national insurance scheme would be allowed to insist upon full recognition of their standard rates.[24]

[23] B. M. Add. Ms. 46327, John Burns' diary, 6 May 1909.
[24] BP, III 39, 'Unemployment Insurance: Special Topics', items 6, 8–15; Cd. 5703/1911, *Tables Showing the Rules and Expenditure of Trade Unions* (compiled by WHB, early 1909).

## III

After discussion with Llewellyn Smith all Beveridge's safeguards against improper claims were inserted into the scheme during the summer of 1909; and many of them have survived in an amended form in the structure of British unemployment insurance up to the present day. The draft bill was now virtually ready for immediate legislation, but on May 19 Churchill told Parliament that there were several reasons why its introduction had to be postponed. The new labour exchanges had first to be set up. Further negotiations had to be conducted with trade unions and employers. The scheme had to be integrated with Lloyd George's plan for sickness insurance. And, finally, the 1909 budget had to be passed before money would be available for new measures of social reform.[25] The budget, in which Lloyd George had proposed to increase land taxes and to introduce surtax, had however been rejected by the House of Lords—thus producing a constitutional crisis which was to dominate British politics for the next eighteen months.

The unemployment insurance scheme was strongly attacked at the conference of the T.U.C. later in the year, and a series of negotiations thereafter took place between the Board of Trade and the T.U.C.'s parliamentary committee.[26] Beveridge, however, appears to have taken little part in these negotiations. From September 1909 onwards his time was fully occupied in galvanizing the new labour exchanges into existence, and for almost a year he gave little concentrated thought to questions of insurance—or to wider issues in the field of social policy. In February 1910 Churchill left the Board and was replaced by Sydney Buxton, the Liberal M.P. for Poplar, whom Beveridge already knew through his friendship with Richard Denman. Buxton, Beveridge recalled, was 'a gentleman and a Radical, a man whom everyone liked and trusted, a man . . . moved by abiding interest in problems of poverty'.[27] But the new President was not a man to force through legislation in the face of political difficulties, and although he circulated the unemployment bill to his Cabinet colleagues in April 1910 the bill again got no further than ministerial discussion.[28] In the summer all prospects of legislation were again postponed, whilst a conference of Liberal and Conservative leaders thrashed out the possibility of resolving the constitutional deadlock by a two-party coalition.

Beveridge himself became increasingly impatient with the delay and confided to Mrs. Dunn Gardner that he was becoming 'bored' with the

[25] H.C. Deb., 5s., vol. 5, cols. 510–11.
[26] Harris, op. cit., pp. 316–18.      [27] *PI*, p. 87.
[28] PRO, CAB 37/102/8, 'Unemployment Insurance Bill', circulated by S. Buxton, 8 Mar. 1910.

tedium of day-to-day administration.[29] In August he addressed a meeting of the Haslemere Labour Exchange and Unemployment Society, at
which he predicted that it would be at least two years before unemployment insurance could be enacted; and he warned his audience that
'unemployment was not going to be abolished in their life-time, and he
very much doubted if it were going to be abolished at all'.[30] The following month he attended a conference on unemployment in Paris, where
he was gratified to find that there was considerable foreign interest in
the British experiment; but he remarked that 'the discussion . . . was to
say the least dull, being enlivened only by the determination of Mr.
Joseph Fels (of Fels Naptha and a notorious land reform theorist) to
insist upon discussing land reform as a branch of unemployment statistics'.[31] Back at the Board of Trade, Beveridge again had little time to
think about unemployment insurance. Throughout the autumn of 1910
he was absorbed in the departmental struggle with the Board of Education, in planning decasualization schemes, in devising a new system of
unemployment statistics, and in sacking a divisional officer who had
allowed exchanges to be used for breaking strikes.[32] In November he
was very disappointed at the collapse of the constitutional conference,
fearing it meant that national insurance legislation would be yet again
postponed.[33]

In the event, however, the failure of the constitutional conference and
the subsequent passing of the Parliament Act, which severely curtailed
the power of the Lords, proved to be the signal for action on insurance.
Lloyd George was able to pass his much-disputed budget, and in
December 1910 he at last turned his attention to national insurance—
appointing as his chief assistant a young Inland Revenue official,
William Braithwaite, who shared Beveridge's background of Balliol and
Toynbee Hall. Consultations between the two departments began early
in 1911, and Beveridge attended a Treasury conference on health
insurance on 9 January.[34] 'I remember being present,' he recalled of
this occasion, 'when a deputation of Friendly Societies came to see . . .
Lloyd George. The Chancellor did nearly all the talking—with immense
success. He seemed able to understand what the members of the deputation wanted and were thinking, by watching their eyes as he talked.
I should have liked the chance of acquiring the same gift myself by
seeing him oftener in action.'[35]

A few days later Beveridge spent an afternoon with Beatrice Webb
and 'reasoned' with her about insurance[36]—apparently without success,

[29] BP, IIb, R. Dunn Gardner to WHB, 30 June 1910.
[30] *Westminster Gazette*, 10 Aug. 1910.
[31] BP, IIa, WHB to ASB, 20 Sept. 1910.      [32] BP, IIa, WHB to ASB, 12 and 23 Nov. 1910.
[33] BP, IIa, WHB to ASB, 12 Nov. 1910.      [34] Braithwaite Papers, Ia, Diary, 9 Jan. 1911.
[35] *PI*, p. 86.      [36] BP, IIa, WHB to HB, 19 Jan. 1911.

as the Webbs remained adamant in their dislike of the government's proposals. 'The unemployment insurance might bring inadvertently the compulsory use of the labour exchange,' remarked Mrs. Webb. '. . . But the sickness insurance . . . is wholly bad, and I cannot see how malingering can be staved off except that the amount given is so *wholly inadequate* that it will be only the very worst workmen who will want to claim it. . . .'[37] Beveridge, however, was enthusiastic about sickness insurance and shortly afterwards he submitted to the Treasury an unsolicited memorandum, outlining a 'comprehensive compulsory scheme of insurance against sickness, invalidity and allied risks by direct State action, with exemption for certain existing societies'. This rather curious document is of some interest to the historian, not merely as Beveridge's first attempt to devise a general insurance plan, but because the views which he expressed on sickness insurance were so markedly different from those which became associated with his name in later life. He suggested that sickness insurance should be paid for entirely by the worker and the state, since the employer 'already bears the whole cost of accidents, and will bear a considerable share of the cost of unemployment'. He proposed also that under the health scheme workmen should be divided into different classes, characterized by different combinations of public and private insurance. At one extreme would be the 'aristocracy of health', who would pay contributions and draw benefits from 'privileged societies', and benefit-paying unions. These privileged societies would have 'complete powers of self-management', they would employ their own doctors, and their members would not be obliged to register at a labour exchange when unemployed. Their funds would be subject to regular scrutiny by the state; and in return they would receive an annual exchequer subsidy, equivalent to the sum of the state's contribution for all their members. At the opposite extreme would be workmen uninsurable in the private market, whose contributions and benefits would be managed exclusively by the state; and in between would be various grades of insured person, drawing some benefits from the state and some from 'privileged societies'. The administration of such a scheme, Beveridge admitted, would involve a 'certain amount of additional labour for the employer', but he claimed rather optimistically that the 'procedure will really be very simple'. Its great advantage he maintained was that it would encourage private thrift and voluntary organizations whilst at the same time restricting private insurance to schemes that were financially sound.[38]

Whether Beveridge's proposals on this occasion had any influence on

---

[37] B. Webb, *Our Partnership*, p. 468.

[38] Braithwaite Papers, II, item 8, 'Memorandum on Sickness and Invalidity Insurance', by WHB, Jan. 1911.

policy is a matter for conjecture. Certainly his proposal to exempt employers from health contributions was not accepted by the Chancellor of the Exchequer. His suggestions for encouraging private insurance were, however, undoubtedly considered by Braithwaite in February 1910,[39] and these suggestions were in certain respects strikingly similar to the administrative arrangements adopted by the Treasury whereby the majority of insured persons participated in the health scheme through 'approved societies', leaving a residue of bad lives to be insured exclusively by the state.[40] But the approved society system had been agreed some time before Beveridge produced his memorandum, and there seems no reason to suppose that the memorandum had any practical effect. It is significant primarily as an expression of Beveridge's own views—of his enthusiasm for national health insurance, and of his preference at this time (in health if not in unemployment insurance) for a pluralistic, self-managing system rather than a uniform scheme run directly by the state.

In spite of Beveridge's interest in health insurance and his admiration for Lloyd George, relations between the Treasury and Board of Trade were not very harmonious; and the process of integrating the two schemes was soon fraught with interdepartmental rivalry and conflict. In January 1911 the details of the health scheme had still to be worked out, and a wide range of private interests had still to be placated. Unemployment insurance on the other hand had been ready for legislation for nearly two years. Its administrative structure had been carefully worked out, and arrangements had been made to involve both capital and labour in collection of contributions and management of benefits. The decision to separate unemployment insurance from the legislation for labour exchanges had originally been taken to suit the convenience of Lloyd George; and Llewellyn Smith therefore took the view that the Board of Trade's scheme should take priority and that 'Health Insurance must be modified to suit unemployment and give way to it'.[41] It soon became evident however that, far from tailoring health to unemployment insurance, Lloyd George was anxious to take over the unemployment scheme in order to merge it with his own. This was quite contrary to the Board of Trade's original conception of national insurance since, although it was recognized that health and unemployment insurance were complementary, neither Llewellyn Smith nor Beveridge had ever envisaged any structural amalgamation between the two schemes. Certainly Beveridge himself at this stage of his career could see no

[39] Braithwaite Papers, Ia, Diary, 13 Feb. 1911.

[40] H. N. Bunbury, *Lloyd George's Ambulance Wagon. Being the Memoirs of William J. Braithwaite* (1957), p. 25.

[41] Ibid., p. 149.

advantage in welding together the different types of insurance into a single uniform system. 'The best chance for . . . unemployment insurance,' he had written two years earlier, 'is to prevent it from being in any way knit up with other schemes or involved in their fortunes. The arguments in favour are much stronger and the obstacles altogether less in the case of unemployment insurance than in regard to any other form of social insurance, so that the former is strongest when standing alone.'[42]

Lloyd George, however, took a different view. He saw himself as the original author of unemployment insurance, and he claimed—quite inaccurately—that Churchill's sole contribution had been a few rhetorical speeches in Parliament.[43] He hoped, moreover, to palliate the unpopularity of the Treasury's scheme for sickness insurance by bracketing it together with the much less controversial scheme devised by the Board of Trade. He failed to convince the Prime Minister that the Treasury should be given sole political responsibility for both health and unemployment insurance, but he persuaded the Cabinet that the two measures should be introduced as a single bill, prepared jointly by the two departments. Then over the next few months he proceeded to launch a powerful attack on the Board of Trade's scheme. He denounced its narrow coverage, and demanded reductions in the level of unemployment benefit, the state contribution and the projected costs of administration. He made vituperative attacks on the mild and harmless Sydney Buxton, was jubilant when the Board's scheme was referred back by the Cabinet, and at one stage seemed willing to abandon unemployment insurance altogether, on the pretext of placating the Conservative opposition.[44]

In nearly all these controversies the Board of Trade's scheme eventually emerged unscathed, though not until it had been dragged through a series of Treasury conferences and two special cabinet committees. The Board was forced to reduce its estimate of administrative expenses, but in other respects the plan for unemployment insurance remained substantially unchanged. This was largely due to the assertiveness of Llewellyn Smith, who, according to Braithwaite, refused 'to admit that he has been worsted, and indeed he has shown himself a very strong man'.[45] Beveridge himself took little part in this conflict, though he attended Treasury conferences in the wake of his departmental chief.[46] His own work was mainly behind the scenes—drafting memoranda for Llewellyn Smith, negotiating points with Braithwaite, refining

[42] BP, III 39, 'Accident Insurance', by WHB, 8 June 1909.
[43] A. C. Murray, *Master and Brother. Murrays of Elibank* (1945), p. 89.
[44] Harris, op. cit., pp. 323–7.          [45] Bunbury, op. cit., p. 149.
[46] Braithwaite Papers, Ia, Diary, 23 Jan. 1911.

clauses in the draft bill and preparing the President's parliamentary brief.

The two schemes were introduced into the Commons by Lloyd George as Parts One and Two of the National Insurance Bill on 4 May 1911. Most of the Chancellor's two-hour speech was taken up with explaining the immensely complicated provisions for health insurance, but he also outlined the main principles of the scheme for unemployment—claiming that continental precedents proved that unemployment insurance must be compulsory and must be subsidized by the State.[47] Beveridge, who was sitting in the officials' gallery, was disappointed in the Chancellor's speech. He complained that in expounding the unemployment scheme Lloyd George had 'made three serious mistakes and gave a generally wrong impression'; and he himself spent several hours afterwards contacting Fleet Street reporters to ensure that an accurate and favourable account appeared in the press. He was pleased, however, with the general reception of the Board of Trade's scheme, which, as he reported to his mother,

appears to have met with a chorus of approval. In the House it was really remarkable how one leader after another got up and blessed the scheme. It looks as if there might be quite a mass of approval—for doing something big and definite and adequate—as to carry the measure right through before the difficulties and obstacles make themselves felt.[48]

Beveridge after this felt increasingly optimistic that both schemes would be enacted before the end of the year—particularly when he learned from Buxton that the unemployment scheme had been examined by a group of trade union M.P.s, who had come to the conclusion that 'with the exception of one or two somewhat trivial matters, their difficulties and objections had already been met in the Bill, and that they were agreeably surprised to find how carefully it had been drawn and thought out'.[49] Nevertheless, there were still numerous points at issue in the Board of Trade's scheme; and at this stage the onus of defending the scheme fell chiefly upon Beveridge, because Llewellyn Smith and Buxton were both continuously occupied with the surge of industrial unrest that broke out in Britain in the summer of 1911.[50] In July Sir Robert Chalmers, the Permanent Secretary to the Treasury, attacked the proposal that Exchequer subsidies to unemployment insurance should be based on contributions levied rather than, as in the case of health insurance, on benefits paid. It was, Chalmers protested, 'an objectionable characteristic . . . from the point of view of public finance

[47] H.C. Deb., 5s., vol. 25, cols. 64 1–3.    [48] BP, IIa, WHB to ASB, 7 May 1911.
[49] BP, IIa, S. Buxton to WHB, 26 May 1911.
[50] BP, IIa, WHB to ASB, 9 and 15 Aug. 1911.

that public money should be set aside for contingencies which might never occur.[51]

Beveridge argued in reply, however, that as unemployment varied so violently from year to year it would be impossible to estimate in advance for a subsidy based on benefit; and this argument was reluctantly accepted by the Treasury in August 1911.[52] On 15 August Beveridge held a conference with a group of Labour M.P.s, who wanted further safeguards for the interests of the unions. The Labour delegation asked for further assurance that all trade unionists should be free to reject work at less than the standard rate. They urged that refusal of benefit for unemployment caused by a trade dispute should be confined to workmen actually out on strike; and they suggested that unemployment insurance, like the proposed scheme for health insurance, should be managed exclusively through 'approved societies', so as to exclude 'free labour' associations and other black-leg agencies.[53] Beveridge was very anxious to win Labour support, and he recorded that the Labour members 'really were very reasonable and pleasant and will be helpful'.[54] Nevertheless, he did not agree to all their demands. He was perfectly willing to secure for trade unionists full recognition of their standard rates; but he rejected the 'approved society' system, on the ground that it would exclude many insured persons who were not members of trade unions. He insisted also that disqualification from benefit for unemployment caused by a trade dispute should apply not merely to workmen who were actually out on strike but to all workmen in a factory where a dispute was in progress. Such a provision was necessary, Beveridge claimed, because it would be impossible to distinguish in practice between men who were parties to a dispute and men thrown out of work by the actions of their workmates; and to pay benefits to the former would mean using state and employers funds to subsidize measures of 'industrial warfare'.[55]

Meanwhile in Parliament the National Insurance Bill was arousing much hostility—partly from Conservative M.P.s defending commercial insurance interests, and partly from left-wing Labour M.P.s who attacked flat-rate contributions as a form of regressive taxation. Most of this criticism was however focused on Part One of the Bill, and the

[51] PRO, LAB 2/1483/LE 9203, Sir R. Chalmers to the Secretary of the Board of Trade, 26 July 1911.

[52] PRO, LAB 2/1483/LE 9203, letter and memorandum by WHB, revised by Sir H. Llewellyn Smith, 31 July 1911; Sir R. Chalmers to the Secretary of the Board of Trade, 4 Aug. 1911.

[53] PRO, LAB 2/1483/LE (1) 9169, Report on Unemployment Insurance Conference with the Labour Party, by WHB, 15 Aug. 1911.

[54] BP, IIa, WHB to ASB, 15 Aug. 1911.

[55] PRO, LAB 2/1483/LE (1) 11101, Memorandum by WHB, 9 Oct. 1911.

scheme for unemployment insurance met with relatively little opposition.[56] In August 1911 the government's decision to hold an autumn session of Parliament greatly increased the bill's chances of getting through that year.[57] In September Beveridge spent a holiday in Ireland with Denman, who as Buxton's private secretary was also closely concerned with unemployment insurance; and when they returned in October it had been decided to refer unemployment insurance to a Grand Committee of the House of Commons. 'It looks as if Ll. G. will need wonderful seamanship to keep the thing afloat,' commented Denman despondently. 'The enemies of the Bill are many and the enthusiasm for it small.'[58] Beveridge, however, was more optimistic. 'I think that Part II of the Bill . . . will be all right,' he recorded. 'Unless there's deliberate obstruction in committee upstairs it'll have plenty of time to get through without any closure. Sending it to a Grand Committee is earnest of an intention to pass it this session.'[59]

The Grand Committee—composed of ninety M.P.s of all parties, sitting in an upper chamber of the Palace of Westminster—began its deliberations on 1 November 1911. Beveridge observed on the first day of the discussion that unemployment insurance had 'met with no hostility in any quarter'; and he recorded that all significant amendments—defining the duties of the umpire, allowing rebates to regular employers, and setting aside 10 per cent of contributions for costs of administration—had been introduced by the Board of Trade itself.[60] Two weeks later he reported to his mother that 'Part II got through the committee today—after a remarkably smooth passage . . . which makes us really rather pleased with ourselves. The Secretary of the Shipbuilding Federation told me that it was one of the best thought-out measures he had ever come across. A sufficient number of people have been saying this to make it seem quite a general impression.'[61] Part One of the bill had a much stormier reception, but was eventually forced through the Commons by the government's use of the 'guillotine', which effectively curtailed much hostile debate. Both parts of the bill completed their passage through Parliament early in December 1911. The structure of compulsory unemployment insurance, as laid down in Part Two of the National Insurance Act, was 'in all essential particulars' remarkably similar to the original scheme produced by Llewellyn Smith and Beveridge three years before—except that contributions for both workers and employers were now fixed at 2½d. a week and benefits at a flat rate of 7s. a week.[62] In addition, section 105 of the Act allowed trade

[56] Harris, op. cit., p. 329.     [57] BP, IIa, WHB to ASB, 6 Aug. 1911.
[58] BP, IIa, R. Denman to WHB, 26 Sept. 1911.
[59] BP, IIa, WHB to ASB, 23 Oct. 1911.
[60] BP, IIa, WHB to ASB, 1 Nov. 1911; Harris, op. cit., pp. 332–3.
[61] BP, IIa, WHB to ASB, 16 Nov. 1911.     [62] BP, IIb, S. Buxton to WHB, 17 Dec. 1911.

unionists to collect benefits through their unions rather than through an exchange; and section 106 implemented the 'Ghent' system, by authorizing state subsidies to voluntary 'out-of-work funds', run by trade unions both inside and outside the insured trades. Other sections of the Act were designed to reduce the actual incidence of unemployment as well as to assist the unemployed. Section 94 allowed rebates to employers who gave long-term engagements. Section 96 allowed rebates to employers who made 'short-time' agreements; and section 99 provided that, where an employer agreed to hire his workmen exclusively through a labour exchange, all his administrative responsibility for both health and unemployment insurance could be transferred to the exchange.

## IV

After the Act was passed Beveridge spent several weeks in Switzerland ski-ing with Sydney Buxton. He returned in January to prepare for collection of the first contributions on 15 July 1912 and payment of the first benefits on 15 January 1913—deadlines known respectively as 'Joy Day' and 'Judgment Day' to officials of the Board of Trade.[63] During the next few months Beveridge presided over the opening of more than a hundred new exchanges, the issue of two and a half million insurance cards, and the recruitment of fifteen thousand additional staff, and he drafted regulations outlining the procedure for checking claims and making appeals. Of all these tasks by far the most difficult was appointment of staff, which involved a renewal of the earlier conflict between Treasury and Board of Trade. During the course of 1912 the Board received over ninety thousand applications for insurance posts,[64] and the Treasury was determined that the Board should not again enjoy the wide discretion in making appointments which had been allowed for labour exchanges in 1910. 'I have had a gorgeous time with the Treasury and the Civil Service Commission,' reported Rey to Beveridge in January 1912. 'The Treasury wanted us to take all our people by Open Competition, and I saw the possibility of trouble of some magnitude. But I managed to square them and make them agree to our scheme.'[65] Rey's confidence was misplaced, however, for on this occasion the Board of Trade was not allowed to have its own way. The Board was given the final power to reject applicants who were patently unsuitable for work with the unemployed; but the Treasury insisted that as many as possible of the new officials should be recruited from inside the civil service, and that all new candidates should be examined by the Civil Service

---

[63] BP, IIb, J. B. Adams to WHB, n.d. (late 1912).
[64] Cd. 6740/1913, *RC on the Civil Service, Minutes of Evidence*, Q. 16,007.
[65] BP, IIb, C. F. Rey to WHB, 9 Jan. 1912.

Commission.[66] This decision effectively put an end to Beveridge's earlier policy of choosing men not for their academic qualifications but for their experience of the shop-floor and knowledge of industrial affairs.

Beveridge himself spent the early months of 1912 travelling around the country explaining the new system to labour exchange managers, and trying to persuade employers to transfer their administrative duties under the National Insurance Act to their local exchange. His correspondence of this period makes it clear that he found the task of setting up administrative machinery much less exciting and intellectually challenging than the invention of new policies and the framing of legislation. He confided to his mother that he was 'bored with unemployment', and he was increasingly irritated by the constraints imposed by the Treasury[67]—an irritation that later hardened into a lifelong aversion for the whole apparatus of Treasury control. He began to yearn for some new project, but observed with characteristic single-mindedness that 'I don't think I can tackle any serious subject while unemployment insurance is still on the stocks—not from want of energy, but simply because one cannot have two serious subjects at the same time'.[68] In April he was forced to take a rest from insurance, when he suffered from a recurrence of athlete's heart. His doctor prescribed a course of thermal baths, and ordered him to 'rest as much as possible' and to refrain from reading 'metaphysical works involving great concentration'.[69] For the next few months Beveridge took little part in official business, although he received regular reports on the progress of unemployment insurance from C. F. Rey.[70] In June, however, Rey had a nervous breakdown and his place was taken by Stephen Tallents, the young official who had worked closely with Beveridge in the dispute with the Board of Education. Tallents was 'a good young man—much older than his years in office work',[71] but he had not previously held a position of authority and for some weeks there was considerable doubt as to whether the new scheme could possibly start on the appointed day. During those weeks Beveridge unofficially resumed responsibility for preparing unemployment insurance—apparently concealing the fact from his doctor, family and friends.[72] 'On the July Sunday that was the eve of the scheme,' Tallents recorded, 'Beveridge and I spent a hectic day together in the office, and in the evening went round to my home in Warwick Square, threw ourselves down exhausted on the patch of meagre grass that grew

---

[66] *RC on the Civil Service, Minutes of Evidence*, Q. 16,167.
[67] BP, IIa, WHB to ASB, 31 Mar. 1912; WHB to Jeannette Tawney, 16 Aug. 1912.
[68] BP, IIa, WHB to ASB, 29 July 1912.    [69] BP, IIa, WHB to ASB, 29 Apr. 1912.
[70] BP, IIb, C. F. Rey to WHB, 23 May 1912.
[71] BP, IIa, WHB to ASB, 22 Feb. 1912.
[72] Letters to his family and personal friends contain no references to any attendances at the Board of Trade between 29 Apr. and 3 Sept. 1912.

under the plane trees in our garden and wondered what was going to happen all over the country next morning.'[73] The first contributions were, in fact, duly paid into the fund on the following day. Beveridge himself subsequently appraised the new system with rather mixed feelings—blaming its imperfections on the narrow range of staff selected for the new service by the Civil Service Commissioners and on the unimaginative exercise of Treasury control.[74]

Beveridge returned officially to the Board in September 1912, determined that he would 'insist on being a Director and not doing drudgery'.[75] For some months he claimed that he was working less strenuously than usual, 'stopping work at about five and idling at home as much as possible'.[76] Nevertheless, throughout the autumn of 1912 he was continuously occupied in defending the new system before the Royal Commission on the Civil Service, urging Buxton to keep up pressure for additional staff, and preparing elections for the new unemployment insurance advisory committees or 'courts of referees'.[77] In December he recorded that he was now ready to 'put the final touches to the unemployment machine'. He appeared to have overcome his disenchantment of earlier in the year and conjured up in glowing terms his personal vision of the new administrative system, with its elaborate nation-wide arrangements for collection of contributions, payment of benefits, compilation of unemployment statistics and hearing of appeals.

All this, once started, must go like clockwork and with absolute continuity—for there will be a perpetual stream of applications for benefit, sometimes large and sometimes small but never ceasing. Will the machine work? It's really almost as new in type as was the first steam locomotive, and of course one hasn't been able to make experiments and trial runs. Of course, it will work, somehow, but with how much or how little friction and partial breakdown and dislocation, one cannot tell.[78]

Beveridge spent the early weeks of 1913 travelling among the Divisional Offices 'seeing what if anything is wrong and wants altering at once'; and he reported that 'London and possibly Ireland are the only danger spots'.[79] The first benefits were paid on 15 January, and over a hundred thousand workmen—most of them from the building industry —qualified for benefit on the very first day. The new experiment created much less stir in the press than the opening of exchanges, but nevertheless it soon came to dominate the labour exchange system. The checking of claims and payment of benefits rapidly took precedence over finding

[73] Tallents, *Man and Boy*, p. 190.
[74] BP, IIa, WHB to Jeannette Tawney, 16 Aug. 1912.
[75] Ibid.
[76] BP, IIa, WHB to ASB, 3 Sept. 1912.
[77] BP, IIa, WHB to ASB, 27 Oct. 1912.
[78] BP, IIa, WHB to ASB, 31 Dec. 1912.
[79] BP, IIa, WHB to ASB, 18 Jan. 1913.

work for the unemployed; and Beveridge himself told the Royal Commission on the Civil Service that 'the undoubted effect of unemployment insurance is to make our work more akin to the type of an ordinary Government department'.[80] The introduction of insurance also had important repercussions on the internal structure of the Board of Trade. Early in 1913 the contentious Rey quarrelled not merely with the Treasury but with the Board's Finance and Establishment departments—which accused the Insurance Office of monopolizing funds and personnel, cutting itself off from the rest of the Board, and 'heading straight for complete independence'.[81] At the same time Beveridge himself was on increasingly bad terms with George Askwith—complaining in private that he could never persuade Askwith of anything unless he allowed him to claim it as his own idea.[82] Askwith as head of the Labour department was still Beveridge's immediate superior, but he was increasingly hostile to labour exchanges and on several occasions came into conflict with exchange officials over the handling of industrial disputes.[83] The situation clearly required either a readjustment of departmental functions, to take account of the new importance of exchanges and insurance, or a change in the department's leading personnel. C. F. Rey on one occasion hinted strongly that he would have liked Beveridge to take over as Permanent Secretary, 'as soon as we can find a good billet for H. Ll. S.'[84] There is no evidence to suggest, however, that Beveridge himself aspired to replace Llewellyn Smith; and the administrative tension was eventually resolved by hiving off the new services from the Labour department. A separate Labour Exchange and Unemployment Insurance department was set up in May 1913 and Beveridge became its chief official, with the rank of Assistant Secretary and a salary of £1,000 a year. At his own request he was henceforth known as 'assistant secretary and director'—a title designed to emphasize the links forged by the new system between conventional public administration and the business and commercial world.[85]

## V

As was shown in earlier chapters Beveridge's interest in unemployment had first been aroused by the phenomenon of casual labour, which he saw as a potent cause of personal demoralization among workmen and

[80] BP, IIb, J. B. Adams to WHB, n.d. (late 1912); *RC on the Civil Service, Minutes of Evidence*, Q. 15,819.
[81] BP, IIb, C. F. Rey to WHB, 23 Mar. 1913.
[82] BP, IIb, R. Dunn Gardner to WHB, 9 July 1912.
[83] BP, IIb, C. F. Rey to WHB, 19 Oct. 1913.
[84] BP, IIb, C. F. Rey to WHB, 14 May 1913.
[85] BP, IIb, H. Llewellyn Smith to WHB, 8 May 1913; C. F. Rey, unpublished memoirs, p. 98.

of inefficiency and bad management in industry at large. One of his chief ambitions when entering the Board of Trade had been to introduce schemes of decasualization, and he had repeatedly stressed the possibility of such schemes as one of the main justifications for labour exchanges. He was himself prepared to use exchanges to abolish casual employment by compulsion, if voluntary persuasion failed; and although Churchill and Llewellyn Smith rejected compulsory decasualization it was nevertheless envisaged from the start of the new system that exchanges would be widely used to discourage casual engagements and to redeploy the invisible surplus of the 'under-employed'. In 1909 negotiations were opened with the Port of London Authority, with a view to setting up decasualization schemes in the London docks, and in 1910 similar discussions were held with dock employers in Liverpool, Manchester, Glasgow, Bristol and South Wales. All these negotiations foundered, however, on the reluctance of both workers and employers to relinquish traditional methods of hiring; and at the end of 1910 a conference of 'all the important shipowners' resolved that it was 'not prepared to welcome a scheme organized by the Board of Trade'.[86]

The shipowners justified their non-co-operation on the ground that it was not at this stage clear whether dock labour would be covered by compulsory unemployment insurance; and until this question was settled negotiations with casual employers were temporarily suspended. Early in 1911 the possibility of including dockers among the 'insured trades' was the subject of considerable discussion within the Board of Trade. Beveridge in March produced a memorandum strongly supporting the extension of unemployment insurance to dock and wharf labourers—arguing that compulsory insurance would make it possible to introduce decasualization by stealth. This proposal won the support of Llewellyn Smith, and was approved by the Treasury at the end of July;[87] but for reasons which are not clear Llewellyn Smith and Beveridge changed their minds, and dock labourers were not included in Part Two of the National Insurance Act at the end of 1911. An important opportunity of promoting regular employment, by making it a prerequisite of entitlement to benefit, was therefore lost. Nevertheless, the Act provided the Board with several other footholds in the casual labour market. It enabled the Board to pay annual rebates to regular employers and to take over the administrative burden of insurance from any employer who hired his labour exclusive through an exchange. In addition, casual labourers were included in Part One of the Act which

[86] *Labour Exchanges and Unemployment Insurance. Report of the Proceedings of the Board of Trade under the Labour Exchanges Act, 1909, and under Part Two of the National Insurance Act, 1911, to July 1914*, by WHB, paras. 206–25, (copy in BP, III 45).

[87] BP, III 42, Unemployment Insurance: Papers for Conference, 16 Mar. 1911; PRO, LAB 2/1483/LE 9203, Sir R. Chalmers to Sir H. Llewellyn Smith, 26 July 1911.

stipulated that contributions to health insurance must always be paid for a minimum period of one week—thus potentially penalizing employers who hired workmen by the day or by the hour.

Beveridge himself was determined to use insurance as an instrument of decasualization, and he resumed negotiations with casual employers in the summer of 1911. In July he inspected an experiment in Manchester, whereby all dock labourers were to be registered by the labour exchange and the exchange was to take over payment of wages and collection of national insurance contributions—wages being paid in a single lump sum to each workman at the end of every week.[88] This scheme was extended to cover 50 per cent of Manchester casuals, but was eventually terminated by a strike of waterside labourers in September 1913. In the autumn of 1911 an attempt was made to introduce a similar scheme in Glasgow, but this was sabotaged by the refusal of Clydeside dockers—whose whole domestic economy was tied to daily and hourly earnings—to wait for their wages until the end of the week. A few months later the Board tried to make a section 99 arrangement with the Clydeside shipbuilding industry, but this was strongly opposed by shipbuilding employers and the attempt was abandoned in October 1912.[89]

Similar opposition was encountered in Bristol and South Wales, but some progress towards decasualization was made on Merseyside. This largely stemmed from the initiative of R. F. Williams, the Divisional Officer of the North Western region. Williams was 'a keen-faced intellectual looking young gentleman, with the Oxford manner strongly developed . . . gifted with a wonderful flow of words and a clever analytical mind'.[90] He had carefully studied Beveridge's works on unemployment, and to a certain extent shared Beveridge's own vision of the future pattern of labour organization.[91] Indeed the two men had much in common and were for a time on intimate terms. During Beveridge's visit to Lancashire in July 1911 they discussed decasualization with the Liverpool shipowners, Charles and Allan Booth;[92] and a few months later Williams informed Beveridge that he had drawn up a plan for abolition of casual labour based on Beveridge's own proposals in *Unemployment: a Problem of Industry*. This plan had been successfully submitted to Liverpool waterside employers who were now 'all absolutely pledged'. 'The Dockers' Union too is alright,' Williams reported, 'but we shall need some propaganda among the men—especially if Master Tom Mann gets going . . . the poor old B. of T. seems d---d

[88] BP, IIa, WHB to ASB, 26 July 1911.
[89] *Labour Exchanges and Unemployment Insurance. Report . . . to July 1914*, paras. 207–11.
[90] *MP*, 22 Oct. 1911.
[91] BP, IIb, R. F. Williams to WHB, n.d. and 13 Aug. 1912.
[92] BP, IIa, WHB to ASB, 26 July 1911.

unpopular here . . . you've no idea of the underhand methods that have been used to smash the scheme.'[93]

Williams's plan came into operation in Liverpool in July 1912. It had gained the support of both sides of industry—possibly because Williams had spent nearly £500 in wining and dining employers and workers and in bribing newspapers to give favourable publicity.[94] The scheme consisted of four main provisions. Firstly, dock employment was confined exclusively to men registered by the local labour exchange, who carried metal 'tallies' to prove their registration. Secondly, 'stands' were set up for the hire of workmen 'who had failed to get work at their ordinary place of employment'. Thirdly, all wages were paid by employers into a labour exchange 'clearing house' and were paid out again to each worker in a lump sum at the end of the week. And, fourthly, the administrative burden of collecting contributions for national health insurance was lifted from the employers and transferred to the local exchange.[95] The objects of the scheme were threefold—to exclude surplus labour from dock employment, to give employers a positive incentive to use their local labour exchange, and to give to each dock labourer as close an approximation as possible to a full week's employment and a full week's pay.

Williams in August 1913 claimed that within five years there would be no more casual labour in Liverpool. He was anxious to make Liverpool 'a pattern for further legislation', and he hinted strongly to Beveridge that he should be given responsibility for promoting a similar scheme in London.[96] Beveridge himself, however, was by no means entirely satisfied with the Liverpool scheme. He learned from Humbert Woolf that the dockers themselves strongly resented the 'tally' system, and Williams's own calculations showed that far too many men had been registered and that a third of Liverpool dockers still took home earnings of less than 15s. a week.[97] When the question arose of extending decasualization to other ports, Beveridge therefore recommended a system rather different from that which Williams had introduced on the Mersey.

The issue of extending decasualization was raised in March 1913 when both the Board of Trade and the National Health Insurance Commission were reviewing the National Insurance Act for possible amendments. The Commission reported that under Part One of the Act many casual labourers had been forced to stamp their own insurance

[93] BP. IIb, R. F. Williams to WHB, n.d. (late 1911).
[94] BP, IIb, R. F. Williams to WHB, 9 Mar. 1912.
[95] *Unemployment: a Problem of Industry* (1930 edn.), p. 314.
[96] BP, IIb, R. F. Williams to WHB, 8 Aug. 1913 and 30 Jan. (1913 or 14).
[97] PRO, LAB 2/1484/LE 23987, 'Objections', by Umberto Wolff, 28 May 1911; *Unemployment: a Problem of Industry* (1930 edn.), pp. 315–16.

cards and to pay for their employers' contributions as well as their own—since without a fully-stamped card it was impossible to get employment in the latter days of the week.[98] Among casual workers the Act was thus reinforcing the poverty it was supposed to relieve; and the Commission therefore proposed to introduce a cut-price daily stamp for casual labourers, and to levy their contributions by the day rather than the week. This proposal was, however, strongly attacked by Beveridge, who claimed that a daily stamp would take away all incentive from employers to engage workmen on a regular basis.[99] He admitted, however, that 'it is high time that we began to get something done . . . in regard to casual labour' and suggested instead a scheme which would heavily penalize casual employers. He proposed that in certain scheduled industries employers who refused to give regular employment should be compelled to bear the cost of workers' contributions as well as their own, and that this burden should be pooled between all employers who hired an individual labourer during the course of a week. Such a system, Beveridge claimed, would relieve the casual labourer of the cost of buying his own stamps; and at the same time it would give 'employers a direct and substantial motive for improving the regularity of dock labour', and would force them to join together in syndicates to guarantee regular work.[100]

Beveridge's plan met with approval in the Insurance Commission, but it evoked a strong protest from R. F. Williams who claimed that, if applied to his own division, it would disrupt his harmonious relationships with Liverpool employers. 'I have not the slightest objection,' he told Beveridge, 'to penalising those employers . . . who will not make any attempt to decasualise, but . . . at Liverpool you have a large body of employers who are genuinely trying to do their best for their men under most disheartening circumstances.'[101] Beveridge retorted rather high-handedly that Williams should 'put his mind' to the subject and 'consider how best this . . . principle can be applied to Liverpool, on the assumption that it probably *will* be applied in one way or another'.[102] Williams in return claimed that many dockers did not want to work for more than two days a week, and that by relieving them of contributions the proposed scheme would merely encourage their irregular habits.[103] Beveridge's reply to this objection revealed his growing determination

[98] PRO, LAB 2/1484/LE 23987, 'A Suggested Casual Labour Amendment to the Act', by E. F. Wise, 22 Apr. 1913.

[99] Ibid., 'Notes on the Difficulties of 2*d*. Daily Stamp Scheme', by WHB, 16 June 1913; WHB to H. Llewellyn Smith, 3 July 1913.

[100] Ibid., WHB to H. Llewellyn Smith, 24 May 1913, and 'Notes on Outline of Scheme for Dealing with Casual Labour', 3 May 1913.

[101] PRO, LAB 2/1484/LE 23989, R. F. Williams to WHB, 4 June 1913.

[102] Ibid., WHB to R. F. Williams, 5 June 1913.

[103] PRO, LAB 2/1484/ LE 23987, R. F. Williams to WHB, 6 June 1913.

to eliminate casual labour at all costs, without regard to the varying circumstances of different trades and localities. 'I admit', he told Williams,

that having regard to the characters of the workmen, this may appear in the first instance like penalising the employer for the casual habits of the workman. . . . However . . . so long as the workmen are allowed to retain their casual habits without appreciable penalty the evils of casual labour will continue . . . but the only effective way of curing them of such habits is through the employers refusing to employ men of such habits, and the best way of getting the employers to take this attitude is to make them pay extra for employing purely casual men . . .[104]

Beveridge's formula was eventually included on a voluntary basis—'subject to consent from local employers'—in the National Health Insurance Amendment Act of July 1913;[105] and a scheme of this kind was tentatively planned by the Port of London Authority later in the year. Voluntary decasualization made little progress elsewhere however and towards the end of 1913 Llewellyn Smith and Buxton reluctantly came round to the view which Beveridge had held all along—that dock labour should be organized by some measure of compulsion. 'I have been considering the question of legislation since I saw you, and my own ideas on the subject are gradually clearing,' wrote Llewellyn Smith on 10 November; and a few days later he instructed Beveridge to prepare a scheme which would include casual labourers within the scope of unemployment insurance.[106] Later in the month Buxton told the Cabinet that no voluntary decasualization scheme had so far been successful, and that 'it has been proved by their experience that compulsion is necessary if any real progress is to be made'. He therefore intended to introduce legislation, empowering his department

to schedule by Special Order trades and localities in which the evil of irregular or intermittent employment is specially prevalent, and . . . in such scheduled trades and districts it shall be an implied condition of every hiring that the workman shall be employed for a week at least.[107]

Buxton's proposal was approved by the Cabinet and negotiations with interested parties began in the following year. Perhaps not surprisingly, however, little progress had been made on this immensely complex and explosive issue by the outbreak of war. Looking back on the policies of

[104] Ibid., WHB to R. F. Williams, 7 June 1913.
[105] BP, IIa, WHB to ASB, 26 July 1913.
[106] BP, III 47, H. Llewellyn Smith to WHB, 10 Nov. 1913; IIb, H. Llewellyn Smith to WHB, 17 Nov. 1913.
[107] PRO, CAB 37/117 'National Insurance Act (Part II) Unemployment', by S. Buxton printed 22 Nov. 1913.

this period, Beveridge viewed the casual labour market as an area of almost unmitigated failure and frustration.[108] A little had been learned about the nature of the problem. A little had been done to promote understanding between employers and workers. But nothing had yet been done in fulfilment of the ambition he had conceived ten years earlier—the conversion of the casual labourer into an efficient, regular and organized member of the industrial working class. 'It cannot be claimed' he wrote in 1915

that any substantial progress has yet been made with the decasualisation of labour in the principal centres where such labour is employed. The powers of the Board have not proved adequate to secure that change in the methods of engagement which alone appears to offer a prospect of real improvement.[109]

## VI

Beveridge's career in public administration during the years prior to the First World War was in some ways typical and in some ways unique among English reforming intellectuals of his own and earlier generations. On the one hand, as Philip Abrams has pointed out, since 1834 a 'recurrent and insistent theme' of English politics and government had been 'the diversion of the most promising sociologists early in their careers away from social analysis and research and toward administration, party politics or one or another kind of institutional innovation'. Among those enticed into government in this way, Abrams notes that 'Beveridge himself was a conspicuous example'.[110] In this respect Beveridge stood squarely within a tradition that included Benthamite utilitarians, social Darwinists, Fabian socialists and radical empiricists like Llewellyn Smith. He represented a phenomenon of which he himself wholeheartedly approved—the capacity of British government and society to contain and integrate the forces of critical dissent. At the same time, however, his career was in certain respects unusual, even within this well-established tradition of institutional reform. 'He had to his credit,' recalled Lord Salter, 'a four-fold achievement perhaps never equalled before or since by a social reformer'; he had studied social problems at first-hand, he had produced a major work of socio-economic analysis, he had 'created an inner circle of supporting opinion by his leading articles', and he had himself 'both established and directed' a new administrative system which embodied his own proposals for social reform.[111] Beveridge was therefore both representative of and outstanding among the large number of Edwardian intellectuals who were

[108] *Unemployment: a Problem of Industry* (1930 edn.), p. 132.
[109] *Labour Exchanges and Unemployment Insurance. Report . . . to July 1914*, para. 225.
[110] Philip Abrams, *The Origins of British Sociology* (Chicago, 1968), pp. 148–9.
[111] Lord Salter, 'Lord Beveridge 1879–1963', *Procs. Br. Acad.*, XLIX, 1963, pp. 419–20.

recruited by both Liberal and Conservative governments into various branches of public administration. For this reason it is worth reviewing in some detail his whole approach to the governmental process and his view of his own role in the bureaucratic machine.

Beveridge's political philosophy, as was shown in an earlier chapter, consisted at this time of a rather uneasy mixture of idealism and positivism; and this mixture was very clearly reflected in his approach to public administration. He saw the goals of administration as idealist goals—the enchancement of the powers of a beneficent state, the harnessing of feelings of social benevolence, and the reconciliation of antagonistic social forces. But at the same time he had a highly positivist conception of administrative methods and of the potentially unlimited scope of administrative action. He tended to perceive all social problems as administrative problems, believing that 'all problems are soluble given enough staff'.[112] And, like the Benthamites eighty years earlier, he thought that the same administrative techniques and solutions were invariably applicable 'all the world over'.[113] This approach undoubtedly contributed to his forcefulness and ingenuity in planning ambitious schemes, and to his 'exceptional administrative flair in translating a general policy into action'.[114] But, as he himself later admitted, it also misled him into attempting to impose administrative remedies on problems that were largely incapable of administrative solution—such as the cultural and psychological aspects of the problem of casual labour and the economic problem of inadequate labour demand.[115] Llewellyn Smith on one occasion gently chided him for becoming 'hypnotised' with the word 'scheme';[116] and this criticism pointed to a basic weakness in Beveridge's administrative philosophy—a tendency to disregard or brush aside inconvenient political realities and to over-estimate the organizing power of the administrative machine.

On a personal level it is clear that Beveridge viewed his position in the Board of Trade mainly as a means of getting things done and not in any sense as a permanent vocation. I have found no evidence to support the view that he regarded other civil servants of this period with 'profound contempt';[117] and in a lecture given in 1922 he observed that 'in his experience civil servants were often very imaginative and full of initiative'.[118] But nevertheless he was frequently impatient with both

---

[112] Harold Wilson, *Beveridge Memorial Lecture* (1966), p. 6.
[113] *RC on the Civil Service, Minutes of Evidence*, QQ. 15,975–6.
[114] Salter, p. 421.
[115] *Full Employment in a Free Society, A Report by William H. Beveridge* (1944), pp. 90–2.
[116] BP, IIb, H. Llewellyn Smith to WHB, 17 Nov. 1913.
[117] Harold Wilson, p. 6.
[118] *The Civilian*, 1 July 1922, report of a lecture by WHB on 'The Civil Service and its Critics'.

superiors and subordinates, and he was critical of the narrow cross-section of experience conventionally recruited by Open Competition. He complained also that, although opportunities did arise for the reforming official to act on his own initiative, these were too often counter-balanced by Treasury 'tightfistedness' and by 'departmental jealousy, lack of decision and readiness to take responsibility, lack of initiative and lack of humanity, or to put it more positively, a tendency to pedantry'.[119]

Beveridge's criticisms of official life were, as we have seen, frequently reflected in feelings of boredom and frustration with his own work in the Board of Trade, and it is clear from his correspondence of this period that, although he welcomed the chance to mould public policy, he by no means relished the life of a professional administrator. He was often perceived by contemporaries as a 'born bureaucrat in his outlook';[120] but he was in many ways too impatient, too idiosyncratic, and too contemptuous of a pre-conceived routine to fit comfortably into the structure of public administration. Paradoxically, for one who imposed so many rationalizing schemes on others, he intensely disliked the personal consequences of administrative rationalization. In his early days at the Board he felt that he was 'creating all the time', but as the years went by and as his plans were successfully implemented he complained that his work was 'less and less work purely with ideas' and more and more with administrative minutiae. As early as September 1909 he had remarked that official duties left him with little energy for anything except 'sitting by the fire', and he clearly missed the freedom to engage in a wide range of public activities that he had enjoyed at Toynbee Hall. He was conscious that the Civil Service was having a 'dulling' effect on his character—an effect which he tried to counteract by frequent pilgrimages to mountains, and by holidays 'spent in playing or working with ideas . . . sometimes fanciful and sometimes serious'. 'There are certain things in me,' he insisted, 'which don't get satisfied with Labex alone, now that Labex is only creative at rare moments.'[121]

These feelings of frustration showed themselves in various ways—most notably in a recurring desire to resume some kind of academic or literary activity. During a visit to Cambridge in 1910 he had 'much discussion' with professional economists and 'was inclined as a consequence to start studying for a book on the eternal subjects of socialism or the limits of state action and the psychology of individual incentive'.[122] Early in 1912 he conceived an ambition to write a 'serious work' on the

[119] W. H. Beveridge, *The Public Servant in War and Peace* (1920), p. 33.

[120] *Pall Mall Gazette*, 5 June 1922.

[121] BP, IIa, WHB to ASB, 30 Sept. 1909 and 26 May 1913; ms. conversations with ASB, 1912.

[122] BP, IIa, WHB to ASB, 24 Jan. 1910.

'woman's question', comparable in scope with his study of the unemployed.[123] During his illness in the summer of 1912 he composed a rather premature autobiography, and, encouraged by his editor at Longman's, he toyed with the idea of further excursions into writing fiction. 'I have a hankering,' he told his sister, 'after imaginative and human and comic work (in the sense of Meredith) and let stories and plots simmer in my mind with some pleasure—when the baths let me have any mind at all.'[124] In the following year he wrote an unpublished short story about a young man named Edward who was 'criticized by Mrs. Barton for not finding a wife'. Edward protested strongly against the blanket assumption of the Mrs. Bartons of this world that 'the main reason why a man doesn't marry is in himself'—an accusation that presumably had often been levied at Beveridge.[125] This story has unfortunately not survived, but it was sternly criticized by Annette Beveridge and Mrs. Dunn Gardner as lacking in both taste and wit.[126] At the same time Beveridge revived his earlier interest in the Toynbee Hall Enquirers' Club and in research on the unemployed. In 1914 he produced an article for the *Economic Journal* on a labour exchange experiment under the Cromwellian Protectorate, and he planned to carry out further research into the labour market of seventeenth-century France.[127] Whether any of these projects would eventually have come to fruition is not clear, but they were in any event eclipsed in the summer of 1914 by the outbreak of the Great War.

[123] Lady Beveridge Papers, WHB to J. Mair, 4 Feb. 1912.
[124] BP, IIa, WHB to ASB, 3 Sept. 1912; WHB to Jeannette Tawney, 16 Aug. 1912. The manuscript of the autobiography is preserved in BP, IXa 35.
[125] *PI*, pp. 111–12; BP, IIa, WHB to ASB, 26 May 1913.
[126] BP, IIa, ASB to WHB, May 1913; IIb, R. Dunn Gardner to WHB, 26 May 1913.
[127] W. H. Beveridge, 'A Seventeenth Century Labour Exchange', *Econ. J.*, XXIV, no. 95, Sept. 1914; BP, IIa, WHB to ASB, 28 Oct. 1914.

# 9

## Labour and War

### I

In July 1914 Beveridge attended a dinner given by Lady Lyttleton, at which the conversation turned upon prediction of the future. 'I told them,' Beveridge recorded, 'that I knew only one really good thing about the Future—theirs or mine or anyone else's—viz. that it was unknown. I did not propose to take that charm from the future. It has indeed been said that if we could all see the future as well as we can see the past, there would be no future. We should all commit suicide through terror or boredom at the prospect.'[1]

These light words, bandied around at a fashionable party, had in retrospect a certain painful irony, for to Beveridge as to most Englishmen of the period it seemed that the era of peace and progress could never come to an end. 'It seemed a time full of event and high endeavour,' recalled Beveridge twenty years later, '[of] working with great allies and leaders to make a better world. . . . Peace had become a habit and war unbelievable to us as to 99 people in 100 of all ages in Britain.'[2] To a few more prescient observers there were threatening signs on the political horizon—in the form of recurrent diplomatic incidents, the international arms race and endemic labour unrest. But to Beveridge and most of his circle in the spring of 1914 the only flaw in an otherwise tranquil political landscape was the problem of Ulster and Home Rule. Even on the Irish question Beveridge was optimistic. He was a convinced supporter of Asquith's Home Rule Bill; and after the Curragh mutiny in March 1914 he recorded hopefully that 'this last crisis has probably done good in bringing us all near enough to civil war to see what it really means (in moving troops and arms etc.). In fact it's been like a mild attack of the same disease—an inoculation—which may help to make us immune from the real disease later and prevent it from attacking us.'[3]

On a personal level the year before the war was for Beveridge a period of marking time. 'I feel curiously unchanged,' he remarked, 'though so much has been changed in my corner of the state.'[4] In July 1913 he had suffered once again from dilation of the heart and travelled with his

[1] BP, IIa, ms. conversations with ASB, 23 June–27 July 1914.
[2] BP, Ic 50, notes for WHB's diary, 29–30 Dec. 1934.
[3] BP, IIa, WHB to ASB, 6 Apr. 1914.    [4] BP, IIa, WHB to ASB, 7 Jan. 1914.

mother to Bad Nauheim, where he underwent a 'cure' at the hands of the great Dr. Schott—the medical adviser to the crowned heads of Europe, who was reputed to identify patients by the beat of their hearts. Back in London he spent his most leisurely winter for years, having little to do except prepare amendments to the National Insurance Act. He kept bare office hours and attended numerous social functions—mixing, through his friendship with Denman, with leading radical Liberals, like the Buxtons, the Holroyds and the Lyttletons, and with prominent literary figures like Henry James, George Birmingham and Mrs. Humphrey Ward. In the spring of 1914 he spent a series of long week-ends walking in the Lake District and sailing in the Channel, and he attended an 'epidemic' of fashionable weddings—including that of Stephen Tallents, who caused a stir in the Board of Trade by 'bolting' with a rich heiress. In June 1914 after the remarriage of Denman Beveridge decided to set himself up in a house of his own, and he moved to 27 Bedford Gardens—a Georgian 'gentleman's residence', staffed by a cook, a boots and a charlady and leased for eight years at a rental of £80 a year. He resolved to spend his holidays on the continent, first in Sweden to observe an eclipse of the sun and then in Bad Nauheim for further treatment from Dr. Schott.

Throughout this period Beveridge continued to suffer from fits of despondency about the unsatisfying nature of his work and the interminably slow progress of labour organizations. These feelings were not assuaged when in April 1914 John Burns replaced Buxton as President of the Board of Trade. The new President, Beveridge soon discovered, was as suspicious as ever of the labour exchange experiment, dilatory in the transaction of business, and 'not very good at explaining complicated provisions' to the House of Commons.[5] Beveridge himself spent much of June and July briefing the President for the highly technical Unemployment Insurance Amendment Bill—only to see his work frustrated by the concentration of parliamentary time on Ireland and the budget.[6] Not until the session was drawing to a close, however, did it become clear that there was another and more ominous threat to normal peacetime legislation. In the last week of July the Austrian ultimatum to Serbia called into play the network of alliances that had encircled Europe during the previous twenty years. For several days the future of Europe hung in the balance. 'London sights and streets have . . . been very strange', Beveridge recorded:

All day today the crowds there have been thick—standing in the roadway, sitting on the railings opposite the Houses of Parliament, and sitting in tiers on the base of Nelson's column. . . . I myself have been largely concerned with drafting U.I. Regulations and signing official letters. Which is better than

[5] BP, IIa, WHB to ASB, 14 June 1914.    [6] BP, IIa, WHB to ASB, 23 June 1914.

thinking—for of course there's nothing very pleasant to think about in the world just now.[7]

Beveridge did not share the illusion of many of his countrymen that a war, once started, would be a short sharp war with rapid victory for one side or the other. 'One sees no reason', he observed on 3 August, 'why all the nations having started war with no reason (except mutual fear) should ever stop war, till one side has nothing to fear from the other.'[8] Nor did he share the feelings of war euphoria that swept the country at the time. On the evening of 4 August he dined with Denman and Humbert Wolfe at the Union Club in Piccadilly, where they 'watched the mob go roaring and cheering past brandishing flags'. 'I of course, shared the delirium,' recorded Wolfe, 'but Beveridge stood silent, fidgeting with his hands.'[9] And to his mother Beveridge wrote:

I can't of course, like most of us I imagine, help feeling relieved that apparently we are to join in (because it seems necessary and in a sense our duty) but it's all against the grain with me to go in against Germans with French and Russians. I can only hope that if we do go in we shall understand and that the Germans will also understand that there is no rancour in it, and that our readiness will always be for an early peace.[10]

## II

Many historians have commented that the rulers of Britain in 1914 were both intellectually and practically completely unprepared for a total war. The dominant liberal ideology was strongly opposed to any curtailment of individual liberties and to more than a minimum of interference by the state. The armed forces were small, there was no tradition of conscription, there was scarcely any government-sponsored scientific research, and strategy was geared to a naval blockade rather than to a long-drawn-out military struggle. Over the previous thirty years there had been a considerable increase in government intervention in social and economic matters, but this had largely occurred on a piecemeal basis with little sense of a common policy between different government departments.[11] The adaptation of peacetime governmental machinery to the demands of war—and the mental realignment which this entailed—was to produce a revolution in public administration in some ways as drastic and far-reaching as the war itself. 'We have . . . under the stress of war,' commented Beveridge several years later, 'made practical discoveries in the art of government almost comparable

---

[7] BP, IIa, WHB to ASB, 3 Aug. 1914.    [8] Ibid.
[9] Humbert Wolfe, *Portraits by Inference* (1934), pp. 95–6.
[10] BP, IIa, WHB to ASB, 3 Aug. 1914.
[11] Humbert Wolfe, *Labour Supply and Regulation* (1923), pp. 7–12.

to the immense discoveries made at the same time in the art of flying.'[12]

For Beveridge himself the intellectual readjustment required by the war was in some ways less profound than for many of his contemporaries. As we have seen, he had long believed that the interests of the state and community should take priority over the interests of individuals. He believed also in the virtually unlimited capacities of rational bureaucracy. He therefore had few inhibitions about the extension of state power for war purposes—a view which was to bring him into considerable conflict both with organized labour and with his political masters during the course of the war. It was a view also that clearly distinguished him from some of his closest associates, notably Denman and Tawney. Tawney at first decided not to volunteer, and then enlisted as a private; but he continued to view the war with profound misgivings, seeing it as a projection of the endemic conflicts of capitalist civilization.[13] Richard Denman came out as one of the few political critics of the war. Although he enlisted in the Army he strongly favoured a negotiated peace—a view that eventually led to his resignation from the Liberal party and the loss of his parliamentary seat.[14]

From the start there was little doubt about Beveridge's own role in the prosecution of the war. He made 'one or two half-hearted moves towards "joining up" . . . but having regard to my enlarged heart . . . it was so clear that the Army could and would use me only on clerical work, that I thought I might as well stay where I was'.[15] He admitted, however, to feeling 'wildly jealous' of a colleague admitted to the Duke of Cornwall's Light Infantry, and remarked that 'the first thing in my life that has made me feel really old is that I should be past the age and unfit'.[16] His work during the early days of war was mainly concerned with military recruitment, with arranging bankers' advances to dislocated industries, and with preparing relief measures for the widespread unemployment which it was believed the war would entail.[17] Beveridge threw himself into these tasks with characteristic energy—setting up beds for his staff in Whitehall and keeping them at work till midnight for days on end. In private, however, he was much perturbed at the lack of a coherent labour policy and pessimistic about the long-term consequences of the war. In mid-August he had a meeting with the Webbs and discussed with them the problems of co-ordinating labour

[12] W. H. Beveridge, *The Public Service in War and Peace* (1920), p. 5.

[13] BP, IIa, Jeannette Tawney to WHB, 8 Sept. 1914; *R. H. Tawney's Commonplace Book*, pp. 81–3.

[14] BP, IIb, R. Denman to WHB, 21 Oct. 1914; AHBP, Mss. Eur. C. 176/203, R. Denman to WHB, 1 May 1916.

[15] BP, Ic 50, notes for WHB's diary, 29–30 Dec. 1934.

[16] BP, IIa, WHB to ASB, 31 Aug. 1914.      [17] BP, IIa, WHB to ASB, 13 Aug. 1914.

exchanges with the emergency relief committee set up by the L.G.B.[18] A few days later he wrote to Jessy Mair:

I've no news and no brain and no interest in man, woman or the world. I detest my work and see no chance of getting any leave and should hate it, if I got it. All the things I've been working at will be swamped in militarism for the next ten years, and I shall be too busy with them to have any part in any of the new movements for disarmament etc. that may come from this war. Meanwhile the whole Civil Service has gone mad and is governed by two simple rules. (1) That any officer may give any instructions to any other to do anything, provided that (a) the thing to be done is no part of the normal duties of either; (b) the officer instructing is not the official superior of the officer instructed. (2) That anything worth doing by anybody is worth doing six times by six separate persons under the directions of not less than three Cabinet committees.[19]

This frustrating sense of chaos was soon replaced by an even more frustrating sense of calm, and a few weeks later Beveridge was bemoaning the fact that he and his department had too little responsibility. 'We chiefly do odd jobs,' he complained. 'help a little with recruiting; help a little with relief; help with supplies of timber and pit-props; concern ourselves a little with refugees and so on. It would be more satisfactory to have one biggish job.'[20] Throughout 1914, however, the Board took a minor and rather indeterminate role in the management of the war; and the initiative, in labour as in military affairs, lay with the War Office under Lord Kitchener. Beveridge and Llewellyn Smith had several meetings with George Booth, the dynamic Liverpool businessman, at which they discussed 'Labour and supply problems', and concluded that the antiquated War Office machinery was 'entirely incapable of coping with its evident duty'.[21] A Cabinet Committee on Munitions was set up, and the War Office appointed a National Labour Advisory Committee under the chairmanship of Arthur Henderson, to assist with recruitment and deployment of labour. But nothing was done to expand the functions of the Board of Trade, and Beveridge found that official demands on his time were extraordinarily limited. In October 1914 he took a month's leave and underwent a further course of thermal baths at his new home in Bedford Gardens. For much of November and December he was looking after his mother, who was convalescing from a major operation; and during this period his only contribution to the war effort was to draw up a rather premature plan for military demobilization.[22] So remote were the pressures of war that

[18] BP, IIa, WHB to ASB, 17 Aug. 1914.
[19] Lady Beveridge Papers, WHB to J. Mair, 19 Aug. 1914.
[20] BP, IIa, WHB to ASB, 23 Sept. 1914.
[21] Duncan Crow, *A Man of Push and Go. The Life of George Macauley Booth* (1965), pp. 72, 87.
[22] BP, IV, 14, draft scheme for post-war demobilization, late 1914.

he found time to invent a new war game, called 'Naval Tipperary'; and he contemplated a visit to the libraries of Paris and Rouen, to carry out research in seventeenth century economic history.[23]

This period of artificial calm was, however, abruptly terminated early in 1915 by the growing crisis in the market for skilled labour. With the onset of recruitment and war manufacture, the fear of widespread unemployment had rapidly given way to the opposite problem—a nation-wide shortage of labour, and particularly of skilled labour, to man the production of munitions. The shortage was caused, partly by the enormous expansion of armaments production, and partly by indiscriminate recruitment for Kitchener's army, which absorbed nearly 20 per cent of skilled engineering manpower during the first twelve months of war.[24] At the end of 1914 the Board of Trade was asked to assist the War Office in recruiting more labour for government arsenals and on 4 January 1915 Beveridge issued a circular to Labour Exchange Divisional Officers, urging them to persuade private employers to release skilled workers for employment on munitions.[25] At the same time the Board proposed that recruiting should be stopped in vital occupations, and that agreements should be made with trade unions 'whereby the existing supply of labour might be more economically and productively used'.[26]

This policy foundered on a number of obstacles. The War Office refused to give a firm undertaking not to recruit skilled men, and continued in many areas to enlist workmen who were essential for production of munitions.[27] Engineering employers demanded that, instead of releasing men for armaments work, they should themselves be allowed to tender for government contracts; and it was discovered that many of them were already indirectly engaged on armaments work through the widespread practice of sub-contracting.[28] A third obstacle was the attitude of the trade unions, who were extremely reluctant in any way to impair their collective bargaining position—particularly at a time when prices were rapidly rising and manufacturers were making large profits from production for war.[29]

During the early months of 1915 various attempts were made to solve these problems. Beveridge himself organized a nation-wide survey of engineering firms, to discover how many had spare labour capacity and

[23] BP, IIa, WHB to ASB, 28 Oct. 1914.

[24] *History of the Ministry of Munitions* (cited hereafter as *HMM*), I, I, p. 122.

[25] Ibid., p. 129; Bev. Coll. Misc. 144, I, I, circular on 'Supply of Armaments Workers', by WHB, 4 Jan. 1915.

[26] *HMM*, I, II, p. 13.

[27] Ibid., pp. 10–11.

[28] Bev. Coll. Misc. 144, I, ff. 41–6, WHB to Sir George Gibbs, 11 Jan. 1915; *HMM*, I, II, p. 26.

[29] *HMM*, I, II, pp. 37, 55–6, 69.

how many could be adapted for production of armaments.[30] He also arranged a special 'Register of Women for War Service', to release male workers for enlistment and work on munitions.[31] In February Board of Trade conferences were held with shipbuilding and engineering trade unions and employers, to discuss the import of foreign labour, the provision of housing for munitions workers, and the postponement of production on private commercial work.[32] A special Committee on Production was set up under Sir George Askwith, who recommended that restrictive practices should be relaxed and collective bargaining suspended on all government contracts for the duration of the war.[33] Finally, during the latter half of February, Llewellyn Smith and Beveridge drafted an amendment to the Defence of the Realm Act, empowering the government to requisition factories not engaged on war production and to prohibit employment on non-essential work.[34]

The Defence of the Realm Amendment Act was passed early in March. It came too late, however, to avert a serious crisis in munitions production. From the front came continuous complaints of inadequate ammunition supplies; from employers there were numerous reports of lack of discipline among workers; and throughout the country the rising cost of living was causing widespread industrial unrest. It was therefore decided to hold a series of confidential meetings with leading trade unionists, to discuss 'certain matters of importance to labour arising out of the recent decision of the Government . . . to take further steps to organise the resources of the country to meet naval and military requirements'. These meetings, presided over by Lloyd George, Balfour and Walter Runciman, were held at the Treasury on 17–19 March, and were attended by representatives of the engineering, shipbuilding, boiler-makers and pattern-makers unions. Lloyd George, opening the discussion, urged the unions to suspend restrictive practices and stoppages of work in all establishments engaged in production for war. In return he undertook to introduce a new system for settlement of disputes, and to restore trade union privileges after the war.[35] An agreement to this effect was drafted by Beveridge, Llewellyn Smith and Henderson and signed by many of the unions on 19 March.[36] A week later a further conference was held with the Amalgamated Society of Engineers at

[30] Bev. Coll. Misc. 144, I, ff. 137–8, WHB to Major General Von Donop, 26 Jan. 1915.
[31] BP, IIa, WHB to ASB, 17 Mar. 1915.
[32] Bev. Coll. Misc. 144, I, ff. 149–158, 'Agenda of Conference on Armaments and Shipbuilding Labour', by WHB, 12 Feb. 1915.
[33] Ibid., ff. 139–43, paper by G. R. Askwith, 28 Jan. 1915.
[34] *HMM*, I, II, pp. 58–65.
[35] Ibid., pp. 81–4.
[36] Bev. Coll. Misc., 144, I, item 14, ff. 363–4.

which Lloyd George promised to control excess profits in firms producing munitions of war.[37]

The Defence of the Realm Amendment Act and the Treasury agreement of March 1915 involved a series of fundamentally new departures, both in relations between trade unions and the state and in government control over management of the war. To exercise this control two new committees were set up—a War Office 'Armaments Output Committee' under Kitchener, and a Treasury 'Munitions of War Committee' under Lloyd George. The two committees were linked together by Llewellyn Smith's friend George Booth, and both Llewellyn Smith and Beveridge were co-opted on to the Munitions of War Committee in April 1915. Over the next two months the two new committees rapidly took on the functions of an embryonic government department. The Armaments Output Committee started a nation-wide campaign to recruit skilled labour, and workmen who volunteered for munitions employment were enrolled in a special 'industrial corps'.[38] The Munitions of War Committee, which was much the more dynamic of the two committees, set out from the start to push official policy in the direction advocated by the Board of Trade.[39] It encouraged the spread of government contracts, discouraged indiscriminate recruiting, laid plans for new government factories, carried out a survey of 'the actual and prospective state of munitions supplies', and tried to harmonize the numerous competing government bodies that now had a finger in the munitions pie. In the work of the committee Beveridge at first found that he was 'rather on the fringe of the centre of things than at the centre itself'; but he was soon employed in drawing up schemes for release of skilled workmen from the Army and for demarcating the spheres of influence of the War Office and Board of Trade.[40] Two weeks later he recorded that he was 'choked up with work' and able to think of nothing else.

Which perhaps is well [he added], for the war has not been pleasant to think of. For the first time (since the gas and the Lusitania) I began to feel depressed not about our success in the war (I'm determined enough about that) but how any good life will ever be re-established in this world. The German methods make the war so bitter, that it is hard even to see the way to friendliness again. At least I begin to postulate, as a condition of friendliness, an absolute destruction of the German government.[41]

Others beside Beveridge in the early summer of 1915 were depressed about the war, and many were less confident about its ultimate

[37] *HMM*, I, II, pp. 93–4.
[38] On the work of the Armaments Output Committee, see *HMM*, I, III, pp. 43–53.
[39] Ibid., pp. 33–5; PRO, MUN 5/8/172/1, 'Munitions of War Committee; Note on Co-ordination' by H. Llewellyn Smith, 16 Apr. 1915.
[40] BP, IIa, WHB to ASB, 30 Apr. 1915; *HMM*, I, III, pp. 37–8, 92.
[41] BP, IIa, WHB to ASB, 11 May 1915.

conclusion. In Europe the British and French Armies were retreating at Ypres and the Russians were collapsing on the eastern front. On the domestic front the War Office was still flagrantly recruiting skilled engineers, and employers proved reluctant to release skilled workmen for transfer to the factories of their erstwhile commercial rivals. Moreover, it was soon clear that the Treasury agreement was not working successfully and that many union leaders were powerless to enforce the agreement among their rank and file—not perhaps surprisingly, in view of the dilatoriness of the government in fulfilling its promise to limit employers' profits.[42] The failure to improve output and continuous military setbacks precipitated the shell scandal of May 1915, which was largely responsible for forcing the Liberal government to give way to a coalition. In the ensuing carve-up of offices a new department was created—the Ministry of Munitions under the direction of Lloyd George.

## III

The political crisis of May 1915 and the formation of a coalition have been interpreted by historians in various lights. They have been seen as the result of a conspiracy by a pro-Lloyd George faction; as evidence of a deep-seated ideological conflict between traditional liberals and supporters of conscription; and as a mainly pragmatic response to the many intransigent problems that confronted the Asquith government at nearly every political level.[43] Whichever of these views is correct, the creation of a single ministry to direct all aspects of munitions production necessarily reinforced the trend towards more state control. This trend was further strengthened by the personal views of several leading members of the new department. Lloyd George himself had proposed a statutory prohibition on strikes during the drafting of the Defence of the Realm Amendment Act in February 1915, and he frequently implied that he had no theoretical objection to conscription if this should prove necessary for the national safety.[44] Llewellyn Smith in the early days of war had strongly opposed any 'frontal attack' on the unions; but by June 1915 he had become convinced that industrial discipline had broken down and that it was necessary to find a political substitute for the traditional economic constraints.[45] Sir Percy Girouard, who was in charge of the technical side of the new ministry, was strongly in favour of prohibiting strikes, and several other members of the Ministry appear

[42] *HMM*, I, IV, pp. 5–6.
[43] Ibid., pp. 26–7; Cameron Hazlehurst, *Politicians at War, July 1914 to May 1915, A Prologue to the Triumph of Lloyd George* (1971), pp. 232–59.
[44] *HMM*, I, II, pp. 63–4; I, IV, p. 27.
[45] *HMM*, I, II, p. 43; Bev. Coll. Misc. 144, I, 6, ff. 292–4, 'Memorandum on Labour for Armaments', 9–10 June 1915.

to have favoured industrial 'mobilisation'.[46] Beveridge himself had no
objection in principle to state direction of the labour force or to statutory
restriction of free collective bargaining—particularly since he was
coming to believe that the war had given workers a position of economic
dominance unparalleled since the time of the Black Death.[47]

The new ministry, which was set up at the end of May, took over
responsibility for munitions production from the War Office, Admiralty
and Board of Trade. Llewellyn Smith was appointed General Secretary,
and to staff the central department Lloyd George imported a large
contingent of businessmen, headed by Girouard, Eric Geddes and
George Booth. Lloyd George was convinced that production of munitions could best be organized on the lines of big business, but Llewellyn
Smith stipulated that the new organization must contain at least a core
of permanent officials experienced in the principles and procedures of
Whitehall:

> As regards Beveridge I am quite unwilling to dispense with his assistance, and
> in particular I must have his help and advice on labour matters as to which
> he is really the technical 'expert' while Girouard and Booth are amateurs . . .
> He would be the officer I should rely on for all matters relating to the
> Secretariat, and as in this event I should have to be responsible for labour
> myself, I should naturally seek his counsel on a subject which he has made his
> own.
>
> I doubt if either Girouard or Booth has any idea of the pitfalls in any 'new
> labour policy' and personally I am not prepared to face any such develop-
> ment without having by me an experienced adviser whom I trust.[48]

In the event Llewellyn Smith, Beveridge, Rey, Wolfe and Adams
were all transferred to the Ministry of Munitions—Beveridge taking
charge of 'general office organisation' and the supply and regulation of
labour.[49] Llewellyn Smith, Beveridge and Rey all held their new posts
jointly with their old positions in the Board of Trade, thus ensuring a
high degree of continuity between the policies of the two departments.
A plan for the administrative structure of the new ministry was drawn
up by Beveridge on 28 May; and in it he emphasized the need for the
closest possible relationship between local munition officials and the
Labour Exchanges department of the Board of Trade.[50]

[46] Lloyd George Papers, D1/2/3, H. Llewellyn Smith to D. Lloyd George, 31 May 1915;
D3/3/12, Leonard Llewellyn to Sir Percy Gironard, 24 July 1915; C. F. Rey, unpublished
memoirs, pp. 109–131.
[47] W. H. Beveridge, 'The Scale of Life Needed for a Standard Budget', *Pall Mall Gazette*,
16 Sept. 1919.
[48] Lloyd George Papers, D1/2/3, H. Llewellyn Smith to D. Lloyd George, 31 May 1915.
[49] BP, IIa, WHB to ASB, 30 May 1915.
[50] PRO, MUN 5/10/200/14, Notes by Mr. Beveridge relating to the formation of the
Ministry of Munitions, 28 May 1915.

Nevertheless, Beveridge's chief work for the Ministry of Munitions was less concerned with labour exchanges than with promoting the more economical use of the labour force and with the discovery and utilization of new sources of labour. From the start officials of the new ministry were involved in preparing legislation to enforce the principles embodied in the voluntary Treasury agreement of three months before. Llewellyn Smith advised Lloyd George that 'any further attempt on merely voluntary lines unsupported by legislative enactment will only break down and lose valuable time';[51] and on 1 June Beveridge drafted proposals for legislation which would give the Ministry powers over industrial labour comparable with those exercised by the War Office over the armed forces. These included 'compulsory arbitration and prohibition of strikes', 'prohibition of restrictions on output and employment', and 'mobilisation of all armament and shipbuilding works' engaged in war production. In all such works a 'military commandant' would be placed in charge, 'certain provisions of military law' would be applied, and workmen would be 'compulsorily enrolled' and issued with uniforms and medals for good service. In addition Beveridge suggested that 'all or most munitions workers' should be mobilized into a corps of King's Munitions Workers, who would be prepared to work wherever they were sent and to accept a system of quasi-military discipline.[52]

These proposals formed the core of the Munitions of War Bill, which was drafted by Beveridge and Llewellyn Smith in a series of week-end sessions at Llewellyn Smith's home in Ashtead during June 1915. The bill was introduced ostensibly to further 'the efficient manufacture, transport and supply of munitions'; but, as the official history of the ministry made clear, its widely-understood real purpose was to limit collective bargaining, and to extend 'Government control over the workman's normal freedom . . . as far as the exigencies of war production demanded and the state of feeling in the Labour world would allow'.[53] After negotiations with the unions some of the more coercive elements in the bill were modified; the plan for compulsory 'mobilisation' was dropped, and 'every feature suggestive of compulsion or of military organisation and authority' was abandoned.[54] Nevertheless, the Act as passed on 1 July imposed compulsory arbitration and prohibited strikes and lock-outs in all factories engaged in production that was 'required for a satisfactory completion of the war'. The Minister of Munitions was empowered to declare all such factories 'controlled

---

[51] Bev. Coll. Misc. 144, I, 15, f. 365, 'Labour Policy—Preliminary Note', by H. Llewellyn Smith, May–June 1915.

[52] PRO, MUN 5/49/300/38, 'Labour Policy. Suggestions by Mr. Beveridge, with draft of Defence of the Realm Amendment Bill', 1 June 1915; BP, IV, 1, Notes by WHB on 'Munitions of War Act', n.d.

[53] *HMM*, I, IV, p. 1.          [54] Ibid., pp. 36–7.

establishments'—in which case excess profits would be paid to the Exchequer, restrictive practices suspended and workers forbidden to leave their jobs without a certificate to prove their employer's consent. Finally, the Act established a War Munitions Volunteer scheme to recruit additional labour from private employment. This scheme was merely a pale shadow of the one initially proposed by Beveridge, since it was to cover only a small minority of the munitions labour force and enlistment was limited to a period of six months. Workers who volunteered for the scheme would agree to work away from home and to accept direction from 'commandants wielding disciplinary powers'. In return they would receive badges, to show that they were working on essential war service, and when employed away from home they would be entitled, in addition to normal wages, to a government-financed subsistence allowance of 17s. 6d. a week.[55]

Although it passed through Parliament with scarcely a protest, the Munitions of War Act created a furore throughout the industrial world. Among trade unionists generally the Act was seen as a challenge to collective bargaining and to the right of the worker to seek the highest price for his labour. To the craft unions in particular it presented a threat to the intricate network of customary rules—governing demarcation of skills, control of apprenticeship and restriction of overtime—by which they had built up their privileged position in the labour market over a long period of years. To anti-conscriptionists the Munitions of War Volunteers Scheme seemed the thin end of the wedge of industrial conscription; and to many liberally-minded people the Act seemed to embody a dangerous and unnecessary degree of government control. To Lloyd George and his subordinates on the other hand the Act was a prerequisite of raising industrial output to the level required by a total war. Lloyd George in public speeches repeatedly affirmed that it was the only alternative to thorough-going industrial conscription, of the kind imposed since the start of the war by many of Britain's allies.[56] To Beveridge himself the Act appeared not merely practically expedient but fundamentally consistent with his basic political beliefs. 'What I have always said', he recorded eighteen months later,

. . . was that I stood for the impartial state. In peacetime the employers were generally top dog and so my business was chiefly to prevent the employer from exploiting his advantage unduly. In wartime the workman is top dog, and therefore my business (for the State) is to prevent the workman from exploiting his advantage unduly.[57]

In this respect Beveridge clearly distinguished himself from many progressive Liberals—most of whom looked with apprehension on the Act's

[55] Ibid., pp. 55–65.    [56] *HMM*, I, IV, p. 27; II, I, pp. 7–9.
[57] BP, IIa, WHB to ASB, 1 Feb. 1917.

curtailment of personal liberties and the substantial accretion of the wartime powers of the state.[58]

Throughout the summer of 1915 Beveridge was working on the recruitment of munitions volunteers, on scheduling factories as 'controlled establishments' and on securing the release of skilled workmen from the forces. In two reports compiled early in September he was cautiously optimistic about the impact of the Munitions of War Act, claiming that 100,000 volunteers had been enrolled, that a start had been made in curtailing restrictive practices, that many disputes had been settled by tribunals and that in many cases 'it has been found that the mere declaration of an establishment as controlled has often produced an excellent effect on the output and feeling of the men'. There were, nevertheless, some areas of conspicuous failure. Pressure on the War Office for 'release of skilled men from the colours' had produced only 5,500 men, and of the 100,000 volunteers it was soon found that the majority were already engaged on work of national importance and that only about 5,000 were in fact available for transfer to munitions. Beveridge therefore concluded that further measures were necessary. He estimated that the munitions industry had a shortage of 280,000 workers; and he argued strongly that the shortage could only be met by measures of 'dilution'—by upgrading semi-skilled workmen and the widespread substitution of women for men. To secure these ends he proposed that munitions recruitment should be greatly 'decentralised', so as to make more use of the machinery of labour exchanges. He suggested that enlistment as a munitions volunteer should be made 'a legally enforceable undertaking', and he urged that 'some form of compulsion' in the transference of skilled labour was 'probably essential'.[59]

Beveridge's suggestions were 'generally approved at a meeting of Departmental Officers' on 3 September.[60] Outside the Ministry, however, they caused a great deal of alarm and unease. Many trade unionists were suspicious that dilution would be used to undermine skilled wage-rates, and that the government would neglect its promise to restore trade union privileges after the war. It was feared, moreover, that the intrusion of semi-skilled workers and the consequent acceleration of mass-production would set in train certain long-term technological developments that no well-meaning post-war legislation would be able to reverse. To this extent the war was merely an episode, though

[58] P. F. Clarke, 'The Progressive Movement in England', *Transactions of the Royal Historical Society*, 5s., 24, 1974, p. 177.

[59] PRO, MUN 5/57/320/34, 'Heads of Proposed Scheme. The supply of Skilled Labour', by WHB, 3 Sept. 1915; Lloyd George Papers, D1/3/8, 'Review of the Work of the Secretariat in Regard to Labour', by WHB, 13 Sept. 1915.

[60] PRO, MUN 5/57/320/34, ms. note by WHB, 3 Sept. 1915.

doubtless an important episode, in the skilled workman's prolonged struggle against the erosion of status differentials and displacement by the machine.

An attempt was made to deal with these fears in Lloyd George's speech to the T.U.C. on 9 September—a speech that had been prepared by Beveridge, though it seems unlikely that the minister adhered very closely to his original brief.[61] Speaking at the T.U.C.'s annual conference, Lloyd George claimed that the government was making a series of revolutionary innovations in restriction of profits and control of the national economy. He chided the unions for not pulling their weight in this process, cited many examples of continuing restrictive practices and urged trade unionists to feel a greater sense of solidarity with soldiers at the front. In return he promised that in no case should dilution be allowed to depress the standard rate, and he re-affirmed the government's promise to restore collective bargaining after the war. The speech met with a mixed but largely sympathetic reception, and the T.U.C. agreed to discuss dilution with Lloyd George and his advisers at a conference held the following week. At this conference Arthur Henderson urged Lloyd George not to alienate the union movement by further measures of compulsion; and it was agreed to set up a Central Committee of officials, businessmen and trade unionists, 'to secure the most productive use of all available labour supplies in the manufacture of Munitions of War'. This committee pledged itself to enforce the Treasury agreement, to promote industrial reorganization and to enter into negotiation with local shop stewards and the industrial rank and file.[62]

The Central Munitions Labour Supply Committee, under the chairmanship of Henderson, began work on 22 September—the ministry being represented by Beveridge and Rey. The Committee drew up a model scheme to advise employers on the process of dilution, and it drafted a questionnaire to manufacturers asking them to indicate how much skilled labour they had available for transfer and what degree of dilution was practically feasible.[63] The Committee also appointed two sub-committees, to deal with wages of female workers and the encouragement of dilution at local level. The women's wages committee drew up a scale whereby all female munitions workers would be paid a minimum of £1 a week and all women doing the work of skilled craftsmen would be paid the full standard rate. Beveridge regarded this provision with a certain amount of suspicion, fearing that it had been designed by union representatives 'rather to keep women out than to bring them in';[64]

[61] *PI*, p. 130.     [62] *HMM*, IV, I, pp. 37–42, 45–50.
[63] BP, IV 4, memorandum on 'Report of Munitions Labour Supply Committee', probably by WHB, n.d.
[64] Bev. Coll. Misc. 144, III, 10, ff. 63–4, WHB to G. R. Askwith, 4 Oct. 1915.

but in an interview with the Amalgamated Society of Engineers on 27 October he agreed that the government should not enforce dilution in any firm until the employer had agreed to pay women at the prescribed minimum and standard rates.[65] The second sub-committee, which was presided over by Beveridge himself, tried to establish a network of local Labour Advisory Boards in all major industrial centres. These Boards, composed entirely of trades unionists, were empowered to investigate workers' complaints, to report on employers who refused dilution, to record changes in workshop practice, to conciliate disputes and generally to promote co-operation between local munitions officials and workers on the shop floor.[66]

The Central Committee's directives were issued to employers in a series of ministerial circulars in October 1915. Beveridge, however, was convinced that circulars were not enough and insisted that they should be followed up by an 'organised series of visits' from departmental officials.[67] At the same time he tried to rationalize certain aspects of the labour supply, by urging employers to make estimates of their future labour requirements and by promoting special training-classes for potential munitions volunteers. Early in December he reported to Lloyd George that many aspects of the Munitions of War Act were working well—that industrial discipline had markedly improved, that workers generally had welcomed the setting-up of controlled establishments and that compulsory arbitration had been 'eminently successful'. He concluded, however, that this catalogue of success did not include the lifting of restrictive practices and the progress of dilution. 'There is a good deal of conservatism', he recorded, 'both on the part of employers and on the part of work people . . . the result is that, generally speaking, while suspension of restrictions and dilution of labour is undoubtedly taking place to some extent, it is taking place too slowly for the necessities of the situation.'[68]

## IV

The enforcement of the government's dilution policy involved a great deal of controversy and conflict both inside and outside the Ministry of Munitions. Beveridge himself had long believed that law without sanc-

---

[65] BP, IV 4, Central Munitions Labour Supply Committee, minutes of conference A.S.E. executive, 27 Oct. 1915.

[66] Bev. Coll. Misc. 144, IV, 9, ff. 54–5, Constitution and Functions of Local Labour Advisory Boards, 28 Sept. 1915.

[67] Bev. Coll. Misc. 144, III, item 19, ff. 128–30 'Report on Progress with Regard to Labour Supply', by WHB, n.d. (4–11 Oct. 1915); item 25, f. 166 J. Mair to Mr. Carter, 27 Oct. 1915.

[68] Bev. Coll. Misc. 144, II, item 8, ff. 71–148, draft and final versions of 'Report of the Labour Department', by WHB, 2 Dec. 1915.

tions was pointless; and he was greatly concerned, once the Defence of the Realm and Munition of War Acts had been passed, that their provisions should be effectively enforced. This view appears to have been shared by other Ministry officials, particularly Llewellyn Smith and C. F. Rey; but it was not fully endorsed by Lloyd George, whose approach to the process of implementing these Acts was in many ways highly ambivalent. Lloyd George, as we have seen, had been one of the first to advocate statutory curtailment of the unions' powers, and in private he constantly berated his officials for not applying the Munitions of War Act effectively and for not prosecuting enough 'test cases' to bring the industrial world to heel.[69] At the same time, however, he tended to treat the Act in public as part of an ongoing process of bargaining rather than as an established law. In August 1916 under pressure from the mining unions he had allowed the coal industry to contract out of the Munitions of War Act—a decision that was 'bitterly criticized by his department which alleged that he had conceded more (to the miners) than ever they had asked'.[70] In treating the Act in this flexible way Lloyd George's political instincts were probably correct, but to his permanent officials it seemed that the minister was evading responsibility for his own unpopular policies. It meant also that within the Ministry there was continual uncertainty about how far and with what severity the prohibition of strikes and pressure for dilution were to be practically enforced. In dealing with this uncertainty Lloyd George often seemed to his officials devious and unreliable, while they in turn seemed to the minister politically unimaginative, stiff-necked and doctrinaire.

These differences of emphasis became increasingly apparent in the autumn of 1915, when Lloyd George was under continual pressure from the unions to amend the Munitions of War Act—in particular the 'leaving-certificate' clause, which in certain cases had been used by unscrupulous employers to dismiss workmen without a character. Beveridge himself was convinced that the grievances stemming from this clause had been grossly exaggerated and he recommended that, if any change was made, it should simply involve the transfer of control over leaving-certificates from employers to public officials.[71] Nevertheless, the clause constituted a major stumbling-block in relations between government and unions throughout the latter half of 1915, and at the end of November Lloyd George agreed with the A.S.E. that the clause should be substantially modified—a decision which Beveridge believed would

[69] Lloyd George Papers D/3/2/7, D. Lloyd George to H. Llewellyn Smith, 24 Sept. 1916; D3/2/49, D. Lloyd George to W. Layton, 22 Feb. 1916.

[70] Lady Beveridge Papers, ms. on 'Whitehall in Wartime', by J. Mair, n.d.

[71] PRO, MUN 5/49/300/23, 'Report of the Labour Department with General Secretary's Minute', 2 Dec. 1915.

seriously hamper labour reorganization and positively encourage further 'unreasonable' demands. The Minister also agreed to repeal the section of the Act which made strikers liable to imprisonment; and both these measures were included in the Munitions of War Amendment Bill in December 1915. Beveridge observed somewhat tartly that, in promoting the Amendment Bill, 'the Minister had stuck to his principles . . . as he said, the Bill consisted wholly of concessions'.[72]

Beveridge's criticisms of the failure to enforce the Act were made clear in his report on the Labour department in December 1915. In this report he strongly defended leaving-certificates and claimed that, in the few cases where strikers had been prosecuted, this had 'had a very steadying effect not merely with respect to the men actually in fault but with respect to discipline in the shops generally'. He emphasized that the level of dilution was still totally inadequate, and was non-committal about the prospects for future policy.[73] This paper drew upon Beveridge the wrath of Lloyd George, who complained that 'the Labour Paper [is] the most disappointing of all the Reports that have come in' and that it supplied him with 'neither figures nor facts to demonstrate to the House of Commons whether the Act has been a success or failure'. 'I shall have to say', he stormed angrily,

that we created a separate Department, brought together a considerable staff, borrowed experienced men from the Board of Trade to advise and direct it . . . and that after six months all we had to show for it was a colossal failure called the 'Munitions Volunteers' . . . Is there no man who will take the trouble to sit down to give me a complete and comprehensive account of what the Department has done, is doing and proposes to do in this most vital aspect of our work?[74]

In fact Beveridge's reports were by far the most comprehensive of all the reports submitted to the Minister by the various departmental heads, and they were accompanied whenever possible by a mass of statistical data. Lloyd George's complaints were so manifestly unjustified that it seems reasonable to infer that what he was really objecting to was not quality of Beveridge's reports but their substantive content—which contained many implied criticisms of Lloyd George's policy of concessions. Beveridge was indeed increasingly convinced that dilution was being steadily undermined, not by failures of administration, but by the Minister's compliance with external political pressures. This belief was all the more galling because Lloyd George in private continued to chide

---

[72] *PI*, p. 132; *HMM*, IV, II, ch. 3.

[73] PRO, MUN 5/49/300/23, 'Report of the Labour Department, with General Secretary's Minute', 2 Dec. 1915.

[74] Lloyd George Papers, D/3/2/23, D. Lloyd George to W. Layton, 29 Dec. 1915.

his officials for the 'insignificant and unsatisfactory' pace of dilution, and to urge upon them the need for exemplary prosecutions and a more energetic enforcement of the law.[75] This curious relationship between Minister and officials—in which each blamed the other for weakness in law-enforcement—is of singular importance in explaining the erratic mixture of concession and coercion that characterized government policy on dilution during the winter months of 1915–16. Nowhere was this more evident that in the Ministry of Munitions' dealings on the Clyde. The Clyde episode will be considered in some detail, partly because it was of central importance in the history of dilution and partly because of the continuing controversy that sixty years later still surrounds the part played by Beveridge himself.

The resistance to dilution on Clydeside involved the Ministry in a series of prosecutions under the Munitions of War and Defence of the Realm Acts; in protracted negotiations with officials of the A.S.E.; in the suppression of three Glasgow newspapers, the *Forward*, the *Vanguard* and the *Worker*: in the dispatch of special commissioners to expedite dilution; and finally in the deportation from Glasgow of a group of socialist workmen who had been prominent in the anti-dilution struggle, known as the Clyde Workers Committee. The role of Beveridge and other officials in enforcement of dilution was first drawn to public attention by the youthful Ernest Bevin at the annual conference of the T.U.C. in 1916. Behind the Minister, declared Bevin, was a 'sinister crowd in the Civil Service who are preparing documents to be used against us . . . I refer to the chief officials of the Labour Exchanges'.[76] This was not the first time that Beveridge had been denounced at a meeting of the T.U.C.; but the events of 1915–16 seem to have been largely responsible for a certain latent hostility between Beveridge and the union movement that lasted for the next twenty-five years. More recently, the role of Beveridge and other officials has been scrutinized by several historians, whose conclusions leave both the events that occurred and the underlying motives of the Ministry still a matter of dispute. In an essay published in 1971 Dr. James Hinton focused attention on the break-up of the Clyde Workers' Committee, and argued that the suppression of the C.W.C. was 'the result of a well-planned offensive directed by the Labour Department of the Ministry of Munitions . . . an offensive remarkable for its clarity of aims, its flexibility, its ruthlessness, and for the careful planning of its means'. The purpose of this offensive was the 'progressive isolation of this militant vanguard in the munitions factories' from the rest of the rank and file. Hinton claimed, moreover,

[75] Lloyd George Papers D/3/2/49, D. Lloyd George to W. Layton, 22 Feb. 1916 (copies to Addison, Llewellyn Smith and Beveridge).
[76] *Report of the Annual Conference of the T.U.C.* (1916), p. 189.

that the existence of this plot had lain concealed 'for more than fifty years' and that 'the clearest evidence of the government's repressive intent is in the Beveridge Papers, a fact which leads one to speculate that Beveridge himself was the original censor'.[77] A similar emphasis has been placed on the role of the C.W.C. by Terence Brotherstone, who concludes that the Ministry's suppression of the non-revolutionary socialist-pacifist *Forward* was merely a smoke-screen 'to divert attention from the serious business in hand, the defeat of the Clyde Workers Committee'.[78] The findings of both Hinton and Brotherstone have, however, been challenged by Dr. Iain McLean, who argues that there was no 'plot' against the C.W.C., who were in any case peripheral to the main dilution struggle. Officials of the Ministry, McLean maintains, were far more concerned with the mainstream of opposition to dilution expressed by the A.S.E. executive than with a small and unrepresentative group of revolutionary socialists. He claims, moreover, that far from being suppressed, the facts of the Clyde episode have been publicly available in the Ministry of Munitions official history for the past fifty years.[79]

This controversy may be distilled into three main questions. Firstly, was the evidence relating to Ministry of Munitions policy on the Clyde officially censored, and was Beveridge himself involved in the censoring? Secondly, did munitions officials see the revolutionary-syndicalist C.W.C. or the labour-aristocratic A.S.E. as their real opponents in the dilution struggle? And thirdly, did Beveridge and other officials engage in a 'plot' to suppress the Clyde Workers' Committee?

Firstly, the alleged suppression of the facts. This is the aspect of the dispute that can most easily be dealt with, since it lends itself most clearly to the weighing of conventional historical evidence. Is Dr. Hinton correct in referring to 'the success with which the government covered its tracks' in its dealings on the Clyde?[80] Hinton rests his case for departmental concealment on the fact that Beveridge preserved his own collection of munitions papers separately from the official archives; and certainly it is true that Beveridge, like many other politicians and administrators, kept in his possession papers which ought legally to have been deposited among the public records. But that he did this to 'cover his tracks' either from critical contemporaries or from the judgement of

[77] James Hinton, 'The Clyde Workers' Committee and the Dilution Struggle', *Essays in Labour History 1886–1923* ed. Asa Briggs and John Savile (1971), esp. pp. 153, 158, 177n., 184.

[78] Terence Brotherstone, 'The Suppression of the "Forward"', *The Journal of the Scottish Labour History Society*, no. 1 (May 1969), p. 18.

[79] Iain McLean, 'The Ministry of Munitions, the Clyde Workers' Committee, and the Suppression of the "Forward", an Alternative View', *The Journal of the Scottish Labour History Society*, no 6 (Dec. 1972), pp. 3–25.

[80] Hinton, loc. cit., p. 177.

history seems highly implausible for two reasons. Firstly, Beveridge himself deposited his munitions papers in the British Library of Political Science, where they have been available to historians since 1941—twenty-seven years before the opening of munitions archives in the Public Record Office. Secondly, on several occasions Beveridge had ample opportunity to delete from the official history all mention of his department's policies on the Clyde, but on none of these occasions does he appear to have done so—in fact, rather the reverse. On the first occasion in 1916 he drafted a skeleton outline of the Ministry's activities up to that date, for the guidance of the official historians. In this outline he specifically drew attention to the 'Clyde agitation', the 'Scottish prosecutions', the C.W.C. deportations and the work of the dilution commissioners as important historical events.[81] A few months later he was appointed to a departmental committee set up to advise the official historians; but there is no evidence to suggest that he interfered with the writing of the history in any way—except in so far as he allowed himself to be interviewed for his 'oral reminiscences'.[82] Finally in 1919 the completed draft of the history was submitted for comment to both Beveridge and Llewellyn Smith. Neither of them appears to have made any criticisms or substantive alterations.[83]

The suggestion that Beveridge deliberately concealed his department's involvement with the Clyde Workers Committee therefore seems ill-founded. Indeed it greatly exaggerates both the importance which he attached to the episode and his awareness of the possibly contentious nature of his own actions. As shown in earlier chapters, it is certainly arguable that Beveridge had an inflated vision of the virtues of state control and that he was basically unsympathetic to the aspirations of organized labour; but to imply that he would have tried to conceal these attitudes is entirely to misread his character and philosophy. He was absolutely—and often tactlessly—frank about his own political opinions at this and every other stage in his public career; and he would not have concealed his policies on the Clyde, because he would never have conceived that it was either necessary or desirable to do so.

The other two points at issue—whether the C.W.C. or the A.S.E. executive were the main opponents of dilution, and whether there was a 'plot' to suppress the C.W.C.—require an analysis of munitions policy from the first anti-dilution strikes in August 1915 through to the deportation of the C.W.C. leaders in the following spring. The workers involved in the Clyde controversy were mainly engaged in heavy engineering and

---

[81] PRO, MUN 3/37/263.2/1, 'Records of the Ministry', by WHB, n.d.
[82] BP, IV 2, Ministry of Munitions, Mr. Beveridge's reminiscences etc.
[83] PRO, MUN 5/4/6/1, History of Ministry of Munitions, Editorial Advisory Committee, Minutes of Meetings, p. 151.

their most important union was the Amalgamated Society of Engineers, one of the most powerful of the old craft unions. The A.S.E. executive had been closely consulted on the drafting of the Munitions of War Act, and they were strongly represented on the Central Munitions Labour Supply Committee. Nevertheless, the A.S.E. had for many years past been involved in a struggle to prevent the devaluation of their craft privileges; and throughout the autumn and winter of 1915 the A.S.E. leaders were in continuous negotiation with Lloyd George to modify the Munitions of War Act and to safeguard their members' interests against dilution.[84] This pressure on the Minister was in many respects successful; but in course of negotiations with the government, the A.S.E. leaders lost the confidence of many of their rank and file. On Clydeside, and to a lesser degree in other heavy industrial areas, the initiative in local union policy passed out of the hands of union officials and into the hands of shop stewards, many of whom denounced the Act as an instrument of industrial slavery.[85] Workers on the Clyde refused to establish local Labour Advisory Boards to implement the policies of the Central Munitions Labour Supply Committee. The result was a struggle against dilution on two distinct levels—one waged by the official A.S.E. executive, the other by local shop stewards and workers on the shop floor.

The first Clydeside anti-dilution strike, against the employment of female labour, occurred at the factory of Lang and Johnstone in August 1915. A second and more serious strike—against abuse of leaving certificates by employers—broke out at Fairfields' shipyard in the following month. The strike-leaders were fined by local munitions tribunals, and three who refused to pay their fines were imprisoned—an action which spread the strike to other Glasgow yards.[86] Local officials appealed to the minister to intervene, and it was from this point that a clear breach became apparent in the views of Beveridge and Lloyd George. Beveridge conceded that the strikers had a legitimate grievance; but he took the view that the Munitions of War Act did not merely prohibit 'unjust strikes', it forbade all strikes whatsoever. Lloyd George, however, took a different view. He made stern speeches about the need for repression and then dispatched to the Clyde a Commission of inquiry under Lord Balfour of Burleigh. This commission persuaded local union officials to pay the prisoners' fines, and then recommended that the A.S.E.'s demands should be met—that leaving-certificates should be modified and imprisonment for strikers abolished.[87] These recommendations, as we have seen, were embodied in the Munitions of War Amendment Bill in December 1915. To Beveridge and other ministry officials these con-

[84] *HMM*, IV, I, ch. 4.
[85] James Hinton, *The First Shop Stewards Movement* (1973), esp. chs. 3–6.
[86] *HMM*, IV, II, pp. 50–6.     [87] *HMM*, IV, pp. 64–5.

cessions seemed fatal to the drive for an increase of output on Clydeside, particularly when it was learnt that the government's conciliation of the unions was being used as an excuse for abandonment of dilution among Clydeside employers. 'The action taken . . . by the Government . . . has been interpreted as concessions wrung by force from weakness', commented Beveridge bitterly,

and the same interpretation will undoubtedly be placed upon many of the concessions of the Munitions of War (Amendment) Act. . . . It seems problematical whether any of the necessary dilution of labour on the Clyde will be obtained by agreement, and postponement of dilution will again be interpreted as weakness on the part of the Government.[88]

Beveridge's belief that the government had capitulated to the unions was not, however, shared by many workers on the shop floor; and the Clyde Workers Committee was set up in October 1915, to protest at the conciliatory policies pursued by the A.S.E. The Committee's best-known members were its Chairman, Willie Gallagher of the British Socialist Party; John Maclean, the Glasgow teacher and revolutionary theorist; and David Kirkwood, the Parkhead shop steward and a leading member of the Glasgow I.L.P. Within the Committee there was little discernible ideological unity; some were committed pacifists, some were mainly concerned with protecting craft unions, whilst others were aiming at the breakdown of craft barriers and the creation of a common revolutionary front. The members were united, however, by a common rejection of the Munitions of War Act and of the readiness to negotiate shown by the official A.S.E. The policy which they advocated was not outright opposition to dilution, but dilution within a context of workers' control.[89]

The attention of the government was first drawn to the Committee in November 1915 when Gallagher published a pamphlet denouncing the Munitions of War Act as 'an act of treachery to the working class'. A Glasgow employer referred the pamphlet to the Admiralty, which passed it on to the Ministry of Munitions. 'I am inclined to think,' commented Beveridge, 'that this Clyde Workers' Committee could [perfectly well] be prosecuted under the Defence of the Realm Regulations, and that it would be worthwhile doing so. Shall we refer it to the Scottish Law Officers for their advice?'[90] The question was submitted to the Lord Advocate and the Scottish Solicitor-General early in December. The Solicitor-General advised that the pamphlet constituted a criminal offence, and that the authors should be prosecuted; but the Lord Advocate, although agreeing that the pamphlet was technically in

[88] PRO, MUN 5/70/24/18, 'Suppression of the "Forward"', by WHB, 6 Jan. 1916.
[89] Hinton, loc. cit., pp. 167–8.
[90] Bev. Coll. Misc. 144, III, item 15, f. 102, WHB to H. Llewellyn Smith, 30 Nov. 1915.

breach of the law, was doubtful about obtaining a conviction since the pamphlet did not actually threaten a strike. Beveridge, Wolfe and Llewellyn Smith appear to have been anxious for a prosecution; but early in January Christopher Addison, the Ministry's parliamentary secretary, advised Lloyd George against further action—in view of 'the very qualified' opinion of the Lord Advocate, the forthcoming amendment of the Munitions of War Act, and the 'lapse of time' since the alleged offence.[91]

Labour department officials were nevertheless increasingly convinced that 'definite and strong measures' would have to be taken to enforce dilution—although they appear to have been in doubt about what such measures should involve.[92] As Beveridge himself pointed out, it would be manifestly impossible to imprison the entire labour force if the whole of the Clyde went on strike.[93] On 18 December, however, Lynden Macassey—a member of the Balfour Commission—reported to the Ministry that hostility to dilution was not universal on Clydeside, but was being artificially fomented by a small group of men. Macassey had himself once served an apprenticeship on Clydeside and was acquainted with some of the engineering workers. He claimed that many workmen 'came to see me personally and unburdened their souls' about the troubles on the Clyde; and he concluded that 'the present state of mind is not the spontaneous product of the workmen's own cogitation . . . It was first created by two or three local Trade Union officials who deliberately and for their own purposes, circulated, only too effectively, untrue statements as to the origin of the Act and garbled and misleading versions of its effect'. It was this small group of agitators, Macassey argued, who were causing disaffection among Glasgow workmen— 'workmen who judged by conventional standards are honest, industrious operatives, are elders in the Kirk, and have their boys fighting at the Front'. Macassey did not recommend prosecution of the trouble-makers, partly because it would turn them into martyrs, and partly because none of his informants dared to give evidence in court. He did suggest, however, that the leaders of the agitation should be dispatched 'to some official post remote from Clydeside, where their activities, which are immense, could be controlled and diverted to the useful services of the community'.[94]

Macassey's memorandum did not refer to the Clyde Workers' Com-

[91] Ibid., ff. 104–7.
[92] PRO, MUN 5/73/324/15/2, 'Material Supplied to Mr. Lloyd George before his visit to the Clyde and Tyne', Dec. 1915.
[93] PRO, MUN 5/70/24/18, 'Suppression of the "Forward"', by WHB, 6 Jan. 1916.
[94] PRO, MUN 5/73/324/15/2, Memorandum on 'Certain Causes of Unrest among Munition Workers on Clyde and Tyneside which are Peculiar to those Districts', by Lynden Macassey, 18 Dec. 1915.

mittee by name, but almost certainly they were the group to whom he was referring; and this memorandum helps to account for the eagerness of the Labour department to proceed with prosecution of the C.W.C. It must, however, be seen in the context of the general failure of the dilution campaign in December 1915 and January 1916—a campaign which according to the Prime Minister fell 'lamentably short of the national requirements'.[95] On 31 December Lloyd George and Asquith had a further meeting with the leaders of the A.S.E. The A.S.E. reiterated their promise to promote dilution in return for protection of their standard rate, but Lloyd George rather bitterly prophesied that this promise would be broken like all their previous pledges.[96] Lloyd George's bitterness was probably linked with his experiences in Glasgow a few days before, when he had appealed to Clydeside workers to sink their grievances for the sake of the national emergency. In a speech to three thousand workers on Christmas Day he had evoked the threat of the triumph of German despotism, but his speech had been punctuated by continuous hostile or derisive interruptions and the meeting eventually 'broke-up in disorder'.[97] Lloyd George's meeting had been officially closed to the press, but a few days later an unauthorized report—emphasizing the hostile reception of the speech—was published by the Glasgow *Forward*, an independent newspaper linked with the I.L.P. Lloyd George discussed the matter with Addison, Llewellyn Smith and Beveridge on 31 December—with the result that the *Forward* was suppressed under the Defence of the Realm Regulations on 3 January 1916. On the presses of the *Forward* the authorities discovered proofs of a more 'rabid' paper, the *Vanguard*, and this was suppressed at the same time.[98]

What was the significance of this incident in the campaign to enforce dilution? As the official history pointed out, the *Forward* was a moderate socialist newspaper with pacifist leanings; it was critical of the war, but in no sense treasonable or revolutionary, and since the outbreak of war it had preserved a policy of strict impartiality in trade disputes.[99] Beveridge himself recorded that Lloyd George justified his action to Parliament mainly by linking the *Forward* with the much more militant *Vanguard*.[100] Why then was the *Forward* suppressed? The official history ascribed the incident to a tactical error of judgement. But Brotherstone has suggested that 'such an irrelevant mistake' on so explosive an issue was inherently unlikely; and he concludes that the seizure of the *Forward*

[95] Bev. Coll. Misc. 144, II, item 17, f. 223.

[96] PRO, MUN 5/73/324/15/8, Extract from Minutes of Proceedings at a Deputation of the A.S.E. to the Prime Minister and The Minister of Munitions, 31 Dec. 1915.

[97] *HMM*, IV, IV, p. 109.

[98] PRO, MUN, 5/70/24/18, 'Notes on the Suppression of the "Forward"', and 'Particulars of the "Vanguard"', by WHB, n.d.

[99] *HMM*, IV, IV, pp. 113–14.  [100] *PI*, p. 133.

was merely a foil for the government's real objective, which was suppression of the C.W.C. 'Llewellyn Smith and Beveridge,' Brotherstone comments, '. . . were both acute and intelligent men, and highly successful administrators. They must have known that the *Forward* was nowhere near the root of the trouble on the Clyde.'[101]

This interpretation gains some credence from Beveridge's declared willingness to take legal action against the C.W.C. It is supported also by the fact that in his brief on the *Forward* Beveridge referred to the C.W.C. as 'the heart of this agitation', and remarked that 'as regards the general position on the Clyde, it is abundantly clear that there is a relatively small but vigorous body organising revolt both against the Munitions of War Act and against official Trade Union leaders, and, further, that this has been gathering strength for some time'.[102] Nevertheless, Brotherstone's view is open to question on a number of grounds. Firstly it is not at all clear by what process of reasoning munitions officials could conceivably have concluded that repression of a moderate, constitutional-socialist newspaper would be more politically palatable than repression of the revolutionary-syndicalist C.W.C. Secondly, Brotherstone greatly overestimates both the political awareness and the practical objectivity of Labour department officials—at least in so far as these can be judged from their writings at the time. Beveridge himself had no very clear understanding of the many subtle variants of 'socialist' and 'labour' thought engaged in the Clyde controversy, and his memoranda on dilution made little distinction between the different political stances of self-protective skilled craftsmen, the Clyde Workers' Committee and the Glasgow I.L.P. Moreover, his notes on the *Forward* were written in a tone, not of cold political calculation, but of highly emotional indignation—in strong contrast to the closely-reasoned and dispassionate memoranda that he usually produced for his departmental chiefs. He admitted that there was 'practically nothing' in the *Forward* 'that can be described as deliberately seditious', but concluded nevertheless that 'there can be no question at all of its directly mischevious tendency'.[103] 'There is no doubt of the thoroughly harmful *effects* of the "Forward",' he wrote on 9 January, 'it is not so easy to show the harmful intention.'[104]

Beveridge's main objections to the *Forward* seem to have been threefold. Firstly, he claimed that it was 'perfectly obvious' that the paper was linked to the agitation on the Clyde 'even if the two things could not be shown directly connected'. Secondly, the report of the Christmas

[101] Brotherstone, loc. cit., p. 12.
[102] PRO, MUN 5/70/24/18, 'Notes on the Suppression of the "Forward"', by WHB, n.d.
[103] Ibid.
[104] PRO, MUN 5/70/24/18, 'Regulations under which "Forward" was suppressed', by WHB, 9 Jan. 1916.

day speech was 'permeated by a spirit of gloating' and of 'obvious glee' over the 'hostile reception stated to have been accorded to Mr. Lloyd George'. And, thirdly, an article in the paper two months earlier had claimed that in settling the Fairfields' dispute the government had 'yielded under pressure of a threat to strike'—a view which Beveridge himself privately both shared and deplored. These offences scarcely constituted a case for suppression of a newspaper; but even if not justifiable Beveridge's reaction is comprehensible in highly personal terms. As we have seen, he was under constant pressure from Lloyd George to produce results from dilution, and yet at the same time felt that the minister was continually letting him down. He had been greatly affected by rumours of German atrocities, and his earlier detachment had been replaced by a passionate commitment to winning the war. He had himself no ideological scruples about control of the labour force in wartime, and he was increasingly baffled by the prevailing opposition to both military and industrial conscription. A further factor which may have influenced his judgement was a letter he received in the midst of the *Forward* crisis from Harry Tawney, who described with graphic insight the bizarre horrors of Christmas on the western front. 'I suppose munitions are going ahead,' wrote Tawney in conclusion:

I don't envy you the job. What can be done is I suppose to effect a great improvement in organisation and this you have no doubt done. May it be sufficient. Probably it will be. The further problem of making the B. Workman and Employer decently public-spirited and less totally selfish can't I imagine, be handled under a generation or two. A year with the former has taught me a good deal—among other things that his philosophy, as much as that of his masters, is 'get as much and give as little as you can'. He has been brought up in that creed—though of course very many rise above it—and one can't change the habits of four or five generations in a year or two. (It is like the old game of decasualising a man who has been carefully taught to be casual) . . .[105]

These personal and emotional pressures, rather than rational analysis of the Glasgow situation, seem to have determined Beveridge's attitude to suppression of the *Forward*, and this is borne out by the fact that he adopted an identical tone of exasperated indignation against the official A.S.E. 'The suggestion that the government is not entitled to carry out an agreed policy of dilution without consultation with the Amalgamated Society of Engineers at every point is ridiculous,' he wrote angrily on 11 February 1916. The A.S.E. had published a pamphlet describing their conference with the Prime Minister on 31 December and denouncing the government for breaking promises given at that meeting about

[105] BP, IIa, R. H. Tawney to WHB, 22 Dec. 1915.

the wages and conditions of diluted labour. This, Beveridge argued, was totally 'inaccurate and misleading'. It was the A.S.E. themselves, he claimed, who had

continually gone back on their agreements and had withdrawn co-operation at a moment's notice, because of some difference with the Minister, that is to say, have themselves gone on strike. Their proper course, if at any time they have a difference with the Government, is not to begin by 'downing tools' i.e. breaking their own pledges, but to continue their co-operation to negotiate as to the points of difference.[106]

On 21 January the Ministry held a further conference with the A.S.E. and with engineering employers, but the A.S.E. pronounced the conference 'a complete failure'.[107] It was undoubtedly the successful resistance of the A.S.E. executive at this point that persuaded the Ministry to dispatch special commissioners to the Clyde to enforce dilution. Beveridge himself drafted the commissioners' terms of reference and the measures of support they were to receive from the government. They were to consult with shop stewards and local union officials, who would be given three days to reach a voluntary agreement—after which dilution would be enforced by compulsion. In the event of a strike the government would take action under the Defence of the Realm Act against those who were 'inciting' the strike; it would 'secure (by an injunction if necessary) that trade union funds are not used to support the strikers'; and it would 'guarantee adequate police and military protection to all who are willing to work'.[108]

The dilution commissioners, headed by Macassey, arrived on Clydeside on 24 January. Within a few days they had negotiated agreements with several important firms—including Parkhead Forge, where Kirkwood 'broke the front' with his C.W.C. colleagues by submitting a scheme for craftsmen-dominated dilution that was enthusiastically received by the commission.[109] At the end of January, however, a dispute arose at Langs' yard over the wages paid to women who did part but not all of the work of skilled craftsmen. The dispute was referred to the Ministry, which ruled that a woman who took over only part of a man's job should receive only part of the man's rate. This ruling was rejected by local A.S.E. officials, and the majority of Lang's workmen went out on strike. Macassey on 5 February reported bitterly on the unco-

---

[106] PRO, MUN 5/73/324/15/8, 'Notes for Minister's Meeting with A.S.E. Executive Council', by WHB, 11 Feb. 1916.
[107] *HMM*, IV, IV, p. 116.
[108] Bev. Coll. Misc. 144, III, item 37, ff. 250–72, drafts of 'Summary of Dilution Programme as Based (with Modifications) on Mr. Weir's Memorandum', by WHB, 22 Jan. 1916.
[109] McLean, loc. cit., pp. 14–15.

operative attitude of both local employers and union officials; but he advised against prosecution of the strikers, and the men returned to work on 7 February, pending further discussions between the Ministry and the A.S.E.[110]

For most of February 1916 Lloyd George and the Labour department were in continuous negotiation with the executive of the A.S.E. Beveridge on 11 February defined the main objectives of negotiation as settlement of the Lang's dispute and 'the securing of the continued co-operation of Mr. Bunton [the local A.S.E. district secretary] in dilution on the Clyde'.[111] On 24 February the A.S.E. finally agreed to proceed with dilution, provided that the agreement on women's wages was made mandatory and that all disputes arising from it should be referred to a special tribunal.[112] In the meantime, however, the C.W.C. had once again sprung into the limelight. Its newspaper, the *Worker*, had published an article entitled 'Should the Workers Arm?' and although the answer given was 'No' the inflammatory tone of the article was thought to justify prosecution. At the instigation of the Ministry of Munitions the paper was seized by the military authorities, and three members of the C.W.C. were prosecuted for 'attempting to cause sedition and dis-affection among the civilian population'.[113] From this time onwards the Clyde commissioners were increasingly anxious to take action against the remaining members of the C.W.C.; and their opportunity came with a dispute at Parkhead Forge, which resulted in the dismissal of Kirkwood. The ensuing strike was repudiated by the A.S.E., but it nevertheless spread to other works and was ascribed by the Ministry to incitement by the C.W.C. According to the official history 'the situation grew worse from day to day' and on 24 March the commissioners recommended a policy similar to that suggested by Macassey three months earlier—the 'deportation' of the C.W.C. leaders from the Clyde. This policy was approved by Lloyd George, who was becoming irritated and bored with labour questions; and Kirkwood and four other members of the committee were arrested and deported to different parts of the country. Thirty strikers were fined by munitions tribunals, and the strike ended and the men returned to work during the following week.[114]

How far does this sequence of events illuminate the two points at issue—namely, what was the main source of opposition on the Clyde,

[110] *HMM*, IV, IV, p. 121.

[111] PRO, MUN 5/73/324/15/8, WHB to H. Llewellyn Smith, 11 Feb. 1916.

[112] *HMM*, IV, IV, p. 123.

[113] McLean, p. 13, quoting Addison's diary for 10 Feb. 1916 (C. Addison, *Politics from Within 1911–18*, vol. I, p. 190) states that the initiative came from the Foreign Office. But the Ministry of Munitions had pressed for the seizure of the *Worker* ten days before (*HMM*, IV, IV, p. 125).

[114] *HMM*, IV, IV, pp. 130–4; C. Addison, *Politics from Within 1911–18*, vol. I, p. 190.

and were Beveridge and other officials implicated in a 'plot' to destroy the C.W.C.? The deportation of Kirkwood and his colleagues provided a dramatic climax to the Clyde struggle; but much of the evidence of munitions archives suggests that the main struggle had already ended a month earlier, with the agreement reached on 24 February with the leaders of the A.S.E. After that date it seems clear from the commissioners' reports that dilution began to bite immediately—several weeks before the final suppression of the C.W.C. On 29 February Macassey recorded that several dilution schemes were already working successfully; he had had 'very satisfactory meetings' with Clydeside shipbuilders and foresaw 'no insuperable difficulty' in putting the rest of his programme into operation. On 1 March he reported enthusiastically on the successful training of women workers, the upgrading of semi-skilled male workers and the release of skilled craftsmen to form the nucleus of additional night shifts.[115] All these points seem to support the view that it was the official A.S.E. rather than the Clyde Workers' Committee that was chiefly responsible for the long-drawn-out resistance to dilution on the Clyde.

What of Dr. Hinton's suggestion that there was a carefully planned official conspiracy against the Clyde Workers Committee? As we have seen, both Beveridge and Macassey in official documents had suggested proceedings against the C.W.C. as early as November and December 1915—more than three months before the government finally took action. Both these documents suggest that official concern about the C.W.C. was more prolonged and serious than is allowed by Dr. McLean. There are, however, certain major objections to the conspiracy thesis as formulated by Hinton and Brotherstone. As indicated above, they greatly overestimate the degree of insight into the Clyde situation displayed by Munitions officials. And, if suppression of the C.W.C. was the officials' main objective, there seems no reason why they should have tried to conceal it by prosecuting the relatively harmless *Forward*—or, for that matter, by incessant negotiations with the A.S.E. Moreover, far from being 'remarkable for its clarity of aims . . . ruthlessness and . . . careful planning',[116] the Ministry's policy towards the C.W.C. seems to have been throughout spasmodic and confused. Beveridge himself during the winter of 1915–16 singularly failed to convince his superiors that any dangers were posed by the C.W.C. By February 1916 his fears of the Committee had apparently been forgotten—or more probably eclipsed by his greater concern over the unco-operative attitude of the A.S.E. It was not until mid-March that Macassey persuaded Chris-

---

[115] PRO, MUN 5/73/324/15/9, 'Dilution of Labour in the Clyde District', Lynden Macassey to D. Lloyd George, 29 Feb. and 1 Mar. 1916.

[116] Hinton, loc. cit., p. 184.

topher Addison that the C.W.C. was undermining the authority of
A.S.E. officials and ought to be suppressed. These facts scarcely indicate
a continuous departmental policy, let alone a carefully planned and
premeditated departmental plot.

More must be said of the role and attitude of Beveridge himself. Of
all the Ministry's officials Beveridge was undoubtedly the most vehement in his denunciation of the C.W.C.—as he was also of the A.S.E.
executive. This was not perhaps surprising, as he was the official who
took the blame when dilution failed. His objections to the C.W.C. were
not based on their revolutionary ideology, since on other occasions
while working in munitions Beveridge helped to shield revolutionary
theorists from demands for prosecution by the military authorities.[117]
Moreover, he made little intellectual distinction between the C.W.C.
and other opponents of dilution—they were all equally 'incorrigibles'
and 'irresponsibles' who were sabotaging the successful prosecution of
the war.[118] His objections stemmed rather from what he believed to be
the C.W.C.'s disastrous practical influence on production of munitions;
and to this extent his attitude must be seen as a pragmatic response to
the frustration of his own policies. On a more fundamental level, however, his support for stern measures to enforce dilution was entirely
consistent with his general political convictions at this time—with his
belief that laws once passed should be enforced to the letter, that the
interests of the state should be paramount over sectional interests and
that curtailment of civil liberties was required by the pressures of war.
Whether such attitudes were in fact justified by the circumstances of the
time is clearly a matter for personal judgement rather than for formal
historical proof.[119]

V

Throughout the period of the Clyde controversy Beveridge was dealing
with a 'ceaseless stream of work' on general office reorganization.[120]
A separate department for munitions recruitment had been set up in
December 1915, but the Labour department was still left with a wide
variety of functions that ranged from settlement of disputes and fixing
of wages to provision of housing for munitions workers and control of

[117] BP, IV, 2, P. J. Hannon to Sir Graham Greene, 19 July 1915; WHB to Sir Graham
Greene, 4 Aug. 1915.

[118] BP, IIa, WHB to ASB, 18 Oct. 1915; PRO MUN 5/49/300/23, 'Report of the Labour
Department with the General Secretary's Minute', 2 Dec. 1915.

[119] For further discussion of the Clyde controversy, see James Hinton, 'The Suppression of
the "Forward"—a Note', *Journal of Scottish Labour History Society*, no. 7, July 1973, pp. 24–9;
and Roger Davidson, 'War-Time Labour Policy 1914–16: A Reappraisal', *Journal of the
Scottish Labour History Society*, no. 8, June 1974, pp. 3–20.

[120] BP, IIa, WHB to ASB, 12 Mar. 1916.

excess profits. The staff contained a large number of temporary civil servants recruited during the war—among them Jessy Mair, who became Beveridge's private secretary. As the Ministry's only woman administrator she was relegated to a tent on the balcony of what had once been Mrs. Gladstone's drawing-room—from which position she dealt with thousands of inquiries from the public, soothed fractious recruiting officers and made endless cups of tea for the permanent officials. She did not get on well, she recalled, with the Ministry's Parliamentary Secretary, Christopher Addison, who was 'overwhelmed with the importance of the job . . . and was *de haut en bas* to anyone in my humble way of work. . . . On one occasion I dropped a fatal brick by inviting him to have a cup of tea with me. He gave me an outraged and prolonged glare, and hurried back to the shelter of his enormous room.'[121] Beveridge himself was responsible for all the work of the Labour department, which by March 1916 was dealing with a correspondence of sixty thousand letters a week. He was particularly involved in measures for expanding the labour force—promoting the employment of female workers, discouraging bad timekeeping, persuading employers to give a 'fair trail' to hastily-trained labour and finding work for discharged soldiers.[122] He was also concerned with forcing employers to submit to arbitration, and with preventing skilled workers in other essential industries—such as mining and agriculture—from leaving their jobs for more highly-paid work in munitions.

Beveridge was therefore working at high pressure throughout the winter of 1915–16; and, as he told Llewellyn Smith, he had 'no regular organisation for dealing with these matters, and, as a consequence, have to do an undue proportion of the work myself'.[123] As dilution began to bite, however, the pressure slackened, and in March 1916 he told his mother that he would 'like to read economics and poetry again . . . which I take as a sign that I am getting a little over the oppression of the Ministry'.[124] He began to spend more time at the Board of Trade—a change probably facilitated by his undeniable connection with some of the more unpopular policies of the Ministry of Munitions. During the next few months he witnessed personally some of the revolutionary changes in methods of production that had been brought about by war. In April he visited Liverpool for a series of meetings with shipping employers and trade unionists, and he inspected the Liverpool Dock

[121] Lady Beveridge Papers, ms. on 'Whitehall in Wartime', by J. Mair, n.d.

[122] Bev. Coll. Misc. 144, V, item 28, f. 223, WHB to M. Delevigne, 19 Feb. 1916; ff. 224–7, 'Draft Appeal by Home Secretary—President of Board of Trade',—by WHB, 21 Feb. 1916; ff. 248–50, 'Engagement of Semi-Skilled and Unskilled Labour', by WHB, 27 Feb. 1916.

[123] Bev. Coll. Misc. 144, II, item 13, ff. 169–72, 'Office Organisation for Miscellaneous Questions', by WHB, 13 Apr. 1916.

[124] BP, IIa, WHB to ASB, 12 Mar. 1916.

Labour Battalion which had been set up by R. F. Williams the year before. The battalion consisted of 1,200 dockers, 'all fully enlisted and subject to military discipline', employed on loading supplies for the front. In August 1915 Williams had reported that 90 per cent of dockers were physically unfit for regular work;[125] but now Beveridge found the situation radically changed. 'Most of the men are by now fully disciplined.' he recorded, 'and the battalion works with quite remarkable regularity—entirely disproving the theory that the average docker is physically incapable of doing more than two days' work a week, so that it is a kindness on the part of the employer to employ him casually.[126] A few weeks later Beveridge visited Coventry, where he found the local labour exchange working in close co-operation with a new government ordnance factory. The labour exchange had recruited female labour from all parts of the country, set up special hostels, 'inspected and approved' local lodgings and opened creches for the babies of married women. 'Altogether I had a most interesting time and from the point of view of the Labour Exchange a most encouraging one,' Beveridge recorded. '. . . A number of girls are being brought all the way from Aberdeen. They are fish curing girls . . . have been trained in a technical school at Aberdeen—and are now very much in demand. About 1,000 girls are already at work—and very beautiful work the fuse work is. It's nearly all done with marvellous automatic or semi-automatic machines. . . .'[127]

In May 1916 the Board of Trade was again reorganized, and Beveridge was placed in charge of a new 'Employment Department'. Throughout the summer he was working to expand the role of labour exchanges in industrial and military recruitment, and to revive the dominant role in labour questions formerly occupied by the Board of Trade. In response to a memorandum from Askwith on the need for greater co-ordination in labour policy, he urged that responsibility for all labour issues should be concentrated under one single ministry, the Board of Trade. At the same time he was determined to reinforce 'that recognition as the official source of labour supply' which had been gained by labour exchanges during the war. He continually emphasized the need for improving labour exchange publicity, for recruiting better staff, for making advisory committees more representative, and for preparing exchanges for the major industrial readjustment that would be required at the end of the war. In particular he was anxious 'to get into closer touch again with Trade Union leaders. . . . Many of them are constantly criticising and objecting to the labour exchange and we ought to ask them to make these criticisms specific . . .' In July 1916 he rejected

[125] BP, IIb, R. F. Williams to WHB, 23 Aug. 1915.
[126] BP, IIa, WHB to ASB, 9 Apr. 1916.          [127] BP, IIa, WHB to ASB, 4 May 1916.

proposals for using exchanges as instruments of industrial conscription, arguing that 'it is better for them to depend for custom on their efficiency, backed by public opinion rather than law'.[128] A few months later, however, both he and Llewellyn Smith gave evidence to a new Manpower Distribution Board under the chairmanship of Austen Chamberlain, and they proposed 'among other things the compulsory use of labour exchanges' to control distribution of manpower for the duration of the war.[129]

Beveridge's appearance before the Manpower Distribution Board proved to be virtually his last contribution to official labour policy during the First World War. His influence in Munitions had clearly been in decline for some time. Twice in the summer of 1916 he was annoyed to find that Humbert Wolfe and possibly also C. F. Rey had been conspiring to oust him from direction of labour policy; and although Wolfe apologized for his 'stupid and childish egotism', Beveridge interpreted this action by two of his former protégés as a sign that 'my welcome in the Ministry of Munitions was coming to an end'.[130] In June he was awarded a C.B., in respect of his work not for the Ministry, but for the Board of Trade; and in September his position in the Board was potentially greatly strengthened by an expansion of the Employment department to cover not merely exchanges and insurance but trade boards, cost-of-living questions and post-war reconstruction. Board of Trade officials hoped that this expansion was the prelude to a much more ambitious take-over of labour policy from other Whitehall departments, including the Manpower Distribution Board and Ministry of Munitions.[131] But the new arrangement proved to be short-lived. Three months later, when Lloyd George replaced Asquith as Prime Minister, a new Ministry of Labour was set up to take over all the labour functions of existing government departments, including the Board of Trade. For political reasons many senior posts in the new Ministry were given to trade unionists; but Beveridge was clearly hoping for a position and actually suggested to John Hodge, the new Minister of Labour, that he should be made joint-Permanent Secretary. John Hodge, 'round and fat and slow and humorous' and himself an ex-steel worker, was much more in sympathy with Beveridge's views on labour than most of the trade union movement.[132] Nevertheless, he 'apparently took umbrage' at Beveridge's suggestion, and replied that 'under no

---

[128] Bev. Coll. Misc. 144, VI, item 3, ff. 35–6, minutes by WHB, 23 and 28 July 1916.
[129] *PI*, p. 139.
[130] BP, IIa, WHB to ASB, 26 Sept. 1916; IIb, U. Wolff to WHB, 3 June and 29 Sept. 1916; Lady Beveridge Papers, J. Mair to WHB, 22 July 1927; *PI*, pp. 137–8.
[131] Rey Papers, 'Memorandum on Employment Department of the Board of Trade', n.d. and 'Revised Draft', 22 Apr. 1916; BP, IIb, S. Tallents to WHB, 22 Sept. 1916.
[132] BP, IIa, ms. conversation with ASB, 30 Dec. 1916.

circumstances can I agree to dual responsibility. Moreover, your suggestion as to being co-secretary . . . would make the position one of an embarrassing character were I to offer you any other position.'[133] 'I fear that the new Government changes do not work out well for me,' Beveridge recorded. 'I am to be cut off from the Exchanges and Labour questions altogether . . . and shall probably be off to the Ministry of Food. . . . I fear the powers that now be are not very fond either of Sir H. Ll. S. or me—we are both out of Labour questions for a bit.' And in private, Beveridge was given to understand that his appointment had been vetoed by certain trade unionists who saw him as 'a personal force that . . . would be against them during the course of the war'.[134]

[133] BP, IIb, John Hodge to WHB, 21 Dec. 1916.

[134] BP, IIa, WHB to ASB, 21 Dec. 1916 and 1 Feb. 1917. For an assessment of the subsequent history of the policies transferred from the Board of Trade's Labour Department, see Rodney Lowe, 'The Ministry of Labour, 1916–24: A Graveyard of Social Reform?', *Public Administration*, winter 1974, 52, pp. 415–38.

# 10

# Rationing and Reconstruction

## I

BEVERIDGE's career in the Ministry of Food was personally significant in several ways. His experience as one of the chief architects of rationing and price control between 1916 and 1919 strongly influenced his subsequent views on the scope of administrative action and economic policy. The impact of this experience was crystallized in the mid-1920s when he wrote the official history of the Ministry of Food; and it was in his reflections on wartime food control that he first clearly articulated the deep mistrust of state-controlled welfare capitalism that was to characterize his thinking for much of the inter-war years. His work for the Ministry must therefore be seen in several distinct though interlocking dimensions. Firstly, he was the impatient protagonist of governmental action, devising and sponsoring particular lines of policy. Secondly, he was, or was trying to be, a detached professional historian, patiently recording facts and trying to extract general principles from a complex pattern of historical events. And, thirdly, for many years afterwards he tended to use food control as a crucible of personal experience —a practical standard by which to measure the soundness and viability of social, economic and political ideas.

The organization of food supplies, to which Beveridge was drafted in December 1916, was in many respects as controversial and explosive an issue as organization of labour. By 1914 nearly two-thirds of the food eaten in Britain was imported from abroad, and maintenance of these supplies was ultimately as important to the war programme as the supply of ammunition for British troops. Because of Britain's commanding naval position, however, it was not envisaged at the start of the war that feeding the civilian population would pose any serious logistical problems. Beveridge as a Board of Trade official had been concerned with drawing up a food price index in August 1914;[1] but the Board's President, Walter Runciman, was firmly opposed to state interference in the food industry, and, when pressed to introduce statutory control of food supplies, he poured scorn on the notion of a 'minister of gastronomic munitions'.[2] For more than two years of war, therefore, the import, manufacture and distribution of food was left almost exclusively

[1] BP, IIa, WHB to ASB, 13 Aug. 1914.      [2] BFC, p. 23, n. 1.

to private enterprise. The only exception was made for sugar, which was placed under a specially constituted Royal Commission—an arrangement made necessary by the fact that the bulk of Britain's pre-war sugar supplies had been imported from Germany, Austria and Hungary.[3]

Between 1914 and 1916, however, many factors conspired to frustrate the expectation of the government that the war would not unduly disrupt normal supplies of food. Competition for food supplies among the many belligerent nations drove up prices in world markets; and this inflation was strongly reinforced by a rising home demand, caused by the decline in unemployment and rise in money-wages brought about by war. At the same time the transport of troops and munitions led to a serious shortage of cargo-space for imported foods. Moreover, the protection afforded by the Navy proved less impenetrable than had been hoped, and many food-cargoes were sunk in the German submarine attacks of 1915 and 1916.

All these factors had serious repercussions on the supply and distribution of British food. Although there seems to have been no overall deficiency in food supplies there were serious local shortages of particular commodities, and retail food prices rose by 59 per cent between June 1914 and June 1916.[4] Rising prices led to speculation in food stocks, and to hoarding on the part of private traders. They led also to serious industrial discontent and to pressure for further wage increases—pressure which employers were often reluctant to oppose in the booming conditions of war. The government early on in the war positively encouraged the payment of higher wages as the only means of encountering rising prices.[5] It thereby accelerated the spiral of inflation, and created a burden of war debt which was to prove one of the most harmful economic legacies of the First World War.

Throughout 1916 there was increasing pressure for state control over food supplies, both from organized labour and from interventionist Conservatives headed by Lord Milner. The demand for a more positive food policy formed one of the main spearheads of the attack on the Asquith coalition, which was eventually to lead to its downfall in December 1916.[6] Within the Board of Trade Runciman continued to resist proposals for state interference, but his officials were becoming increasingly sceptical about the continued viability of policies of *laissez-faire*. Beveridge himself began to inquire into cost-of-living problems after the Board of Trade reorganization in September 1916, though he was uncertain whether he would be allowed to proceed to any kind of

[3] *BFC*, p. 6.       [4] *BFC*, p. 19.       [5] *BFC*, p. 9.
[6] *BFC*, pp. 26–31; J. O. Stubbs, 'Lord Milner and Patriotic Labour 1914–1918', *English Historical Review*, Oct. 1972, p. 720.

action.[7] In the following month Runciman announced the setting up of a special Wheat Commission, to co-operate with other allied countries in wholesale purchase of wheat; but during a debate in the Commons he refused to contemplate any further extension of government control. Beveridge, who attended the debate with Llewellyn Smith, 'went back to the Board of Trade wondering if the food problem was really so unimportant as it seemed, and if the alleged popular discontent could be side-tracked as easily as a House of Commons debate'.[8] His secretary, Jessy Mair, was in no doubt about the matter. 'There wasn't a housewife in England,' she vehemently assured him, 'who wasn't in the greatest difficulties owing to the increase of prices, and that was where the trouble would come from if nothing was done . . . if there had been a single woman in the House of Commons Runciman would have been made to come to the real point.'[9]

Circumstances in the autumn of 1916, however, forced Runciman to shift from his dogmatically non-interventionist position. After a temporary lull in submarine warfare German attacks were renewed, resulting in serious losses among merchant ships. A major political scandal began to rage around the issue of spiralling prices. On 18 October Beveridge suggested that the Board of Trade should acquire extensive powers of control over food supplies, to be used if the need should arise; and he tentatively drafted a bill to this effect. His proposals met initially with a cool reception from the President, but a few weeks later Runciman announced in Parliament that he was considering the possibility of controlling the price of food. In mid-November an extension of the Defence of the Realm Acts enabled the Board to exercise control over the production, price and distribution of food supplies; and a new ministerial post of Food Controller was created within the Board to exercise these powers. Runciman failed, however, to find anyone willing to take on the job of Food Controller—possibly because the leading protagonists of food control were all by this time secretly committed to bringing down the Asquith government. When Lloyd George became Prime Minister in December the Board of Trade's administrative empire was broken up and food questions were hived off to an entirely new department—the Ministry of Food. A Liberal businessman, Lord Devonport, took office as Food Controller; Beveridge himself became second secretary; and the post of Permanent Secretary was given to a civil servant from the Board of Agriculture Sir Henry Rew.[10]

---

[7] BP, IIa, WHB to ASB, 26 Sept. 1916.
[8] *BFC*, p. 23.
[9] Lady Beveridge Papers, J. Mair to WHB, 22 July 1927.
[10] *BFC*, pp. 24–32.

## II

The first six months of Beveridge's period with the Ministry of Food were in many ways the most frustrating of his Civil Service career. On 15 December he drafted a programme for the new department, advocating centralized purchase of imports, regulation of prices, prohibition of luxury consumption and measures of rationing both voluntary and compulsory.[11] He soon found, however, that the Lloyd George ministry once in office was no more prepared for positive measures of food control than its predecessor under Asquith.[12] Moreover, he strongly resented the dominance in the field of food control of a large contingent of wholesale and retail traders, who had been brought into the new ministry in pursuit of Lloyd George's vision of efficient 'business' government. Beveridge soon came to the conclusion that the more closely a man's private interests were linked to a particular commodity the less likely he was to administer that commodity efficiently as a public official—not necessarily because of corruption, but because too great a knowledge of one aspect of the market tended to distort understanding of the market as a whole.[13] Such an outlook, Beveridge believed, contrasted strongly with the wider perspective of the professional civil servant, who was trained to look at a problem from all points of view. 'For the time being, however,' he commented bitterly, 'not only the last Government, but the whole Civil Service is out of office, and much of the subordinate government of the country is in the hands of amateurs.'[14]

Beveridge's greatest opprobrium was reserved for his new minister, Lord Devonport. The owner of a retail grocery chain, Devonport owed his advance in Liberal politics mainly to his donations to party funds. Beveridge at first treated him with mild contempt—he was 'a big grocer', he observed, 'quite good-humoured but quite unbusinesslike . . . if he were more competent, the job would be very enjoyable'.[15] As the months went by, however, a violent mutual antipathy grew up between the two men, and Beveridge came to look upon Devonport as the embodiment of all that was wrong in wartime public administration. Devonport's shortcomings in Beveridge's eyes stemmed in particular from two highly personal characteristics. Firstly, he persisted in looking at food control through the eyes of a retail trader, rather than from the point of view of the community at large. He tinkered with a large number of trivial measures such as rules against hoarding and 'meatless days', but he failed to grasp the relation of food control of wider issues of economic

[11] BP, IV, 20, 'Heads of Action for Food Supplies Department', by WHB, *c.* 15 Dec. 1916.
[12] *BFC*, pp. 45–6.     [13] *BFC*, pp. 335–6.
[14] BP, IIa, WHB to ASB, 14 Jan. 1917.
[15] BP, IIa, ms. conversation with ASB, *c.* 30 Dec. 1916.

policy. The result was 'a period of food control without principle on practical lines, a scurrying hither and thither in chase of the unapprehended consequences of ill-considered actions'.[16] Devonport's second fault was his obsessive refusal to delegate. He insisted on dealing personally with routine questions and treated his staff as 'office-boys' rather than responsible officials—thus creating a permanent bottleneck in the Ministry's affairs. This problem was exacerbated by the fact that the new Ministry's officers were located in Grosvenor House, the town residence of the Duke of Westminster, at a considerable distance from Parliament and Whitehall. 'My phrase for the office is "Delay and Delirium"'—that hits it exactly,' commented Beveridge with rising irritation after a few weeks experience of the Devonport regime.[17]

Beveridge was joined in the Ministry by his former colleague, Stephen Tallents, and by his friend Andrewes Uthwatt, who became the Ministry's legal adviser. He got on well with the permanent secretary, Sir Henry Rew; but Rew was an elderly man with little energy for new schemes, whose main contribution to food control seems to have been maintaining the peace between Beveridge and Devonport. It was with Tallents and Uthwatt that Beveridge began to press for more radical state intervention, and for several months the three of them fumed together in private about Devonport's pointless exertions and lack of coherent policy. In December 1916 Beveridge and Tallents in the face of rising sugar shortages drew up a scheme for the wholesale purchase and rationing of sugar, which they pressed on Devonport's attention; but no action was taken, and over the next few months the scheme was referred to no less than seven official committees of inquiry—at a time when there was widespread public anger about unfair sugar distribution in many parts of the country.[18] In February 1917 Beveridge drafted a 'memorandum of general policy as to Food'; but this seems merely to have confirmed Devonport in his dislike and suspicion of Beveridge. 'His distrust of me arises from the fact that I've been accustomed to do things and to take responsibility,' Beveridge complained. 'D. hates even to have a suggestion made to him for his consideration. . . . My crowning offence was that knowing we might have to ration, I actually thought out a draft scheme for rationing. He was furious—practically tore it up . . .'[19]

Throughout the early months of 1917 Devonport's only major innovation was to fix the price of potatoes—an action which merely intensified the potato shortage, since he refused at the same time to assume control

[16] *BFC*, p. 342.
[17] BP, IIa, ms. conversations with ASB, *c.* 30 Dec. 1916 and Spring 1917; BP, IV, 20, typed notes by WHB, n.d.; *BFC*, p. 47.
[18] *BFC*, pp. 45–54.
[19] BP, IIa, WHB to ASB, 1 Feb. 1917, and ms. conversation, spring 1917.

of wholesale potato supplies. He started a campaign for 'voluntary rationing', and issued a handbook prescribing what people should eat, which was condemned by nutritionists as being totally unrelated to scientific notions of diet. He also drastically curtailed grain supplies to brewers—a policy that almost certainly helped to exacerbate the prevailing industrial unrest. His officials meanwhile were employed not on contingency plans but on an endless stream of trivial correspondence— on letters to 'householders in trouble with servants' and to 'clergymen concerned as to the propriety of parish teas'.[20] As the months went by Beveridge himself was increasingly unable to conceal his indignation. 'Lord Devonport has no more idea of running a business than I have of loading a 17mm. gun,' he stormed with more truth than discretion in December 1916.[21] 'I hope Lloyd George now he's back from his travels, will put some of his freaks in their places,' he remarked caustically a few weeks later on the Prime Minister's return from a visit to France.[22] To his mother he wrote at the end of March:

I'm . . . just sticking things out and doing what work comes to hand. Of course many others are in the same sort of position. My special trouble is that I'm conceited enough to think I see more clearly than most what needs to be done, and therefore fret the more. But that's just my conceit.[23]

Beveridge in retrospect was more generous to Lord Devonport than he was prepared to be in 1917. He conceded in his official history that Devonport while doing little positive good could not be accused of doing very much harm. He admitted also that in many respects the minister's lack of policy merely reflected the negative view of food control that prevailed in the War Cabinet—a view which Beveridge ascribed partly to fear of revealing to the Germans just how effective their attacks had been and partly to a mistaken belief that the British public would refuse to tolerate further state regulation.[24] In the spring of 1917, however, several factors gradually combined to force a more positive policy on public control of food. On 18 April Herbert Hoover, the food representative of the United States Government, attended a meeting of the War Cabinet at which it was agreed to establish far-reaching co-operation between the Allied governments in wholesale purchase of food.[25] Public discontent continued to smoulder, and a parliamentary committee recommended rationing of sugar and wheat.[26] On 25 April Devonport

[20] *BFC*, pp. 34–5, 42, 46–9, 100–3.
[21] BP, IIa, ms. conversation with ASB, 30 Dec. 1916.
[22] BP, IIa, ms. conversation with ASB, Spring 1917.
[23] BP, IIa, WHB to ASB, 30 Mar. 1917.
[24] *BFC*, pp. 42 and 46.
[25] *War Memoirs of David Lloyd George* (1938 edn.), vol. I, pp. 796–7.
[26] *BFC*, p. 45.

announced at last that he was planning to set up machinery to introduce rationing, if and when the need should arise. 'I have suddenly had a time of violent business,' wrote Beveridge to his mother.

Considerable developments are brewing in the Ministry of Food, and I have been helping to brew them. You'll have seen from the papers that compulsory rationing is coming nearer. It is now on the cards that if it comes I shall have a great deal to do with running it—which would of course mean a dramatic change from my relative idleness of the last three months to a time of absolutely unparalleled activity and delirium.[27]

Meanwhile Devonport's failure to deal with shortages was increasingly attacked in Parliament and the press, and he resigned on 30 May. He was succeeded by Lord Rhondda, the President of the Local Government Board, who agreed to transfer to food control in return for Lloyd George's pledge of support for a new Ministry of Health.[28] Rhondda came to food control intending 'to make a complete sweep and start again'; and he brought with him as Permanent Secretary, Ulick Wintour, an ex-Board of Trade civil servant who had been working as director of War Office contracts. Beveridge himself initially hoped to return to the Board of Trade to work on questions of post-war reconstruction, but at Wintour's personal request he was retained for the time being in the Ministry of Food.[29]

## III

Rhondda like Devonport was a Liberal businessman, but Beveridge soon discovered that he was in many ways the antithesis of his predecessor. Almost alone among politicians of the day he was seriously troubled by the problem of uncontrolled inflation, and as soon as he was appointed he brought the issue of rising prices before the War Cabinet.[30] He chose as his parliamentary secretary the Labour M.P., John Clynes, to represent the interests not merely of organized labour but of the poorest section of the working class. He established close liaison with the Board of Agriculture, the Wheat and Sugar Commissions and the military authorities, and he moved his Ministry's headquarters out of Grosvenor House and into less imposing but more functional premises closer to Whitehall. From the point of view of a forceful and creative administrator like Beveridge he was an ideal political superior, 'because he trusted absolutely his chosen subordinates' and delegated to them wide discretionary powers.[31] 'You can use my authority as you think necessary,' he told them, 'but do be careful to let me know exactly what you have said.'[32] He continued to employ professional traders, but used them mainly as technical advisers, leaving planning and policy-making almost exclusively in the hands of permanent officials.[33] He also appointed a Consumers' Council, to make suggestions, to hear complaints and to represent both the 'unorganised consumer' and the 'organised working class'. As a prerequisite of effective food control he introduced public auditing of retail traders' accounts. To supervise rationing and price control he established throughout the country fifteen regional food commissioners and hundreds of local Food Control committees representing the interests of workers, farmers, traders and co-operative organizations. He soon realized, however, that rationing and price control were pointless unless the government could guarantee supplies and prevent hoarding; so he therefore introduced bulk purchasing of imports and control of wholesale supplies. At the same time he laid down the principle that so far as possible 'the existing channels of trade' should be maintained. The machinery of food control was therefore superimposed upon the existing commercial structure of production and distribution; and Rhondda went to great lengths to accommodate both large and small traders and to disrupt as little as possible the normal methods of supply. In this whole gigantic operation, which eventually controlled 85 per cent of civilian food supplies, the Ministry of Food went into the market on a quasi-commercial basis. It bought and sold at a profit nearly all major items of food without cost to the taxpayer— the only important exception being the subsidy introduced in September 1917 to keep down the price of bread.[34]

Beveridge in his official history described Rhondda's regime as the 'heroic age of food control'; and he ascribed the move towards a more dynamic style of administration partly to Rhondda himself but more particularly to Rhondda's chosen confidant, Ulick Wintour.[35] In private, however, he portrayed Wintour mainly as a brilliant mediator of other men's ideas, and indicated that he himself had been mainly responsible for Rhondda's programme—together with Stephen Tallents and a young official from the National Health Commission, E. F. Wise.[36] The accuracy of this private account is largely corroborated by contemporary records. Certainly it was Beveridge himself who, even before the retirement

[31] BP IIa, WHB to ASB, 7 July 1918; *BFC*, pp. 53–4.

[32] *D. A. Thomas, Viscount Rhondda, by his Daughter and Others* (1921), p. 254.

[33] E. F. Wise, 'The History of the Ministry of Food', *Econ. J.* XXXIX, no. 156, Dec. 1929, pp. 570–1.

[34] *BFC*, ch. 5.     [35] *BFC*, pp. 51–3.

[36] BP, IIb, WHB to Christopher Addison, 9 Nov. 1923; Ib 23, 'A Day of Encounters, 26 April 1955', in WHB's ms.

of Devonport, urged upon the government the 'elementary principle of economic administration . . . that prices could only be controlled
if distribution was also undertaken'.[37] Similarly it was Beveridge who
devised the plan for central, local and regional rationing machinery—a
plan combining 'central initiative with decentralized execution',[38] that
was in many ways strikingly similar to his plan for labour exchanges
eight years before. This plan, 'which almost certainly saved the country
from revolutionary riots, was worked out mainly by Sir William Beveridge when he was second secretary', recorded one of Rhondda's successors, George Roberts, in 1919.[39] It was Beveridge who collected statistics
and consulted nutrition experts about diets and family budgets, so as to
draw up rationing scales related to physical needs; and it was Beveridge
also who designed special rationing scales for workers in heavy industry,
for children of different ages and for nursing and pregnant mothers.[40]
It was he who suggested that to make rationing enforceable every citizen
should register with a single retailer for each rationed commodity; and
during the serious shortages of December 1917 it was he who urged
local authorities to introduce schemes of 'rationing by local option',
pending the introduction of rationing throughout the country.[41]

During the winter of 1917–18 the shortage of imported food was
temporarily intensified by the diversion of merchant shipping to transport of American troops across the Atlantic. The Ministry of Food was
assured by the Board of Trade that the shortage of cargo space would
only be of short duration;[42] but nevertheless there was widespread
public anxiety about food supplies, and the police reported long queues
in many parts of the country. Beveridge himself was convinced that the
sense of crisis was a false one and that there was no aggregate deficiency
in food supplies, merely maldistribution caused by panic buying.[43]
Throughout the winter months therefore he and his assistants were
'drowned in work', striving to complete the new rationing machinery
and to avert what they believed to be a purely artificial emergency.[44]
A nation-wide scheme for sugar rationing was introduced on 31 December, based on Beveridge's and Tallent's plan of the previous year.
In February a general rationing order, covering meat, butter, bacon and
ham, was issued for London and the Home Counties; and on 25 February Beveridge issued a meat rationing order for the whole country.

[37] E. F. Wise, loc. cit., p. 567.
[38] *BFC*, p. 335.
[39] *Lloyd George Papers*, F/44/1/11, G. Roberts to D. Lloyd George, 4 July 1919.
[40] BP, IIa, WHB to ASB, 8 Feb. and 28 Nov. 1917; draft of Ministry of Food Meat Rationing Order, 1918.
[41] BP, IIa, WHB to ASB, 22 Dec. 1917.
[42] BP, IIb, H. Llewellyn Smith to WHB, 29 Dec. 1917.
[43] *BFC*, p. 208.
[44] BP, IIa, WHB to ASB, 25 Jan. 1918.

The new system made an immediate impact on food supplies and the behaviour of consumers, and by early March the number of people in food queues had fallen from 1,300,000 to less than 200,000 a week.[45]

The national and local rationing machinery was virtually complete by July 1918. It applied universally to sugar, meat, bacon, jam, butter, margarine and lard; and tea and cheese were rationed on a basis of local option. Food queues virtually vanished and a 'ruthless equalitarianism' was imposed on the whole community—backed up where necessary by exemplary prosecutions and fines.[46] To achieve this end, however, Beveridge appears to have brought himself to the verge of a breakdown.[47] He later admitted that it was a period of 'the greatest possible anxiety';[48] and, as had often happened before, his single-minded pursuit of objectives brought him into recurrent conflict with departmental colleagues and political superiors. With Rhondda and Wintour his relations were extremely harmonious, but elsewhere in Whitehall he appears to have been regarded with considerable suspicion and hostility. At the eleventh hour of the rationing scheme Lloyd George himself had threatened to dismantle the new machinery and urged Rhondda to replace Beveridge by a 'director-general of rationing'. This proposal came to nothing, but only because the Prime Minister could find no one willing to take on so arduous a job; and Beveridge and Tallents continued with their work in the depressing knowledge that they were under continual 'sentence of supersession'.[49] A few weeks later Beveridge observed sardonically that 'the Prime Minister has been spying out the land at the Ministry of Food—which may portend changes and troubles for some or all of us'.[50] These suspicions were substantially correct for shortly afterwards the Labour M.P., George Barnes, reported to Lloyd George that he had inspected the administration of food control at the Prime Minister's request. 'I believe Lord Rhondda is getting on very well with the businessmen,' reported Barnes,

and Clynes . . . is also doing very well with the new Consumers' Council which has had to be humoured a good deal, however, but is now doing much better. The organisation of the office is giving trouble and I think the source of the trouble is twofold—first that there are quite a number of smart men from other offices, most of whom have been troublesome in those offices and they cannot get on together in the office of the Food Controller. There is friction between them. And second, that there is a sort of bottleneck set up by Wintour and Beveridge through which everything has to pass and through which a good deal doesn't pass at all, to use an Irishism. Wintour is a very

[45] BP, IIa, WHB to ASB, 6 Mar. 1918; *The Times*, 15 Mar. 1918.
[46] *BFC*, pp. 234–40.　　　　　　　　　　[47] BP, IIa, WHB to ASB, 27 Jan. 1918.
[48] D. A. Thomas, *Viscount Rhondda*, p. 238.　　[49] *BFC*, p. 204.
[50] BP, IIa, WHB to ASB, 24 Feb. 1918.

strong-willed person but is, I am told, very clever. Perhaps he is not altogether suitable for the position in which he is. . . . Beveridge is, I believe, a failure in administration which had caused a great deal of trouble.[51]

It seems unlikely that Beveridge was aware of this report, which was in any case much more revealing of the narrow-minded mediocrity of George Barnes than of any faults or virtues in Wintour and himself. There was, however, at least an element of truth in the charge that he did not get on well with some of his departmental colleagues. In order to launch the rationing schemes he had forcibly overridden the views of many junior executive officers—an action which, however circumstantially justified, did nothing to modify his reputation for high-handedness.[52] He annoyed Charles Bathurst, the chairman of the Sugar Commission, by failing to consult him on the issue of statutory orders;[53] and he did not conceal his anger when in May 1918 the scheme for bacon rationing was disrupted by the failure of those in charge of imports to make provision for cold-storage.[54] He also offended Sir John Beale, the City businessman who chaired the Wheat Commission, by his insistence on the need for forward planning and preparation for contingencies. The dispute between Beveridge and Beale, which arose over bread rationing, was significant not merely because of the clash of personalities involved but because it revealed a fundamental conflict of opinion over the whole issue of state intervention. On 11 March the Wheat Commission reported to the Food Controller on the serious shortage of cereal supplies, and urged him to give priority to production of bread.[55] Within the Ministry this was interpreted as a sign that bread might soon have to be rationed; but on 13 March Beale told Beveridge that there was no need to prepare for such a measure since rationing would not be necessary before May at the earliest.[56] After consultation with Wintour and Rhondda, however, Beveridge took the precaution of printing rationing-cards well in advance. The result was an explosion of indignation and fury from Sir John Beale. 'I can only express astonishment,' wrote Beale,

that you should have thought it right, without further consultation with me, to ask Lord Rhondda for a decision in favour of immediate printing of cards, nor can I understand how Lord Rhondda can have given you the authority you asked for without consulting me, since I am supposed to be in charge of

[51] Lloyd George Papers, F/4/2/25, G. Barnes to D. Lloyd George, 11 Mar. 1918.
[52] *D. A. Thomas, Viscount Rhondda*, p. 239.
[53] BP, IV 27, WHB to Sir Charles Bathurst, 4 Apr. 1918.
[54] BP, IIb, WHB to ASB, 3 May 1918.
[55] BP, IV 27, memorandum by the RC on Wheat Supplies for Consideration by the Food Controller, 11 Mar. 1918.
[56] BP, IV 27 Sir John Beale to WHB, 13 Mar. 1918.

the bread supply. You and I approach this question from an entirely different standpoint. You appear to regard bread-rationing by ticket as a thing inherently good. In my opinion, the introduction of bread tickets would do the greatest possible harm to the national effort as a whole, and I think the maintenance of the bread supply ought to be one of the first charges on the entire national manpower; and if this principle is accepted it should with reasonable foresight be possible to postpone the introduction of bread tickets indefinitely.[57]

Beveridge in reply claimed that he had acted on instructions from Rhondda and Wintour, and that he had given Beale every opportunity to express his views in advance. The issue had been fully discussed in Parliament, and a public commitment to bread rationing had been definitely accepted if the need should arise. 'As to the general question of bread rationing,' Beveridge protested,

I certainly differ from you in thinking that you over-estimate entirely the objections and difficulties; and I differ profoundly from your idea that we should postpone bread rationing till we are certain of an acute shortage and then introduce a starvation ration. But I don't in the least want bread rationing for its own sake and I don't want a decision now to ration bread. It is simply one of how much warning one can have. Can you guarantee us against a strike, or a fire in a printing establishment, or against a strike in Argentina, or against a mere delay. . . ? But I am sure I need not waste your or my time in any sort of recrimination. . . . I think, as a measure of insurance, we clearly ought to go ahead with the scheme up to this point. It will not cost anything except a few hours or your and my time.[58]

In the circumstances of the day Beveridge was almost certainly right in principle, even though eventually it proved unnecessary to ration supplies of bread. But his quarrel with Beale clearly illustrated the kind of reaction he not infrequently provoked among departmental colleagues. He aroused resentment by his militant efficiency and by his ill-concealed contempt for the ethic of 'muddling through'; and, even when he was trying to be conciliatory, his tone towards those who opposed him was often brusque and ironic. At the same time he aroused suspicion among people like Beale, who were fundamentally hostile to state intervention, that he wished to subject the whole of social and economic life to bureaucratic control. In the case of food control this suspicion was in fact unfounded, since Beveridge was firmly opposed to public regulation of food supplies except in time of war;[59] but nevertheless such a misunderstanding did not make for harmonious relationships with a group of men whose normal peacetime activity was commercial trading in food.

[57] BP, IV 27, Sir John Beale to WHB, 19 Mar. 1918.
[58] BP, IV 27, WHB to Sir John Beale, 20 Mar. 1918.
[59] Below, p. 249.

By June 1918 Beveridge's rationing work was virtually complete, and he was impatient to start on some new venture. Rhondda had fallen ill, however, and for nearly two months the future of food control hung in a state of uncertainty. Rhondda died in July and his post passed to Clynes, the former Parliamentary Secretary. As the summer progressed the question of food control became increasingly bound up with plans for an Allied peace settlement. Herbert Hoover again visited Europe, and an Inter-Allied Food Council was formed, composed of the food controllers of Britain, the United States, Italy and France. Beveridge himself was involved in bargaining with Hoover over maintenance of British food supplies and was made chairman of a Programme Committee to assess Britain's future needs. 'If it had only been done two months ago, we might have been ready in time,' he observed; 'as it is our "programme" will be a rather sketchy affair.'[60] In September Sir John Beale was appointed chief executive of the Inter-Allied Food Council, and this appointment caused a 'bitter domestic crisis' in the Ministry of Food, because Beale refused to work with Wintour and demanded the latter's resignation. Clynes pressed for Beveridge to replace Wintour, but Beveridge himself drew up a plan for an equal division of authority between the two contesting officials. Beale refused to accept this, however, and the War Cabinet intervened in the person of the Chancellor of the Exchequer, Bonar Law, who gave the permanent secretaryship to Beale himself.[61]

Beveridge's actions on this occasion were patently against his own self-interest, since prior to the intervention of Bonar Law he had every reason to hope that he himself would replace Wintour as Permanent Secretary. His attempt to foster harmony between Wintour and Beale is significant evidence both of his conception of the role of a permanent civil servant and of his personal loyalty as a departmental colleague—a loyalty that was warmly acknowledged by Clynes. In several respects, however, the incident was less important for its personal than its political implications. As Beveridge himself pointed out in his autobiography, this was the first occasion on which the Treasury asserted what subsequently became its accepted right of appointing permanent secretaries to all Civil Service departments;[62] and, as has been shown in earlier chapters, Beveridge was never very sympathetic towards the wider aspirations of Treasury control. Far worse than this, however, was the suspicion that Beale was the nominee not so much of the Treasury as of the Conservative wing of the Coalition Government—a fact which

[60] BP, IIa, WHB to ASB, 18 July 1918.
[61] BP, IIa, WHB to ASB, 13 and 14 Sept. 1918; copy of WHB to J. R. Clynes, 13 Sept. 1918, 'Ministry of Food Imports Organization', memorandum by WHB, 13 Sept. 1918.
[62] *PI*, p. 144.

seemed to make nonsense of the principle of a non-partisan Civil Service pursuing the interests of an ideologically neutral administrative state. The whole incident seemed to Beveridge dangerously typical of the widespread corruption of accepted constitutional principles which, in the eyes of many civil servants, had set into Whitehall since the start of the war.[63]

## IV

Although nominally only second secretary Beveridge found himself from this time onwards increasingly forced to take on the responsibilities of the permanent head of the Ministry of Food. Beale was almost entirely engrossed in international problems, and it fell to Beveridge to take charge of domestic food control—to deal with recurrent shortages, to advise the Food Controller, and to ward off a series of Treasury attacks on the Ministry's staffing and accounts.[64] Beveridge himself, however, was increasingly ambitious to do 'something inter-Allied and inter-national',[65] and shortly after the Armistice he was sent to Berne as British delegate of an Inter-Allied Mission on the Relief of German Austria. It was a depressing mission, to a Europe ravaged by influenza, starvation and political disintegration. The delegates spent Christmas 1918 negotiating with representatives of the defeated Austrian government, and they found themselves 'listening to a story of utter and hopeless disaster and beggary'. 'I believe it is literally true,' wrote Beveridge to his mother,

that people are starving in Vienna just now. They would *all* starve soon if the Allies didn't help them. They've no food and no money with which to buy any—no money that is which is any use outside German Austria itself. Unfortunately we—especially the Americans—came here with the idea of *selling* them food and with no authority to *give* it or send it on credit. So we've spent four—to me as to the Austrians—miserable days wrangling about finance, till at last we were all stampeded into the conclusion (which I reached days ago) that we must simply send the food and chance being paid for it. So we've sent off tonight 4000 tons of wheat from Trieste, and have told our Government that they've got to send along a lot more without payment.

I can't describe to you the impression of disaster which these German-Austrians have made for me. They're the saddest men I ever saw. German Austria . . . is now a province of 8,000,000 people of whom 2¼ million live in Vienna—a head obviously too large to be fed by such a small body. They're not allowed to join on to Germany and they're threatened on all sides by

[63] BP, IIa, WHB to ASB, 20 and 25 Sept. 1918.
[64] BP, IV 27, J. R. Clynes to Bonar Law (drafted by WHB), 17 Dec. 1918; Notes on Report of Committee on Staff, by WHB, n.d.
[65] BP, IIa, WHB to ASB, 20 Oct. 1918.

enemies . . . one and all join in oppressing German Austria and depriving it of food and coal.[66]

From Berne the mission travelled to Vienna, where they found a 'place that is literally starving', full of black marketeers, corrupt public authorities, children dwindling from malnutrition and 'women customers . . . twittering around us like ghosts in Hades, saying that they wanted food'.[67] At first the mission hoped to obtain supplies from neighbouring countries, but visits to Czechoslovakia and Hungary soon revealed that conditions there were almost as bad. Moreover, in both Prague and Budapest economic breakdown was compounded by serious political unrest. 'The shortage of food is little more than a symptom of a social and economic disintegration, so complete and so strange as to make adequate description almost impossible,' reported Beveridge to the Allied headquarters in Paris:

Wherever the Commission went . . . they found a constantly repeated fear of Bolshevism, arising both out of the hardship which the workmen were being subjected to and as the result of agitation fostered from Russia . . . Buda-Pesth, at the time of our visit, was in the throes of a political crisis and . . . the spectre of Bolshevism was always present in the minds of everybody. The only publicly armed force in Hungary now is entirely in the hands of the Social Democrats and entirely undisciplined. At any moment there is fear that the extreme social democrats may become Bolshevists or the soldiers themselves may go over to a party of robbery [and] violence. There seems little doubt that if Budapest is left to itself it will sooner or later explode and the only difference of opinion that I have heard is as to whether the explosion was likely to take place in a few days or a few weeks.[68]

Beveridge's response to this situation was to demand from his political superiors swift and uncompromising remedial action. He brushed aside contemptuously the arguments of those who claimed that Austria and Hungary should be left to fend for themselves as righteous punishment for their part in an unjust war. The war was finished so completely, he asserted, that 'wartime standards of inhumanity are no longer applicable'. Instead he recommended that the Allied Governments should intervene, by force if necessary, not merely to guarantee food supplies, but to revive financial institutions, to provide machinery and raw materials, and to restore as soon as possible the normal processes of trade.[69] On his return to Paris he pressed these proposals on representa-

[66] BP, IIa, WHB to ASB, 27 Dec. 1918.

[67] BP, IIa, WHB to ASB, 30 Dec. 1918; *PI*, p. 153; W. H. Beveridge, *Peace in Austria* (pamphlet published by the Fight the Famine Council, 7 Feb. 1920).

[68] Lloyd George Papers, F/97/5/1, Inter-Allied Commission on Relief of German Austria. Interim Report by British Delegate (Sir Wm. Beveridge) to the Earl of Reading, 17 Jan. 1919, S.II.

[69] Ibid., S.III.

tives of the British government, and urged Robert Cecil, the Foreign Office under-secretary, that he should be sent back to Hungary to organize reconstruction. This suggestion met with some approval in Foreign Office circles, but was coldly received by Robert Cecil himself. Beveridge's views, reported Cecil to the Prime Minister, were 'altogether wild and injudicious'; he was unduly sympathetic to the defeated nations, and 'did not give one the impression that he had any real understanding of the political situation'. He was 'strongly imbued', Cecil complained, 'with the idea that peace is already practically concluded and that all trade restrictions . . . ought to be promptly removed'. Moreover, he wanted to use food control to promote 'all sorts of political and political-economic schemes, which in my opinion should be beyond the scope of any relief schemes', Cecil grudgingly acknowledged that it might be desirable to send a British observer to Austria and Hungary, but he urged that Beveridge 'would not be a competent or reliable adviser on political matters; and that, should it be decided to send someone, another selection should be made'.[70]

Beveridge's plea for a humane and constructive policy was tragically vindicated by the history of central Europe over the next twelve months —not to mention the next quarter of a century. On a visit to Vienna at the end of 1919 he found poverty and malnutrition even more prevalent than they had been a year before—in spite of the injection of nearly fifty million dollars in emergency relief.[71] His colleague, E. F. Wise, discovered similar conditions and recommended similar policies in the industrial regions of Germany.[72] As J. M. Keynes remarked, however, in his classic critique of the peace negotiations, 'the fundamental economic problems of a Europe starving and disintegrating before their eyes' was 'the one question in which it was impossible to arouse the interest' of the Allied heads of government.[73] Beveridge was one of the few participants in the Paris conference who tried to penetrate this economic miasma. His role at the conference was a minor one, however, and his share in the negotiations was short-lived. In December 1918 Clynes had resigned as Food Controller and his place was taken by George Roberts, one of the few Labour M.P.s to remain in the Lloyd George coalition after the end of the war. Shortly afterwards Beale also resigned, to work exclusively for the Inter-Allied Food Commission as direct representative of the British Cabinet. Beale continued, however, to make use of his former Ministry of Food subordinates—a situation

[70] Lloyd George Papers, F/49/3/1, memorandum by R. Cecil.
[71] W. H. Beveridge, *Peace in Austria*, 7 Feb. 1920.
[72] Lloyd George Papers, F/8/3/26, copy of letter from G. H. Roberts to W. S. Churchill, 3 Mar. 1919.
[73] J. M. Keynes, *The Economic Consequences of the Peace* (1920), p. 226.

that evoked a strong protest from George Roberts, who accused Beale of undermining his ministerial authority. Roberts complained to Lloyd George that Beale was enticing away the services of Beveridge and other senior officials and that 'his proposals have unsettled them and made them reluctant to return to their duties in London'.[74] Beveridge as a result was recalled to Whitehall, and his appointment as Permanent Secretary was announced in January 1919.

Beveridge thereafter played no official part in the peace negotiations, although he continued in private to press for a liberal settlement and to canvass contributions to famine relief.[75] In March 1919 he arranged a meeting at his own house between Robert Cecil and the Czech Prime Minister, Kramarsch; but Cecil remained apparently unmoved by the mounting crisis in central Europe.[76] When civil war broke out in Hungary Beveridge regarded it as a direct indictment of the selfish and supine policies of the Allied powers. 'I am bound to say I fully understand their joining the Bolshevists,' he remarked angrily after reports of an uprising in Budapest.[77] And to Sir John Beale he wrote: 'I can quite understand the Hungarians giving up hope and turning from the Entente to the Bolsheviks when all they know is that the Entente takes four and a half months before it gives them any help either in food or economics, and is spending the interval in carving their territory about without consulting them.'[78]

Beveridge's own work, however, was once again concerned with food administration at home—and, in particular, with the problem of when and to what extent the vast machinery of wartime controls should be dismantled. It soon became clear that this was by no means a simple question, and that there was a powerful lobby in favour of perpetuating government control over food. Members of the labour movement, fearful of a recurrence of soaring prices, pressed for continuing control, and even among commercial traders there was a small but significant minority who were reluctant to lose the guaranteed customers and prices that wartime controls had entailed.[79] Within the Ministry itself Beveridge's colleague, E. F. Wise—who had been converted to socialism by his wartime administrative experiences—argued for permanent maintenance of control by the state. Wise claimed that 'in nearly every European country proletarian opinion is moving strongly in favour of communal trading'; and he urged his minister that 'the psychological results on labour in all European countries of the abandonment at this moment of

---

[74] Lloyd George Papers. F/44/1/6, G. H. Roberts to D. Lloyd George, 20 Jan. 1919.
[75] *The Times*, WHB to the Editor, 8 Dec. 1919 and 21 Jan. 1920.
[76] BP, IIa, WHB to ASB, 12 Mar. 1919.       [77] BP, IIa, WHB to HB, 25 Mar. 1919.
[78] BP, IV 27, WHB to Sir John Beale, 25 Mar. 1919.
[79] *BFC*, pp. 277, 295–6.

international co-operation in dealing with the common problem of the high cost of living cannot be overlooked'.[80]

Beveridge himself, however, did not share this view—though largely for pragmatic rather than ideological reasons. He believed that, in order to be effective, food control had to be more all-embracing than was politically acceptable in peacetime; and his visits to the continent had convinced him that the first priority of economic policy should be a rapid revival of normal channels of trade. In memoranda to the Food Controller in May and June 1919 he argued that international co-operation had already broken down, and that other allied governments were refusing to continue with the joint purchase of wholesale supplies that was an essential prerequisite of effective control of food. He claimed, moreover, that food prices had already fallen by 10 per cent since the end of the war, and that in so far as they did not fall further this was caused by a depreciation in the value of money which no measures of food control could counteract. He concluded therefore that control should be abandoned for most commodities, and that government policy should henceforth concentrate simply on increasing merchant-shipping space and supplies of imported food.[81] Some months later in a report to the Consumer Council he ascribed high prices mainly to the growth of monopolies, and he urged that under peacetime conditions cheap food could best be guaranteed by a revival of free trade. The same remedies were, he believed, the main solution for the European famine. Before an audience of businessmen in March 1920 he denounced the stupidity of 'governments obsessed with the madness of control'; and he claimed that the only way to restore prosperity to Central Europe was by a revival of the 'principles of the Manchester School'.[82]

The machinery of food control was in fact retained for a further year, largely in response to continuing inflation and industrial unrest. Powerful pressure for decontrol came, however, from the Treasury and from the Conservative wing of the Lloyd George Coalition, and the Ministry of Food was eventually abolished in 1920, its residual powers passing back to the Board of Trade. Beveridge himself played little further part in food policy after May 1919. Since his return from Paris he had been increasingly convinced that there was no permanent role for food control in peacetime; and he began seriously to review his own future career. In April he received from Sidney Webb the unexpected suggestion that he should leave the Civil Service and allow his name to be put forward for the vacant directorship of the London School of Economics. For

[80] Lloyd Papers, folder on Frank Wise, 1934; Notes on Draft Memorandum entitled 'International Food Control', by E. F. Wise, 20 June 1919.

[81] *BFC*, pp. 282–4; Lloyd Papers, 'International Food Control', by WHB, June 1919.

[82] *Daily News* and *Manchester Guardian*, 13 Mar. 1920.

some weeks Beveridge hesitated. He sounded out Llewellyn Smith on the prospect of a return to the Board of Trade; but Llewellyn Smith replied that the future of the Board was 'nebulous', and advised him to accept the position at the L.S.E.[83] His appointment was confirmed by the L.S.E. governors early in July, and he resigned from the Civil Service in September 1919.

V

Throughout the latter half of the war Beveridge, like many other Whitehall officials, had also been continuously involved in plans for post-war reconstruction. The reconstruction movement dated back to the early days of war, and Beveridge himself had drawn up a scheme for the use of labour exchanges in military demobilization as early as December 1914.[84] As hopes of an early peace faded, reconstruction policies had gradually acquired a broader and more radical dimension; and by 1916 it was widely felt that the prolonged destruction and damage of war must be compensated for, not merely by restoration of peace, but by the creation of a better and more 'just' society.[85] This impulse towards social reconstruction was embodied in a series of innovations in the machinery of central government. A Cabinet committee on Reconstruction Problems was first appointed by Asquith in the spring of 1916. It was superseded a year later by a committee of experts under Lloyd George and Edwin Montagu; and finally a full-scale Ministry of Reconstruction was set up in July 1917. The movement covered a wide spectrum of economic, social and political issues, ranging from administrative reform and improvement of industrial relations to enhancement of the status of women and prevention of unemployment after the war.

Beveridge himself first became seriously involved in reconstruction problems in 1916, after his virtual withdrawal from munitions and return to the Board of Trade. He found himself for several months with time on his hands, and he spent this time in doing what he most enjoyed—in looking beyond short-term administrative questions and devising general strategies for economic and social policy.[86] From the start he took the view that the reconstruction movement should not be 'too philanthropic', but should concentrate on measures of 'social organisation', of the kind he had advocated before the war.[87] He became convinced that in any programme of national reconstruction the Board of Trade and

[83] BP, IIb, H. Llewellyn Smith to WHB, 21 Mar. 1919.

[84] BP, IV, 14, 'Demobilization. Draft Scheme for the Return to Civil Employment of Men Leaving the Colours', Dec. 1914.

[85] Arthur Marwick, *The Deluge* (1973 edn.), p. 239.

[86] W. H. Beveridge, 'An Economic General Staff', *Nation and Athenaeum*, 29 Dec. 1924.

[87] BP, IV, 15, WHB to Vaughan Nash, 27 July 1916.

its officials should play a crucial role. He urged that the Board rather than the Ministry of Munitions should be chiefly responsible for resettling workers in peacetime occupations,[88] and as head of the Employment Department he himself became particularly concerned with three major policy issues. These were, firstly, the development of long-term economic forecasting; secondly, the promotion of industrial efficiency and prevention of industrial conflict; and, thirdly, the preparation of measures to deal with the widespread unemployment that seemed likely to occur at the end of the war.

Beveridge composed his first papers on reconstruction problems in April 1916. He circulated notes to his Board of Trade colleagues on the need for detailed planning of the transition from war to peace; and he made a systematic survey of the probable industrial situation after the war.[89] On 27 April he had a long interview with Vaughan Nash, the secretary of the Cabinet's reconstruction committee, at which they discussed problems of demobilization and the re-settlement of soldiers and workers in munitions. Beveridge informed Nash that the Board of Trade was already planning to extend unemployment insurance to all munitions workers, so as to ease the return to normal peacetime production; and he suggested that a special committee should be appointed to forecast patterns of unemployment, to draw up plans for post-war public expenditure and to supervise the distribution of counter-depressive public works.[90] A few weeks later he submitted to Nash's committee a paper proposing certain reforms of post-war industrial structure. In this he recommended the widespread introduction of schemes of 'profit-sharing', not between employers and individual workmen but between employers and trade unions or other kinds of workers' association. Such schemes, Beveridge suggested, would promote solidarity between the two sides of industry, they would discourage strikes and restriction of output, and they would mobilize support among trade union officials for 'discipline and efficiency'. They would at the same time radically transform the nature of trade unions, turning them from restrictive protectionist organizations into profit-making 'business concerns'.[91]

It was soon clear that, at least in the field of labour policy, Beveridge was reluctant to relinquish all the greatly enhanced administrative powers acquired by central government during the course of the war. In a brief for the Prime Minister early in May he recommended that the

---

[88] BP, IV, 15, WHB to H. Llewellyn Smith, 26 June 1916.

[89] Webb Reconstruction Papers, vol. I, ff. 46–9, 'Notes on Preparation for Post-War Conditions', by WHB, early 1916; BP, IV, 15, ms. and typescript notes on Post-War Conditions, n.d.

[90] Webb Reconstruction Papers, vol. I, ff. 93–9, 'An Interview with Mr. Vaughan Nash and Mr. Dale', report by WHB to II. Llewellyn Smith, 28 Apr. 1916.

[91] BP, IV, 15, 'Profit-Sharing between Employer and Trade Union', by WHB, 8 May 1916.

Munitions of War Act should be retained for at least a year after the
war; and he urged that trade union privileges should be restored only
where they were the subject of a definite agreement capable of arbitration. He suggested that wherever possible union leaders should be
'persuaded . . . to forego strict restoration of pre-war conditions, which
in many cases are clearly harmful'; and he proposed instead that 'compulsory profit-sharing' should be widely substituted for voluntary collective bargaining.[92] A few weeks later Beveridge embodied these proposals
in a draft bill, under which 'liberal profit-sharing schemes' would be
introduced in return for the permanent suspension of 'any rule, practice
or custom certified by the Board of Trade . . . to be restrictive of output
or employment or contrary to the national interest'.[93] These proposals
were widely circulated among reconstruction enthusiasts, but they met
with a cool reception from Beveridge's friends and colleagues. Llewellyn
Smith feared that any attempt to evade the restoration of pre-war trade
union practices would provoke union hostility and 'make them suspicious of our good faith'.[94] Vaughan Nash objected that 'to invite the
unions to participate in any such arrangement is to place them in a false
position and to weaken their functions as agencies dealing with wages
and conditions of labour'; and he claimed that there was 'no case in
justice or expediency for sharing profits between capital and labour'.[95]
Beatrice Webb remarked that Beveridge's memorandum was 'the most
notable' of current reconstruction proposals, but that she and Sidney
thought it 'both unworkable and undesirable'. She inferred, moreover,
that 'the formulation of it by the Board of Trade signifies that the
permanent officials desire to undermine the strength of trade unionism
and that they have sufficient contempt for the alertness and intelligence
of trade union officials to believe that they will fall into the trap'.[96]

After this hostile initial reaction profit-sharing schemes played little
further part in Beveridge's plans for reconstruction, although for many
years afterwards he continued to tinker with similar ideas for fostering
co-operation between capital and labour.[97] Whether his proposals had
any practical outcome at the time is not entirely clear. A few weeks
later Nash's committee appointed a 'capital and labour sub-committee';
but the sub-committee's discussions proceeded on very different lines

[92] BP, IV, 15, 'Demobilisation after the War, Notes on Resolutions from the Triple Trades
Union Alliance', ms. and typescript by WHB, May 1916.

[93] BP, IV, 15, 'Labour Reconstruction', and 'Heads of Labour Reconstruction Bill—Part
I', by WHB, n.d. (late May/early June 1916).

[94] BP, IV, 15, 'Demobilization after the War. Notes on Resolutions from the Triple Trade
Union Alliance', annotations by H. Llewellyn Smith, n.d.

[95] BP, IV, 15, 'Profit-Sharing with Trade Unions', by Vaughan Nash, n.d.

[96] Passfield Papers, B. Webb's diary, 8 June 1916.

[97] BP, IIb, WHB to Aneurin Williams, 16 July, 1921; WHB to R. H. Brookings, 21 Apr.
1925; *The Times*, 8 June 1923.

from those envisaged by Beveridge, and eventually led not to profit-sharing schemes but to the wage-settlement system for public employees known as the Whitley Councils. There is, moreover, no evidence to support Beatrice Webb's fear that Beveridge's memorandum represented an official Board of Trade offensive against the trade unions. As he himself assured her, in thinking about profit-sharing he had 'never even in my own mind got beyond the point of exploration'.[98] The proposal was therefore primarily significant, not for its practical influence but because of its personal ideological implications. It was evidence of how far Beveridge was prepared to go at this time in subordinating industrial relations to statutory control; and it may perhaps be seen as the high-water-mark in his personal commitment to the concept of a corporate state.

Beveridge's attention was soon diverted, however, to other and more pressing aspects of post-war labour policy. In June 1916 a further sub-committee was appointed on Army Demobilization; and as a member of this sub-committee Beveridge put in a strong bid for the expansion of his own department. He urged that labour exchanges should be used as the main instrument for resettling soldiers in civilian employment, and he recommended that all discharged soldiers should be given a year's free unemployment insurance under the Act of 1911.[99] On the advice of the Board of Trade the government had in fact already committed itself to providing unemployment insurance for ex-soldiers;[100] but this decision had been strongly criticized by the Treasury, on the grounds that free insurance policies would be prohibitively expensive and that extension of the right to refuse work at less than the customary rate would be subject to 'grave abuse'. Beveridge in reply pointed out that unemployed ex-servicemen would have to be supported somehow; and he claimed that insurance was the 'most organized and scientific' form of relief, and that payments through a labour exchange would keep the recipients in constant touch with opportunities for employment.[101] These arguments were accepted by the Demobilization sub-committee in its first interim report in October 1916. The report recommended that all discharged soldiers should be entitled to certain 'war gratuities', to four weeks' furlough with pay, and to a year's free unemployment insurance entitling them to benefit for up to twenty weeks. Benefits were to be administered by labour exchanges, working in close conjunction with local demobilization committees. The report observed that

[98] Passfield Papers, IV, 7, WHB to B. Webb, 14 Mar. 1917.

[99] BP, IV, 15, 'Post-War Problems. Employment Department', n.d.

[100] W. H. Beveridge, 'Unemployment Insurance in the War and After', in *War and Insurance*, ed. James T. Shotwell (1927), p. 233.

[101] BP. IV, 15, 'Note on Treasury Memorandum on Unemployment Insurance for ex-Soldiers', by WHB, 14 June 1916; 'Unemployment Insurance for ex-Soldiers', by WHB, n.d.

exchanges were still unpopular with certain sections of the working class; but it ascribed this unpopularity to the prevalence of the myth that exchanges were still primarily institutions for dealing with casual labour. It would be 'bad in principle' and socially divisive to have two different methods of finding work—one for civilians and the other for discharged soldiers. The committee concluded, moreover, that 'the State cannot and should not abdicate the control of so large and important an operation, conducted at the cost of public funds, and transfer it to unpaid committees under no direct responsibility to Parliament and the nation'. It recommended also that labour exchanges should henceforth be known as 'employment exchanges', to symbolize the enlargement of their economic and social functions.[102]

Beveridge himself had begun to prepare for the implementation of these measures nearly two months before the Demobilization sub-committee eventually reported.[103] At the same time he began to think once again about the problem of casual employment, and he and other Board of Trade officials prepared a scheme for decasualization of dock labour—a scheme whereby after the war dock employment would be exclusively confined to registered dockers, working for a guaranteed minimum wage.[104] In October and November 1916 he wrote a series of papers on the post-war re-settlement of labour; and there seems little doubt that at this time Beveridge was hoping to be placed personally in charge of both military and civilian demobilization. It was a problem in many ways peculiarly suited to his talents—a problem which by its nature would involve far-reaching policy-formation and which was unlikely ever to subside into a repetitive administrative routine. It was a problem also that would require the invention of precise and watertight administrative rules and machinery, at which perhaps nobody in White-hall was more skilful than Beveridge himself. Demobilization seemed, moreover, to offer a golden opportunity for those measures of comprehensive 'social organization'—decasualization, compulsory insurance, rationalization of the labour market—that Beveridge had espoused so vigorously before the war. For a short time in the autumn of 1916 it seemed that Beveridge's ambition was close to realization. He had the support of Llewellyn Smith and of the committee on Reconstruction; and he successfully warded off a demand from the Local Government Board that demobilization should be managed solely by charitable committees.[105] Towards the end of November, however, Beveridge fell

[102] BP, IV, 15, Reconstruction Committee. First (Interim) Report of the Sub-Committee on the Demobilization of the Army, Oct. 1916.

[103] BP, IV, 15, 'Demobilization Preparations', by WHB, 23 Aug. 1916.

[104] *Unemployment: a Problem of Industry* (1930 edn.), pp. 317–18.

[105] BP, IV, 15, note by WHB, 13 Oct. 1916; 'Riders to Counterblast Mr. Long's Memorandum', 9 Nov. 1916; Reconstruction Committee papers, circulated 19 Dec. 1916.

ill and was away from his office for several weeks. When he returned to work in December 1916 the decision had been taken to transfer demobilization to the new Ministry of Labour. Beveridge, as we have already seen, was excluded from the new ministry by the hostility of certain trade unionists, and his attempts to persuade John Hodge to give him a senior position proved of no avail. Looking back on this incident in later years he saw it as the most important turning point and the greatest missed opportunity of his professional career.[106]

Beveridge no longer hoped to be placed personally in charge of post-war demobilization, but he continued to urge that the demobilization period should be used for introducing a wide range of reforms. Throughout 1916 and 1917 he had frequent discussions with the Webbs and Llewellyn Smith, during which they thrashed out plans for dealing with unemployment, for reforming the machinery of government, and for developing facilities for long-term economic planning.[107] The Webbs like Beveridge were convinced that the war would be followed by a serious recession, and they were keen to promote the policies for meeting unemployment outlined in their Poor Law Report of 1909.[108] Beveridge himself, however, was chiefly interested in measures of decasualization and in the extension of insurance; and he was particularly anxious that provision should be made for discharged munitions workers, comparable with the provision that was already being planned for unemployed ex-servicemen.[109] In view of the high wages paid to munitions workers, however, it seemed reasonable to Beveridge and his Board of Trade colleagues not to grant free policies but to extend contributory insurance. An Act extending unemployment insurance to all workers in munitions had therefore been introduced by the Board in September 1916. This Act was potentially very wide in scope since 'munitions work' was taken to include not merely workers in armaments factories but all workers involved in producing military supplies, such as cotton-workers, tailors, and producers of boots and shoes. The Act met with immediate resistance from many of the employers and workers to whom it applied— particularly among those not engaged in arms production, who could less easily envisage the prospect of redundancy after the war. The textile industries insisted on the issue of exclusion orders, exempting their workers from the new Act, and in the leather trade both employers and workers refused to pay contributions and had to be excluded by retrospective legislation. The result was that the Act of 1916 eventually applied to little more than a million workers; and more than two-thirds

[106] BP, Ic 50, notes for WHB's diary, 29–30 Dec. 1934.
[107] BP, IIb, B. Webb to WHB, 1 July and 7 Nov. 1917.
[108] BP, IIb, 'Memorandum on the Problem of the Able-Bodied', by B. Webb, 1 Nov. 1917.
[109] BP, IV, 15, 'Industrial Demobilization' by WHB, 1 Nov. 1916.

of the labour force were still not covered by unemployment insurance in the last year of war.[110]

Nevertheless Beveridge and other Whitehall officials were convinced that the end of the war would bring 'a general dislocation of industry and the need for practically universal insurance', and this belief was increasingly reflected in discussions of reconstruction.[111] In the spring of 1917 the new Ministry of Reconstruction set up a special committee to examine the problems of civilian workers engaged in war production; and this committee appointed Beveridge as chairman of a sub-committee to consider the future of insurance against unemployment. The report of this sub-committee, issued early in 1918, not surprisingly bore the strong imprint of Beveridges' own current thinking on insurance questions—although he claimed that its recommendations had been strongly endorsed by leading employers and trade unionists.[112] The report stated that the Act of 1916 had been a failure and that any further attempt to insure 'war workers' as a special group would be similarly pointless— partly because of resistance from the trades concerned, and partly because of the difficulty in a total war situation of defining precisely what constituted 'war work'. The report claimed that any attempt simply to extend unemployment insurance to specific industries would present similar difficulties, since it would be impossible either to predict accurately where unemployment was likely to occur or to convince workers in the chosen trades that they were particularly at risk. The report therefore concluded that unemployment insurance should be made universal; and it put forward a plan which combined direct state insurance with a wide degree of scope for special schemes subsidized by the state but managed by voluntary bodies, such as trade unions or joint societies of workers and employers. Such a plan, it was claimed, would harness both public and private initiative, and was 'based on the principle that the State, while prescribing the end to be attained— universal insurance against unemployment during the reconstruction period—should leave the greatest possible freedom as to the means to be adopted for this end, according to the varying conditions of each trade'.[113]

Beveridge was convinced that a universal scheme should be introduced well in advance of the anticipated post-war depression, and he concluded his report by proposing immediate legislation. He himself

[110] PRO, PIN 7/6, National Insurance (Part II) (Munitions Workers) Act, 1916, Summary of Objections; W. H. Beveridge, 'Unemployment Insurance in the War and After', loc. cit. pp. 232–3.

[111] Ibid., p. 233.

[112] PRO, PIN 7/12, WHB to D. Shackleton, 14 June 1918.

[113] PRO, PIN 7/12, Civil War Workers Committee, Unemployment Insurance Sub-Committee—Draft Report.

drew his report to the attention of the Ministry of Labour. He met, however, with a disappointing response. The minister, George Roberts, was sympathetic; but Thomas Phillips, the official now in charge of unemployment insurance, denounced Beveridge's proposals as 'very dangerous'.[114] Phillips objected particularly to the idea of a state subsidy to sectoral insurance schemes, arguing that this would relieve strike funds, isolate workers from contact with a labour exchange and encourage the formation of 'bogus societies'.[115] Beveridge in reply claimed that trade unions with special schemes would continue as at present to lodge their 'vacant books' at local exchanges; and he pointed out that ultimately 'any provision . . . made by the State for unemployment tends to relieve the Union Fund in whatever form it may be'.[116] He failed, however, to persuade Phillips to take immediate action. A few months later he wrote to the Ministry's permanent secretary, David Shackleton, urging him to extend unemployment insurance and offering his own services in the preparation of legislation; but Shackleton replied that the question was already being considered by several departmental committees.[117] The demand for universal insurance was in fact endorsed by a Ministry of Labour committee in June 1918; but again no action was taken, partly for fear that the measure would prove politically unpopular, and partly because of objections from the Minister of Reconstruction, Christopher Addison, who insisted that any universal scheme must contain provision for 'contracting-out'.[118] The upshot was that when the war came to an abrupt end three weeks later the government was forced to fall back on a non-contributory civilian 'out-of-work donation', similar to that already promised for discharged soldiers. To Beveridge this was the end of his hopes that demobilization would be used for a radical reform of the labour market, and it was at the same time a serious blow to those rational principles of insurance administration on which he had worked so assiduously for the previous ten years. Looking back on the scheme twelve years later he conceded that the military out-of-work donation, which had been carefully planned for a clearly defined group of beneficiaries, had worked reasonably well. But the civilian donation, which had been hastily extemporized to cover the failure to extend insurance, had

[114] BP, IIa, WHB to ASB, 24 Feb. 1918; PRO, PIN 7/12, T. W. Phillips to C. F. Rey, 17 Jan. 1918.

[115] PRO, PIN 7/12, Notes by T. Phillips on the Unemployment Insurance Sub-Committee Draft Report.

[116] PRO, PIN 7/12, WHB to T. W. Phillips, 18 Jan. 1918.

[117] PRO, PIN 7/12, WHB to D. Shackleton, 14 June 1918; D. Shackleton to WHB, 17 June 1918.

[118] PRO, PIN 7/36, Ministry of Labour, Extension of Unemployment Insurance Committee, Minutes and Papers, May–July 1917; PIN 7/13, 'Contributory Insurance: Memorandum by the Minister of Reconstruction', 6 Nov. 1918.

let loose a flood of criticism and damaged the whole principle of insurance. Thrust on the exchanges at a few weeks' notice, it allowed no time for framing water-tight regulations or collecting and training staff. . . . No satisfactory definition of those entitled to donation was possible; as a free gift everyone tried to get all he could; casual workers and men on the borderland of being unemployable harvested the benefit. . . . The damage done to the principle and credit of unemployment insurance cannot be doubted. From the donation scheme dates the term 'dole', indiscriminately applied later to insurance benefit also; from it dates the conception of largesse in which all were entitled to share.[119]

# VI

Beveridge's career in the civil service during the First World War was in many ways markedly less successful than it had been before 1914. It is true that he held high positions throughout the war, and early in 1919 he was awarded the K.C.B. and promoted to the rank of permanent secretary—being, at thirty-nine, one of the youngest men ever to reach this position in Whitehall. He was conscious throughout these years, however, of feelings of frustration and failure. He disclaimed any desire for personal recognition; but, nevertheless, he had hoped for both the permanent secretaryship and the K.C.B. several years before they were actually given to him.[120] He felt that he had lost the personal influence which he had enjoyed under Churchill and Buxton, and that he had been systematically excluded from his chosen fields of social insurance and labour organization. The war, he later recorded, had robbed him of his 'vocation': 'The problem of unemployment was changed; the experiments of labour exchanges and insurance were distorted, my personal connection with them were cut.'[121] This experience constituted the first major set-back that Beveridge had encountered in his single-minded attempt to reform and rationalize British social institutions and policy. It coincided with, and was partly responsible for, a fundamental change in his personal philosophy. Beveridge had entered the war a convinced believer in the need for state intervention in social affairs. During the early years of the war his commitment to this view was greatly enhanced, and on several occasions between 1915 and 1917 he advocated policies which in the eyes of many contemporaries seemed not merely interventionist but suspiciously authoritarian. During the next two years, however, he underwent a gradual reaction against his earlier views, and he emerged from the war in 1919 increasingly sceptical of state control and increasingly inclined towards policies of non-intervention. At the same

---

[119] *Unemployment: a Problem of Industry* (1930 edn.), pp. 273–4.
[120] BP, IIa, ms. conversation with ASB, 30 Dec. 1916; WHB to ASB, 6 June 1918.
[121] BP, Ic 50, notes for WHB's diary, 29–30 Dec. 1934.

time he became markedly more conservative in his mental outlook; and like many others of his generation he increasingly hankered after things that were 'pre-war'—an adjective, he recorded, that he was 'coming to use as the highest term of praise'.[122]

The reasons for these changes in Beveridge's attitudes must be to some extent conjectural, but it seems probable that they were closely linked with his personal experience in wartime administration. As we have seen, Beveridge as a young man had conscientiously believed that the interests of the state should always take precedence over those of individuals; and this principle seemed to him to gain added strength from the exigencies of war. Hence his support for policies designed to regulate collective bargaining and to restrict free movement of labour—policies which he believed would improve industrial efficiency even in time of peace. However, the criticisms which such policies aroused—not merely from trade unionists but from personal friends like the Webbs and Llewellyn Smith—seem eventually to have persuaded Beveridge that state regulation of the labour market was not practically feasible. Similarly, his experience of food rationing convinced him that—even when politically popular—state control was an 'all-or-nothing' process; partial control merely ignited a chain of unforeseen reactions which eventually multiplied the problems that control was designed to solve. These reflections seem to have induced in Beveridge a certain loss of faith in the administrative process—or at least in the administrative process as he had conceived of it before 1914. This is not to say that he lost interest in administrative questions; but there was, nevertheless, a noticeable difference between his attitude to administration in the 1900s and that which he adopted after the war. In the 1900s, as was shown in earlier chapters, he tended to regard all social problems as administrative problems—as problems to be solved simply by devising an appropriate piece of governmental machinery. After the war he was by comparison much more sceptical about the nature and limits of governmental action; and at the same time he became much more conscious—perhaps over-conscious—of the inhibiting influence on the would-be reformer of political, economic and ideological constraints.

The war was therefore a watershed in the development of Beveridge's ideas about politics and society; it encompassed both the apogee of his youthful belief in state action and the beginning of his transition to a philosophy of economic liberalism and administrative *laissez-faire*. This transition gathered momentum in the 1920s and was to dominate his social and economic thinking for much of the inter-war years. The influence of war on a particular individual cannot be assessed, however, in purely intellectual terms, and more must be said about the impact of

[122] BP, IIa, WHB to ASB, 3 July 1918.

the war on Beveridge as a human being. Perhaps here the most significant events were not those which Beveridge himself experienced but those
which he did not. Many post-war writers observed that the war had
created a deep imaginative cleavage between those who stayed at home
and those who went to the front, and Beveridge through no fault of his
own found himself on one side of this gulf. Years later, when he read
Vera Brittain's *Testament of Youth*, he was deeply struck by her condemnation of the pre-war generation for failing to prevent the war, and
by her reference to the 'fundamental antagonism which persists to this
day between those who suffered deeply from the war, and the others
who escaped its most violent impacts'. 'I can understand the bitterness
of her feeling against the causers of the war,' Beveridge commented,
'but were there any specific causers? Or were there few enough to
indict? Try as I may, I don't feel able to plead guilty of causing the war
or cynically exploiting the young to death, either personally or as one
of my generation.' He admitted, however, that in certain respects Vera
Brittain's description exactly fitted his own case. Not only was he never
personally involved in fighting but, untypically in that era of death and
telegrams, he lost no one dear to him throughout the four years of war.
The only incident of the fighting that affected him directly was the
wounding of Tawney on the Somme. 'Apart from this one anxiety—
soon over,' Beveridge recorded, 'I hardly felt the war at all personally or
emotionally. My generation was half-way between being in the trenches
itself and having children there; my closest associates were for the most
part civil servants like myself who, rightly or wrongly, stayed behind the
lines.'[123] The closest he came to the scene of warfare was shortly after
hostilities had ended, when he visited the battlefields of Northern France.
At Loos he noted that 'the place is and looks like a murderer—haunted
and really horrible beyond words'. Even in November 1918, however,
the impact of the battlefields derived chiefly from their association with
the fast-receding past. Of the Hohenzollern Redoubt Beveridge observed
that 'the horror of the place—and it is indeed a grisly one—lay simply
in its hopeless hideousness and its memories'. The town of Ypres, he
recorded, was already sliding visibly into history; it had 'the air of
Tintern Abbey, mossy and mellowed'.[124]

Beveridge felt therefore that he had lost his leading role in the pre-war
epic of social reform, and that he had played little part in the ensuing
tragedy. This regret for his lost vocation, uneasily combined with his
curious sense of remoteness from the reality of war, may perhaps help
to explain certain developments in Beveridge's character and personality
during these years—changes that were watched with dismay by some of

[123] BP, Ic 50, notes for WHB's diary, 29–30 Dec. 1934.
[124] BP, IIa, WHB to ASB, 25 and 26 Nov. 1918.

his closest contemporaries. There seemed to be a growing rigidity in certain aspects of his mental outlook, a contraction in the scope of his imaginative sympathies, a certain aloofness from and loss of contact with some of his oldest friends. With Tawney he recorded that he continued to 'discuss as usual the future of the war and the world';[125] but his pre-war intimacy with Tawney was not resumed—presumably because of the widening gulf between their personal experience and political convictions. With Denman he remained on close terms, but they no longer shared the same political aspirations—Denman having become a fierce critic of the war and supporter of the Union of Democratic Control. Even with the Webbs his relationship was less sympathetic than it had once been, although they were to be thrown much together by his work at the London School of Economics. 'Beveridge . . . is too mechanical minded,' observed Beatrice Webb. 'One never comes into contact with either his intellect or his emotions.'[126] At the same time he seemed to lose some of that quality of passionate idealism which in earlier years had persuaded people to forgive or overlook the more abrasive sides of his personality. Before the war he had been deeply involved in his work for the Board of Trade, and both his work and leisure had been welded together by an all-consuming commitment to the cause of reform. By comparison much of his wartime work was a chore. It was necessary and difficult and extremely exhausting, but it was only of transitory significance and it made few demands on Beveridge's personal vision of society. In the few cases where this was not so and where his personal convictions *were* aroused—in famine relief, in reform of industrial structure, and in post-war reconstruction—Beveridge on each occasion was singularly unsuccessful in gaining support for his views. The result was a certain deadening of his enthusiasms, and a waning of his earlier belief in the possibility of 'reasoned progress' and of rational administrative reforms. By the end of the war he felt that he had been employed for five years on work of no permanent importance, and that he had become the slave of a sterile administrative routine. 'I've had quite enough work to make me a very dull little bureaucrat,' he commented wryly in 1918; and a year later he found it a 'glorious relief' to lay down his duties as permanent secretary.[127] He referred to the war in later years as a period of personal 'coma',[128] and his final comments on food control may be read as a bleak epitaph, not merely on the war itself, but on his sense of futility about his own work during the war period. 'Like other civilian departments,' he wrote in his war history,

[125] BP, IIa, WHB to ASB, 3 May 1918.
[126] Passfield Papers, B. Webb's Diary, 4 May 1922.
[127] BP, IIa, WHB to ASB, 20 Oct. 1918 and 15 Aug. 1919.
[128] *PI*, p. 211.

the Ministry of Food to those who worked in it was a refuge, a means to forget in nights and days of overpowering toil what else was happening, in the trenches and on the sea, in the air of heaven, in hospitals and prison camps and ravaged lands. It opened no way of permanent advance; its record is that of one small aspect of the human spirit in its five years' prison, but here upon a treadmill that has ground no corn. The most intricate experiments of the Ministry which culminated in the control of livestock or the rationing system, are those farthest removed from any possible task of peace; little if anything learned in them can be of use again, save in a civilization bent again on self-destruction. The account that has been given here of these particular experiments . . . is no more than a surface gleaning of the archives. There forms and circulars, reports and instructions, schemes and counter-schemes and plans for another war, all so many monuments of toiling ingenuity, are mouldering gently into dust and oblivion—lie buried, please God, forever.[129]

[129] *BFC*, p. 344.

# II

# The London School of Economics

## I

BEVERIDGE took up his post as director of the London School of Economics in October 1919. He was to remain there for eighteen years, and it was to be the scene of some of his greatest personal failures and triumphs. When Beveridge came to the School it already housed a distinguished coterie of scholars; but it was nevertheless a small and rather obscure institution, providing mainly part-time courses for students living in London. By 1937 it had become the largest centre for the study of social sciences in Britain. Its premises had increased threefold and its annual budget sevenfold;[1] it had many teachers with an international reputation and attracted students and scholars from all over the world. Much of this expansion was due to the force, vision and tireless energy of Beveridge himself—a fact that was acknowledged by many of his colleagues.[2] At the same time, however, Beveridge's directorship forcibly demonstrated many of his faults and shortcomings, both as an administrator and as a human being. In a curious way his career at the School mirrored and highlighted the pattern of his earlier career in Whitehall. In both situations he started out as a zealous and dynamic innovator, and in both situations he was eventually rejected by the new institutions that he himself had made. In both contexts he appeared at his best in policy-formation, as the architect of grand visions and designer of far-reaching schemes; he appeared at his worst in day-to-day administration, in accommodating the views of critics or opponents, and in the personal conduct of often trivial aspects of institutional affairs. The next two chapters will consider in some detail Beveridge's contribution to the growth of the L.S.E., his role in the wider history of higher education, and his personal development during his period at the L.S.E. They will analyse also some of the debates and controversies that broke out at the School during Beveridge's directorship—debates that stemmed partly from personal rivalries and partly from more deep-seated issues, such as the distribution of power in college government, the extent of academic freedom, and the nature and content of the social sciences.

[1] Janet Beveridge, *An Epic of Clare Market* (1960), pp. 67–8.
[2] Passfield Papers, B. Webb's diary, 16 Dec. 1933; BP, IIb, B. Webb to WHB, 1 Oct. 1937.

## II

The history of the L.S.E. has been told many times and need not be recounted in detail.[3] Nevertheless, certain features of that history must be mentioned in order to indicate the character of the institution that Beveridge took over in 1919 and the problems that he faced. The school had been founded twenty-four years earlier by a small group of progressive reformers headed by Sidney and Beatrice Webb. It was designed to provide higher education in certain areas of knowledge where the older British universities were notoriously weak—in economics, anthropology, public administration and the study of modern societies. It was implicitly based on a highly rationalist conception of politics and society—on the belief that men would be better governed and institutions better organized if rulers and citizens were better informed about social, political and economic processes. It may perhaps be seen as the most enduring monument to that movement for 'national efficiency' in which the Webbs had been closely involved at the turn of the nineteenth century.[4]

From the start of its history the School had acquired a 'socialist' reputation—partly because it had originally been financed by a bequest to the Fabian Society for 'socialist propaganda', partly by association with the views of the Webbs. This reputation seems, however, to have been singularly unjustified, since Sidney Webb insisted that the School should represent all shades of opinion—believing that its influence would be impaired by blatant political bias and that the inherent superiority of socialism would eventually become manifest through a free exchange of views.[5] Possibly for this reason Webb seems to have gone out of his way to recruit non-socialists to senior positions in the School. Of the first three directors only one was in any sense a socialist—William Pember Reeves, who was a Fabian and a former minister in a New Zealand Labour Government. The first director, W. S. Hewins, had been a Conservative tariff reformer and his successor, Halford Mackinder, was a 'Bismarkian Darwinist of the purest Milnerian water'.[6] Among the teaching staff theoretical socialism was equally uncommon. Of the School's earliest professors the only socialist was the Fabian, Graham Wallas; and by the 1900s Wallas had virtually broken with the Fabians and had drawn closer to the 'new Liberals' in many of

---

[3] Janet Beveridge, *An Epic of Clare Market*; Lord Beveridge, *The London School of Economics and its Problems 1919–1937* (1960); Sydney Caine, *The History of the Foundation of the London School of Economics and Political Science* (1963).

[4] E. J. T. Brennan, *Education for National Efficiency: the Contribution of Sidney and Beatrice Webb* (1975), pp. 34–9.

[5] *An Epic of Clare Market*, pp. 49–50.

[6] Wallas Papers, Box 3, A. Zimmern to G. Wallas, 12 May (?1908).

his views. The School's senior economist, Edwin Cannan, was a leading exponent of unfashionable principles of Gladstonian finance; and the reader in economic history, Lilian Knowles, 'combined outspoken anti-sacerdotalism and anti-snobbery, with violent Toryism'.[7] L. T. Hobhouse, the Professor of Sociology, was a leading philosopher of radical liberalism and the School's Social Science department had been taken over from the School of Sociology, a body founded by the London C.O.S.

The image of the L.S.E. as a socialist institution was therefore largely unfounded. If anything, the bias of its teaching in the early twentieth century leaned, not towards socialism, but towards radical Milnerite conservatism and opposition to Free Trade. Nevertheless, the image persisted of the L.S.E. as an institution devoted, if not actually to socialism, at least to a kind of authoritarian administrative collectivism that in the eyes of many people was much the same thing. 'The new helotry in the servile state run by the archivists of the London School of Economics means a race of paupers in a grovelling community ruled by uniformed prigs,' declared John Burns in 1910; and towards the end of Pember Reeves' directorship the School was undoubtedly regarded as 'a place where socialism is propagated'—a fact which contemporaries, perhaps unfairly, ascribed to the influence of Pember Reeves himself.[8] Whatever its source, it seems that this reputation for socialism was increasingly seen by Sidney Webb as an academic encumbrance. Early in 1917 Webb foresaw that the ending of the war would bring about a greatly increased demand for university training in economics and public administration, and he was determined that the L.S.E. should play a major part in meeting this demand.[9] The expansion of the L.S.E., however, depended on winning the confidence of City businessmen, local authorities and other grant-giving agencies; and in such a process Pember Reeves' dogmatic Fabianism proved more of a liability than an asset. Reeves had shown himself, moreover, to be an indifferent administrator; he had lost the confidence of his staff, and he had shown little interest in the prospects for expansion. Reeves was in fact 'a politician manqué', who saw his directorship as little more than 'a passing job' and as a convenient springboard for advancing his political career.[10]

Early in 1919 Sidney Webb was appointed trustee of a fund set up by Sir Ernest Cassel to endow a new Commerce degree in the University

---

[7] 'Professor Lilian Knowles 1870–1926', obituary by Graham Wallas, *Economica*, VI, 17 June 1926, p. 121.

[8] Burns Papers, B.M. Add. Ms. 46301, f. 121, J. Burns to H. G. Wells, 16 May 1910; Samuel Papers, A/155, XI, A. Carr Saunders to H. Samuel, n.d.

[9] Letters of Sidney Webb to the Director, S. Webb to W. Pember Reeves, 11 Mar. 1917.

[10] B. P. IIb, S. Webb to WHB, 14 July 1919; Samuel Papers, A/155, XI, A. Carr Saunders to H. Samuel, n.d.

of London; and he was determined that the lion's share of this money should go to the L.S.E.[11] He came to the conclusion that Pember Reeves, with his 'pathological vanity' and lack of interest in the School's development was manifestly unsuited to supervise this expansion; and he 'had to undertake the unpleasant task of telling an old friend . . . that the time had come for him to resign the directorship'.[12] Beveridge was not the Webbs' first choice as Pember Reeves' successor. The post had been previously offered to Professor W. G. Adams, who had just been elected warden of All Souls. Apart from Adams, however, no other candidates were seriously considered by the L.S.E. authorities. Beveridge seemed to Sidney Webb to offer to the School precisely the talents and perspectives that were needed for a period of massive and rapid expansion. He was a highly efficient organizer, he had an instinct for publicity, he had wide contacts with public officials, and he had the capacity for self-commitment that Pember Reeves had conspicuously lacked. He shared Webb's belief in the need for more formal training in economics and government, and since the 1900s he had been a powerful advocate of those 'modern studies' in which the Webbs were pioneers. He had himself been a part-time student at the School, and had been offered a post on the staff as early as 1906.[13] At the same time he was a man of powerful intellect, he could deal on an equal footing with academics, politicians and civil servants, and in Sidney Webb's view his study of unemployment was 'perhaps the most brilliant and original contribution to economics of the present century'.[14] Beatrice Webb appears to have been more doubtful, but soon acquiesced in her husband's judgement. 'Beveridge was Sidney's choice and has been accepted by the Governors,' she recorded. 'He has his defects—he is not the sweetest-tempered of men and has a certain narrowness of outlook. But he is a good administrator—an initiator of both ideas and plans and a man who will concentrate his energies on the School. Our relations with him are pleasant and friendly—his views are slightly anti-labour but pro-collectivist and he is an innovator, not a conventional-minded man. He is also "well seen" by the Government Departments.'[15]

## III

When Beveridge accepted his new post in 1919 he was therefore confronted with a multitude of tasks and problems. He was to revive the flagging morale of lecturers and professors, to win the financial con-

[11] Wallas Papers, Box 6, S. Webb to G. Wallas, 16 Nov. 1918.
[12] Passfield Papers, B. Webb's Diary, 29 Apr. 1919 and 29 Nov. 1920.
[13] BP, IIa, WHB to ASB, 22 June 1906.
[14] Letters of Sidney Webb to the Director, S. Webb to C. Mactaggart, 21 June 1919.
[15] Passfield Papers, B. Webb's diary, 23 June 1919.

fidence of politicians and businessmen, to develop new branches of academic learning and to secure for the L.S.E. a central and permanent place in British higher education. Whether he initially realized that this was what lay in store for him seems unlikely. The Webbs had rather disingenuously assured him that the School would 'run itself'; and he himself clearly hoped that the post would give him scope for fulfilling his long-cherished ambition of becoming a 'scientific economist'.[16] This desire was reflected in his research on prices and the trade cycle which increasingly occupied much of his spare time. It was reflected also in his earliest lectures to L.S.E. students, when he spoke to packed audiences on unemployment.[17] Almost immediately, however, this aspect of his work was eclipsed by questions of college administration. As early as July 1919 he mapped out a programme for the School's development, concentrating particularly on the growth of the new Commerce Degree, on 'research into state control', on courses of training for civil servants, and on 'making the School a place to which the press can come and editors send their young men to get economic facts and opinions'.[18] When he took up his directorship in October he was instantly absorbed in plans for acquiring new buildings, promoting the new Commerce Degree, recruiting staff, and raising funds from the Treasury and the Unemployment Grants Committee. The result was that his interest in research was thwarted from the start. 'I don't have time to write anything and that rather grieves me,' he commented several years later, '. . . I have no time to be a philosopher or an economist but [am] absolutely an administrator.'[19] In 1923 when he was offered the post of Chief Education Officer to the L.C.C., he declined on the ground that 'the only post for which I should ever wish to leave my present one, would be a post of a Professor with no students and a large grant for research. I am not really in the market for more administration'.[20]

Beveridge's new job was not therefore precisely what he had expected, but nevertheless he threw himself into it 'with characteristic zeal and energy'.[21] When he arrived at the School many students were being taught in huts on the neighbouring Aldwych building site, and over the next few years his chief priorities were the acquisition of land and erection of new college buildings. Even before the war the School's premises had been totally inadequate for its student body, consisting merely of the Passmore Edwards building on the corner of Clare Market—a building that forcibly reminded its beholders 'that economics has been called

[16] *PI*, pp. 168–9; above, p. 62.
[17] BP, IIa, WHB to ASB, 26 Nov. 1920.
[18] BP, IIa, WHB to ASB, 13 July 1919.
[19] BP, IIb, WHB to Arthur Lord, 20 Nov. 1923.
[20] BP, IIb, WHB to Sir Edwin Cooper Perry, 19 Sept. 1923.
[21] Lord Chorley, 'Beveridge and the L.S.E. Part One', *L.S.E.*, no. 44, Nov. 1972, p. 7.

the gloomy science'.[22] The slums of Clare Market had once bustled with thieves and prostitutes, but it was now a desolate area awaiting redevelopment, and on the surrounding wilderness of graveyards, tenements and workshops Sidney Webb and Beveridge cast keen and calculating eyes. Already in 1918 Webb had resolved that part of the Cassel donation should be used for new buildings; and this use of the fund was fully endorsed by Beveridge, who was determined that each member of staff should have his own room for teaching and private research.[23] A site was acquired in Houghton Street running south from Clare Market to the Aldwych. An appeal for £150,000 was launched, the foundation stone was laid by King George V in 1920, and the new building was opened in May 1922. This was merely the beginning of the unprecedented expansion that occurred at the L.S.E. during Beveridge's directorship. Throughout the 1920s he was continually making plans to take over the rest of Houghton Street, urging the L.C.C. to use its powers of compulsory purchase on the School's behalf and threatening the remaining residents with private Acts of Parliament to secure their dispossession. The east side of Houghton Street was acquired in 1926, and St. Clements Press was eased out on very favourable terms in 1927— the owner of the press generously donating £3,000 towards the cost of purchase. Two disused schools were taken over from the L.C.C. in 1929, and as early as 1924 Beveridge and Webb were holding a watching brief for the W. H. Smith Memorial building in neighbouring Portugal Street —a property that did not ultimately pass into the possession of the School until nearly fifty years later.[24] Further buildings were commissioned in 1929 and additional storeys were added to the existing premises. 'Resplendent in new stone and cedar panelling', the new L.S.E. was a 'direct expression of Beveridge's own personality' commented a civil servant in 1924. 'It appears as a working College of London University and it is destined more and more to strike the imagination of London and the world as the representative college of the great Metropolitan University. Its very appearance reminds one that its full title is The London School of Economics and Political Science.'[25]

Beveridge's most ambitious property venture centred not on the School, but on the creation of a central building for London University. The University of London had developed in the nineteenth century mainly as an examining body, awarding only external degrees. In the

[22] J. H. Macrae-Gibson, 'Civil Servant to University Director, Sir William Beveridge, K.C.B.', *Red Tape*, Sept. 1924, p. 457.

[23] *The London School of Economics and its Problems*, pp.18-19.

[24] L.S.E. Papers, minutes of the Emergency Committee, 5 Nov. 1924, 21 Jan. 1925, 2 Feb. 1926, 22 Feb. and 5 July 1927, 19 Nov. 1929; Letters of Sidney Webb to the Director, WHB to S Webb, 11 Nov. 1924.

[25] J. H. Macrae-Gibson, loc. cit., p. 457.

1890s, however, the Royal Commission on the University of London had recommended the development of teaching as well as examining functions, and this had resulted in the incorporation into the University of many colleges in the London area, including the L.S.E. Since 1900 both 'internal' and 'external' sides of the University had undergone rapid expansion—though with a considerable amount of rivalry and hostility between the two. By the end of the war the University's head-quarters in South Kensington had become manifestly inadequate to cope with this expansion; and in 1919 the Board of Education had proposed to set up a new centre for London University, on a site in Bloomsbury purchased from the Duke of Bedford. This proposal had been strongly denounced by the 'external' interests, who feared that it would shift the balance of power in favour of the teaching colleges, and no agreement was reached among the main contending parties for the next five years. Beveridge himself from the start of his directorship threw in his hand with the proponents of the Bloomsbury site. He strongly favoured the development of a closer and more formal relationship between the colleges and the university. The existing structure, he remarked caustically, reminded him of 'a turn in a workmen's social club . . . the Fat Girl of Bethnal Green'. He was equally opposed both to a mere extension of the South Kensington site and to the building of the new University in some remote London suburb. He believed that London needed a true 'civic' university, organically related to the centres of government, commerce and population; and he claimed that the size of the proposed Bloomsbury site would give scope for the construction of a magnificent, spacious, multi-purpose building, worthy of the metropolis whose needs it would serve.[26] His main motives in supporting the Bloomsbury scheme, however, were to increase the power of the teaching colleges and to improve the status and significance of the L.S.E. As part of a system centred in South Kensington, L.S.E. was rather on the periphery of university affairs; as part of a system centred in Bloomsbury it would be one of the most important colleges in London, able to share and perhaps to dominate university policy, administration and finance.

Early in 1926 the Board of Education despaired of persuading the university authorities to reach any agreement, and the Bloomsbury site was sold back to the Duke of Bedford for £425,000. This spurred the supporters of Bloomsbury to take desperate action. In May 1926 Beveridge was invited to stand for election as Vice Chancellor, in opposition to Dr. Ernest Graham Little, the representative of medical, legal and other 'external' interests, who sat as M.P. for London University. The

[26] W. H. Beveridge, 'The University of London and its Colleges', *The Education Outlook*, May 1925, pp. 169–72.

election quickly resolved itself into a battle for the Bloomsbury site. It coincided with the General Strike, and was fought out in an atmosphere of considerable tension. Beveridge himself accused his opponent of buying support with free dinners, while the supporters of Little claimed that Beveridge was an 'advanced socialist' and that it was contrary to all precedent for the head of a college to hold office as Vice Chancellor.[27] Beveridge was, however, duly elected as Vice Chancellor of 25 June. His election, he commented, 'was a recognition of the position of the School and to some extent of my assumed fair-mindedness'. It was also, he believed, a dramatic opportunity to rescue the Bloomsbury scheme.[28]

Almost immediately Beveridge led a deputation to the Chancellor of the Exchequer, Winston Churchill, and persuaded him to set aside part of the proceeds of the sale of the Bloomsbury site for the purposes of London University. Then in December 1926 he paid a visit to the Rockefeller Foundation in New York. The primary purpose of this visit was to raise money for the L.S.E., but during the course of negotiations he persuaded the Foundation to make available up to £400,000 for re-purchase and development of the Bloomsbury site. At first the Duke of Bedford refused to re-sell, but in February 1927 Beveridge put pressure on him through the Board of Education and the British Museum Trustees.[29] On 23 March he had 'a remarkable and complete success' in the University Senate, when he persuaded the senators by an overwhelming majority 'to buy the whole of the Bloomsbury site and to authorise me formally to ask the Rockefeller people for a grant to supplement what we have from the Government'.[30] The deal was concluded with both the Duke and the Treasury early in May. 'The Duke has now written saying he will take £550,000,' Beveridge recorded. 'Winston Churchill came to dinner at the School last night, to meet a dozen of the teaching staff and sat talking till midnight.'[31]

Beveridge served as Vice Chancellor for the next two years, and during this time plans were confirmed for the building of the new University. In 1928 he was urged by his supporters to stand again, but he insisted that he needed more time for the L.S.E. and 'more time for living a reasonable life for myself'.[32] His views on the nature of the new centralized University were, however, personally revealing and are worthy of further comment. They suggest perhaps more clearly than anything else the curious mixture of pragmatism and utopianism that characterized much of his thinking about university education. The new

[27] BP, V, 22, correspondence about WHB's election as Vice-Chancellor, May–June 1926.
[28] BP, IIa, ms. conversation with ASB, June 1926.
[29] *PI*, pp. 194–5; BP, IIa, ms. conversation with ASB, Feb. 1927.
[30] BP, IIb, WHB to G. Wallas, 1 Apr. 1927.
[31] BP, IIa, ms. conversation with ASB, 6 May 1927.
[32] BP, V 22, WHB to Lord Dawson, 7 June 1928.

university, he insisted, must not attempt to ape the traditions of Oxford and Cambridge. It must be practical and cosmopolitan and functionally related to modern city life. Nothing should be allowed on the Bloomsbury site that was not 'characteristic of London and of this time'. When challenged with the criticism that this would destroy many eighteenth-century garden squares, he replied impatiently that London had many gardens but only one university.[33] At the same time, however, he dreamt of a building that would lift the eyes of students above the pressures of everyday life—a building with a tower, a bell, a clock and a muezzin, that would embody 'the lightheartedness and solemnity of youth', conjure up 'the enchanted garden of the arts' and express the character of London University as a 'romance of modern times'.[34] To execute this vision Beveridge and his colleagues chose Charles Holden, the well-known designer of underground railway stations. The ambiguity of the vision—and the problems of reconciling romanticism and functionalism—were evident in Holden's Senate House, which hangs heavily over Bloomsbury at the present day.

Beveridge's efforts in acquiring new sites and buildings were matched by many other kinds of academic expansion. During his directorship the total number of students at the L.S.E. remained fairly steady at about three thousand, but of these an increasingly high proportion were full-time students working for three-year degrees. The number reading for higher degrees increased ninefold between 1919 and 1937.[35] During the same period there was a considerable expansion in teaching staff, and new chairs were created in Economics, Law, International History, Anthropology, Social Biology and Banking. Special courses were provided for civil servants, army officers, colonial administrators, and railway managers, and the School began to publish its own learned periodicals—*Economica* from 1921, the *London and Cambridge Economic Service* from 1922, and *Politica* from 1934. The British Library of Political Science became one of the leading specialist libraries in the world, and in 1924 a gift from the daughter of Richard Cobden was used to endow the School's Cobden Library on International Trade.[36] At the same time many eminent scholars were attracted to the school in a variety of subjects. Beveridge's old B.C.L. tutor, Edward Jenks, became Professor of English Law, and Harry Tawney joined the School in 1920 first as Reader and later as Professor of Economic History. In 1926 the Harvard economist, Allyn Young, succeeded Edwin Cannan as Professor of Political Economy; and other distinguished members of the Economics

[33] BP, IIb, WHB to T. L. Humberstone, 29 Dec. 1937.
[34] W. H. Beveridge, *The Physical Relation of a University to a City*, Nov. 1928.
[35] *The London School of Economics and its Problems*, pp. 31–2, 118.
[36] L.S.E. Papers, minutes of the Emergency Committee, 23 Oct. 1923.

department included Theodore Gregory, Hugh Dalton, Lionel Robbins and F. J. Hayek. Sociological theory was taught by L. T. Hobhouse and Morris Ginsberg, Anthropology by Malinowski and Raymond Firth. Harold Laski came to the School from Harvard in 1921 and eventually succeeded Wallas as Professor of Political Science. Legal history was taught by T. C. Plucknett, and mediaeval economic history by the brilliant and beautiful Eileen Power.

It would be wrong to suggest that Beveridge himself was personally responsible for gathering together this distinguished collection of scholars, and perhaps equally wrong to suggest that a similar growth would not have occurred under any other director. Nevertheless, it was he who determined the scale and pace of change, and it was he who laid the financial groundwork for academic expansion. As soon as he arrived at the School he wrote numerous 'begging letters' asking for funds,[37] and over the next eighteen years he proved highly successful in raising money from businessmen, public authorities and charitable foundations. In 1923 he made his first application to the Rockefellers and was awarded a capital grant of £6,000 for building, plus £5,000 per annum over the next four and a half years for the expansion of teaching and research. By 1925 the School had an income of over £77,000 and an annual surplus of £2,000 a year.[38] It became the first college in London to raise Professors' salaries to a minimum of £1,000, and special education and child endowment schemes were set up to supplement the salaries of staff with dependent children.[39] Beveridge was, nevertheless, ambitious for further expansion, and at the end of 1925 he made another application to the Rockefellers, outlining a programme for more new buildings, for an additional chair in economics and for the development of studies relating to the 'natural basis' of the social sciences.[40] The Rockefeller trustees were greatly impressed by the 'very forward-looking basis' of Beveridge's programme, and early in 1926 they awarded the School £200,000 for building, £8,000 for the Library and £1,000 a year for a new chair of political economy. Later in the year Beveridge paid a personal visit to New York, where he persuaded the Foundation to allocate a further £35,000 for building and £145,000 for the development of social sciences and international studies.[41]

Not perhaps surprisingly the rapid growth of the L.S.E. and the development of new areas of academic activity were attended by some

---

[37] Lady Beveridge Papers, WHB to J. Mair, 7 Apr. 1920.
[38] L.S.E. Papers, minutes of the Emergency Committee, 21 Jan. and 20 Oct. 1925.
[39] *The London School of Economics and its Problems*, pp. 46–87.
[40] L.S.E. Papers, 'Memorandum from the London School of Economics and Political Science', submitted to the Rockefeller Trustees, drafted July 1925.
[41] L.S.E. Papers, minutes of the Emergency Committee, 25 Jan. 1926 and 27 Jan. 1927; BP, WHB to ASB, 15 Jan. 1927.

severe institutional strains. Beveridge himself was initially conscious of this danger, and in 1925 he produced a paper on 'The School of Economics in the Stationary State' in which he suggested that there was a limit to the size of any institution 'informed with a single corporate life'. He concluded, however, that in spite of the expansion of the previous five years, the School was still 'underhoused, under-staffed, under-equipped with books, instruments and the material means of artistic and social activities';[42] and in the years that followed his sense of caution was gradually blunted by the seemingly limitless generosity of the Rockefeller trustees. In the pursuit of expansion he appeared to become increasingly autocratic and increasingly reluctant to balance the need for expansion against other academic goals. The expansion was therefore accompanied by a continuous series of conflicts over academic policy and government, and a gradual deterioration of relationships between Beveridge and his staff. During the first year of his appointment Beatrice Webb had recorded that 'the L.S.E. is going ahead at a great rate and Beveridge is universally liked by the staff and says he has never been so happy in his life'.[43] Three years later she observed that Beveridge had 'done wonders in the way of organisation. Sidney has the utmost confidence in him and is always congratulating himself on having got him as Director.'[44] Over the next sixteen years, however, she recorded a tortuous history of decline in Beveridge's popularity and of recurrent friction with members of his staff. 'The directorship of the School is a post in which the holder gets quickly worn out,' she observed, shortly before Beveridge's retirement in 1937. 'The last time Sidney lunched at the School, Beveridge was sitting absolutely alone at the directors' table, whilst the two others were crowded. He had in fact been boycotted. There were unpleasant scenes during his farewell address too; a marked coldness in the audience.' She concluded sadly that Beveridge's position 'had become impossible—he had got to dislike his staff and they were tired of him'.[45] The causes of this decline in Beveridge's popularity may be sought in a number of factors—in his own character and personal development; in his controversial relationship with Jessy Mair, who became the School's secretary early in 1920; and in the nature of some of the policies that he pursued at the L.S.E.

## IV

The complexities of Beveridge's character have been discussed in earlier chapters, and these became more marked as he moved into middle age.

[42] L.S.E. Papers, 'The School of Economics in the Stationary State', by WHB, circulated to the Emergency Committee, 1 Apr. 1925.
[43] Wallas Papers, Box 6, B. Webb to G. Wallas, 21 Nov. 1919.
[44] Passfield Papers, B. Webb's diary, 14 May 1922.
[45] Ibid., 1 May and 27 Aug. 1937.

As a man in his forties and fifties he presented to contemporaries a rather baffling image—a curious mixture of high-mindedness and hard-headed worldliness, of quick sympathy for suffering combined with frequent insensibility towards the feelings of others, of strong commitment to 'liberal values' combined with a highly dogmatic perspective on the world. To some he appeared as a 'complex of Ariel, a Professor and a scientist'; to others he was a 'born bureaucrat' incapable of appreciating 'the importance of freedom from the continuous and oppressing official-dom of the state'.[46] In moments of relaxation he was engagingly unself-conscious. At his cottage in Avebury he 'played like a schoolboy' in tattered dungarees given to him by miners during his work for the Coal Commission; he referred to himself by such names as Sir William Beetroot, and he would converse by the hour 'with a young lady of five and her two dolls'.[47] He enormously enjoyed the informality and friendli-ness that he encountered on his visits to America, and he took an almost childlike delight in Disneyland, Hollywood, Hell's Angels and other curiosities of the North American scene.[48] In professional life, however, he was imperious, quick-tempered and frequently sarcastic. He found it hard to conceal his impatience with people less efficient than himself and would turn purple with anger at those who tried to cross him. He had few close intellectual relationships and to some observers he seemed to lead a 'secret life', pursuing certain ideas and ideals largely in isolation from those around him.[49] 'One very seldom sees anybody who bears so plainly the marks of spirit and intellect,' remarked one acquaintance;[50] yet at the same time he had a certain rigidity of outlook that did not fit well into an academic environment. 'One of Beveridge's failings is that he is too contemptuous of other experts,' complained Beatrice Webb. His intellect, she commented, was 'strangely energetic but arid; he dealt with problems by narrowing them and isolating them from the main-stream of human activities'.[51] 'In Sir William's odd composition there is a streak of the fantastic, but of imagination no trace,' commented an anonymous critic in 1921:

there is in him nothing of the artist, and this limitation of his intellectual horizon, combined as it is with an inordinately strong sense of fact, produces a stiffness in his alignment to ideals of any sort. . . . Sir William's is an impatient

[46] BP, IIb, Annie Davison to B. Webb, 3 Oct. 1934; *Pall Mall Gazette*, 5 June 1922; *The Times*, Lord Askwith to the Editor, 4 Nov. 1919.
[47] Lady Beveridge Papers, WHB to J. Mair, n.d. (1925); 30 July and 16 Sept., 1930; interview with Miss Eve Evans.
[48] Lady Beveridge Papers, WHB to J. Mair, 30 July, 7 and 13 Aug. 1930.
[49] Passfield Papers, B. Webb's diary, 30 Apr. 1928; Turin Papers, L. Turin to Jeannette Tawney, n.d. (*c.* June 1937).
[50] BP, IIb, Annie Davison to B. Webb, 3 Oct. 1934.
[51] Passfield Papers, B. Webb's diary, 10 Mar. 1936 and 10 Aug. 1938.

temper. His own hard and clear intelligence, with its quick apprehension and ready arrangement and co-ordination of data, makes it natural for him to leave out the imponderables; to despise the intelligence of others, where that intelligence is of a different character from his own. . . . He has devoted friends, but he does not as a rule get on easily with other people. He is apt to tread on their corns, not the less painfully, to them, because he has not even noticed their feet. Though mentally abnormally quick, he is psychologically insensitive, unobservant, and this, in conjunction with his extreme self-centredness, makes him unaware of the reactions and even of the characters of others to a degree that is a real hindrance, since it represents an exposure both to flattery and to simple dislike.[52]

Standing on its own, this judgement was neither accurate nor fair, since it ignored many of Beveridge's more attractive qualities—his selflessness in working for causes in which he believed, his abundant financial gene-rosity to friends and charitable causes, his undoubted desire to make other people happy, and the vitality and gaiety with which he often charmed even his sternest critics.[53] Nevertheless, it is indicative of the rather forbidding impression that Beveridge made on some of his con-temporaries, and helps at least partially to explain his difficulties in dealing with the L.S.E. These deficiencies of character must, however, be seen in the light of his personal history during this period and, in particular, the growth of his family responsibilities after the First World War. His mother had been living in his house in Bedford Gardens almost continuously since her operation in 1914. After the war it became clear that neither of his parents could any longer look after themselves and virtually the whole responsibility of caring for them now fell upon Beveridge. His sister, Jeannette Tawney, had become a semi-invalid, and, far from sharing the task of looking after Annette and Henry, she herself constantly leaned on Beveridge for emotional and financial sup-port. Both the Beveridge parents therefore came to live with their son; and in 1921 he moved to a larger house at 51 Campden House Road, where they could each have bedrooms and private studies.

Looking after two aged parents, both of whom were infirm and one now totally deaf, might have been difficult under any circumstances; but Beveridge's task was complicated by the growing cantankerousness of his mother's personality. Annette had never been an easy person to live with, but in old age she became increasingly unreasonable in her attempts to dominate both her husband and her son. Henry Beveridge in his eighties was an eccentric and endearing old man, 'a mixture of

---

[52] 'Personalities and Powers. William H. Beveridge, K.C.B.', *Time and Tide*, 20 May 1921.
[53] Beveridge sometimes posed as a miser and cynic; but his personal records for the 1920s and 30s reveal that nearly half his income was spent on donations to good causes and gifts and loans to family and friends.

extreme shrewdness and extreme childlikeness'.[54] His mind was still actively engaged in oriental scholarship, but he was increasingly confused about day-to-day affairs and at times imagined that he was still living in India.[55] For several years he tried to placate his wife's difficult behaviour and took refuge in silence when Annette was 'on the warpath'.[56] But eventually in 1924 he insisted on returning to Pitfold, which had by that time been up for sale for several years. Annette tried unsuccessfully to stop local tradesmen from serving him and protested that he had no right to live there, since the house had been purchased in her name. 'You have an overwhelming idea of your own importance,' Henry retorted, 'and reject with contempt any suggestion of others, especially if they be made by me. . . . I believe you had some affection for me when you married me. But we have drifted now far away from that and you seldom or never have allowed our love to interfere with your love for getting your own way.'[57]

The Beveridge parents thereafter lived mainly apart, and Beveridge had to maintain two separate establishments for them—one for his mother in London, the other for his father in the country. He employed a long series of nurses and housekeepers to look after them, and made heroic efforts to maintain the peace between them, to rescue his mother from the isolation of deafness and to soothe and enliven her stormy old age. The voluminous notebooks of written conversations that survive from this period are evidence of his unflagging devotion in discussing with her his daily work, involving her in a round of social events and generally keeping her in touch with the outside world. It is not therefore surprising that he was often under considerable strain, nor that the intensity of his concern for his parents should have produced a corresponding insensitivity in relations with his colleagues. The demands of his domestic life and its wearying influence were apparent in other ways —in a certain deadening of his intellectual faculties, and in a tendency to treat both work and leisure as a form of 'escape'. As we have seen, Beveridge as a young man had been a voracious if not very discriminating reader of books of all kinds—poetry, novels, plays, history and works of natural science. This habit continued until the First World War, after which it became increasingly rare for him to engage in intellectual activity that was not in some way related to his work. Towards the end of the war he had expressed a desire to resume his earlier ambition of writing creative fiction, but his only idea for the subject of such a work

[54] Lady Beveridge Papers, J. Mair to WHB, Christmas 1926.
[55] AHBP, Mss. Eur. C. 176/36, HB to ASB, 17 Feb. 1925.
[56] BP, IIa, HB to WHB, 20 Dec. 1915, 25 June 1916; Turin Papers, Jeannette Tawney to Lucia Turin, 22 Oct. 1933.
[57] AHBP, Mss. Eur. C.176/34, HB to ASB, 17 Oct. 1924; C 176/35, HB to ASB, 25 Nov. 1924.

was a literary life-history of the 'statistically average man'.[58] His leisure hours were increasingly spent, not in reading and writing, but in crosswords and games of bridge. Even his work on the trade cycle he approached as a rather mechanical exercise, 'like solving an acrostic set by nature'.[59] In the late 1920s he recorded that he read little for pleasure except detective novels, and that 'soon I shall read nothing but the Bell Ringers Gazette . . . there is such a paper and I've read it, though not since I ceased loving my fellow men'.[60]

Beveridge's family life was not therefore calculated to improve his irascible temper, and for much of his time at the L.S.E. he was under continuous domestic strain—a fact that at least partially accounts for Lord Robbins' observation that Beveridge was 'fundamentally an unhappy man'.[61] There were, moreover, other causes of Beveridge's unhappiness—the most important being a deep sense of regret that he had never married. He felt 'an agony of frustration' that he had never 'had the fulfilment of young love';[62] and throughout the 1920s he thought much about marriage and relationships with women, as he had done twenty years before. At least three times in the 1920s he appears to have toyed with the idea of matrimony, on each occasion with a woman much younger than himself.[63] On the third occasion, which occurred shortly after the death of his parents in 1929, he received a severe rebuff —an event which left him greatly shattered and depressed.[64] Thereafter he seems to have abandoned hope of finding a congenial marriage-partner—though for many years afterwards he continued to collect quotations about other people's marriages. During a lonely week-end in 1934 when he had been reading the memoirs of Vera Brittain he wrote:

I was struck by her saying on the one hand that 'the noblest and profoundest emotions that men experience—the emotion of love—of marriage and fatherhood—come to them and can come to them only through women' and on the other hand that for women as for men marriage is irrelevant to the main purpose of life. For a woman as for a man, marriage might enormously help or devastatingly hinder the growth of her power to contribute something

---

[58] *Daily Telegraph*, 13 Mar. 1923, report of WHB's address to the Authors' Club on 'Economics and Literature'.

[59] BP, IIa, ms. conversation with ASB, n.d. (1921).

[60] BP, IIa, ms. conversation with ASB, Apr. 1927; Lady Beveridge Papers, WHB to J. Mair, 19 Aug. 1928.

[61] Lionel Robbins, *Autobiography of an Economist* (1971), p. 135.

[62] BP, IIa, WHB to ASB, 6 Sept. 1926; Lady Beveridge Papers, J. Mair to WHB, 17 Feb. 1931.

[63] Lady Beveridge Papers, J. Mair's diary, 4 Dec. 1929, J. Mair to WHB, 12 and 14 Aug. 1924 and 21 Jan. 1931; Dodd Papers, extracts from a letter from John Dodd, Aug. 1924.

[64] Lady Beveridge Papers, J. Mair to WHB, 21 Jan. 1931.

impersonally valuable to the community in which she lived, but it was not the same as that power and could not be regarded as an end in itself. Nor, even, were children ends in themselves.[65]

V

One of the main barriers to Beveridge's choosing a wife was the influence of Jessy Mair, and no analysis of his personal development nor of his career at the L.S.E. would be complete without an account of his relationship with this formidable woman. Mrs. Mair's character and early friendship with Beveridge have already been discussed. She had provided Beveridge as a young man with an hospitable family circle, and he in turn had alleviated the boredom of her life as a suburban housewife. Their relationship grew closer during the war, when Mrs. Mair became a temporary civil servant—working first as Beveridge's private secretary and later as an administrator in the Ministry of Food. Like many middle-class women of her generation she had never had a job in her life before, and she found working in Whitehall 'a kind of incredible romance'.[66] She rose to the rank of acting principal, was personally responsible for the system of bacon-rationing, and in 1919 became the first woman ever to sit in the Officials' box in the House of Commons. Throughout the war she and Beveridge were thrown by their work continuously in each other's company and they increasingly shared their leisure hours. As Beveridge took on more responsibility for his parents, it was Jessy Mair who chose his servants, assisted in nursing his mother and helped him to find a new house. She frequently entertained on his behalf and it was in her home that Beveridge sought refuge from his own rather exhausting domestic life—a fact that was strongly resented by Annette Beveridge, who was deeply suspicious of this rival source of influence over her son.[67] When in 1919 Sidney Webb was considering his choice of a new director he had remarked that Mrs. Mair was 'the price he would have to pay' for attracting Beveridge to the L.S.E.[68] Nevertheless, there seems no reason to suppose that when Beveridge first accepted the job he intended to bring with him his cousin and colleague. Early in 1919 Mrs. Mair had rejected a job as factory inspector in 'the Home Office harem' on the ground that it was 'well known to be hidebound by potty little Home Office rules'. But in September 1919 she had accepted on Beveridge's advice a post in the

[65] BP, Ic 50, notes for entry in WHB's diary, 29–30 Dec. 1934.

[66] Lady Beveridge Papers, folder on 'Whitehall in Wartime', and fragments of ms. autobiography by J. Mair.

[67] AHBP, Mss. Eur. C. 176/34, HB to ASB 8 Feb. 1919; Turin Papers, Jeannette Tawney to Lucia Turin, 13 June 1937.

[68] Interview with Miss Eve Evans.

department of National Kitchens, from which it seemed likely that she should shortly be transferred to the new Ministry of Health.[69] It was not until the end of 1919 that she took on the position of administrative secretary at the L.S.E.—Miss Mactaggart, the existing secretary, having been promoted to Dean of Admissions. A few months later Miss Mactaggart fell ill and Mrs. Mair took over all her administrative functions, combining in her own person the posts of both secretary and dean.

From the start Mrs. Mair's position at the School was the subject of controversy—a fact which must be ascribed partly to her own personality and partly to what was seen as her undue influence over Beveridge. She was, according to her Civil Service superiors, a woman with an 'intense desire to work' and 'natural powers of organisation'. She had 'a strong and capable mind', a 'liking and aptitude for administration', a 'vivid femininity behind administrative capacity' and a 'willingness to sacrifice the frivolities, and subordinate even the normal pleasures, of a civilized life to the particular public task of the time'.[70] Nevertheless, she had acquired in the Civil Service certain administrative habits that were not altogether suited to an institution like the L.S.E. She had perhaps been spoiled by being the only woman in an office of male administrators, and she was used to getting her way by flattery and cajolery rather than reasoned argument.[71] She was proud of recalling how she had once dealt with a blasphemous admiral by refusing to speak to him until he stopped behaving like a naughty boy; but the same technique did not work with the professors of the L.S.E. She was, as we have already seen, an insecure person, who longed for admiration and approval, and this appears to have made her both highly susceptible to flattery and hypersensitive to criticism. 'Adverse criticism depresses me too far,' she once admitted, 'and I just go down with a bang.'[72] She had strong likes and dislikes, and regarded the staff of the L.S.E. as 'composed pretty equally of a brilliant group gathered together to make between them an experiment in learning . . . and a random sample of elderly women with bees in their bonnets'.[73] She could be charming, generous and helpful to people who did not threaten her; but she became hostile and domineering if her authority was called in question or her views were opposed.

Upon Beveridge her influence was undoubtedly powerful, but it was

[69] Lady Beveridge Papers, J. Mair to WHB, 3 and 16 Jan. 1919; WHB to J. Mair, 6 Sept. 1919.

[70] Lord Salter, 'Lord Beveridge 1879–1963', *Procs. Br. Acad.*, vol. XLIX, 1963, p. 421; BP, Ib 16, T. C. Witherby to WHB, 1 Dec. 1942.

[71] Lady Beveridge Papers, folder on 'Whitehall in Wartime', by J. Mair.

[72] Ibid., J. Mair to WHB, 8 Apr. 1942.

[73] Ibid., fragments of ms. autobiography by J. Mair.

less all-pervasive than was often supposed. In his autobiography Beveridge generously gave her credit for many of the reforms in which he had been involved.[74] With the sole exception of food-rationing, however, there is little evidence to show that she had any major influence either on his intellectual attitudes or his contribution to public policy. Certainly she shared many of his views on academic and administrative questions, but she merely echoed opinions that he held already and does not seem to have determined them to any great extent. He often disagreed with her both in public and in private, and his discussions with her on questions of policy were considerably less profound than similar discussions that he had with Mrs. Dunn Gardner or with Beatrice Webb.

Similarly, Beveridge's recurrent interest in other women suggests that Mrs. Mair's emotional hold over him was less powerful than many people assumed. He was undoubtedly strongly attached to her, and allowed her to dominate his social life; but their diaries and correspondence suggest that she was more emotionally dependent on him than he was on her. Beneath a veil of self-assertion she relied very heavily on Beveridge for emotional and professional support, and during Beveridge's frequent trips abroad she often felt that without his protective presence she could not face her work at the L.S.E. She was also excessively jealous of his other female friends. When in 1924 she heard a rumour from Ernest Barker that Beveridge was about to be married, she took to her bed and wrote him bitter, frenzied letters—in much the same way as Annette had done many years before.[75] 'Do be content not to ask questions across the Atlantic to which nobody knows the answer,' replied Beveridge, who was at the time in North America. '. . . Barker, as you know, for all his virtues is the very worst type of old gossip. Can't we have a league of reticence against him, and Knowles and Cannan and *id genus omne ferarum*. To love and trust and help one's friends without asking them to live naked in glass cases, is that really beyond our powers. . . . No more of this, dear, please till I get back.'[76]

Throughout the 1920s and 30s the tone of Beveridge's letters to Mrs. Mair was affectionate and conciliatory rather than romantic. Nevertheless, the relationship between them not unnaturally aroused considerable speculation both inside and outside the L.S.E. 'There is today complete anarchy in opinion about sex relations,' complained Beatrice Webb in the privacy of her diary. '. . . As an instance I take the relation of Beveridge—the Director of the London School of Economics—to Mrs. Mair, the secretary. Whether they are or have been technically "lovers" I really don't know. But they are inseparable and have all the appear-

---

[74] *PI*, pp. 169, 307, 314.
[75] Ibid., J. Mair to WHB, 14, 15, 16, 19, 24 and 27 Aug. 1924.
[76] Ibid., WHB to J. Mair, 7 Sept. 1924.

ance of being more than friends. . . . We like both Beveridge and Mrs. Mair and they have been charming to us; but from the standpoint of a large educational establishment, with three thousand students of both sexes and mostly young, this relationship of the Director and the Secretary is not a desirable example. And yet we all turn away and say "it is their affair".'[77] Three years later she decided 'it is, I am pretty certain, a platonic relationship—but in spite of their mature age it is far too romantic to be comfortable for the institution over which they preside, as Director and Secretary, or agreeable to her husband or children . . . For Beveridge and Mrs. Mair obviously "belong to each other" and cannot keep apart in work or in play.'[78]

Beatrice Webb's concern about the harmful moral example of 'the Beveridge–Mair entanglement' does not seem to have been shared by their academic colleagues—many of whom believed that Beveridge was in any case incapable of active sexual relationships.[79] What annoyed people about Mrs. Mair was not her private relationship with Beveridge so much as her attempts to dominate the running of the School. She appeared to encourage Beveridge in his autocratic habits, she aspired to be treated as deputy director and she pushed herself forward on public occasions—such as the visit to the L.S.E. of the Prince of Wales in 1928.[80] She also interfered with questions on which she was not competent to judge—such as assessments of the professional competence of academic staff.[81] The result was a growing dislike for her that began with Cannan and Wallas and eventually spread to many members of the academic body. In fairness to Mrs. Mair it must be stated that her unpopularity was never so universal as her enemies liked to suggest. Many students and members of the junior staff found her sympathetic and tireless in her efforts to promote their interests; and she was warmly admired by Hogben and Malinowski, who saw her as a consistent champion in their campaign for a more 'scientific' social science.[82] 'She had dignity and style and she got things done,' recalled one of her colleagues many years later; and others admitted that, although quick to anger, she was equally quick to forget and forgive.[83] But nevertheless she undoubtedly antagonized many of the School's teachers and professors. She was accused of 'ruining Beveridge's influence', of 'coming between Beveridge and his staff' and of poisoning his mind against certain of his

---

[77] Passfield Papers, B. Webb's diary, 20 Aug. 1925.
[78] Ibid., 30 Apr. 1928.
[79] Dalton Papers, Hugh Dalton's diary, vol. 10, 6–8 July 1929.
[80] Interview with Miss Eve Evans.
[81] e.g. Lady Beveridge Papers, J. Mair to WHB, 26 July 1927.
[82] Letter from Professor Lancelot Hogben to the author, 25 July 1974; Lady Beveridge Papers, B. Malinowski to J. Mair, 22 and 23 Feb. 1936. Below, pp. 284–90, 306.
[83] Interview with Miss Enid Chambers; Lord Chorley, loc. cit., p. 6.

colleagues.[84] Beveridge himself, however, angrily repudiated these allegations and sprang quixotically to Mrs. Mair's defence. In a long letter to Steel-Maitland, the chairman of the L.S.E. governors, he claimed that Mrs. Mair was universally liked by her clerical subordinates, by members of other colleges, by University administrators and by the public at large. Her help had been invaluable in dealing with architects, builders, public authorities and charitable trustees. The feeling against her among the teaching body he ascribed partly to institutional growing pains, partly to the malice of several elderly professors, and partly to the 'Curzonesque attitude uniformly adopted in all London colleges towards administrative staff'.[85]

Resentment against Mrs. Mair gathered momentum throughout Beveridge's directorship, and made itself apparent in many different ways. In 1928, for example, Graham Wallas reported to Sidney Webb that Mrs. Mair 'without consulting the Emergency Committee or anyone else with power to authorise' had built for herself a 'flat' on the School's premises, which had been 'extravagantly furnished and fitted up' out of the grant from the L.C.C. Wallas claimed that the whole School was 'buzzing' with anger and demanded an inquiry.[86] 'It is always useful to have gossip brought to notice, though it is seldom accurate and always exaggerated,' commented Webb rather tartly; and Beveridge, when called upon to furnish an explanation, pointed out that the so-called 'flat' was in fact a 'rest-room' for the use of female visitors and administrative staff. 'The whole thing is a storm which cannot fill even a tea-cup,' he protested indignantly.[87] Nevertheless, the degree of conflict generated by such an apparently trivial incident was an indication of the depth of feeling involved, and this feeling grew stronger as the years went by. Mrs. Mair was increasingly seen by many of her colleagues as an 'intriguer', a 'dictator', a 'hard-faced administrator' and as the resident 'devil' of the L.S.E.[88]

In the late 1920s both the Beveridge parents grew more helpless and senile, and Mrs. Mair was undoubtedly a great source of strength to Beveridge in caring for their last days. In 1929 both his parents died, and his acute sense of loss combined with release from the strain of looking after them induced in him a period of prolonged loneliness, introspection and depression. During this period he longed to leave the L.S.E. and to accept one of the numerous professorships that were offered him by other universities; but he was dissuaded from doing so by the

[84] Passfield Papers, B. Webb's diary, 14 May 1922.
[85] BP, IIb, WHB to Sir Arthur Steel-Maitland, 10 Feb. 1924.
[86] Passfield Papers, X, 2(1), 227–8, G. Wallas to S. Webb, 13 June 1928.
[87] Wallas Papers, Box 8, S. Webb to G. Wallas, 18 June 1928; Passfield Papers, X, 2 (1), 229, WHB to S. Webb, 2 July 1928.
[88] Ibid., B. Webb's diary, 14 May 1922, 7 Feb. 1927, 23 Sept. 1931.

Webbs, who argued that he was mainly responsible for the 'brilliant success' of the L.S.E., and that 'no other director would treat us so well as you have done'.[89] At the same time he appears to have made several attempts to lessen his dependence on Mrs. Mair. Early in 1931, when he seems finally to have despaired in his hopes of finding a wife, he refused to accept the comfort and sympathy proffered by Mrs. Mair.[90] She in turn became ever more suspicious of his other female companions— including Lucia Turin, Beveridge's faithful and effusive Russian secretary, who lived in constant fear that Mrs. Mair's jealousy would oust her from her job. 'Treat Mrs. Mair kindly and considerately, as a mentally afflicted person, over whom you have no control,'[91] Mrs. Turin was advised by Beatrice Webb, who was still anxious that nothing should provoke Beveridge into resignation. Beveridge himself meanwhile spent much time in the company of his sister, who shared her mother's jealousy of the influence of Mrs. Mair.[92] He passed many week-ends alone, working on his history of prices, sorting his parents' papers, milling over his past career and making 'good resolutions' for the future.[93] In 1934 he sold his house in Campden Hill, moved into a bachelor flat in the Temple, and transferred to Mrs. Mair his cottage at Avebury 'in order to regain his freedom during the recess'. Mrs. Mair, however, 'followed him to a flat within sight of his new abode in the Temple, from which she spies on his movements'. 'The plight of our old and loyal friend worries me,' observed Mrs. Webb. 'I don't see any way out for them— Mrs. Mair has become a Fury and is in control of his house and his workplace.' And she concluded, sadly and reluctantly, 'that for his own and the students' sake, Beveridge would do well to move off to other work'.[94]

[89] BP, IIb, B. Webb to WHB, (? Apr.) 1929; Passfield Papers, B. Webb's diary, 16 Dec. 1933.

[90] Lady Beveridge Papers, J. Mair to WHB, 21 Jan. 1931.

[91] Passfield Papers, B. Webb's diary, 18 Aug. 1933 and 25 Aug. 1934.

[92] Turin Papers, Jeannette Tawney to Lucia Turin, 13 June 1937.

[93] BP, Ic 50, notes for WHB's diary, 4 and 6 Aug. 1933; 29–30 Dec. 1934.

[94] Passfield Papers, B. Webb's diary, 18 Aug. 1933 and 25 Aug. 1934.

# I 2

# Social Science and Academic Freedom

## I

MRS. MAIR's influence was frequently blamed for the disputes that occurred at the L.S.E. particularly during the latter years of Beveridge's directorship, and undoubtedly her powerful and assertive personality helped to fan the flames of academic discontent. Nevertheless, it is difficult to avoid the impression that she was often the excuse for rather than the cause of academic dissension. On each major issue she was one among many dimensions of controversy and it seems probable that serious disagreements would have arisen without her presence. It is therefore necessary to look around for other and less personal explanations for the series of internal conflicts that divided the L.S.E. for much of the 1930s. The most important of these conflicts concerned the nature and method of the social sciences, the question of academic freedom, the internal government of the L.S.E., and the balance of power between director and professors.

## II

The debate on the nature of the social sciences was the most prolonged and all-pervasive of the subjects in dispute. As we have seen, Beveridge as a young man had firmly attached himself to the 'empirical' tradition in social science, represented by Llewellyn Smith and the Labour department of the Board of Trade. When he came to the L.S.E. he was convinced that the social sciences were still 'too theoretical, deductive, metaphysical' and that 'the way ahead' lay in empirical studies of social phenomena rather than in deductions based on analytical postulates about the nature of human behaviour.[1] This was made clear in his lecture on 'Economics as a Liberal Education', which he delivered at the L.S.E. in October 1920. In lecture he re-affirmed his discipleship of the biologist, Thomas Huxley, and called for social inquiries based on 'observation and experiment, comparison and classification'. Only through such inquiries, he argued, was it possible to realize Huxley's vision of a truly scientific 'science of society'. The development of such a science, he believed, would not merely transform academic studies; it

[1] BP, IIb, WHB to J. Chandler Cobb, 3 June 1925.

would transform man's ability to control his social environment, as natural science had transformed his ability to control nature. Men would 'gradually bring themselves to deal with political as they do with scientific questions . . . and to believe that the machinery of society is at least as delicate as that of a spinning jenny and as little likely to be improved by the meddling of those who have not taken the trouble to master the principles of its action'.[2]

These beliefs were sharply distinguished from both the 'pure' and 'applied' traditions of sociological inquiry established at the L.S.E. On the one hand, Beveridge's conception of social science was clearly opposed to the highly abstract, speculative sociology practised by L. T. Hobhouse. And, on the other hand, it was equally remote from the studies of social welfare carried out by the Department of Social Administration, since Beveridge's main aim as an academic social scientist was not to solve social problems, but to discover social laws. These two principles – inductionism, combined with a search for ulti-mate generalizations – were to dominate his attitude to social research for the next forty years, and can most clearly be seen in his monu-mental and unfinished study of the history of prices.[3] It is difficult to find fault with his desire for a more rigorous approach to social investiga-tion, or for a closer relationship between theory and fact. Nevertheless, his views on how these were to be brought about were, and are, open to a number of objections. The most serious objection was Beveridge's in-ability to see that the very process of choosing a subject for observation necessarily entailed a set of assumptions about the significance of that subject and why it should be observed. A second objection was that social facts never do 'speak for themselves' in the way that Beveridge seemed to imply; they only become intelligible either by reference to 'theory' or by making theoretical connections with other sets of facts. It is difficult, for example, to think of a *less* empirically based cognitive device than Beveridge's own image of society as a kind of spinning-jenny. A third objection was that Beveridge's conception even of empirical inquiry was unduly limited and narrow. It did not include, for example, the kind of descriptive studies of institutions carried out by the Webbs, which Beveridge regarded as mere historical narrative and not truly 'scientific' in the proper sense of the term.[4] Yet it was precisely the lack of an historical perspective that made his own work on prices much less valuable than it might otherwise have been. Beveridge started work on

[2] W. H. Beveridge, 'Economics as a Liberal Education', *Economica*, no. 1, Jan. 1921, pp. 2–19.

[3] W. H. Beveridge and others, *Prices and Wages in England from the Twelfth to the Nineteenth Century*, vol. 1 (1939).

[4] BP, IIb, WHB's notes on the Webbs' *Methods of Social Study*, 25 July 1932; Passfield Papers, B. Webb's diary, 10 Mar. 1936.

his price history in 1919, and over the next forty years he extracted price data from a wide range of archive sources all over the world. He examined records going back to the twelfth century, relating to fairs and markets, monasteries and manors and other large estates. His hope was that he would reveal the mechanism of the trade cycle by discovering the determinants of changes in the price of wheat – the secret of which he believed to lie in the realms of astronomy and meteorology.[5] In this he was not just a crank, though he was often regarded as such by academic contemporaries. Important work of a similar kind was being developed in the 1920s and 30s by continental scholars; and certainly it would be a rash historian who from the perspective of the 1970s would state categorically that movements of wheat prices make little impact on the world economy. Nevertheless, Beveridge's collections of prices were less important than they might have been, because he made no attempt to link them to specific structural and institutional factors. It is perhaps significant that his figures have subsequently been most useful, not to analysts of the trade cycle, but to analysts of particular institutions and economies who have made the excursion into a specific historical context that Beveridge himself regarded as suspiciously 'unscientific'.[6]

Beveridge's opinions on the nature of social science might not have become controversial if he had not tried to impose them on his academic colleagues, and if he had not become increasingly intolerant of all other kinds of social research. Early in the 1920s he made it clear that he wanted the L.S.E. as a research institution to develop 'the very interesting borderland' between natural and social science, and this emphasis was initially welcomed by many of his colleagues.[7] In 1925 he was informed by the Rockefeller Trustees that the Foundation would look favourably upon requests for funds for any striking new departure in social research; and in response to this invitation Beveridge drew up an ambitious programme for development of research into 'the natural basis of the social sciences'. In this he argued that the social sciences were already well advanced in the spheres of 'economic' and 'political' studies. 'To complete the circle of the social sciences a third group of studies is required, dealing with the natural bases of economics and politics, with the human material and with its physical environment, and forming a bridge between the natural and the social sciences.' The

[5] BP, IIb, WHB to R. Denman, 9 Jan. 1921; WHB to W. D. Spring Rice, 3 Feb. 1922; W. H. Beveridge, 'Wheat Prices and Rainfall in Western Europe', *JRSS*, LXXXV, part III, May 1922, p. 412.

[6] e.g. W. G. Hoskins, 'Harvest Fluctuations and English Economic History 1480–1619', *Agricultural History Review*, XII (1964), pp. 44–6; F. J. Fisher, 'Influenza and Inflation in Tudor England', *Economic History Review*, 2nd s., XVIII, no. 1 (1965), pp. 120–9.

[7] BP, IIb, WHB to Sir Richard Gregory, 23 Nov. 1922; L.S.E. Papers, Minutes of Professorial Council, 1 Dec. 1926.

main components of this new area of knowledge, Beveridge envisaged, would be Anthropology, Social Biology, Physiology, Geography, Meteorology and Public Health. In particular, he emphasized the need for development of Social Biology – by which he meant 'genetics, population, vital statistics, heredity, eugenics and dysgenics'. For this purpose Beveridge hoped to appoint 'a man of biological training to learn economics and politics', to 'apply himself to economic and social problems' and to develop links with other areas of research.[8]

Beveridge's programme met with a certain amount of criticism from L. T. Hobhouse, who protested that the Sociology Department had not been consulted, that he himself had been linking sociology with biology and psychology for the past twenty years, and that 'the non-sociological teacher in these subjects is indifferent and in nearly all cases ignorant of the sociological point of view'.[9] Beveridge replied in conciliatory tones that 'what I want most is to develop just that side of the social sciences which stands nearest to your own work', although privately he believed that the tradition represented by Hobhouse 'does not necessarily go with "social science"'.[10] Apart from Hobhouse, however, Beveridge's programme met with little but approval from the L.S.E. staff. It was strongly supported by Malinowski, and Laski declared that he was 'in complete sympathy' with Beveridge's scheme.[11] In February 1926 the School's Emergency Committee asked Beveridge to consult with a representative group of professors and lecturers, and this group pronounced itself in favour of developing research on the lines Beveridge had laid down. Again the only serious doubts seem to have come from Hobhouse, who complained that Social Biology was 'an odd name' and that Anthropology was really a form of Sociology.[12] Beveridge's proposals were, however, approved by the Professorial Council, and a grant of nearly £200,000 was made by the Rockefeller Foundation. 'It's a wedding of natural and economic science,' declared Beveridge exultantly, 'the difficulty will be to find men to break this new ground. Rockefeller will provide the money. I've got to find the men and the scheme.'[13]

Beveridge's programme was put into operation in 1927, when the Professorial Council agreed that the Rockefeller grant should be equally divided between Anthropology, Social Biology, Modern Social

[8] L.S.E. Papers, 'Memorandum from the London School of Economics and Political Science', submitted to the Laura Spelman Rockefeller Trustees, July 1925.
[9] BP, IIb, L. T. Hobhouse to WHB, 20 Jan. 1926.
[10] BP, IIb, WHB to L. T. Hobhouse, 20 Jan. 1926; WHB to Sir George Adami, 2 Mar. 1923.
[11] L.S.E. Papers, minutes of Professorial Council, 1 Dec. 1926.
[12] BP, IIb, L. T. Hobhouse to WHB, 21 Feb. 1926.
[13] BP, IIa, ms. conversation with ASB, early 1926.

Conditions and International Studies. New chairs were created in Social Anthropology and International Relations, and research and teaching rapidly developed in both these fields. The 'modern social conditions' grant was used to commission an up-dated version of Charles Booth's survey of London, planned and directed by Hubert Llewellyn Smith. It proved more difficult, however, to develop studies in social biology, which Beveridge himself saw as the key discipline in the complex no-man's-land between natural and social science. The creation of a chair in Social Biology was approved by London University in 1929, and the post was given to Lancelot Hogben, the Professor of Zoology at the University of Cape Town. Beveridge recorded approvingly that Hogben was 'an enormously amusing and clever creature' with 'a critically constructive mind and ferocious scientific conscience'.[14] He brought with him to the L.S.E. a distinguished group of young researchers, including his demographer wife, Enid Charles; and over the next five years his department produced an impressive series of monographs on heredity, population control, statistical method and human reproduction. Nevertheless, from the start the social biology experiment was fraught with dissension and conflict – difficulties which stemmed partly from the lack of facilities for experimental research, partly from the personalities involved, and partly from the inherently controversial nature of social biology as an academic subject. In spite of the lavish Rockefeller endowment, Hogben's work was carried out under very cramped and unsuitable conditions, and to the discomfort of his colleagues the air of Houghton Street often echoed with the cries of animals in his underground laboratories. Hogben himself was an extremely contentious and mercurial personality, who made no secret of his contempt for the unscientific character of much of what passed for social research. These practical and personal difficulties might not in themselves have been very significant, but they were accompanied by the growth of controversy among the L.S.E. staff about the aims and methods of the social sciences – a conflict in which the role of the department of Social Biology came to be the central issue. As we have seen, Beveridge's plans for the development of empirical research had been looked on with suspicion by Hobhouse, as the leading representative of the 'metaphysical' school. Hobhouse died in 1929, but in the early 1930s the gulf between the methodological traditions reasserted itself in various ways. On the one hand, the economics department under Robbins and Hayek became increasingly deductive and analytical and increasingly hostile to 'problem-oriented' research; and on the other hand the department of government under Laski became increasingly associated with the teaching of Marxist political theory. Hogben himself furiously opposed both

[14] BP, IIb, WHB to R. Denman, 23 Dec. 1931.

the 'unscientific' commitment to Marxist dogma which he perceived in the followers of Laski, and the 'secular Platonism', 'ostentatious useless- ness' and devotion to the 'idol' of academic purity which prevailed in the study of theoretical economics.[15]

Hogben's views were strongly supported by Beveridge who was in- creasingly hostile both to 'pure theory' and to partisan commitment in academic research. In terms of political ideology Beveridge himself in the early 1930s was very close to the school of Robbins and Hayek; but nevertheless, he strongly attacked their deductive methodology as 'fantastically unreal' and not corresponding 'to anything taking place in men's minds'.[16] When Robbins proposed a new course on 'pure theory', Beveridge himself in the 'role of intelligent business man . . . argued for theory and laboratory' – by which he meant a 'course on current problems'.[17] As the bias of his colleagues moved away from empiricism, he himself became all the more determined to develop empirical studies, and with this end in view he diverted an increasing proportion of the Rockefeller funds to his own research on prices and to the department of Social Biology. 'Partly because of his anti-Marxism and anti-politics [Hogben] has got on the right side of Beveridge and even of Mrs. Mair,' commented Beatrice Webb; '[He] gets all the money and freedom he wants for his and Enid's investigations.'[18] This situation was increas- ingly resented by many of Beveridge's colleagues, who complained that indefinite expansion of Social Biology had never been contemplated in the programme of 1925. Beveridge retorted, however, that the Rocke- feller grant had specifically been given for study of the 'natural bases of the social sciences', and that the grant had been accepted after full consultation with the teaching staff.[19] Hogben himself meanwhile was clearly unhappy at the L.S.E. He rarely entered the Senior Common Room, made few friends among the staff, and frequently attacked the 'purism' of his colleagues in learned journals and the press. Matters came to a head in 1935–6 when prolonged economic recession forced the Rockefeller Foundation to reduce its commitment to social research. Beveridge was informed that no more funds could be promised for the time being, except in the form of 'tapering grants' with which to con- clude current projects.[20] Then at the end of 1936 Hogben resigned from

---

[15] Passfield Papers, B. Webb's diary, 17 Dec. 1931 and 19 Jan. 1935; Lancelot Hogben, 'The Contemporary Challenge to Freedom of Thought', *Freedom: its Meaning*, ed., Ruth Nanda Anshen (1942), pp. 120–30. Philip Abrams, *The Origins of British Sociology 1834–1914*, p. 147.

[16] BP, IIb, WHB's ms. comments on J. R. Hicks' *Wages*.

[17] BP, Ic 9, WHB's diary, 6 Jan. 1934.

[18] Passfield Papers, B. Webb's diary, 19 Jan. 1935.

[19] L.S.E. Papers, 'Origin of Social Biology in the School of Economics', by WHB, 16 July 1935.

[20] Lady Beveridge Papers, Tracy Kittredge to WHB, 29 Dec. 1934. Possibly also the

the L.S.E. and the School's Emergency Committee refused to commit itself to appointing a successor. Hogben's chair was left vacant, and his department was dismantled after Beveridge's own resignation later in 1937. To Beveridge the eclipse of social biology was a crushing blow – an end to his hopes of establishing a new 'science of society', based on cross-fertilization of disciplines and inductive methods.[21] Among his colleagues the end of the experiment was generally greeted with relief, though some at least thought that it had never been given a fair trial.[22] Many of them blamed the failure on Beveridge's own mismanagement – on his hostility to pure theory, his resistance to criticism and his failure to consult his staff. Hogben himself, however, saw the failure as a victory for a factious and traditional academic establishment, obsessed with age-old battles between worn-out metaphysical creeds. 'As Principals and such like go I don't think Beveridge was a bad sort,' he wrote to Beatrice Webb;

and if there had been four people in the place with the determination to make a realistic programme of social studies I am sure he would have played ball. The trouble was that the Left Wingers were just as dialectical as the Right, and the few who (like Robson) were sympathetic to realistic research (as opposed to tautological necromancy and belles letters) were not in powerful positions. . . .

That will end an inglorious and rather humiliating chapter of my life. Just now I am on top of the world again. The biological opportunities are stupendous. But if what is called social science is what is done at the L.S.E. thank Heaven I am still a biologist. . . .[23]

### III

The debate on the nature of the social sciences was closely linked with another major issue of Beveridge's directorship – the issue of 'academic freedom' and of how far university teachers should become actively engaged in political controversy. As a journalist in the 1900s Beveridge had written eloquently in favour of total academic freedom, and had strongly denounced the exclusion of socialists and anarchists from teaching posts in German Universities.[24] When he accepted the directorship

---

[21] *PI*, p. 252.

[22] Lord Chorley, 'Beveridge and the L.S.E. Part One, *L.S.E. Magazine*, 44, Nov. 1972, pp. 9–10;

[23] Passfield Papers, II, 4, k, 52, L. Hogben to B. Webb, 30 Sept. (? 1937).

[24] Review of Friedrich Paulsen, *The German Universities and University Study*, presscutting in BP, XII, 2, ff. 64–5.

---

Rockefeller Trustees were alarmed at the amount being spent on Social Biology, but the evidence on this point is inconclusive (BP, IIb, Tracy Kittredge to A. Carr Saunders, 31 Jan. 1938; WHB to A. Carr Saunders, 16 Feb. 1938).

of the L.S.E. he had stipulated that he should have 'complete freedom of speech and writing' and that 'the tenure of the post would not exclude my becoming a candidate or member of Parliament'.[25] Before the general election of 1922 he was invited to stand as Liberal candidate for Oxford University, and was only deterred from doing so because Oxford Liberals could not raise the money to finance his campaign.[26] He was, however, active for a time in the Liberal Summer Schools movement, where he urged the Liberals to make themselves the party of expertise and 'public service', as distinct from the sectional interests represented by Labour and Conservatives.[27] When members of the L.S.E. staff were elected to Parliament they were required to resign their full-time appointments; but they continued to lecture on a part-time basis and to contribute to the life of the School – the most notable examples being the reader in economics, Hugh Dalton, and the reader in government, Herbert Lees Smith.[28]

During his early years at the L.S.E. Beveridge was therefore strongly in favour of close links between academic life and the world of public affairs. He positively encouraged the development of research that was relevant to politics and government, and he urged politicians and administrators to make more use of academic research.[29] At the same time – contrary to what has sometimes been suggested – he seems to have supported complete freedom of political thought and action for members of his staff. Kingsley Martin, who was an assistant lecturer at the L.S.E. from 1924 to 1927, implied in his memoirs that Beveridge had blocked his promotion to a permanent lectureship, because he and Beveridge had clashed in their views on the General Strike.[30] But I have found no shred of evidence to corroborate Martin's statements, and his whole account of what went on at the L.S.E. in the 1920s is so riddled with inaccuracies as to be scarcely a reliable record.[31] It is certainly true that Beveridge disagreed with Martin politically, and probably disliked him personally, but this in no sense proves that he discriminated against him professionally – particularly as there were many other members of the L.S.E. staff who shared Martin's views. There is, moreover, positive

---

[25] BP, IIb, WHB to S. Webb, 6 June 1919.

[26] BP, IIb, 22, WHB to Lancelot Phelps, 7 Nov. 1922.

[27] See below, pp. 312.

[28] L.S.E. Papers, minutes of Emergency Committee, 5 Nov. 1924.

[29] BP, IIb, WHB to Lord Haldane, 5 Nov. 1923; WHB to A. W. Flux, 28 Jan. 1924.

[30] Kingsley Martin, *Father Figures, A First Volume of Autobiography 1897–1931* (1966), pp. 163–4.

[31] e.g. he ascribed the ideological battles during his period at L.S.E. to the *laissez-faire* influence of 'Professors Robbins, Plant and Hayek' (*Father Figures*, p. 158). But Martin left in 1927; Robbins was in Oxford during most of Martin's time at the School, and did not become a professor until 1929. Plant and Hayek were respectively in Cape Town and Vienna throughout the period in question.

evidence to show that Beveridge on numerous occasions staunchly defended the political freedom of members of his staff. When a group of the School's businessmen governors demurred against the promotion of Harold Laski to a readership, Beveridge replied that Laski's political convictions were irrelevant, and that the appointment had been made at his own recommendation purely on the basis of 'the technical eminence' of the teacher concerned.[32] He replied in a similar way to accusations of bias from members of the public. 'I have been advised by two or three friends to write and ask you whether it is true that the London School of Economics has a distinctly *Socialist* influence,' wrote a lady from Hampstead in 1923.

I have been told that the teaching is very socialistic and that particularly in the Welfare Workers' Department it turns out young people with revolutionary ideas. . . . I have read Mr. Tawney's books and also Prof. Dalton's on the Capital Levy published by the Labour Publishing Co. I have heard a good deal about Mr. Laski and I cannot help asking you whether it is *right* that such an important subject as *Political Ideas* should be dealt with in a *London University* by a foreigner? . . . When I was at Oxford I had the great advantage of attending Mr. A. L. Smith's lectures on Political Science and should like to think that the London students had someone as thoroughly *English* as he was.[33]

Beveridge replied reassuringly that there was no foundation for such accusations of bias, that Mr. Laski was not a foreigner, and that political subjects were taught at the School by many lecturers of widely varying points of view. 'I am sure,' he concluded, 'that Mr. A. L. Smith, who is the master of my and Mr. Tawney's old college, would be one of the first to advise you to listen to both Mr. Tawney and Mr. Laski.'[34]

At the outset of his directorship Beveridge was therefore strongly committed both to individual freedom of expression and to providing a forum for many conflicting political views. For private citizens he continued to adhere to these principles through his life; but during the 1920s he gradually came round to the view that total freedom of expression for University teachers might in certain circumstances be incompatible with pursuit of academic truth. This modification of his views seems to have been brought about by a number of factors. One of these was his own growing political agnosticism, which led him as a private individual to look with increasing suspicion on all forms of political and governmental activity.[35] A second factor was his growing concern to

[32] BP, IIb, J. Wilson Potter to WHB, 22 Feb. 1923; WHB to J. Wilson Potter, 23 Feb. 1923.
[33] BP, IIb, M. A. Clay to WHB, 7 Apr. 1923.
[34] BP, IIb, WHB to M. A. Clay, 12 Apr. 1923.
[35] Below, p. 311–23.

establish social research on a scientific basis, and his fear that objectivity would be impaired by a strong prior commitment to political beliefs. A third factor may possibly have been the influence of Steel-Maitland, the chairman of the L.S.E. governors. Steel-Maitland, a former chairman of the Conservative pa.ty, in principle favoured complete freedom of expression; but he was strongly opposed to involvement of the School in current political debate. On several occasions he intervened to dissuade Beveridge from giving a platform to speakers on explosive political issues—a policy which, to give him his due, Steel-Maitland pursued against speakers of the 'right' and 'centre' rather than speakers of the 'left'.[36] The fourth and almost certainly the crucial factor was the position of Harold Laski, who was chiefly responsible for the revival of the School's reputation for socialism. Laski was by no means the only socialist at the L.S.E., nor was he ideologically the furthest to the 'left'; but with his flair for publicity, his brilliance as a lecturer and his frequent excursions into left-wing journalism, it was he who most regularly and most flamboyantly caught the public eye.

Laski had come to the L.S.E. from Harvard at the specific invitation of Beveridge in 1920. He had had a stormy career in Boston, where he had been accused of political anarchism, of exercising undue influence over students, and of being a person who 'loved to be in the limelight, which is not conducive to profound scholarship'.[37] Nevertheless, for several years he and Beveridge were on the best of terms. When offered the post at the L.S.E. Laski had rejoiced like 'a mad excited Indian', and he told Graham Wallas that Beveridge's 'plans and manner delight me'.[38] On his return to England he immediately became active in Labour politics, and soon made a name for himself as a socialist orator. These activities attracted a certain amount of criticism but, as has been shown, Beveridge consistently defended Laski and sponsored his promotion to a readership in 1923. The first sign of serious disquiet about Laski's extra-mural activities came not from Beveridge but from Sidney Webb. On the retirement of Wallas in 1926 Webb in a confidential letter to Beveridge urged that Laski should be discouraged from applying for Wallas's chair. If he *did* apply for it, Webb admitted, he must undoubtedly be appointed as the most distinguished candidate; but he implied that Laski was already neglecting his teaching duties, and that the difficulties this caused would become much more pronounced if Laski became head of a large department. Webb therefore suggested that Laski should be given a part-time personal professorship, which

[36] BP, IIb, Sir Arthur Steel-Maitland, to WHB, 22 Nov. 1926 and 2 Aug. 1927.

[37] Wallas Papers, Box. 6, H. Laski to G. Wallas, 30 Sept. and 21 Dec. 1919; Box 7, A. L. Lowell to G. Wallas, 18 Jan. 1921.

[38] Wallas Papers, Box 7, Frida Laski to G. Wallas, 26 Mar. 1920; H. Laski to G. Wallas, 4 June 1920.

would leave him free for his political interests and 'for dealing with those individual students with and for whom he happens to be fertile and stimulating, though not for the mass, or even for other individuals. . . . I am sure he would be unhappy if he knew and felt that he *had* to be "full-time", and unable conscientiously to give his mind to (a) adult education (b) the miners' cause (c) any other "crisis" that arrives!'[39]

No record has survived of Beveridge's response to Webb's proposal. It is possible that Laski himself caught the wind of some hostile move against him, because shortly afterwards he wrote to Beveridge a rather challenging letter, claiming that there was 'grave doubt and confusion' about the School's appointments procedures and asking Beveridge to make a statement about 'the status of younger members of staff and their advancement'.[40] Nevertheless, as Laski subsequently applied for and was duly appointed to Wallas's chair, it seems improbable that Beveridge was at this stage unduly alarmed by Sidney Webb's misgivings. As Professor of Political Science, Laski's radical opinions attracted even more publicity than before, but Beveridge was still strongly opposed to any kind of suppression. In 1928 whilst on a fund-raising visit to the Rockefellers he heard that Laski had written an article in *Harpers Magazine*, denouncing the role of capitalist philanthropy;[41] but although annoyed and embarrassed Beveridge did not on this occasion question Laski's right to express such opinions. Within the L.S.E. the main criticism of Laski's activities seems to have come from Hugh Dalton—a personal rivalry that probably concealed a more fundamental antagonism between the Labour 'right' and 'left'. Laski made no secret of the fact that he regarded Dalton as 'the Devil in the British Labour Party',[42] whilst Dalton on one occasion publicly denounced Laski at an L.S.E. dinner. When Laski complained against Dalton to Mrs. Mair, she had a 'very friendly' conversation with him and was clearly inclined to take his side. 'Dalton had been in fact unbelievably silly and swelled-headed,' she recorded. 'I told Prof. Laski how much I liked one side of Dalton and how sure I was that punishment would come for his present indiscretions. Later, having thought it all over again, I saw Laski for a minute and told him I'd try to drop a hint.'[43]

Neither Beveridge nor Mrs. Mair was therefore at all disposed to be personally hostile to Laski; but, nevertheless, relations between them gradually deteriorated as Laski's politics grew more radical and as Beveridge became more insistent on preserving a neutral front. When

[39] BP, IIb, S. Webb to WHB, 15 May 1926.
[40] BP, IIb, H. Laski to WHB, 25 Nov. 1926.
[41] Lady Beveridge Papers, WHB to J. Mair, 22 Aug. and 6 Sept. 1928.
[42] Passfield Papers, B. Webb's diary, 30 May 1934.
[43] Lady Beveridge Papers, J. Mair's diary, 29 Nov. 1929.

in 1928 the School commissioned a portrait of the Webbs, Beveridge deliberately recruited sponsors of all shades of political opinion, so as to 'avoid any association of the London School of Economics with the Political Labour Party and the Socialist Creed'.[44] In the following year Mrs. Mair recorded with approval that a conference of lawyers meeting at the School had agreed in condemning the involvement of academics in political action—the sole dissenter being the School's own leading international lawyer, Professor H. A. Smith.[45] Early in 1930 a member of the Governors wrote to Beveridge urging that greater control should be exercised over members of staff who held joint L.S.E. and university appointments—a suggestion that was almost certainly directed against Harold Laski.[46] Beveridge replied at the time in distinctly negative terms;[47] but a few weeks later an incident occurred which may well have been the turning-point in his relationship with Laski. He recorded in his diary that at a students' dinner Laski had made a 'rather savage speech' and had turned the occasion into a 'protest meeting' against the School.[48] Relations between Beveridge and Laski thereafter grew noticeably cooler. They continued to correspond with each other, to dine together, and even on occasion to visit each other's homes; but there was a perceptible note of artifice in the rather strained joviality of Beveridge's letters and the feline politeness of Laski's. In 1932 the situation worsened when Laski became a regular columnist for the *Daily Herald*. The L.S.E. was frequently attacked in the conservative press, and Beveridge found his efforts to raise funds for the School increasingly hampered by charges of militant socialism. Early in 1932 he recorded that he had had to give 'life histories of Laski and Tawney' and to defend the compatibility of socialism and scholarship, whilst negotiating a grant from the Leverhulme trustees.[49] Shortly afterwards the question of 'political activities' was discussed at length by the School's Professorial Council. At this meeting it was decided that, although the School's constitution guaranteed to its teachers 'absolute freedom in both speaking and writing, they should nevertheless regard it as a personal duty to preserve in such writings or speeches a proper regard for the reputation of the School as an academic centre of scientific teaching and research'.[50]

The growth of controversy about Laski must, however, be seen in the context of wider developments in the intellectual history of the L.S.E. As we have seen, the School had long had a reputation for socialism—

[44] Passfield Papers, B. Webb's diary, 31 Mar. 1928.
[45] Lady Beveridge Papers, J. Mair's diary, 10 Dec. 1929.
[46] BP, IIb, Frank Pick to WHB, 29 Jan. 1930.
[47] BP, IIb, WHB to Frank Pick, 30 Jan. 1930.
[48] BP, Ic 5, WHB's diary, 18 Feb. 1930.
[49] Ibid., 19 Jan. and 1 Feb. 1932.
[50] L.S.E. Papers, minutes of Professorial Council, 1932.

a reputation that sheltered a very catholic cross-section of opinion, as it continued to do throughout Beveridge's directorship. In the early 1930s, however, what had previously been a forum for the mutual exchange of conflicting ideas became for a time an embattled institution polarized into two hostile and non-communicating ideological camps. The reasons for this change were complex and must to a certain extent be a matter for conjecture. An important factor was almost certainly the rapid transformation of the L.S.E. from a small closely-knit community where everyone knew everybody else, into a larger and much more anonymous body in which it was literally impossible to know the names and faces of all one's colleagues. A second factor was the intellectual impact of the world crisis of 1929–31, which seemed to many people totally to discredit the system of capitalism modified by welfare that had grown up in Britain and Western Europe during the previous fifty years. To some, like the Webbs and Laski, the prolonged depression seemed to prove the need for a planned socialist economy; to others, like Beveridge, it seemed to prescribe a thorough-going restoration of free market economics. This movement of ideas and Beveridge's share in it will be considered in more detail in the following chapter; here it is sufficient to say that, within the L.S.E. and among intellectuals generally, there was a conspicuous hardening of opinion on both left and right. An additional and complicating factor was Beveridge's personal quest for a non-ideological inductive social science. His initial concern for mutual exchange between scholarship and government gradually gave way to the belief that academics should refrain from prescriptive statements about practical issues of policy. 'Can anything we say or do affect the acts of millions?' he wrote. 'Probably not. That is not my problem. Economics is not an art but a science. A study and explanation of facts, not a compendium of practical reforms.'[51]

The new climate of opinion gradually became evident within the L.S.E. Hugh Dalton, writing in 1932, foresaw 'the possibility of intellectual friction at the School'. He ascribed it, perhaps surprisingly, not to Laski but to his own former pupil, Lionel Robbins, who had recently been appointed Professor of Political Economy. Robbins, complained Dalton, had 'stiffened in an old-fashioned laisser-faire attitude' towards current economic problems, and was exercising a powerful influence over the attitudes of both students and staff.[52] A year later Beatrice Webb, far advanced on her 'pilgrimage to Moscow', observed that communications between 'the rival schools of economic individualism and economic communism' had completely broken down, and that it had become imposs-

---

[51] BP, III 19, ms. notes on 'The Problem of Human Control', in material for revision of *Unemployment: a Problem of Industry.*
[52] Dalton Papers, Dalton's diary, 16–18 Jan. 1932.

ible to talk about serious subjects with Beveridge 'or any other old friend of the other side . . . Apparently the lively and brilliant Laski is feeling the cold wind of intolerance blowing—even in his direction. But it will be a polite and silent intolerance; a subject to be avoided—sometimes persons to be avoided; not more than that.'[53] Shortly afterwards, when serious political dissension broke out at the School, Beveridge urged that all debate on current politics should be ruled out of the conversation of staff and students, as 'inconsistent with the scientific outlook and therefore improper subjects for discussion!' But, commented Mrs. Webb, 'seeing that Laski is University Professor of political science and that Robbins is University Professor of economics, and that they each accuse the other of being unrelenting propagandists, Beveridge's naive suggestion is not likely to be accepted'.[54]

The political antagonisms at the School came to a head over several issues—the most serious being the acquisition of the library of the Frankfurt Institut für Sozialforschung, and the question of Laski's work for the *Daily Herald*. Early in 1933 Beveridge had become actively involved in the movement for assisting refugee scholars expelled from Nazi Germany.[55] Many members of the School made donations to this movement, and several distinguished German scholars joined the staff of the L.S.E. In June 1933 Beveridge informed the School's Emergency Committee that he was negotiating with Dr. Pollack, the head of the Frankfurt Institute, for transfer to the L.S.E. of the Institute's library and several of its staff.[56] The institute was well-known as a centre of Marxist studies, and the library was threatened with confiscation by the German government on the ground that it was 'advancing communistic and other activities contrary to the well-being of the People and the State'. The Emergency Committee agreed to the acquisition of the library, and authorized Sir Josiah Stamp, the Vice-Chairman of the Governors, to arrange the transfer with the government in Berlin.[57] 'It is proof of Beveridge's open-minded tolerance,' acknowledged Beatrice Webb, 'that he is willing to absorb this hostile school of thought.'[58] Stamp reported two months later that the matter had been transferred from the Prussian Secret Police to the German Foreign Office and that 'he was hopeful that either the whole library or a great part of it would eventually reach the School'. The Emergency Committee 'passed a vote of thanks to Sir Josiah Stamp for his effectual help in this matter'.[59]

[53] Passfield Papers, B. Webb's diary, 18 June, 1933.
[54] Ibid., 12 Mar. 1934.
[55] Lord Beveridge, *A Defence of Free Learning* (1959), esp. ch. 1.
[56] L.S.E. Papers, minutes of Emergency Committee, 8 June 1933.
[57] Ibid., 25 Jan. 1934.
[58] Passfield Papers, B. Webb's diary, 29 May 1933.
[59] L.S.E. Papers, Minutes of Emergency Committee, 22 Mar. 1934.

In May 1934 Beveridge reported that as the library now legally belonged he was considering the possibility of pursuing the matter in the German High Court. The Emergency Committee authorized him to do this, provided that Pollack could guarantee the expenses of such an action.[60] Two months later Beveridge reported that, as Pollack had agreed to this condition, he was instructing solicitors to proceed with the case.[61] At this point, however, the proposed acquisition of the library came to the notice of Professor Robbins, who objected strongly to the incorporation of such a manifestly partisan body into the L.S.E. Such an action, he complained to Mrs. Mair 'would be the ultimate and complete ruin of the School as an educational institution', and he invoked the opinion of several German refugees in support of this view.[62] Robbins's arguments apparently convinced the Emergency Committee, and to Beveridge's fury the decision to take legal action was therefore reversed. In his autobiography Robbins recalled that Beveridge afterwards was very contrite and thanked him 'for having saved him from what he himself described as a major mistake'.[63] But Beveridge's contrition was either insincere or short-lived. Eight months later when Sidney Webb under pressure from Pollack inquired whether the subject could be raised again, Beveridge replied that the Emergency Committee were now 'dead set against doing anything' and had refused to proceed with legal action. He himself believed, however, 'that we ought even at this late hour to reverse that decision at the next meeting . . . I should not be surprised to find that Stamp takes the same view.'[64] In the event it was not Robbins but Mrs. Mair who dissuaded Beveridge from taking further action. In a long letter to Beveridge she strongly endorsed Robbins's objections. She reported that the Institute had now been offered accommodation in Geneva, so that the School no longer had a moral obligation to provide it with asylum; and she denounced Pollack as a dishonourable 'cad' for using Beveridge as an instrument in his private feud with the Nazis, and for trying to exploit and batten on the good name of L.S.E.[65]

As Lord Chorley has recently pointed out the library of the Frankfurt Institute was a 'collection of outstanding importance', the acquisition of which would have placed the L.S.E. library 'in important respects far ahead of any other library in the world'.[66] Nevertheless, the practical question of whether or not the library was acquired was probably less important than the questions of principle and ideology that were involved. It seems highly unlikely in the circumstances that the library

[60] Ibid., 31 May 1934.   [61] Ibid., 19 July 1934.
[62] Lady Beveridge Papers, J. Mair to WHB, 16 Mar. 1935.
[63] Lionel Robbins, op. cit., p. 140.
[64] BP, IIb, WHB to S. Webb, 6 Mar. 1935.
[65] Lady Beveridge Papers, J. Mair to WHB, 16 Mar. 1935.
[66] Lord Chorley, 'Beveridge and the L.S.E. Part Two', *L.S.E.*, no. 45, June 1973, p. 8.

would ever have reached L.S.E., and on this point it is certainly possible to question Beveridge's political judgement. As Sidney Webb pointed out, suing the Nazi government in the German courts was rather a pointless venture.[67] It was an ingenious and quixotic thought on Beveridge's part, but really nothing more. On the question of principle, however, it is difficult to understand why Beveridge's desire to acquire the library was seen by Robbins and others as so objectionable. It is true that the library was a centre of Marxist scholarship; but it is hard to see why its amalgamation with the L.S.E. would have been more intellectually compromising than, for instance, the merger with the Charity Organisation Society's School of Sociology in 1912, or the acquisition of the Cobden Library on International trade in 1924. Similarly, whilst it is true that Beatrice Webb—not Sidney—viewed the library as a potential counter-weight to orthodox economics,[68] it is hard to imagine that a small handful of refugee archivists would have been able to undermine the academic integrity of the rest of the L.S.E. The incident was, however, highly significant in three respects. It refutes the suggestion sometimes made that Beveridge's 'impartiality' applied only to the political right.[69] It showed how deeply entrenched ideological positions had become at the School, and how strongly academics of the right feared and resented the activism of the left. And it showed how narrow and undemocratic was the L.S.E.'s system of academic government. As Lord Robbins has pointed out, it was highly unsatisfactory that he should only have heard of the proposal by accident, when the issue had been virtually settled.[70] What was no less unsatisfactory was that likely supporters of the Frankfurt library—such as Laski, Tawney and their followers—took no part whatsoever in making the decision, and were apparently never consulted at all.

The controversy over the Frankfurt library can perhaps best be understood within the context of the more overtly political conflict between Beveridge and Harold Laski, which also came to a head in 1934, and was sparked off by an outbreak of student unrest. In 1933 there had been a series of articles by socialist students in the *Clare Market Review*, accusing the University Senate of planting 'spies' in the students' union. These articles provoked a certain amount of criticism in other London colleges,[71] but Beveridge himself did not take the matter very seriously. He rather prided himself on his good relations with students, and early in 1934 he had a series of friendly discussions with two of the leading student protestors—H. J. Simons, the president of the Marxist

---

[67] BP, IIb, S. Webb to WHB, 5 Mar. 1935.
[68] Passfield Papers, B. Webb's diary, 19 May 1933.
[69] e.g. C. Rolph, *Kingsley* (1973), p. 137; Kingsley Martin, *Harold Laski*, p. 97.
[70] Robbins, op. cit., pp. 140–1.  [71] BP, IIb, E. Dellar to WHB, 21 Dec. 1933.

Society and F. S. Meyer, an American graduate anthropologist who was president of the students' union.[72] At the end of February, however, his attention was drawn to an article in the *Student Vanguard*, in which one of the School's professors was accused by name of 'spying' on students on behalf of colonial governments. Since the article was clearly libellous, Beveridge forbade any further sales of the paper; but this was defied by six students, led by Meyer and Simons, who continued to sell the *Vanguard* 'openly and defiantly' outside the student refectory. Five of the six students were forthwith suspended by the Emergency Committee, and Meyer and Simons were eventually expelled.[73]

Beveridge's actions on this occasion seem to have commanded widespread support among governors, teachers and students. Laski himself had been the first person to draw attention to the libellous passage in the *Vanguard*; and he criticized the actions of the six students as 'indefensible from any angle', although he blamed Beveridge's paternalistic methods of government for the general atmosphere of student discontent.[74] Beatrice Webb recorded that Beveridge had been 'most conciliatory', and that his 'attitude towards these "children" is irreproachable'. She blamed the incident on a 'knot of Marxists led by an odious American Jew', who were trying to promote revolt by personal vilification—a policy that 'eventually damages its own side more than that of its victims . . . it poisons the atmosphere and leads to reaction into fascism'.[75] The L.S.E. students' union appealed for a lessening of the sentences, but carefully disassociated itself from the actions of the six offenders. When a polite deputation of union members was sent to Beveridge to plead for clemency, the leader of the deputation 'emphasised that as one of the prominent members of the Athletic Union' he had himself 'habitually opposed Meyer . . . and was himself a Conservative'. When a group of left-wing students proposed more militant action this was denounced by liberals and moderates as 'merely another example of the deplorable state of affairs now existing in the Union, whereby a minority of members active in Union affairs is driving a dwindling body along a path completely divorced from that which appeals to the students at large'.[76]

These reactions do not suggest that the L.S.E. in 1934 in any way resembled the 'hot-bed of Communism', depicted in the national press. Nevertheless, Beveridge himself had become convinced that student protest had been encouraged and legitimized by the political activities of

[72] BP, Ic, WHB's diary, 8 and 9 Jan. 1934.
[73] L.S.E. Papers, minutes and papers of the Emergency Committee, 5 and 22 Mar. 1934; BP, Ic, WHB's diary, 28 Feb. 1934.
[74] L.S.E. Papers, 'Case of Student Discipline', by WHB, 1 Mar. 1934; Passfield Papers, II, 4, j, 35c, H. Laski to B. Webb, 13 Mar. 1934.
[75] Passfield Papers, B. Webb's diary, 12 Mar. 1934.
[76] L.S.E. Papers, minutes and papers of the Emergency Committee, 22 Mar. 1934.

certain members of staff—especially Harold Laski. Three days after the issue of the libellous *Vanguard*, he wrote to Laski, drawing attention to 'the possible harm that his utterances might be doing to the School'. The letter was followed by a painful interview, at which Beveridge also suggested that Laski's regular articles for the *Daily Herald* were incompatible with his post as a full-time professor. He pointed out that the School had two distinct professorial salary-scales, one for those who drew their incomes solely from teaching, and another for those who had an additional source of earnings outside the School. It was unfair, Beveridge protested, that some professors—such as lawyers with a part-time practice—should be confined to the lower scale, while Laski remained on the higher.[77] Laski agreed at this meeting that both questions should be decided by the Emergency Committee. 'I, too, found our talk of the other night very painful,' wrote Laski to Beveridge a few days later. 'I had not realised until then how profound had become your personal antagonism to me, and it came upon me with all the force of an unexpected blow.'[78]

It was perhaps unfortunate that, because of pressure of other business, Laski's position was not in fact considered by the Emergency Committee until July 1934. In the meantime Laski went on a lecture tour to Moscow as a guest of the Soviet Government. During this tour he reputedly criticized many aspects of the Stalinist variant of communism, but nevertheless the visit attracted much criticism in the British parliament and press.[79] Sir Ernest Graham Little complained in the *Daily Telegraph* that Laski ought to be disciplined by the L.S.E. governors, but that such action was unlikely to be taken since the School was well-known as a centre of Communist doctrine.[80] At the same time the London University authorities issued a statement publicly disassociating themselves from Laski's views—a statement that evoked many protests from University teachers, who objected strongly to the implication that the University had any right either to approve or disapprove the opinions of its staff.[81] Beveridge himself was widely regarded as being either responsible for or closely associated with the University's statement, but this was not in fact the case. Shortly afterwards he wrote to the Vice Chancellor, repudiating the view that either the University or individual colleges had any right to interfere with the opinions of their members. He pointed out that complete freedom of opinion was guaranteed by the L.S.E. constitution, and that abuse of this freedom was guarded against by the Professorial Council resolution of 1932, by which Laski

[77] BP, Ic 9, WHB's diary, 3 Mar. 1934; *The London School of Economics and its Problems 1919–37*, pp. 55–6.

[78] Lady Beveridge Papers, H. Laski to WHB, 19 Apr. 1934.

[79] Kingsley Martin, *Harold Laski*, p. 93.       [80] *Daily Telegraph*, 14 July 1934.

[81] Kingsley Martin, *Harold Laski*, pp. 93–4; C. H. Rolph, *Kingsley*, p. 137.

along with the rest of the School's professors regarded himself as 'fully bound'.[82] Within the School itself, however, Beveridge continued to pursue the discussions he had had with Laski earlier in the year. He visited Laski at the latter's home to try to work out a *modus vivendi*, and the question of Laski's political activities was raised in the Emergency Committee on 19 July. It was decided that Laski's work for the *Herald* was a breach of the School's arrangements about professorial salaries, and the Committee unanimously concluded that 'the development of public opinion concerning Professor Laski's recent more popular utterances was against the best interests of the School'.[83] A few days later Laski wrote to Beveridge agreeing to end his regular articles for the *Herald* and to confine his extra-curricular activities to 'occasional' articles and speeches on 'political topics'.[84]

This formal attempt to shackle Harold Laski proved to be in many respects one of the most mishandled episodes of Beveridge's career. Far from establishing the principle of scientific impartiality, it aroused suspicion in many quarters that Beveridge was an enemy of academic freedom; and, as a result, hostility towards his methods of government was increasingly apparent not merely among extremists of right and left but in the School's large 'moderate' centre.[85] Nor as an act of suppression was it particularly successful, since Laski did not noticeably modify his political activities, and although he ceased to be regularly retained by the *Herald* he continued to write for the paper nearly as often as before. Quite why Beveridge took the action that he did must be a matter for speculation, but it seems probable that the answer should be couched in highly personal terms. Beveridge in 1934 felt himself beleaguered on several fronts—domestic, political, intellectual—and the behaviour of Laski was perhaps the last straw in a period of intense personal strain. Moreover, it is difficult to avoid the impression that what Beveridge objected to was not so much the content of Laski's politics, as their highly emotive and flamboyant style. Laski was a very compelling public orator, a charismatic personality who exercised a great deal of influence over students and colleagues, and he made no secret of his gleeful delight in anticipating the prospect of martyrdom—an attitude in which he as encouraged by such friends as Kingsley Martin.[86] Almost certainly it was these factors, rather than the substantive content of Laski's doctrines, that provoked the hostility and intervention of Beveridge. Certainly it would be quite wrong to suggest that Beveridge wished to suppress Marxism as a school of academic inquiry—as was shown by

[82] L.S.E. Papers, draft of letter from WHB to the Vice Chancellor, 1 Aug. 1934.
[83] L.S.E. Papers, Minutes of the Emergency Committee, 19 July 1934.
[84] L.S.E. Papers, copy of letter from H. Laski to WHB, 25 July 1934.
[85] Passfield Papers, B. Webb's diary, 14 Feb. 1936.
[86] Ibid., 10 May and 13 July 1934.

his attitude to the Frankfurt library. Nor, to the surprise of Beatrice Webb, did he object to the publication of the Webbs' *Soviet Communism*, which was a good deal more uncritically pro-Soviet than anything written by Laski. In practice, however, it proved virtually impossible to draw a fine distinction between Marxist propaganda, which in Beveridge's eyes was objectionable, and academic Marxist analysis, which was not. By September 1935 Beatrice Webb remarked that his 'vehement objection to Laski's propagandist activities' had become an 'obsession'.[87] A few months later R. H. Tawney observed that Beveridge, in his alarm at the growth of student Marxism and at the hostile reaction of the School's city governors, was 'getting more and more autocratic in his manner and bearing towards the professoriate, he is shackling the new-comers among the staff with prohibitions and restrictions and is bitterly resentful of Laski's continuous propagandist articles in the D. H. and elsewhere'. Twelve years earlier Sidney Webb had proudly declared that 'there is not the slightest intention or danger of the School taking up a position in the slightest degree below that of the older English universities as regards freedom of speech and political association'. Now in 1935, Tawney sadly remarked, it was no longer possible for staff to study 'present day problems', and there was 'far more freedom of expression at Oxford today than at the London School of Economics'.[88]

## IV

Beveridge's conflicts with his staff were closely bound up with the method and manner of his government of the L.S.E. In his history of the School, Beveridge recalled that it had once been described by a committee of inspection as a 'benevolent autocracy'. 'I have never discovered what period of the School's history they had in mind,' he added indignantly; 'it certainly did not fit anything that happened in my time there.'[89] Beveridge's perception of his own administrative methods was not, however, shared by many of his colleagues, nor is it borne out by the records of the time. Beveridge came to the L.S.E. with something of a reputation as a classic Whitehall bureaucrat; but this was not in fact a particularly accurate description, since his approach to administration was very much more personal and charismatic than was common Whitehall. Throughout his civil service career he had fretted against the petty rituals of day-to-day public administration; and, in spite of his frequent clashes with 'businessman' administrators, he greatly

[87] Ibid., 16 Sept. 1935.
[88] Ibid., 8 Dec. 1935; Wallas Papers, Box 8, S. Webb to G. Wallas, 11 May 1923.
[89] *The London School of Economics and its Problems 1919–1937*, p. 78.

admired the speed, decisiveness and capacity for firm action that he found in some of the businessmen imported into Whitehall during the war.[90] By the end of the war he had been perceptibly influenced by the entrepreneurial manner, and as director of the L.S.E. he combined the thoroughness and professionalism of a permanent civil servant with the rather high-handed paternalism of the managing director of a large family firm.

Such a combination of attitudes probably greatly facilitated the rapid growth of the L.S.E. but it did not leave much scope for sharing important decisions with members of his staff. As early as 1919 Beveridge recorded that 'some of the professors are afraid of bureaucratic government'; but he claimed confidently, 'I'll have no difficulty I think in putting that right'.[91] During the next two years he set up a series of staff committees to advise him on such questions as appointments, admissions and management of the library; and he increased the meetings of the Professorial Council from two to six a year. Nevertheless, control over important decisions was effectively concentrated in the Emergency Committee of the Court of Governors, set up in 1921. This committee consisted of Beveridge himself, Sidney Webb, four of the School's businessmen governors, and only two (later three) members of the Professorial Council. It was this committee that decided questions about academic policy, acquisition of property, discipline of students and employment of staff. Moreover, even within this committee Beveridge seems for many years to have played an excessively dominant role. The only other member whom he regularly consulted was Sidney Webb; and with Webb's support he continually 'managed' and cajoled the four City governors. When he discussed issues with members of his staff it was usually not through committees but in a highly confidential and personal manner—a manner echoed by Mrs. Mair, who tried to insist that all approaches to the director should be made through herself. This method of administration clearly reflected Beveridge's own personality, but it was not purely idiosyncratic; it was also consciously based on his ideas about how a college ought to be run. He freely admitted that he was against 'excessive democracy' in university administration. His aim at the L.S.E., as he later recalled, was to relieve academic staff of the burden of decision-making, so as to leave them free for their proper tasks of teaching and research.[92]

It is perhaps surprising that in his early days at the L.S.E. Beveridge's administrative tactics aroused so little controversy; but it would clearly

[90] W. H. Beveridge, *The Civil Service and its Critics* (1922).

[91] BP, IIa, ms. conversation with ASB, 5 July 1919.

[92] BP, IIb, WHB to Hector Hetherington, 12 Apr. 1929; *The London School of Economics and its Problems 1919–1937*, p. 82.

be wrong to read into the history of the 1920s the kind of pre-occupation with academic democracy that has been an issue in universities in the 1960s and 70s. Nevertheless, signs of discontent gradually accumulated as the years went by. As early as 1922 some members of the students' union criticized the autocracy of college government in the *Clare Market Review*; but Beveridge was assured by other students that this view was by no means widespread and that 'the attitude of many members of the Students' Union is far more autocratic than that of the authorities'.[93] In 1927 Beatrice Webb referred disparagingly to 'the Beveridge–Mair dictatorship', and Kingsley Martin complained that Beveridge had returned from his visits to the Rockefellers 'with the autocratic manner of the representative of the USA millionaires'.[94] In the following year, as we have seen, there was general indignation that even the Emergency Committee had not been consulted over Mrs. Mair's rest-room. There was also increasing criticism of Beveridge's single-handed management of the Rockefeller donations and of the 'altogether disproportionate' share that he was thought to be spending on his own research.[95]

These discontents about L.S.E. government became much more articulate in the 1930s, as controversy grew over major items of academic policy. On many issues the School was split into two or more factions; but on occasion, when Laski and Robbins united their influence, Beveridge was forced to submit.[96] Members of staff became increasingly weary of wasting time on powerless committees, and in 1934 Laski blamed the growth of student protest on a 'long history in which Beveridge and Mrs. Mair have a serious responsibility. To run a place like the School on a policy of favouritism and benevolent autocracy must result in an expulsion somewhere.'[97] Matters came to a head at a meeting of the Professorial Council in February 1934—in the midst of the *Student Vanguard* episode—when professors of all shades of opinion united to protest about lack of consultation. At this meeting Beveridge's wishes were overridden, and a committee was set up to revise the constitution of the School.[98] Over the next two years this committee 'discussed at length various proposals for reform'. In 1936, with the approval of inspectors from the University, it recommended certain changes to the L.S.E. constitution—as a result of which a good deal of power was shifted away from the director to the senior teaching staff. The Professorial Council was to cease to be a largely token body, and was hence-

[93] BP, IIb, J. Bruce to WHB, 23 June 1922.
[94] Passfield Papers, B. Webb's diary, 7 Feb. 1927.
[95] Lady Beveridge Papers, J. Mair's diary, 29 Nov. 1929.
[96] BP, Ic 5, WHB's diary, 9 and 10 Oct. 1930.
[97] Lord Chorley, 'Beveridge and the L.S.E. Part Two', loc. cit., p. 5; Passfield Papers, II, 4, j, 35c, H. Laski to B. Webb, 13 Mar. 1934.
[98] L.S.E. Papers, Minutes of Professorial Council, Feb. 1934.

forth to consider 'all important questions of policy on academic matters' —such as appointments, methods of teaching, and development of research. In addition the Council was to set up a General Purposes Committee, to act as 'an organ for the formative discussion of academic policy'.[99]

The triumph of the professors in reforming the constitution revealed just how vulnerable Beveridge might be when all factions in the School combined against him. Whether he himself realized that this was so is not clear, but he was certainly hurt and bewildered by the actions of his colleagues, and was increasingly anxious to resign from the L.S.E. He spent much time on his price history, and in June 1934 it was agreed that in the following year he should have two days' leave a week to devote to research. Then a month later he accepted a post as Chairman of the newly-created Unemployment Insurance Statutory Committee— a job which he planned to hold while continuing on half-pay as director of the L.S.E. He was strongly advised against this arrangement by Steel-Maitland, who pointed out that it might seriously hamper his efforts to curb the extra-mural activities of the L.S.E. professors.[100] Beveridge's rejection of this advice was curiously inconsistent with his view that academics should not meddle in questions of public policy; and it was a reflection also of his apparent insensitivity to the fact that in certain quarters employment by the government might be seen as just as academically compromising as active political propaganda.

The next three years, 1934 to 1937, were in many respects the unhappiest period of Beveridge's life. At the School, as we have seen, his administrative methods were increasingly criticized by all parties, and controversy continued to rage over the issues of academic freedom and methods of social research. Among the senior staff Beveridge's policies seem to have been supported only by Hogben and Malinowski—both of whom saw Beveridge as the champion of empirical studies against a rising tide of pure theory, and both of whom complained that the combined professoriate was even more autocratic than Beveridge himself.[101] This loss of control over the L.S.E. was accompanied by, and perhaps partially responsible for, something of a crisis in Beveridge's personal and intellectual life. Although outwardly a highly successful man, in moments of pessimism he looked back on his past career as a crater of dust and ashes. His civil service career, he told himself, had been a failure; and his work at the L.S.E. had meant '14 years in one

---

[99] L.S.E. Papers, 'Interim Report of Constitution Committee on Establishment of a General Purposes Committee', 18 Nov. 1936.

[100] BP, IIb, Sir Arthur Steel-Maitland to WHB, 11 July, 1934; L.S.E. Papers, minutes and papers of the Emergency Committee, 19 July 1934.

[101] Lady Beveridge Papers, B. Malinowski to WHB, 22 Feb. 1936; B. Malinowski to J. Mair, 23 Feb. 1936; Lancelot Hogben, 'The Contemporary Challenge to Freedom of Thought', loc. cit., p. 126.

administrative groove, reasonably productive but narrow. Looking back
. . . I seem to have missed ever so much of interest and importance that
was happening in the world and in the minds of men; I haven't really
used my opportunities of learning what the coming generation was
planning to do.'[102] This sense of personal futility was reinforced by a
loss of political hope and conviction. He was greatly depressed by his
visits to America in 1933–4, which destroyed his belief in the superior
efficiency of free market capitalism; he was distressed at the conversion
to Soviet Communism of his old friends and mentors, Sidney and
Beatrice Webb; and yet he was highly sceptical of the *via media* of modified
welfare capitalism, preached by interventionist liberals like F. D.
Roosevelt and J. M. Keynes.[103] 'He is restless and unhappy about the
present trends in capitalist countries,' recorded Beatrice Webb, 'especially so about the USA—which he admits is the key country and
which he thinks is heading for disaster, cultural, political and economic.
Intellectually he can find no resting place and no group of thinkers or
social reformers, with whom he can act for the betterment of men.'[104]

Beveridge's response to these gloomy reflections was to throw himself
more doggedly than ever into his daily work; and throughout 1935 he
poured a ceaseless stream of energy into the collection of price data, the
preparation of reports for the Statutory Committee and the running of
the L.S.E. The result was a serious strain on his health and temperament, and a series of debilitating infections in his teeth, nose and throat.
Early in 1936 Eileen Power reported to the Webbs that Beveridge was
'breaking down in health' and that his influence on his staff was nil.[105]
The Webbs, greatly concerned, persuaded him to accompany them on a
cruise to Majorca, where they spent several pleasantly contentious weeks
discussing soviet communism, sociological method and J. M. Keynes'
new *General Theory*. Beveridge was 'very good company', remarked
Beatrice Webb, '. . . to those whom he likes personally and even to those
he meets casually he is a charming companion'. During this holiday
Beveridge revealed that he was planning to accept the directorship of
a new social research institute, which was to be founded in Britain by the
Rockefeller Foundation. 'He has decided to spend the remainder of his
energies on scientific research' Mrs. Webb recorded with mingled
feelings of relief and regret. '. . . In this intention he has our blessing.'[106]

Beveridge's desire to devote himself to full-time research competed,
however, with a growing desire to return to government service. As
early as 1934 he had been apprehensive that developments in Germany

[102] BP, Ic 50, ms. notes for WHB's diary, 29–30 Dec. 1934.
[103] Passfield Papers, B. Webb's diary, 23 Sept. 1934; Below, ch. 13.
[104] Passfield Papers, B. Webb's diary, 16 Sept. 1935.
[105] Ibid., 15 Feb. 1936.     [106] Ibid., 10 Mar. 1936.

must inevitably lead to war; and he had asked himself, 'ought I, for the rest of my active time before becoming a spectator, to do anything but try to help in preventing this calamity?'[107] Whilst he was relaxing with the Webbs in Palma, German troops marched into the Rhineland, and he returned home convinced that the government of Britain must be persuaded to prepare for war. In 1936 he drafted a scheme of contingency food rationing for the Committee of Imperial Defence;[108] and a few months later he was invited to become administrative head of a new Ministry for Coordination of Defence, to draw up plans for organizing the home front in the event of war. This invitation, Beveridge later recalled, seemed to offer a perfect opportunity not merely for planning food control, but for creating the nucleus of an Economic General Staff —a body which would plan all the non-military aspects of the war and explore 'the unchartered seas of civilian mobilisation'. The invitation came to nothing, however, because in spite of pressure from the Cabinet Office, the Treasury refused to allow him pension rights comparable with those which he enjoyed at the L.S.E.[109]

Beveridge was therefore hoping to find a new vocation for some time before he eventually resigned from the L.S.E. In the summer of 1936, however, a further breach occurred with members of his staff—on this occasion over the future of Mrs. Mair. Mrs. Mair, as we have seen, had rarely played an important part in the various conflicts that shook the L.S.E., and it is difficult to imagine that similar conflicts would not have happened without her. Nevertheless, like the question of college government, hostility to Mrs. Mair was a potentially unifying force among certain members of staff who could not agree upon substantive issues of policy. In the early 1930s her habits of self-assertion became even more pronounced—possibly as a reaction against Beveridge's recurrent efforts to escape from her influence. She became increasingly possessive towards Beveridge himself, and increasingly capricious in her behaviour to others —bestowing favouritism where it was not requited, and pursuing feuds against those whom she believed to have offended her. It was not therefore surprising that when in 1936 she asked for an extension of her appointment beyond the normal retiring age, this was opposed by the professorial body. 'My heart is nearly broken by the thought of the intrigue against me,' she wrote despairingly to Beveridge[110]—who angrily threatened to resign himself if the extention were not granted. In reply, professors of both right and left joined together to threaten 'scandal and wholesale resignation if Mrs. Mair is retained'. Sir Josiah

[107] BP, Ic 50, ms. notes for WHB's diary, 29–30 Dec. 1934.

[108] BP, VIII, 12, Committee of Imperial Defence, Sub-Committee on Rationing, *Report*, Oct. 1936.

[109] *PI*, pp. 239–43; BP, VIII, II, correspondence on Rationing and Food Plans, 1936–7.

[110] Lady Beveridge Papers, J. Mair to WHB, 30 May (? 1936).

Stamp, now chairman of the governors, paid a visit to Passfield Corner to consult the Webbs—who pointed out that, since Beveridge was planning to leave the L.S.E. in any case, his threat of resignation was an empty threat. 'Sidney and I,' recorded Beatrice, 'in spite of our warm liking for Beveridge, and desire not to break with him, agree that the crisis must be ended and *Mrs. Mair must go.*'[111]

The final decision about Mrs. Mair's future was delayed until the end of the year—during which period she herself threatened to resign and to refuse her pension.[112] Then in December 1936 a meeting of the governors was called by Sir Josiah Stamp, and Beveridge's plea for an extension of Mrs. Mair's appointment was definitely rejected. Beveridge was highly indignant and announced that 'if they were guilty of "breaking the heart" of this admirable woman he could no longer associate with them!' 'He came down here to talk it over,' recorded Beatrice Webb. 'He and Sidney had a long interview during which Sidney spoke of the "impossible situation" at the School. Beveridge said he had never heard of the "scandal"!! But he looked tragic after the interview, and though there was no further discussion and I was not involved, the rest of the visit was painful.'[113] Shortly afterwards, however, Stamp informed Sidney Webb that Beveridge was now far more 'reasonable'. He had proposed a compromise solution, whereby Mrs. Mair would be retained for another year, followed by a year's leave with pay; and this compromise was eventually accepted by the School's governors and professors and by the Emergency Committee.[114]

The revolt against Mrs. Mair appeared to strengthen Beveridge's own resolve to leave the L.S.E., and in April 1937 he allowed his name to go forward for election to the mastership of University College, Oxford. It was a post, he hoped, that would leave him plenty of time for research on prices and unemployment; and he planned to combine it with the unpaid chairmanship of the new National Institute of Social and Economic Research. He resigned from the L.S.E. early in May, and Alexander Carr Saunders, the Professor of Social Science at Liverpool University, was chosen as his successor. In his final address to staff and students in June 1937 Beveridge dwelt at length on two themes which had preoccupied much of his time at the School—the need for political detachment among university teachers, and the need for more empirical social studies.[115] This speech was very clearly directed against some of his erstwhile adversaries in the School, and at the time was the

[111] Passfield Papers, B. Webb's diary, 12 July 1936.
[112] Lady Beveridge Papers, J. Mair to WHB, 6 Nov. 1936; D. Mair to WHB, 15 Nov. 1937
[113] Passfield Papers, B. Webb's diary, 31 Dec. 1936.
[114] Passfield Papers, X, 2(1), 336–7, note by B. Webb, Apr. 1937.
[115] W. H. Beveridge, 'The Place of the Social Sciences in Human Knowledge', *Politica*, II, 9 Sept. 1937, pp. 459–79.

cause of considerable embarrassment—though more recently it has been seen as a classic plea for 'social scientists to develop a responsibility to their profession which could counteract the pull of politics and government'.[116] 'Poor Beveridge,' wrote Beatrice Webb, in her epitaph on Beveridge and his eighteen years of directorship, 'he has always been so kind to the old Webbs, and he is so able and disinterested; if only he had better manners and was more sensitive to other mortals' conventions, creeds and aspirations . . . I doubt whether [Carr Saunders] is as able, either intellectually or administratively as Beveridge; far less power of initiative and fulfilment; but he has more judgment and far better manners, "the manners that maketh man". To be head of the London School of Economics—with its 120 professors and its 3,000 students, in these tumultuous times of mutually hostile political and economic creeds, held with religious fervour, is a difficult business. . . .'[117]

[116] Philip Abrams, op. cit., p. 148.
[117] Passfield Papers, B. Webb's diary, 27 Aug. 1937.

# 13

# Liberalism, Socialism and Economic Planning

## I

SOME indication has already been given of the changing pattern of Beveridge's ideas on politics and society in the 1920s and 30s. It has been shown that his administrative experiences in wartime had sown seeds of doubt in his mind about just how far it was possible to proceed with government-inspired social reforms. Opposition to control of the civilian labour market had shown him, perhaps for the first time, just how strong was popular hostility to bureaucratic regulation. The resistance of workers to the extension of compulsory insurance and the subsequent introduction of the 'civilian out-of-work donation' threw him for a time into a state of cynical despair about what he perceived as the selfishness and short-sightedness of the labour movement and the negligent indifference of governments towards rational social planning. The contrasting regimes of Devonport and Rhondda had made him more than ever suspicious of piecemeal policy-innovation, and had convinced him that state intervention should be thorough and all-embracing if it was to occur at all. He himself had no objection in principle to a wide degree of government control; but he came to the conclusion that in many spheres of policy such control was neither politically acceptable nor pragmatically desirable in time of peace. These views seem to have been reinforced during the 1920s and early 1930s. 'I think there is perhaps a tendency,' he told the Royal Commission on Unemployment Insurance in 1931, 'to think that the Government has greater responsibilities than the Government or any Government can possibly fulfil.'[1] As his faith in the processes of government waned, he turned more and more to social science—and in particular to economics—as the tool that would solve the problems of society. He was increasingly influenced by orthodox political economy, and for a time in the late 1920s and early 1930s a belief in the laws of the 'free market' seems to have at least partially displaced his earlier belief in a benevolent administrative state.[2] This faith in free market economics was in turn shattered by certain historical events of the 1930s, and Beveridge went through a period of prolonged political uncertainty—during which he once again began

---

[1] *RC on Unemployment Insurance, Minutes of Evidence*, Q. 5,944.
[2] BP, IIb, WHB to Lionel Robbins, 3 Oct. 1930.

to think in terms of central government planning for comprehensive social reform. It would be wrong to suggest too stark a contrast between these two phases, since there is of course no imperative connection between support for the free market and hostility either to social welfare or to measures of state control. And, moreover, there were numerous occasions in the earlier phase when Beveridge favoured paternalistic state intervention, just as there were numerous occasions in the later phase when he supported the retention of some form of market economy. But, nevertheless, there was a significant difference of emphasis between the two periods. In the 1920s and early 30s it is fair to say that Beveridge was mainly concerned with economic solutions to economic problems. From 1934 onwards he gradually returned to his youthful concern with questions of welfare and social planning. This chapter will look briefly at some of the main developments in Beveridge's political attitudes in the 1920s and 30s and at his views on certain specific socio-economic questions. It will examine also the fundamental realignment of many of his opinions that seems to have begun in 1932–4 and which was still taking place at the beginning of the Second World War.

## II

As in earlier years Beveridge's political views in the 1920s and 30s could not be consistently identified with those of any political party. In 1922 he was invited to stand for Parliament as Liberal candidate for Oxford University, and although he did not accept this invitation it seems to have brought him at least for a short time into the Liberal fold.[3] In the last week of 1922 he attended a conference in Cambridge of the Liberal Summer Schools committee—a 'gathering of youngish Liberals (mostly defeated candidates) setting out to discover a policy that should be neither Conservative or Labour, but mortally afraid of being connected with the existing official Liberal organisation'.[4] At this conference he supported a demand from Ernest Barker for a revival of the philosophy of social and political integration once preached by T. H. Green; but he was highly sceptical about whether such a programme in an economically polarized society could ever be successful in winning popular votes. 'In his view,' he argued, mounting his favourite hobby-horse, 'Liberalism in the economic sphere ought to stand for empirical study of social questions; for this task Liberals ought to qualify them-selves, but it was a difficult task and the prospects of any large measure of support were problematic.'[5]

[3] BP, IIb, Sir John Simon to WHB, 6 Dec. 1922.
[4] BP, IIa, WHB to HB, 1 Jan. 1923.
[5] BP, IIb 21, Notes on Liberal Summer School conference at Caius College, Cambridge, 28–31 Dec. 1922.

A year later Beveridge published a Liberal pamphlet entitled *Insurance for All and Everything*, and he drafted a private members' bill for the introduction of widows' and orphans' insurance and contributory old-age pensions. The bill was temporarily adopted as part of official Liberal policy; but it soon fell foul of the prevailing rivalry between the followers of Asquith and Lloyd George. Beveridge was filled with irritation by this glimpse of party in-fighting, and the episode seems to have ended his brief flirtation with the parliamentary Liberals. Even at the time he would have preferred his bill to be put forward on a non-party basis, 'just for propaganda and for discussion . . . on its merits',[6] and from this time onwards he was increasingly reluctant to be publicly identified with any political group. Already in 1923 he had asked for his name to be expunged from the official literature of the Liberal Summer Schools Committee;[7] and he took little part in this intellectually fertile but politically barren movement after 1924. In 1926 when standing for the Vice Chancellorship of London University he claimed that 'I am as nearly non-political as anybody can be, but when I have any politics I am a Liberal'.[8] This rather vague and negative commitment was characteristic of his attitude for many years afterwards, both to the Asquithian Liberals and to the followers of Lloyd George. In the late 1920s and early 1930s he paid several visits to Lloyd George's home at Churt, and relations between them were noticeably more cordial than they had been during the war.[9] But nevertheless, Beveridge was not involved with Keynes, Henderson and other radical Liberals in the preparation of Lloyd George's famous policy documents, *Britain's Industrial Future* and *We can Conquer Unemployment*; nor was he in sympathy with their unorthodox notions of expansionist public finance. Throughout the period he refused to take part in, or even to endorse, spasmodic 'Liberal revivals', and he held himself free 'to advise any party which wants my advice on any subject on which it thinks my opinion important'.[10]

For most of the inter-war years therefore Beveridge tended to adopt a self-consciously neutral stance on questions of party politics—an attitude that may be explained, partly by a fear of compromising his position at the L.S.E. and partly by his long-standing preference for the role of the expert rather than that of the party politician. Nevertheless, it would be wrong to take Beveridge at his own assessment of himself as an

[6] BP, IIb, WHB to E. D. Simon, 27 Feb. 1924; IIa, ms. conversations with ASB, Apr.–May 1924.
[7] BP, IIb, WHB to Thomas Tweed, 24 Apr. 1923.
[8] BP, V 22, WHB to Sir H. J. Waring, 31 May 1926.
[9] BP, Ic 4 and 5, WHB's diary, 3 July 1929, 3 Nov. and 25 Dec. 1930, 16 Feb. and 13 Nov. 1932.
[10] BP, IIb, WHB to J. C. Maxwell Garnett, 20 Mar. 1934; WHB to Ramsay Muir, 21 Oct. 1935 and 18 May 1936.

almost wholly non-political animal; and it is possible to discern in his writings of the 1920s certain coherent principles that were relevant to his ideas on economic and social policy. These basic principles were in many respects not very different from those which he had held as a young man, though they were much less clearly articulated than in the columns of the *Morning Post*. As in earlier years he believed that the 'national interest' should nearly always take precedence over the interests of groups or individuals; and by the term 'nation' he seems to have meant not merely a political but a biological entity—'not the material resources, not even the generation of today, but the race, the inheritance, is the nation', he told a British Association conference in Toronto in 1924.[11] He was strongly opposed to 'economic nationalism' in the form of protective tariffs; but at the same time he had a strong sense of Anglo-Saxon identity, and he was distressed to find on his visits to North America just how few Americans and Canadians were of English—or British—descent.[12] As in earlier years he disliked doctrines of social conflict; and in so far as the existence of such conflict was undeniable, he thought that its main arena was consumer *versus* producer rather than capital *versus* labour. His own sympathies in such a situation lay decisively with the consumer. He thought 'it was absolutely certain in one way or another that the state would have to come into industry in the interests of the consumer'; and he thought that contracts of employment should in certain circumstances be enforceable at law.[13] His conception of government was still dominated by a belief in an impartial, benevolent, educated élite; and he was still highly suspicious of all kinds of 'direct democracy'—in particular, the new forms of industrial syndicalism preached by the disciples of G. D. H. Cole. He still feared that the most dangerous aspect of the British labour movement was its penchant for 'sloppy democracy', rather than its support for socialism or policies of state control.[14] Perhaps the most significant change in Beveridge's attitudes between the 1900s and the 1920s was that he became markedly less 'bureaucratic' and more 'technocratic' in his approach to public policy. As we have already seen he had been perceptibly influenced by his contacts with businessmen, and they in turn regarded him as one of the few academic economists who was not a 'crank'. 'Sir William's plain common sense suited City men,' commented a speaker at a Mansion House conference in 1924.[15] At the

[11] Lady Beveridge Papers, WHB to J. Mair, 15 Aug. 1924.

[12] *The Civilian*, 20 Nov. 1920; BP, IIb, WHB to J. C. Maxwell Garnett, 29 May 1927.

[13] BP, IIb, WHB to E. Hubback, 9 Nov. 1922; IXb 21, 'Does Britain want a New Deal?', lecture by WHB to L.S.E. Sociology Club, 14 Feb. 1934.

[14] Bb, IIb, WHB to W. W. Astor, 27 Feb. 1932.

[15] WHB, IIa, WHB to ASB, 1 May 1921; *The Social Service Bulletin, London Supplement*, June 1925.

same time he was greatly impressed during his visits to North America by the advance of automation and 'business management', and by the 'limitless possibilities for human development' which seemed to be created by the booming free market economy of the United States.[16] These new perspectives were reflected in a shift of emphasis in his thinking about the purposes of government. In the 1900s he had been mainly concerned with persuading governments to undertake measures of 'social organisation'—but this term was conspicuously absent from his writings of the 1920s. Instead, he was now much more concerned with persuading governments to improve their organs of financial and commercial 'intelligence'—in particular, by setting up what he described as an Economic General Staff. His proposals for an Economic General Staff, first expounded in the *Nation* in 1923, were characteristic of and central to the new technocratic phase of Beveridge's political ideas. In his *Nation* articles he criticized the lack of public spending on economic research, and deplored the fact that the government's Chief Economic Adviser—a post now held by Llewellyn Smith—was mainly employed in representing Britain at international conferences. To remedy this situation he called for the setting-up of a staff of professional economists, to carry out 'comprehensive technical investigation' of the 'main economic problems of the day'. The staff would be headed by a 'person of high authority in the science of economics' and would draw for assistance on economists working in universities. It would have no administrative and policy-making functions, but would review the economic implications of all items of public policy, and would advise the government on such major issues as unemployment, tariffs and revival of foreign trade. The cost of such a venture, Beveridge optimistically predicted, would be amply offset by the forestalling of economic disasters, the avoidance of *ad hoc* crisis measures and the provision of a rational and scientific basis for major policy-decisions.[17]

## III

Beveridge's views on specific areas of policy had changed much more markedly by the 1920s than his underlying assumptions about political power. His interest in social welfare had waned, and he was now much more inclined to give priority to economic rather than to social goals. He refused, for instance, to support the movement for raising the school-leaving age, on the ground that—in a time of inflated wage-costs—this

[16] Lady Beveridge Papers, WHB to J. Mair, 4 Aug. and 6 Sept. 1934.
[17] W. H. Beveridge, 'An Economic General Staff', *The Nation and the Athenaeum*, 29 Dec. 1923 and 5 Jan. 1924.

would deprive industry of a source of cheap labour.[18] This change of emphasis may be explained partly by Beveridge's personal desire to gain recognition as a professional economist, and partly by the fact that economic questions seemed in the 1920s to be inherently more urgent and problematic than they had been twenty years before. Another significant difference was that in the 1900s Beveridge's views on policy had been relatively uninhibited by the constraints of economic theory. By the 1920s he was much more conscious of debates among professional economists; and, for better or worse, his new ideas were much more directly influenced by the prevailing assumptions of orthodox economics. He was also noticeably less sympathetic to the needs of labour and more concerned with the interests of savers and investors—a change of priorities which he believed was justified by the large-scale destruction of capital and rapid advance of real wages that had occurred during the war. He was apprehensive that any further redistribution of existing resources might seriously impede the process of investment; and he urged that any future increase in wages must be derived from increased production rather than from 'living off capital' as had happened during the war.[19] He was highly sceptical of all forms of minimum wage theory —arguing that such theories took no account of fluctuations in industrial progress, of individual variations in size of family, and of local variations in labour demand.[20]

The area of economic policy with which Beveridge was most passionately concerned during the post-war period was the debate between protectionists and supporters of free trade—a debate in which he had taken relatively little interest twenty years before. During the war British producers had lost many markets to foreign rivals, and after the war obsolete plant and relatively high wage-costs made the prices of many British products uncompetitive in both home and foreign markets. Many British manufacturers and a large section of the Conservative party demanded protection—a remedy which was, however, rejected by the British electorate in 1923. Beveridge himself strongly opposed this panacea for Britain's industrial stagnation—though unlike many free market economists he based his arguments primarily on practical rather than analytical grounds. His views were formed during his visits to Austria in 1919 and 1920, when the crippled state of the central European nations and the breakdown of international food control had convinced him that the first priority of economic policy should be a revival of free trade.[21] He was highly critical of Allied reparations policy

[18] BP, IIb, WHB to E. Hubback, 15 Dec. 1932.
[19] BP, IIb, WHB to Mark Requa, 16 Dec. 1932; WHB to A. Charles, 28 Mar. 1933.
[20] BP, IIb 24 (1), WHB's notes on Walter Layton's 'Fair Wage' paper, 18 Nov. 1924.
[21] *Daily News*, 13 Mar. 1920.

and of proposals to make Germany pay for the war by an indemnity tax on German exports; and he condemned the Americans for demanding repayment of war loans yet by their hostile tariff barriers preventing debtor nations from earning the currency that might make such payments possible.[22] He criticized proposals for taxing imports—reiterating the traditional free trade argument that British exports could best be encouraged not by limiting foreign competition, but by stimulating the purchasing power of foreign customers.[23] He was not in principle opposed to preferential agreements between Britain and the dominions; but he was convinced that such a compromise would never be accepted by the dominion governments, except on terms unfavourable to Britain.[24] He concluded therefore that government interference in international trading relationships should be confined to functions broadly similar to those envisaged by the nineteenth-century Manchester economists— namely stabilization of currency and control of facilities for credit.

The protectionist movement made little headway in Britain throughout the 1920s, although tariffs were imposed in certain key industries under the Safeguarding of Industries Act of 1921. The situation was changed, however, by the impact of the world crisis of 1929. As unemployment rose above two million powerful demands for protective tariffs were put forward by the T.U.C.; and under pressure from Beaverbrook and Rothermere the Conservative opposition committed itself to imperial preference, and to tariffs on foreign manufactures and certain kinds of imported food. Then in February 1931 J. M. Keynes in his evidence to the Macmillan Committee on Finance and Industry announced his conversion to qualified measures of protection, as the only means of reducing real wages and thus increasing the volume of employment.[25] A few months later Keynes as chairman of a committee of the Economic Advisory Council recommended a combination of tariffs on imports and bounties on exports—a policy that evoked a furious protest from Lionel Robbins, who as a member of the committee objected strongly both to the principle of protection and to Keynes' high-handed attempts to secure a unanimous report.[26] As a result, Robbins recorded, 'Beveridge, Clay, Plant, Layton and myself and one or two others have formed a sort of Committee of Public Safety and are getting out a book on the question which we hope will do something to check the landslide of public opinion and if necessary to counterbalance the effect of the Report'.[27] This committee met several times

[22] BP, IIb, WHB to Mark Requa, 16 Dec. 1932.
[23] *The Times*, 27 Nov. and 5 Dec. 1923.
[24] BP, IIb, WHB to Sir Sydney Russell-Wells, 16 Oct. 1923.
[25] R. F. Harrod, *The Life of John Maynard Keynes* (Pelican edn., 1972), pp. 500–2.
[26] Cannan Papers, vol. 1,030, f. 197, L. Robbins to E. Cannan, 17 Oct. 1930.
[27] Ibid., f. 202, L. Robbins to E. Cannan, Nov. 1930.

during the next few months, and Beveridge recorded that most of his spare time was being spent in writing about tariffs.[28] In the autumn he gave a broadcast talk in reply to Lord Beaverbrook, in which he complained that tariffs on food were the most regressive form of taxation. He claimed that unemployment in protectionist countries was even higher than in Britain; and he argued that withdrawal of custom from Argentinian farmers would do nothing to create work for unemployed riveters in Jarrow.[29] These arguments were reiterated at greater length in *Tariffs: the Case Examined*, a collection of essays refuting the protectionist position, which he produced in collaboration with the other members of Robbins's committee. This book restated the classic case against tariff barriers, arguing that only free trade could achieve an optimum distribution of international resources and that tariffs would produce a permanent decline in real living standards. Unemployment was blamed partly on the continuing disorganization of the labour market, partly on the failure of international credit arrangements, and partly on an over-generous insurance system and inflated money-wages.[30]

In spite of a fairly large sale and translation into several languages, *Tariffs: the Case Examined* was one of Beveridge's least successful works. Politically it did nothing to stem the tide of protection, which culminated in the imposition of a wide range of tariffs under the Ottawa agreements of 1932. As an essay in political economy the book bore all the signs of a committee production, its contents varying widely in logical subtlety and technical sophistication. It suffered from the fact that its authors had originally planned to write a 'popular refutation of some elementary fallacies', and only half-way through had the decision been made to challenge the arguments of academic protectionists like Keynes and Josiah Stamp.[31] The transition from a popular to an academic medium was not successfully accomplished—with the result that the book was too elementary for an academic audience, too dry and technical for political propaganda. Beveridge himself was unfamiliar with many theoretical aspects of the subject, and he found the work of trying to master them an 'appalling toil'.[32] Moreover the authors of the book were not in full agreement about the arguments they were trying to put forward. Robbins, for instance, appeared to favour an undiluted

---

[28] BP, Ic 5, WHB's diary, 24, 25 and 31 Oct., 3 and 29 Nov. 1930.

[29] W. H. Beveridge, *Empire Free Trade: a Reply to Lord Beaverbrook* (published by the Free Trade Union, Jan. 1931).

[30] *Tariffs: the Case Examined* (1931), pp. 62–6, 239–40.

[31] Bev. Coll. Misc. 11, vol. III, pp. 125–6, 'Tariff Book—Progress Report' by WHB, 12 Apr. 1931; Keynes Papers, WHB to J. M. Keynes, 21 Apr. 1931.

[32] Lionel Robbins, *Autobiography of an Economist*, p. 158; BP, Ic, WHB's diary, 29 Nov. 1930.

free trade system and total flexibility of money wages.[33] Beveridge on the other hand thought that there was a minimum standard below which wages should not be allowed to fall—as 'an indispensable bulwark against a return to barbarism'. He was also 'prepared to explore, not a protective tariff on manufacturers . . . but the totally different (and opposite) plan of preferential arrangements with countries producing food and raw materials' so as to create 'an artificial United States for ourselves, an area large enough to use all Britain as its principal work-shop'. Such a policy, he admitted, might be seen as a surrender to economic nationalism, 'but it is of no use to stick the flag of Cobdenism on a melting ice-floe, and that may be a true account of Britain's posi-tion today'.[34] These differences of emphasis between the authors were not resolved in the text of the book, which nowhere contained a clear definition of what social and economic policies the maintenance of Free Trade in a world of universal mercantilism would practically entail. Moreover, as J. M. Keynes pointed out, Beveridge and his colleagues nowhere proved that a fall in money-wages would in fact improve the distribution of 'productive resources', nor did they substantiate their claim that a high volume of imports necessarily entailed a high volume of exports. 'It would seem to follow from your argument,' wrote Keynes to Beveridge with a hint of irony, 'that one need not be afraid of Lloyd Georgian expansionist schemes, on the ground that they might cause an increase of imports, because on your argument this would be balanced by an increase of exports. Do you hold this? If not, it needs explaining.'[35]

The other major area of economic debate in which Beveridge was involved in the 1920s was analysis of the causes of mass unemployment. Beveridge's share in this debate was in no sense original, but it must be considered in some detail as providing the intellectual framework for his contribution to policies of unemployment insurance. It was also in many ways a touchstone to changes in the rest of his economic and social ideas. As we have seen, Beveridge in the 1900s had not seriously questioned the classical assumption that there could be no permanent failure of demand for labour; but nor had he regarded it as a serious obstacle to the study of unemployment as a practical question. He had ascribed unemployment, partly to frictional factors that could be cured by 'labour organisation', and partly to cyclical fluctuations which he believed were largely outside the sope of rational human control.[36] During the 1920s, however, a new kind of unemployment emerged. After a brief post-war boom, many of Britain's basic industries—mining,

[33] BP, IIb, L. Robbins to WHB, n.d. (1930).
[34] BP, IIb, WHB to L. Robbins, 3 Oct. 1930.
[35] Keynes Papers, J. M. Keynes to WHB, 23 Mar. 1931.
[36] Above, ch. 6.

shipbuilding, textiles and heavy engineering—were plunged into prolonged recession. In all these trades unemployment throughout the
1920s rarely fell below 10 per cent and was often above 20 per cent. It
could not therefore be ascribed to cyclical fluctuation—nor to lack of
organization, since these industries comprised the most highly organized
section of the labour force. Nevertheless, Beveridge was for some time
reluctant to concede that this new type of unemployment could not be
accounted for by the analysis he had put forward in 1909. At the end of
the war he hoped to produce a statistically up-dated but substantially
unrevised edition of *Unemployment: A Problem of Industry*, and was only
prevented from doing so by pressure of other work.[37] He still insisted
that unemployment was basically incurable without a total reconstruction of the existing industrial system, and he still believed that the best
palliatives were labour exchanges and contributory insurance. As in the
1900s he favoured the Webbs' policy of concentrating public works into
periods of high unemployment, but he was strongly opposed to all
'artificial' methods of creating work for the unemployed.[38]

As the depression lengthened, however, Beveridge was gradually
forced to take account of the apparently irreducible core of the long-
term unemployed. He came to the conclusion that *Unemployment* could
not be satisfactorily revised; and he decided to reprint the original
edition intact, together with an appendix reviewing trends in unemployment and the growth of new theories and policies since 1909. This
appendix was an amplified version of a collection of lectures that
Beveridge gave to a variety of audiences—the L.S.E., the British Association and the University of Chicago—between 1923 and 1930. Early
in 1930 he submitted it to London University for the degree of Doctor
of Science, and it was published by Longman's later in the year. In it he
developed his earlier analysis of unemployment in four different ways.
Firstly, he summarized the expanding body of literature on trade
fluctuations, and he endorsed the view which ascribed them to lack of
monetary liquidity and the 'inherent instability of credit'. He had no
suggestions to offer, however, about how these factors might be reduced
or removed.[39] Secondly, he traced the history of labour exchanges and
unemployment insurance over the previous twenty years. He was
highly critical of successive governments for neglecting the need for
decasualization, and for allowing the job-placement functions of
exchanges to be swamped and obscured by administration of insurance.[40]
He deplored also the gradual erosion of the underlying principles of

---

[37] *Unemployment: a Problem of Industry* (1930 edn.), p. vii.
[38] BP, IIb, Notes on Liberal Summer School Conference at Caius College, Cambridge, 28–
31 Dec. 1922.
[39] *Unemployment* (1930 edn.), pp. 324–44.      [40] Ibid., pp. 305, 317–23.

social insurance—in particular, by the granting of benefit for extended periods and by divorce of an individual's entitlement to benefit from his contribution record. Such relaxations, he contended, were tending to exacerbate the unemployment problem, by removing incentives to labour mobility, by reducing the fear among trade-unionists of putting fellow workmen out of work, and by enabling casual industries to 'batten on the taxation of other industries or of the general public in place of reforming their ways'.[41] Thirdly, he examined and rejected the view that unemployment was caused by overpopulation—claiming that there was no evidence of exhaustion in productive resources, and pointing to the dramatic fall in the birth-rate that had occurred in Western Europe during the previous fifty years. He suggested, however, that an artificial equation between unemployment and overpopulation *might* be created, if people refused to work except in return for an unrealistically high 'minimum standard of life'.[42] Fourthly, Beveridge examined the relationship between unemployment and wages; and it was on this point that his views had changed most fundamentally since before the First World War. Just before the war Beveridge had written a review in the *Economic Journal*, strongly criticizing the Cambridge economist, A. C. Pigou, for restating the classical view that unemployment was caused by the failure of money wages to adjust to a decline in labour demand. Such a view, Beveridge argued, was a mere 'paradox of the lecture room' and bore no relation to the real industrial situation, where men frequently found that there was 'no demand for their services at any price at all'.[43] This review and its rejection of the orthodox position won favourable comment from Pigou's Cambridge colleague, J. M. Keynes.[44] During the 1920s, however, Beveridge was fully won over to the theory of 'wage-rigidities'—a conversion that seems to have taken place during his work for the Coal Commission in 1925, when he gradually became convinced that stagnation in the mining industry was being largely caused by the relatively high level of miners' wages.[45] Between 1913 and 1925, Beveridge argued in the new edition of *Unemployment*, real wages in all industries had risen by an average of 17 per cent. Over the same period there had been some increase in productivity, but this has been virtually swallowed up by a simultaneous shortening of hours. The rise had therefore been brought about, firstly by the artificial scarcity of labour created by the war, and secondly by the failure of money-wages to fall in conjunction with the decline in retail prices, which had been occurring in Britain since the summer of

[41] Ibid., p. 294.  [42] Ibid., pp. 373–400.
[43] *Econ. J.*, XXIV, no. 94, June 1914, pp. 250–2.
[44] BP, IIb, J. M. Keynes to WHB, 25 Mar. 1914.
[45] Below, p. 338.

1920. This persistence of high money-wages was caused, Beveridge suggested, partly by a 'natural sluggishness' in the process of wage-adjustment and partly by the growth of organized collective bargaining. Secure in the knowledge that their unemployed members would be supported by insurance, trade union leaders had refused to accept any downward adjustment in wage-rates. The result, Beveridge believed, had been to drive marginal workmen out of the labour force and to price British products out of world markets. Hence the creation of a hard core of long-term unemployment and an artificial imbalance between labour supply and demand.[46]

The publication of the 1930 edition of *Unemployment: a Problem of Industry* revealed just how far Beveridge had moved towards belief in a self-regulating market economy. In this he was almost certainly influenced by Lionel Robbins, who had acted as research assistant, collaborator, supervisor and examiner at various stages of his work.[47] In his conclusion, Beveridge still emphasized the need for labour organization and for scientifically administered social insurance—backed up by a reformed Poor Law and by the timing of public expenditure to counteract depression.[48] But such policies were irrelevant, he contended, in cases where unemployment was caused by labour offering itself at too high a price. In such cases 'the remedy must be sought in restoring the equilibrium thus disturbed. It cannot be found elsewhere.' Equilibrium might be restored either by reducing wages or increasing productivity; but in either case the cost of labour must be adjusted downwards. Otherwise the employed would be exploiting the unemployed and 'the high standard of life of those who are in regular work' would be 'won at the cost of the unemployment of those who are not'.[49]

Beveridge's conversion to free market economics dominated his reaction to the crisis of 1929–31. In a series of broadcast talks he ascribed mass unemployment to the collapse of credit, and argued that credit could only be restored by increasing profits and lowering wages.[50] At the same time he was increasingly critical of the social services, and in particular of unemployment insurance, for subsidizing workmen 'on the borderland of being unemployable'.[51] In 1931 C. M. Lloyd, the head of the L.S.E.'s Social Science department, told the Webbs that 'owing to Beveridge's powerful personality the dominant tone among the younger economics lecturers at the School of Economics is almost virulently anti-labour, against socialistic services and in favour of the whip of starvation being applied all round, to force the manual workers to accept lower

[46] *Unemployment* (1930 edn.), pp. 366–72.     [47] Ibid., p. xi.     [48] Ibid., pp. 406–15.
[49] Ibid., pp. 416–17.
[50] Passfield Papers, B. Webb's diary, 13 June 1931.
[51] BP, IIb, WHB to W. S. Churchill, 5 Feb. 1930.

wages and to work longer hours'.[52] This was perhaps an exaggeration of Beveridge's views; but he himself told Beatrice Webb that the limits of redistribution had now been reached, that 'the profit-making capitalist will not "play" unless given a stupendously unequal amount of the national income', and that 'this raising of the National Minimum had now overstepped the limit'. He was more inclined to lower wages than to reduce social services; but he favoured social welfare only '*in so far as consistent with maximum profits* for the business world'.[53] In support of these principles he approved the cuts in social expenditure imposed by the National Government in 1931, and he rather reluctantly endorsed the decision to go off the gold standard—on the ground that this would indirectly force wages to fall.[54] At the same time he was highly sceptical of the 'controlled capitalism' and state regulation of economic policy that was being proposed by radical Liberals like Arthur Salter and J. M. Keynes. 'The first essential is to restore the price-machine—in wage fixing and elsewhere,' he wrote to Lionel Robbins. 'Food Control experience in the war is more relevant than I had ever thought it would be, since all the world is trying to be Devonport today.'[55]

Beveridge's attitudes during the crisis had clearly swung a very long way from his attitudes during the Edwardian period; and in many respects it is difficult to conceive of a more striking contrast than that between the optimistic young social reformer of the 1900s and the implacable free marketeer of 1929–32. It would be wrong, however, to over-emphasize this contrast, since there was a certain underlying consistency between the Beveridge of youth and the Beveridge of middle age. In both periods he was totally opposed to 'sentimental' criteria in the provision of welfare. In both periods his conception of policy was basically holistic—it was primarily directed towards the interests of the economy, or of the nation, and only secondarily towards those of the individual citizen. And in both periods he was highly suspicious of piecemeal state intervention—believing that such policies would merely create worse problems than those they were designed to solve. Moreover, Beveridge's spell as a committed free marketeer was of relatively short duration. As the crisis lengthened his reforming spirit reasserted itself. He found that he was unable to accept some of the more extreme positions of the free market economists—such as their neglect of the phenomenon of 'involuntary' unemployment.[56] And he began to wonder

---

[52] Passfield Papers, B. Webb's diary, 13 June 1931.

[53] Ibid., 28 Aug. 1931 and (? 23) Feb. 1932.

[54] BP, IIb, WHB to R. Denman, 27 Aug. 1931; Passfield Papers, B. Webb's diary (23?) Feb. 1932.

[55] Ibid., 23 Sept. 1931 and (23?) Feb. 1932; BP, IIb, WHB to L. Robbins, 30 Oct. 1930.

[56] BP, IIb, WHB's 'Notes on Professor Robbins' Essay on the Nature and Significance of Economic Science', 30 Nov. 1932.

whether a short sharp conversion to a totally planned economy might not be preferable to the long-drawn-out agony of capitalism in decline. The result was a period of violent oscillation in Beveridge's social philosophy that lasted for several years—from which he was eventually to emerge as one of the leading exponents of the new liberal *via media* that in its early stages he so forcibly denounced. The evolution of this third stage will be considered in some detail, since it formed the intellectual background to his most important contribution to the making of social policy—the 1942 Beveridge Report.

## IV

The first indications of Beveridge's loss of faith in an undiluted free market date from 1932—possibly as a reaction against his failure to influence prevailing fiscal policies, possibly as a symptom of the general malaise and disillusionment that seemed to afflict him in many of his activities during his final years at the L.S.E. After his unsuccessful attempt to resist protectionism he refused to involve himself in further pressure-group activity, and confessed himself baffled by the underlying causes of the economic crisis.[57] Even his faith in applied social science seemed to falter, and he recorded that he had 'given up trying to understand the modern world' and was concentrating on 'the history of prices before Waterloo'.[58] He was, moreover, increasingly irritated by what he understood of the doctrines advanced by leading exponents of orthodox economics. He dismissed as 'pedantic' the view put forward by Robbins that redistribution of incomes could not be justified on grounds of marginal utility, because one man's satisfaction could not be compared with another's.[59] He rejected the argument of the Austrian economist, von Mises, that a planned economy would necessarily entail the destruction of efficiency and individual freedom. Instead he suggested that public-spirited bureaucrats were just as capable as capitalists of making rational decisions and dynamic innovations; and he reflected that 'if (as is possible in England) we are threatened by stationary or falling standards, the free system may prove incompatible with democracy'. He concluded also that the price-mechanism was an inadequate device for making decisions about questions of social quality—such as the allocation of welfare or the desirability of clean air.[60] At the same time, however, he was greatly depressed by what he perceived as the disastrous consequences of misguided deviations from economic laws by

[57] BP, IIb, WHB to Charles Mallet, 9 Apr. 1932; WHB to Roy Harrod, 2 Mar. 1933.
[58] BP, IIb, WHB to Edmund Johnstone, 27 Sept. 1932.
[59] BP, IIb, WHB's 'Notes on Professor Robbins' Essay on the Nature and Significance of Economic Science', 30 Nov. 1932.
[60] BP, IXa 99, WHB's notes on a paper by Ludwig von Mises, n.d. (1933–4).

successive British governments. 'Frankly the more I see of the favouring of vested inefficiency by the Conservatives and the sloppy democracy of the Labour party, the more I incline to become a sensible Russian socialist,' he wrote half-humorously, half-seriously in February 1932.[61]

The possibility of a Marxian socialist alternative to capitalism was forcibly thrust upon Beveridge at this time by the growing interest in Soviet communism shown by Sidney and Beatrice Webb. During the early 1930s Beveridge seems to have been more intimate with the Webbs than at any other period—a fact which probably reflected the relative loneliness of this phase of his personal life. The Webbs were the only people with whom at this time he habitually discussed basic political principles; and much of his quest for a new social philosophy seems to have been worked out in conversation and correspondence with one or other of the famous partnership. The Webbs themselves in the early 1930s were also anxiously searching for a new philosophy. The events of the late 1920s had convinced them that capitalism was doomed, and at the same time had undermined their long-standing belief in the inevitability of gradualism. They paid their first visit to Russia in 1932, and were greatly impressed, not so much by Marxist–Leninist ideology as by Soviet planning machinery and by the selflessness and puritanism which they discovered in many communist officials. They returned to England convinced that what they had seen in Russia constituted the only viable future for industrial societies, and spent the next two years preparing the detailed description of Russian institutions that appeared as *Soviet Communism: a New Civilisation?* in 1935.

The Webbs first discussed their new beliefs with Beveridge in August 1932. Together they deplored the latest in a series of international swindles, and agreed that contemporary capitalism was in a state of ethical decline—a fact which they concurred in ascribing to the dwindling of religious faith and 'the loss of any recognised code of conduct'. But, concluded Beveridge, 'there is no alternative to capitalist enterprise —so we must make the best of it'. 'What about the scientific materialism of Karl Marx tempered by the religion of humanity of Auguste Comte?' replied Mrs. Webb, '. . . need the denial of God entail the denial of man?'[62] Beveridge was unconvinced, and was to remain unconvinced by the political aspects of Russian communism for the rest of his life. 'It is impossible for me,' he wrote several months later, 'irrespective of any views that I may hold upon their economic policy, to appear to condone the attitude of the Russian government in regard to liberty of thought and speech.'[63] Beveridge had 'deliberately turned away from considering

[61] BP, IIb, WHB to W. W. Astor, 27 Feb. 1932.
[62] Passfield Papers, B. Webb's diary, 24 Aug. 1932.
[63] BP, IIb, WHB to Winifred Smith, 7 Nov. 1932.

this new social order', complained Beatrice Webb towards the end of
1933. 'He won't even visit his old friends for fear that they might refer to
the horrid beast, and then his anger and contempt might break loose in
unseemly fashion.'[64]

In spite of his political objections, however, Beveridge did not wholly
reject the economic and administrative aspects of the soviet experiment.
The features of the Russian system that the Webbs most emphasized—
namely comprehensive planning machinery and management by a
corps of public-spirited officials—were precisely the features most calculated to appeal to Beveridge himself; and he was clearly intrigued by
the prospect of a planned economy on the Russian model. 'Both
economic conditions and thought about them are in a state of lamentable disorder,' he wrote in March 1933:

There is an unresolved conflict of opinion between the planned economy
(such as the Russians are trying to work out, though with many unnecessary
mistakes of their own) and an automatic system using the mechanism of
prices and the motive of profit to adjust production to the wishes of the consumers through their use of purchasing power. Frankly, for myself, I am an
agnostic on this issue, that is to say I see the dangers and difficulties alike of
complete socialism and complete *laisser-faire* and at the same time I am not
sure that there is any practicable half-way house between the two.[65]

Beveridge's political uncertainty was intensified by the course of
world events during 1933. The triumph of National Socialism in
Germany and the onset of the Jewish persecution strengthened his
dislike of political totalitarianism;[66] but at the same time a further visit
to America reinforced his doubts about the viability of economic liberalism—both the free-market liberalism of Robbins and Hayek, and the
interventionist liberalism of Salter and Keynes. In November 1933 he
visited the United States to make a report for the Rockefeller Foundation on the early stages of Franklin Roosevelt's 'new deal' legislation—
in particular, the National Industrial Recovery Act (NRA) and the
Agricultural Adjustments Act (AAA) passed by Congress earlier in the
year. There he was thrown into the depths of gloom by the intensity of
the contrast between the booming economy of the 1920s and the
present economic collapse. A few years earlier, he recalled, the Americans had 'derided dole', had 'lectured the world on the wickedness of
unbalanced budgets' and had championed unbridled business enterprise as the main precondition of economic growth. Now in 1933,
fourteen million people were unemployed, twenty-one million on

[64] Passfield Papers, B. Webb's diary, 27 Nov. 1933.
[65] BP, IIb, WHB to the Rev. C. J. Shebbeare, 10 Mar. 1933.
[66] BP, Ic, WHB's diary, 24 Aug. 1933, 4 Jan. 1934.

welfare, public authorities were crippled by debt, and there was a general 'moral breakdown and loss of faith in business leadership'. At the same time, however, he was highly sceptical of the numerous contradictions and inconsistencies—the mixture of inflation and deflation, expansion and contraction—that characterized the reforms introduced by Roosevelt during the first year of his presidency. He approved of Roosevelt's public works programmes, which he saw as a 'natural' way of alleviating trade depression; and he described the AAA, which endeavoured to raise prices by limiting agricultural output, as a 'constructive attempt to deal with a real problem'. But he was very critical of Roosevelt's attempt to encourage inflation by purchasing gold—a policy which, he argued, would merely devalue the dollar, upset the international exchanges and impede rather than encourage recovery of trade. In particular he condemned those aspects of the NRA programme which imposed minimum wages, maximum hours and restrictions on industrial output—policies which, he believed, would merely increase costs of production and further reduce demand.[67] The result, he suspected, could only be a total collapse of capitalist enterprise and might ultimately destroy American democracy. 'If the Roosevelt policy were to be continued as a paramount policy, the game was up with capitalism,' he reported to Mrs. Webb, 'for it meant a mass of contradictions and inhibitions and would destroy the efficient working of the profit-making impetus.' 'I agreed with him,' she recorded, 'and suggested that he should read S's chapter on USSR planning. . . . Given his scale of values, I think he is right in his conclusions—far more straightforward, scientific and practical than other theoreticians of the capitalist order such as Keynes, Salter and Stamp.'[68]

Beveridge's vacillation between rival systems persisted for several years. He duly read the draft version of Sidney Webb's chapter on Russian planning, and he acknowledged the success of the Soviet government in abolishing unemployment—a success which he thought was the 'strongest case to date for planning . . . as unemployment itself is the longest nail in the coffin of capitalism'. But he challenged the Webbs' claim that a planned economy would eventually achieve higher output as well as better distribution than free-market capitalism—arguing that there was no conclusive evidence either way.[69] At the same time he remained highly sceptical of the liberal-collectivist 'Halfway House'; and yet he continually toyed with the hypothetical possibility of a 'new deal' for Britain. In a lecture to the L.S.E. Sociology Club early in 1934

[67] BP, IXb 21, 'A Terrific Smash of Extravagent Hopes', paper by WHB to the Marshall Society, Cambridge, 26 Jan. 1934; 'Some Aspects of the American Recovery Programme', *Economica*, Feb. 1934, n.s., no. 1. pp. 1–12.
[68] Passfield Papers, B. Webb's diary, 16 Dec. 1933 and 5 Jan. 1934.
[69] BP, IIb, WHB to S. Webb, 29 Jan. 1934.

he outlined his own conception of such a new deal—which involved government control of credit, public ownership of heavy industries, a national population policy, and economic planning to secure maximum employment rather than a 'theoretical maximum standard of life'. He suggested also a massive housing and slum clearance programme, which would involve 'sending all trade union leaders in the building industry to a concentration camp or the House of Lords'.[70] Some months later in a lecture entitled 'My Utopia' he argued that in an ideal world there would be a variety of competing governmental systems, with complete freedom of movement across national boundaries, so that each individual could select his own ideal state. He himself, he admitted, would prefer a society where parliaments and dictators had both been superseded by enlightened professional administrators, who would control the psychological and physical environment through education, housing, transport, and town and country planning.[71] The main problem for these experts, he thought, would be ultimately not economic but political—'it is really the question of how Plato's Republic could be induced to accept government by his philosopher governors'.[72] 'I am particularly interested in your profession of administrators,' commented Beatrice Webb, '[it is] rather similar to Wells' Samurai, and his "open conspiracy". It is also analogous to the Communist Party in the USSR as a vocation of leadership.'[73]

By 1935 Beveridge had clearly moved a long way from the rather extreme free market position that he had adopted some years before. Moreover, in purely economic terms he seemed more inclined to favour a socialist model of planning than the mixture of state control and free enterprise prescribed by Roosevelt and Keynes. In his Herbert Spencer lecture at Oxford University in May 1935, he dismissed the view that socialism could not invent substitutes for the price-mechanism —arguing that precisely the same problem arose under monopoly capitalism. He suggested that in certain respects socialist planning might widen rather than restrict consumer choice and occupational freedom; and he claimed in rather Popperite terms that the only 'certain advantage which planning under capitalism appears to possess over planning under socialism is that it would be less difficult to abandon if it failed'.[74]

Beveridge was convinced, however, that in the last resort the merits and demerits of planning would have to be judged on political criteria— with reference not to economic efficiency but to 'the problem of the constitution and the powers of the supreme authority in the State'.[75] It

[70] BP, IXb 21, 'Does Britain want a New Deal?', ms. paper by WHB, 14 Feb. 1934.
[71] Sir William H. Beveridge, *Planning under Socialism and Other Addresses* (1936), pp. 130–42.
[72] Passfield Papers, II, 4, j, 50, WHB to B. Webb, 15 Nov. 1934.
[73] BP, IIb, B. Webb to WHB, 13 Nov. 1934.
[74] *Planning under Socialism*, pp. 1–31.     [75] Ibid., p. 2.

was this point that divided him most fundamentally from the Webbs and that constituted an insurmountable stumbling-block to his acceptance of Soviet-style planning. This difference of emphasis was clearly brought out in March 1935 during a passage of arms with Beatrice Webb over *Russia's Iron Age*, a book by an American journalist W. H. Chamberlin who had lived in Russia for the previous twelve years. In a review for the *New Statesman* Mrs. Webb challenged Chamberlin's assertion that there had been widespread famine in Russia in 1931–3. She claimed that his statements were based on totally inadequate statistical data and that, in so far as there *had* been famine, it had been deliberately caused by counter-revolutionary conspiracies. She complained, moreover, that Chamberlin had entirely ignored Lenin's 'great economic discovery' whereby unemployment had been abolished by gearing production to mass consumption.[76] Beveridge was provoked into writing a reply to the *New Statesman*, where he defended Chamberlin's statistics and ascribed their admitted inadequacies to the exclusion of journalists from the famine areas—a fact which he regarded as 'proof that the Soviet rulers had something more than usual to conceal'.[77] His objections were spelt out in more personal terms in a private letter to Mrs. Webb:

As you know I personally have an open mind as between the respective merits of a planned and a price economy with a sneaking desire to see a planned economy fairly tested out. But it does hurt me to think of any cause in which I could be interested or any persons for whom I care being associated with the kind of brutality represented by the present Russian regime, or appearing in any way to condone or make light of it.

The facts are not really questionable by any open-minded person. You do not have to believe Chamberlin's own statements (though I do not know of any grounds for questioning them), you have only to look at the official announcements of the Soviet rulers: at their 'pardoning or remitting sentences' of 71,000 slaves employed on the Baltic canal, (how many hundreds of thousands are there now in Siberia and elsewhere?); at their law prescribing savage penalties for the innocent children of anyone attempting to escape from Russia; at their odious caste and class system; at their censorship and refusal to face publicity; etc. etc.

During the earlier days of the revolution I happened to read something about Siberia under the Tsars. I remember saying to myself 'Thank Heaven, that'll come to an end now'. Do you think there would be the faintest chance of the Soviet rulers allowing a League Commission of Enquiry or any other impartial person to find out and tell the world what is inside Siberia now?

I know this won't move you not to regard Russia as a new civilisation, but I do hope that you will manage to put something in your book to make it clear that you do not make light of hateful things.

[76] *New Statesman*, 9 Mar. 1935.　　　[77] Ibid., 16 Mar. 1935.

You know I don't believe in Lenin's 'economic discovery', but that's quite a different and academic and unimportant point as compared with my hating to think of you and the G.P.U. as friends.[78]

Throughout 1935–6 Beveridge was feverishly and rather fruitlessly searching for an economic philosophy that would help to resolve his intellectual dilemmas and at the same time solve some of the practical problems of modern industrial societies. 'He likes Robbins and Co. best,' observed Beatrice Webb, '. . . but he admits that they and their credo are side-tracked, without influence or even relevance to the present state of the world'.[79] He spent much time examining the concept of an 'economic calculus' and pondering ways in which planners might devise effective substitutes for the price-mechanism.[80] Early in 1936 he was reluctantly impressed by Roosevelt's success in passing the first federal Social Security Act; but he continued to be critical of many other aspects of the New Deal legislation.[81] A few months later the ambivalence of his views was expressed in a review of the Webbs' *Soviet Communism* for the *Political Quarterly*—a review which the Webbs themselves admitted was 'masterly and very fair'.[82] In it he criticized the Webbs for nowhere comparing living standards in Russia with what they might have been under capitalism. He criticized their claim that mass unemployment had been abolished by 'universal distribution of effective demand' rather than by expansion of demand from the state. At the same time, however, he conceded that abolition of unemployment by whatever means was a crushing indictment of what had *not* been done in Britain over the previous ten years. British governments, he suggested, were 'inhibited' from taking preventive action by fear of crippling private enterprise—not realizing that private enterprise was in any case a 'fair weather' vessel, unsuited for periods of prolonged crisis. The central question posed by the Webbs' study, he asserted, was whether the abandonment of these economic fallacies was worth the political price. 'Is it possible,' he asked, 'to obtain release from such inhibitions without the Marxist operation? If this is not possible, can the gains of such release outweigh the losses and dangers of the operation itself? These, on the economic side, are the two vital issues raised by the Webbs' descriptions of Soviet Communism. They transcend in importance all disagreement on minor matters.' What was now required, he concluded, was much more 'detached' research into the rival

---

[78] Passfield Papers, II, 4, j, 54, WHB to B. Webb, 13 Mar. 1935.
[79] Passfield Papers, B. Webb's diary, 16 Sept. 1935.
[80] Passfield Papers, II, 4, i, 26, WHB to B. Webb, 28 Mar. 1935; BP, IIb, B. Webb to WHB, 29 Mar. 1935.
[81] *Planning under Socialism*, pp. 40–4, 123–9.
[82] Passfield Papers, B. Webb's diary, 22 Apr. 1936.

systems, so as to identify the best features of both capitalism and communism and to solve the 'common problem' of both.[83]

From its note of judicious compromise this review might have been thought to mark Beveridge's conversion to a liberal-collectivist *via media*; but that this was not so was shown by his reaction to J. M. Keynes' *General Theory of Employment*, also published early in 1936. Beveridge made copious notes on Keynes' new work, he read a paper on it to Hayek's seminar and he publicly denounced it in his farewell oration to the L.S.E.[84] The heightened tone of these comments suggests that his reading of the *General Theory* was for Beveridge a rather shattering experience: it was a work that seemed to challenge many of his most cherished beliefs about both the nature of social science and the direction of public policy. In general he took strong objection to Keynes' reliance on deductive reasoning and to his reduction of economic concepts to a high level of abstraction. Terms like 'unemployment' and 'demand' were meaningless, Beveridge protested, unless studied empirically and broken down into their constituent parts. The 'unemployed' were not a homogenous mass who would respond uniformly to changes in demand; they were a highly differentiated group, whose behaviour varied enormously according to age, skill, personal history and geographical location. More particularly, Beveridge was highly critical of Keynes' comments on 'involuntary unemployment', the concept of the 'multiplier', and his views on interest and wages. He hotly challenged Keynes' assertion that in orthodox economics 'involuntary unemployment' simply did not exist—pointing out that he himself and many others like him had spent their lives exhaustively studying the 'involuntary unemployed'. He was clearly baffled by the idea of the multiplier; 'digging holes in the ground is a reductio ad absurdum', he noted solemnly, 'why not merely pay people for doing nothing or pay people for being over sixty?' And if wages were raised and interest rates lowered as Keynes proposed, Beveridge objected, then saving would cease and the price of labour would henceforth be totally independent of labour demand.[85]

The publication both of *Soviet Communism* and of the *General Theory* intensified Beveridge's sense of estrangement from current economic and political thought. Politically he sympathized with the Keynsian liberals, but he found their economic policies not merely objectionable but virtually incomprehensible. 'I have tried to understand Mr. Keynes,' he recorded sadly, 'I have probably failed. Hicks' review in the E. J. seems

[83] Sir William Beveridge, 'Soviet Communism', *Political Quarterly*, vol. II, no. 3 July–Sept. 1936, pp. 346–67.

[84] 'The Place of the Social Sciences in Human Knowledge', *Politica*, Sept. 1937.

[85] BP, IXb 23, ms. by WHB on 'Employment Theory and the Facts of Unemployment', early 1936.

to be almost about another book.'[86] Conversely, he was impressed by the economic policies favoured by the Webbs, but found their politics totally unacceptable—a feeling that was strengthened during the winter of 1936–7 by the Moscow treason trials and by the Webbs' rather tortuous justification of Stalinist oppression.[87] The result at an intellectual level was an almost total withdrawal into political agnosticism—an agnosticism which dovetailed with Beveridge's growing conviction that academic social scientists should refrain from dabbling in current politics. A comparison of the gradual economic revival that was taking place simultaneously in both Britain and America convinced him that the contrasting policies pursued by the two governments had made 'surprisingly little difference in the course of economic events'; and in his farewell address to the L.S.E. he predicted that it might be another hundred and fifty years before social scientists could arrive at an accurate diagnosis of the ills of society.[88] He moved back to Oxford determined to concentrate not on the solution of current problems, but on the discovery of basic economic laws. 'He is going to devote the rest of his thinking life, apart from his University duties, to a scientific study of the facts of British capitalism,' noted Beatrice Webb after Beveridge had spent a week-end at Passfield Corner. In the course of this week-end she and Beveridge went for several long walks together over the Hampshire downs—during which they talked at length about his loss of confidence in applied social science and his scepticism of prevailing political ideologies. Mrs. Webb's account of their discussions must be treated with some reserve since it is clear from other sources that Beveridge's ideas at this time were still in a state of violent flux. Nevertheless, her recollection of their talk is worth quoting in some detail, since it portrays Beveridge in a mood of almost total pessimism about the possibility and even the desirability of radical social reform.

He stresses the word *scientific* [she recorded], 'which he defines as the quantitative study of facts; he also insists that it must be free from any prejudged scale of values as to these happenings. Thus today he thinks he has discovered one fact about cyclical depression, concerning the *season of the year* in which the depression or recovery occurs, this depends on a good or bad harvest. When I asked whether this discovery would help to discover how to prevent unemployment, he said that was irrelevant; or whether this seasonal variation had any connection with the relative *depth of continuance* of depression that question was also irrelevant. . . . The only reform besides labour exchanges, sound administration of insurance and of public assistance that he believes

---

[86] BP, IXb 23, 'Supplementary Notes on Keynes', by WHB, 8 June 1936.

[87] BP, IIb, 'What do you think of the Moscow trials?' by B. Webb, Feb. 1937.

[88] *Planning Under Socialism*, p. 129; 'The Place of the Social Sciences in Human Knowledge', loc. cit., p. 479.

might diminish unemployment, was a general lowering of wages, so as to increase demand, home and foreign. He however expressed the desire to see family allowances introduced which would enable wages to be lowered, without endangering the birthrate or the health of the rising generation. . . . He admitted almost defiantly that he was not concerned with the condition of the common people. His human sympathies were satisfied by the family group at the College and his pleasant relations with his fellow dons and his college undergraduates; his intellectual activities were fully employed in applying the statistical method to *discovering* facts without regard to political or economic values. He declared he had no *living philosophy*—he was a thoroughgoing materialist agnostic about man's relation to the universe; and he had no particular credo or ideal as to man's relation to man. If men were fools in not accepting sound economics—and the common people represented by the Labour party might be fools—there would be universal poverty and war.'[89]

[89] Passfield Papers, B. Webb's diary, 10 Aug. 1938.

# 14

## Social Policy Between the Wars

### I

In view of Beveridge's conversion to free-market economics in the 1920s, and his profound scepticism of interventionist liberalism in the 1930s it was not perhaps surprising that for most of the inter-war years he was much less concerned than he had previously been with questions of social policy. He refused many invitations to take part in social policy inquiries, and he regarded his involvement with welfare as a thing of the past.[1] He recognized a need, however, for a certain basic minimum of welfare, partly on humanitarian grounds and partly in order to preserve economic efficiency.[2] This mixture of social and economic goals can clearly be seen in three important areas of policy in which he did become involved—the Royal Commission on the Coal Industry, the movement for 'family endowment', and the development and refinement of the system of social insurance.

### II

The Royal Commission on the Coal Industry was set up in 1925 under the chairmanship of Sir Herbert Samuel, the former Liberal Home Secretary. Its other members were Beveridge himself, the soldier and banker Sir Herbert Lawrence, and a Lancashire cotton manufacturer, Mr. Kenneth Lee. The commission was assisted by a panel of experts, and all its meetings were attended by representatives of the mine-owners and of the main mining trade union, the Miners' Federation. It was the second inquiry of its kind in six years, a previous commission under Lord Sankey having recommended that coal mines should be taken over by the state. The immediate cause of the appointment of a new commission was the decline of the coal-exporting trade since 1924. The industry had been saved from total collapse by a temporary government subsidy, but employers were also demanding a reduction in miners' wages and a longer working day. The Commission was faced with two major problems—the immediate problem of lack of profitability, and the more fundamental problem of how the coal mines should be managed and organized so as to serve the needs of other sectors of

[1] BP, Ic 50, ms. notes for WHB's diary, 6 Aug. 1933.
[2] Passfield Papers, B. Webb's diary, 23 Feb. 1932.

industry. The mining employers, who were mainly concerned with the short-term problem, ascribed the industry's difficulties to declining productivity and to the refusal of the unions to accept lower wage-rates during periods of recession. The Miners' Federation on the other hand concentrated mainly on the long-term problem. They blamed declining output on the owners' mismanagement and on the fragmentation of the industry into nearly three thousand small and ill-co-ordinated collieries, often working side by side on the same seams of coal. They claimed that real wages had fallen since 1914, and they accused the owners of deliberately concealing their profits by selling coal cheaply to non-mining subsidiaries. As a solution to the industry's problems they put forward a plan drafted by R. H. Tawney for nationalization of both mines and mineral royalties. Under this plan, management of the industry would be vested in a National Coal and Power Production Council, subject to the ultimate authority of councils of producers and consumers. Such a scheme, it was argued, would secure for the industry state financial backing without subjecting it to excessive bureaucratic control. The aims of the new management would be to improve working conditions, to restore the industry to a sound financial footing, and to rationalize the production, transport and marketing of coal in all parts of the country.[3]

Between September and November 1925 the four Commissioners interviewed numerous witnesses, compiled statistics on wages, hours, profits and output, and visited collieries in all the main coal-producing districts—severely embarrassing mine managers by their insistence on descending in person to the depths of the coalface.[4] Beveridge got on well with Herbert Samuel, who shared a similar background as a Balliol-educated, Fabian-influenced Liberal reformer; and between them Beveridge and Samuel seem to have dominated both the interrogation of witnesses and the composition of the Commission's final report. Because of their similarity of outlook it is not always easy to distinguish which parts of the inquiry should be ascribed to Beveridge and which to Samuel; but the main features of Beveridge's contribution can be pieced together from the Commission's minutes of evidence and internal correspondence.[5] Almost certainly it was Beveridge himself who insisted on checking oral statements against statistical data, since much of the statistical material used by the Commission was painstakingly written out in Beveridge's own minute and meticulous manuscript.[6] Similarly it was he who suggested that many of the witnesses should be 'practical

---

[3] Cmd. 2600/1926, *RC on the Coal Industry, Report*, ch. 6.

[4] Lady Beveridge Papers, WHB to J. Mair, 23 Apr. 1925.

[5] *Coal Commission 1925–6*, twenty-six volumes deposited by WHB in the British Library of Political Science (Coll. T.).

[6] BP, VIII 2, working notes and statistics about coal industry, 1925–6.

colliery people'—managers, engineers and foremen—as well as representatives of the unions and employers.[7] It was Beveridge also who
collected information on the highly complex structure of the industry—
on the different practices prevailing in different coalfields, on the
interdependence of mining with transport, gas, electricity and engineering, on developments in fuel technology, and on the relative efficiency
of the industry's foreign competitors.[8]

The four coal Commissioners had all been deliberately chosen for
their lack of previous contact with any aspect of mining, in the hope
that they would produce a unanimous and impartial report acceptable
to both management and workers. This coincided precisely with
Beveridge's own conception of how a public inquiry ought to work, and
it was not perhaps surprising that he looked back on the Commission in
after years as a model of its kind.[9] His own share in the Commission's
work demonstrated very clearly his confident belief in the inherent superiority of the role of the impartial expert. His manner towards both coal-
owners and miners' leaders was more than usually abrasive and
peremptory. The inflexibility of the Miners' Federation filled him with
irritation, and he described their militant secretary A. J. Cook as having
a mind with 'the motions of a drunken dragon-fly'.[10] At the same time
his attitude towards many of the colliery-owners was one of profound
contempt. He made no secret of his belief that the industry was badly
managed, and he was sarcastic to the point of rudeness about the
employers' fear of left-wing agitation. In spite of his arrogant manner,
however, Beveridge proved to be extremely effective in cross-examination
of witnesses, usually to the detriment of the owners' rather than the
miners' case. It was he who produced unpublished figures compiled by
the Registrar-General showing that, whereas before the war mortality
among miners had been lower than among the general population, it
was now considerably higher. It was he who revealed that diminishing
returns in the coal industry were mainly due to the increased proportion
of surface workers rather than to a decline in productivity at the coalface. It was Beveridge who extracted the information that something like
two-thirds of coal produced in Britain was transferred to subsidiary
industries at less than the market price, thus artificially deflating the
employers' profits. He also argued strongly against a lengthening of the
miners' working day, arguing that far from increasing output it would
almost certainly have a 'psychologically depressing effect'.[11]

[7] BP, VIII 2, WHB to C. S. Hurst, 20 Oct. 1925.
[8] BP, VIII 1, working notes and statistics about coal industry, 1925–6; VIII 2, 'Inquiries
to be put in hand', ms. by WHB, n.d.
[9] *PI*, p. 221.          [10] Ibid., p. 220.
[11] *RC on the Coal Industry*, Minutes of Evidence, QQ 5,787–90; 6,520–35; 6,602–4; 6,541;
6,588; 12,260–1; 12,960; 13,247; 14,964–5.

In view of Beveridge's manifest contempt for the mining management and his success in reinforcing the miners' case, it might have been expected that he would support the proposals put forward by the Miners' Federation. He did not do so, however, for two reasons. Firstly, although he endorsed the demand for nationalization of royalties, he could not accept the model for public ownership of the mines themselves which had been drawn up by Tawney. His objection was almost certainly not to nationalization *per se*, but to direction of the industry by a system of producers' and consumers' councils. He was afraid that working-class representatives, even on a consumers' council, would nearly always identify with producer rather than consumer interests; and, even if this were not so, he was convinced that producer-control would always outweigh consumer-control, because producer councils could back up their decisions with the power to strike. He feared also that the goal of economic efficiency could not always be reconciled with the goals of better working conditions and job security, and that in a popularly managed industry the latter would always prevail.[12] His own preference therefore was for the rationalization of coal mining under private management—for the grouping together of contiguous mines into large combines, which would do away with inefficient boundaries, invest in new technology and close uneconomic pits. He seemed to envisage that this grouping together of private mines might eventually compel a transition to state management—but it was to be management by a public corporation or civil service department rather than management by any form of direct popular control. It was to come about, moreover, by a process of slow evolution rather than by an act of once-and-for-all intervention by the state. This was brought out very clearly in Beveridge's cross-examination of Tawney, who appeared on behalf of the Miners' Federation. Tawney argued for immediate nationalization on the ground that otherwise the problems of the industry would go from bad to worse 'Is not history against you?' asked Beveridge. 'In this country, are not all our revolutions gradual?' History, replied Tawney with uncharacteristic purism, merely recorded what had actually happened, it did not tell people what they ought to do.[13]

Beveridge's second disagreement with the miner's case was over wages. The Federation claimed that between 1914 and 1925 the cost of living had risen by 75 per cent, whereas miners' wages had risen by only 61 per cent, so that miners had suffered a substantial decline in real income. With the help of Arthur Bowley and E. A. G. Robinson, Beveridge analysed the basis of these estimates and came to the conclusion

[12] Cmd. 2,600/1926, *RC on the Coal Industry Report*, ch. 6. On Beveridge's share in drafting this chapter, see *PI*, pp. 219–20.

[13] *RC on the Coal Industry, Minutes of Evidence*, Q. 16,975.

that although superficially correct they were in fact misleading. He argued, firstly, that the miners' figures took no account of the much higher proportion of unskilled workers now employed in the industry; and secondly, that 1914 was an unsuitable base for comparison since it had been for the coal mines an unusually prosperous year. If the index was weighted to take account of the changing composition of the work-force, and if wages in 1925 were compared, not with those of 1914 but with average wages between 1909 to 1913, then a very different picture emerged. On that basis, Beveridge claimed, miners' wages had risen by 78 per cent.[14] He therefore accepted the employers' contention that rising wages were a significant factor in rising costs of production. He was, moreover, greatly impressed by the argument put forward by Josiah Stamp that rigidity of wages was directly responsible for the current recession—an argument which, as we have seen, rapidly came to dominate his own approach to unemployment.[15] Beveridge admitted that a third of the mining community was still living in poverty, but he claimed that this was confined to workers with large families. He con-cluded therefore that the cure for the miners' grievances was not higher wages but family allowances, to be paid for by a levy on mining employers. Such a solution he argued, would make possible wage-reductions during periods of depression, without endangering the health of the rising generation or penalizing those in greatest need. It would divert resources from the single and childless, for whom even low wages were adequate, to those with large families, for whom even high wages could never be entirely sufficient. It would cut production costs, cheapen British coal in world markets, and enable employers to retain a much higher proportion of their labour force during periods of slack demand. Moreover, by reducing the earnings of single and childless workers it would penalize the group who were most frequently guilty of 'absenteeism', and who could most easily make up their wages by working longer hours.[16]

Many of Beveridge's arguments were contained in the Commission's report, published in March 1926. As a remedy for the industry's short-term problems the Commissioners rejected the employers' demand for longer hours, on the grounds that this would seriously impair the miners' quality of life and was in any case pointless when the mines were already producing an unsaleable coal surplus. They condemned also the temporary expedient of a government subsidy, seeing it as a positive bar-rier to more drastic permanent reforms. They suggested instead a tem-porary reduction in the minimum wage-rates of higher-paid workers—

[14] *RC on the Coal Industry, Report,* Annex S.7., pp. 280–4.
[15] *RC on the Coal Industry, Minutes of Evidence,* QQ.5,061–8.
[16] BP, VIII 2, WHB to E. Rathbone, 15 Dec. 1925.

combined with the extension of piece-rates and profit-sharing, so as to secure to the miners an immediate increase of income as soon as trade revived. They proposed also that wage-rates of all kinds should be negotiated nationally rather than on a local basis. 'What we contemplate,' the Commissioners claimed, 'is not a permanent lowering of wage standards but a temporary sacrifice by the men in the industry, other than the worst paid, in order to avoid the possible unemployment of hundreds of thousands of men.'[17] To deal with the long-term problem the Commission favoured nationalization of mineral royalties and state-financing of technological research; but it rejected the demand for nationalization of mines, proposing instead that the industry should be reorganized under private enterprise, and that 'joint pit committees' should be set up to improve consultations between management and men. In addition the commission recommended a wide range of welfare measures—family allowances for miners' children, baths at every pit-head, better housing in mining villages, improved facilities for finding new employment and the introduction throughout the industry of annual holidays with pay.[18]

The Report of the Coal Commission may perhaps be seen as a classic example of the long tradition of utilitarian public inquiries that had informed governments in Britain over the previous hundred years. It had all the strengths and weaknesses of that particular tradition; and an assessment of those strengths and weaknesses may help to throw some further light on Beveridge's own conception of the process of social reform. The authors of the report were all drawn from the economic and political establishment, but they were strongly committed to an ethic of impartiality and even critics on the far left admitted that the commission was in no sense biased in favour of employers.[19] The report itself was precise, accurate, logical, well-documented and almost completely non-historical in its method of approach. It seemed to assume that both employers and workers were a set of totally rational men, capable of harmonizing their conflicting interests at the price of a little deferred gratification—ignoring the fact that if such were the case the need for such an inquiry would scarcely have arisen. The Commissioners dismissed in half a paragraph the long history of risk, exploitation, suspicion and struggle that had fashioned relationships in the mining industry time out of mind; and instead they devoted themselves to a judicious analysis of faults and imperfections in the current situation. The result was a report which was widely acknowledged to be 'very good from a scientific point of view',[20] but which was totally unacceptable to

[17] *RC on the Coal Industry, Report*, p. 229.  [18] Ibid., pp. 163, 185, 199–210.
[19] Passfield Papers, II, 4, h, 39, H. Laski to B. Webb, 9 Oct. 1925.
[20] Samuel Papers, A/159, item 4, B. Webb to H. Samuel, 27 Mar. 1926.

either of the warring parties. Its conclusions were 'sound but ineffectual', commented Mrs. Webb, 'sound in doctrine but ineffectual in practice'.[21] The miners' leaders clung to their slogan of 'not a minute on the day, not a penny off the pay', convinced that any compromise would prove the thin end of the wedge. The mine-owners meanwhile refused to take part in national wage agreements and continued to press for a longer working day. The Conservative government under Baldwin made a half hearted offer to implement the Report, and then backed the employers in demanding both reduction of wages and lengthening of hours.[22] The result was the miners' lock-out of 30 April 1926 and the nine days General Strike.

Beveridge took no formal part in the flurry of negotiations surrounding the General Strike, although Herbert Samuel, who was employed by the government to negotiate with the T.U.C., tried at one stage to reconvene the Royal Commission.[23] From a document in the Samuel papers, however, it seems probable that it was Beveridge who composed the first draft of what subsequently became known as the Samuel memorandum. On 6 May 1926 Beveridge sent to Samuel, a 'Note of Suggestions', recommending the setting up of a National Wages Board to arbitrate on miners' wages, the temporary continuance of the government subsidy, and the appointment of a committee to implement the Commission's proposals for mining reorganization.[24] These suggestions formed the core of Samuel's discussions with the T.U.C., as a result of which he eventually persuaded them to call off the General Strike.[25] The proposals were not, however, accepted by the miners' leaders and their intransigence was used by the government as an excuse for consigning the Coal Commission's report to virtual oblivion. No effective action was taken on its suggestions for structural reform, and in June 1926 an Act of Parliament increased by an hour the miners' maximum working day. Beveridge was highly critical of the government's policy and of the complacent inefficiency of the mining employers; but at the same time he was baffled by the attitude of the miners' leaders, which he thought was playing into the hands of the diehard opponents of reform.[26] Three years later he had apparently come to the conclusion that mining reorganization could only be brought about by some form of public

[21] Passfield Papers, B. Webb's diary, 28 June 1926.

[22] C. L. Mowat, *Britain between the Wars* (1968 edn.), pp. 298–302.

[23] Ibid., p. 324. For a detailed account of Samuel's contacts with Beveridge during the strike, see BP, Ic 7, WHB's diary, 5–9 May 1926.

[24] Samual Papers, A/66, 'A Note of Suggestions from Sir W. Beveridge', *c.* 6 May 1926; and WHB to H. Samuel, 12 May 1926. See also BP, VIII 2, WHB to H. Samuel, 12 May 1926.

[25] Mowat, op. cit., pp. 324–6.

[26] BP, IIb, WHB to Arthur Henderson, 15 Mar. 1926; *The Times*, 21 Oct. 1929, WHB to the Editor.

control. In a letter to the Cambridge lawyer, Arnold McNair, he revealed that he now favoured the transfer of retail coal distribution to 'local public monopolies' and the amalgamation of coal mines into 'six or seven public district companies'. These companies, he suggested, should reorganize coal production and enjoy a 'statutory monopoly' over home and foreign trade.[27]

## III

The aspect of Beveridge's work for the Coal Commission that was to prove of most lasting significance was his espousal of family allowances. His support for family allowances stemmed initially from his interest in population, but it gradually became linked with his ideas on wages and insurance. Beveridge's views on the population problem were, as we have already seen, highly ambivalent. He accepted the logic of the neo-Malthusian argument that, without artificial restraint, population even in an advanced economy would eventually outrun resources; and he once admitted that in his private dream of Utopia the population of Britain would be reduced to five millions.[28] In his role as a labour economist, however, he strongly denied that there was any evidence of a permanent labour surplus; and he was much less concerned with over-population than with the decline in the birth-rate and the differential impact of that decline among different nations and different sectors of society. It was this concern that promoted his lecture on 'Population and Unemployment' to the British Association in 1923. In this lecture Beveridge criticized Keynes for his pessimistic account of the problems of pre-war Europe in *The Economic Consequences of the Peace*, and he accused Keynes of having revived the Malthusian spectre of over-population. Beveridge pointed out that in nearly all European countries over the previous fifty years there had been a 'revolutionary fall in fertility'—a fall which he ascribed to artificial methods of family limitation. 'The questions now facing us,' Beveridge argued,

are how far the fall will go; whether it will bring about a stationary white population after or long before the white man's world is full; how the varying incidence of restriction among different social classes or creeds will affect the stock; how far the unequal adoption of birth control by different races will leave one race at the mercy of another's growing numbers, or drive it to armaments and perpetual aggression in self-defence.[29]

[27] BP, IIb, WHB to A. D. McNair, 22 July 1929.
[28] W. H. Beveridge, 'My Utopia', in *Planning under Socialism*, p. 132.
[29] Sir William Beveridge, 'Population and Unemployment', reprinted in R. L. Smyth, *Essays in the Economics of Socialism and Capitalism* (1964), pp. 241–71.

Beveridge's speech was strongly attacked by Marie Stopes, the pioneer of birth control, who accused him of 'apparently forgetting the physiological facts of life'. 'At the present time,' she claimed, 'the nation was spending £100,000,000 per year on unemployables, including the maintenance of diseased, enfeebled persons whom the proper use of birth control would have prevented from ever existing.' Beveridge replied that he had no objection to 'constructive birth control', but that until its effects had been scientifically tested it should not be preached indiscriminately to 'all and sundry', since 'all and sundry were not unfit'.[30] This interchange between Beveridge and Dr. Stopes flashed across the headlines of the national press. In the *Daily Herald* Beveridge was dismissed as a 'scientist totally remote from reality', but he was warmly praised by the *New Statesman* which denounced birth control as 'one of the most dangerous movements ever to threaten our civilization'.[31] Keynes himself chided Beveridge for lending to 'ignorance and prejudice the shelter of his name'. He complained also that Beveridge had seriously distorted or misinterpreted his views: he had not diagnosed 'overpopulation' or even a decline in living-standards but merely a growing 'precariousness' in the economic situation—a precariousness that was signalled in Britain by a declining volume of exports and increasingly unfavourable terms of trade.[32]

The dispute between Beveridge and Keynes was really rather artificial since in the last resort they both accepted the Malthusian analysis and both were in favour of 'rational' family planning. Nevertheless, Beveridge clearly had reservations about the limitation of fertility if left solely to the discretion of private individuals. These reservations seem to have stemmed from three sources; firstly, from a fear of the ultimate eclipse of the most 'advanced' races; secondly, from a desire to avoid producing a society over-loaded with old people; and, thirdly, from a belief that birth control was mainly practised by the most 'responsible' sectors of society and might therefore be harming the 'national stock'.[33] A solution to the second and third of these problems seemed to present itself in the form of family allowances, which were first proposed by Eleanor Rathbone, the Liverpool philanthropist, during the First World War. In her book *The Disinherited Family*, published in 1924, Miss Rathbone argued that in spite of rising incomes there was still a large concentration of poverty among children in large families. This she ascribed to the fact that the wage-system took no account of depend-

---

[30] *Manchester Guardian*, 18 Sept. 1923; *The Scotsman*, 18 Sept. 1923.

[31] *Daily Herald*, 18 Sept. 1923; *New Statesman*, 22 Sept. 1923.

[32] J. M. Keynes, 'A Reply to Sir William Beveridge', reprinted in Smyth, pp. 272–83; Keynes Papers, J. M. Keynes to WHB, 16 Feb. 1924.

[33] *The Times*, 15 Aug. 1924; BP, III 19, ms. notes on 'Unemployment Twenty Years After', by WHB.

ants; and she proposed a remedy that had already been adopted in France, Belgium and Poland—a system of *per capita* family allowances, payable for all children irrespective of family income and irrespective of whether the breadwinner was in or out of work. The allowances would be modelled on the system used for supporting children of servicemen during the war, including payment direct to the mother—a system that was believed to have resulted in a marked improvement in juvenile nutrition and physique.

Beveridge reviewed Miss Rathbone's book for the *Weekly Westminster* and was greatly impressed. 'I've been reading . . . "The Disinherited Family", he, wrote to Graham Wallas, 'i.e. the case for distributing part of the total national income not as profits, interest, salaries and wages, but as "family allowances". The book has converted me, and if you read it, will, I believe, convert you and others.'[34] In June 1924 he became a member of the Council of the newly founded Family Endowment Society, and later in the year he introduced a system of children's allowances for the staff of the L.S.E.[35] His motives in supporting the movement were not, however, precisely the same as those of Eleanor Rathbone. Undoubtedly he shared her concern to abolish family poverty, but an important secondary motive was his hope that family allowances would help to arrest the decline in the birth-rate.[36] From this time forward he advocated a combined policy of family allowances and birth control—on the not altogether logical assumption that their eugenic effects would cancel each other out and that trends in fertility would achieve some kind of equilibrium.[37] Another secondary motive not shared by Miss Rathbone was his hope that family allowances would help to keep down wages—an argument which he urged upon the Balfour Committee on Trade and Industry in 1926.[38]

Beveridge drafted his first concrete proposals on family allowances for a conference of the Family Endowment Council in June 1924. He proposed that allowances should be financed by contributory insurance and should be payable for all children whose parents were covered by national health insurance, which included most working persons earning less than £250 a year. He estimated that weekly allowances of three shillings per child would cost £78 million a year—to be paid for by weekly contributions of one shilling from the worker, one shilling from

[34] Wallas Papers, Box 8, WHB to G. Wallas, 29 Apr. 1924.
[35] L.S.E. Papers, minutes of the Emergency Committee, 17 July 1925.
[36] Miss Rathbone argued that family endowment would tend to decrease rather than increase the birth-rate, by raising the living-standards and aspirations of working-class parents (*The Disinherited Family* (1924), pp. 242–3, 247).
[37] *The Times*, 15 Aug. 1924; *Daily Telegraph*, 21 May 1926; *Manchester Guardian*, 6 Dec. 1924.
[38] BP, IIb, WHB to Walter Carter, 19 Feb. 1926.

the employer and ninepence from the state. Allowances would not be paid for children on poor relief, nor for children of parents drawing unemployment benefit, for whom dependants' allowances had been payable since 1922. The scheme would not include illegitimate children unless their parents were living together in 'a relatively permanent union'. In addition to the state scheme, voluntary and occupational family endowment schemes should be encouraged for self-employed and professional groups.[39]

Beveridge's proposals formed the basis of the conference discussion, and most of them were accepted by the Family Endowment Council— although it was decided that allowances ought to be payable at all times whether or not the father was in work, and that special dependants' allowances under unemployment insurance should therefore be abolished. The Council would have preferred a universal scheme, on the ground that 'a scheme confined to the working classes would encourage an increase of population from inferior stocks'. It was thought, however, that the practical difficulties in the way of such a scheme would be too great.[40] A few months later, Beveridge wrote to Edward Marsh, Winston Churchill's private secretary, urging that family allowances should be included in the new Conservative pensions legislation; and he advised the Liberal Summer Schools movement to 'hitch its wagon' to the cause of the child.[41] In the following year he persuaded Miss Rathbone to give evidence to the Coal Commission in favour of family allowances for miners; and, as we have seen, he himself submitted proposals for an occupational scheme of family allowances as a palliative for lower rates of pay. Although Beveridge and Miss Rathbone worked closely together on this occasion there was once again a perceptible difference between their views. Miss Rathbone refused to associate herself with wage-cuts; and she based her recommendations for both family allowances and minimum wage-rates on Seebohm Rowntree's 'human needs scale', which was considerably more generous than Rowntree's other and more famous scale of subsistence-level poverty.[42] Beveridge on the other hand was convinced that payments on the more generous scale could only be made at the price of abolishing wage-differentials between different grades of miners—a price which he thought would be both economically undesirable and politically unacceptable. He therefore proposed that both family allowances and minimum wages should be based on the mean between the two Rowntree scales, so as to 'show simultaneously a

[39] Bev. Coll. Misc. 9, items 41–8, 'Family Allowances Points for Discussion', by WHB, 11 June 1924, and supplementary papers.

[40] Bev. Coll. Misc. 9, items 67–9, report of a discussion held on 17 June 1924.

[41] BP, IIb, WHB to E. Marsh, 8 Dec. 1924; Lady Beveridge Papers, WHB to J. Mair, 29 Dec. 1924.

[42] BP, VIII 2, E. Rathbone to WHB, 1 Dec. 1925.

saving on the wages bill and an improvement of the standard of living of persons with families, combined with leaving the present graduation of workers untouched'.[43]

Beveridge's proposals were contained in the Commission's report, but as we have seen they were not adopted by the government. Not perhaps surprisingly the proposals were looked on with suspicion by labour leaders, although Eleanor Rathbone claimed that there was a good deal of support for family endowment among the labour rank and file.[44] Two years later Beveridge returned to the theme of providing family allowances via national insurance—once again linking them with a reversal of the prevailing decline in fertility. In a lecture to the Family Endowment Society he argued that national income, if distributed equally amongst all adult workmen, would now provide adequately for a husband, wife and three dependent children. Even if equal distribution was economically desirable, however—and Beveridge clearly implied that it wasn't—it would do nothing to prevent poverty among families with more than three children, and would mean extravagant overpayment of single workmen and childless couples. He therefore argued for insurance-based family allowances as 'the only way of preventing the passage through poverty of a substantial part of the rising generation'. Such a policy, he claimed, would also have a constructive eugenic effect —not by penalizing the feckless, but by encouraging fertility among the responsible and prudent, who limited their families according to their means.[45]

At the end of this lecture Beveridge called for more research into both family limitation and family endowment, and in the following year he was involved in setting up a new British Population Society, which was affiliated to the International Union for the Study of Population Problems. In 1931–2 he took part in a series of B.B.C. programmes on Changes in Family Life, which involved circulating a questionnaire to radio-listeners on such topics as family size and structure, choice of marriage-partners, sharing of housework, use of leisure and pooling of family income. The response to this questionnaire was predictably too selective to form a reliable basis for sociological analysis, but nevertheless the experiment provoked much discussion of family and population questions in the national press.[46] For some time thereafter Beveridge was too busy to take an active part in the family endowment movement; but nevertheless he continued to take a passionate interest in all kinds of 'family problems—an interest which possibly stemmed as much

[43] BP, VIII 2, WHB to E. Rathbone, 30 Nov. 1926.
[44] Bev. Coll. Misc. 9, item 29, 'Opinions of Miners' Secretaries on Family Allowances'.
[45] Ibid., items 12–21, notes for speech on 'Family Allowances as Redistribution of Total Product of Industry', by WHB, 14 Oct. 1927.
[46] Sir William Beveridge, *Changes in Family Life*, B.B.C. pamphlet, Feb. 1932.

from his devotion to an ideal of family life as from detached scientific curiosity. He was increasingly convinced, moreover, that family allowances offered the single most effective cure for the problem of poverty, and this conviction was strengthened by his work for the Unemployment Insurance Statutory Committee. From 1934 onwards there was a perceptible change in his approach to family allowances; he became much less concerned with their relevance to size of population, and much more concerned with their role as an adjunct to the system of social security. To understand the nature of this change we must now turn to the third main area of policy in which Beveridge was involved during the inter-war years—the development of social insurance and, in particular, the provision of maintenance for the unemployed.


IV


Beveridge's share in policies of social insurance during the 1920s and 30s was in marked contrast to the role that he had played in the years before the war. Between 1908 and 1914 he had been personally responsible for one of the major areas of insurance, and he had been strikingly successful in getting his ideas accepted by the government of the day. During the inter-war years, however, he was rarely close to the centre of policy-formation, and he was far more often the critic than the architect of new insurance schemes. Nevertheless, his criticisms are worth analysing in some detail, since it is possible to discern in them certain basic principles that were to be of considerable long-term significance in Beveridge's philosophy of social security. The most important of these principles were, firstly, his increasing emphasis on 'universalism'; secondly, his anxiety to protect the contributory basis of insurance; and, thirdly, his desire to achieve an administrative balance between self-governing pluralism and bureaucratic centralization.

As was shown in an earlier chapter Beveridge towards the end of the war had strongly favoured the universal extension of insurance against unemployment. In his report for the Civil War Workers' Committee he had recommended a combination of direct state insurance and state-subsidized occupational schemes, managed by trade unions or by joint committees of employers and workers.[47] In May 1919 he had a chance to elaborate this plan when he was appointed to a committee under the chairmanship of E. C. Cunningham, set up by the Minister of Labour to draft proposals for legislation. On this committee Beveridge pressed for a threefold mixture of direct state insurance, 'segregated schemes' for particular industries, and state-subsidized schemes run by non-profit-

[47] Above, p. 256.

making voluntary organizations. He also recommended the setting-up of a special scheme for dock labourers; and he persuaded the government actuary, Sir Alfred Watson, to reduce his estimate of average future unemployment from 8.6 per cent to 6.6 per cent.[48] These proposals were embodied in the report of the Cunningham committee in August 1919—together with a proposal, which does not appear to have emanated from Beveridge, that unemployment and health insurance should henceforth be administratively unified.[49] No action was taken on these proposals for some time—partly because the trade unions were demanding a non-contributory scheme, and partly because the Treasury objected strongly to the payment of government subsidies to 'segregated industries' and voluntary organizations.[50] Rising unemployment, however, eventually forced the government to take remedial action, and a new Unemployment Insurance Bill was rushed through Parliament in February 1920. This Bill extended unemployment insurance to all employees earning less than £250 a year, with the exception of servants and agricultural labourers. It allowed also for the management of state unemployment insurance by voluntary organizations. These included trade unions, as under the original Act of 1911, and also, for the first time, national health insurance 'approved societies'. The Act also allowed industries with a negligible risk of unemployment —such as railways and banking—to contract out of the state scheme into special schemes of their own.[51]

The Unemployment Insurance Act of 1920 bore in certain respects a close resemblance to Beveridge's proposals on the Cunningham committee; and certainly he must be held at least partially responsible for what have subsequently been seen as some of its worst features—notably the unrealistically low prediction of average unemployment and the provision for 'contracting out'.[52] Nevertheless, there were some important differences of principle between Beveridge's proposals and those embodied in the Act. Firstly, he had not envisaged that 'voluntary associations' would include the approved societies, whom he regarded as at best inefficient and at worst corrupt. He had not intended that participation in management of the state scheme should be confined solely to trade unions, as was advocated by many members of the Labour Party; but he had hoped for the setting up of a new form of statutory insurance association, involving co-operation between management and workers.

[48] PRO, PIN 7/36, Extension of Unemployment Insurance Committee, Minutes of fourth and fifth meetings, 4 and 5 June 1919.
[49] Ibid., 'Summary of Proposed Scheme', n.d., and 'Interim Report', 8 Aug. 1919.
[50] Ibid., Minutes of eighth meeting, 1 July 1919; Draft Cabinet Memorandum on 'Unemployment Insurance', 26 Aug. 1919.
[51] Bentley B. Gilbert, *British Social Policy 1914–39* (1970), pp. 67–74.
[52] Ibid., pp. 73–4.

A second and more important difference was his conception of 'contracting out'. He had not intended that this should be applied solely to industries with a low rate of unemployment. Rather, he had hoped that it would be particularly applied to highly organized industries, such as those included in the original scheme of 1911. It may be recalled that in the planning stages of the first National Insurance Act he had proposed a scheme by which unemployment funds would be pooled on an occupational rather than a national basis;[53] and his motives for supporting such an arrangement in 1919 were precisely the same as they had been ten years before. He believed that feelings of social solidarity were much stronger within a particular industrial sector—such as engineering or mining—than they were throughout industry as a whole. He therefore argued that both workers and employers were much more likely to take rational steps to prevent unemployment if they were thereby relieving their own sectoral insurance fund, than if they were merely relieving a fund shared by the whole community. He hoped, moreover, that it would be possible to encourage such feelings of group self-interest by differentiating rates of weekly contribution—by raising them in industries where unemployment was high and reducing them where unemployment was correspondingly low.[54]

Beveridge continued to favour industry-based unemployment insurance, rather than a uniform national scheme, for several years thereafter. He frequently implied that a uniform flat-rate contribution, levied indiscriminately throughout the industrial labour force, was a 'tax on employment' that positively encouraged employers to discharge marginal workmen.[55] In 1922 he outlined a plan for insurance by industry to the Liberal Summer Schools committee, proposing that in each industrial sector employers should group themselves together into mutual insurance guilds. Unemployment benefit would be paid by the employment exchanges and recovered from the guilds—thus penalizing industries in direct proportion to their prevailing level of unemployment.[56] This scheme attracted the notice of the Conservative Minister of Labour, Sir Montague Barlow, who was preparing a further amendment to the Unemployment Insurance Acts; and at Barlow's request Beveridge submitted his proposals in an official memorandum.[57] They were not, however, adopted by the Ministry of Labour, and Beveridge's

---

[53] Above, p. 171–2.

[54] PRO, PIN 7/36, 'Compulsory Segregation by Industry', by WHB, n.d.

[55] BP, III 24, WHB to Leonard P. Adams, 20 Mar. 1934; *RC on Unemployment Insurance, Minutes of Evidence*, Q 5,861.

[56] BP, II 21, Notes on Liberal Summer School Conference, held at Caius College, Cambridge, 28–31 Dec. 1932.

[57] BP, II b, Sir Montagu Barlow to WHB, 18 Jan. and 26 Feb. 1923; WHB to Sir Montagu Barlow, 22 Jan. 1923.

own enthusiasm for industry-based insurance seemed thereafter to wane. A year later he had come to the conclusion that, however desirable in theory, it would in practice be very difficult to organize and was unlikely to gain serious political support.[58]

Baulked on this particular issue, Beveridge turned his attention to the prevailing movement for 'all-in' insurance—a movement that stemmed partly from a desire for administrative rationalization, partly from an abhorrence of means tests, and partly from the Economy Drive that swept through Whitehall during the depression of 1921–2.[59] As we have seen, the Cunningham committee of 1919 had floated the idea of administrative integration between health and unemployment insurance. Two years later this was endorsed by the government actuary, in an appendix to the Geddes Report on National Expenditure—the notorious 'Geddes Axe' of December 1921. From this time onwards the possibility of unified social insurance was increasingly canvassed by a widely varying group of reformers, who hoped in this way to abolish poverty without significantly enlarging the burden of public expenditure. A Liberal pamphlet advocating 'all-in' insurance was published in September 1923, and both Liberal and Conservative parties included promises about integrated social insurance in their election manifestos at the end of the year.[60]

Beveridge's contribution to the 'all-in' insurance debate was embodied in his pamphlet, *Insurance for All and Everything*, published in 1924. In this pamphlet he proposed that contributory flat-rate national insurance should be extended to cover, not merely sickness and unemployment, but old age, industrial accidents and the support of orphans and elderly widows. Contributions would be collected through a single weekly stamp, and administration of the different schemes would be unified, in so far as this was compatible with functional efficiency. Beveridge did not envisage total amalgamation, since he conceded that the local employment exchange could not take over the functions of the friendly society sick visitor or panel doctor. Possibly also he was reluctant to challenge the power of the approved societies, although, as we have seen, he was vehemently opposed to any further extension of their administrative control. *Insurance for All and Everything* was in many ways a logical development of the views which Beveridge had expressed seventeen years earlier as a leader-writer for the *Morning Post*. It was an attempt to introduce into Britain a system of social insurance coverage

[58] BP, IXa 59, 'Unemployment Insurance in England', typescript article by WHB (written for Neue Freie Presse of Vienna), 20 Dec. 1924.

[59] P. M. Williams, 'The Development of Old-Age Pensions Policy in Great Britain 1878–1925', London Ph.D. 1970, ch. 14.

[60] Ibid., pp. 397–401.

even wider in scope than the system invented by Bismarck. It was designed to reduce to a minimum the need for discretionary relief and to supersede the system of non-contributory old-age pensions, which Beveridge in 1908 had denounced so strongly for penalizing thrift. The pamphlet has also frequently been seen as the germ of Beveridge's later contribution to the structure of the welfare state;[61] and comparison should be made with his report on *Social Insurance and Allied Services* of eighteen years later. Certainly there were many striking similarities between the pamphlet of 1924 and the famous Beveridge report of 1942. In both works Beveridge emphasized the concept of 'interruption of earnings' as the factor that linked together all the different contingencies that could be relieved by insurance. In both he portrayed insurance as not merely the most economical but the most psychologically desirable form of public relief. Both schemes were designed to extend insurance coverage, and at the same time to prevent wasteful duplication: 'their edges must fit, neither overlapping, nor leaving holes through which people can drop undeservedly into destitution'. Both schemes were designed to provide for 'perfectly normal persons' facing 'disorders endemic in modern society'; they took little account of the deviant, the incurable and the down-and-out—an emphasis which directly reflected the self-confessed bias of Beveridge's social conscience, and his conception of priorities in social reform.[62]

There were, nevertheless, some important differences in method, scope and underlying principle between *Insurance for All and Everything* and the Beveridge report of 1942. *Insurance for All and Everything* was composed at top speed as a piece of party propaganda. It contained many loose ends and, unusually for a work by Beveridge, its arguments were not backed up by statistical research. Its conception of benefits was the same as that in the Act of 1911: benefits were not to meet subsistence needs but merely to act as a threshold for voluntary private saving. Its definition of 'all' did not in fact mean 'all', but persons with incomes below a certain limit.[63] There was very little discussion of, or provision for, the needs of families—a problem that was to be of central concern in the report of 1942. Most strikingly of all, the pamphlet of 1924 showed very little awareness of the overwhelming seriousness of the problem of unemployment. Eighteen years later Beveridge was to see full employment as an absolute precondition of any successful system of national social security.[64] In February 1924, however, when over two million people were out of work, he paid curiously little attention to the massive

---

[61] Ibid., p. 414; Janet Beveridge, *Beveridge and his Plan*, p. 75.
[62] *Insurance for All and Everything* (1924), pp. 4–5, 7–8, 30–1.
[63] Ibid., p. 35. The limit was 'the present scope of Health Insurance'.
[64] Below, chs. 16 and 17.

financial problem of supporting the unemployed. He clearly supposed
that prevailing unemployment could be mainly ascribed to one of those
'cyclical fluctuations', that had been a familiar feature of economic life
before the war. It was to protect workmen against this kind of sporadic
unemployment that the 1911 insurance scheme had been specifically
designed, and in the winter of 1923-4 Beveridge seemed confident that
the scheme was working well. So confident was he, indeed, that he
predicted an imminent surplus in the unemployment fund of £25
million a year. It was with this surplus that he proposed to finance the
new benefits for widows and orphans. 'There is no reason at all,' he
wrote, 'why unemployment after the war should be permanently at a
higher level than it was before the war; if we are prepared to contemplate
its continuance at anything like its present level, we might as well contemplate national decay at once.'[65]

Beveridge's pamphlet, as was shown in the last chapter, was briefly
adopted as official Liberal policy in the House of Commons. In July 1924
an official committee under Sir John Anderson reported unfavourably
on 'all-in' insurance, and in particular criticized Beveridge's scheme for
exaggerating the yield of the unemployment fund, ignoring the difficulties of insuring females, and generally underestimating the problems
of administrative simplification.[66] In the following year, however, a
Widows', Orphans' and Contributory Old Age Pensions Bill was introduced into Parliament by Neville Chamberlain. This fell far short of
total 'all-in' insurance, since it ignored unemployment and workmen's
compensation; but it linked the new benefits very closely with the
existing system of national health insurance. Moreover, the new
measure was in certain respects very similar to Beveridge's own scheme
—although, as he himself admitted, there was no evidence whatsoever
that his ideas had had any direct influence. Beveridge thought that
Chamberlain's proposals were excellent, particularly in their provision
for contributory old-age pensions.[67] He was critical, however, of certain
aspects of the bill; and these criticisms are of some significance, not
because they had any immediate impact but because they were to be
echoed many years later in the Beveridge report. At a conference of the
London Council of Social Service he condemned the granting of pensions to young, childless widows—who should he thought be encouraged
to re-enter the labour market rather than to live off public funds. He
criticized Chamberlain's decision to lower the pension age from 70 to
65, arguing that the decline in fertility and mortality ought to lead to a
lengthening rather than shortening of the working life. He thought that
the projected benefits (10s. for pensioners and widows, 3s. to 7s. for

[65] *Insurance for All and Everything*, p. 23.    [66] P. M. Williams, op. cit., p. 416, fn. 2.
[67] BP, IIa, ms. notes on 'Widows and Orphans Insurance Scheme', early or mid 1925.

orphans) would be too high in the countryside and too low in the towns. More provocatively, he suggested that no true system of 'all-in' insurance would ever be achieved until some attempt was made to regulate the surpluses of rich approved societies, and to utilize those surpluses for the community at large.[68]

Beveridge from this time onwards was widely regarded as an expert not merely on unemployment insurance but on all aspects of social security. He was invited to take part in numerous inquiries on social insurance questions, and was frequently consulted by representatives of foreign governments.[69] Yet, as he himself acknowledged, his reputation in this area was not really justified. He had little time to keep abreast of changing ideas in social security or to master the increasing intricacy of social insurance programmes. He declined to take part in the 1925 Royal Commission on National Health Insurance, on the ground that he had 'no direct knowledge' of this area of social administration.[70] At one stage he was pressed by a group of Liberals to support a proposal from Seebohm Rowntree for earnings-related insurance; but he replied that he was 'too busy' to consider Rowntree's scheme.[71] Moreover, as the depression lengthened Beveridge was increasingly concerned less with the extension of social insurance than with resisting the erosion of the basic insurance principles that he had helped to lay down in 1911. Those principles had prescribed that a man's entitlement to benefit should be arithmetically linked to the number of his contributions. Benefits were to be paid for a strictly limited period, and they were always to be preceded by a test of willingness to work. The history of unemployment insurance throughout the 1920s consisted of a series of largely futile attempts to adapt these cautious principles to the procrustean bed of chronic depression. It involved a prolonged struggle between the unemployed and the national exchequer, between voters and taxpayers, and between rival conceptions of social welfare—between relief modelled on the actuarial logic of private insurance and relief paid unconditionally as a citizen right. The result of this struggle was a series of grudging concessions to the unemployed, which gradually transformed the basic structure of the system set up in 1911. 'Uncovenanted benefit' for those who had exhausted their formal entitlement was introduced in 1921. It was initially discretionary and confined to a limited period, but three years later it was made non-discretionary and unlimited in duration. The level of unemployment benefit was gradually raised

---

[68] *The Social Service Bulletin*, London Supplement, June 1925.
[69] BP, IIb, T. Mayeda to WHB, 29 Nov. 1922; Joseph Cohen to WHB, 19 Nov. 1924; C. Matthews to WHB, Mar. 1925; Joseph Chamberlain to WHB, 7 Aug. 1930 and 22 June 1931.
[70] BP, IIb, WHB to E. Hackforth, 13 Jan. 1925.
[71] BP, IIb, WHB to Walter Isaac, 18 Feb. 1924.

considerably higher than sickness benefit, and allowances for dependants were introduced in 1922. In 1927 a committee under Lord Blanesborough recommended the abolition of any formal relationship between a man's contributions and entitlement to benefit. Benefit was henceforth to be payable for an unlimited period to any unemployed person who had paid a minimum of fifteen weeks' contributions in the previous year; and for those who could not meet even this requirement, a system of 'transitional' benefits was recommended, as a temporary expedient until trade revived. These proposals were enacted by the Conservative government in 1927, and further extended by Labour in 1929 and 1930. The result was an enormous deficit in the unemployment fund, which was at least partly responsible for the economic and political crisis of 1931.[72]

Until 1924 Beveridge had been optimistic about the capacity of unemployment insurance to cope with new conditions. From 1924 onwards, however, he was increasingly alarmed at the continuous retreat from orthodox insurance principles. He was highly critical of the first Labour government for indefinitely extending uncovenanted benefit without providing compulsory re-training for the long-term unemployed.[73] At the same time he denounced the introduction of the notorious 'genuinely seeking-work clause', arguing that the clause made 'compulsory that hawking of labour at the factory gates which was emphatically condemned by the Poor Law Commission twenty years ago'.[74] He was even more critical of the Conservative government which in 1927 'on the bad advice of the rather stupid Blanesborough Committee . . . formally divorced the claim to benefit from payments of contributions'. Beveridge was convinced that unlimited benefit was potentially highly demoralizing, not merely to recipients, but to trade unionists, employers, governments and the community at large. It encouraged reckless wage-demands and lack of concern about throwing fellow-employees out of work. It fostered the view that a workman had an inalienable right to a place in a particular industry, regardless of any demand for his services, as a kind of feudal fief. And, worst of all in Beveridge's eyes, it acted as an anodyne against more drastic reforms. 'The trouble with the insurance system today', he wrote to Winston Churchill in 1930,

is not merely or mainly the maintenance of people [who are] unemployable, but the fact that with its flat rate of contributions for an unlimited benefit, it

[72] Bentley B. Gilbert, op. cit., pp. 75–97, 162–75; Robert Skidelsky, *Politicians and the Slump* (1970 edn.), ch. 13.

[73] BP, IIb, Hubert Henderson to WHB, 7 Nov. 1930.

[74] W. H. Beveridge, *The Past and Present of Unemployment Insurance*, Sidney Ball Lecture, 7 Feb. 1930.

subsidises the casual and disorganised industries (dock labour, building, works of construction, cotton) at the expense of other industries, and this perpetuates measures of industrial disorganisation. All unemployment policies of 1909 which aimed at diminishing unemployment, such as de-casualisation and organisation of the labour market, have been neglected in favour of extension of benefit, and now adoption is made harder by it.[75]

Beveridge's own prescription for the relief of unemployment was not a strict return to actuarial principles of the kind that governed the private market. He acknowledged that unemployment insurance was not precisely analogous to private insurance, since unemployment was not a calculable risk and its relief involved social as well as commercial goals.[76] Instead he argued that insurance should be supplemented by the policies that he and the Webbs had advocated twenty years earlier—in particular, the concentration of public works into periods of slack demand, the development of the 'job-placement' functions of labour exchanges, and reform of the Poor Law to cope with the 'unemployable' and the long-term unemployed. Such policies, he claimed, would increase labour mobility and discourage workmen from clinging to industries in which there was no demand for them. They would enable the authorities to detect and punish the small minority of habitual malingerers, who were battering on the insurance fund and giving the unemployed an undeservedly bad name. And they would enable the insurance system to be restored to its original function of 'spreading wages over good times and bad' and relieving regular workmen during temporary fluctuations. These views were clearly spelt out in his comments on a draft of the Webbs' *History of the Poor Law* in 1928. 'I've read the unemployment chapter with greatest interest and ninety-nine per cent agreement,' he wrote to Beatrice Webb.

Most particularly do I agree on the main final conclusion as to the need to fit Labour Exchanges and Unemployment Insurance into a general Framework of Prevention. Not doing so has meant that insurance gets diverted from its primary purpose of tiding over temporary idleness and gets strained into a general provision for every varying type of unemployment. It's the evil of the General Mixed Workhouse again.[77]

There were, however, a number of obstacles to applying the policies of 1909 to the problem of unemployment as it appeared twenty years later. Contra-cyclical public expenditure, however desirable as a device for stabilizing labour demand, could not cure unemployment that was not cyclical but permanent. Beveridge does not appear to have supported the kind of public works programmes advocated by Lloyd George and

---

[75] BP, IIb, WHB to W. S. Churchill, 5 Feb. 1930.
[76] BP, IIb, WHB to Glenn Bowers, 16 Mar. 1927.
[77] BP, IIb, WHB to B. Webb, 23 Apr. 1928.

Oswald Mosley, which were designed not merely to regulate but to increase employment by massive 'deficit-spending'. In the absence of such policies, however, the 'job-placement' functions of labour exchanges became little more than a farce; labour exchange officials could not streamline the labour market nor test 'willingness to work' if no work was available. More fundamentally, it was highly questionable just how far and in what manner the Poor Law could be 'reformed' in a political democracy. The Webbs themselves were increasingly conscious of this problem, which they had largely ignored in 1909, and it was partially responsible for their ultimate conversion to Soviet communism. The relaxation of both Poor Law and insurance, wrote Mrs. Webb to Beveridge in 1929, had come about 'not from any process of thought but from a vague drift into what is considered "philanthropic" and "advanced"'.[78] Four years later she had come to the conclusion that any attempt to stiffen the conditions for insurance and to transfer the able-bodied to the Poor Law would merely 'intensify the evil effects of democratic electorates and . . . will end in a sort of Class War'.[79]

Beveridge, however, continued to hope that a rigorous demarcation between insurance and relief could be achieved within the context of the existing political system. Rather paradoxically he now adhered even more closely to the views expressed in the Minority Report on the Poor Laws than he had done in 1909—when he had hoped that labour exchanges would obviate the need for many of the coercive residual policies suggested by the Webbs. His proposals for reform were spelt out in detail in his evidence to the Holman Gregory Commission on Unemployment Insurance in March 1931. He made a number of suggestions for preventing unemployment, of which the most notable were the provision of public works in depressed areas and the extension to manual workers of the kind of job-security enjoyed by salaried employees— although he thought that the latter principle was 'too revolutionary' to be applied instantaneously throughout industry. The main burden of his evidence, however, concerned the prevailing crisis in the system of insurance, which he ascribed to the fact that many different types of unemployment—structural, cyclical, casual and voluntary—were in practice being treated as one. The remedy, he suggested, lay in classification of the unemployed into three different groups, and the provision of maintenance by three strictly-demarcated administrative systems. The first group, consisting of men who had every hope of regaining work, would be relieved by an insurance system administered according to the principles laid down in 1911. In other words they would draw benefit as a contractual right, limited only by the number of their

[78] BP, IIb, B. Webb to WHB, 4 May 1927.
[79] BP, IIb, B. Webb to WHB, n.d. (*c.* Aug. 1931).

contributions. In addition, Beveridge proposed that the level of contributions within a particular industry should be adjusted according to its prevailing level of unemployment, so as to convert insurance from a 'tax on employment' into a 'tax on dismissals'. In industries where dismissals were abnormally frequent, the Ministry of Labour could intervene— via the local employment exchange—to compel decasualization and prevent any further recruitment of labour. The second group of unemployed would consist of those who had exhausted their benefit rights and had little immediate prospect of regaining employment. Such men were to be relieved not as a matter of contractual right but as a matter of administrative discretion. They would not be entitled to insist on work at their former wages or in their former trade, and might be required to undergo industrial training. The third group would consist of men who, either through infirmity or because they had 'lost their taste for work', were unlikely ever to regain regular employment. Of these men the infirm would be relieved by public assistance committees; the able-bodied who refused work would be handed over to penal labour colonies and other forms of corrective institution. The administration of these three different types of relief should, Beveridge suggested, be entrusted to three entirely separate authorities. The third group, consisting of the infirm and the work-shy, should be dealt with by the reformed Poor Law. The first and second groups should be dealt with by two statutory commissions, each attached to the Ministry of Labour but not directly responsible to Parliament. These commissions would have the constitutional status of public corporations, such as the Central Electricity Board and the B.B.C. Their powers and functions would be defined by legislation, but their treatment of individual cases would not be subject to parliamentary scrutiny and their levels of benefit would not be affected by swings of government policy or changes of the party in power.[80]

Quite how far Beveridge's evidence to the Royal Commission influenced subsequent policy is a matter for conjecture. Several members of the Commission were clearly startled by the stern and uncompromising character of some of Beveridge's proposals,[81] and though some of his ideas were embodied in the Commission's final report, others were rejected. The report recommended that unlimited insurance rights should be abolished and that a statutory commission should be set up to restore the insurance fund to financial solvency. For workmen who had exhausted their right to benefit, the report suggested discretionary relief through local authority committees. Encouragement was given to government re-training centres, but no mention was made of compul-

---

[80] *RC on Unemployment Insurance*, Paper 42, and *Minutes of Evidence*, QQ. 5,838–6,097.
[81] Ibid. QQ 5,882, 6,057–8, 6,081–97.

sory labour colonies either for habitual malingerers or for the long-term unemployed.[82] The Holman Gregory report came too late, however, to make much impact on government policy, and by the time it was published the Treasury and Ministry of Labour were already preparing legislation to separate insurance from non-contractual relief.[83] The new legislation bore a certain resemblance to Beveridge's evidence before the Royal Commission;[84] but ideas of this kind had been put forward by a number of different authorities in Whitehall over the previous ten years.[85] The Act restored the contractual basis of insurance and created two new authorities—an Unemployment Insurance Statutory Committee which was to manage the insurance fund, and an Unemployment Assistance Board, which was to administer discretionary relief. Under the Unemployment Assistance Board means-tested relief to the able-bodied became a charge on the national exchequer, although payments were made through local offices and subject to local tribunals. The Unemployment Insurance Statutory Committee was more limited in its powers and functions; it was merely to advise the Minister of Labour on questions relating to unemployment insurance, and to suggest changes in levels of benefit and contribution that would maintain the solvency of the fund.

Beveridge was at first rather sceptical of the value of a statutory committee with a purely advisory rather than administrative role.[86] In June 1934, however, he was offered the post of part-time paid chairman of the new Statutory Committee—a post which he accepted and was to hold for the next ten years. The rest of the Committee consisted of six unpaid 'lay members', and a full-time secretary from the Ministry of Labour. In spite of Beveridge's initial misgivings he soon found that even in an advisory capacity the Committee was able to wield considerable power. The Minister was not obliged to accept the Committee's advice, but nor was he allowed to let the Fund run into debt—with the result that only once was the Committee's advice rejected, throughout the ten years of Beveridge's chairmanship.[87] The Committee was fortunate in that it started its work during a mild trade boom; and the upward trend of employment was maintained throughout the 1930s, first by the housing programme and later by rearmament. The result was that the fund enjoyed an annual surplus of income over expenditure,

[82] Cmd. 4185 (1932), *RC on Unemployment Insurance, Final Report*, pp. 162, 169–71, 332–4.

[83] Bentley B. Gilbert, op. cit., pp. 178–9.

[84] John D. Millett, *The Unemployment Assistance Board. A Case Study in Administrative Autonomy* (1940), p. 30.

[85] e.g. by the Anderson Committee of 1924. Beveridge himself was doubtful whether his proposals had been at all influential (*PI*, p. 225).

[86] BP, IIb, WHB's replies to a questionnaire from the National Liberal Federation, 5 Jan. 1933.

[87] *PI*, p. 227.

and the Committee was able to recommend a long series of extensions in the scope of insurance benefit. Basic benefits were restored to their 1931 level in 1935, and further increased in 1938. The 'benefit year' was increased to thirty weeks in any one year, and the 'waiting period' before which a person became entitled to benefit was reduced from six days to three. Large sums were allocated to repayment of the fund's pre-1934 inheritance of capital debt. Agricultural labourers were brought into unemployment insurance for the first time under a special scheme started in 1936; and plans were made for extension of insurance to certain groups of the self-employed.[88]

By its terms of reference the Statutory Committee was only required to balance the fund on a yearly basis, but Beveridge soon persuaded the other members that they should plan ahead for periods of depression.[89] He devised estimates of future expenditure, based on the assumption of an eight-year cycle of trade; and in order to gear the fund to this cycle the committee applied to the Minister of Labour for wider powers than they had initially been given under the Unemployment Act. Late in 1934 they were allowed to build up a 'depression reserve', and to invest part of their income in high-yield long-dated investments as well as in Treasury bonds.[90] The aim of this policy was to build up 'a working balance of not less than half the sum required for the worst emergency', and to obviate the need to lower benefits and raise contributions during the slump that was expected in 1941.[91] In the event such precautions were rendered unnecessary by the outbreak of war, but the logic behind the policy deserves comment. On one level, Beveridge's policy had an almost Gladstonian ring of old-fashioned financial orthodoxy. It was forcibly opposed to the new heresy of deficit-spending—a point on which members of the Committee took pride in being even more traditional than the Treasury itself.[92] On another level, however Beveridge's policy may be seen as foreshadowing later proposals that insurance benefit should be used as a form of economic regulator. He did not suggest that benefits should be raised to offset trade depression; but he did suggest that it would positively reinforce depression if benefits were lowered during periods of slack demand.[93]

Beveridge's work for the Statutory Committee was highly significant in several ways—of which perhaps the least important was his eventual

[88] *Reports of the Unemployment Insurance Statutory Committee*, 1935–9.

[89] PRO, PIN 7/212, 'Preparation of Report on the Financial Condition of the Unemployment Fund', by WHB, n.d. (late 1934).

[90] Ibid., WHB to Oliver Stanley, 15 Oct. 1934; Oliver Stanley to WHB, 31 Oct. 1934.

[91] Ibid., 'Finance of the Unemployment Fund—Experience and Prospects', by WHB, 14 Jan. 1935.

[92] Mary Stocks, *My Commonplace Book* (1970), p. 169.

[93] PRO, PIN 7/212, 'Finance of the Unemployment Fund—Experience and Prospects', by WHB, 14 Jan. 1935.

success in restoring financial solvency. Each year before advising the minister the Committee canvassed opinion among trade unionists, employers, and social welfare agencies on how the fund should be administered and whether contributions and benefits should be lowered or raised. On several occasions the Committee carried out on-the-spot inquiries into social insurance problems. In 1936 for instance Beveridge and Mary Stocks—one of the Committee's two 'statutory women'—toured fishing ports in Scotland, Devon and Cornwall to investigate the question of providing insurance for self-employed 'share fishermen'. They visited fish-markets, interviewed fishermen and discussed the problem with local insurance officials.[94] Beveridge himself, as chairman of the Committee, was frequently invited to broadcast on social security questions for the B.B.C.; and his talks attracted a shoal of letters from members of the public, including unemployed workers and their wives. 'I am asking you if a surplus is available to remove the six waiting days,' wrote a typical correspondent from Suffolk,

In my opinion they are quite as big a curse as the Means Test. I wishes sometimes my husband didn't like work, a sinful thing to wish I know, but if he was constantly unemployed we should get a weekly income; half a loaf is better than none at all, Rent, Rates, light, fire and clubs etc., have all got to be met during the 6 waiting days. . . . I might have asked for a letter to be sent to you through some political organisation, but I thought I could explain to you how these waiting days affects the home and makes a man afraid of work. Hoping I have made the facts clear to you. Thanking you in anticipation of their removal.[95]

This direct contact with popular attitudes towards social security perceptibly modified the rather doctrinaire approach that Beveridge had adopted before the Holman Gregory Commission in 1931. He was greatly impressed by the strength of support for insurance among the organized working class, and by their willingness, even eagerness, to pay larger contributions for broader coverage—in striking contrast to the widespread hostility to insurance that he had found in 1916.[96] He was impressed also by evidence of growing pressure for extension of insurance to the 'excluded classes'—particularly white-collar workers and the self-employed. He gradually became convinced that the problems of malingering and refusal of suitable employment were much less

[94] Mary Stocks, op. cit., p. 170.
[95] PRO, PIN 7/216, Mrs. A. Allborough to the U.I.S.C., 12 Nov. 1936. See also BP, IIb, H. Clifton to WHB, Apr. 1935; Mary Smith to WHB, 30 Oct. 1936; E. Watts to WHB, 1 Nov. 1936.
[96] *Oxford Times*, 29 Apr. 1938, report of speech by WHB to Oxford and District Local Employment Committee.

widespread than was frequently imagined.[97] And, for the first time, he gained direct practical insight into the impact of job insecurity upon working-class budgets and the structure of family life.

These experiences help to explain Beveridge's gradual transformation from the narrowly orthodox economist of 1931 to the radical social reformer of eleven years later. He himself recorded that they 'carried me back to my first love in social problems'. They helped also to foster a greatly improved relationship between Beveridge and some of the leaders of the trade union movement—a relationship that was to form 'an admirable foundation for the discussions of social insurance that were to follow in 1942'.[98] Another important aspect of his work for the Statutory Committee was that it focused his attention on many of the practical administrative problems that he tried to resolve in the 1942 Beveridge Report. Commenting on a draft insurance bill in 1932 he had remarked rather ruefully that he was 'increasingly ignorant of an increasingly complex subject';[99] but over the next few years he was continually grappling with some of the underlying problems of extending and rationalizing the system of social security. His efforts to make insurance independent of fluctuations in employment have already been discussed. He was highly critical of the anomaly that basic unemployment benefit was now more than twice as high as sickness benefit—even though the needs of the sick were often greater than those of the unemployed.[100] He was increasingly conscious of the problems posed by the relationship between benefit and wages, and by the fact that in low-paid industries a man with a family might get more when unemployed than his earnings when in work.[101] Beveridge was reluctant to impose a 'wage-stop' of the kind used by the U.A.B.; and he therefore came to the conclusion that a proper margin between benefits and wages could only be ensured by universal family allowances, paid irrespective of whether a worker was employed or unemployed. It was for this reason that in his annual report for 1937 Beveridge endorsed the view of the Family Endowment Society that insurance benefits should henceforth be considered, not in isolation, but in relation to all aspects of the total problem of poverty.[102]

In all these ways Beveridge's work for the Statutory Committee foreshadowed his work for the Committee on Social Insurance and Allied

---

[97] PRO, PIN 7/214, 'Enquiry as to whether Difficulty has Arisen in Low Wage Areas in Getting Men with High Weekly Rates of Benefit to take Employment', n.d.; BP, IIb, WHB to Sir James Lithgow, 19 Jan. 1938.

[98] *PI*, p. 226.

[99] BP, IIb, WHB to T. W. Phillips, 14 Dec. 1932.

[100] BP, IIb, WHB to Mary Smith, 2 Nov. 1936.

[101] PRO, PIN 7/217, 'Early Thoughts on Agriculture', by WHB, 28 Nov. 1938.

[102] *Report of the Unemployment Insurance Statutory Committee,* for the year ending 31 Dec. 1937, p. 24.

Services, which produced the Beveridge Report of 1942. Moreover, on both committees Beveridge forcefully imposed the unmistakable imprint of his own personality. On both committees he went far outside the terms of reference initially laid down for him. On both committees he was avidly concerned not merely with shaping political decisions but with 'educating the public and arousing discussion'.[103] And on both committees he tended to brush aside the views of members who disagreed with him—such as Mary Stocks' proposal in 1936 that benefits should be equalized for both men and women.[104] 'Nothing in the world will ever deter you from writing the Report of the Unemployment Insurance Statutory Committee . . . before you have heard a scrap of evidence, or before any ordinary member has begun to think about it,' commented a Ministry of Labour official with friendly sarcasm in 1938.[105] 'Seeing Beveridge at work week by week was a memorable experience,' recorded Mary Stocks.

. . . he could take the bit between his teeth and plunge forward into wider regions than anything foreseen by those who designed his harness . . . during the ten years of my membership Beveridge transformed the Statutory Committee from an annually reporting watchdog intended to keep the fund decently in balance . . . into a policy making body with a long-term plan relating to the whole problem of unemployment in relation to public finance.[106]

[103] PRO, PIN 7/214, WHB to M. Stocks, 16 May 1935.
[104] Mary Stocks, op. cit., p. 169.
[105] PRO, PIN 7/217, A. C. Reeder to WHB, 28 Nov. 1928.
[106] Mary Stocks, op. cit., pp. 168–9.

# 15

## Oxford and War

### I

THE late 1930s, Beveridge observed in his memoirs, saw the gradual eclipse of various illusions that had amused the world and me, since the Armistice of 1918'.[1] At the time, however, it seemed to him at least briefly a period of hope and of considerable personal happiness.[2] He took on a new lease of life from his return to Oxford, and he found the fellows of University College highly congenial—in particular, the reader in politics, G. D. H. Cole. Beveridge had previous regarded Cole as an unsound and dangerous eccentric,[3] but now in his late fifties he began to develop a close intellectual sympathy and warm regard for this lifelong critic of the over-bureaucratized administrative state. At the end of his first year in office he was reported by Cole to be 'a great success as Master and very happy'. He derived great pleasure from some of the more personal aspects of college government, such as the election of scholars and presentation of clerical livings; and he was delighted with his new students who 'welcomed him as a father and adviser' and 'all rose and greeted him respectfully and affectionately' when he entered a room! He was delighted also with the 'perfect physical surroundings' of the Master's lodging—a 'Victorian Tudor manor-house', where he was looked after by Mrs. Mair's youngest daughter, Elspeth. From the outbreak of war Mrs. Mair herself moved into the lodgings, thereby reputedly outraging the 'lady censors of the University world'. She also antagonized many of Beveridge's colleagues by her attempts to interfere in college affairs. But Beveridge himself would brook no criticism of Mrs. Mair. The slight estrangement that had arisen between them in the early 1930s had vanished, and as in earlier years he was happy for her to dominate his social life. He was 'in high spirits', recorded Beatrice Webb, 'thoroughly enjoying his new life as Master of University College, Oxford; an easy job, within a cultured and well-mannered group; dignity and prestige without any particular responsibility or hard work; able to concentrate on his statistical investigation of prices and trade cycles. . . . What a change from the

[1] *PI*, p. 167.
[2] Passfield Papers, II, 4, k, 65, WHB to B. Webb, 21 Dec. 1937.
[3] BP, IIb, WHB to A. J. Carlyle, 21 July 1924.

turbulent atmosphere and continuous work and friction of the London School of Economics.'[4]

Beveridge's satisfaction with his life in Oxford was reflected also in a revival of his confidence in academic social science. He was involved in the planning of Nuffield College and had great hopes that Nuffield would succeed in establishing a neutral and empirical social science tradition where the L.S.E. had failed.[5] For the first time for years, moreover, he was able to concentrate on his long-cherished ambition of unlocking the secrets of the trade-cycle. The first volume of his price-history was ready for publication in 1938, and he started work on a new study of trends in unemployment—a study that was purposely designed to correct the methodological heresies of Keynes' *General Theory*. To assist him in these inquiries Beveridge employed a young economist from Jesus College, Harold Wilson—who, Beveridge recorded approvingly, 'has a good head, is extremely methodical and is prepared to work really hard'.[6] Wilson compiled an immense mass of unemployment statistics, toured labour exchanges to extract information about filling of vacancies, and confirmed Beveridge's favourite hypothesis that fluctuations in employment were linked with the price of wheat. 'Your forecast of the nature of the elephant upholding the world thus appears to be vindicated,' Wilson reported to Beveridge in September 1938. 'The next step will be the tortoise on whom the world stands—in other words the cause of the fall in agricultural purchasing power.'[7] Wilson's conclusion—that depressions were sparked off by a decline in employment in exporting industries, which in turn was caused by a decline in demand among primary-producing countries—was ultimately to form an important part of Beveridge's study of *Full Employment* which appeared in 1944.[8] Beveridge himself meanwhile was off on another tack. 'I am enjoying myself immoderately with proving the periodicity of the weather,' he wrote to Wilson '. . . I have discovered within the last few days what seems to me convincing evidence of the reality of a weather cycle which I discovered seventeen years ago, affecting the harvests at least of the Eastern hemisphere and I am very much excited about it.'[9] The explanation of this periodicity Beveridge believed might lie in the Jevonian theory of 'sun-spots'; and Harold Wilson has put on record a humorous description of his frantic and ultimately successful efforts to lure Beveridge away from this statistical red-herring. Wilson has also given us an illuminating picture of their work together at Mrs.

[4] Passfield Papers, B. Webb's diary, 1 May 1937, 5 July and 10 Aug. 1938.
[5] Passfield Papers, II, 4, k, 65, WHB to B. Webb, 21 Dec. 1937.
[6] BP, VII 49, WHB to H. A. L. Fisher, 25 Nov. 1937.
[7] BP, VII 49, H. Wilson to WHB, 20 Sept. 1938.
[8] *Full Employment in a Free Society*, pp. 294–306.
[9] BP, VII 49, WHB to H. Wilson, 10 Sept. 1938.

Mair's cottage in Avebury. Beveridge would rise at six and take an icy
bath, before putting in two hours work before breakfast. He was viewed
by his research assistants as a mingled source of inspiration and terror;
and he made no secret of the fact that any 'slackness during working-
hours' was a 'form of sinful self-indulgence'. At the same time he was
'utterly self-sacrificing' in his search for the solution of problems and for
objective statistical truth.[10]

## II

In view of Beveridge's stern criticism of academics who engaged in
political action, and in view of his oft-expressed desire to devote himself
exclusively to research, it might have been expected that his return to
Oxford would have marked the end of his involvement in questions of
public policy. That this was not so may be explained in a number of
ways. Firstly, in spite of his frequent protestations to the contrary,
Beveridge did not really have a calling for a life of scholarship. Men's
desires may not be judged entirely by their actions, but no one who
rejected the opportunity of a life of pure scholarship so frequently as
Beveridge did can be seen as having a vocation in that direction.
He was always much happier when directly involved in practical
problems; and, in spite of his devotion to the trade-cycle, he soon found
that as a master of an Oxford college many of his most positive faculties
were frustrated and under-engaged. He continued to act as part-time
Chairman of the Unemployment Insurance Statutory Committee—even
during the autumn of 1938 when he was ill for several months with a
viral infection and had to conduct the affairs of the committee from a
hospital bed. But these activities by no means exhausted his desire for
practical action, and from the start of his career at University College he
was constantly looking round for further opportunities to influence
public affairs. The second point to be emphasized is that Beveridge's
actions were by no means always consistent with his political beliefs.
He was rarely inhibited by his own doctrine that social scientists should
refrain from prescribing a course of political action, and his anxiety
about the inherent contradictions of middle-of-the-road welfare
capitalism was increasingly tempered by a burning personal desire to
'get things done'. As we have seen, during the late 1930s his work for the
Statutory Committee gradually revived his earlier interest in questions
of social welfare; and at the same time his scepticism of state planning
was gradually eroded by the growing threat of war.

Beveridge's transformation from critic of welfare capitalism in the

---

[10] Harold Wilson, *Beveridge Memorial Lecture*, pp. 3–5, 16.

mid-1930s to its most archetypal exponent in the early 1940s must be directly related to the context of war. Since 1934 he had been a consistent though regretful opponent of appeasement; and, as was shown earlier, he had hoped in 1936 to be placed in charge of organizing the 'home front'. These hopes had come to nothing; but since that time Beveridge had continually pressed both in public and private for more constructive official preparation for the outbreak of war—in particular for measures to secure civilian welfare in the likely event of massive aerial bombardment. He denounced the 'Laodicean permanent secretaries and ministers' who dominated Whitehall, and supplied them with a stream of unsolicited advice on such questions as the evacuation of London, the dispersal of food storage, strategic weaknesses in transport and communications and the transfer of the British aircraft industry to North America.[11] At the same time he wrote a series of articles for *The Times*, once again urging the government to prepare plans for food control and mass evacuation and to appoint an Economic General Staff.[12] His ultimate though still reluctant conversion to a philosophy of 'planning' was signalized by an essay in a book on *Constructive Democracy*, published in 1938. In this he argued that planning had ceased to be a matter of ideological preference and had become a prerequisite of national survival. There was, he still thought, a 'natural incompatibility' between planning and democracy, but this should be overcome by the artificial development of new political and research institutions; planners must learn to adapt to democracy like swimmers under water and patients in iron lungs.[13] *Constructive Democracy* was based on a series of public lectures given by a wide range of well-meaning intellectuals in politics, from Lord Halifax to Clement Attlee, and was generally dismissed by critics as 'unbearably gentle and genteel'.[14] Beveridge's contribution was, however, singled out by commentators of both right and left as challenging the stagnant complacency of the Chamberlain government. 'Across this galaxy of high-minded agreement Sir William Beveridge shoots like an angry comet,' observed Richard Crossman, in an otherwise scathing review. '. . . Here at last, you feel is someone talking and talking angrily, out of his experience. For the moment you feel the swish of controversy before you see once more the pallid steady light of Mr. Henderson of All Souls.'[15]

Beveridge's conversion to centralized planning was reinforced by the outbreak of war in 1939. As in the First World War he was

[11] BP, IIb, WHB to Sir Edward Grigg, 25 Feb. 1937; WHB to Sir Thomas Inskip, 13 Apr. 1938.

[12] *The Times*, 22–4 Feb. 1937.

[13] Sir Ernest Simon et al. *Constructive Democracy* (1938), pp. 125–43.

[14] Review by Denis Brogan, *Fortnightly Review*, Apr. 1938.

[15] R. H. S. Crossman, 'Sedatives, Mild and Strong', *New Statesman*, 19 Feb. 1938.

convinced of the need for government control of all national resources—human, economic and financial—and from the start of the war he pressed for the adoption of a number of policies which he believed were justified by the experience of 1914 to 1918. In this he was actively encouraged by Jessy Mair, who urged upon him the need for a 'Bolshie policy' of 'national service' and 'equality of sacrifice'.[16] In a series of articles and letters to leading civil servants he called for radical changes in the structure of wartime government—in particular for a small War Cabinet of ministers free from departmental duties and advised by an Economic General Staff.[17] He urged the new Ministry of Food to avoid half-measures and to learn from the historical example of Devonport and Rhondda.[18] He was more cautious than he had been in the previous war about government control of labour; but nevertheless, he called for compulsory arbitration, statutory control of wages and prohibition of strikes. To reconcile the trade union movement to this loss of peacetime privileges he proposed a wide range of emergency social policies—family allowances, extension of school meals, subsidies on food and highly progressive taxation.[19] Finally, he advocated the advance planning of an ambitious programme of post-war reconstruction. Such a programme, he claimed, would avert the economic catastrophies of the 1920s, provide psychological encouragement to soldiers and workers, and help people to know not merely 'what they were fighting against but what they were fighting for'.[20] It was to be a programme, moreover, considerably more egalitarian and collectivist than anything he had been prepared to consider in the pre-war years. 'I don't think Communism as such is an evil,' he wrote to Beatrice Webb early in 1940. 'I would very much like to see Communism tried under democratic conditions.' 'Beveridge is today a Socialist,' commented Mrs. Webb a few months later; 'He agrees that there must be a revolution in the economic structure of society.'[21]

From the start of the war Beveridge hoped that he himself would be recalled to Whitehall to take part in wartime government; and, in particular, he hoped that he might be placed in charge of either distribution of manpower or economic planning. For a long time, however, his hopes were doomed to disappointment. During the early months of war he

[16] Lady Beveridge Papers, J. Mair to WHB, 3 Apr. 1939.

[17] BP, IIb, WHB to Lord Hankey, 4 Sept. 1939; WHB to Sir Horace Wilson, 3 Oct. 1939; *The Times*, 3 Oct. 1939 and 6 Feb. 1940.

[18] BP, IIb, WHB to W. W. Astor, 19 Oct. 1939; WHB to Alan Lennox-Boyd, 23 Oct. 1939; WHB to Sir Henry French, 9 Apr. 1940.

[19] BP, IXb 54, Script of broadcast on 'The Economic War' for B.B.C. Home Service, n.d.; *The Times*, 12 Jan. 1940.

[20] BP, IIb, WHB to Lord Halifax, 4 Mar. 1940.

[21] Passfield Papers, II, 4, L, 74, WHB to B. Webb, 21 Feb. 1940; B. Webb's diary, 11 Aug. 1940.

bombarded government departments with offers of assistance, but all these offers were politely but firmly rejected.[22] This rejection was a severe blow to Beveridge, not merely because he was anxious to be useful but because he was convinced that 'the present crew have no conception at all of how to plan for war'.[23] Beveridge's experience was shared by other veterans of First World War administration such as Keynes, Layton and Salter; and throughout the autumn and winter of 1939–40 this group of 'ancient warhorses' met together at Keynes' house in Bloomsbury, where they denounced the Chamberlain government's lack of coherent policy, criticized the dispersal of Whitehall departments to the provinces, and devised alternative strategies for prosecution of the war.[24] From these discussions emerged Keynes' important little book on *How to Pay for the War*, in which he warned the government against the temptations of fiscal drag, and called for policies of high taxation, family allowances, subsidies on food and compulsory wartime savings. At the same time Beveridge became active in the Federal Union—a movement among radical intellectuals for prevention of future wars by the creation of some form of international government among the European and English-speaking countries. Beveridge's ideas on how to avert war were spelt out in a pamphlet on *Peace by Federation*, published in February 1940. In this he assumed that Britain and France would win the war and would be able to dictate the terms of the peace. He proposed that after the war a federation should be formed of the British dominions and European nations—excluding Russia, but possibly including the United States. Each member of the federation would relinquish a large measure of national sovereignity to a federal government, which would exercise supreme control over defence and foreign affairs. Parliamentary democracy would be imposed, by force if necessary, on Germany, Italy and other totalitarian regimes.[25]

Beveridge made numerous speeches on the theme of federation throughout the winter of 1939–40, and in April 1940 he flew to Paris with Lionel Robbins and Barbara Wootton for an international conference of the Federal Union. There he recorded that he found 'nothing but friendliness and great readiness to take the subject most seriously'.[26] With the collapse of the Allied Armies, however, the aims of the Federal Union seemed increasingly academic and Beveridge's criticisms were

[22] BP, IIb, WHB to Ernest Brown, 4 Sept. 1939; WHB to Lord Hankey, 4 and 8 Sept. 1939; WHB to Sir Horace Wilson, 4 and 7 Sept. 1939.
[23] BP, IIb, WHB to Sir Herbert Morgan, 4 Oct. 1939.
[24] BP, IIb, J. M. Keynes to WHB, 30 Sept. 1939 and 15 Apr. 1940; WHB to Walter Layton, n.d. (Oct. 1939); Roy Harrod, *Life of John Maynard Keynes*, pp. 577–8; Lord Salter, *Slave of the Lamp; A Public Servant's Notebook* (1967), p. 88.
[25] *Peace by Federation*, Federal Tracts, no. 1 (1940).
[26] Lady Beveridge Papers, WHB to J. Mair, 13 Apr. 1940.

once again focused on the immediate running of the war. He was increasingly convinced that Whitehall would only be galvanized for wartime measures by a radical change of government—preferably by a coalition with a strong infusion of ministers from the left. He was therefore delighted when Chamberlain resigned to make way for an all-party coalition under Winston Churchill in May 1940. This change he saw as a necessary prelude, both to the more dynamic prosecution of the war and to his own return to Whitehall.[27] A few days after the change of government he wrote to Churchill, reminding him of their 'old association' and of his own special talent for 'devising new types of Government machinery (like unemployment insurance and food rationing) for dealing with new problems'.[28] At the same time he wrote to the new Labour ministers, Attlee, Bevin and Morrison, once again offering his services and spelling out the need for an Economic General Staff.[29] Once again, however, Beveridge's hopes were frustrated. One by one the other old war-horses were absorbed into government—Keynes into the Treasury, Salter into the Admiralty, Layton into the Ministry of Supply—but once again there seemed to be no place for Beveridge. Beveridge was more hurt by this rejection than he cared to reveal to any but his closest friends. Mrs. Mair recorded that he was 'bitterly disappointed' at receiving a 'very damping reply' from Churchill, and 'heartbroken when he heard from Bevin that there was no room for him at the Ministry of Labour.'[30] 'Poor Beveridge was in a state of collapse,' observed Beatrice Webb. 'I have never seen him so despondent about public affairs, so depressed about his own part in bettering them. The collapse of France and the obvious incompetence of our own government and governing class . . . [have] overthrown his old confidence that the Allies would win the war and dictate the peace. What is even more personally depressing is that he has been ignored; his services as an administrator have not been requisitioned.'[31]

Coming at a time when academics of all kinds were flooding into Whitehall, the neglect of Beveridge's services should probably be explained in highly personal terms. One problem was that as an ex-permanent secretary he was much more difficult to place than the average temporary civil servant, since he could scarcely be given less than a fairly senior position. Another problem was that Beveridge himself had fixed ideas about what he wanted to do. He refused, for instance, an invitation from Bevin to take charge of a new welfare department in the Ministry of Labour. 'I didn't feel that welfare was up my street,'

[27] BP, IXa 107, WHB to the Editor of *The Times*, 9 May 1940 (not published).
[28] BP, IIb, WHB to W. S. Churchill, 23 May 1940.
[29] BP, IIb, WHB to C. Attlee, 13 May 1940; WHB to H. Morrison, 13 May 1940.
[30] Lady Beveridge Papers, J. Mair's diary, 27 May, 6 and 7 June 1940.
[31] Passfield Papers, B. Webb's diary, 11 Aug. 1940.

Beveridge significantly recorded, '. . . organisation of manpower was my goal.'[32] Equally important were Beveridge's clumsiness in handling personal relationships, his manifest contempt for many conventional administrative procedures, and his inability to wrap his criticisms of government in a palatable disguise. Thus he annoyed Attlee and Dalton by treating them as though they were still junior lecturers and he the director at the London School of Economics.[33] He made the serious mistake of underestimating Bevin, regarding him merely as a 'powerful personality without any intellect or comprehension of the facts'.[34] He wrote to Sir Horace Wilson, the Permanent Secretary to the Treasury, demanding a return to the dynamic administrative tradition of Morant and Llewellyn-Smith—a demand that may well have been justified but was scarcely calculated to endear him to the most high-ranking official in the British Civil Service.[35] With Churchill his relations had been cordial throughout the inter-war years, but intellectually the two men had travelled along very different paths since their youthful involvement in Edwardian social reform. The war reinforced the divergence in their views, for it confirmed Churchill in his fundamental commitment to traditional values, whereas it induced in Beveridge an almost extrasensory consciousness of revolutionary change. And, much as he welcomed the change of government Beveridge made no secret of his belief that 'we shall need something more revolutionary before very long'.[36] He was, moreover, convinced of the need for an effective opposition, even against an all-party government, to keep ministers on their toes. There was therefore no possibility that Churchill would employ him as a personal adviser as he had done thirty years earlier; and it is clear that Churchill increasingly regarded Beveridge as an impractical visionary, whom the passage of years had rendered 'very long in the tooth'.[37]

## III

Beveridge therefore resigned himself to fighting the war as a private citizen. With other Federal Unionists he took part in a series of conferences in Oxford, which discussed the post-war government of

[32] BP, IIb, E. Bevin to WHB, 5 June 1940; *PI*, p. 272.
[33] Interview with Sir Norman Chester.
[34] Passfield Papers, B. Webb's diary, 11 Aug. 1940.
[35] BP, IIb, 'Note on Planning and Co-ordination' by WHB, 10 June 1940, pp. 11–12.
[36] BP, IIb, WHB to J. L. Garvin, 13 May 1940.
[37] Dalton Papers, Hugh Dalton's diary, 12 May 1942. Churchill's view of Beveridge as an unreliable eccentric may well have been coloured by an ill-timed letter that Beveridge wrote to him in the spring of 1940—predicting on the basis of his research into meteorology that wheat-shortage in Central Europe was about to force the imminent retreat of German troops. (BP, IIb, WHB to W. S. Churchill, 2 May 1940.)

Germany, the drafting of humane peace terms, the creation of a
Federal Europe and measures for the 'disintoxification of the German
mind'.[38] He wrote a series of memoranda and letters to the press, criticizing the Keynsian view that specific direction of manpower was unnecessary, since surplus labour would be automatically absorbed into
the war effort by a mere expansion of aggregate demand.[39] He strongly
attacked the rigid departmentalism of Whitehall and the lack of any
overall planning machinery; and he urged the need for 'drastic measures of taking over businesses on to State account (whether it should be
called State socialism or not) in order to deal with wage and income
problems'. He tried to persuade Hugh Dalton to send him on a mission
to America,[40] and when Dalton did not respond he resolved to visit the
United States in a private capacity to canvass support for American
entry into the war. Then came, however, the opening that Beveridge had
been hoping for and the visit to America was first temporarily and then
indefinitely delayed. In July 1940 Ernest Bevin asked him to carry out a
brief survey of the government's wartime manpower requirements, and
two months later Beveridge was appointed chairman of the Manpower
Requirements committee of the Production Council. Neither of these
posts was particularly important and neither of them carried executive
responsibility, but they gave Beveridge a foothold in his chosen area of
policy. He was furnished with an office in New Scotland Yard, and he
took up residence in the basement of the Reform Club, where he lived
throughout the blitz. He acquired the services of Harold Wilson as
secretary of the manpower committee, and much of the local fieldwork
was done by G. D. H. Cole. Beveridge and Cole were 'working together
and modifying each others' views', commented Beatrice Webb;[41] and it
seems probable that the influence of Cole was at least partially responsible for the marked radicalization of Beveridge's attitudes during this
period. Certainly, as the Webbs remarked, it was a curious alliance, for
twenty years earlier Beveridge had dismissed Cole as a brilliant but
unbalanced revolutionary, whilst Cole as a guild socialist had been a
leading critic of Beveridge's policies at the Ministry of Munitions.
Now, however, Cole showed himself almost as anxious as Beveridge for
total mobilization of the civilian labour market; and Beveridge himself
under Cole's influence became increasingly committed to policies of
radical change.

    [38] *Report of a Conference on the Re-education of the German Mind*, University College, Oxford,
14–15 Dec. 1940. I am grateful to Professor R. Klibansky for lending me his copy of this
report.
    [39] BP, IIb, draft of a letter from WHB to *The Times*, 15 June 1940; typescript note by WHB,
11 June 1940.
    [40] BP, IIb, WHB to Hugh Dalton, 22 June 1940.
    [41] Passfield Papers, B. Webb's diary, 29 June and 11 Aug. 1940.

Almost immediately Beveridge and Cole began to press upon Bevin the need for a clearer definition of essential occupations, for dilution of skilled labour and for a national register of skilled engineers.[42] They urged him also to put pressure on the supply departments to locate new factories in areas with surplus labour capacity and to spread government contracts more widely so as to make optimum use of national manpower supplies.[43] Beveridge's report to Bevin, submitted in October 1940, was a passionate plea for an extension of state control not merely over the civilian labour market but over many other aspects of civilian life. Workers transferred to new government factories must, Beveridge argued, be given facilities for taking their families with them. Those working in high-risk bombing areas should be given adequate protection against air-raids. Special arrangements should be made by the state for feeding and housing those whose work forced them to stay in London, which should henceforth be regarded as part of the 'front line'. 'On no other terms can the continuance of work be demanded or expected,' Beveridge asserted, '. . . the front line is not a fit environment for family life.' The main thrust of his report, however, was reserved for a veiled attack upon the government's lack of a wages policy and the minister's reluctance to exercise control over manpower—a reluctance that Beveridge privately ascribed to Bevin's personal history as a veteran trades unionist and to his continuing identification with trade union interests. 'The actual use of available manpower in Britain today is less complete than it need be,' Beveridge concluded:

mainly because the peace-time economic and political structure of the country has been carried on with too little change into war. There has been too much reliance on individual capitalism with its accompanying machinery of wage bargaining even though the excess profits tax and other financial relations between the state and managers of businesses have deprived both private capitalism and wage bargaining of their logical basis. There has been needless reliance upon the motive of personal gain as the sole basis upon which workmen can be expected to render service to the State.[44]

These arguments were presented in a slightly different form a month later in Beveridge's interim report to the Production Council on behalf of the Manpower Requirements committee. In this report Beveridge estimated that nearly two million additional men and women would be required by the armed services in the following year and that an additional 700,000 workers would be required for war production. Such

[42] BP, VIII 20, 'Industrial Registration, Priorities and Transfer Instructions', by WHB, 24 July 1940.

[43] BP, VIII 20, 'Unused Industrial Capacity', by WHB, 30 July 1940; WHB to E. A. Hitchman, 30 July 1940.

[44] BP, VIII 15, 'Report by the Commissioner for Man-Power Survey', 5 Oct. 1940.

demands could, he thought, be met, but not without a 'revolutionary change in the attitude of managements and in the speed of administrative action'. The essential prerequisites for meeting such demands were widespread dilution, a great expansion of women's employment, an end to the 'hoarding' of skilled labour, the dispersal of factories to areas with surplus labour, and an acceptance by employers of responsibility for on-the-job training of the unskilled. In addition, Beveridge suggested, there should be communal food and sleeping arrangements for all working in dangerous areas, 'combined with similar provision for their families by removal elsewhere'.[45] In the committee's second report, issued in December, Beveridge proposed that 'reserved occupations' should be largely confined to those in which men could not be replaced by women. At the same time he recommended as a general principle of wartime manpower policy that no one should be 'called up' for military service without provision being made for an equivalent expansion in production of weapons. There should be no repetition of the suicidal 'shell scandals' of 1915.[46]

Beveridge's proposals were discussed by the Production Council under the chairmanship of Arthur Greenwood in November and December 1940.[47] The Council consisted of a small nucleus of Cabinet ministers attended by a large contingent of civil servants from the various departments engaged in war production. It was in theory a powerful body, but Greenwood was a notoriously weak chairman and its meetings resulted in little effective discussion. No decisions were reached on Beveridge's reports, and the Council itself was dismantled soon afterwards in response to public criticism of its failure to accelerate industrial expansion.[48] Beveridge's work was not without effect, however, for early in the new year the War Cabinet announced its commitment to the principle that conscription of soldiers should be carefully geared to supply of munitions.[49] Moreover, in December 1940 Beveridge himself became once again a full-time civil servant. He was appointed to an Under-Secretaryship in the Ministry of Labour, in charge of its military service department, and was given the special brief of preparing a schedule of reserved occupations. He spent the next few weeks interviewing representatives of a large number of fringe organizations—such as Jehovah's Witnesses and moral rearmers—who wished to claim

[45] Lloyd Papers, 'Interim Report of the Manpower Requirements Committee', 8 Nov. 1940; and 'Memorandum by the Chairman of the Man Power Requirements Committee on the Practical Problems of Man Power and the Conditions for their Solution', 8 Nov. 1940.

[46] BP, VIII 15, 'Man Power Requirements Committee, Draft Second Report', 4 Dec. 1940.

[47] Lloyd Papers, copy of 'War Cabinet Production Council and Economic Policy Committee', 18th meeting, 12 Nov. 1940.

[48] M. M. Postan, *British War Production* (1952), pp. 141–2.

[49] *PI*, p. 278.

exemption from call-up on conscientious or practical grounds. 'I've no fondness for their form of mental aberration,' he recorded after a meeting with the Moral Rearament movement, 'but a sort of feeling that we oughtn't to make it—or any other form of harmless lunacy— impossible.'[50] His schedule of reserved occupations was approved by Bevin in April 1941, and formed the basis of the call-up for the rest of the war.[51]

Beveridge undoubtedly hoped that in his new post he might soon be placed in charge, not merely of military recruitment but of civilian mobilization. Throughout the early months of 1941 he urged upon Bevin the need for a stringent wages policy, conscription of women and the exercise of detailed state control over direction of labour.[52] To achieve the latter aim he proposed a system of leaving-certificates, similar to those introduced during the First World War, but issued by Ministry of Labour officials rather than individual employers.[53] Once again, however, he was doomed to disappointment. 'I'm being kept firmly to my own job of National Service,' he recorded in February: 'On all the rest of labour policy, Bevin having swallowed it whole and undigested from me has never since asked my opinion.'[54] A few days later he complained that Bevin was 'more anxious to revolutionise the wage system than to do his job of organising labour to win the war. That being so, he'll not use me on labour organisation—apart from the military side—because I wouldn't fit into that aim of his.'[55]

In his private correspondence Beveridge ascribed his exclusion from civilian labour problems to Ernest Bevin's autocratic personality and fear of rivalry from others more capable than himself. He was also highly critical of Bevin's extreme caution in exercising the authority conferred upon him by the Emergency Powers (Defence) Act, and of the slowness and reluctance with which he implemented Beveridge's suggestions about subjecting the civilian labour market to state control.[56] In Beveridge's criticisms there was a grain of truth; yet in making them he was less than just to Bevin, and it is difficult to share his conclusion that Bevin's handling of labour problems in 1940 was markedly inferior to that of Lloyd George in 1915. Bevin, as Beveridge admitted, had accepted in principle virtually all Beveridge's recommendations, and in the discussions of the Production Council in November 1940 he had

---

[50] Lady Beveridge Papers, WHB to J. Mair, 12 Feb. 1941.

[51] H. M. D. Parker, *Man Power, A Study of War-Time Policy and Administration* (1957), pp. 145–6.

[52] Lady Beveridge Papers, WHB to J. Mair, 12 Feb. 1941; *PI*, pp. 279–81.

[53] *PI*, p. 280; Donald Tyerman and Sir William Beveridge, 'The War in the Workshop', *The Listener*, 6 June 1940, p. 1,096.

[54] Lady Beveridge Papers, WHB to J. Mair, 6 Feb. 1941.

[55] Ibid., WHB to J. Mair, 12 Feb. 1941.     [56] *PI*, p. 281.

been the only minister to support Beveridge in his demand for a decisive policy.[57] It is true that he used his statutory powers with great circumspection, but in doing so he successfully avoided many of the bitter conflicts that had bedevilled labour relations during the First World War. Moreover, there were reasons other than Bevin's jealousy of rivals to account for his reluctance to employ Beveridge. It is difficult to know just how far Bevin still blamed Beveridge for the coercive policies of the First World War; but almost certainly he still associated him with policies of wage-control and direction of labour.[58] Moreover, in the light of Beveridge's temperament and past career there was much to be said for the minister's action in using Beveridge to draw up a policy and then firmly excluding him from its detailed execution. As Dalton discovered in rather similar circumstances a year later, it was typical of Beveridge's approach to a problem that, having discovered what he believed to be the best solution, he should demand its immediate and thorough implementation—regardless of any personal and institutional barriers that might stand in the way.[59] Logically it was true, as Beveridge argued, that if total control of the labour market was necessary to deal with the current emergency then it was desirable to introduce it without delay. But politically and historically there was much to be said for Bevin's approach of treating labour problems, not as a question of strict logic, but as a question of continuous diplomatic negotiation.

It was this fundamental difference of approach to policy, at least as much as Bevin's autocratic personality, that stood in the way of Beveridge's realizing his ambition of gaining control of manpower. Moreover, Beveridge himself was temperamentally no more easy to deal with than Ernest Bevin. He found it impossible to conceal his dislike of Bevin, whom he regarded as the personal embodiment of narrow sectarian interests in politics. He was unable to sympathize with Bevin's motives for caution, and he bemoaned the fact that labour policy was getting 'more like Devonport every day'.[60] He tended also to underestimate the tremendous difference which Bevin's mere presence in government had made to labour relations—a difference that could not be measured simply by the scale and pace of administrative innovation.[61] A further complicating factor was the difficulty that Beveridge seemed to find in accepting a subordinate position, and in particular in working under Sir Thomas Phillips, the Ministry's permanent secretary. Phillips had originally been one of the 'bright young men' brought into

[57] Lloyd Papers, 'Conclusions of a Joint Meeting of the Production Council and the Economic Policy Commitee', 12 Nov. 1940, pp. 1–2; H. M. D. Parker, op. cit., p. 107.
[58] Alan Bullock, *The Life and Times of Ernest Bevin*, Vol. II (1967), p. 70. 47–8, 87.
[59] Dalton Papers, Hugh Dalton's diary 8 May, 1942; below, p. 377.
[60] Lady Beveridge Papers, WHB to J. Mair, 12 Feb. 1941.
[61] M. M. Postan, op. cit., p. 145.

labour exchanges by Beveridge himself in 1909, and he had been one of the few senior labour exchange staff to be retained by the Ministry of Labour in 1916. As an administrator he was Beveridge's opposite in almost every possible way—cautious, patient, unimaginative, an excellent agent of other men's ideas. Possibly conscious of this contrast, Phillips throughout his career tended to be unduly squashing of proposals put forward by Beveridge,[62] and it seems unlikely that he advanced Beveridge's interests within the Minister of Labour. Beveridge himself, however, did little to advance those interests either with Phillips or with Bevin himself. He wrote to Churchill behind their backs, complaining about the 'wrong selection' of departmental heads and the dominance in labour policy of 'safe men embedded in the ways of peace rather than dangerous men ready for the rapid decisions required by war'.[63]

I've a little war on with Bevin and Phillips [he recorded], about where I should sit to do my work. They had the neck to meet and decide without reference to me that I was to stay in the Ministry main building and not with my staff. So I went at once to the Minister and told him that he really mustn't decide these things without reference to me—that in the past six months he had sent for me on precisely four occasions nearly all trifling—that I was just as firm in my views as he could possibly be, etc. etc. All this he took in perfectly good part, and it's left either that I shall get my way or he will speak to me again. But of course I shall get my way, and work with my staff—after I've made plain to Phillips how *not* to behave to me.[64]

In view of these personal conflicts it was not perhaps surprising that Bevin, far from employing Beveridge as director of manpower, seems to have been increasingly anxious to get rid of him. In April 1941 Phillips suggested that Beveridge should become the Ministry of Labour's 'thinking department', without executive responsibility—a role very similar to that which had been proposed for Beveridge in the early days of labour exchanges. Beveridge was no more impressed by this suggestion than he had been thirty years before. 'I said I didn't think much of that,' he recorded. 'One couldn't have one man giving ideas to a staff and another giving them orders. I wait for the next move.'[65] Shortly before this, Beveridge had been approached by Lord Nathan with a proposal from Clement Attlee that he should accept a Labour peerage in the birthday honours; and for some weeks he was deeply torn by the advantages and disadvantages afforded by such a move. He was strongly attracted by the forum which he believed the House of Lords would

---

[62] See above, p. 257, and below, p. 422.
[63] BP, IIb, WHB to W. S. Churchill, 27 Apr. 1941.
[64] Lady Beveridge Papers, WHB to J. Mair, 6 Feb. 1941.
[65] Lady Beveridge Papers, WHB to J. Mair, 29 Apr. 1941; above, p. 156.

give him, both for criticizing the wartime government and for influencing the direction of post-war Labour policy. He was intrigued also by a hint thrown out by Nathan that he might well expect to be appointed Minister of Reconstruction. At the same time, however, although he was not at this time a member of the Liberal Party he felt a deep reluctance to abandon his 'Liberal friends'. He was, moreover, embarrassed by the rather crudely implied suggestion that he should join Labour in order to gain a peerage; and he privately confessed that he felt 'no respect for anybody in the present Labour Party—least of all the peers'. He explained some of his difficulties to Attlee at a private meeting in July, and indicated that, although he would be happy to accept a peerage, he could not do so if joining the Labour Party were a necessary prior condition. Once in the Lords, he thought that he would have no difficulty in supporting Labour on most issues and even in joining the Party; but, even so, he stipulated that he should retain his freedom to dissent if necessary from the official party line. Attlee, Beveridge recorded, seemed sympathetic to his misgivings, but not unexpectedly his conditions proved unacceptable to the Labour leader and the question was quietly dropped.[66]

Ernest Bevin, however, was by now determined to remove Beveridge from the Ministry of Labour. In June 1941 he appointed another man as Director-General of Manpower—thus finally excluding Beveridge from the job he had coveted since the outbreak of war. At the same time Beveridge was removed from administrative work and placed in charge of an investigation into the use of skilled manpower in the armed services.[67] Then a few weeks later he was offered the job of chairman to an interdepartmental inquiry that was about to be set up on co-ordination of social insurance. The social insurance inquiry had initially been opposed by Ernest Bevin, but he changed his mind when he saw that it was a chance of ridding himself of Beveridge.[68] Beveridge himself was bitterly disappointed and was under no illusions about what was happening to him. It is recorded that tears stood in his eyes when the new appointment was offered to him, and twenty years later he recalled that Ernest Bevin 'pushed me as Chairman of the Social Insurance Committee by way of parting with me. . . . My removal in 1941 from the Ministry of Labour to Social Insurance was a "kicking upstairs".'[69] Thus almost inadvertently, and at a time when he was being ousted

[66] Lady Beveridge Papers, WHB to J. Mair, 31 Mar. 1 and 5 Apr. 9 June 1941; BP, IIb, WHB to C. Attlee, 12 June 1941; C. Attlee to WHB, 17 June 1941.

[67] Lady Beveridge Papers, WHB to J. Mair, 29 May 1941.

[68] PRO, PIN 8/85, 'Workmen's Compensation and Social Insurance', report of meeting at War Cabinet Offices, 16 May 1941.

[69] Information from Professor Arthur Goodhart; BP, IIb, WHB to Lord Longford, 9 Aug. 1961.

from his chosen area of policy, there came to Beveridge the opportunity of doing what was eventually to prove the most important work of his life.

## IV

Beveridge's appointment to the committee on Social Insurance attracted a good deal of comment in both Parliament and the press; but by Beveridge himself the Social Insurance inquiry was for some months given rather low priority. He gradually became convinced that an inquiry into the social insurance system was potentially far more significant than it had seemed at first sight. But, nevertheless, his attention was still focused on wartime manpower problems, and throughout the autumn of 1941 he was touring military and airforce bases gathering material for his report on skilled manpower. He found that many skilled workers, especially engineers, were being used on routine military duties; and he found also that whereas some service units had a severe shortage of skilled technicians others had a surplus which they did not know how to use. This maldistribution of manpower was particularly severe in the Army—a fact which Beveridge ascribed to the recruitment of soldiers into individual regiments rather than into the Army as a whole. He therefore proposed a system of 'general enlistment' by which men would enter the Army and then be allotted to regiments that had a special need for their skills.[70] Beveridge's proposal was accepted by the War Office in February 1942; but his reports on the armed services provoked a good deal of public criticism of defence arrangements and did not increase his popularity with the government, particularly with Mr. Churchill.[71] Two months later, in April 1942 Beveridge accepted an invitation from Hugh Dalton to draw up a scheme for rationing fuel. He devised what Dalton privately admitted was a 'very clever and perfect plan', based on 'a points system with interchangeable coupons'.[72] The plan proved very unpopular with Parliament, however, and Dalton found himself increasingly embarrassed by Beveridge's stubborn refusal to modify his scheme either to meet practical administrative objections or to take account of Dalton's own political interests in the Labour Party.[73] The issue of full rationing was therefore postponed and Beveridge's plan was quietly dropped. It was not until this stage—May 1942—that Beveridge turned his undivided attention to the problems of social insurance—and, indirectly, to the much wider question of post-war social reform.

[70] Cmd. 6333/1942, *Committee on Skilled Men in the Armed Services, Second Report*, pp. 14–19.
[71] *PI*, pp. 286–91.
[72] BP, VIII 25, *Report of the Fuel Rationing Enquiry*, 1942; Dalton Papers, Hugh Dalton's diary, 7 Apr. 1942.
[73] Ibid., 8 and 12 May 1942.

# 16

# The Making of the Beveridge Report

## I

THE Committee on Social Insurance and Allied Services was set up in June 1941 to inquire into the wide range of anomalies that had arisen as a result of the haphazard and piecemeal growth of the social security system over the previous fifty years. In 1941 no less than seven government departments were directly or indirectly concerned with administering cash benefits for different kinds of need. Thus workmen's compensation was supervised by the Home Office, unemployment insurance by the Ministry of Labour, national health insurance by the Ministry of Health and the Department of Health for Scotland. Non-contributory old-age pensions were administered by the Customs and Excise, contributory old-age pensions by the Ministry of Health and 'supplementary pensions' by the Unemployment Assistance Board—which also dealt with the long-term unemployed. War victims and their dependants were relieved by the Ministry of Pensions, while the civilian disabled, widows and orphans were insured by the Ministry of Health. In addition there was a nation-wide network of local authority committees— the heirs of the old Poor Law guardians—which paid means-tested public assistance to persons in need. Benefits under these various systems were financed in a number of different ways. Thus, workmen's compensation was paid for by the employer; war pensions, non-contributory old-age pensions and unemployment assistance by the taxpayer; public assistance by the ratepayer; and health, unemployment and old-age pensions insurance by tripartite contributions from employers, workers and the state. Moreover, as Beveridge had discovered as chairman of the Unemployment Insurance Statutory Committee, the benefits payable under the various systems varied widely in size and scope. Thus, a man entitled to workmen's compensation received a benefit proportionate to previous earnings. A man supported by unemployment insurance received a benefit related to subsistence needs, plus an allowance for wife and children. A man out of work through sickness, on the other hand, received no statutory allowance for dependents; and his benefits were deliberately fixed below subsistence in order to encourage voluntary thrift.[1]

[1] In 1940 the average weekly insurance benefit for a man with a wife and two children was 20s. 6d. for sickness, 38s. for unemployment, and 42s. 6d. for workmen's compensation (PRO, CAB 87/76, 'Basic Problems of Social Security with Heads of a Scheme', by WHB, 11 Dec. 1941).

Such a variety of systems gave rise to much overlapping and duplication of services, and at the same time it failed to make provision for many people in need, particularly children and certain sections of the aged. In 1940 for example 28.8 per cent of children in L.C.C. schools were still living below the Ministry of Health's prevailing definition of a 'poverty line';[2] yet such children received no help from the social security system unless their father was dead or out of work. Moreover, even within the separate compartments of the system there were many anomalies and inequalities. A man entitled to workmen's compensation, for example, might receive no benefit if his employers went bankrupt or had failed to insure. Under national health insurance there were wide variations in benefits received from the same rate of contribution. Thus a workman insured through a prosperous approved society might receive a wide range of 'additional benefits'—such as nursing-home fees and dental and ophthalmic treatment—whereas a man insured through a poor approved society might receive only the basic statutory sickness benefit guaranteed by the state. Even more serious though outside the terms of reference of Beveridge's committee, were the anomalies that existed in the private sector, particularly in the field of 'industrial assurance'—that is, working-class life assurance primarily designed to cover the costs of a 'decent burial'. By 1941 industrial assurance companies held over a hundred million policies for this kind of insurance, yielding a premium income of £74 million a year. It was notorious, however, that nearly 40 per cent of this sum went in 'management expenses' and that a third of such policies never matured. Industrial assurance agents were regular visitors in more than three-quarters of working-class homes; and they were frequently accused of 'swelling their books' by deliberately selling policies to people too poor to pay for them—knowing that such people would fall into arrears and that their right to benefit would eventually 'lapse'.

Throughout the 1930s there had been a growing body of criticism of the social welfare system—a movement in which Beveridge himself to a certain extent had shared. Rowntree's study of York in 1936 found that, whereas thirty-seven years earlier poverty had been mainly caused by low earnings, it was now mainly due to unemployment and to inadequate provision for childhood and old age.[3] An official inquiry into Industrial Assurance had severely criticized the commercial insurance companies for their extravagant administrative costs and the high incidence of 'lapsing'.[4] The family endowment movement had continually

[2] BP, VIII 28, 'The Extent and Causes of Poverty among Families in London containing Elementary and Secondary Schoolchildren', by E. Bransby, n.d.
[3] B. S. Rowntree, *Poverty and Progress* (1941), p. 116.
[4] Sir Arnold Wilson and Hermann Levy, *Industrial Assurance* (1937), pp. 113–16.

drawn attention to the fact that lack of any regular provision for large families meant that for many workers their earnings whilst in work might well be lower than their benefits whilst unemployed.[5] There had been many criticisms of the very limited provision for medical treatment that was available from the 'panel system' under national health insurance; and various proposals had been put forward for a much more extensive health service, which would provide specialist as well as general practitioner treatment and cover not merely employed persons but the whole community.[6] Within the Labour movement there had been much discontent about the different levels of benefit paid for different types of misfortune—which meant, for instance, that a worker who fell sick whilst unemployed had suddenly to face a severe drop in income. There was even more discontent about the limited coverage of contributory insurance, and the imposition of a strict 'household means test' on those applying for public relief.[7]

This growing desire for some kind of major reform of the social welfare system was strongly reinforced by the outbreak of war. As we have seen, Beveridge himself from the start of the war had pressed for family allowances to mitigate the impact of high taxation and compulsory wartime saving. At the same time he had urged the need for far-reaching policies of 'social reconstruction'—partly to give the British people something worth fighting for and partly to ease the eventual transition to peace. In pressing for such measures, however, Beveridge was in no sense a voice crying in the wilderness; he was merely articulating a view that already had widespread political support. Thus from the beginning of the war backbenchers of all parties had supported the demand for family allowances—some with the aim of promoting economic equality, others with the more traditional motive of enhancing 'national efficiency' in time of war.[8] Before the Beveridge committee was set up officials in the Ministry of Health were already scrutinizing proposals for an improved health service, and officials in the Home Office were discussing with the trade union movement certain far-reaching reforms of workmen's compensation.[9] Outside Whitehall bodies like the Fabian Society and P.E.P. were pressing for social reform as an essential ingredient of the war effort; and in Oxford G. D. H. Cole had founded the Nuffield College Reconstruction Survey, a body devoted to drawing up plans for

---

[5] Above, pp. 360.

[6] Brian Abel-Smith, *The Hospitals 1800–1948. A Study in Social Administration in England and Wales* (1964), esp. chs. 18 and 27.

[7] C. L. Mowat, *Britain the Wars between 1918–1940* (1968 edn.), pp. 483–4.

[8] PRO, PIN 8/163, papers on 'A System of Family Allowances', 1940–2.

[9] PRO, PIN 8/85, 'Workmen's Compensation and Social Insurances', notes of a meeting at the Offices of The War Cabinet, 16 May 1941; CAB 87/76, S.I.C. minutes, 8 July 1941.

economic and social policy after the war. Already by June 1941, therefore, there was a large body of reforming opinion interested in, and with well-formed views upon, the range of problems that Beveridge and his committee were to examine in detail over the next eighteen months.

This surge of interest in social questions forms an essential backcloth to the work of the Social Insurance committee, and helps to explain the enthusiastic popular reception eventually accorded to the Beveridge report. The causes of such a movement are difficult to catalogue precisely, and must to a certain extent be a matter for speculation. Undoubtedly at a purely pragmatic level there were good reasons for encouraging social reform in wartime—not least the need to foster morale in the armed forces and to keep the support of organized labour, as essential prerequisites of winning the war. A second factor was that stressed by Richard Titmuss in *Problems of Social Policy*—that the tremendous disturbance of civilian population during the bombing of 1940 underlined the defects of existing services, and areas of neglect which had lain concealed in peacetime were glaringly exposed by the impact of war. In particular, mass evacuation had revealed to many middle-class people just how severe was the problem of poverty among children in great cities; and at the same time it had drawn attention to the widely varying quality of many social services—to the bad conditions prevailing in many old Poor Law hospitals and to the grossly uneven distribution of doctors and hospital beds.[10] A third factor was the sense of social solidarity induced by the war and the consequent muffling of ideological conflict.[11] This sense of solidarity was clearly reflected in discussions of social policy, and their influence was particularly noticeable upon Beveridge himself. Under the impact of war many of his earlier fears about undermining incentives and damaging investment seemed to recede; and in the midst of a world war he clearly found it much easier to identify with those in need than he had done during the world slump. A fourth important factor was that the Second World War, like the First World War, brought about a tremendous expansion in state control and economic management; and many reformers, including Beveridge himself, were not slow to argue that these experiments could be seen as creating precedents for peacetime social administration.[12] This argument was strengthened by recollections of the withdrawal of government from social and economic life after the First World War—a withdrawal that had been accompanied by, if not

[10] R. M. Titmuss, *Problems of Social Policy* (1950), pp. 66–73, 114–33.

[11] Ibid.; pp. 506–8, 514–16; R. M. Titmuss, *Essays on the Welfare State* (1963 edn.), pp. 84–6; Lionel Robbins, *Autobiography of an Economist*, p. 169.

[12] BP, VIII 27, 'Reconstruction Problems: Five Giants on the Road', by WHB, 3 June 1942.

necessarily responsible for, prolonged depression and unemployment.[13] A fifth and more nebulous factor was the effect of the economic climate produced by the war in redefining the nature of social distress. As surplus workmen were absorbed into the services or into war production and as wages spiralled upwards in key industries, the concern of social reformers shifted away from the unemployed and focused instead upon the problems of low wage-earners, of those on fixed rates of benefit and those with large families. For the first time for twenty years the relief of poverty from whatever cause rather than relief of unemployment became the major problem and first priority of social administration.

## II

The Beveridge committee on Social Insurance and Allied Services was therefore set up in an atmosphere that was highly favourable to discussion of social reform. Nevertheless Beveridge was correct in believing that his new appointment was not seen by the government as an important one, and certainly not as the prelude to a massive programme of social reconstruction. In fact, the decision to appoint a Social Insurance committee had been taken almost by accident and had come about in the following way. Since 1938 a Royal Commission had been investigating trade union complaints about the prevailing system of workmen's compensation. This Commission had virtually folded up in July 1940 because employers claimed that they could not prepare evidence on such a subject in wartime. Nevertheless, the Home Office was reluctant to offend the unions by abandoning the inquiry, and early in 1941 Home Office officials were looking around for some alternative way in which to continue the discussion of workmen's compensation. At the same time the Ministry of Health was under pressure to extend the scope of health insurance and to increase the level of sickness benefit. A bill to this effect was being prepared by the Ministry in the spring of 1941; but it was felt that the bill was a 'minimum bill' and could 'only be supported if the Minister of Health could at the same time give a definite undertaking that a fuller inquiry was being made'.[14] Moreover, the Ministry was being urged to start planning for a major extension of medical services; and its officials argued that this should not be done in isolation from reform of social security, since 'there is no problem of public health which does not have a common frontier with the treat-

---

[13] R. H. Tawney, 'The Abolition of Economic Controls', *Econ. Hist. Rev.*, XIII, I (1943), pp. 1–30.

[14] PRO, PIN 8/85, 'Workmen's Compensation and Social Insurances', notes of a meeting held at the Offices of the War Cabinet, 16 May 1941.

ment or rehabilitation side of social insurance'.[15] It was to deal with these practical problems that in April 1941 the Minister of Reconstruction, Arthur Greenwood, proposed that a special committee should be set up to survey the whole area of workmen's compensation and social insurance.[16] This suggestion was warmly welcomed by Ministry of Health and Home Office officials; and it was proposed that the committee should consist mainly of civil servants together with a few 'outside experts', presided over by Sir Hector Hetherington, the chairman of the Commission on Workmen's Compensation.[17] Bevin, as we have seen, originally opposed the scheme, on the ground that 'a Committee consisting partly of civil servants and partly of outsiders would be no good',[18] but he apparently capitulated when it was suggested that Beveridge rather than Hetherington should be appointed chairman. Nevertheless, Bevin insisted that the inquiry should not be a 'policy enquiry', but should concern itself merely with technical details—a condition which senior officials privately admitted to be quite unrealistic, in view of the controversial nature of many of the financial issues and 'questions of major policy' to be raised.[19] The Treasury indeed was anxious that the committee should be a secret committee, fearing that its inquiries would be interpreted as an indication of future policy.[20] The committee's terms of reference were in fact never officially disclosed to Parliament, although M.P.s soon extracted from Greenwood the information that a special inquiry on the social services had been set in hand.[21] It was Greenwood who announced Beveridge's new appointment to the House of Commons on 10 June 1941.

## III

Beveridge met his new committee early in July 1941. In terms of its contribution to social policy-formation this committee has often been compared to the Royal Commission on the Poor Laws of 1905-9, but it would be hard to conceive of two official inquiries more dissimilar in composition and general outlook. The Royal Commission on the Poor Laws had been deliberately chosen to include a wide spectrum of

[15] PRO, PIN 8/85, Report of a Preliminary Conference on Workmen's Compensation and Social Insurances 29 May 1941.

[16] PRO, PIN/85, Arthur Greenwood to Ernest Brown, 10 Apr. 1941.

[17] PRO, PIN 8/85, 'Survey of Social Insurance, etc.', note of conclusions reached at a conference on 24 Apr. 1941.

[18] PRO, PIN 8/85, 'Workmen's Compensation and Social Insurances', notes of a meeting at the offices of the War Cabinet, 16 May 1941.

[19] PRO, PIN 8/85, 'Survey of Social Insurance, etc.', notes of conclusions reached at a conference on 24 Apr. 1941.

[20] PRO, PIN 8/85, Sir George Chrystal to Sir John Maude, 2 July 1941.

[21] H.C. Deb., 5s., vol. 371, col. 1575; vol. 372; col. 45.

political views and its members had been drawn from the civil service, the churches, the medical profession, academic life, radical politics, the trade union movement and organized philanthropy. The Social Insurance committee on the other hand was drawn—apart from Beveridge himself—entirely from the Civil Service; and the tone of its discussions was studiously non-partisan. The committee consisted of a middle-ranking official from each of the seven departments concerned with social insurance, together with the Government Actuary and representatives of the Treasury, Assistance Board, Registry of Friendly Societies and Ministry of Reconstruction. Its secretary was a young official from the War Cabinet Office, D. N. Chester, who in peacetime had been a lecturer in government at Manchester University. Apart from Beveridge himself the only member of the committee at all known to the public was Mary Agnes Hamilton—a former Labour M.P. for Blackburn and now a civil servant in the Reconstruction Secretariat. Mrs. Hamilton had once been a lecturer at the L.S.E. and was an old friend of both Beveridge and Mrs. Mair. Peering through her pebble-dash spectacles and chain-smoking Turkish cigarillos, she had the kind of forceful and articulate personality that Beveridge appeared to admire in women; and other members of the committee soon found that in order to persuade Beveridge to listen to their views it was useful to get them put forward by Mrs. Hamilton. Of the other committee members the most active were R. A. Bannatyne, Edward Hale, Sir George Reid, Miss Muriel Ritson, and Sir George Epps, the government actuary. Bannatyne, the Home Office representative, had worked on the Commission on Workmen's Compensation and in Beveridge's eyes was the member of his committee most strongly committed to radical reform.[22] Edward Hale, the Treasury representative, was regarded by his colleagues as a classic exponent of the Whitehall virtue of 'soundness'. He played an important part on the committee in focusing Beveridge's attention on administrative and financial reality and in persuading him to think about how general principles were to be practically enforced. Reid, the secretary of the Assistance Board, was perhaps the most conservative of the committee members and staunchly defended the virtues of means tests and discretionary relief. Miss Ritson, the Department of Health for Scotland representative, was described by Mrs. Mair as 'interesting and delightful but non-committal—the Compleat Civil Servant'.[23] Her main task on the committee was to express Scottish interests; but next to Beveridge himself she was the most prolific in putting her ideas on paper and the most experienced in handling a wide range of problems in social administration. She was the author of many of the memoranda jointly

[22] *PI*, p. 306.
[23] Lady Beveridge Papers, J. Mair to WHB, 6 Apr. 1942.

submitted by the Ministry of Health and Department of Health for Scotland; and both in her grasp of problems and thoroughness in solving them she appeared to eclipse the rather negative Ministry of Health representative, R. Hamilton Farrell. Beveridge himself was very pleased with the calibre of his committee. They were 'very forthcoming and progressive', he recorded after their second meeting[24]—a judgement echoed by Mrs. Hamilton, who found her lifelong prejudice against bureaucracy being eroded as the committee began its work. 'I found the meetings a fascinating and most enriching experience,' she recorded; 'my respect for the "higher civil servant" went up and up, as I grew to realise the entire objectivity and selfless readiness to put all they had into a common pool of a range of extremely able individuals.'[25]

Nevertheless, in spite of the high quality of the official members it was soon clear that the proceedings of the committee were going to be dominated and even monopolized by Beveridge himself. After only one meeting he drafted a paper on 'Social Insurance—General Considerations', in which he mapped out the main lines of his inquiry, and hinted at many of its eventual conclusions, without reference to his colleagues. This action set the tone for the committee's proceedings over the next eighteen months. The official members were all heavily engaged on other aspects of wartime administration, most of them had been evacuated out of London, and none of them had the time to prepare detailed alternatives to Beveridge's proposals. Beveridge himself was not very tolerant of those who disagreed with him, and although some of the committee found him highly receptive, others found him rather intimidating and unwilling to consider any views but his own. The result was that the committee's discussions centred mainly on questions chosen by Beveridge, and these tended to be primarily technical in character. At no stage did Beveridge discuss with his committee the general scope of the inquiry and the goals to be attained. Moreover, outside the formal meetings there was much less contact between the members than is sometimes found in such inquiries. There was little of that behind-the-scenes discussion of first principles which can be found in the correspondence of the Royal Commission on the Poor Laws. Beveridge consulted individual members mainly about their special areas of expertise—such as workmen's compensation or actuarial prediction—rather than about questions of general policy. At the same time the committee had no significant 'social' dimension. A year earlier,

[24] Lady Beveridge Papers, WHB to J. Mair, 25 Sept. 1941.
[25] Mary Agnes Hamilton, *Uphill All the Way. A Third Cheer for Democracy* (1953), p. 81. The remaining members of the committee, other than those mentioned above, were P. Y. Blundun of The Ministry of Labour, B. K. White of the Registry of Friendly Societies and A. W. Mackenzie of the Board of Customs and Excise. Miss Marjorie Cox of the Ministry of Pensions was added in September 1941.

when Beveridge was working on his manpower survey, he had invited his assistants and their wives for several long week-ends at University College, where they had been graciously entertained by Mrs. Mair and had thrashed out labour problems with a group of government economists. There were no such long week-ends for the Social Insurance Committee—possibly because Mrs. Mair had gone to Scotland to stay with relatives, and was no longer available to act as Beveridge's hostess. The meetings of the committee were rather formal; Beveridge himself usually left immediately without engaging in further conversation; and they were never preceded or followed by those intimate working breakfasts and lunches that were an integral part of policy-formation in many areas of Whitehall throughout the war.[26]

A second point which soon became clear was that Beveridge intended to place a very ambitious interpretation on the Committee's terms of reference—which were merely to make a survey of 'existing national schemes of social insurance and allied services, including workmen's compensation, and to make recommendations'. The official members themselves varied considerably in their expectation of what these rather vague words might be taken to mean. The Treasury representative, for example, expected merely 'a sort of tidying up operation—e.g. perhaps relieving the Customs and Excise of their administration of the Lloyd George non-contributory old-age pension'.[27] The Home Office and Ministry of Health representatives were hoping for something more far-reaching; but none of them was quite prepared for the panoramic review of national social policy which it soon became evident that Beveridge had in mind. As we have seen, in the early years of war Beveridge had been reluctant to involve himself in social welfare, hoping for some more immediate share in running the war. At the same time, however, he had consistently argued that the war effort would be greatly strengthened by a positive government commitment to social reform. He gradually became convinced that the Social Insurance Committee gave him a chance to provoke such a commitment; and he determined to use the inquiry not merely to rationalize the existing insurance system, but to lay down long-term goals in many areas of social policy. In this he was greatly encouraged by Jessy Mair. There is no evidence to suggest that Mrs. Mair was responsible for any of Beveridge's substantive proposals; but much of his report was drafted after weekends with her in Edinburgh, and it was she who urged him to imbue his proposals with a 'Cromwellian spirit' and messianic tone. 'How I hope you are going to be able to preach against all *gangsters*,' she wrote, 'who for their

[26] D. N. Chester, 'The Wartime Machine', *Policy-Making in Britain*, ed. Richard Rose (1969), pp. 342–3; interviews with Miss Muriel Ritson and Dame Marjorie Cox.
[27] Sir Edward Hale to the author, 13 June 1972.

mutual gain support one another in upholding all the rest. For that is really what is happening still in England . . . the whole object of their spider web of interlocked big banks and big businessmen [is] a frantic effort to maintain their own caste.' And she urged Beveridge to concentrate on three main policy objectives—'prevention rather than cure', 'education of those not yet accustomed to clean careful ways of life', and 'plotting the future as a gradual millennium taking step after step, but not flinching on ultimate goals'.[28]

Beveridge's radical interpretation of the scope of his inquiry was soon revealed at the committee's early meetings. At these meetings he refused to confine himself merely to consideration of cash benefits. He brushed aside impatiently the assumption that any aspects of the existing system should necessarily be continued; and he brushed aside also the suggestion that the committee should concentrate on difficult marginal problems—such as the right to benefit of the 'unmarried wife'. 'If that was the sort of thing that they dealt with in the Ministry of Pensions then he wanted nothing more to do with it,' he asserted, when the 'unmarried wife' question was tentatively raised by the war pensions representative, Miss Marjorie Cox.[29] Instead he insisted from the start of the inquiry that all of the insurance system should be fundamentally re-assessed, and that this re-assessment should be extended to include many other areas of policy—such as medical treatment, prevention of unemployment and provision for large families. In 'Social Insurance—General Considerations' he proposed that all the separate compartments of social insurance, including workmen's compensation, should be administratively unified, and that cash benefits should be standardized at subsistence level. Such a reform he envisaged would almost certainly entail the suppression of approved societies; and it would be backed up by universal family allowances, and by a local authority health service supplying all forms of medical treatment to the whole population. 'The time has now come,' Beveridge argued,

to consider social insurance as a whole, as a contribution to a better new world after the war. How would one plan social insurance now if one had a clear field, that is to say if one could plan an ideal scheme, using all the experience gained in the past, but without being hampered by regard for vested interests of any kind? The first step is to outline the ideal scheme; the next step is to consider the practical possibilities of realising the ideal and the changes of existing machinery that would be required.[30]

Almost certainly a majority of Beveridge's committee were in sympathy with this radical approach, but at the same time it placed them in an

[28] Lady Beveridge Papers, J. Mair to WHB, 21 Mar., 4 June and 20 Aug. 1942.
[29] PRO, CAB 87/76, S.I.C. minutes, 8 July 1941; interview with Dame Marjorie Cox.
[30] BP, IXa, 37 (2), 'Social Insurance—General Considerations', by WHB, July 1941.

awkward position. None of them had any instructions from their ministers about what line to take on the wider issues raised by Beveridge;[31] and the various social policy departments were at this stage extremely reluctant to commit themselves to promises of post-war reconstruction, particularly since the war was still a long way from being won. It was increasingly feared, however, that the signatures of a group of permanent civil servants at the bottom of Beveridge's proposals might well be interpreted as such a promise; and early in 1942 Arthur Greenwood informed Beveridge that the official representatives on his committee were to be down-graded from being full members to being merely 'advisors and assessors'.[32] The committee's eventual conclusions would therefore be signed by Beveridge alone. Beveridge was forced to acquiesce in this decision, but he accepted it only with reluctance, presumably realizing that it might seriously diminish the political weight of his report. In the first complete draft of his Report Beveridge in fact implied that it was the joint production of his whole committee; but this was amended at the request of the official members, who felt that even as mere advisers and assessors their views had not been adequately considered. 'Beveridge cannot properly expect to have "the best of both worlds",' commented the Ministry of Health representative, 'viz. a free hand as to the contents of the Report, coupled with the implication . . . that his advisers and assessors agree with his conclusions.'[33]

## IV

In spite of his resolve to produce far-reaching proposals, Beveridge was for some time uncertain about the form they should take. During the autumn of 1941 he was still hard at work on his armed services inquiry and the social insurance committee met only at infrequent intervals. At these occasional meetings there appeared to be general agreement with Beveridge's own view that the principle of contributory insurance as the chief means of financing cash benefits should be retained and extended. Brief consideration was given to the possible alternative of a system financed purely out of taxes—but this was quickly rejected, partly on the ground that a tax-financed system would involve an extension of means tests and partly for fear that it would arouse traditional Treasury hostility against the principle of 'ear-marked funds'.[34] Whether there was in fact any justification for these two assumptions was never further considered. There was general agreement also with

[31] Sir Edward Hale to the author, 13 June 1972.
[32] PRO, CAB 87/79, Arthur Greenwood to WHB, 27 Jan. 1942.
[33] PRO, PIN 8/87, R. Hamilton Farrell to E. Hale, 3 Sept. 1942.
[34] PRO, CAB 87/76, S.I.C. minutes, 15 Oct. 1941.

Beveridge's proposal that benefits should be standardized for different kinds of 'interruption of earnings'—although the officials were dubious about total amalgamation of the separate insurance funds, fearing that this 'would make it difficult to maintain that there was an insurance basis to any particular scheme'.[35] The committee's work in these early months, however, consisted mainly in surveying the existing system; and papers were produced by the official members summarizing the schemes administered by their respective departments. Among these papers those produced by the Home Office, Ministry of Health and Department of Health for Scotland stood out from the rest in showing just how far these departments were already considering major social reforms. The Home Office paper was a severe indictment of the system of workmen's compensation that had developed in Britain since 1897—whereby workmen suffering from sickness or disablement 'arising out of and in the course of employment' were entitled to benefits from their employers. The system had given rise to a welter of litigation concerning both the interpretation of the Workmen's Compensation Acts and the degree of disablement in individual cases. Moreover, in many cases where employers had failed to insure themselves they could not keep up payments; and often workers themselves were unable to afford the legal costs of pursuing their claims. Provision for the treatment and rehabilitation of injured workmen was virtually non-existent. The result was that although in theory the system provided complete coverage against industrial injury, in practice many injured workers were dependent on public assistance and many were forced to return to work before they were fully fit. The proposals for reform currently under consideration by the Home Office included compulsory private insurance for all employers, transfer of workmen's compensation to contributory social insurance, and the setting up of a special industrial injuries assistance board modelled on the U.A.B.[36] The memoranda produced by the Ministry of Health and Department of Health for Scotland judiciously surveyed both the advantages and disadvantages of the existing pensions and national health schemes. They defended the approved society system as embodying the principles of participation and self-government but they pointed also to the severe financial inequalities that these principles had produced. They defended the principle of 'flat-rate' insurance, on the ground that it encouraged additional private saving; but at the same time they criticized the regressive impact of flat-rate contributions on the incomes of the poor. They condemned the lack of 'prevention' on the treatment side of health insurance, and suggested

[35] PRO, CAB 87/76, S.I.C. minutes, 29 Oct. 1941.
[36] PRO, CAB 87/76, 'Committee on Social Insurance. Memorandum on Workmen's Compensation', Aug. 1941.

that the time had come either to extend medical benefit to dependants of insured persons or to set up a universal medical service 'divorced from insurance and administered by the State or by the Local Health Authority and financed from public funds'.[37] An additional paper by the Department of Health for Scotland representative called for the 'regionalisation, rationalisation and specialisation of hospital services'; and it suggested also that all personal social services should be concentrated in one single local authority committee—a proposal that anticipated the Kilbrandon and Seebohm proposals on social work of a quarter of a century later.[38]

Beveridge himself did not begin to think seriously about insurance until the end of the year. He 'professes himself to be not at all in a hurry', observed G. D. H. Cole, 'and is not himself very clear about what he intends to do'.[39] In December 1941 and January 1942, however, he drafted two papers which outlined many of the assumptions and proposals that were eventually to be embodied in his final report. Beveridge claimed that he was putting forward these assumptions and proposals in the light of the surveys of existing schemes carried out by the official members; but in fact they embodied many of the favourite principles of social insurance that he himself had evolved over the previous thirty years. Beveridge's first paper, on 'Basic Problems of Social Security with Heads of a Scheme' was circulated to the committee in mid-December 1941. In it he assumed that reform of social security must be accompanied by the setting up of a 'national health service for prevention and comprehensive treatment available to all members of the community'. The details of such a service, Beveridge conceded, were outside the ambit of his committee; but he suggested that the social insurance fund should make a donation towards the cost of the new service, and that the administrators of social insurance 'as representing the consumer of medical services, should have a definite status to represent the view of those consumers to the Health Administration'. Secondly, he assumed that tax-financed children's allowances should be paid in respect of all children, whether or not their father was out of work. Such a measure, Beveridge argued, would remove the single main cause of poverty in Britain. At the same time it would help to reverse the decline in the birth-rate, and it would remove the anomaly that a man's income from benefit might be larger than his earnings from employment. Thirdly, Beveridge assumed that 'full use' should be made of 'the powers of the State' to reduce unemployment to a minimum. At a

[37] PRO, CAB 87/76, 'Problems which have arisen in the Administration of the Schemes of Health Insurance and Pensions', Aug. 1941.

[38] PRO, CAB 87/76, 'Outline of Scottish Services. Health. Public Assistance', Aug. 1941.

[39] Cole Papers. G. D. H. Cole to Joan Clarke, 9 Oct. 1941.

later stage in the committee's proceedings Beveridge argued that maintenance of full employment was necessary to avoid bankrupting the insurance fund; but in this early paper he was mainly concerned with its relevance to the treatment of individual workmen. Prolonged cash benefits, he argued, were an inappropriate means of assisting an able-bodied citizen of working age—whose primary need was not for welfare but for work. Moreover, a reduction of unemployment was necessary to protect the scheme from exploitation. Only by the offer of a job could a man's 'willingness to work' be tested; and only if such a job was likely to be quickly available would it be safe to abandon the old Poor Law principle of deterrence and to meet a man's subsistence needs. Some residual element of deterrence would, Beveridge thought, be necessary for those who failed to find work even in conditions of full employment, but he firmly laid down the principle that such deterrence should 'not take the form of an inadequate cash allowance'. Instead it should consist of compulsory re-training, prior to a man's return to normal work.

Having postulated these 'basic assumptions', Beveridge proceeded to outline his ideas about the future structure of social security. As a first principle he laid down that the whole system, including compensation for industrial injury, should be financed by equal contributions from the worker, the employer and the State. There was, he admitted, no inherently logical basis for such a principle; but he argued that each of these parties had an interest in maintaining an effective welfare system and that 'equality of shares offers one less point for criticism than inequality'. Secondly, he suggested that for reasons of 'simplicity, economy and efficiency', the different compartments of social insurance should be administratively unified. Approved societies would be abolished and control vested in a Social Security Board, which would 'combine responsibility to Parliament with freedom from parliamentary pressure about individual cases'—an arrangement similar to that which he had proposed for unemployment insurance before the Holman Gregory Commission in 1931. Such a reform, he argued, would avoid demarcation problems and duplication of benefits, it would reduce costs of administration, it would ensure that all needs were effectively covered and it would make possible the rapid detection of 'fresh needs', if in the course of future social change these should arise. Thirdly, he laid down that benefits and contributions should be paid at a flat rate and—with certain exceptions—should be standardized for different kinds of social need. At the start of the inquiry Beveridge had proposed that the committee should examine foreign systems in which benefits and contributions were graduated according to earnings; but he himself was of the opinion that such a system was inappropriate to Britain—where national insurance was complemented by a vast network of institutions for private saving. It had been found in the 1930s that even among the long-term unemployed no less than three-quarters had some form of private insurance; and Beveridge estimated that friendly societies alone had an income as large as the income of state health insurance. He himself fully endorsed this pervasive ethic of voluntary private thrift. Once subsistence needs had been secured, he argued, there was 'no reason for the State to deprive the better paid workman of the responsibility and opportunity of making his own provision for higher standards'.

Within the context of this standardized framework of insurance, Beveridge proposed a system of benefits and contributions that was not in fact uniform for the whole insured population. To Beveridge the archetypal insurance contributor was the kind of person that he had always dealt with in unemployment insurance—the adult male worker whose income was derived solely from earnings and who needed protection when such earnings were interrupted by unemployment, accident or disease. Beveridge's perception of social need was in fact dominated by the concept of 'interruption of earnings'; but he recognized that such a concept could not be realistically applied to those outside the labour market. He therefore proposed that there should be seven different categories of persons covered by social security—employees, the self-employed, housewives, those above working age, those below working age, the 'blind and other incapables', and 'others of working age fit for work'.[40] Within these seven categories people would be entitled to seven different kinds of cash benefit—namely, family allowances, old-age pensions, disability benefit (including both sickness and industrial injury), unemployment benefit, funeral expenses, 'loss grants' for the self-employed who suffered theft or bankruptcy, and 'special provision' for the 'marriage needs of women'. In this last category Beveridge included an ambitious range of benefits, ranging from a 'furnishing grant' for setting-up house, maternity benefit and widowhood and separation allowances, to a dependant's allowance during a husband's unemployment or sickness, old-age pensions at sixty and provision of domestic help to housewives who fell ill. In addition to these general proposals Beveridge made various detailed suggestions about protecting the scheme from abuse. The employers' contribution should be converted into a 'tax on dismissals'—thus achieving his long-standing aim of penalizing employers who refused to give regular work. The 'three-days waiting-period' before benefits became payable should be retained, so as to discourage trivial or frivolous claims. The whole insurance system should be underpinned by a system of means-tested public assistance, which Beveridge hoped would in future be drastically

---

[40] The last two categories were amalgamated in the final Report as 'others of working age not gainfully occupied'.

reduced in scope. He hoped also that with a comprehensive system of contributory insurance, the conditions for residual assistance could be made correspondingly more severe. 'An assistance system,' he asserted, 'which does not in one way or another leave the person assisted with an effective motive to avoid the need for assistance and to rely on earnings and insurance, undermines the Security Scheme. Further, an assistance scheme which makes those assisted unamenable to economic rewards or punishments, while treating them as free citizens, is inconsistent with the principle of a free community.'[41]

Beveridge's second key memorandum was circulated to his committee a month later, and consisted of a detailed defence of the view that poverty could henceforth be abolished and that it could best be abolished through the medium of social insurance. Beveridge first surveyed the conclusions of a number of 'standard-of-living inquiries' which had been carried out during the previous fifteen years. In particular he concentrated on Llewellyn Smith's *New Survey of London Life and Labour*, which had repeated Booth's inquiries of the 1890s, and on Seebohm Rowntree's *Poverty and Progress*, which repeated Rowntree's own York survey of 1899. These surveys showed, Beveridge argued, that since the beginning of the century average real living-standards in working-class families had risen by 30 per cent. 'Primary poverty' had fallen from 38 per cent to 14 per cent in East London, and from 15.5 per cent to 6.8 per cent in York. In York in 1936 the total surplus income of working-class families living above the poverty line was eight times as great as the total deficiency of those below it. Poverty could now be abolished, Beveridge therefore concluded, 'by a re-distribution of income within the working-classes, without touching any of the wealthier classes. This is said not to suggest that re-distribution of income should be confined to the working-classes, but as the most convincing demonstration that abolition of poverty is within the financial power of the community.' Moreover, in the 1890s primary poverty had been mainly caused by low earnings, the solution for which was largely outside the scope of contributory insurance. By the 1930s five-sixths of primary poverty was caused by unemployment, sickness, old age and death— all of which, Beveridge argued, were suitable for relief by social insurance. The other main cause of poverty was 'the misfit of wages and family needs' arising from the 'fact that the average family is a statistical myth'. Poverty in large families could not be cured by higher wages or insurance; hence the need for family allowances paid at subsistence rates. For his definition of 'subsistence' Beveridge again looked to Seebohm Rowntree. In his 1936 survey Rowntree had used not merely a

[41] PRO, CAB 87/76, 'Basic Problems of Social Security with Heads of a Scheme', by WHB, 11 Dec. 1941.

'primary poverty' scale—which covered such items as were nutritionally necessary for survival—but also a 'human needs' scale—which took into account changing perceptions of a decent standard of life. The earlier and more stringent scale Beveridge argued, would 'be rejected decisively by public opinion today'; and he concluded that insurance benefits must be related to the wider concept of 'human needs'.[42] This latter concept, although still comparatively spartan and austere, became the basis of his definition of poverty throughout his Report.

These two papers, produced by Beveridge in December 1941 and January 1942, outlined many of the main proposals that were to be embodied a year later in the Beveridge Report. During the next few weeks he made several further suggestions designed to enhance the scope and simplify the administration of the new scheme. Social insurance was to be extended to cover the whole population, regardless of income.[43] The special schemes introduced since 1920 for industries with low unemployment were to be abolished. The cost of public assistance was to be transferred to the national exchequer, and its administration combined with that of social insurance. Old-age pensions were to be conditional on retirement, and would be paid at a higher level to those who deferred retirement beyond the minimum age—a rule which Beveridge hoped would encourage elderly people to go on working as long as they were physically fit.[44] It was significant that all these principles were laid down before more than a small fraction of witnesses had given evidence; and most of them were not substantially altered by discussion with the committee's official members. The latter indeed found that although Beveridge was happy to accept advice on matters of detail he was extremely reluctant to modify any of the basic principles that he himself had devised. Several members, for instance, were extremely critical of the retirement condition for pensions, and thought that such a condition would be impossible to enforce.[45] The Ministry of Labour representative, P. Y. Blundun, was doubtful whether lower-paid workers could afford the necessary contributions; and he was sceptical

[42] PRO, CAB 87/79. 'The Scale of Social Insurance Benefits and the Problem of Poverty' by WHB, 16 Jan. 1942.

[43] PRO, CAB 87/79, 'The Problem of an Income Limit', by WHB, 10 Mar. 1942.

[44] The retirement condition was first suggested to Beveridge on 14 Jan. 1942 by the T.U.C., who believed that it would encourage the elderly to *leave* the labour market, thus creating work for younger men. Beveridge strongly rejected the view that the elderly should be *kept out* of the labour market, but adopted the retirement condition (in conjunction with higher pensions for deferred retirement) as a means of *keeping them in*. It is not clear at what point he first formulated this proposal, but it was referred to in several memoranda by his advisers in Apr. 1942. (PRO, CAB 87/77, S.I.C. minutes, 14 Jan. 1942, QQ. 357–9; CAB 87/79, 'Retirement Pensions. Practicability of Enforcing Conditions', by P. Y. Blundun, 17 Apr. 1942, with Appendices by A. W. McKenzie and Sir George Reid.)

[45] PRO, CAB 87/79, 'Retirement Pensions. Practicability of Enforcing Conditions', by P. Y. Blundun, 17 Apr. 1942; 'Retirement Conditions', by E. Hale, 24 Apr. 1942.

also about the political viability of Beveridge's proposal that the long-term unemployed and the 'workshy' should be dealt with by compulsory training rather than by withdrawal of cash relief.[46] These objections do not appear to have been considered by Beveridge, however, and their merits were never discussed.

V

Nevertheless, the plan drawn up by Beveridge in the winter of 1941–2 was still far from complete, and many important questions both of principle and practical detail remained to be settled. These concerned particularly the administrative structure of the new scheme, the definition of 'subsistence', the assimilation of workmen's compensation to social insurance, and the treatment of groups with special needs—such as married women, 'domestic spinsters', unsupported mothers and 'unmarried wives'. Most fundamentally there remained the question of how the new scheme was to be paid for, since the Government Actuary estimated that it would nearly treble the burden of social services expenditure on the national exchequer.[47] These basic problems formed the main topics for discussion in the committee throughout 1942. The attempts to deal with them will be considered in some detail, since they show how some at least of Beveridge's proposals were modified by his official advisers and by pressures from outside the Social Insurance committee. They illustrate also some of the basic dilemmas involved in the planning of a social security system—many of which were not fully resolved in the committee's final report.

The question of administrative machinery was hived off in February 1942 to a small sub-committee consisting of Hale, Reid, Blundun, Miss Ritson and Hamilton Farrell. The correspondence between members of this sub-committee gave vent to much suppressed resentment at Beveridge's neglect of his colleagues' views and at his attempt to drive them to decisive conclusions before the relevant evidence had been heard or discussed. There were complaints also about Beveridge's rather cavalier dismissal of routine administrative problems, such as how contributions from the self-employed and non-employed classes could be practically enforced.[48] Blundun in particular was strongly opposed to Beveridge's proposal for vesting control, not in a Minister but in a non-Parliamentary Board. 'It would be as improper as it would be futile,' Blundun

[46] PRO, PIN 8/87, 'Observations on First Draft of Social Insurance Committee Report', by P. Y. Blundun, n.d.

[47] PRO, CAB 87/79, 'Finance of the Chairman's Draft Proposals', by G. S. W. Epps, 22 Apr. 1942.

[48] PRO, PIN 8/86, M. Ritson to R. Hamilton Farrell, 9 and 10 Apr. 1942; M. Ritson to Sir George Reid, 24 Mar. and 14 May 1942.

argued, 'to try to "take" the Social Security Scheme, dealing with millions sterling, "out of politics";' and he suggested instead that there should be a new Ministry of Social Security, assisted by a non-executive advisory body modelled on the Unemployment Insurance Statutory Committee.[49] Miss Ritson was highly critical of Beveridge's plan for combining the administration of insurance and assistance. Such an arrangement, she argued, ran entirely counter to popular sentiment, it would arouse suspicion that social security was primarily concerned with 'doles to social misfits', and it would undermine the psychological distinction between benefit according to means and benefit as of right.[50] In the sub-committee's report in June 1942 compulsory contributions from persons not under contract of employment were condemned as unjust and impracticable; and it was recommended instead that insurance for such persons should be subject to upper and lower income-limits, outside which they would be entitled to voluntary exemption. The sub-committee agreed that approved societies should be abolished, but suggested that friendly societies might be retained as government agents for paying benefit, checking fraud and visiting the sick. Finally, the sub-committee dissented from Beveridge's proposals for a 'loss benefit' for the self-employed and for a special policy to meet the needs of married women. In the former case it was claimed that 'the loss benefit is a mere frill for which there was no demand', and in the latter that the average housewife would pay so few contributions in return for such a wide range of benefits that all semblance of true insurance would be lost.[51] Most of these objections were overruled by Beveridge; but he accepted Blundun's argument that social security should not be removed from the arena of parliamentary politics, and should be placed under a Ministry rather than a Board. He welcomed the suggestion that friendly societies should continue to share in the management though not the financing of social insurance; and he agreed also that non-employed persons below a certain income limit—mainly students, spinsters and invalids—should be allowed the option of 'contracting out'.[52]

The second main area of discussion within the committee centred upon the definition of 'subsistence level'. There was general agreement among the official members that benefits should be adequate to cover subsistence needs. But as D. N. Chester pointed out, such needs might

[49] PRO, PIN 8/86, 'Social Insurance Committee, Machinery Sub-Committee', note by P. Y. Blundun, 18 Feb. 1942.

[50] PRO, PIN 8/86, M. Ritson to Sir George Reid, 14 May 1942.

[51] PRO, PIN 8/86, 'Draft Provisional Conclusions of Committee on Administration', n.d., paras. 4, 40–3; 'Report of the Sub-Committee on Administration', May 1942, paras. 23–30, 40–3; E. Hale to Sir George Reid, 18 Mar. 1942.

[52] PRO, PIN 8/87, 'First Draft of Report by Sir William Beveridge', 10 July 1942.

vary widely according to the sex, age, number of dependants and rent-liability of the insured person. They would be affected also by periodical variations in prices, by regional variations in living-costs and by the season of the year.[53] During the 1930s there had been several attempts—by Seebohm Rowntree, R. F. George, the B.M.A. and the Ministry of Health—to devise a scientific subsistence scale, linked to the needs of men and women at different ages and in different areas, for food, clothing, heating, lighting, minor luxuries and rent. But as George Reid argued, in a paper based on Assistance Board experience, any practical definition of 'subsistence' was largely dependent not merely on what was necessary but also on what was customary—and in the world of administrative reality these two criteria might well not coincide. All the theoretical studies of subsistence, for example, assumed that a woman's 'need' for clothing was a third less than the 'need' of a man; but nearly all empirical studies of how people actually spent their money showed that the average working-class female spent considerably more on clothing than the average working-class male. Reid concluded that subsistence needs should take account of clothing 'which conforms more or less to prevailing fashion'; and similarly it should include food that was not merely nutritionally adequate but 'of a kind and variety which satisfy current tastes'.[54]

Beveridge, as we have seen, was sympathetic to the view that an administrative definition of 'subsistence' should take account of changing social perceptions of human needs. He recognized also that there were many variable components in the needs of different individuals. At the same time, however, he disliked Reid's view that all definitions of subsistence were in the last resort arbitrary; and he was determined to keep benefits at a level that would continue to encourage voluntary thrift. In his early papers on benefit-levels he tentatively suggested a flat-rate weekly benefit derived from Rowntree's 'human needs' scale, and including the sum of ten shillings for rent. He hinted, however, that some kind of regional adjustment of benefits would probably be necessary in order to take account of wide local variations in the level of rent.[55] This suggestion drew an immediate protest from Muriel Ritson, who complained that it would be grossly unfair to low-paid, low-rent areas like Scotland, and would mean that the contributions of poor highland crofters would subsidize the rents of affluent workers in the South-East.[56] It was pointed out also that rents varied widely not merely between regions but between similar accommodation in the same town

[53] BP, VIII 37, 'Fixing Rates of Benefit', by D. N. Chester, 5 Jan. 1942.
[54] BP, VIII 37, 'The Subsistence Level', by Sir George Reid, 20 Feb. 1942.
[55] BP, VIII 28, 'Subsistence Standards for Social Insurance Benefits', by WHB, 29 Dec. 1941.
[56] BP, VIII 27, Muriel Ritson to WHB, 19 Jan. 1942.

and even the same street. The problem was discussed at a meeting on 21 January and it was decided to refer the whole question of subsistence to a special sub-committee composed of Seebohm Rowntree, the statistician Arthur Bowley, and a doctor and nutritionist from the B.M.A.[57]

The sub-committee on subsistence met several times during the spring of 1942 and compiled a mass of data on working-class living standards, on the nutritional minimum for 'health and working capacity' and on regional average rents. Beveridge himself extracted statistical data from the Ministry of Labour, and discovered that average working-class rents varied from more than fifteen shillings a week in London to considerably less than ten shillings in Wales, Scotland, the Midlands and the North-East.[58] In the discussions of the sub-committee it was soon clear that the weight of expert opinion favoured a definition of subsistence that was in some way adjusted to take account of rent. Rowntree in particular urged Beveridge that a flat rate of ten shillings for rent would be excessively generous in some areas and grossly inadequate elsewhere; and he proposed instead that insurance claimants should receive a flat-rate benefit for food, heating and clothing, plus their *actual* rent. Only by such a provision, Rowntree argued, was it possible to combine equality of treatment with adequate provision for subsistence needs.[59] This proposal was strongly endorsed by the Fabian Society and by the Association of Municipal Corporations, and Beveridge himself was clearly attracted by the undeniable logic of Rowntree's scheme. In a paper circulated in July he rejected the idea of rent variations for old age pensioners, on the ground that long-term claimants could adjust their living standards by moving to cheaper housing; but he suggested that 'actual rent' might be paid for short-term claims.[60] This proposal was, however, strongly opposed by several of the official members. Reid objected that it would 'introduce a discordant note' into a scheme that was supposed to be free from means tests; and he urged that relief of excessive rents should be left to public assistance. Hale protested that the problem of rent was a question for post-war housing policy rather than social security; and Miss Ritson once again emphasized the injustice to Scotland and to poor people living in cheap accommodation.[61] Rowntree in reply claimed that it would be good public policy to

[57] PRO. CAB 87/77, S.I.C. minutes, 21 Jan. 1942.
[58] BP, VIII 28, E. Ramsbottom to WHB, 19 Jan. 1942.
[59] BP, VIII 28, 'Calculation of the Poverty Line', by B. S. Rowntree, n.d.; 'Replies to Queries raised by WHB in the Memorandum S.I.C. (42) 55', by B. S. Rowntree, 1 July 1942.
[60] BP, VIII 28, 'Possible Variation of Benefit Levels for Rent', by WHB, 20 July 1942.
[61] BP, VIII 28, G. Reid to D. N. Chester, 27 July 1942, and attached note; E. Hale to D. N. Chester, 24 July 1942, enclosing 'Observations on S.I.C. (42) 115'; PRO, PIN 8/87. Note by M. Ritson on 'Objections which may be urged against the payment of differential benefits based on rent variations', Aug. 1942.

encourage people to move to better accommodation; and he was frankly cynical about the supposed injustice to poor persons with low rents. 'The case would be more clearly and accurately stated,' Rowntree argued, 'if reference was made to the fact that a large number of families that are earning good money are living in the slums and paying low rents because they choose to spend their money on drink and gambling rather than a decent house.'[62] Beveridge, however, was for once swayed by his official advisers—especially by the suggestion that a variable rent allowance would infect social insurance with the taint of a means test. In a letter to Rowntree on 18 August he revealed that he had definitely decided against payment of individual rent. 'The difficulty is,' he explained, 'that it is of the essence of insurance benefit that being given as of right it should not take too detailed account of how individuals spend their income. Freedom to spend is part of essential freedom.'[63] He therefore reverted to his original proposal for a flat-rate benefit which included a notional ten shillings for weekly rent; and he thus allowed himself to be stuck with the paradoxical proposition that benefits should be based on subsistence needs and yet should be uniform for all parts of the country. This paradox was acknowledged in the Beveridge Report; but it was nevertheless seized upon in government circles as an excuse for rejecting the principle of subsistence.[64] In future years it was to prove a continuing Achilles' heel in Beveridge's scheme for the elimination of means tests and abolition of primary poverty.

A third important question discussed at length by the Committee was the integration of social insurance with workmen's compensation. Beveridge, as we have seen, proposed to put an end to the system whereby benefits for industrial injury were paid exclusively by the employers—who either bore the risk themselves or arranged insurance through mutual indemnity guilds and commercial insurance companies. Beveridge's argument was that the causes of physical disability were irrelevant, and that a workman's needs were the same whether his earnings were interrupted by industrial injury or by some other form of accident. He was strongly opposed to the 'lump-sum' settlements often paid to industrial injury victims—which he believed had turned workmen's compensation into a form of 'lottery' rather than scientific social security. He was highly critical also of the continuous litigation to which the system gave rise, and the high management costs incurred by insurance firms that dealt with industrial accidents. He therefore

[62] BP, VIII 28, B. S. Rowntree to WHB, 20 Aug. 1942.
[63] BP, VIII 28, WHB to B. S. Rowntree, 18 Aug. 1942. See also Asa Briggs, *Social Thought and Social Action, A Study of the Work of Seebohm Rowntree* (1961) pp. 307–8.
[64] Cmd. 6404/1942, *Social Insurance and Allied Services*, p. 84, para. 216; below, p. 422.

proposed that industrial injuries should be dealt with like other forms of sickness and should be covered by contributory national insurance.[65] His aim, he claimed, was that of 'converting workmen's compensation from a lawyers' paradise into a "social service"'.[66]

Beveridge's proposals on industrial injuries won a certain amount of support from employers;[67] but not surprisingly they aroused much opposition from commercial and mutual insurance interests and from the trade unions. The insurance companies claimed that Beveridge had greatly exaggerated both their management costs and the extent of litigation, and that the 'absence from the system of all competitive interest would not be conducive either to economy or to efficiency'.[68] The trade union movement was dismayed at the prospect that earnings-related industrial injuries payments (which could be as high as 48 shillings a week) might be reduced to a flat-rate subsistence level; and they pressed for the continuance of a separate workmen's compensation system, still financed solely by the employers.[69] Moreover, many witnesses to the Beveridge committee—including the T.U.C., the Fabian Society and the Cooperative Congress—argued that the aim of workmen's compensation was the prevention and punishment of negligence as well as the relief of financial need. They feared that the transfer of industrial injuries benefit to social insurance would remove the incentive from individual employers to take precautions against accidents and avoid unnecessary risks.[70]

Beveridge was unsympathetic to the protests of the accident insurance companies, but he was anxious to conciliate trade union opinion and he spent a considerable amount of time negotiating with the T.U.C. and trying to meet their demands. Some of the T.U.C.'s objections had been anticipated in his 'Basic Problems of Social Security with Heads of a Scheme'—where he acknowledged the difficulty of reducing industrial injuries benefit to the level of subsistence, but claimed that to raise other benefits to the levels prevailing under workmen's compensation would totally destroy incentives to thrift. He was doubtful also about how far it

[65] BP, IXa, 37(2), 'Social Insurance. General Considerations', July 1941; PRO, CAB 87/76, 'Basic Problems of Social Security with Heads of a Scheme', by WHB, 11 Dec. 1941.

[66] *The Times*, WHB to the editor, 16 Oct. 1945.

[67] PRO, CAB 87/78, S.I.C. minutes, Q. 4,927, evidence of the Shipping Federation and Liverpool Steamship Owners' Association.

[68] *Social Insurance and Allied Services*, Memoranda from Organisations, Paper 26, pp. 139–48. See also Papers 24, 25 and 27. Beveridge himself subsequently admitted that he had exaggerated the high administrative costs of workmen's compensation insurance, which varied from 45 per cent of premiums in a few notorious cases to less than 10 per cent in some of the occupationally based mutual indemnity schemes (BP, VIII 32, 'Further Thoughts on Workmen's Compensation', by WHB, 17 July 1942).

[69] PRO, CAB 87/77, S.I.C. minutes, 14 Jan. 1942, QQ.375–6.

[70] Ibid., QQ.377–81; 11 Mar. 1942, pp. 8–10; 28 July 1942, QQ.6,416–17.

was reasonable to penalize employers with a high rate of accidents—arguing that accidents stemmed from the inherently dangerous nature of certain types of enterprise (such as mining), rather than from the specific negligence of individual employers. A possible compromise, Beveridge suggested, might be to make a distinction between long- and short-term industrial injury. Short-term injuries he thought should be completely assimilated to flat-rate, subsistence-level sickness insurance; but he was prepared to accept that an earnings-related system should be retained for long-term injuries—thus conceding that popular morality required an element of compensation for such injuries as well as mere relief of financial need.[71]

Beveridge's compromise was tentatively accepted by the T.U.C. at a meeting in February 1942; but trade unionists were clearly unhappy with his proposals, and in April the T.U.C. returned to its original demand for retention of a totally separate, employer-financed system of workmen's compensation.[72] Beveridge however, was reluctant to make any further changes in his basic scheme. Over the next few months he received many alternative suggestions on the future of workmen's compensation—including a proposal from Marjorie Cox that industrial injuries benefit should be based on the concept of 'degree of disability' rather than 'interruption of earnings'. This was the principle that had always been followed in the payment of war pensions; and as Miss Cox pointed out it had the great advantage of not discouraging the partially disabled from seeking paid employment.[73] This idea was not considered by Beveridge, however, and the final version of his proposals in December 1942 was virtually identical with the compromise that he had put to the T.U.C. eleven months before. Workmen's compensation was to be abolished, and the first thirteen weeks of industrial injury were to be covered by flat-rate sickness benefit. Thereafter injured workmen would be entitled to long-term disability benefit at two-thirds of their previous earnings, up to a ceiling of £3 a week. Both benefits would be financed out of tripartite national insurance contributions—but the employers' contribution for industrial injury would contain an element of

[71] PRO, CAB 87/76, 'Basic Problems of Social Security with Heads of a Scheme', by WHB, 11 Dec. 1941.

[72] BP, VIII 32, R. A. Bannatyne to WHB, 10 Feb. 1942; PRO, CAB 87/79, 'Trades Union Congress. Replies to Questions submitted by Sir William Beveridge', 3 Apr. 1942, p. 3.

[73] Cox Papers, M. S. Cox to WHB, 4 July 1942. Miss Cox's letter does not appear to have been circulated to the Committee, but she made the same point at a meeting a few days later (PRO, CAB 87/78, S.I.C. minutes, 7 July 1942, QQ. 5,344). Four years later 'degree of disability' rather than loss of earnings was adopted as the basis of the National Insurance (Industrial Injuries) Act. Beveridge commented approvingly on this change of principle and complained that 'degree of disability' had never been suggested by any of his advisers on the Social Insurance committee. But his memory was clearly at fault (*The Times*, WHB to the Editor, 16 Oct. 1945).

'merit-rating', so as to retain some degree of incentive for the promotion of industrial safety. 'Merit-rating' was to be assessed, however, not on the basis of an individual firm's accident record, but on the degree of risk generally involved in the industry to which it belonged.[74]

A fourth important problem area discussed by the committee was the treatment of various kinds of women—employed women, housewives, widows, *divorcées*, deserted and unmarried mothers, 'domestic spinsters' and 'unmarried wives'. The provision for women under existing insurance arrangements demonstrated very clearly the tangle of contradictory principle and inadequate coverage that stemmed from the piece-meal developments of the previous fifty years. At one end of the scale was the employed single woman, who enjoyed virtually the same rights as a male contributor—provided that she did not marry. At the other end of the scale was the *divorcée*, the deserted mother and the spinster caring for elderly relatives—for whom there was no social security provision except public assistance. Beveridge in 1942 was determined to rationalize the position of women and to give each category of women a foothold in social insurance. In particular, he was concerned with improving the position of housewives and mothers, who in the next thirty years would 'have vital work to do in ensuring the adequate continuance of the British race and British ideals in the world'.[75] His interest in insurance for housewives went back to 1924, when his draft bill for 'all-in' insurance had included proposals for giving women benefit rights derived from contributions paid by their husbands.[76] Now eighteen years later he returned to the same theme, and in the early discussions of the committee he proposed that women's insurance should henceforth be provided in five different ways. Employed single women would contribute like men for comprehensive insurance. Married women would be entitled to the special housewives' policy, based on the contributions of their husbands, which would entitle them to furnishing benefit, maternity grants, dependants' benefits, funeral benefit, widowhood and separation allowances, domestic help during sickness and pensions in old age. Employed married women would have the choice of relying on their housewives' policy or contributing separately as employed persons—but in the latter case their benefits would be lower than those of men, on the assumption that free lodging was provided by their husbands. 'Unmarried Wives' would be entitled to certain items of the housewives' policy, but not to the furnishing grant or widows' pension.

---

[74] *Social Insurance and Allied Services*, paras. 100, 360. For a fuller discussion of this issue, see Helen Bolderson, 'Compensation for Disability. The Social and Economic Objectives of Disability Benefits', *Journal of Social Policy*, vol. III, no. 3, 1974, pp. 193–211.

[75] *Social Insurance and Allied Services*, p. 53, para. 117.

[76] Above p. 313, 351.

Other groups of women, such as 'domestic spinsters' would be classed as unoccupied persons and would contribute solely to gain an old-age pension.[77]

Beveridge's early proposals for women had a deceptive air of comprehensiveness about them, but it soon became clear that they bristled with practical difficulties and raised many fundamental questions about contemporary social structure and women's rights. Over the next few months they were subject to a wide range of criticisms both from the official members and from several leading women's organizations. As we have seen the sub-committee on administration condemned the idea of a housewives' policy as a departure from true insurance; and this criticism was echoed from a different angle by Edith Summerskill's Married Women's Association, which urged that married women should become full contributors in their own right quite separately from their husbands.[78] The National Council of Women proposed that female employees both married and single should receive the same benefits as men; and they suggested that, in addition to family allowances, married women should be paid a housewives' allowance like a wage for an ordinary job.[79] Mary Agnes Hamilton urged upon Beveridge the need for more generous treatment of the spinster caring for aged parents; and Beveridge himself was clearly dissatisfied with this aspect of his plan. The problem of the 'domestic spinster', he assured Mrs. Hamilton in March 1942, 'was very much in his mind'.[80] The most controversial of Beveridge's proposals on women, however, was his suggestion that the housewives' policy should include a benefit for the end of marriage by divorce or separation. The break-up of a marriage, Beveridge argued, was one of the hazards that a woman faced in the occupation of matrimony and was therefore in theory a legitimate insurable risk.[81] On the other hand—unlike widowhood and sickness—divorce and separation were to a certain extent under the control of the parties involved; and there was a danger of 'collusive desertion' and of 'exploitation by the anti-social elements in the community'.[82] There was the problem also that the deserted wife had a right to maintenance enforceable against her husband through the courts; and it was a cardinal principle of

[77] PRO, CAB 87/76, 'Basic Problems of Social Security with Heads of a Scheme', 11 Dec. 1941, paras. 9, 22–3.

[78] BP, VIII 35, Juanita Frances (Chairman of the Married Women's Association) to WHB, 21 Sept. 1942.

[79] PRO, CAB 87/77, S.I.C. Minutes, 11 Mar. 1942, QQ. 1,361, 1,366–7, 1,420–1.

[80] BP, IXa 37(2), ms. extracts from S.I.C. correspondence, WHB to M. A. Hamilton, 16 Mar. 1942.

[81] PRO, CAB 87/76, 'Basic Problems of Social Security with Heads of a Scheme', by WHB, 11 Dec. 1941.

[82] BP, VIII 27, 'Preliminary Notes on The Organisation of a Scheme of Social Security', by M. Ritson, Jan. 1942.

Beveridge's scheme that a person should not receive two different benefits for the same social misfortune.

These objections were discussed several times during the spring of 1942 with the official members and with groups of female witnesses.[83] On the question of a special housewives' policy Beveridge refused to be moved. Against his official advisers he argued that housewives were doing work of national importance and therefore needed insurance as much as men; but at the same time he resisted the demand of the women's organizations that women should be placed on the same footing as men. It was an economic fact, Beveridge argued, that seven-eighths of married women were dependent on their husbands; and, whether or not this was a good thing, social insurance should be geared to the needs of the majority and not to the needs of an atypical minority.[84] He defended also the payment of lower benefits to married women employees—claiming that all social surveys showed that their needs were less than those of single women, and that their motivation for returning to work after sickness and unemployment was considerably weaker than that of married men. Beveridge also dismissed as not 'practical politics' the demand from the National Council of Women for a universal 'housewives' allowance' in addition to allowances for children.[85] In this he was supported by Eleanor Rathbone, who recalled that in the early days of the family endowment movement she also had pressed for state provision for both children and wives. She had come to the conclusion, however, that it was better to concentrate such support solely upon children—partly because the childless wife could take paid employment, and partly because single people had to incur the expense of housekeeping no less than married couples.[86]

On the 'domestic spinster' and the deserted mother, however, Beveridge's views were much less clearly defined. He urged the various women's organizations to submit detailed proposals on the treatment of these two groups, and he was clearly hoping to include them within the ambit of social insurance.[87] No such proposals were forthcoming, however, from any of the women's organizations—presumably because of the inherent difficulties of including either group within a contributory system. The only concrete proposal for extending insurance coverage of 'domestic spinsters' came from Muriel Ritson, who suggested that women caring for aged parents should be treated like married housewives.[88]

[83] PRO, CAB 87/77, SIC minutes, 11 Feb. and 11 Mar. 1942.
[84] *Social Insurance and Allied Services*, p. 49, para. 108.
[85] PRO, CAB 87/77, SIC minutes, 11 Mar. 1942, QQ. 1,368, 1,387, 1,394, 1618–20.
[86] PRO, CAB 87/77, SIC minutes, 2 June 1942, QQ. 3,021–4.
[87] PRO, CAB 87/77, SIC minutes, 11 Mar. 1942, QQ. 1,614, 1,627.
[88] BP, VIII 27, 'Preliminary Notes on The Organisation of a Scheme for Social Security', by Muriel Ritson, Jan. 1942.

Beveridge himself reluctantly rejected this proposal as impossible to justify within the context of contributory insurance. Married women's benefits could be financed by contributions from their husbands, but benefits for non-employed spinsters could only be financed by public funds. No change was therefore made in Beveridge's original proposals; and in his final report the 'domestic spinster' was left—as she was left for the next thirty years—as one of the most neglected figures in the field of social security. Non-employed spinsters with an income of over £75 were to be insured for an old-age pension; and those without an income were to be left to public assistance.[89]

The deserted mother presented similar difficulties. Beveridge, as we have seen, had included divorce and separation in his first draft scheme as risks to be covered like widowhood and old age. He was anxious, however, about the extent to which the fact of separation could be accurately verified; and this doubt was shared by several members of his committee. Miss Cox from her experience of war pensions thought that such problems as co-habitation could best be dealt with by sympathetic 'casework', but Beveridge himself was anxious to devise a system as free as possible from any kind of personal supervision.[90] In discussions with the National Council of Women he remarked that 'I am inclined to think that [the deserted wife] ought to be allowed to declare off marriage, as it were. The difficulty is that she may go and declare it on again. It is not her fault, because there is the husband and his changes of mind may vary. I am not saying it against her, but you do not quite know what she will do.'[91] Two months later in his first complete draft report he had apparently come to the conclusion that provision for separation through insurance was impracticable; and he recommended that the deserted wife should be relieved by the public assistance authorities, which would pursue her right to maintenance from her husband through the courts.[92] This proposal evoked a vigorous protest, however, both from public assistance authorities, and from the Married Women's Association. A highly articulate delegation from the Association of Municipal Corporations argued that deserted wives should not be excluded from insurance and that the unpleasant task of pursuing defaulting husbands should lie with the Ministry of Social Security and not with public assistance officers.[93] A few weeks later Edith Summerskill urged Beveridge that the 'same allowances as received by widows be granted to non-gainfully occupied housewives who have been deserted

---

[89] *Social Insurance and Allied Services*, p. 127, para. 317.
[90] Interview with Dame Marjorie Cox.
[91] PRO, CAB 87/77, SIC minutes, 11 Mar. 1942, Q. 1,458.
[92] PRO, PIN 8/87, 'First Draft of Report by Sir William Beveridge', Part III, July 1942, para. 45.
[93] PRO, CAB 87/88, SIC minutes, 29 July 1942, QQ. 6,910–14.

by their husbands, pending court proceedings'.[94] Beveridge in reply suggested that deserted mothers might be given a guardians' benefit, but that in making any more generous provision the 'practical difficulty was one of proof'.[95] That he was anxious to make such provision, however, became clear in his discussions with the Corporation of Edinburgh in August 1942. 'Why should you not have a benefit for a deserted wife?' he suggested.

I want to put this to you; actually I had left the deserted and separated wife out and said she ought to be dealt with by assistance, but on talking this over with a very able man indeed, he told me, 'You are quite wrong. You ought to provide a benefit for the deserted wife'. I said 'Well, ought not the husband to pay for it,' and he said, 'Yes, you look after the wife and then you can pursue the husband'. Do you see why you should not have a benefit for the deserted wife? It is like being widowed.

This proposal clearly did not commend itself, however, to the baillies and burghers of Edinburgh. 'I think probably that class of person would be very difficult to cater for,' remarked the convenor of the public assistance committee. 'Might one not put it that it would be subsidizing an illegal and immoral act?' objected the town clerk. 'I wonder if it is,' replied Beveridge. 'I think it would be if you did not pursue the husband. On the other hand, I feel myself that every person doing useful work— and most housewives are doing useful work—ought to be secured against the risks of their calling. It is like an industrial accident.'[96]

Over the next few weeks Beveridge was searching for ways in which his comments to the corporation of Edinburgh might be translated into policy.[97] He raised the question of deserted wives at a meeting of his committee on 23 September, and re-affirmed his desire to include them in the scope of insurance. 'The great administrative problem,' he admitted, 'was to have sufficient check on the authenticity of the desertion; the husband might be merely working some distance from home or might be a sailor on a long voyage.'[98] A possible solution to this dilemma was outlined in a paper by D. N. Chester, who suggested that desertion should be treated like industrial accidents—where an injured party had rights both from social security and from the common law. In both cases benefit would be paid by the Ministry of Social Security, which would recover the cost through the courts from the offending party—the employer in the case of industrial injury and the husband in the case of

[94] BP, VIII 35, Edith Summerskill to WHB, 18 Sept. 1942.
[95] BP, VIII 35, notes in WHB's ms. entitled 'Widow', n.d.
[96] PRO, CAB 87/78, SIC minutes, 31 Aug. 1942, QQ. 8,270–82.
[97] BP, VIII 43, notes in WHB's ms. (n.d., Aug. 1942).
[98] PRO, CAB 87/78, SIC minutes, 23 Sept. 1942.

the deserted wife.[99] During discussion of this paper the problem was raised of what was to be done in cases where the wife rather than the husband was responsible for desertion; but it was objected that great administrative difficulties would arise 'if an attempt was made to restrict payment of benefit to cases where the man was the guilty party'.[100] Nevertheless, the raising of this question placed Beveridge on the horns of a dilemma and brought into conflict two of his most deeply-held beliefs about social insurance. On the one hand, payment of benefit to a 'guilty wife' would mean covering a contingency which was under the control of the insured individual; and on the other hand the withholding of benefit from a 'guilty wife' would entail personal inquiry into the behaviour of the insured. Probably for these reasons Beveridge at this point came to the conclusion that his plan for a separation benefit was administratively unworkable. In a further draft later in September he envisaged that such a benefit could be paid only in the case of divorce or legal separation.[101] In other cases deserted wives would have to rely on public assistance or maintenance proceedings through the courts. This rather anticlimatic conclusion was reinforced in the autumn of 1942 by revelations of difficulties encountered by the Ministry of Pensions in the payment of separation benefit to soldiers' wives. 'Did you see the article in the *Evening Standard* of yesterday in regard to Soldiers' Marriage Troubles?' commented R. A. Bannatyne. 'That article seems to me to confirm the view that however much one might desire to make special provision for a deserted wife, the practical difficulties are too formidable.'[102]

## VI

The most serious question left unsettled by Beveridge's early memoranda was how comprehensive insurance, family allowances and a universal health service, were to be financed. Sir George Epps estimated that the total cost of Beveridge's proposals in their first year of operation would be £535 million, of which £402 million would be devoted to social insurance and £302 million would fall on the Exchequer. This latter estimate was nearly three times as high as Exchequer expenditure on equivalent services in 1941; and Epps predicted that the cost of the new scheme would increase rapidly after it was introduced, because of the

---

[99] PRO, CAB 87/82, 'The Problem of Alternative Remedies', by D. N. Chester, 21 Sept. 1942.
[100] PRO, CAB 87/78, SIC minutes, 23 Sept. 1942.
[101] PRO, PIN 8/87, 'Draft Report by Sir William Beveridge', Part V, para. 47, 29 Sept. 1942. *Social Insurance and Allied Services*, para. 347.
[102] BP, VIII 43, R. A. Bannatyne to WHB, 13 Oct. 1942.

rising population of pensionable age.[103] Such a heavyweight addition to the annual budget threatened to undermine the political plausibility of Beveridge's plan; and members of his committee, particularly Hale and Chester, urged him to tailor his proposals to fiscal reality.[104] To deal with this problem Beveridge sought advice from outside his committee. In March 1942 he wrote to Maynard Keynes, now a high-ranking Treasury adviser, enclosing copies of his proposals and suggesting a talk 'about some of the general problems that will arise, including particularly the question of how such services should be financed'.[105] Keynes replied that he was 'in a state of wild enthusiasm' about Beveridge's scheme, which he thought was 'a vast constructive reform of real importance' and much less expensive than he had originally feared. Keynes at this stage made four suggestions for strengthening the financial aspects of Beveridge's plan. Firstly, he advised him to take into account the effects of wartime inflation. 'As a matter of drafting,' he wrote, 'the whole question of adjustments to the value of money needs perhaps to be made a little clearer. It is also important to make it clear, I think, that it is not intended in future to have frequent adjustments of this kind or put the benefits and the contributions on a cost of living scale, but only to make such adjustments when there have been major disturbances, as for example between pre-war and probable post-war values.' Secondly, he urged him to consider the possibility of financing pensions, not out of an accumulated fund, but out of current income. It was a 'severe burden', Keynes argued, 'to meet simultaneously pensions against which no funds have been accumulated and to accumulate funds for future pensions. The future can well be left to look after itself. It will have more resources for doing so than the immediate present.' Thirdly, he was 'very keen' on the proposed 'tax on dismissals'—suggesting that in cases of 'outright dismissal' the tax should be considerably higher than Beveridge had proposed. And, finally, he urged Beveridge to be more radical in his attack on vested interests.

I feel you have been a little weak-kneed about voluntary industrial insurance. I should like to be much more drastic about this, thereby releasing substantial working-class funds. Indeed, I should like to see the new State Fund take over Employers' Liability Insurance by employers and Industrial Insurance by employed. I agree with you, on the other hand, in wanting to encourage Friendly Societies and similar organisations by which a man makes provision for more than his minimum relief.[106]

---

[103] PRO, CAB 87/79, 'Finance of the Chairman's Draft Proposals', by G. S. W. Epps, 22 Apr. 1942, paras. 22, 56–8.
[104] Interviews with Sir Edward Hale and Sir Norman Chester.
[105] BP, IXa 37(1), 'Dealings with Keynes on Beveridge Report', by WHB, p. 1.
[106] BP, IXa, 37(1), J. M. Keynes to WHB, 17 Mar. 1942.

The co-operation of Keynes was to be of great importance to Beveridge over the next few months, both in enhancing the financial viability of his report and in smoothing the way for its reception in official circles. In contrast to his relations with his committee Beveridge's dealings with Keynes were highly convivial, and their discussions took place over lunch and dinner in a series of West End Clubs. Initially, however, Beveridge was reluctant to make any major changes in his basic plans. He apparently rejected Keynes' suggestion that pensions should be paid for out of current income; and the only signs of Keynes' influence in Beveridge's first draft report were a proposal for state-management of industrial life assurance and the addition of 25 per cent to the proposed level of benefits in order to take account of wartime inflation.[107] This latter change, far from pruning the cost of Beveridge's scheme, raised the projected social security budget to £500 million—a figure that caused considerable concern both to Beveridge's official advisers and to government financial experts. At a meeting of the committee on 23 June it was urged that the proposed benefits should be treated as merely provisional, and that cuts should be made in maternity grants, dependants' benefits and rates paid to workers under twenty-one. In particular it was suggested that subsistence-level old-age pensions should be introduced only gradually over an extended period, 'during which time the pension received would have some relation to the contribution records of the applicant, including contributions made since 1926'.[108] Similar concern was expressed by Lionel Robbins in a discussion between the Beveridge committee and members of the Economic Section of the War Cabinet Office. Robbins was apprehensive that the proposals as they stood would require a level of taxation unacceptable in peacetime and might seriously hamper post-war investment. He was particularly alarmed by the projected expenditure on pensions, which might preclude expenditure on other more important social objectives, such as technical education, relief of child poverty, and post-war reconstruction. Robbins proposed therefore that the plan should be developed by gradual stages, 'full implementation being deferred until it could be seen that the rate of recovery and the trend of national income were favourable'.[109]

Beveridge was still reluctant to modify his scheme, but on 25 June he received a further note from Keynes, asking for a copy of his latest proposals and inviting him to lunch at the Atheneum. 'From the criticism made,' commented Keynes, 'I am rather alarmed lest it is being overwhelmed by the pensions part, for it seemed to me the least

---

[107] PRO, PIN 8/87, 'First Draft of the Report by Sir William Beveridge', part II, para. 23; part III, para. 50; part IV, p. 9.
[108] PRO, CAB 87/78, S.I.C. minutes, 23 June 1942.
[109] PRO, CAB 87/78, S.I.C. minutes, 24 June 1942.

interesting and least essential of the whole.'[110] A few days later Beveridge was approached by Sir Richard Hopkins, the deputy secretary to the Treasury, who had been warned by Hale about the far-reaching financial implications of Beveridge's plan.

I have seen a copy of the note which was furnished to you by the Economic Section [wrote Hopkins], and while I have a very high appreciation of the work which Robbins and his colleagues have done in connection with reconstruction, I do not personally feel that this particular note gives you an adequate picture of the financial problem—at any rate as we see it here. The issues involved in your great topic are so far-reaching and bear on so many aspects of our future life that I should like very much to have an informal talk with you before you circulate any draft to the Departments principally concerned.[111]

Beveridge replied on 9 July that he had talked the matter over with Keynes and had simplified his proposals, 'leaving a large number of cracks suitable for the insertion of Treasury wedges . . . I would now like as soon as possible to get down to a serious business talk about finance. Some form of Sub-Committee with the Treasury and Epps seems to me the right thing.'[112]

Beveridge's rather vague reassurances did not quieten the alarm in Treasury circles; and there was much discussion of his proposals among Treasury officials throughout July and August 1942. Early in July Keynes put forward detailed proposals for a gradual transition to subsistence-level old-age pensions—which would involve no increase in existing pension rates for the first five years of the scheme, and an annual increase of 6d. a week thereafter. During the transitional period pensions would be graduated according to the individual pensioners' contribution record. The idea of a transitional scheme was strongly supported by Beveridge's Treasury adviser, Edward Hale—who thought, however, that it would be impossible to combine such a scheme with Beveridge's insistence on making pensions conditional on retirement.[113] These and other insurance problems were discussed at a meeting between officials of the Treasury and the various social policy departments on 22 July. The meeting was attended by several members of Beveridge's committee, but not by Beveridge himself; and during the discussion considerable alarm was expressed, not merely at the cost of Beveridge's proposals, but at his apparent desire to stampede the government into an over-hasty commitment to post-war social reform. It was feared that

[110] BP, IXa 37(1), J. M. Keynes to WHB, 25 June 1942.
[111] BP, IXa 37(1), Sir Richard Hopkins to WHB, 30 June 1942.
[112] BP, IXa, 37(1), WHB to Sir Richard Hopkins, 9 July 1942.
[113] PRO, PIN 8/87, 'Beveridge Old-Age Pensions—Transitional Arrangements', by E. Hale, 18 July 1942.

if the various departments suggested detailed amendments these 'would be brushed aside by Sir William Beveridge' and yet at the same time would be interpreted as a definite sign of future government policy. These fears were partially assuaged by Keynes, who claimed that Beveridge was 'not finally committed to the whole plan as set out in his report and, if approached, would be ready and willing to be co-operative'. Keynes urged the departments, including the Treasury, to render Beveridge every possible assistance; and he undertook to persuade Beveridge to divide his report into two distinct parts—a definition of ultimate Utopian goals and a less ambitious statement of the gradual stages by which those goals might be attained.[114]

Thanks to Keynes' intervention, Beveridge at the end of July received a letter from Sir Horace Wilson, offering him the services of both Keynes and Robbins in modifying the financial aspects of his insurance plan.[115] 'There followed,' Beveridge recorded, 'a series of discussions and interchange of notes, between Keynes, Robbins, Epps and myself, with the finance of the scheme coming ever more clearly to depend on what we did about pensions for those at or near the pensionable age.' In these discussions Beveridge eventually agreed with Keynes that the additional cost imposed on the exchequer should not exceed £100 million a year for the first five years with no fixed limit thereafter.[116] The two men dined together at the Gargoyle Club on 12 August, and Keynes influence was clearly apparent in a paper which Beveridge composed a week later, entitled 'The Problem of Pensions'. In this memorandum he outlined his reasons for 'sticking to adequate retirement pensions as the ultimate goal'; but he now thought that 'in view of the vital need of conserving resources, particularly in the aftermath of war, it is impossible to justify giving, as from the first day of the plan for social security, full subsistence pensions to people who have neither contributed for them nor are in need'. He therefore proposed that subsistence-level pensions should be introduced by stages over a period of sixteen years. During the interval, insurance pensions would be paid at less than subsistence-level and supplemented where necessary by public assistance. Such an arrangement, Beveridge admitted, would involve continued reliance on a means test; but the disincentive to thrift would be reduced to a minimum, because it would affect only those nearing retirement, who had never previously expected subsistence-level pensions. It would not affect those in lower age-groups, who had the rest of their working lives in which to save. At the end of sixteen years, Beveridge envisaged, pensions would become fully adequate for

[114] PRO, PIN 8/87, 'Beveridge Report, Meetings at the Treasury', 22 July 1942.
[115] BP, IXa 37(1), 'Dealings with Keynes on Beveridge Report', by WHB, p. 6.
[116] *PI*, p. 309.

subsistence and, except for an insignificant minority, the need for public assistance would eventually wither away. Subsistence-level pensions, when eventually attained, were to be conditional on recipients retiring from full-time work. 'It would be reprehensible and unjustifiable,' Beveridge argued, 'to give a full subsistence-level income to every citizen, as a birthday present on his reaching a particular age.'[117]

Beveridge's discussions with Keynes and Robbins also resulted in a modification of his family endowment proposals—although the motive for this change was less a reduction in the total budget than a concentration of resources upon those in special need. In his earlier memoranda Beveridge had assumed that allowances would be paid universally in respect of all children at a rate of five shillings a week. Studies of working-class incomes, however, suggested that even in the lowest-paid groups wages were normally adequate to support a man, a wife and one child. In August 1942 Beveridge therefore modified his scheme by proposing that no allowance should be paid for the first child in a family, but more generous provision should be made for second and further children. In a letter to Keynes explaining his new proposals he claimed that the higher level of allowance was in accord with advice from nutrition experts, and that exclusion of the first child would enable him to keep within the agreed limit of £100 million.[118] Keynes in reply urged him to be very specific in his final report about the projected level of contributions and benefits, partly because 'it would be impossible to expect Parliament to discuss the scheme on a purely hypothetical basis' and partly to underline the determination of the Treasury to keep a strict control on money values after the war. In the same letter Keynes admitted that he was now converted to Beveridge's plan for making pensions conditional on retirement, though he was doubtful whether such a condition would gain political support.

After reading this further instalment [Keynes concluded], I feel confirmed in the feeling I expressed the other day that this is a grand document. You can scarcely expect it to be adopted just as it stands, but it seems to me that you have got it into an extremely workable shape, and I should hope that the major and more essential parts of it might be adopted substantially as you have conceived them.[119]

## VII

Beveridge's Report was virtually complete and ready for publication early in October 1942. Except for its financial provisions the final draft

[117] BP, IXa 37(1), WHB to J. M. Keynes, 20 Aug. 1942; VIII, 33, 'The Problem of Pensions', by WHB, 19 Aug. 1942.
[118] BP, IXa 37(1), WHB to J. M. Keynes, 20 Aug. 1942.
[119] BP, IXa 37(1), copy of letter from J. M. Keynes to WHB, 14 Oct. 1942.

was in most respects remarkably similar to the first complete draft of four months earlier—a fact which reflected both the reluctance of the departments to suggest substantive alterations and Beveridge's own unwillingness to modify his key ideas. The report reiterated the ambitious series of proposals that he had outlined in numerous memoranda over the previous nine months—a free national health service, policies of full employment, family allowances for second and further children, and abolition of poverty by a comprehensive system of social insurance, with benefits paid at subsistence-level and as a statutory right. The different compartments of social insurance were to be unified under a single Ministry, which would also take over responsibility from local authorities for residual public assistance. Approved societies would be abolished, although friendly societies and other voluntary organizations would continue to act in an administrative capacity as agents of the state. The hallmarks of the new system, Beveridge claimed, were to be economy in administration, adequacy in benefits, universality in scope. Before looking in detail at the final stages of the report and its political reception, however, some comparison should be made with some of the alternative proposals that were submitted to Beveridge during the course of his inquiry but were ultimately rejected. More must be said also about the underlying themes of Beveridge's Report, their intellectual origins and their significance in his wider social philosophy.

It has already been emphasized that many of Beveridge's ideas had been formulated and much of his report drafted before more than a fraction of evidence had been received. Nevertheless, Beveridge's discussions with witnesses are of considerable interest, both in revealing the degree of popular concurrence with his views and in suggesting the range of alternative ideas that were current at the time. Evidence was submitted on behalf of more than a hundred organizations with interests in social welfare—trade unions, employers, friendly societies, insurance companies, research institutes, local authorities and professional groups. Representatives of fifty of these bodies appeared in person and were cross-examined on the views expressed in their written memoranda. Beveridge himself took a very lively part in these discussions, sometimes acting as 'devil's advocate', and sometimes using them not merely to extract information but to expound and publicize his own favourite ideas. 'Perhaps I am giving evidence on this,' he joked with a delegation from the T.U.C., after he had spent a morning trying to convert them to family allowances.[120] To witness after witness he made clear his own biases and convictions—his dislike of means tests and administrative 'police supervision', his belief in the psychological value of contributory insurance, his concern at the administrative expenses incurred by

[120] PRO, CAB 87/77, S.I.C. minutes, 14 Jan. 1942, Q.498.

commercial insurance, his desire to encourage voluntary action and thrift. He shocked a delegation from the Co-operative Congress by suggesting that, if a man with a family was so badly paid that he got less from wages than from benefit, then it was his moral duty to apply for the latter;[121] but at the same time he was scathing in his rejection of all forms of 'Santa Claus state'. 'Go away and think over what is best,' he urged witnesses, 'not as a matter of history, not as a matter of vested interests or anything of that kind, but what is best for the workmen of the country when they are incapacitated . . . and also how it is to be paid.'[122]

One of the most striking features of the evidence submitted to the Beveridge Committee was the very widespread expectation among witnesses that the inquiry was going to lead to radical, even 'Utopian' social change.[123] Quite where this expectation came from is not entirely clear, but it may well have derived from Beveridge himself and from his frequent references in articles and broadcasts to the abolition of poverty and to post-war social reform. A second striking feature was the very wide degree of support among witnesses for the kind of reform that Beveridge already had in mind—a measure of the extent to which Beveridge himself was interpreting rather than creating the spirit of the times. Again and again witnesses pressed spontaneously and independently for measures which afterwards became the main policy proposals of the Beveridge Report—namely, family allowances, full employment, a universal health service, a uniform system of contributory insurance, subsistence-level benefits and the reduction or abolition of public assistance. In so far as witnesses dissented from these policies it was mainly on points of detail rather than on general principle. Many friendly societies, for example, endorsed the need for universal medical care and more comprehensive statutory benefits—with the reservation that sickness insurance should continue to be managed through approved societies.[124] Even the industrial assurance companies claimed to favour a great expansion of existing statutory services, provided that they could continue to act as agents for national insurance and retain the commercially valuable right of 'door-to-door collection'.[125] In certain cases witnesses in their anxiety for reform were highly critical of their own roles in the prevailing system of welfare. Public assistance officers, for example, unanimously called for a repeal of the Poor Law, denounced the 'meanness of the means test', and condemned existing public assistance provision as 'inadequate, overlap-

[121] PRO, CAB 87/77, S.I.C. minutes, 11 Mar. 1942, p. 11.
[122] PRO, CAB 87/77, S.I.C. minutes, 14 Jan. 1942, Q. 630.
[123] PRO, CAB 87/78, S.I.C. minutes, 17 June and 25 Aug. 1942, QQ. 4,677–8 and 7,463.
[124] *Social Insurance and Allied Services. Memoranda from Organisations*, Paper 13.
[125] PRO, CAB 87/77, S.I.C. minutes, 25 Mar. 1942, QQ. 693, 1,871, 1,877.

ping, ungenerous and inefficient'.[126] Politically perhaps the most significant evidence came from the T.U.C., who in spite of initially declaring their refusal to compromise, ultimately agreed with Beveridge on every major issue—with the sole exception of workmen's compensation.[127] Beveridge spent more time negotiating with the T.U.C. than with any other witnesses; and his cordial relations with them at this time were a striking contrast to the mutual mistrust and hostility that had existed between him and the trade union movement during the First World War.

Beveridge was therefore articulating ideas which already commanded a good deal of popular support. Nevertheless, it would be wrong to suggest that there was a universal consensus among witnesses in favour of his proposals. The relative mildness of the commercial insurance interests was a reflection of the fact that they had had little time to organize themselves against Beveridge's attack. A year later, when his Report was under consideration by the government, the big insurance companies were vociferous in condemning him as a 'Professor of Economics' whose proposals were based on 'book lore' and a complete lack of knowledge of working-class life.[128] The British Employers' Confederation, while vaguely assenting to the need for reform, thought that the whole question of reconstruction should be postponed until after the war.[129] Moreover, among those who supported Beveridge's general scheme, there were many varied suggestions about the precise form it should take. Some of these alternatives are of particular interest, because although rejected by Beveridge, they have been revived and in some cases acted upon in subsequent phases of British social policy. The economists Robbins and Meade proposed that social insurance could in itself be used to maintain full employment, by variation of contribution and benefit rates to regulate consumer demand. This proposal was mentioned in passing in the final report; but Beveridge himself remarked disparagingly that he 'had invented too many such devices in the early days of unemployment insurance to have retained much faith in their practical value'.[130] Several witnesses proposed that contributory insurance should be abolished and benefits financed as a surcharge on the

---

[126] PRO, CAB 87/81, memoranda from the Local Government Clerks' Association, the Assistance Board Departmental Whitley Council and The National Association of Relieving Officers, July–Aug. 1942.

[127] PRO, CAB 87/79, 'Trades Union Congress, Replies to Questions Submitted by Sir William Beveridge', 3 Apr. 1942.

[128] PRO, PIN 8/89, 'Interview with Sir William Jowitt', notes by J. A. Jefferson, Chairman of the Industrial Life Offices Association, 10 Feb. 1943.

[129] PRO, CAB 87/77, S.I.C. minutes, 20 May 1942, QQ. 2,844, 2,849, 2,854.

[130] BP, VIII, 29, 'Internal Measures for the Prevention of General Unemployment' by the Economic Section of the War Cabinet Secretariat n.d.; PRO, CAB 87/78, S.I.C. minutes, 24 June 1942; *Social Insurance and Allied Services*, pp. 164–5; *PI*, p. 305.

income tax;[131] but as was shown earlier, this possibility had already been rejected by the Beveridge committee as likely to fall into the forbidden category of an 'earmarked fund'. Others, notably the International Labour Office, commented favourably on the kind of 'earnings-related' system commonly found on the Continent;[132] but this was turned down as administratively complex and liable to intrude upon the sphere of voluntary saving. A third alternative, favoured by P.E.P. and the Association of Approved Societies, was the payment of flat-rate benefits in return for contributions graduated according to income; but this proposal was condemned by Beveridge himself as the epitome of the 'Santa Claus state'. 'I believe there is a psychological desire,' he argued, 'to get something for which you have paid . . . the tradition of the fixed price is very strong in this country. You do not like having to pay more than your neighbours.'[133] A fourth alternative, also proposed by the Association of Approved Societies, was that social insurance should be managed, not by bureaucrats in Whitehall, but by small, highly personalized welfare societies rooted in local communities. These welfare societies would be subject to control by meetings of contributors and would be advised by public relations officers 'whose sole function it would be to keep in touch with the trend of public opinion on the administration of the Fund'. In each area the needs of contributors would be the subject of 'continuing care' by local 'welfare officers', who would pay benefits, deal with claimants' personal problems and advise them of their rights. Such an arrangement, it was argued, would bring to bear 'humanising influences' on the social security system.[134] Beveridge and his officials, however, were resolutely unimpressed. Miss Ritson thought that many grievances would arise if people were not treated on a uniform basis, and Mrs. Hamilton objected to the 'sinister' and 'terrifying' power that would be exercised by the welfare officer over his clients' private lives. 'You know I am a little frightened of your picture of going to the welfare officer,' Beveridge himself commented; and he concluded that the scheme would involve 'an amount of supervision, and police supervision, which makes the thing unworkable'.[135]

The underlying themes of the Social Insurance report may be seen as a mixture of principles that were both old and new. On the one hand it was the culmination of certain ideas that Beveridge had been evolving

[131] BP, VIII 27, J. E. Meade to D. N. Chester, 28 Aug. 1941; *Memoranda from the Organisations*, Paper 7, 'Summary of Memorandum of Evidence by P.E.P.', p. 35.
[132] PRO, CAB 87/77, S.I.C. minutes, 6 May 1942, QQ.2,464–71.
[133] PRO, CAB 87/78, S.I.C. minutes, 17 June 1942, QQ.4,719–26.
[134] *Memoranda from the Organisations*, Paper 19, pp. 110–18. The Association of Approved Societies was a small body representing 'intellectual' interests in the friendly society movement; it was in no sense representative of approved societies as a whole.
[135] PRO, CAB 87/76, S.I.C. minutes, 26 Nov. 1941, QQ.27–8, 182, 298, 311, 314.

over the previous thirty years; and on the other hand it contained certain radical innovations that reflected the heightened consciousness of social change and social solidarity induced in Beveridge by the Second World War. The central emphasis upon insurance went straight back to his days on the *Morning Post* and to his youthful denunciation of means tests, behavioural tests, and all forms of relief that stigmatized the recipient and discouraged personal saving. The practical details of insurance management—the stamping of books by employers, the conditions proposed for verification of sickness and unemployment, the system of appeals to an umpire, the imposition of a three days' waiting period—all rested firmly on the structure originally invented for the first National Insurance Act of 1911. The integration of different sectors of insurance went back to Beveridge's involvement in the 'all-in' movement of the 1920s—although both the scope and degree of rationalization envisaged in the Report went far beyond anything Beveridge had envisaged in 1924. The central role of family allowances was the fruit of Beveridge's growing concern throughout the 1920s and 30s with the problem of family poverty and with the antagonistic relationship between social security and wages. The transfer of public assistance to the national exchequer was an expression of his long-standing bias towards administrative centralization. His attempt to retain an active role for the friendly societies may be seen as a reflection of his lifelong concern to harness the spirit of 'voluntary action' to a system organized and underwritten by the state.

Superimposed upon these long-standing themes were a number of new ideas that distinguish Beveridge's views in the 1940s from those which he had held in earlier years—though in certain respects the difference was one of emphasis rather than basic principle. For the first time he envisaged that unemployment could be abolished within the context of the existing political system. For the first time he suggested that insurance should be applied uniformly to the whole community and not merely to manual workers or those below a certain income limit. For the first time he proposed that state benefits should provide not merely a platform for private saving but a subsistence income—a subsistence income, moreover, that was geared not merely to physical survival but to current perceptions of 'human needs'. In the Report of 1942 he laid much greater emphasis than he had previously done on insurance as an instrument of redistribution—as a means not merely of 'spreading wages over good times and bad'—but of effecting a positive re-allocation of resources from single people to families and from the rich to the poor.

Another important change—which contrasted strongly with his *laissez-faire* attitudes of the early '30s but which harked back to his ideas in the Edwardian period—was his view of social insurance not merely as an isolated system but as part of a spectrum of co-ordinated social planning. The proposals contained in his Report, Beveridge emphasized, should be seen merely as an integral stage in a much wider programme, covering transport, housing, education, employment and health. A further and less tangible change was in Beveridge's perception of the relationship between measures of social welfare and the overall structure and temper of society. Thirty years earlier, as we have seen, he had first supported social insurance, as a means not simply of meeting needs but of promoting social solidarity and of bringing institutions and individuals into partnership with the state. This emphasis on social cohesion was still powerfully present in the Beveridge Report, but now it was a cohesion that was ethical rather than organizational. It was to be based on a common freedom from the demoralizing pressures of poverty, and a common condemnation of 'the scandal of physical want'.[136]

[136] *Social Insurance and Allied Services*, pp. 165–6, 170–2.

# 17

# Aftermath of the Beveridge Report

## I

At the end of October 1942 Stafford Cripps informed Beatrice Webb that the Beveridge Report was now complete, but that publication was being postponed 'as some of the Cabinet object to it as too revolutionary'.[1] Anxious questions were asked in Parliament, and rumours of the report's suppression began to circulate in the press. For several days, recorded one of Beveridge's assistants, 'the atmosphere was not only obscure but unpleasant'.[2] The report was, however, eventually published as '*Social Insurance and Allied Services—Report by Sir William Beveridge*' on 1 December 1942. The report set out the long series of proposals that Beveridge had devised over the previous twelve months—for a national health service, family allowances, full employment and a comprehensive system of social insurance designed to cover the whole community. Approved societies were to be abolished, though voluntary associations would continue to act as administrative agents of the state. Benefits were to be paid at subsistence-level except for long-term industrial injury benefits, which would be based on previous earnings, and old-age pensions which would build up to subsistence over an interval of twenty years. Public assistance was to be transferred to the national exchequer and industrial assurance taken over by the state. The whole system of income maintenance was to be supervised and co-ordinated by a new Ministry of Social Security.

Clothing the bare bones of these proposals was a highly emotive and eloquent account of Beveridge's vision of the new society that was to emerge in Britain after the war. The report was designed, Beveridge asserted, not merely to abolish physical want, but to give a new sense of purpose to democracy, to promote national solidarity and to define the goals of the war. If the Allies could 'plan for a better peace even while waging war,' he argued, 'they will win together two victories which in truth are indivisible.'[3] The report was inspired, Beveridge claimed, by three 'guiding principles'. The first of these was the blending of the 'experience of the past' with a sweeping attack on vested interests

---

[1] Passfield Papers, B. Webb's diary, 26 Oct. 1942.
[2] Frank Pakenham, *Born to Believe* (1953), p. 132.
[3] *Social Insurance and Allied Services*, p. 172.

'established in the gaining of that experience'. 'Now, when the war is abolishing landmarks of every kind, is the opportunity for using experience in a clear field,' Beveridge proclaimed. 'A revolutionary moment in the world's history is a time for revolutions, not for patching.' The second principle was that of comprehensive social planning. The report was to be seen as merely a stage in a 'comprehensive policy of social progress' against the 'five giants on the road of reconstruction—' whom Beveridge defined as Want, Ignorance, Squalor, Idleness and Disease. The third principle was the principle of 'co-operation' between voluntary and public action and between the individual and the state. Such co-operation, Beveridge argued, would be uniquely embodied in his proposals for flat-rate insurance, which would guarantee to all citizens an adequate income and at the same time satisfy popular instincts for privacy, independence and thrift. His plan was

first and foremost, a plan of insurance—of giving in return for contributions, benefits up to subsistence level, as of right and without means tests, so that individuals may build freely upon it. Benefit in return for contributions, rather than free allowances from the State is what the people of Britain desire.[4]

Beveridge's report received maximum publicity in the press and was instantly seized upon by the Ministry of Information as a means of fostering wartime morale.[5] Within a month the 'Beveridge Plan', as it was widely called, had sold over a hundred thousand copies and a special cheap edition was printed for circulation in the armed services. On the Continent abbreviated copies of the plan were circulated among underground movements in Nazi-occupied countries; and in Germany itself the Plan was interpreted by propagandists as 'an especially obvious proof that our enemies are taking over national-socialistic ideas!'[6] The report aroused widespread discussion among journalists, backbenchers, social workers, public assistance officials and the public at large; and as Beveridge himself had anticipated, it was interpreted in many quarters as a token of the government's commitment to post-war social reform. Many of its proposals were warmly endorsed by the trade union movement, and in industrial areas like Clydeside meeting after meeting of workers passed resolutions of support.[7] The principles of the report were enthusiastically debated in universities, churches, rotary clubs, social welfare organizations and educational bodies like the W.E.A. Among women's organizations some were critical of Beveridge's

[4] Ibid., pp. 6–7, 11.
[5] BP, IXa 37, ms. notes on S.I.C. correspondence by WHB, report of phone-call from Bracken, 29 Nov. 1942.
[6] BP, VIII 59, translations of German documents about Beveridge Report (1943), found in Hitler's bunker in Sept. 1945; IIb, L. de Jong to WHB, 19 Apr. 1945.
[7] BP, IXa 37(i), 'Clydeside Workers and the Beveridge Plan', by A.W.S., 18 Mar. 1943.

failure to give all women an independent status, but others thought that he had 'gone a very long way towards establishing the rights of a married woman as a worker and as a partner in the home'.[8] A national conference of free churchmen claimed that the Beveridge Report was nothing less than 'practical Christianity'—marred only by its lack of reference to the Giant Sin.[9] Many of these discussions ended in demands for the Report's immediate implementation. 'It must be the Plan, the whole Plan and nothing but the Plan,' wrote a local correspondent of the reconstruction survey to G. D. H. Cole.[10]

This euphoric popular reception for the Beveridge Plan was a matter partly of luck and partly of careful calculation. The report was published a few days after the battle of Alamein, which to many people seemed like a turning-point in the war; and Beveridge was fortunate in that his mingled tone of optimism, patriotism, high principle and pragmatism exactly fitted the prevailing popular mood. It suited also the feeling of national solidarity that seems to have been engendered in all sections of the community by the Second World War. Nevertheless the groundwork for the reception of the report had been carefully and consciously prepared for many months before. Beveridge himself throughout 1942 had referred in numerous articles and broadcasts to the need for 'equality of sacrifice' and the possibility of abolishing poverty after the war.[11] And without precisely 'leaking' advance information, he had contrived to create the expectation that his Report would be far-reaching in scope and radical in tone. In this he has helped by his friend Frank Pakenham, who acted as a kind of unofficial public relations officer and assiduously fostered Beveridge's relations with the press.[12] He had been given a standing invitation to contribute material to *The Times* by the paper's deputy editor, his old Balliol contemporary R. Barrington Ward. Popular discussion of Beveridge's ideas had also been actively fostered by G. D. H. Cole. At an early stage in his inquiry Beveridge had decided that he must consult 'consumer' opinion, as well as producer and professional groups, and he had asked Cole to carry out a survey of attitudes to welfare among the working-class.[13] Cole was forbidden by the government to conduct a house-to-house inquiry on the ground that this might arouse suspicions of 'snooping'; and he therefore fell back upon a mass of impressionistic data, compiled for him

[8] Lady Beveridge Papers, Edith Summerskill to WHB, 2 Dec. 1942.
[9] BP, IIb, cutting from *Lytham Times*, sent to WHB by the Rev. H. Williamson, Sept. 1943.
[10] Cole Papers, B3/4/E, Box 5, Bernard Hickson to G. D. H. Cole, 28 Mar. 1943.
[11] e.g. *News Chronicle*, 19 Mar., 31 July, and 14 Oct. 1942; *The Times*, 23 Mar., 31 July and 23 Nov. 1942.
[12] Interview with the Earl of Longford.
[13] PRO, CAB 87/76, 'Nuffield College Reconstruction Survey', to WHB, 11 Dec. 1941.

by trade unionists, clergymen, social workers and officials of the W.E.A. The results of this survey came too late to have much influence on Beveridge's proposals, and in fact they merely confirmed many of the assumptions about 'popular attitudes' that Beveridge already held.[14] But the survey was of considerable importance in airing discussion of social policy questions; and in 1943 many of the people who had supplied information to Cole became active members of the movement for implementation of the Beveridge Report.

Among politicians and administrators, however, the reception of the Report was much more cautious than among the public at large. Within Whitehall itself there was considerable interest in social reform, but at the same time much resentment at Beveridge's high-handed treatment of official advice, and at his attempts to force an official commitment to post-war reconstruction. There was also much scepticism about the practical viability of Beveridge's proposals. As soon as the Report was published it was submitted to the scrutiny of a committee of officials under Sir Thomas Phillips—who, as has already been remarked, tended to make a point of pouring cold water on suggestions coming from Beveridge. The Phillips committee accepted the principles of universalism and of a comprehensive health service; but its members were highly critical of several important aspects of Beveridge's scheme. They were understandably doubtful about the long-term possibility of maintaining full employment. They queried the need for family allowances, and suggested that, if paid at all, they should be given in 'kind' rather than in 'cash'—an approach that Beveridge himself had specifically rejected. They argued that there was an irreducible helpless and feckless class, whose existence meant that a deterrent Poor Law could never be abolished. And, most fundamentally, they rejected the principle of 'subsistence', on the ground that universal flat-rate benefits could never accurately be based on subsistence requirements, because of widespread local and personal variations in liability for rent.[15]

Similar doubts were expressed in the Treasury, where despite Beveridge's 'deal with Keynes' officials continued to be seriously alarmed about the possible effects of the Plan on the post-war fiscal situation. A Treasury memorandum in the autumn of 1942 expressed the fear that the Plan would require an excessively high level of peacetime taxation which would discourage saving and hinder post-war expansion—'for experience shows that over-heavy public levies have a depressing effect upon the community and an adverse reaction upon industrial activity

[14] Cole Papers, B3/4/C, Box 1, 'A Memorandum on Wartime Surveys', by G. D. H. Cole, 14 Nov. 1941; PRO, CAB 87/80, Nuffield College Reconstruction survey, memoranda on 'National Health Insurance', 'Contributory Old Age Pensions', 'The Assistance Board', 'Public Assistance' and 'Workmen's Compensation', June 1942.

[15] PRO, PIN 8/85, Report of the Official Committee on the Beveridge Report, early 1943.

more especially in anxious times'.[16] A fierce attack on the Plan was made by Hubert Henderson, the Oxford don and former editor of *The Nation*, who was employed by the Treasury as a wartime economic adviser. Henderson claimed that Beveridge's remedy for poverty did not match his diagnosis, because a majority of people relieved by the scheme would not in fact be 'in need'. He objected that Beveridge's claim to have devised a uniform and comprehensive Plan was in fact spurious, since Beveridge had invoked the principles of 'comprehensiveness' and 'uniformity' when they suited him and ignored them when they did not. A cheaper and more logical alternative, Henderson suggested, would be to pay benefits to those in need out of direct taxation—the same 'means test' as was imposed on taxpayers being applied to recipients of public relief. He complained also that flat-rate benefits could not take account of local variations in the cost of living; and he denounced flat-rate contributions as an 'employment tax' on employers and a poll-tax on the employed. 'The Beveridge Plan,' Henderson concluded, '. . . conveys insidiously the suggestion that a good time can be had by all the moment the last shot is fired; and the substantial adoption of Beveridge would confirm this impression and greatly militate against an austerity psychology.'[17] These objections were answered by Keynes, who thought that Henderson had failed to do justice to Beveridge's earnest efforts to produce an economically viable and politically realistic scheme. Keynes admitted that in strict logic there was much to be said for Henderson's objections to the social insurance principle; but he thought that the kind of alternative Henderson proposed would require a prior reform of the system of direct taxation, which was not at the time a practical possibility. Keynes maintained, moreover, that con-tributory insurance was a useful 'fiction', both for making employers share the costs of welfare and for dispelling popular myths of the Exchequer's bottomless purse.[18] Keynes was in fact convinced that Beveridge's Plan was 'the cheapest alternative open to us' and that 'the 'suggestion that is being put about in some quarters that there are financial difficulties is quite unfounded'.[19] This view was supported by D. N. Chester, who pointed out that the government was already under heavy pressure to extend the scope of existing schemes, and that the Treasury might well find itself involved in a costly process of 'buying off sectional interests, which will not produce the maximum of human

---

[16] Henderson Papers, 'The Social Security Plan. Memorandum prepared in the Treasury', n.d. (Nov. 1942).

[17] Henderson Papers, 'The Principles of the Beveridge Plan', by H. D. Henderson, 4 Aug. 1942; 'Draft Memorandum on the Social Security Plan', by H. D. Henderson, 22 Dec. 1942.

[18] Henderson Papers, memorandum on 'The Beveridge Proposals', by J. M. Keynes, 20 July 1942.

[19] Passfield Papers II, 4, n, 11, J. M. Keynes to B. Webb, 3 Mar. 1943.

welfare, will bring little credit to the Government, and will involve the Exchequer in as much, if not more expenditure than is contemplated in the report'.[20]

The report evoked an equally mixed response in political circles. It was unanimously endorsed by the Liberal Party and by Liberal M.P.s in the House of Commons.[21] In the Conservative Party a group of business-men came together to oppose the Plan, but at the same time a group of backbench Tory M.P.s pledged themselves to its support.[22] It was strongly endorsed by many Labour constituency organizations, and the principles of the report were warmly praised by many Labour intellec-tuals such as Tawney, Cole and Laski. 'Your Report is the test of whether we can make democracy viable,' wrote Laski, generously for-getting past differences in his enthusiasm for the Beveridge scheme. '. . . do fight for your principles; their enemies are the enemies of light.'[23] Among the rank-and-file of the Labour party there were some reserva-tions about Beveridge's emphasis on the contributory principle; but Beveridge's only major critic on the left proved to be Beatrice Webb. Before the Report was published Mrs. Webb told the London corre-spondent of *Izvestia* that it would be 'a bomb thrown into the political arena, which will hit the Tories and Liberals who want to go back to the status quo'; but having read it, she concluded that Beveridge had fallen into the same trap—of reform within a context of capitalism—that had ensnared herself and Sidney in 1909. 'If carried out (which I think unlikely),' she commented, '[it] will increase the catastrophic mass unemployment, which could happen here as in the U.S.A. The better you treat the unemployed in the way of means, without service, the worse the evil becomes; because it is better to do nothing than to work at low wages and conditions.'[24]

Within the government there were perhaps many who secretly agreed with Mrs. Webb. Churchill himself thought that planning for recon-struction should be substantially left until after the war, and he claimed that he could not commit himself to the Beveridge proposals without a general election to test popular support.[25] The Chancellor of the Exchequer, Kingsley Wood, was doubtful whether the necessary re-sources would be available in the post-war economic climate; and he was sceptical about the willingness of the public to countenance extra

[20] 'Finance of the Proposals in the Beveridge Report', by D. N. Chester, 18 Nov. 1942. (I am grateful to Sir Norman Chester for lending me his copy of this paper.)
[21] *Liberal Party Organisation Bulletin*, no. 37, Dec. 1942.
[22] BP, IIb, Hugh Molson to WHB, 9 Oct. 1943.
[23] BP, Ib 16, H. Laski to WHB, 30 Nov. 1942 and 6 Jan. 1943.
[24] Passfield Papers, B. Webb's diary, 30 Nov. 1942; Fabian Society Papers, Box 3, B. Webb to Reginald Pott, 14 Dec. 1942.
[25] PRO, CAB 66/34, Note on 'Beveridge Report' by the Prime Minister, 15 Feb. 1943.

taxation, once released from the constraints of war.[26] These financial forebodings were brushed aside by Lord Cherwell, Churchill's personal friend and adviser, who thought that 'on balance the scheme should improve rather than worsen our economic position' and that it was 'not altruistic but worth its cost'. But Cherwell had reservations on other grounds; he was afraid that increased social services expenditure might give a bad impression in America and reduce American willingness to shoulder the cost of the war.[27] Brendan Bracken, the Minister of Information, had initially welcomed the Report as a powerful instrument for boosting military morale. But he was acutely embarrassed by the attitude of his colleagues and was forced to withdraw the popular version of the Beveridge Report that had been circulated among the troops for 'compulsory discussion'. Early in 1943 Bracken refused to supply official speakers on the Report, complaining that his staff were already addressing forty thousand such meetings a year and that 'the passion of the British people for oratory is growing to most monstrous proportions'.[28] Among Labour ministers Bevin declared that many parts of the Report were unacceptable to the unions[29]—even though, as we have seen, it was warmly welcomed by many trade unionists and had been drawn up in close consultation with the T.U.C. Herbert Morrison argued strongly in favour of the Plan, but his views were overridden by the newly founded Lord President's Committee on Reconstruction Priorities, which advised the government to avoid any firm commitment.[30] Attlee and Dalton welcomed the Plan, but were lukewarm in pressing for its implementation. Dalton in particular feared that demand for its acceptance by impatient backbenchers might drive Churchill to act upon his threat of going to the country—in which case Dalton foresaw a landslide victory for the Prime Minister and the eclipse of the parliamentary Labour movement for the whole foreseeable future. During the Commons debate on the Beveridge Plan he was horrified by the sight of 'Master Shinwell rushing about with a maniacal look in his eye' whipping up Labour support.[31] Of Labour frontbenchers, only Sir

[26] Cherwell Papers, Off. 45.6, 'The Financial Aspects of the Social Security Plan', n.d.; Paul Addison, *The Road to 1945: British Politics and the Second World War* (1975), p. 220.

[27] Cherwell Papers, Off. 42.1, memorandum on 'Economic Effects of the Beveridge Plan'. 22 Jan. 1943; Off. 32–B, Lord Cherwell to W. S. Churchill on 'The Beveridge Report', 25 Nov. 1942 and 11 Feb. 1943.

[28] H.C. Deb., 5*s*., vol. 387, col. 1614.

[29] Dalton Papers, Hugh Dalton's diary, vol. 28, 18 Feb. 1943; Bevin's attitude met with considerable criticism from the rank and file of the labour movement (Bevin Papers, Box 18, L. Washington to E. Bevin, 20 Feb. 1943; E. Wear to E. Bevin, 20 Feb. 1943; V. Steed to E. Bevin, 7 Mar. 1943.)

[30] Bernard Donoghue and G. W. Jones, *Herbert Morrison: Portrait of a Politician* (1973), pp. 314–15; Paul Addison, op. cit., pp. 222–3; PRO, CAB 66/34, 'The Beveridge Plan. Interim Report of the Committee on Reconstruction Priorities', 11 Feb. 1943.

[31] Dalton Papers, Hugh Dalton's diary, vol. 28, 16, 18 and 24 Feb. 1943.

William Jowitt, the Minister for Reconstruction, seemed keen to proceed with converting the plan into legislative proposals; and even Jowitt was careful to reassure his colleagues that the Report had nothing to do with 'the framing of Utopias' and was thoroughly consistent with the reforming traditions of 'parties of all political complexions'.[32]

## II

For Beveridge himself the publication of his Report on Social Insurance was perhaps the most important public event of his life. It transformed him overnight from a rather obscure and academic figure, best known as a broadcaster on 'thought-raising subjects', into a much-feted national hero. He addressed packed meetings on the principles of his report, and was widely portrayed as a personal symbol of the kind of society that people in Britain were hoping for after the war. He was summoned to an audience with George VI, who wanted to hear, not about national insurance, but about the doings of the 'queer people' reputed to inhabit the L.S.E.[33] He was invited to dine with the Russian ambassador, who was greatly impressed with his unemployment proposals—particularly with the prospect of 'training-camps' for those 'suspected of malingering'.[34] He was hailed as a new Bentham, and in its significance for social policy his report was compared with the classic reports on the Poor Law of 1834 and 1909.[35] It was 'a queer result of this strange and horrible war', wrote Beatrice Webb rather sourly, that Beveridge—of all people—should have 'risen suddenly into the limelight as an accepted designer of the New World Order'.[36] Quite how far Beveridge was genuinely seen in this light by the public at large, and how far it was an impression deliberately fostered by the media is difficult to say. Certainly the image of Beveridge as the embodiment of popular reforming ideals seems to have been carefully projected by the press and the B.B.C.; and pictures of Beveridge, looking prophetically white-haired and benign, were flashed by Pathe News into every cinema in the country. But that Beveridge's impact was more than just a trick of wartime propaganda is suggested by the vast sales of his Report, by the apprehension it aroused in government circles and by his massive mail bag from members of the public—asking for his advice on social questions, urging him to press for

[32] PRO, CAB 66/30, 'Outline of Statement on Reconstruction Problems', by the Paymaster-General, 14 Nov. 1942.
[33] Lady Beveridge Papers, fragment of diary, 9 Dec. 1942.
[34] Passfield Papers, B. Webb's diary, 14 Jan. 1943.
[35] A. D. K. Owen, 'The Beveridge Report: its Proposals', *Econ. J.*, LIII, no. 209, Apr. 1943, pp. 1–9; BP, Ib 16, John Maude to WHB, 1 Dec. 1942.
[36] Passfield Papers, B. Webb's diary, 19 Dec. 1942.

immediate legislation, and assuring him that 'the spiritual forces of the Nation are on your side'.[37]

Beveridge's report coincided with another major event in his life. His cousin David Mair had died in the early summer of 1942, and in October Beveridge and Mrs. Mair informed her family of their intention to marry—Mrs. Mair at the same time announcing her wish to be known as 'Janet', her true baptismal name. They were married at Caxton Hall on 15 December—followed by a service of blessing in a bombed church, conducted by Archbishop William Temple, and by a reception at the Dorchester Hotel. On her marriage lines the new Lady Beveridge with forgivable human frailty knocked three years off her age. Beveridge himself, when asked why he had waited until the age of sixty-three to marry, replied that 'My lady was married to my friend and cousin and I had to wait for her'.[38] 'Today Beveridge marries Mrs. Mair,' recorded Beatrice Webb. 'He wrote some time ago to tell me of the coming event and I sent him our warmest greetings on his marriage to his life-long companion and long continued colleague in research and administration . . . I think he will, like Keynes, be made a Peer—so she will be The Lady Beveridge and will appear at Court in a scarlet velvet robe.'[39]

Immediately after his marriage Beveridge was invited by the Rocke-feller Foundation to go on a tour of America to explain and publicize his report. The tour had been suggested by the British Minister in Washing-ton who thought it would 'help Anglo-American relations through the labour movement here'.[40] Beveridge and his new wife sailed in the *Queen Mary* in May 1943, and during the next three months he made over a hundred speeches on his report—defending it as a practical embodiment of the Atlantic Charter of 1941, which had defined social security as an essential human freedom. To Americans who objected that social security would destroy incentives to enterprise and adventure Beveridge replied that the great buccaneers of English history—Hawkins, Raleigh, Drake—had all been born into well-established or wealthy families. Each of them had 'anticipated the Beveridge Plan by choosing his parents well; each from birth had social security'.[41] His tour was a spectacular publicity success, and throughout North America people appeared to mistake him for the unofficial 'goodwill' ambassador of the British government. The American edition of his report sold fifty

[37] BP, IIb, A. P. Young to WHB, 2 Feb. 1943.

[38] Lady Beveridge Papers, fragment of diary, 9 Dec. 1942.

[39] Passfield Papers, B. Webb's diary, 15 Dec. 1942; 115, M939, additional letters, no. 215, B. Webb to R. H. Tawney, 29 Dec. 1942.

[40] BP, IIb, Brendan Bracken to WHB, 8 Dec. 1942.

[41] *Beveridge on Beveridge, Recent Speeches of Sir William Beveridge*, ed. Joan S. Clarke (published ˌ Social Security League, 1943).

thousand copies within six months. He had several friendly interviews with Franklin Roosevelt and he was warmly welcomed by the American Minister of Labour, Frances Perkins, who was herself strongly committed to the extension of social security.[42]

After so many years of having his services rejected the adulation that he received in America acted upon Beveridge like a heady wine. He clearly loved every moment of the speechmaking, autograph-signing, appearances before cine-cameras and meetings with American administrators, trade unionists and philanthropic millionaires. Everywhere he went he was received with extravagant enthusiasm and praise. 'Photographed by a lady to whom all I did was automatically perfect,' he noted with evident satisfaction on 17 May 1943.[43] Nevertheless, Beveridge was not content to spend the rest of the war merely making speeches on social policy—particularly since the government had been so guarded in its reception of his report. Pressure in the Commons forced a debate on the Beveridge Plan in February 1943, and the refusal of ministers to commit themselves wholeheartedly to Beveridge's proposals led to a revolt among Labour and Liberal backbenchers and the largest anti-government vote of the war.[44] Two months later a group of Whitehall officials, headed by Mr. Thomas Sheepshanks, began to consider the implementation of Beveridge's proposals, and eventually produced the government's White Paper on Social Security of 1944.[45] Beveridge himself, however, was carefully excluded from these discussions; and he made no secret of his belief that the government under Churchill would 'not do more for Social Progress than they are driven to by opposition and pacemaking'.[46] His own ambitions increasingly revolved around two main objectives—to carry out an inquiry into full employment, and to marshal political pressure for the implementation of the Beveridge Report. It was these two objectives that dominated his public career for the rest of the war.

## III

As we have seen, one of the three basic assumptions on which Beveridge had based his plan was the assumption that the government should maintain 'full employment' after the war.[47] Of his three assumptions

---

[42] Janet Beveridge, *Beveridge and his Plan*, pp. 173–4, 191; BP, IIb, F. D. Roosevelt to WHB, 22 Dec. 1944.

[43] Lady Beveridge Papers, notes by WHB in Lady Beveridge's diary, 13, 14 and 17 May 1943.

[44] Angus Calder, *The People's War: Britain, 1939–1945* (1971 edn.), p. 614.

[45] The papers of this group of officials are in PRO, PIN 8/1 and 8/2.

[46] BP, IIb, WHB to R. Barrington-Ward, 14 Dec. 1943.

[47] By 'full employment' Beveridge meant not total abolition of unemployment, but a margin of unemployment of not more than 3 per cent.

this was the one that most defiantly offered a hostage to fortune, since few people in Britain in 1942 were convinced that full employment in peacetime could in fact be maintained. It was also the one of his three assumptions whose presence in the Beveridge Report is most difficult to explain. His assumption of family allowances was clearly derived from his own active espousal of the family endowment movement over the previous eighteen years. His assumption of a national health service directly reflected current thinking in the medical profession and Ministry of Health. The origins of Beveridge's assumption of full employment, however, are less easy to trace. It is true that by 1941 Keynes and other government economists were beginning to formulate policies of post-war economic management, but there is no evidence to suggest that Beveridge was familiar with the thinking of this group; and his Treasury adviser, Edward Hale, was not employed on this side of Treasury activities. Lord Robbins has implied that Beveridge's interest in full employment stemmed from a 'chance remark' passed by Robbins himself during his evidence to the Beveridge committee, when he happened to mention a paper on remedies for unemployment composed for the Economic Section of the War Cabinet by his colleague, James Meade. But this impression cannot be correct, since Robbins and Meade gave evidence in June 1942, and Beveridge had already postulated his assumption of full employment more than six months before.[48] A possible source of influence was obviously Keynes himself; but as was shown in an earlier chapter Beveridge five years earlier had scornfully rejected Keynes' analysis of unemployment and there is no documentary evidence to suggest that he had changed his mind at this time. We cannot of course know what transmission of ideas may have taken place in those intimate little meetings at the Gargoyle Club. But Beveridge certainly did not give the impression to his assistants that he was familiar with the Keynsian system; and we have Harold Wilson's testimony that Beveridge was not in fact converted to Keynsianism until after the publication of his Social Insurance Report.[49]

If it was not derived from the Keynsians then how can Beveridge's new-found belief in the possibility of full employment be explained? How did he come to abandon his earlier view that unemployment was caused by wage-rigidity or that it was inevitable without an 'entire reconstruction of the economic system'? The answer may be found in two factors. Firstly, at the time of writing his report on Social Insurance Beveridge was in fact prepared to contemplate a very much more

---

[48] Lionel Robbins, *Autobiography of an Economist*, pp. 187–90. Above, p. 390–91. Robbins also states that Beveridge was denied access to Meade's paper; but a copy of this paper is preserved in Beveridge's papers and was clearly used by him in preparing his Report (BP, VIII 29, 'Internal Measures for the Prevention of Unemployment', July 1941).

[49] Interview with Lord Longford; Harold Wilson, *Beveridge Memorial Lecture*, p. 3.

extensive reconstruction of the economy than at any previous stage in his career. And secondly, his views on how employment might in practice be maintained seem to have owed less to Keynes than to socialist writers like the Webbs and G. D. H. Cole. Cole in the 1920s and 30s had frequently advanced the view that unemployment could be abolished if governments in peacetime exercised the same control over production as they did in war.[50] The Webbs over thirty years earlier had put forward proposals for reducing unemployment by concentration of public expenditure into periods of depression. They had subsequently concluded that such policies were unworkable within a capitalist economy; but in *Soviet Communism* they had described in detail the abolition of unemployment in Russia by what they had described as 'planned production for community consumption'. Beveridge, as we have seen, had been greatly impressed by this aspect of the Soviet system, but he had been repelled by the degree of political coercion that comprehensive state planning seemed to entail. At the time of writing his Report, however, Beveridge's reservations about state planning appear to have faded away. He had become convinced that some form of planning was no longer an option but a sheer practical necessity; and his hope that planning could be made compatible with democracy seems to have been greatly strengthened by the experience of war. The war entailed an enormous extension of state control over production without apparently destroying democracy or straining the political consensus, and at the same time it brought about a considerable advance in planning techniques.[51] Beveridge hoped that these same techniques could be used to maintain full employment after the war. Thus his conception of how to cure unemployment in 1942 was in many respects very similar to that advanced by the Webbs in *Soviet Communism* and by Cole in his evidence to the Holman Gregory commission in 1931. It was a cure based on state control of production and on detailed planning of deployment of labour rather than on monetary and fiscal regulation of consumer demand. Where Beveridge chiefly differed from the Webbs was in his belief that full employment could be maintained without massive coercion; where he differed from Cole was in his rejection of the view that it would require no coercion at all.

The clearest evidence for this interpretation of Beveridge's ideas on unemployment—and of his wider views on the future structure of society—lies not in his discussions with the Social Insurance committee but in his contributions to the Advisory Panel on Home Affairs. This panel, consisting of administrators, businessmen and social scientists,

[50] *RC on Unemployment Insurance, Minutes of Evidence*, Paper 43.

[51] Margaret Gowing, 'The Organisation of Manpower in Britain during the Second World War', *Journal of Contemporary History*, vol. VII, nos. 1–2, pp. 147–67.

was convened by Jowitt during the summer of 1942. It was designed to bring together 'the large body of thought and research' which was being developed on social and economic questions outside the inner circles of government.[52] It was at the first meeting of this panel that Beveridge first conceived of the 'five giants'—Idleness, Want, Squalor, Ignorance and Disease—who were later to appear as the five villains of his report on Social Insurance. At this meeting

he warned the Panel that although it was possible to plan attacks on Want, Disease and Ignorance, the fight against Idleness and Squalor raised vast political issues which would certainly strain national unity. . . . Their defeat could not be secured without on the one hand state planning and on the other relaxation of Trades Union restrictions; two things which together would forfeit all the votes in the country.[53]

A few days later Beveridge sent to Jowitt a brief memorandum on 'Reconstruction Problems—Five Giants on the Road', in which he outlined an overall strategy for the reconstruction of society after the war. In this he proposed that Want should be abolished by social insurance, family endowment and a statutory minimum wage. Disease was to be prevented and cured by a free medical service, by better housing, sanitation and nutrition, and by the systematic development of applied science. Ignorance was to be overcome by raising the school-leaving age, 'widening the educational ladder to Universities' and development of 'adult education on an immense scale'. Idleness was to be prevented by the maintenance of 'fluidity of labour and resources' and by 'state planning' to maintain full employment—modelled on the kind of comprehensive control over the economy exercised by governments in time of war. 'Squalor' Beveridge defined as 'the irrestible disorderly growth of great cities . . . the daily waste of life and human energy in needless travel, bad housing and ill health, needless exhausting toil for the housewife in struggling with dirt and discomfort, habituation of the population to hideous surroundings'. It was to be met by reorganization of local government, by 'imaginative centralised direction of transport and public utilities' and by strict controls on the location of industry and use of land. It would involve severe restrictions on 'private enterprise and private ownership', which had hitherto been the 'inseparable accompaniment' of conurbation. 'Here,' Beveridge concluded, 'is a giant indeed.'[54]

Accompanying his paper on the 'Five Giants' Beveridge sent a letter urging Jowitt that 'the maintenance of productive employment' should

[52] BP, VIII 45, circular note from Sir William Jowitt, 29 Apr. 1942.
[53] BP, VIII 45, Advisory Panel on Home Affairs, minutes of a meeting on 2 June 1942.
[54] BP, VIII 45, 'Reconstruction Problems; Five Giants on the Road', 3 June 1942.

be seen as the most fundamental of reconstruction problems. 'Without such maintenance,' he argued, 'all else is futile and our reconstruction will be held to have failed. With such maintenance all other problems become soluble.'[55] Jowitt agreed, and a month later an extended version of Beveridge's paper was circulated to the Advisory Panel as a basis for discussion. In this revised version of the 'Five Giants' Beveridge spelt out in greater detail his conception of how 'Idleness' might be abolished and full employment maintained. Unemployment had vanished in war-time, he argued, partly because the government exercised total control over production and consumption and partly because sectional barriers to the most efficient deployment of manpower were broken down.

Can we hope to accomplish the same full use of resources in the aftermath of war, except on something like the same conditions? Maintenance of productive employment means adjustment of productive resources to real needs. In times of peace in all countries other than Russia, this adjustment has been carried out in the main by the price mechanism. In so far as the price mechanism has failed to do what was desired, most states have limited themselves to seeking remedies of a general financial nature, that is to say they still worked through the price mechanism, endeavouring to manipulate the volume of purchasing power in general, but not to direct it down particular channels. In times of total war adjustment of resources to needs is carried out by complete state planning. Shall the aftermath of this war be treated by the former methods of peace or by the methods of war? On the face of it, the experience of 1920–39 suggests that the former methods of peace are unlikely to accomplish the object in view with even tolerable success, and that there are probably two unavoidable conditions for the maintenance of productive employment after the war, namely (a) fluidity of labour and (b) national planning.

To achieve these two objectives, Beveridge maintained that existing barriers to the movement of labour would have to be dissolved; trade unions and professional bodies would not be allowed to limit occupational recruitment, and unemployed workers would not be able to insist on re-employment in their former line of trade. A national planning authority would have to be set up, to prepare schedules of national resources and of 'things that are required in the national interest in the aftermath of war—houses, schools, transport, education, hospitals, exports and other means of securing purchasing power abroad'. The planning authority would be required to draw up a national plan for state control of industry in one of three different ways: either through 'direct nationalisation of a large number of important industries'; or through 'public utility corporations'; or through 'continuance of profit-making private enterprise in production, while directing production not

[55] BP, VIII 45, WHB to Sir William Jowitt, 3 June 1942.

simply by manipulating purchasing power in general, but by control of investments'. The first two alternatives, Beveridge suggested, would mean 'making up our minds to becoming a community in which undertakers' profit as the guide to production disappears permanently over a large part of the whole field of economic activity'.[56]

Beveridge's paper was discussed by the Advisory Panel on 15 July, and met with considerable trepidation among the other members. Several of the business representatives objected that 'before making revolutionary changes in our pre-war economic system it was desirable to examine the possibilities of improvement'; and Seebohm Rowntree feared that 'once it was begun there was no stopping place before a complete system on Russian lines had been achieved and with it a total sacrifice of freedom'. Beveridge's proposals, were however, strongly supported by the Labour M.P., John Wilmot, who argued that 'State planning did not in the least imply the Russian system and loss of liberty. . . . The things we dislike in Russia are mainly concerned with political and not economic organisation.' Beveridge himself stated even more forcibly his conviction that the free market system had irretrievably broken down and that without the intervention of war the international economy would once more have been plunged into a depression. He made clear also his own belief that, of the three alternative strategies he had outlined, some form of public ownership of land and essential services would almost certainly be necessary for coping with Idleness and Squalor. He conceded that

the costs of planning must be considered but did not believe that the loss of liberty need be one of them. The worker need only be made to choose other employment if his own failed. If the State sees that minimum needs are satisfied consumers can spend their surplus income as they will. As for deprivation of the individual's right to control capital, if this should prove necessary, it was a loss of freedom which would affect very few people.[57]

'Ownership of Means of Production,' Beveridge asserted, was 'not one of the essential British liberties' and could not be allowed to stand in the way of social reconstruction after the war.[58]

Beveridge's contribution to this discussion is of considerable significance—partly because it shows just how far he had travelled from his earlier reservations about state planning, and partly because it suggests that his view of 'full employment' in 1942 was essentially a socialist rather than a Keynsian conception. It was a conception that centred, not upon state regulation of consumer demand, but upon state control of

[56] BP, VIII 45, 'Reconstruction Problems: Five Giants on the Road', revised draft, 25 June 1942.
[57] BP, VIII 45, Advisory Panel on Home Affairs, minutes, 9 July 1942.
[58] BP, VIII 45, ms. notes by WHB, n.d.

the means of production. Indeed, both of Beveridge's memoranda on the 'Five Giants' suggest that the so-called Beveridge Plan was merely the iceberg tip of a very much larger and more ambitious plan that he had in mind at the time—the full extent of which was only briefly hinted at in the Beveridge Report. The Report was 'only a very small part of all that is wanted for social reconstruction,' wrote Beveridge early in 1943; it was merely the prelude to a much more ambitious programme of industrial reorganization and economic planning.[59] The chief objective and chief justification for such a programme Beveridge saw as the prevention of mass unemployment; but he claimed that state action to prevent unemployment could not be divorced from state control of industry, housing, transport and the use of land.

IV

In his report on Social Insurance at the end of 1942 Beveridge acknowledged that, however fundamental to the success of his scheme, maintenance of full employment could not be discussed in detail within the context of social security. Nevertheless, he was hoping to be asked to carry out a further inquiry into this aspect of his Plan, and in November he asked University College to appoint a Vice-Master, in anticipation of the fact that he himself would be fully engaged in government service for the rest of the war. To Beveridge's great disappointment however, the expected invitation to carry out further official investigations never came. Early in 1943 the Minister of Production, Oliver Lyttleton, suggested to the War Cabinet that Beveridge should be commissioned to follow up his report by an inquiry into full employment; but Lyttleton's suggestion was not acted upon and Beveridge was never consulted by the government on this or any other aspect of the Beveridge Plan.[60]

The background to Beveridge's exclusion from any further share in the reconstruction programme has never been fully explained, but reasons for his exclusion are not difficult to find. As was shown in earlier chapters Beveridge was not very skilful in handling relationships with ministers and senior officials. He had acquired a reputation as a brilliant inventor of model schemes, but as imperious and unrealistic in translating them into action—characteristics that had been underlined by his share in the abortive fuel-rationing scheme of May 1942.[61] Throughout his period as chairman of the Social Insurance committee he had con-

[59] BP, Ib 16, WHB to Sir Richard Paget, 23 Jan. 1943.
[60] PRO. CAB 66/33, 'Social Security', Note by the Minister of Production, 13 Jan. 1943. The Government was advised against Lyttleton's proposal by Lional Robbins, on the ground that Beveridge was not a genuine expert on the unemployment question (PRO, CAB 123/43, Lionel Robbins to Sir John Anderson, 14 Jan. 1943).
[61] Above, p. 377.

tinued to deplore the lack of a parliamentary opposition; and according to Dalton his name 'was mentioned in the Cabinet as one who criticizes the government too much'.[62] 'Don't go around denigrating Winston.' he was cautioned by Mrs. Mair, after one of the numerous occasions on which he had unfavourably compared Churchill's management of the war with that of the small War Cabinet introduced by Lloyd George in 1916.[63] Probably the chief barrier to Beveridge's further employment, however, was the way in which he had courted massive advance publicity for his report on Social Insurance. Whether without such publicity the report would have made the impact that it did is a matter for conjecture; but Beveridge's behaviour was seen by many people inside government as a flagrant breach of Whitehall conventions and as an attempt to usurp the powers and functions of the regular policy-making machine.[64]

Beveridge therefore played no official part in policy-formation for the rest of the war. He was determined, however, to proceed with an inquiry into full employment and in 1943 he accepted an offer from a group of progressive businessmen to finance such an inquiry out of private funds.[65] To assist him in this inquiry Beveridge gathered together a small 'technical committee' consisting of Frank Pakenham, Barbara Wootton, Joan Robinson, E. F. Schumacher, Nicholas Kaldor, and Lady Beveridge's youngest daughter, Elspeth Mair. The economists on this committee were all to the 'left' of Beveridge in their political views; but nevertheless it seems to have been their influence that converted him to a Keynsian conception of unemployment and to the advocacy of full employment policies based not so much on state-ownership as on state regulation of demand. The first sign of this new departure in Beveridge's thinking came at one of the Nuffield Reconstruction Conferences in September 1943, when he gave a paper on 'full productive employment in a free society' which he frankly acknowledged was based on ideas supplied to him by E. F. Schumacher. In this he accepted the Keynsian analysis of factors governing the demand for labour and Keynes' rejection of the classical view that there was an automatic self-regulating relationship between the level of wages and labour demand.

Following Schumacher he rejected the idea that unemployment should be abolished simply by expansion of private consumption; but at the same time he rejected his own view of a year earlier that full employment could best be attained by wholesale nationalization. Instead he outlined a programme for maintaining full employment which

[62] Dalton Papers, Hugh Dalton's diary, 8 Apr. 1942.
[63] Lady Beveridge Papers, J. Mair to WHB, 11 May 1942.
[64] Cherwell Papers, Off. 32–B, Lord Cherwell to the Prime Minister 25 Nov. 1942.
[65] *PI*, p. 328.

he claimed was based on 'socializing demand rather than production', and which may be seen as a classic formula for the kind of mixed economy that was to emerge in many Western countries after the Second World War. This programme involved state investment in certain 'socialized industries', notably transport and power; state spending on a wide range of 'non-marketable' goods and services, such as roads, hospitals, schools and defence; state subsidies to housing, medical services, food and fuel; and state regulation of private investment through interest rates, taxation policy and redistribution of income.[66]

This paper set the tone for the discussions of Beveridge's technical committee throughout the autumn of 1943. A majority of the committee clearly desired a more 'socialist' kind of society, but they emphasized that from the technical point of view full employment was now possible within a system of private enterprise. Beveridge himself now agreed that the 'main way to full employment was not by socialism, although good reasons for socialism exist'.[67] He was urged by Pakenham to commit himself for or against socialism as a matter of principle; but the rest of the committee thought that such a commitment was unnecessary, and Beveridge himself argued that the future organization of industry should be decided on pragmatic grounds. 'If in fact full employment did produce Socialism,' he remarked, 'that should not stop the pursuance of the policy although it would remove an inessential freedom. Whether that should be done would depend upon how this freedom of private enterprise was being used'.[68]

Beveridge's central concern in his full employment inquiry was not merely how unemployment could be abolished, but how it could be abolished without infringing 'basic freedoms'—which he defined as freedom of speech, worship and association, freedom to choose an occupation and freedom in spending a personal income.[69] This concern was particularly apparent in the committee's discussions of the possible effect of full employment upon industrial discipline and free collective bargaining. Beveridge stipulated that a policy of full employment 'should not remove the right to strike and that the free society would not imprison a man for refusing to work, either singly or collectively'. At the same time, however, he and several members of his committee were apprehensive that the creation of a 'sellers' market' for labour might encourage excessive wage-demands and lead to severe inflation. 'There was a grave danger,' it was remarked, 'from the new phenomenon of the

[66] BP, IXa13, 'Full Productive Employment in a Free Society', by WHB, 8 Sept. 1943.
[67] BP, IXa 13, Employment Investigation Minutes, 30 Sept. 1943.
[68] BP, IXa 13, Employment Investigation Minutes, 11 Nov. 1943.
[69] BP, IXa 15, Employment Investigation, report of a meeting with the Economic Committee of the T.U.C., 10 Nov. 1943.

monopoly employer co-operating with his workers to raise prices as in the coal trade. The producers were lining up against the consumers.'[70] Beveridge himself suggested that the best antidote to inflation was price control, combined with compulsory arbitration in trade disputes; and Barbara Wootton proposed that machinery should be evolved to confine collective bargaining to industries where it would not result in a rise in prices. Neither of these proposals met with any enthusiasm in the trade union movement, whose leaders assured Beveridge that 'the common sense of the unions could be relied upon to restrain wild inflation' and that any element of 'regimentation' was unacceptable in peacetime.[71] In general, however, Beveridge and his committee were not unduly alarmed by the prospect of inflation. Kaldor suggested that 'a collective treaty with all workers would result in a fixing of relative prices and wages', and both Kaldor and Schumacher envisaged that removal of the disciplinary effects of unemployment could be compensated for by a greater degree of workers' control.[72] 'Everything depends on the moral atmosphere,' wrote Joan Robinson to Beveridge. 'If the workers feel that genuine progress towards social justice is being made it will not be hard to solve the problem. But so long as the economic system presents itself as a dogfight they will naturally take advantage of every increase in their bargaining power.'[73] Beveridge himself was inclined to be cautiously optimistic on this point. He urged that the unions should accept responsibility for encouraging arbitration and restraining the prices of monopolies; but he thought that 'the people were not profiteers by nature' and that, subject to these safeguards, 'the right to strike should be retained'.[74]

Beveridge began his full employment inquiry with the help of several senior civil servants; and as in his Social Insurance inquiry he was hoping for advice and criticism from Keynes. In the autumn of 1943, however, instructions were issued from the Treasury that no official assistance was to be given to Beveridge, and his civil service advisers were forced to withdraw.[75] Beveridge himself was never officially informed of the Treasury's intervention and only learnt about it when it attracted adverse criticism in the press. It was a significant commentary on Beveridge's changed position in the eyes of the world that he who in earlier years had often been condemned as a repressive Whitehall

---

[70] BP, IXa 13, Employment Investigation Minutes, 11 Nov. 1943.
[71] BP, IXa 15, Employment Investigation, report of a meeting with the T.U.C., 9 Feb. 1944.
[72] BP, IXa 13, Employment Investigation Minutes, 11 Nov. 1943 and 17 Feb. 1944.
[73] BP, IXa 16, Joan Robinson to WHB, 23 Sept. (1943).
[74] BP, IXa 13, Employment Investigation Minutes, 11 Nov. 1943.
[75] BP, IIb 43, W. Eady to WHB, 11 Nov. 1943; G. L. Watkinson to WHB, 17 Nov. 1943.

bureaucrat was now portrayed in radical and left-wing journals as the popular victim of heavy-handed bureaucracy.[76] Thereafter followed what Beveridge in his memoirs described as the 'White Paper Chase'— the attempt by the government to publish its proposals on full employment before Beveridge himself should produce his private report.[77] Beveridge sometimes implied that it was only the rivalry of his own inquiry that forced the government to consider the problem of full employment—a view that is clearly incorrect, since full employment had been under consideration by economists in the Treasury and the War Cabinet Office since 1941. Nevertheless it is clear from Cabinet records that official commitment to full employment was greatly speeded up by awareness of Beveridge's private inquiry; and the government's Full Employment White Paper of 1944 was deliberately designed to distract attention from Beveridge in the popular press.[78]

The government's White Paper appeared in June 1944, Beveridge's *Full Employment in a Free Society* not until five months later. Both outlined a programme for maintenance of full employment but the report produced by Beveridge and his committee was much more ambitious and far-reaching in scope. The White Paper proposed to maintain employment and regulate demand by adjusting the level of social insurance contributions and local authority public expenditure.[79] *Full Employment in a Free Society* on the other hand proposed a totally new kind of annual budget, which would use taxation, borrowing and deficit-financing to determine the levels of public expenditure, business investment and consumer demand. The first priority of this budget would be, not the balancing of income and expenditure, but adjustment of production to the total supply of labour. The budget would be managed by a new Ministry of National Finance, thus reducing the Treasury to its traditional function of merely supervising the expenditure of other departments.[80] Regulation of demand would be backed up by a series of subordinate policies—such as planned location of industry and measures to encourage mobility of labour.[81] Both public and private investment would be supervised by a National Investment Board which would

---

[76] *Daily Worker*, 5 Nov. 1943; *Daily Herald*, 5 Oct. 1943.

[77] *PI*, p. 330.

[78] PRO, CAB 66/42, 'Reconstruction Plans. Memorandum by the Paymaster-General', 29 Oct. 1943.

[79] Cmd. 6527/1943–4, *Employment Policy*, pp. 21–3. The White Paper also considered the possibility of regulating demand by varying taxation rates, but concluded that such a policy 'would come into operation more slowly than an effective policy demands'. If such variations *were* found necessary, the White Paper preferred 'deferred credits'—i.e. high taxation in periods of boom repayable to taxpayers during periods of high unemployment. For the background to the White Paper, see Paul Addison, op. cit., pp. 243–6.

[80] *Full Employment in a Free Society, A Report by William H. Beveridge*, pp. 135–42.

[81] Ibid., pp. 166–75.

make available low-interest loans to private enterprise and bridge the Keynsian hiatus between decisions to save and decisions to invest.[82] Demand for labour would be adjusted so as always to exceed supply— although Beveridge envisaged that even in 'full employment' 3 per cent of the labour-force would always be unemployed at any one time, as a natural consequence of technical innovation and labour mobility.[83] The report emphasized that full employment could be maintained in a variety of ways—by remission of taxation so as to increase consumption, by public expenditure financed out of loans, or by public expenditure financed out of taxation. Similarly full employment was compatible with either a socialist or a capitalist system or a liberal-collectivist *via media*. As a matter of policy Beveridge and his advisers hoped that the emphasis would be placed on public expenditure—on state replenishment of capital equipment and provision of social services. They envisaged also that only about 25 per cent of 'total national investment' would remain in private hands.[84] But these were seen as desirable ends in themselves rather than as prerequisites of full employment—in contrast to the view that Beveridge had taken on the Advisory Panel on Home Affairs two years before. His central emphasis now was not upon state control of production but on the very different goal of state management of aggregate demand. 'The policy outlined in the Report by-passes the socialist–capitalist controversy', he concluded.

It can be accepted by persons holding many different views on that controversy —by those who desire socialism at once, by those who oppose socialism at any time, and by those who are prepared to judge private enterprise and public enterprise on their merits in the light of experience. . . . It could be done in a United States which remained capitalist as in a Soviet Russia which was wholly collectivised or in a Britain which took a middle course.[85]

Beveridge's Full Employment report, as he himself acknowledged, was based in its economic aspects on ideas supplied to him by other people. In particular, its proposals for a new kind of budgetary control of the economy were directly based on a paper drafted by Kaldor in November 1943.[86] Beveridge's own contribution to the report seems to have been mainly one of synthesis and exposition; it was he who linked Keynsian economics with an overall strategy for post-war social planning, and it was he who translated the ideas of his economic advisers into lucid layman's prose.[87] It was Beveridge also who supplied the

[82] Ibid., pp. 177–8, 271.     [83] Ibid., pp. 125–9.

[84] Ibid., pp. 142–6, 177, 185–7; BP, IXa 13, Employment Investigation Minutes, 9 Dec 1943.

[85] *Full Employment in a Free Society*, pp. 190–2.

[86] BP, IXa 13, 'A Note on Alternative Ways of Influencing the Level of Employment by Budgetary Measures', by N. Kaldor, 30 Nov. 1943.

[87] BP, IXa 16, B. Wootton to WHB, 20 Jan. 1944.

report with its moral rhetoric—invoking once again the Bunyanesque conception of the war against the five giants. Nevertheless, *Full Employment in a Free Society* was more than just an exercise in the popularization of economic theory; it was also the clearest expression—clearer even than his Social Insurance Report—of Beveridge's mature political convictions and of his vision of the character of the post-war world. Its central theme was abolition of unemployment; but it also ranged in detail over the fundamental problem with which Beveridge had been grappling throughout the 1930s—the question of how far 'liberal freedoms' were ultimately compatible with collectivist social planning. As we have seen, Beveridge's views on this point had been drastically revised since the late 1930's—largely because the war had narrowed his definition of essential freedoms and at the same time greatly broadened his sense of political cohesion and social solidarity. By 1942 he had come to the conclusion that a highly collectivist planned society was both consistent with personal freedom and a prerequisite for combating major social ills. His report of 1944 marked a slight retreat from this position. In *Full Employment in a Free Society* Beveridge was still prepared for a wide measure of state socialism if this should prove a practical necessity; but for the first time he saw Keynsianism as a possible alternative route towards similar goals.

The highly collectivist character of Beveridge's political ideas at this time raises the question of how far he should actually be seen as a 'socialist' in any of the many senses of that word. I think there is no doubt that in terms of social and economic policy Beveridge's views between 1942–4 were virtually indistinguishable from those of many people in the Labour Party who called themselves 'socialists'. On questions such as public ownership, redistribution of income and extension of social services he did not fundamentally disagree with socialist politicians like Aneurin Bevan and Stafford Cripps. It is true that he did not contemplate total economic equality, and it is true that his ideas contained large residual traces of liberal individualism, but the same may truly be said of the mainstream of English socialist thought at the time. Several of his advisers on the full employment inquiry were socialists; and in the eyes of the official members of his Insurance committee Beveridge seemed 'virtually labour' and 'rather Left by the standards of the day'.[88] On a more theoretical level Beveridge seems to have entirely abandoned the intellectual reservations about neglecting the laws of the free market that had troubled him ten years before. When in 1944 he read F. J. Hayek's classic critique of centralized planning, *The Road to Serfdom*, he remarked that 'Professor Hayek . . . is not I think a man who understands British mentality . . . I did not find his book in the least

[88] Interviews with Sir Edward Hale and Miss Muriel Ritson.

convincing.'[89] By contrast with his political agnosticism during the 1920s and 30s he had now reverted to his youthful belief that 'human institutions were made by men and could be infinitely improved by them'.[90] Where Beveridge differed most profoundly from orthodox socialist thinking was not on substantive issues of policy but on how such policies were to be brought about. As in earlier years he saw reforms as coming about through the power of abstract ideas or through pragmatic administrative adjustments rather than through historical movements; and he envisaged that a more 'socialistic' organization of society would be achieved, not through working-class pressure, but through an enlightened, bureaucratic, public-spirited élite. He insisted moreover that socialism was a technique rather than a principle and a question of means rather than ends; it should be invoked on a pragmatic basis when other methods were found wanting, and it should be pursued where it worked successfully and abandoned where it failed.

## V

The euphoric popular reception of his Social Insurance report and the subsequent official boycott of his services led Beveridge for the first time in forty years to take an active role in organized politics. He was convinced that his Report should be acted upon before the end of the war, and he was convinced also that the government was unlikely to take such action except in response to external political pressure. Early in 1943 he was active with Cole in setting-up a nation-wide Social Security League to canvass support for social reform and to press for the Report's immediate implementation.[91] In demanding immediate action Beveridge commanded much popular support; but his attitude gave rise to considerable irritation among ministers and officials, to whom it seemed that Beveridge thought 'that the war ought to stop while his plan was put into effect'.[92] Undoubtedly there was much to be said for the view that social reform could not be given immediate priority; but in pressing for rapid action Beveridge was not being entirely unreasonable. He remembered only too clearly the contrast between the rosy promises of reconstruction during the previous war and the grim reality of the post-war depression. He believed that the government should take advantage of the prevailing full employment and high wages to start financing the new insurance system before the end of the war. And he feared also that

---

[89] BP, IIb, WHB to J. B. A. Boyle, 6 Dec. 1944.
[90] BP, IIb, WHB to H. Prain, 14 Feb. 1944.
[91] Cole Papers, Bs/4/4, Box 5, papers and correspondence of Social Security League 1943–4.
[92] Francis Williams, *A Prime Minister Remembers* (1961), p. 56.

the morale-raising impact of his Report would be lost, if its implementation were deferred until some indefinite future date.[93]

Almost certainly it was these considerations that persuaded Beveridge to go into active politics. Another contributory factor was the sensation of personal popularity, which Beveridge undoubtedly enjoyed and which he seemed to believe would carry him to political success regardless of party ties. Letters from the public frequently urged him to enter politics, and during the winter of 1942–3 there were rumours among his acquaintances that he was beginning to see himself as a possible future Prime Minister.[94] There is no direct evidence that Beveridge's ambitions were in fact running in this totally unrealistic direction, but the rumours were so widespread that they cannot be entirely ignored. From Beveridge's correspondence of the time it seems highly unlikely that he consciously aspired to rival Churchill, since in spite of his criticisms of some of Churchill's policies he was acutely conscious of the Prime Minister's tremendous powers of leadership and charismatic appeal.[95] What is far more likely is that Beveridge hoped to become either Minister of Social Security or Minister of Reconstruction—an idea that had been implanted by the Labour peer Lord Nathan in 1941 and that was enthusiastically fostered by Beveridge's supporters in the Social Security League.[96]

Almost as soon as the insurance report was published, Beveridge was invited to stand as a Liberal candidate for the parliamentary seat at Dunfermline. The election would be uncontested, since the previous member had been a Liberal and the three major parties had agreed not to contest each other's seats as long as the Coalition should last. 'I am certain,' wrote Lady Glen-Coats, an official of the Scottish Liberal Federation, 'that in view of the very good work you have done for the country you would find election a very easy matter.' Beveridge at this stage was still hoping for further government employment and did not reply for some weeks; but he eventually replied to Lady Glen-Coats showing some interest in her offer, provided that he could stand 'with sufficient independence of position'. By that time the chance of Dunfermline had passed, but Lady Glen-Coats promised to look out for another Scottish constituency—assuring him that, far from imposing constraints upon its members, the Liberal Party was if anything suicidally free.[97]

[93] BP, IIb, WHB to Hubert Hills, 9 June 1945.
[94] Dalton Papers, Hugh Dalton's diary, vol. XXVII, 16 Dec. 1942; Harold Nicolson, *Diaries and Letters 1939–45* (1967), p. 282; Francis Williams, op. cit., p. 56.
[95] Lady Beveridge Papers, WHB to J. Mair, 19 Mar. 1941; Lloyd George Papers, G/3/94, WHB to Frances Stevenson, 4 Mar. 1942.
[96] Lady Beveridge Papers, WHB to J. Mair, 5 April 1941; BP, IIb, Joan Clarke to WHB, 29 Jan. 1944.
[97] BP, IIb, Lady Glen-Coats to WHB, 18 Dec. 1942 and 19 Jan. 1943; WHB to Lady Glen-Coats, 14 Jan. 1943.

Nevertheless, although Beveridge was increasingly interested in standing for Parliament, it was by no means a foregone conclusion that he would stand as a Liberal. As he recalled in his memoirs he toyed with the idea of standing as Liberal, Labour, Independent or as a candidate for one of the University seats.[98] He had several invitations to contest by-elections as an Independent; but in spite of his demand for effective parliamentary opposition he felt a psychological reluctance to breach national unity by standing against the government of Churchill. The same objection probably applied to Sir Richard Acland's Common Wealth Party, which won several by-elections on a pro-Beveridge plat-form in 1943–4. It is perhaps surprising that Beveridge did not show more interest in the wartime Common Wealth Party, since at least superficially it bore all the marks of his spiritual home. Like Beveridge the Common Wealth believed in the force of moral ideas and like Beveridge at this time it preached a brand of socialism based on the leadership of an intellectual aristocracy rather than the working class.[99] Joining the Common Wealth would have meant opposing the Coalition, however, and this in the last resort Beveridge was not prepared to do. Probably the alternative which he most favoured, at least for a time, was the possibility of joining Labour. He had several meetings with senior Labour politicians, and almost certainly would have joined the Labour Party of its leaders had shown themselves a little more willing to accommodate his desire for freedom of conscience and a little more anxious to win his support.[100] As it turned out, however, it was the Liberals who most assiduously wooed and flattered Beveridge and eventually won him. From the start the Liberals had enthusiastically endorsed the Beveridge Report, which had been warmly praised by Liberal elder statesmen like Lloyd George and Herbert Samuel and by the younger generation of radicals led by Clement Davies and Dingle Foot. For the next eighteen months Lady Glen-Coats and Lady Violet Bonham Carter were urging Beveridge to throw in his hand with that section of the 'Left' which rejected the 'narrow sectarianism' of Labour;[101] and in August 1944 Beveridge agreed to stand as Liberal candidate for Berwick-on-Tweed.

Beveridge's adoption as Liberal candidate for Berwick provoked something of a crisis in his relations with the fellows of University College—several of whom complained that he had been neglecting his

[98] *PI*, pp. 336–7.

[99] Angus Calder, op. cit., pp. 631–5; D. L. Prynn, 'Common Wealth—A British Third Party of the 1940s', *J. Cont. Hist.*, vol. 7, nos. 1–2, Jan.–Apr. 1972, pp. 169–79.

[100] Interview with Lord Longford; *PI*, p. 337; BP, IIb, C. Attlee to WHB, 3 Feb. 1943.

[101] BP, IIb, Lady Glen-Coats to WHB, 2 Oct. 1943; Lady Violet Bonham Carter to WHB, 8 Dec. 1943; VI 20, Lady Violet Bonham Carter to WHB, 7 Oct. 1944; *PI*, p. 337.

duties as Master, and that the administration of a College could not be combined with the work of an M.P. Beveridge himself hotly denied that this was so. He claimed that the writing of his reports had never interfered with his conduct of College business, that many other academics were similarly engaged in public work, and that the proceeds of his extra-collegiate activities—royalties, income from journalism and payments from the government—had all been paid into College funds. He claimed, moreover, that there was nothing inconsistent in the roles of Master and Member of Parliament, and that there was no reason why he should not combine both positions at least until the end of the war. In this Beveridge was arguing directly against the stand that he had taken at the L.S.E. in the 1930s, when he had come to the conclusion that political action was basically incompatible with an academic career. He had always been rather blind, however, about the application of this principle to his own political activities, and he was deeply hurt and disappointed when a majority of the fellows decided that it was necessary for him to resign.[102]

In standing for Parliament therefore Beveridge was not merely embarking upon a new career; he was incurring a considerable loss of income and security—forfeiting both his salary of £1,800 as Master of University College and the £1,000 a year that he was paid as nonpolitical chairman of the Unemployment Insurance Statutory Committee. It was a bold venture for a man of sixty-five; but as Beveridge himself later admitted the full extent of his rashness was not apparent at the time.[103] Berwick-on-Tweed in 1944 seemed like one of the few surviving invincible Liberal strongholds. It was a far-flung border constituency of sheep-farmers and small tradesmen, who had consistently voted Liberal throughout the Liberal twilight of the 1920s and 30s. Beveridge himself had frequently been assured that his personal prestige would make it possible for him to win virtually any constituency in the country, and he had no doubt of his power to hold Berwick for the rest of his active life. He had an easy by-election victory, polling more than six times as many votes as his only opponent, a right-wing Independent. Early in 1945 he and Lady Beveridge moved to Tuggal Hall, an attractive border manor-house; and they planned to live permanently in the constituency, devoting themselves partly to a nation-wide revival of Liberalism and partly to local affairs.

Beveridge's decision to join the Liberals was taken, as we have seen,

---

[102] *PI*, pp. 290, 337–9. The Treasury had paid £100 a month to University College while Beveridge was employed on the Social Insurance inquiry (BP, IIb, C. Davidge to WHB, 3 June 1942). After his resignation his plans to endow the college with the royalties from *Full Employment* were abandoned, but a substantial part of these royalties was given to the Social Security League and the Webb Memorial Fund.

[103] *PI*, pp. 339–41.

largely on personal grounds, but nevertheless his decision was not
entirely fortuitous. He had always seen the Liberals as the 'Party of
ideas' and of 'national interests'—as opposed to the sectionalism of both
Conservatives and Labour. His belief in the possibility of pursuing goals
by reasoned argument, and by consensus rather than conflict, appears to
have been strengthened by the sense of national unity created by the
war. The very contradictions of Liberalism—the tensions between individualism and collectivism, radicalism and traditionalism—appealed to
Beveridge's own personal slant upon the world. He was quite the last
person to submit happily to party discipline; and, as Lady Glen-Coats
had admitted, Liberal control over the views of members was notoriously weak. Beveridge tended, moreover, to idealize the Liberal past,
and he looked back in particular upon Edwardian Liberalism as a
golden age of radical innovation and as the period of his own most
spectacular success.[104] All these factors combined to make him feel at
home within the Liberal Party, and once he had made the commitment
he flung himself into the cause of 'Liberal revival' and into restoring the
image of the Liberals as the party of reform.

Beveridge took his seat in the Commons in October 1944 and was
greatly moved to be personally welcomed by Churchill. He made his
maiden speech on the government's Social Security White Paper—welcoming the commitment to universal insurance, but deploring the
government's reluctance to accept the principle of subsistence.[105] Over
the next few months he spoke frequently in the House—supporting
electoral reform and the development of small-scale industry, and
criticizing the powers of the new Security Council proposed for the
United Nations.[106] In particular, he and other radical Liberals condemned the conferment of the right of veto upon the five permanent
members of the Security Council—predicting that this would be used by
the Russians to reduce the assembly to deadlock.[107] 'Soviet Russia is the
Devil I incline to think,' wrote Beveridge during the Yalta peace talks—
emphasizing that his admiration for Soviet planning machinery had in
no way dispelled his earlier fear that Russia was the chief menace to
world peace.[108] He dealt also with a flood of letters from his Berwick
constituents. Many of these dealt with social welfare, but they reflected
also the more localized concerns of a remote, rural constituency—the
lifting of restrictions on agricultural building, the scarcity of rural
housing, the repeal of the Witchcraft Acts and the shortage of Wellington

---

[104] BP, IIb, V. Markham to WHB, 12 June 1941.
[105] H.C. Deb., 5s., vol. 404, cols. 1,121–33.
[106] Ibid., cols. 633–4; vol. 407, cols. 647, 712–13; vol. 408, cols. 1,313–16.
[107] Samuel Papers, A155, XI, Sir A. Sinclair to Lord Samuel, 10 Mar. 1945; H.C. Deb..
5s., vol. 410, cols. 89, 103–9.
[108] Lady Beveridge Papers, WHB to Janet Beveridge, 11 May 1945.

boots.[109] On matters of general policy Beveridge firmly identified himself with the Party's left wing—routing the Liberal 'bow and arrow brigade', calling for an uncompromisingly radical programme, and urging his colleagues to admit the pragmatic necessity for certain measures of state control.[110]

The chance to test out a radical programme came much sooner than Beveridge had envisaged. He and many other Liberals hoped that there would be no change of government until after the war. But by March 1945 it was clear that the Coalition was breaking down, and two months later a general election was called for July. Beveridge himself was regarded by many Liberals as their chief electoral asset and he was rather precipitately placed in charge of the Liberal campaign— regardless of the fact that his only formal experience of electioneering was at Toynbee Hall more than forty years before. Literal implementation of the Beveridge Report became the central item in the Liberal manifesto—backed up by an attack on monopolies and by policies of international arbitration and federation. Beveridge rather belatedly urged his colleagues to develop a 'first-rate organisation';[111] and between April and July 1945 he made more than a hundred and fifty speeches in all parts of the country. Everywhere he went he was greeted by large and enthusiastic audiences, and like many hopeful Liberals before and since he was seduced into believing that he was taking part in the long-awaited Liberal revival. His efforts, however, proved unavailing. At the end of July Liberals were elected to only twelve seats, and Beveridge himself was defeated by the Conservative candidate at Berwick in a three-cornered fight.

Many explanations have been put forward for the Labour victory of 1945, for the defeat of the Conservatives and for the virtual eclipse of parliamentary Liberalism. The Labour success has been ascribed to popular memories of the inter-war depression, to the radicalism of the troops, to an incoherent desire for 'change for its own sake', and to the fact that—at a time when all parties were promising radical innovations —it was Labour that managed to identify itself most convincingly with the cause of reform. The continued decline of the Liberals has been ascribed to their lack of funds and organization, to their lack of connection with any major class or sectional group, and to the growth of a new voting generation among whom for the first time there was no hereditary Liberal tradition. Their failure has been blamed also upon their mistaken emphasis on the Beveridge Report. Surveys of opinion after the election found that even among those who had voted Liberal

[109] BP, VI 21, *passim.*

[110] BP, IIb, WHB to Lady Glen-Coats, 8 Jan. 1945; Elliott Dodds to WHB, 4 Feb. 1945; WHB to A. H. Hansen, 15 Mar. 1945.

[111] BP, IIb, WHB to Lady Glen-Coats, 8 Jan. 1945.

only 8 per cent put implementation of Beveridge at the head of their political priorities; and the enthusiasm that had greeted the report two and a half years earlier appeared to have been swallowed up in a more generalized desire for radical social change.[112]

All these factors help to explain the events of July 1945. Nevertheless, they do not fully explain Beveridge's defeat at Berwick; nor do they take account of the crisis in Liberal ideology and leadership that emerges from the pages of Beveridge's correspondence with other Liberal politicians. Beveridge's defeat at Berwick cannot be ascribed to Labour's success in cornering the radical vote, since the constituency swung to the Conservatives—with Labour trailing a very poor third. Moreover, Berwick had a flourishing Liberal tradition and an active Liberal organization; it had certainly not 'lost the habit' of voting Liberal—as subsequent history was to show. From Beveridge's correspondence with his supporters and party workers his defeat seems to have turned at least partly on much more personal factors. The Liberalism of Berwick was the Liberalism of nonconformity and of rugged individualism, and many of Beveridge's constituents were clearly mistrustful of his support for 'social planning'.[113] Beveridge did his best to placate the *laissez-faire* tradition and to minimize the role of state interference, but he admitted that he did not find it easy 'to make a vote-catching appeal out of individualism and personalism'.[114] Another factor was that, in his efforts to inspire the whole campaign, Beveridge spent much time away from Berwick; and his agent wrote warningly that many of his supporters were feeling neglected—'personal contact means so much in this constituency'.[115] A third factor that is difficult to weigh precisely but that was certainly present among Berwick Liberals was a psychological reluctance to vote against Churchill and to damage the structure of political consensus. Some of Beveridge's erstwhile supporters were clearly indignant that the election had been called before the war had ended, and—even though it was Churchill who had called it—they simply refused to oppose Churchill for the duration of the war. This ambivalence among Beveridge's constituents was reflected among the Liberal leaders.[116] The leader in the Commons, Sir Archibald Sinclair,

[112] R. B. McCallum and Alison Readman, *The British General Election of 1945* (1947), pp. 266–71; Bentley B. Gilbert 'Third Parties and Voters' Decisions: The Liberals and the General Election of 1945', *Journal of British Studies*, XI, May 1972, 2, pp. 131–9; Henry Pelling, *Britain and the Second World War* (1970), pp. 230–6.

[113] BP, IIb, correspondence between WHB, A. Smart and C. D. Smedley (editor of *Alnwick and County Gazette and Guardian*), June–Aug. 1945; VI 17, W. S. Morris to WHB, 30 June 1945.

[114] BP, IIb, WHB to Elliott Dodds, 10 Mar. 1945.

[115] BP, IIb, M. A. Gregson (agent of Berwick-on-Tweed Liberal Association) to Enid Chambers, 2 June 1945.

[116] BP, IIb, WHB to James E. Allen, 30 May 1945; Samuel Papers, A155, XI, Hamilton of Dalziel to Lord Samuel, 19 Apr. 1945, and Marquis of Reading to Lord Samuel, 31 May 1945.

was clearly troubled by the party's radical wing, and tried to insist that the only difference between Liberals and Conservatives was the now extinct issue of international free trade.[117] Sinclair also shared the reluctance of many rank-and-file Liberals to oppose the Prime Minister; and Beveridge was horrified when Sinclair publicly implied that, whatever the result of the election, Churchill should be asked to carry on as Prime Minister until the war was ended and negotiations for a peace complete.[118] Yet Beveridge himself seemed at times to share exactly the same assumption. On several occasions during his campaign he referred rather cryptically to the possibility of keeping Churchill without his more objectionable followers—a remark which presumably pointed towards a radically oriented multi-party coalition. 'We can have Winston without the Tories,' he declared in one of a number of speeches that have survived on gramophone records among his private papers. These speeches are remarkable for their clarity, earnestness and precision in dealing with factual details; but they are totally lacking in that sense of personal righteousness, that absolute conviction of the unworthiness of all opponents, that seems to be one of the hallmarks of a successful election campaign.

## VI

Beveridge's defeat at Berwick marked the end of his hopes that he would be personally involved in implementing the Beveridge Report. It marked also the end of his brief career in the Commons. In the following year he was invited to stand again as independent candidate for the Northern Universities, but was dissuaded from doing so by the rump of Liberal M.P.s[119] A few months later he accepted a Liberal peerage and took his seat in the upper house as Baron Beveridge of Tuggal, becoming leader of the Liberals in the House of Lords. From this dignified but in no sense powerful position he took part in many debates on the legislation which created the structure of the modern 'welfare state'—a phrase that he personally disliked and never used, because of what he believed were its 'Santa Claus' and 'brave new world' connotations.[120] At no stage was he involved in the policy discussions of the wartime coalition or the post-war Labour government, and at no stage can he be seen as personally responsible for any of the great social policy statutes of this period—the Family Allowances Act of 1945, the National Insurance and National Health Service Acts of 1946 and the National

---

[117] Ibid., Sir A. Sinclair to Lord Samuel, 2 June and 9 Aug. 1945.
[118] Lady Beveridge Papers, WHB to Janet Beveridge, 3 June 1945.
[119] Samuel Papers, A 155, XII, WHB to Lord Samuel, 27 Jan. 1946.
[120] H.L. Deb., 5s., vol. 190, col. 532.

Assistance Act of 1948. Paradoxically, however, Beveridge's Plan was acted upon much more quickly and thoroughly than the vast majority of comparable public inquiries. It is true that there were some important deviations from Beveridge's proposals. Family allowances were introduced at a much lower rate than Beveridge had suggested; old-age pensions were introduced at a slightly higher level but with no commitment to build up towards subsistence; industrial assurance was never nationalized; and some of Beveridge's fringe-benefits—such as the furnishing allowance and domestic service benefit for sick housewives— were quietly dropped. But the main structure and many of the principles of the welfare legislation of 1945–8 were those which Beveridge had laid down in 1942. In devising these principles, Beveridge's role had been mainly that of a synthesizer and publicist rather than that of an innovator and it is difficult to claim that he had made any inherently original contribution to subsequent social policy. But, nevertheless, it was Beveridge who interpreted the mainstream of public opinion and who transformed an incoherent mass of popular feeling into a blueprint for social reform.

It is clearly impossible within the limits of a biography to weigh the full impact of Beveridge's Report upon subsequent developments in social welfare. Nevertheless, in order to assess the significance and influence of Beveridge himself, an attempt must be made to consider how far his proposals were an adequate solution for the problems they were trying to cure, and how far they have weathered the test of subsequent social history. The British social security system has been considerably modified since the legislation of the 1940s—most notably by the introduction of the principle of 'earnings-relation'; but it is still recognizably the system recommended by Beveridge in 1942, and the question must be asked—how far has that system been successful in 'slaying the Giant Want'? A Beveridge who surveyed the map of poverty in Britain in the mid-1970s would probably be struck by two dominant features. Firstly by the persistence of a major role for means-tested 'supplementary benefit', fulfilling a similar function to the old 'public assistance' system. And secondly, by the prevalence of a kind of poverty that falls outside the scope of the social insurance system—of poverty among low wage-earners, the chronically sick and disabled, and children in large or one-parent families. In this latter respect the problem of poverty today might strike the observer as rather remote from the problem that struck Beveridge in 1942—as perhaps rather more closely akin to that described by Seebohm Rowntree in his classic study of York in 1899.

Does this therefore mean that Beveridge's diagnosis was inaccurate, and that his remedy for poverty—primarily through the mechanism of insurance—was therefore wholly inadequate? Clearly some of the components of modern poverty are created by changes in social structure—by, for instance, the increasing prevalence of divorce and separation and the failure of social insurance to take sufficient account of these trends. To do Beveridge justice I think it is undeniable that he himself would have been the first to argue that no welfare system was immutable and that his own principles should be constantly revised, extended and modified to take account of structural change. One of these modifications might well have been a recognition of the fact that he had almost certainly exaggerated the degree of need that could be fitted into the context of contributory insurance—a fact that was acknowledged by pro-Beveridge writers such as D. N. Chester as early as 1946.[121] Beveridge's desire to get rid of means tests was an understandable response to the experience of the 1930s, and a very popular response at the time. But it was not wholly realistic in the fast-changing conditions of an advanced industrial society, where it is often difficult to predict in advance the precise nature and location of material human needs.

In other respects, however, an advocate for Beveridge might well defend both him and his system in a number of different ways. Firstly, it is arguable that much of the inadequacy of modern social security in Britain stems not so much from the inherent defects of the Beveridge scheme as from the failure to implement some of its important features. The introduction of subsistence-level family allowances as Beveridge recommended would long ago have prevented and cured vast tracts of family poverty. Similarly—whilst one must acknowledge the economic pressures which militated against his superannuation proposals—if Beveridge's 'build-up to subsistence-level pensions' had been adopted, then inadequate old-age pensions might have been phased out as long ago as 1965. Secondly, it is arguable that much more reliance has been placed on the social security system than was ever intended by Beveridge. As was shown earlier in this chapter his insurance proposals were merely the first instalment of a much more far-reaching programme of radical reform. An essential component of that programme was minimum-wage legislation which would bring all wages to the level of subsistence for a man, a wife and one child—assumed in Beveridge's proposals on family allowances.[122] Going far beyond this were Beveridge's proposals for rationalization of the labour market, industrial training-schemes, strict control of prices, statutory limitation of free collective bargaining, public ownership of land and essential services

[121] D. N. Chester, 'Social Insurance Legislation. Some Issues raised by the National Insurance Bill', *Social Welfare* (published by the Manchester and Salford Council of Social Service), VI, 7 July 1946, pp. 191–6.
[122] BP, IIb, WHB to Leonard Behrens, 10 Mar. 1945.

and, if necessary, the phasing out of private ownership of most of the means of production. Whether such a programme was in fact appropriate to the British political tradition is clearly a matter for personal opinion and judgement. But it was undoubtedly seen by Beveridge as a necessary supplement to his proposals on social welfare; and in view of how little of it has ever been acted upon, it is not perhaps surprising that Beveridge's proposals for the abolition of poverty have met with only qualified success.

# 18

## Beveridge in Old Age

### I

Beveridge's defeat at Berwick and elevation to the peerage did not put an end to his official career. From 1947 to 1951 he was chairman of the Development Corporation at the 'new town' of Newton Aycliffe in County Durham—a post which he combined after 1949 with the chairmanship of a second new town at Peterlee. From 1949–50 he was also chairman of an official committee on broadcasting, which inquired into the monopoly status of the B.B.C. Nevertheless, the eclipse of the Liberals and his elevation to the Lords effectively destroyed what had become his dearest ambition—the hope that he would be personally involved in implementing the Beveridge Report. In Britain and abroad he was increasingly seen as the 'father of the welfare state' and as the presiding genius of British social policy. But in fact his role in the new welfare system that emerged after 1945 was that of critic, interpreter and moralist rather than architect of official government policy.

### II

Beveridge was invited to become chairman of the Newton Aycliffe corporation by the Minister of Housing in 1947; and in this position he resumed a cause that he had espoused forty years earlier, when he had condemned conurbation and pressed for devolution of industry in the leader columns of the *Morning Post*. Early in the 1940s he had strongly supported the Barlow and Uthwatt Reports on land use and town and country planning; and his belief in the need for strict control over the location of housing and industry had been reflected in his papers on the Five Giants. Beveridge therefore brought to Newton Aycliffe a lifelong conviction that both industry and population should be decentralized and that communities should be planned on 'rational' lines. He threw himself into the new movement with characteristic energy—selling Tuggal in order to move to Newton Aycliffe, visiting many housing experiments on the continent, corresponding with town planners and frequently expounding the 'new towns' philosophy in the House of Lords.[1]

[1] H.L. Deb., 5s., vol. 152, cols. 1,134–9; vol. 190, cols. 991–5.

Beveridge's early days at Newton Aycliffe appear to have been one of the most satisfying episodes of his public career. He saw in the new towns movement the most hopeful sign that the government intended to adopt his own formula for comprehensive planning. He took an active part in local affairs, pressing for local amenities, setting up local societies and trying to develop a corporate community life. He had a 'very friendly' reception from the Newton Aycliffe corporation, and a similar welcome two years later in Peterlee; and he was pleased and flattered when a local trades unionist assured him that 'we don't want a squire but we do want intellectual leadership'.[2] He was on good terms with Lewis Silkin, the Labour Minister of Housing, who allowed the new town corporations a good deal of independence and discretion in the management of their affairs.

Nevertheless, like so much of his experience in practical administration, Beveridge's career in new towns proved in many respects a disappointment to him. He was acutely conscious of the dangers of building a community marred by 'the complete absence of anything except houses';[3] but nevertheless, the pressures of the post-war housing shortage, coupled with the lack of funds for non-essential services, meant that this was the pattern that inevitably emerged. Again and again his two corporations were unable to build libraries, health-centres, playgrounds and schools because of chronic shortage of funds.[4] Moreover, Beveridge brought to his two new towns the ideals and aspirations of the Edwardian town planning movement. He dreamt of a new community rich in cultural and occupational diversity—modelled on Henrietta Barnett's ill-starred vision for Hampstead Garden Suburb. Hence he was totally unprepared for the uniform community of young married couples with small children, drawn almost exclusively from the skilled working class, that rapidly developed at Newton Aycliffe and Peterlee. Beveridge was not a snob, but he was and felt himself to be 'a gentleman' in the pre-1914 conception of that word; and it was strange and rather uncomfortable for him to live in a small box-like house without a library and without resident domestic help. 'A really new town cannot have all classes in it,' he confided ruefully to Richard Denman, '. . . there's no real society for J. at Newton Aycliffe. The people are nice and the troops of children are lovely, but there's no conversation.'[5]

Beveridge's dissatisfaction with life at Newton Aycliffe was intensified by the change of government in 1951. The new Housing minister, Harold Macmillan, had committed himself to building half a million

[2] BP, IIb, WHB to R. Denman, 19 Sept. 1950.
[3] H.L. Deb., 5s., vol. 190, col. 994.
[4] Ibid., vol. 186, col. 1,100; vol. 190, cols. 994–5.
[5] BP, IIb ms. notes of conversations with R. Denman, n.d.

houses a year. The new towns were pressed to increase their housing output, and social amenities were given an even lower priority than before. Moreover, Macmillan allowed the new towns much less autonomy than had been allowed by Silkin, and he infuriated Beveridge by his 'meticulous interference' in Newton Aycliffe affairs.[6] Beveridge regarded Macmillan with deep suspicion, attributing to him a basic lack of sympathy with the new towns movement; and he found himself for the first time in his life acting as the champion of local initiative and autonomy against interference from Whitehall.[7] Not perhaps surprisingly, Macmillan became the last in a long line of ministers determined to dispense with Beveridge's services, and in 1952 he was informed by the Minister that he was too old to continue at Peterlee and Newton Aycliffe and was asked to resign. Beveridge was indignant and denounced Macmillan as a 'Pompous Ass' with 'no manners' and 'no idea of delegation from Whitehall'. But privately he was rather relieved to have an 'honourable release' from what had become an increasingly frustrating and onerous position. 'And he's quite right in one sense,' he recorded, 'I'm not too old to be Chairman. But I am too old and too distinguished to be subordinate to his third-rate officials.'[8]

Beveridge's Report on Broadcasting, composed with the assistance of a committee of eleven members, proved to be the last of the many official reports that he had composed for successive ministers since 1911. The committee was convened to inquire into the monopoly enjoyed by the B.B.C. and to consider the alternative of a commercial broadcasting system. Beveridge himself had for twenty years been a successful broadcaster on serious radio programmes. He had appeared on television during the first year of transmission in 1936, and he regarded himself as something of an expert on mass communication. Consequently he took up his post as chairman of the Broadcasting committee in 1949 with certain well-defined ideas about the future role and purpose of television and radio. He was convinced that both media should have a strongly 'elevating' and 'educative' function, and he had been greatly repelled by what he had seen of commercial broadcasting in the United States.[9] He was therefore anxious that broadcasting should be protected against any form of commercial control. At the same time, however, he was inclined to be critical of the existing powers and structure of the B.B.C. One of the members of his committee, Lady Stocks, has suggested that Beveridge was at this time nursing a grudge against the Corporation because he had not been invited to participate in the

[6] BP, IIb, WHB to Lewis Silkin, 18 and 31 June 1953.

[7] BP, IIb, WHB to Daisy Hobman, 25 Mar. 1953.

[8] BP, II, WHB to J. Mair, 28 Apr. 1952; IIb, WHB to R. Denman, May 1952; ms. notes of conversation with R. Denman, n.d.

[9] H.L. Deb., 5s., vol. 188, cols. 244–9.

B.B.C.'s Wordsworth Centenary.[10] There were, however, other and more substantial grounds for his dislike of the B.B.C. monopoly. He was in principle opposed to state monopoly in mass communications, frequently citing examples from Eastern Europe to prove how such monopoly was open to abuse. He believed that the B.B.C. in the past had not in fact abused its powers; but in discussions of broadcasting he was fond of quoting Thomas Huxley's dictum that 'the devoted leaders of revolution in one generation can and do become tyrants in the next'. His second major objection was to the general tone and character of B.B.C. programmes and policy, which he condemned as 'beginning with Londonisation, going on to secretiveness and self-satisfaction and ending up with the danger of a sense of mission becoming a sense of divine right'.[11]

As chairman of the Broadcasting Committee Beveridge's initial aim was therefore to devise a formula that would avoid commercial control of broadcasting and yet at the same time put an end to the monopoly enjoyed by the B.B.C. He was not in principle opposed to raising funds through advertising, arguing that even the best newspapers took advertisements and that this did not necessarily contaminate editorial policy.[12] His committee considered various schemes for financing programmes through commercial 'sponsorship' while vesting control of the actual content of programmes in an independent board. Beveridge regretfully concluded, however, that 'money speaks' and that the commercial and cultural aspects of an independent system could never be successfully divided in this way.[13] The committee also examined various proposals for breaking the B.B.C.'s monopoly by creating several rival corporations, all financed out of licenses; but such schemes proved administratively highly complex and were eventually rejected.[14] Beveridge and a majority of his committee therefore concluded that, in spite of the dangers of a statutory monopoly, there was no real alternative to the concentration of broadcasting under the B.B.C. They recommended, however, that there should be much more scope for regional broadcasting, much greater emphasis on cultural programmes, and that both radio and television should henceforth play a major part in adult education. They proposed also that B.B.C. government should become much more 'open', that more attention should be paid to the views of outsiders, and that there should be a much greater degree of consumer representation.[15] This report was signed by the whole of

[10] Mary Stocks, *Still More Commonplace* (1973), pp. 54–5.
[11] H.L. Deb. 5s., vol. 172, cols. 1,251–61.
[12] BP, IIb, WHB to Stephen Taylor, 13 July 1953.
[13] Cmd. 8116/1950–51, *Report of the Broadcasting Committee*, pp. 100–7; H.L. Deb., 5s., vol. 586–8.
[14] *Report of the Broadcasting Committee*, pp. 41–6.      [15] Ibid., pp. 189–200.

Beveridge's committee except for Mr. Selwyn Lloyd, the future
Conservative Chancellor of the Exchequer, who produced a minority
report favouring the introduction of an independent commercial network.[16] Beveridge himself and two other members of his committee also
put forward a minority proposal suggesting that a limited amount of
advertising might be allowed on the B.B.C.—as a legitimate means of
assisting people to exercise the consumer choice that was one of their
rights in a 'free society'.[17]

Beveridge's report was welcomed by the Labour government, but its
implementation was postponed by the 1951 general election, and the
incoming Conservative government preferred the commercial alternative proposed by Selwyn Lloyd. Beveridge thereafter became a fierce
critic of commercial broadcasting, claiming in the Lords that some of
the programmes put out by the new commercial television channels
conformed to the worst standards of the gutter press. He continued to
advocate the use of radio and television as aids to learning—arguing, in
terms reminiscent of his days at Toynbee that the working class were
now not merely a governing class but a 'leisured class' and needed education appropriate to their leisure. His last speech in parliament was on
the Pilkington Report on Broadcasting of 1961, when he warmly
welcomed the idea of a 'University of the Air', but strongly condemned
both commercial television and the corrupting influence that he
believed commercial competition was having on the B.B.C. In watching television, he remarked, he saw 'a good many things as beautiful
and thought-provoking as anyone could desire. I saw other pictures so
disgusting to decent minds, so corrupting to clean minds, that they were
a disgrace to the inventors.'[18]

## III

Beveridge never fully recovered from his bitter disappointment at being
excluded from government service. In a personal sense, however, his old
age—at least until the death of Lady Beveridge—was in many respects
one of the happiest periods in his life. He was a devoted husband, hating
to be parted from his wife and writing to her the kind of tenderly
chivalrous and romantic letters that he might have written as a young
man of twenty. He generously ascribed to her many of his own ideas,
and always pushed her forward when he was asked to address public
gatherings—such as the meeting of the International Social Security
Association in 1959. 'Janet . . . has never had the publicity that she

16 Ibid., pp. 201–10.           17 Ibid., pp. 226–8.
18 H.L. Deb., 5s., vol. 184, cols. 586–8; vol. 221, col. 688; vol. 242, cols. 630–6.

should have had,' he commented to a friend.[19] Lady Beveridge in turn idealized her husband, referring to him as 'my dear Socrates' and regarding him as the source of all wisdom and knowledge.[20] They shared all their activities together, from writing books to household chores—the latter a necessity in the strange new servant-less world of the 1950s, to which neither Beveridge nor his wife could ever become quite accustomed. In 1948 they sailed together on a round-the-world tour, giving lectures on social welfare and visiting the numerous Beveridge cousins in New Zealand and Australia. In Auckland, Beveridge recorded, he had 'come out as the patron saint of housewives, who certainly get a very raw deal in New Zealand'.[21] On board ship it was observed that Beveridge in his seventieth year had lost none of his physical energy and lifelong zeal for new causes. He rose every morning before six and took a dip in the ship's pool, before putting in two hours' work before breakfast. 'Even in the tropics he thought nothing of playing three or four strenuous games of deck tennis and entered for most of the organized games and sporting events.' He overwhelmed his fellow passengers by his 'amazing vitality' and relentlessly filled idle moments by organizing debates on 'the conditions of world peace'.[22]

Beveridge's 'amazing vitality' lasted into his late seventies, and much of his time in old age was absorbed in writing books, in making speeches on social policy, in further research for his history of prices and in frequent trips abroad. His first post-war book, *India Called Them*, was a history of the marriage of Henry and Annette, based on the rich collection of Beveridge family letters. As a biography Beveridge's portrayal of his parents was too dutifully selective to be altogether successful; but as a social history it was a unique account of the careers and aspirations of two earnest intellectuals in India and of domestic life under the British Raj. The book was also a monument to Beveridge's never-ending delight in family life and his delicate feeling for the smallest details and nuances of family relationships. *India Called Them* was followed two years later by Beveridge's *Antipodes Notebook*, a slight, affectionate memoir of his New Zealand cousins and their round-the-world tour. His autobiography, *Power and Influence*, was published in 1953 together with Lady Beveridge's biographical study *Beveridge and his Plan*. Covering the period from Toynbee Hall to his defeat at Berwick, *Power and Influence* was a curiously ambivalent and in some ways rather tragic book. Beveridge portrayed himself as a consistently cheerful and rather egotistical extrovert—with only an occasional hint of the self-doubt

---

[19] Mary Stocks, *Still More Commonplace*, p. 63; BP, IIb, WHB to Hugh Bell, 6 Oct. 1961.
[20] Lady Beveridge Papers, J. Beveridge to 'Anny', 7 Jan. 1944.
[21] BP, IIa, WHB to P. Mair, 10 May 1948.
[22] BP, IIa, press-cuttings from the *Weekly Scotsman*, May 1948.

and intellectual uncertainty that had characterized long periods of his inner life. The book pursued his long-standing vendetta against social scientists who involved themselves in political action—with no hint of recognition of the fact that Beveridge himself was one of the leaders of the tribe. The central theme of the book, as suggested by its title, was an expression of Beveridge's passionate belief that the human condition could be improved, not simply by the use of power but by the beneficent influence of 'reasonable' ideas. Yet his conclusions on this point were depressing. The world as Beveridge saw it in 1953 was governed not by 'reason' but by antagonistic military powers. 'The world is an unhappy place; the picture of yesterday's hopeful collaboration in curing evils of want and disease and ignorance and squalor, as I have tried to draw it here, looks like a dream today.'[23]

From the point of view of social policy Beveridge's most significant post-war work was his study of *Voluntary Action*, published in 1948. This work was commissioned by the National Deposit Friendly Society, and was undertaken by Beveridge as a form of protest against the Labour Government's rejection of his proposal that Friendly Societies should be employed as agents for 'humanising and personalising' national insurance. Like his Social Insurance and Full Employment inquiries, the inquiry into voluntary action was carried out with the help of a panel of assessors, but the report was signed by Beveridge alone. Together with his two earlier reports it may be seen as completing his mature philosophy of welfare. In it Beveridge surveyed the history of philanthropic and 'mutual aid' movements in Britain, and he expressed the fear that the motivation for such movements might be in decline—partly because of a decline in religious conviction and partly because of an erroneous belief that all material and social needs were in process of being met by the state.[24] In order to demonstrate the continuing need for voluntary action Beveridge drew attention to many areas of social need that had been ignored or glossed over in his report on Social Insurance—the chronically sick and disabled, the housing of old people, battered and neglected children, discharged prisoners, unmarried mothers, day and night nurseries, and the provision of refuges and rest homes for housewives overwhelmed by large families, ill-health, bad housing and matrimonial strife.[25] This catalogue of problems is of peculiar interest because it was one of the few occasions in Beveridge's writings about welfare when he focused attention, not upon the 'average citizen', but on the special needs of untypical distressed minorities. It is significant also because it lists many of the areas in which, three decades later,

[23] *PI*, pp. 360–1.
[24] Lord Beveridge, *Voluntary Action, A Report on Methods of Social Advance*, chs. 7–9.
[25] Ibid., pp. 226–7.

there is greatest criticism of the inadequate provision made by the 'Welfare State'. Beveridge's view, expressed in *Voluntary Action,* was that the basic financial needs of all these groups should be met by the state; but he claimed that they all had additional needs that could only be met by some form of 'personal service'. Such service, he argued, could not be supplied on a commercial basis and could only be very inadequately supplied by a statutory authority. A 'free society' could not forcibly mobilize the altruistic instincts of individual citizens. Personal service could therefore be provided only by voluntary organizations, working partly through trained social workers and partly through ordinary citizens inspired by 'social conscience'.[26] Beveridge concluded his study by restating his youthful conviction of the need for a working partnership between the state, individuals, and voluntary organizations. The state, he recommended, should encourage all kinds of voluntary association, by legislation to expand their functions, by generous financial assistance, and by the employment of such bodies as agents of public administration. Such co-operation, he argued, was an essential precondition of 'social advance' and of 'experiment, invention, self-criticism'.[27] It would also have an important moral and psychological function; it would harness the energies of 'dynamic individuals with social conscience' and it would provide an ethical substitute for the specifically Christian conviction that had inspired the philanthropy of the past. 'So at last human society may become a friendly society,' Beveridge concluded, 'an Affiliated Order of branches, some large and many small, each with its own life in freedom, each linked to all the rest by common purpose and by bonds to serve that purpose.'[28]

## IV

Beveridge's views on social policy continued to attract a good deal of popular, though not official, attention throughout his old age. He was rather embarrassed by his reputation as 'father of the welfare state'— frequently emphasizing that he preferred the term 'social service state', which implied that citizens had duties as well as rights.[29] He was even more embarrassed when people referred to him as creator of the National Health Service—insisting that this term could only be applied to the Labour Minister of Health, Aneurin Bevan.[30] His own view of the new system of welfare that emerged after 1945 was in many respects ambivalent. He welcomed the introduction of 'universal' insurance and a free national health service; but he was at the same time highly

---

[26] Ibid., pp. 314–15, 320.     [27] Ibid., pp. 305–18.     [28] Ibid., pp. 322–4.
[29] BP, IIb, WHB to Daisy Hobman, 25 Mar. 1953; WHB's comments on Gabrielle Brenne's *Freiheit und Soziale Sicherheit,* 20 July 1961.
[30] H.L. Deb. 5s., vol. 235, cols. 1,143–4.

critical, both of the neglect of certain aspects of the Beveridge Plan and of the reluctance of public authorities to come to terms with certain new problems that had not been apparent in 1942. Beveridge's comments on the social legislation of the 1940s and 50s are of considerable interest, partly because they were an extension of his own personal philosophy of welfare and partly because they provide an important critical perspective on certain aspects of the British welfare state. These comments were not confined to insurance, but ranged over areas of welfare in which Beveridge himself had little personal knowledge or experience. For instance, he warmly welcomed the Children Act of 1948, which defined the circumstances under which local authorities might take children into care; but at the same time he criticized the Act for failing to give social workers adequate powers for 'keeping families together'.[31] He favoured the movement for providing more professional social work training; but at the same time he was apprehensive that 'social work solutions' might be misapplied to problems that were basically economic rather than psychological. Where families were living in bad housing, he argued, 'the remedy is not to send someone to guide them in their marriage; the remedy is to find houses. I do not believe this talk about family disintegration.'[32]

Beveridge's main criticisms of post-war social policy were, however, reserved for the areas covered by his report on Social Insurance. It would be wrong to suggest that he condemned all deviations from his own proposals; but nevertheless, he was highly critical of certain respects in which the Labour government rejected or modified his Report—most notably the rejection of the subsistence principle, the exclusion of friendly societies from administration of benefits, the whittling down of his conception of a 'housewives' policy' and the failure to nationalize industrial assurance.[33] His maiden speech in the Lords in 1946 was on the government's National Insurance Bill, which had been introduced into the Upper House by his former assistant, Frank Pakenham. In general Beveridge welcomed the bill, which he described as asserting his own principle of 'bread and health for all before cake and circuses for any'. But he deplored the lack of any long-term political commitment to subsistence-level pensions; and he strongly criticized the government's decision not to make use of existing voluntary organizations. 'It did frankly send a chill to my heart,' he admitted, 'to realise that it was contemplated that the only way in which most people would get their sickness benefit would be through the post.' He argued

<hr />

[31] Ibid., vol. 153, cols. 9, 35–9.
[32] Ibid., vol. 152, col. 1,135.
[33] Ibid., vol. 142, cols. 208–17; BP, IIb, WHB to Sir Geoffrey Mander, 12 Feb. 1945; WHB to Professor E. Schoenbaum, 8 Mar. 1945.

instead that sickness benefit, maternity benefit, widows' benefit and death grants should all be paid personally by friendly society visitors—who could perform the dual function of discouraging fraudulent claims and, more importantly, of offering personal assistance to the sick, bereaved and dying. Such a system, Beveridge claimed, would 'maintain variety, and from variety, will come experiment, individualization and more humanity ... I am not going to say a word ... to suggest that civil servants are not human. . . . But while civil servants are perfectly human, the unfortunate fact is that anything as big as the Civil Service, merely because of its size, tends to become inhuman.'[34]

Beveridge took an equally ambivalent view of the new National Health Service set up in 1948. He warmly praised the National Health Service Act of 1946, describing it as a 'revolutionary change in values in this country'.[35] He strongly defended the new service when its rising costs came under attack in the mid-1950s—pointing out that they were much lower than the aggregate cost of health care in many other developed countries. He was nevertheless critical of certain aspects of the N.H.S.; and characteristically his criticisms could not be neatly slotted into any pre-ordained niche in the political spectrum. Almost certainly he would have liked a more fully 'socialized' health service, with a 'salaried' medical profession employed on terms similar to teachers in universities.[36] He was one of the first people to draw attention to the problems arising from lack of communication between hospitals, G.P.s and local authority health services; and he urged that this should be overcome by more rapid development of multi-purpose health centres to supersede the lone G.P. He ascribed the service's financial problems largely to the constraints imposed by an annual budget; and he proposed that the N.H.S. should be run like a nationalized industry, with much greater freedom to plan long-term capital expenditure and much less subjection to detailed Treasury control.[37] At the same time, however Beveridge was convinced that there was a continuing need for voluntary and private health care, both inside and outside the N.H.S. He defended the existence of private beds in N.H.S. hospitals, on the ground that the right to spend one's income as one chose was a basic political freedom. When confronted with the argument that this led to 'queue-jumping' he replied that 'the remedy is not to abolish pay-beds but to abolish the queue'. More particularly, he was concerned with the role of voluntary action in supplementing the medical functions of the National Health Service—in financing convalescent homes, entertaining patients, caring for the aged, providing home-help services and 'in

[34] H.L. Deb., 5s, vol. 141, cols. 1,105–11.                    [35] Ibid., vol. 143, col. 92.
[36] Ibid., vol. 143, col. 93–5; BP, IIb WHB to Donald Watson, 19 May 1944.
[37] H.L. Deb., 5s., vol. 186, cols. 1,099–1,104.

doing things which the hospital staff in fact do, but which could be done by a volunteer, thus setting the hospital staff free to do work which only they can do'.[38]

The need to encourage and mobilize voluntary effort was the main theme of Beveridge's criticism of trends in social welfare during the late 1940s and early 1950s. It was with this end in view that he wrote his survey of *Voluntary Action*, pressed for reforms in the law relating to charities, and became involved in bodies like the National League of Hospital Friends. In the mid-1950s, however, his general concern with promoting voluntary action was partially eclipsed by two more specific problems—the social problem of old age and the economic problem of continuous inflation. As Beveridge himself moved into old age he became acutely aware of the multitude of problems faced by many old people—problems of poverty, loneliness, inadequate housing and physical neglect. All these problems were intensified by the sheer growth in numbers of old people and by decline in the size of families; and in his speeches in the Lords Beveridge repeatedly called for a whole new range of old people's services to meet needs that had formerly been catered for within the context of the family. He urged voluntary societies to develop home-visiting and home-help services, and local authorities to give high priority to old people's housing. He himself became President of the Abbeyfield Society, a housing association which provided homes for the elderly; and he pressed the National Health Service to develop geriatric care and to release expensive hospital beds by making better provision for support of the aged in their own homes.[39]

Underpinning all the other problems of old age was the problem of sheer poverty. Beveridge did not share the widespread illusion of the 1950s that poverty had been abolished, and he was increasingly perturbed by the inadequacy of pensions—an inadequacy that he ascribed partly to the rejection of the subsistence principle and partly to erosion of the real value of insurance benefits by continuous inflation. Beveridge was one of the first social commentators in post-war Britain to become seriously alarmed by the phenomenon of inflation; and his fear of the consequences of spiralling prices and wages is perhaps more intelligible in the 1970s than it seems to have been to most people twenty years ago. Beveridge's proposals of 1942 had been framed on the assumption that there would be a wartime inflation of 30 per cent but that after the war the level of prices would be rigorously controlled. Between 1946 and 1957, however, prices of basic commodities rose by more than 50 per

---

[38] Lord Beveridge, 'The Role of The Individual in Health Service', reprinted in *National Health and Hospital Contributory Schemes Conference Addresses, 1950–1961*, pp. 37–43.

[39] H.L. Deb., 5s., vol. 147, cols. 351–3; vol. 186, col. 1,101; vol. 192, cols. 79–90, vol. 236, col. 364–8.

cent. Under the social security legislation of 1946–8, means-tested non-contributory benefits were regularly adjusted to take account of this rise, but national insurance benefits were subject to review only at five-year intervals. This meant that there was a continual decline in the purchasing power of insurance benefits and a widening gap between benefits paid through insurance and those paid through 'National Assistance', which replaced the old Poor Law in 1948. The result was that—far from withering away as Beveridge had predicted—the means-tested sector of social security continued to play an important role not merely in providing for those outside insurance but in supplementing the benefits available from insurance; and by the early 1950s nearly three million people a year were applying for means-tested relief. The inadequacy of benefits was particularly severe among pensioners; and, far from gradually progressing towards subsistence, the real value of the contributory pension in the early 1950s was considerably lower than it had been when the universal system was first introduced in 1946.[40]

Beveridge himself in the mid-1950s campaigned vigorously for a restoration of the adequacy of contributory insurance and in particular for a more generous old-age pension. He denounced the anomaly that national assistance benefits were higher than social insurance benefits, and he was scathing in his attacks on those who favoured a deliberate revival of means tests on grounds of economy. He echoed the arguments he had used fifty years earlier, that means-tested benefits stigmatized poverty and penalized thrift; and he drew attention also to the large number of people who through pride or ignorance failed to make use of a means-tested system and failed to claim necessary relief.[41] In May 1953 he urged the Conservative government to use the forthcoming quinquennial review of benefit rates to implement the subsistence principle —suggesting that the cost might be met out of taxation rather than contributions, so as to avoid imposing further burdens on the low-paid. At the same time, however, he continued to be strongly opposed to the principle of linking benefits automatically to the cost of living—arguing in terms similar to those used by Keynes in 1942, that without prior stabilization of prices such a device would merely reinforce the problem it was designed to solve.[42]

Beveridge was critical also of the new ideas about graduating insurance according to earnings that crept into both Labour and Conservative thinking after 1957. The 1950s saw a rapid growth in occupational pension schemes, arranged by employers for their employees through

[40] Ibid., vol. 175, cols. 1,207–8; vol. 182, cols. 674–80; vol. 185, cols. 787–95, 833–4; vol. 230, cols. 12–14.

[41] Ibid., vol. 190, col. 532–42; vol. 230, col. 14.

[42] Ibid., vol. 182, cols. 674–80; vol. 212, cols. 1,083–90; BP, Ic, WHB's diary, 23 May 1957.

private insurance companies. These occupational schemes varied considerably in adequacy and scope, and there was much criticism of their lack of 'transferability' when workers changed their jobs; but nevertheless by the late 1950s two distinct classes of pensioner had emerged in Britain—those forced to rely on the state scheme, eked out by national assistance, and those covered by some form of occupational pension. It was to extend to the former group some of the benefits enjoyed by the latter that in 1957 the Labour Party put forward its plan for 'National Superannuation'. Under this plan both contributions and benefits for old-age pension purposes would be linked to an insured person's individual earnings; contributions would be transferable if a man changed his job; all contributors would be guaranteed a minimum pension equal to half their average lifetime earnings; and pensions would be 'dynamised' against inflation by linking them to the prevailing cost of living.[43] These proposals were countered in 1958 by a White Paper from the Conservative government, which proposed to introduce earnings-related pensions and to encourage 'contracting-out' into private occupational schemes.[44] Both plans were debated in the Lords, and Beveridge denounced them both as expensive, inefficient and failing to guarantee the principle of subsistence. He objected particularly to the lack of provision for 'transferability' between different pension schemes in the Conservative plan, and to the incitement to higher wage-demands which he believed was contained in the proposals put forward by Labour. 'To me it seems clear that it would encourage inflation,' he asserted: 'It says to the worker, "If you want a really good pension, be sure you get really good wages while you are working." It encourages him to ask for more and more.' Finally he complained that both schemes would reinforce the pattern of inequality imposed by the free market—ignoring perhaps unfairly the far-reaching capacity for redistribution that was at least potentially inherent within a graduated system. 'I am still,' he declared, 'enamoured of the Beveridge principle of treating all the citizens of this country alike and not making an artistocracy of richer workers who will get bigger pensions because they have been richer workers and without lifting a finger to get them.'[45]

## V

Beveridge's public reputation in the years after the war was as great if not greater in Europe and America as it was in Britain. Many foreign social security experts were anxious to emulate the Beveridge system and

---

[43] The Labour Party, *National Superannuation* (1957), pp. 20–30.
[44] Cmnd 538/1957–8, *Provision for Old Age*, pp. 11–14.
[45] H.L. Deb. 5s., vol. 207, cols. 29–36.

he was frequently invited to address foreign audiences on principles of social insurance. He also acted as a kind of roving ambassador for the United Europe movement and other movements for the promotion of international federation. Early in 1946 he went on tours of Spain and Scandinavia, partly to lecture on the new British Social Insurance programme and partly 'to do good work for mutual understanding'.[46] Later in the year he visited Berlin and the British sector of occupied Germany—a visit that was in many ways reminiscent of his visits to Austria–Hungary in 1919. He was appalled by what he saw of homelessness and malnutrition among the German people, by the relative affluence of the invading armies, and by the tragic plight of the million 'displaced persons' in western Germany who refused to return to the Russian zone. He was highly critical also of what he believed to be the vengeful and economically futile policies of the Allied invaders—in particular the destruction of strategic industries, the retribution imposed on minor Nazi officials and the withholding of pensions from wounded German soldiers. 'Our administration of Germany is a mess—our control of Germany is bloody,' he wrote to Lady Beveridge.

Hamburg is tragic—and so is our policy here. 75% of the houses are beyond repair and uninhabitable. We are crowding more of us, and our wives and families into it. We are blowing up shipyards. We are keeping them on impossible rations. And then we expect co-operation . . . The most forbidding sights in Hamburg are the Flak Towers—great concrete towers which resisted all our bombs and from which our lads were shot down. Now they stand in desolation—hideous beasts able to survive in a beastly world.[47]

During the next few years Beveridge made several visits to Germany where he was consulted by federal and provincial officials on social reconstruction.[48] As chairman of Newton Aycliffe he toured German housing developments, and was greatly impressed by the efficiency of the renascent German building industry.[49] Increasingly, however, his trips abroad were devoted not to social policy but to international peace. In Germany he gave lectures on world government, and urged the British authorities to pursue policies of 'reconciliation and re-education.[50] In 1948 and 1949 he lectured in Brussels and Hamburg on the need for European economic integration—arguing that this should be seen as

[46] Lady Beveridge papers, WHB to Janet Beveridge, 25/6 Mar. 1946.

[47] H.L. Deb. 5s., vol. 143, cols. 1,021–5; Lady Beveridge Papers, WHB to J. Beveridge, 1 and 12 Aug. 1946.

[48] BP, XI, 79, Walter Auerbach to WHB 28 Dec. 1951, WHB to Walter Auerbach, 8 Jan. 1952; Otto Neulch to WHB ,19 Nov. 1951; Bruno Richter to WHB, 25 Oct. 1951.

[49] Lady Beveridge Papers, WHB to J. Beveridge, n.d., and 20 Apr. 1952.

[50] Lady Beveridge Papers, WHB to J. Beveridge, 23 Mar. 1949; H.L. Deb., 5ths, vol. 143, col. 1,022.

merely a preliminary stage in the movement towards world government
and international control of defence.[51] In 1954 when he was invited to
New York to address a conference on Welfare and Social Security, he
used the opportunity to press for a revision of the United Nations charter
and control of nuclear arms.[52]

Beveridge's preoccupation with world government and international
security was increasingly reflected in his speeches to the House of Lords.
He frequently emphasized that peace was more important than questions of social policy, and much more important than either socialism
or conservatism. 'Would it be fair to ask whether peace is more important than Liberalism?' he was asked by an ironical Labour peer.
'Certainly it is more important than Liberalism,' Beveridge replied.[53]
Beveridge's concern with international security stemmed primarily
from his fear of Russia—a fear that he shared with the most ardent protagonists of the cold war. He often stressed in his speeches that he
admired Russian economics, and that Russia's internal politics were her
own affair; but he was convinced that Russia's expansionist foreign
policy was the major threat to world peace.[54] To combat this threat he
proposed various short and long-term measures. In the short-term he
pressed for international agreement on the limitation of weapons—of
conventional as well as nuclear weapons, since the banning only of
nuclear weapons would merely open the way to Russian domination.[55]
In the long term he hoped for some form of world government—a
government that would leave most internal affairs in the hands of
national governments, but would take over responsibility for defence
organization and for problems of underdevelopment.[56] On the question
of how either the long- or short-term goal was to be realized Beveridge
was not at all clear; he seems to have relied simply on the kind of
optimism and altruism that he himself as a young man would almost
certainly have dismissed as sentimental and unrealistic. But on the issue
of world peace Beveridge as an old man was frankly and defiantly
Utopian, because he believed that as guides to political action hedonism
and the pursuit of enlightened self-interest had manifestly failed. In a
revealing speech in 1958 he recalled with regret his own rather patronizing contempt for the Utopians of the 1920s:

It seemed so absurd then that anybody should want to go on to another war
that I went about other things and left it to the League of Nations and Gilbert

[51] Lady Beveridge Papers, WHB to J. Beveridge, 9 and 14 Sept. 1948, 23 Mar. 1949.
[52] BP, IIb, WHB to R. Denman, 13 May 1954; X 185, WHB to E. A. Hammesfahr, 21 and 30 Apr. 1954.
[53] H.L. Deb., 5s, vol. 186, cols. 667–8.
[54] H.L. Deb., 5s., vol. 152, col. 1,139; vol. 226, cols. 87–97; vol. 233, col. 735–7.
[55] H.L. Deb., 5s., vol. 186, cols. 665–6; vol. 218, cols. 399–404.
[56] H.L. Deb., 5s., vol. 209, cols. 305–12.

Murray to stop the next war; and we all know that they did not succeed in stopping it. It reminds me of my own foolish past and the past of many of us.[57]

## VI

Beveridge's lifelong physical and intellectual vigour began gradually to dwindle in his late seventies. He still hungered after new ideas and causes, but he was increasingly baffled and to a certain extent repelled by the 'social revolution' that he perceived as going on around him.[58] He was not a poor man, but he had little to live on except his University superannuation, and he was anxious and troubled by the problem of living on a fixed income in an age of continual inflation. He had given away a substantial part of the royalties from his highly successful war-time works to various charitable causes; and the site which he had bought for building a house at Newton Aycliffe was for years frozen by planning blight and not eventually sold until just before his death.[59] After his retirement from Newton Aycliffe he and Lady Beveridge lived for a time in Edinburgh and then retired to Oxford, where they lived in a flat owned by University College at 104 Woodstock Road. But they found Oxford a very different place from the sylvan backwater of the 1930s. 'Oxford as a place to live in,' Beveridge recorded, 'is sadly changed, and damaged by Nuffield and his works and workpeople.'[60] From Oxford he travelled frequently to London to speak in the Lords, but he found himself rather out of touch with new trends in politics and welfare. He still sat on the Liberal benches, but took little part in Liberal organization; and he began to take the view that the Liberals should act as an intellectual pressure group rather than as a party— they should seek, like the early Fabians, not to win elections but to permeate other parties with the force of their ideas.[61] For both Labour and Conservative parties he had little but contempt. He blamed Labour for encouraging inflationary wage-demands, and the Conservatives for clinging to selectivity and means tests; and he condemned both parties for ignoring the need for coherent social planning.[62] He was increasingly distressed by the plight of pensioners, remarking in his diary that 'the conditions under which many old people live in this country are a disgrace to civilization'.[63] He urged leading politicians to press for

[57] Ibid., col. 367–8.
[58] BP, IIb, WHB to Leonard Behrens, 1 May 1953.
[59] BP, IIb, statement of WHB's donations to Webb Memorial Trust, 8 Feb. 1945; WHB to Joan Clarke, 20 Jan. 1945; IIa, R. Burn to WHB 6 Sept. 1962.
[60] BP, IIb, WHB to R. Denman, 31 Dec. 1954.
[61] BP, IIb, ms. conversation with R. Denman, n.d.
[62] H.L. Deb., 5s., vol. 146, col. 580; vol. 152, cols. 1,139–40; vol. 190, cols. 534–6; vol. 212, cols. 1,087–9.
[63] BP, Ib 26, ms. on 'A Study of Legs. Being Eastbourne Re-visited at Whitsun 1960'.

action on pensions; but his views were no more warmly received than they had been in 1942.[64] Thwarted on this issue he immersed himself in his monumental study of prices—more than ever convinced that dislocations in the world economy could ultimately be traced to the shifting price of wheat. This he saw as potentially much more significant than anything he had written on social welfare. 'I have as a first duty,' he wrote in his eighty-second year, 'to complete a vast history of Prices and Wages in England which I began thirty years ago, and which will, in fact, be my main contribution . . . to the understanding of modern problems.'[65]

In 1956 both Beveridge and his wife spent several months in the Acland nursing home, where they corresponded affectionately by letter from their separate rooms. Beveridge thereafter seemed to many of his associates visibly older and more frail. The last years of his life were inevitably overshadowed by the death of some of his closest family and friends. Jeannette Tawney and Richard Denman died in 1957, Lady Beveridge after a brief illness in 1959. The death of his wife left Beveridge lonelier than he had ever felt in his life. He spent much time sorting and re-reading her letters. 'Janet more wonderful than ever,' he recorded in his diary after a day of such sorting in October 1959. A few months later he wrote that sending Christmas cards and doing household chores had been 'great fun with my Janet, but not now I am alone'. 'I am a busy and rather unhappy old man,' he recorded pathetically in September 1960.[66]

In Oxford Beveridge was now looked after by Mrs. Turin, his devoted secretary of former days, who helped with his research, typed his letters and fussed over him like a child. He spent much time with his stepchildren, especially Elspeth Burn, Lady Beveridge's youngest daughter, who had once helped with the research for his study of *Full Employment*. Her house at Carrycoats in Northumberland he now regarded as his second home. In London he stayed at the Reform Club, where he sometimes dined with an equally lonely Harry Tawney. Together they mulled over Edward Caird and Balliol, and recaptured some of their intimacy of fifty years before.[67] As with many old people, Beveridge's mind increasingly flowed back into the past. He paid a nostalgic visit to Eastbourne, where he visited the graves of his brother and sister and recalled the days when he had been persecuted by a bully at Kent House

---

[64] BP, IIb, WHB to Hugh Gaitskell, 26 May 1953; Hugh Gaitskell to WHB, 4 June 1953.

[65] BP, IIb, WHB to Lady Plowden, 5 Oct. 1961.

[66] BP, Ic, 14, WHB's diary, 24 Oct. 1959; BP, IIb, WHB to Norman Cursley, Jan. 1960; IIa, WHB to M. Gwilt, 14 Sept. 1960.

[67] Ross Terrill, *R. H. Tawney and His Times: Socialism as Fellowship* (Harvard U.P., 1973), p. 115.

School.[68] He renewed correspondence with one of his oldest childhood friends, E. M. Forster; and he was thrilled by the dramatized version of Forster's *Passage to India*, which, he observed, was 'full of people just like my father and very well done indeed'.[69] His mind turned also upon spiritual matters, and he spent much time reading the New Testament, the Catholic mystic Tielhard de Chardin, and Longinus' 'On The Sublime'.[70] One of his last speeches in the Lords was a contribution to a debate on Christian Unity when he announced that 'I have no admitted religion' but 'I have some strong beliefs'. He urged factious Christians to forget their differences and to 'make a new and happy Christian world even if it does not admit me to it', by pursuing the 'sweet reasonableness of Jesus Christ'.[71] In a letter to a friend he confided that after a lifetime of secularism and anti-clericalism he was coming to the conclusion 'that Churchmen and the organisation of Churches can do much good'.[72]

Beveridge in his last days threw himself into work to escape unhappiness as he had always done in the past. He delivered to the L.S.E. several further chapters of his history of prices, and he still took an active part in the movements for world government and the settlement of refugees. He became strongly committed to the movement against apartheid, and proposed the encouragement of mixed marriages as a means of dissolving colour prejudice—apparently rejecting his own earlier views about the historic superiority of the Anglo-Saxon race.[73] Early in 1962 he again spent several weeks in the Acland nursing-home, where he still worked away with his slide-rule at changes in the price of wheat. During the next year he had several falls which left him fretful and forgetful, and he was greatly distressed by the death of Harry Tawney; but at the end of the year he took part in several programmes for the B.B.C. and was again planning regular speeches in the Lords.[74] On 16 October he wrote to *The Times* protesting about a report in the Court Circular that 'owing to medical advice' he had had to cancel all engagements. 'I have not accepted any such advice,' Beveridge firmly insisted. On 10 January 1963 he recorded that he was 'still plodding away at Price and Wage History' and was collecting material for a book on 'fellow workers'— which was to be a collective biography of many friends of his youth. Neither work was ever completed, however, for he died in Oxford on

[68] BP, I 26, ms. on 'A Study of Legs. Being Eastbourne Re-visited at Whitsun 1960'.

[69] BP, IIa, WHB to Lucy Mair, 20 Jan. 1960; IIb, E. M. Forster to WHB, 19 Jan. 1962; WHB to E. M. Forster, 16 Mar. 1962.

[70] BP, L III 251, WHB to Helen Sutherland, 4 Sept. 1961; WHB to Philip Rowntree, 4 Sept. 1961; Lady Violet Bonham Carter to WHB, 30 Dec. 1961; Ib 17, ms. notebook of quotations from Longinus, Aug. 1961.

[71] H.L. Deb., 5s., vol. 231, cols. 279–81.

[72] BP, IIb, WHB to Dr. John Badenoch, n.d. (1961–2).

[73] BP, IIb, WHB to H. A. Taylor, Jan. 1961.

[74] BP, IIa, WHB to E. Burn, 23 Nov. 1962.

16 March 1963, during a visit from his stepdaughter, Lucy Mair, and his stepson and daughter-in-law, Philip and Dorothy Mair. His dying words were peculiarly appropriate for a great social reformer, who had spent his life in restless pursuit of manifold ideals and causes. 'He was murmuring to himself when suddenly he said in a clear voice, "I have a thousand things to do". Then he sank back into a deep sleep from which he hardly wakened again.'[75]

[75] *Oxford Mail*, 18 Mar. 1963.

# Conclusion

WILLIAM BEVERIDGE may perhaps be seen as the last of the great line of 'all-round' social reformers who have played a significant part in moulding the institutions of Britain over the past two hundred years. He combined in his own person the roles of social scientist and bureaucrat, journalist and popular moralist, politician and philanthropist—a combination increasingly difficult to achieve in the highly specialized world of the second half of the twentieth century. Temperamentally too he belonged to the tradition of Edwin Chadwick and Florence Nightingale, John Simon and Robert Morant. Like them he was imperious, compassionate, quick-tempered and neurotic, with an almost infinite capacity for selfless and single-minded devotion to a cause. He shared with them a commitment to the philosophy of 'thorough' and a contempt for the ethic of 'muddling through'. Like them he had more than a fair share of personal vanity—a vanity that in Beveridge's case must be seen in part as a wounded vanity, stemming from the frequent and often painful rejection of his services by persons in power. Like many of his Victorian forerunners Beveridge was outwardly opinionated and extrovert, inwardly troubled by doubt and self-reproach. Like them he seemed to live for his work; and like them he was occasionally ruthless in sacrificing people and personal relationships on the altar of public life.

To describe Beveridge simply as a classic 'social reformer', however, tells us little about his underlying philosophy and specific reforming goals. These varied throughout his life and two of the most striking features of Beveridge's career are the frequency with which he changed his mind and his unflagging interest in new problems and new solutions. 'I am still radical and still young enough,' he declared, in Parliament at the age of eighty, 'to believe that mountains can be moved.'[1] His approach to social problems and to wider issues of politics may be seen as falling into three main phases, which roughly coincided with his youth, middle and old age. During the first phase, before the First World War, he believed in far-reaching state intervention in the nation's social life—an intervention which he saw as in no way incompatible with a free enterprise economy. Indeed, like Edwin Chadwick he seems to have believed that, far from damaging the free market, interventionist social policies could streamline and strengthen the free market and render it more efficient than ever before.[2] During the

---

[1] H.L. Deb., 5s., vol. 214, col. 492.
[2] S. E. Finer, *The Life and Times of Sir Edwin Chadwick* (1952), p. 26.

second phase—between the wars—Beveridge was much more troubled by the possibility of a conflict between the promotion of social welfare and the retention of a free market; and for a time he turned his back on questions of social policy and pressed for a revival of economic *laissez-faire*. During the third phase—the Second World War and after—he came to the conclusion that the so-called free market had irretrievably broken down; and he pressed again for far-reaching measures of state intervention—this time not merely in social welfare but in running the economy. For a time he believed that this far-reaching intervention could only come about through some kind of state socialism; but in 1943 he was converted to the view that it might come about also through Keynsian-style economic management. Whichever of these two strategies was adopted, however, he clearly envisaged that the social reforms proposed in the Beveridge Report would be backed up by very extensive measures of economic state control.

In spite of these major shifts in his views on policy there were nevertheless certain key themes in Beveridge's political ideas that consistently recur throughout his career. One of the most important of these themes was a very high esteem for the role and character of the professional bureaucrat—an esteem that transcended his rather low opinion of many of the individuals who held senior positions in Whitehall between the two world wars. Beveridge's ideal society, he confided to an audience at L.S.E. in 1934, would be run not by dictators nor by parliamentary democracy but by professional administrators or 'social doctors', whose sole function would be, 'so to adjust the economic and social relations of his clients as to produce the maximum economic health'.[3] In this respect Beveridge may be seen as a direct heir to the liberal utilitarian tradition and to the administrative ideals of the Indian Civil Service. A second important feature of his political ideas was his continuing concern to promote an organic, interdependent relationship between voluntary organizations, the individual and the state—a concern that first became apparent in his articles on old-age pensions in 1907 and found its fullest expression in *Voluntary Action* more than forty years later. Such a relationship Beveridge saw as the best means of fostering social solidarity and of enabling individual citizens to exercise both their feelings of altruism and their democratic rights. In this respect he may be seen as much more closely akin to the other main stream of the English liberal tradition—the liberal idealism of T. H. Green. A third recurring feature of Beveridge's ideas was an abiding suspicion of organizations of producers. As we have seen, at certain stages of his career he had worked in close co-operation with trade union leaders, and in his old age he came to the conclusion that the rights of the unions

---

[3] 'My Utopia', *Planning under Socialism*, p. 137.

were part of his definition of 'essential freedoms'. But, nevertheless, he was always rather wary of the trade union movement—seeing it, potentially at least, as a refuge for narrow sectarian interests and obsolete class divisions. His ideal 'voluntary association' was not the trade union but the philanthropic or 'social service' organization, which he saw as giving expression to feelings of social conscience rather than economic self-interest. Where it was necessary for people to combine for economic purposes he preferred associations of consumers like the friendly societies rather than associations of producers. He was always much more concerned to promote the interests of the citizen *qua* consumer rather than *qua* producer—a concern that may be seen in his lifelong interest in consumer representation and in extending the powers of consumer groups.

One point that should be stressed about Beveridge's ideas on policy is just how little they were dependent upon his empirical social research. As we have seen, Beveridge as a social scientist laid great stress on the need for observation rather than deduction; but this principle had surprisingly little influence on his work as a social reformer. It is true of course that nearly all his writings on social policy questions were supported by statistical material; and undoubtedly Beveridge's familiarity with statistics enabled him to gauge very quickly the quantitative dimensions of a social problem—a fact that gave him an advantage over many other chairmen of public committees. But he used statistics in a policy context mainly to illustrate a problem or to reinforce an argument; and it is difficult to find any major instance in which empirical research either made him aware of a social problem or suggested a solution that he had not been conscious of before. This is true even of those works in which his academic and policy interests were most closely linked: for instance, in both editions of *Unemployment: a Problem of Industry* Beveridge's policy proposals ultimately rested, not on empirical observation, but on analytical presuppositions about economic relationships—such as the rigidity of wages or the inevitability of trade depressions. It is equally true of Beveridge's official reports. For his Social Insurance report Beveridge gathered together a great deal of empirical data; but he used it in exactly the same way as Edwin Chadwick had used empirical data in the famous Poor Law inquiry of 1834—that is to say, he used it to strengthen the case for policies that he had already chosen on other non-empirical grounds.[4] Whether Beveridge himself was fully conscious of this is not entirely clear, but he seems in practice to have made a fundamental distinction between his work as a social reformer and his work as a social scientist. The first priority of the social

[4] Mark Blaug, 'The Poor Law Report Re-examined', *Journal of Economic History*, XXIV no. 2, 1964.

scientist was not to make prescriptions but to uncover the laws of human society; the first priority of the policy-maker was much more immediate and much more pragmatic—it was, he noted in one of his papers on the Five Giants, 'Action *Now* Not Research'.[5]

How adequate was Beveridge's conception of politics and society as a basis for constructive social reform? It may I think be both criticized and defended on a number of grounds. It may well be objected that Beveridge placed far too much emphasis on the need for political cohesion and social solidarity—ignoring the extent to which political conflict and 'trade-offs' between competing interest groups can in themselves be a fruitful source of innovation and reform. Similarly, within the context of an advanced industrial society, Beveridge's analysis dismissed much too easily the significance of social-class divisions, both in determining the structure of political power and in influencing an individual citizen's aspirations and 'life-chances'. In this respect he shared the perspectives of many social reformers of the 1940s, who appear to have believed that material redistribution would in itself resolve the vast majority of social problems and who at the same time greatly exaggerated the ease with which such material redistribution could be brought about. A third objection to Beveridge's approach is that he tended to overestimate the disinterestedness of public officials and to ignore the possibility that the goals and interests of the bureaucrat might not be the same as those of other members of society. A fourth and more fundamental criticism is that he never considered either the logical or historical limitations on the process of social planning, and that he rarely questioned just how far it was either possible or desirable to bring the whole of social and economic relationships under 'rational' human control.

Against these criticisms Beveridge's political philosophy may be defended in several respects. His preference for a consensus view of politics may be explained in terms of personal experience, since he was usually unsuccessful in situations of conflict and always much more effective in initiating reforms when he managed to project them as politically non-controversial. In spite of his high regard for bureaucrats he was always conscious of the dehumanizing potential of large-scale bureaucracy; and this was one of the main reasons why he wished to develop the self-governing 'voluntary society' as a buffer between the individual and the state. His views, as we have seen, were always changing and often inconsistent and internally self-contradictory; but this in itself was partly a reflection of Beveridge's continuous attempt to comprehend and come to terms with new social and political situations. In this he resembled his youthful mentor, Samuel Barnett—to whom

[5] BP, VIII 45, ms. notes by WHB, n.d.

perhaps more than anyone else Beveridge owed that mixture of high principle and pragmatism that characterized many of his writings on social reform. On the issue of planning, Beveridge's ultimate commitment to a planned society must be seen, not as a reflection of his instinctive preferences, but as a reluctant recognition of what he believed to have become a practical necessity—brought about by the fact that other methods of running complex industrialized societies had manifestly failed. Beveridge's commitment to planning must be set against his spirited defence of personal freedom and against his emphasis on voluntarism and on the crucial role of a wide variety of intermediate organizations. Whether such a mixture of planning and pluralism is in fact feasible—without simply underwriting inequality and privilege—is still a matter for continuing political debate. In this respect Beveridge's attempt to harness state action to individual diversity touches upon one of the most fundamental problems of modern politics—namely, how far the so-called 'liberal freedoms' are compatible with a context of highly collectivized social and economic control.

Beveridge's general political ideas have been unravelled at some length in this study, because without them it is impossible to understand fully his ideas about social welfare. Nevertheless, it is on his work as a framer of practical social policies that Beveridge's reputation must ultimately rest. Of the many areas of policy in which he was involved the two most important must undoubtedly be seen as the organization of the labour market and the planning of social insurance. On the organization of the labour market many of his ideas have either fallen out of fashion or have never really gained political acceptance. For instance, his views on promoting labour mobility and a more 'rational' use of manpower are no more popular with any sector of industry than they were sixty years ago. In certain other respects, however, his ideas on the labour market have a surprisingly modern ring. The erosion of the system of post-war economic management has revived the validity of Beveridge's contention that macro-economic adjustments do not necessarily solve the specific problems of depressed areas, bankrupt industries, the unskilled and disabled and other minority groups. More particularly, the 'new look' for employment exchanges of the 1970s coincides to a marked degree with Beveridge's original version of the labour exchange—as an attractive, purpose-built, business-like institution, catering for the clients' individual needs and used as a matter of course not merely by the unemployed but by all different types of workers wishing to change their jobs. On social insurance many of Beveridge's ideas and assumptions are still the subject of controversy. The Beveridge Report proposals have been criticized in recent years as inadequate in scope, as insufficiently redistributive and as tending to perpetuate obsolete free-market values—although, as has been shown, most of the criticism put forward in 1942 expressed a diametrically opposite point of view. More fundamentally the whole rationale of the insurance system has been called in question, as expensive to administer, psychologically unwarranted, fiscally regressive, and as failing to take account of many varieties of social and financial need. The determination of questions such as these is clearly outside the scope of a personal biography. It seems unlikely, however, that Beveridge himself would have been impressed with such criticisms. On the subject of his Report he would almost certainly have argued that, if carried out in full, it would have been in many respects considerably more 'redistributive' than any social security system yet implemented in Britain. And he might have pointed out that, far from reinforcing free-market values, his report was intended merely as the first instalment of a much more ambitious programme of collectivist reforms. On the general principle of insurance, he was undoubtedly convinced that flat-rate contributory insurance was the most efficient, the most popular and the least expensive method of financing a system of statutory income maintenance. These were not, however, his most fundamental reasons for advocating a system of social insurance. Beveridge's social insurance proposals, from his *Morning Post* articles of 1907 to his report of 1942 were grounded in the belief that social insurance could synthesize and reconcile certain contradictory principles that seemed to be inherent in modern industrial societies. It combined a state-guaranteed income with scope for private saving and freedom of choice. It was a structural embodiment of the social and economic interdependence of modern men. And above all, it seemed to offer practical scope for that organic relationship between the state, the individual and the voluntary organization, that Beveridge prized so highly as a counterweight to bureaucracy and as a medium of citizen rights. Whether such a reconciliation of goals is in fact practically possible is open to question; and the increasing bureaucratization of social welfare suggests that—at least in the form conceived of by Beveridge—in fact it is not. But Beveridge's whole career may be seen in the last resort as a quest for elusive or unattainable solutions; and we may perhaps take as his epitaph his own favourite quotation from Sophocles' *Antigone*: 'When I have ceased to hanker after the impossible I shall have ceased to breathe.'[6]

[6] *Modern Churchman*, Apr. 1941, note by WHB on Dr. Reginald Macan.

# Sources and Bibliography

A UNPUBLISHED SOURCES

1. *Beveridge Papers*
William Henry Beveridge Papers (British Library of Political Science—
B.L.P.S.).
Annette and Henry Beveridge Papers (India Office Library).
Beveridge Collection on the Coal Commission (B.L.P.S.).
Beveridge Collection on Family Allowances (B.L.P.S.).
Beveridge Collection on Munitions (B.L.P.S.).
Beveridge Collection on Tariffs (B.L.P.S.).
Lady Beveridge Papers (these were consulted when in the possession of Mr.
Philip Mair. Most of them have now been deposited in the B.L.P.S.).

2. *Other collections of personal papers*
H. H. Asquith Papers (Bodleian Library).
Samuel and Henrietta Barnett Papers (G.L.C. Library).
W. J. Braithwaite Papers (B.L.P.S.).
Ernest Bevin Papers (Churchill College, Cambridge).
John Burns Papers (British Museum).
Edwin Cannan Papers (B.L.P.S.).
Cherwell Papers (Nuffield College Oxford).
G. D. H. Cole Papers (Nuffield College Oxford).
Hugh Dalton Papers (B.L.P.S.).
John Dodd Papers (lent to the author by Mr. John Dodd).
R. C. K. Ensor Papers (Corpus Christi College, Oxford).
Hubert Henderson Papers (Nuffield College Oxford).
J. M. Keynes Papers (Royal Economic Society, Cambridge).
E. H. Lloyd Papers (B.L.P.S.).
D. Lloyd George Papers (These were consulted when in possession of the
Beaverbrook Library. They have now been transferred to the House of
Lords).
Passfield Papers (B.L.P.S.).
C. F. Rey Papers (Bodleian Library).
C. F. Rey unpublished autobiography (lent to the author by Messrs. Frank
Thorold).
Samuel Papers (House of Lords Library).
R. H. Tawney Papers (B.L.P.S.).
Lucia Turin Papers (some in B.L.P.S., others lent to the author by Mr.
Martin Collier).
Graham Wallas Papers (B.L.P.S.).
Letters from Sidney Webb to the Director (B.L.P.S.).
S. and B. Webb Local Government Collection (B.L.P.S.).

S. and B. Webb Reconstruction Papers (B.L.P.S.).
Unpublished and manuscript material was also lent to the author by Sir
   Norman Chester, Professor R. Klibansky and Dame Marjorie Cox.


3. *Official sources in the Public Record Office*
Board of Education Papers: Ed. 24.
Board of Trade/Ministry of Labour Papers: B.T. 15; LAB 2; PIN 7; PIN 8.
Cabinet Papers: CAB 37; CAB 66; CAB 87; CAB 123.
Local Government Board Papers: HLG 29.
Ministry of Munitions Papers: MUN 5.


4. *Other unpublished sources*
Charity Organisation Society Papers (G.L.C. Library).
Fabian Society Papers (Nuffield College, Oxford).
London County Council Juvenile Advisory Committee records (G.L.C.
   Library).
London School of Economics Papers (L.S.E.).


B PUBLISHED SOURCES

5. *Books by William Beveridge*
*Unemployment: a Problem of Industry* (Longmans, 1909 and 1930).
*John and Irene: an Anthology of Thoughts on Women* (Longmans, 1912).
*British Food Control* (Oxford University Press, 1928).
*Tariffs: the Case Examined*, by a committee of economists under the chairman-
   ship of Sir William Beveridge (Longmans, 1932).
*Planning under Socialism and Other Essays* (Longmans, 1936).
*Changes in Family Life*, by Sir William Beveridge and others (Allen and Un-
   win, 1932).
*Prices and Wages in England from the Twelfth to the Nineteenth Century*, vol. I
   (Longmans, 1939).
*Pillars of Security and Other Wartime Essays and Addresses* (Allen and Unwin,
   1943).
*Full Employment in a Free Society* (Allen and Unwin, 1944 and 1960).
*Why I am a Liberal* (Herbert Jenkins, 1945).
*The Price of Peace* (Pilot Press, 1945).
*India Called Them* (Allen and Unwin, 1947).
*Voluntary Action: A Report on Methods of Social Advance* (Allen and Unwin, 1948).
*The Evidence for Voluntary Action*, Ed. W. H. Beveridge and A. F. Wells (Allen
   and Unwin, 1949).
*Antipodes Notebook*, by Janet and W. H. Beveridge (Pilot Press, 1949).
*Power and Influence* (Hodder and Stoughton, 1953).
*A Defence of Free Learning* (Oxford University Press, 1959).
*The London School of Economics and its Problems* (Allen and Unwin, 1960).

A full bibliography of pamphlets, articles, and official reports by Beveridge and contributions by him to works edited by other people has not been included, since it would cover over a thousand items. For further details of these the reader is referred to works cited in footnotes and to the various Beveridge collections in the B.L.P.S.

6. *Biographical Studies of Beveridge*
Janet Beveridge, *Beveridge and his Plan* (Hodder and Stoughton, 1954).
Lord Chorley, 'Beveridge and the L.S.E., Parts One and Two', *L.S.E.*, nos. 44 and 45, Nov. 1972 and June 1973.
Siegfried Moos, *A Pioneer of Social Advance: William Henry Beveridge 1879–1963* (Durham University, 1963).
Lord Salter, 'Lord Beveridge 1879–1963', *Proceedings of the British Academy*, vol. XLIX, 1963.
Harold Wilson, *Beveridge Memorial Lecture*, Institute of Statisticians, 1966.

# Index